A COMPLETE GUIDE TO
Arctic Wildlife

Richard Sale

Photographs by
Per Michelsen and Richard Sale

FIREFLY BOOKS

A FIREFLY BOOK

Published by Firefly Books Ltd. 2006

First printing

Publisher Cataloging-in-Publication Data (U.S.)
Sale, Richard.
    A complete guide to Arctic wildlife / Richard Sale ;
photography by Per Michelsen and Richard Sale.
[464] p. : col. photos ; cm.
Includes index.
Summary: Includes Arctic geology, geography, speciation,
biogeography with field guide of the region's mammals and
birds species.
ISBN-13: 978-1-55407-178-4
ISBN-10: 1-55407-178-X
1. Birds — Arctic regions — Guidebook. 2. Mammals — Arctic
regions — Guidebook. 3. Arctic regions. I. Title.
591.998 dc22   QL105.S25   2006

Library and Archives Canada Cataloguing in Publication
Sale, Richard, 1946-
    A complete guide to Arctic wildlife / Richard Sale ;
photographs by Per Michelsen and Richard Sale.
Includes index.
ISBN-13: 978-1-55407-178-4
ISBN-10: 1-55407-178-X
1. Animals—Arctic regions. I. Michelsen, Per II. Title.
QL105.S23 2006   591.75'86   C2006-904334-5

Published in the United States by
Firefly Books (U.S.) Inc.
P.O. Box 1338, Ellicott Station, Buffalo, New York 14205

Published in Canada by
Firefly Books Ltd.
66 Leek Crescent, Richmond Hill, Ontario L4B 1H1

Published in the United Kingdom in 2006 by
A&C Black Publishers Limited
38 Soho Square, London W1D 3HB (www.acblack.com)

Design by Pewter Design Associates

Printed and bound in China by Compass Press Ltd

Front cover: Polar Bear and her cubs, Storfjorden,
Svalbard.

Back cover: (top) Ptarmigan, Barren Lands, Northwest
Territories; (middle) Harbor Seal, north Norway;
(bottom) white-morph Gyrfalcon, Nunavut.

Contents

Acknowledgments

▲ Bar-tailed Godwits, north Norway.

This guide is the result of many expeditions to the Arctic spread over a period of years. During that time numerous people and organizations in the Arctic countries have assisted with permissions to travel and to take photographs. To avoid the risk of omitting the names of those that I may have temporarily forgotten, I offer my grateful thanks to you all.

I would particularly like to thank those who have accompanied me on trips — Tom Critchley, Jan von Engel, Chris Hamm, Yevgeni Lobkov, Tony Oliver and, of course, Per Michelsen, whose constant friendship and support has made this book possible. Others have offered invaluable assistance in one way or another — Yuri Artukhin, Petúr Bjornsson, Maria Gavrilo, Alexander Kondratyev, Martha Madsen, Eugene Potapov, Dave Reid, the staff of the EGI, Oxford, Mike Wilson and the staff of Argent, Bristol for the careful handling of my slides.

Special thanks are due to Nathan Sale for his very considerable help in producing the distribution maps. I would also like to express thanks to Nigel Redman and Jim Martin of Christopher Helm for their help in bringing the book to print. Thanks also to editors Patricia Loesche and Ernest Garcia, to designer Reg Cox and to Marc Dando, who painted the superb mammal plates.

Finally, this book would not have been possible without the support of my wife, Susan. Her patient sorting out of occasionally complex travel arrangements allowed me to concentrate on other things, and her continued enthusiasm for the project, despite the occasionally prolonged, anxious absences it required and my occasional low points during the writing, was remarkable.

Richard Sale

I thank those whose companionship and support have made my trips to the Arctic a success, in particular my wife, May Brit, and my son, Mats, for their patience during absences and their interest in my experiences when I returned. I thank my parents, who always have supported me even when they had reason to be anxious. I thank my brother, Kjell Tysdal, Richard Sale for his friendship and for being an excellent companion and also Arnfinn Nielsen, Harriet Backer, Aka Lynge, Sigurdur Adalsteinsson, Bengt Rodin, Mamarut Kristiansen, Lassi Rautiainen, Boyd Warner, Mike Dunn, Brian Kahler, Ray LeCotey, Arild Thorsen, Geir Helland. And, finally, Stavanger Foto for always being helpful.

Per Michelsen

Richard Sale, Per Michelsen and the publishers would also like to express their gratitude to the following photographers, who kindly gave permission for the use of their images: Steve Arlow, Yuri Artukhin, Aurélian Audevard, Alister Benn and Juanli, Daniel Bergmann, Ian Boustead, Vladimir Burkanov, John Cang, Sergey Chårenkov, Dorothea Dallmeijer, Nikhil Devasar, Barwolt Ebbinge, Hanne and Jens Eriksen, Vasily Grabovskiy, Dan Guthrie, Martin Hale, Chris Hamm, Douglas Herr, Kim Hyun-tae, Tuomo Jaakkonen, Arto Juvonen, Alexander Ladygin, Garth McElroy, Nial Moores, Stein Nilsen, Jari Peltomäki, René Pop, Eugene Potapov, Robert Royse, Amano Samarpan, Chris Schenk, Tobias Stenzel, Koji Tagi, Glen Tepke, Kjell Tysdal, Steve Tomlinson, Bas van den Boogaard, Chris van Orden and Natalia Paklina, Markus Varesvuo, Peter S. Weber, and Michelle and Peter Wong.

Preface

The Arctic can appear empty. It can also appear an extremely harsh and unforgiving environment, demanding to all who venture there. It is both those things, but it can also be magical.

This book is a celebration of the Arctic. It deals primarily with its wildlife, but a discussion of birds and mammals cannot restrict itself solely to identification, diet and breeding biology; it must also consider the wider picture. It cannot ignore the geology, the geography and the climate that define the habitat in which those animals and birds live. It cannot ignore the threats currently faced by the region, such as climate change, and the probable outcome for the wildlife if those threats are ignored.

The book starts by defining the Arctic and by considering how animals and plants have evolved to cope with the tough Arctic environment. The adaptations of these creatures are discussed, as are the ways their evolution has been driven by the ebb and flow of polar ice. Next the book moves on to look at the human history of the area, followed by a discussion of the threats posed to the Arctic and its wildlife by human activity.

Following the extensive field guides to bird and mammal species, there is a visitor's guide to the Arctic, which looks in brief at what each region has to offer the wildlife observer, and the ease of travel to it.

Richard Sale, June 2006

Dwarf Caribou, Svalbard.

Defining the Arctic

More than 3,000 years ago, the Chaldeans, living in what is now southern Iraq, wrote that the stars of the northern hemisphere rotated about one fixed star. Though the Chaldeans were the first to record this fact, they were probably not the first to have observed it; humans had doubtless been studying the heavens for millennia before that time. It is likely, too, that ancient observers had noticed that some stars were visible at all times while others rose and set. The Greeks systematized this knowledge. They noticed that the farther north an observer traveled, the greater the number of stars was that were visible at all times. They also saw that the boundary between those stars that were always visible, and those that rose and fell, passed through the constellation they called Arktikos, the Great Bear. And so they called the boundary the Bear's Circle, what is now called the Arctic Circle.

Land of the midnight sun

Earth orbits the sun in an ecliptic orbit. Earth rotates on an axis through the North and South Poles, but this axis is not at right angles to the plane of the ellipse. If it were, then the lengths of day and night would be consistent at all points, and identical at all points on a given latitude north and south of the equator; the seasons would be all but eliminated. But the axis of rotation is at an angle of 23° 27' to the ecliptic. As a consequence, the share of an Earth day of 24 hours taken by day or night varies with the time of year. At the summer solstice, the sun is visible throughout the day at a latitude of 66° 33'N. This latitude corresponds to the celestial Bear's Circle of the ancient Greeks; it is the Arctic Circle. At latitudes to the north of this, the sun is visible throughout the day for increasingly longer periods, until at the North Pole it is visible continuously during the six-month northern summer.

▼ The timberline, Barren Lands, Northwest Territories.

Seen from the North Pole on a given summer's day, the sun circles the sky at a constant elevation. The elevation changes each day, reaching a maximum of 23° 27' on midsummer's day, then dropping until the sun skims the horizon at the autumnal equinox. The sun then rises on the austral polar summer, reaching a maximum elevation, as seen from the South Pole, at the northern winter solstice (i.e., the southern summer solstice) before dropping to the horizon again at the northern spring equinox. The reverse is true during the northern winter, with six months of darkness at the North Pole. The sun does not appear above the horizon throughout the day of the winter solstice at a latitude of 66° 33'N.

In practice, atmosphere refraction causes the sun's image to appear above its true position, by about two times its diameter. The phenomenon of the 24-hour sun, often called the Midnight Sun, can therefore be seen for about 90 mi. (150 km), at sea level, south of the Arctic Circle. Refraction can also cause the curious phenomenon of the sun reappearing above the horizon after it has set for the Arctic night. In both cases the sun usually appears as a distorted, broken image. The most famous of such events, and one of the most extreme, occurred toward the end of the northern winter of 1596–1597 when the Dutch expedition of Willem Barents, wintering on Novaya Zemlya, saw the sun rise almost two weeks before it was due.

In defining the Arctic, the Arctic Circle would seem the obvious choice. North of the Circle, winters are cold and dark, and summers, though light, are also relatively cold. But despite this, the Circle has limited climatic significance, the geography of Earth negating such an attractive and straightforward option. While the Labrador Current brings cold water and hence cold air through the Davis Strait, chilling eastern Canada and western Greenland, the North Atlantic Drift or Gulf Stream, which shifts vast quantities of warm water from the Caribbean to northern Europe, forces back northern chills.

Longyearbyen, the capital of the Svalbard Archipelago, is a town with hotels, and it has an airport used by scheduled aircraft. To the west, at a similar latitude (78°N), Greenland and the islands of Arctic Canada are uninhabitable. North of the Arctic Circle in Norway, the warm waters allow cities to flourish and agriculture is possible. North of the Circle in North America lie Inuit settlements, and hunting represents the only feasible way of life.

Alternative definitions

One proposed definition of the Arctic eliminates such climatic effects. In winter, the lack of sun makes the far north a cold place. In summer, the extra sunlight might be thought to compensate, but this is not so. The sun is always at a low angle in the sky, so light from it traverses more of the atmosphere, losing energy by absorption and scattering as it does so. It also illuminates a larger area of Earth than, for instance, it does at the equator, so energy input per unit surface area is reduced. This reduction in incident energy leads to a definition of the Arctic based on the amount of energy received annually by a unit area of the Earth's surface.

An alternative definition is suggested by considering Antarctica. In the southern hemisphere, the Antarctic Convergence, the boundary between the cold mass of southern polar water and the warmer mass of subtropical water to the north, offers a strong delineation and an excellent definition of "the Antarctic." However, such a neat definition is defeated by geography in the north. Antarctica is a huge landmass entirely surrounded by water, the Convergence clearly marked by sudden changes in water temperature and salinity. The Arctic is an ocean, albeit a largely frozen one, surrounded by continental landmasses. Convergence exists, but it is discontinuous and much less clearly defined.

Another sea-based definition could be the limit of sea ice, but this has the disadvantages of being highly seasonal and of having annual variations, which are not predictable in a way that allows an adequate definition to be formulated. It is also difficult to interpolate the position of the sea ice edge across the continental landmasses and, since they almost entirely surround the Arctic Ocean, such interpolation would be crucial.

The landmasses surrounding the frozen Arctic Ocean offer another potential definition that has been frequently suggested — the timberline or treeline, the northern limit of tree growth. In Europe, the climatic influence of the Gulf Stream allows tree growth well north of the Arctic Circle, while in North America, in general, trees are not encountered well before 60°N is reached. For the purposes of defining a timberline, what constitutes a tree has first to be defined. Normally it is assumed that to be considered a tree it must be about as tall as a human. The definition is not trivial; Arctic Willow (*Salix polaris*) is a true tree, displaying, in particular, wonderful leaf color changes from the green of summer to the red of autumn, while often barely reaching a height of 4 in. (10 cm) because of the effects of wind and cold. While in temperate forests the observer walks beneath the forest canopy, in the "forests" of the Arctic the observer is usually walking on the canopy.

Because of these climatic effects, the timberline is not a precise, easily identified boundary. Local geology and geography play their part in defining the habitability of an area, while ground elevation, drainage, soil composition and the like will also have an effect, so that occasionally patches of forest exist with significant areas of treeless tundra to the south. On paper the timberline is solid and immutable, but on the ground it is more vague, forming a band as much as 125 mi. (200 km) wide. A further confusion is that there are places in which trees grow where propagation through seeds is now impossible, as the Arctic summer is neither long enough nor warm enough for this to occur. These trees grew from seeds, but climatic changes mean that they can now only reproduce by a form of "suckering," whereby branches touch the ground and throw out roots from which a trunk grows, creating a new tree once the original branch has withered and died.

An isotherm solution

Another potential definition is one closely linked to the timberline. This is the 50°F (10°C) summer isotherm, a line that links points on the Earth's surface at which the mean temperature of the warmest month of the year is 50°F. The alliance of the timberline and this particular isotherm is to be expected. Despite the intuitive assumption that it is the cold that prevents trees from progressing northward, that is not the case; in Siberia trees grow in an area that experiences the lowest winter temperatures in the northern hemisphere. What stops trees growing farther north is summer temperature. The abundant light of the Arctic summer can only be used by the tree if its cell temperatures are high enough for the chemical reactions of photosynthesis to take place. This makes maximum summer temperature, and the persistence of adequately high temperatures, critical. However, the 50°F summer isotherm is poorly defined in the waters of the North Atlantic and other northern intercontinental waters. Despite this, the isotherm has been adopted as a useful measure of the border between the Arctic and the sub-Arctic by many specialists since it was first suggested in the late 19th century. One drawback of its use is that it can make no allowance for winter cold, leading to the anomalous situation in which the point in the northern hemisphere where the lowest temperature was measured, in the Siberian forest, is south of the 50°F isotherm. This anomaly was addressed by the Swedish scientist Otto Nordenskjöld, a nephew of the first man to sail the Northeast Passage and himself a noted Antarctic explorer, who suggested a formula that allowed a modification of the strict 50°F limit by considering the mean temperature of the coldest winter month. Nordenskjöld's formula allows regions in which the mean temperature of the warmest month varies from 48°F (9°C) to 55°F (13°C), while that of the coldest month varies from 32°F (0°C) to -40°F (-40°C).

In practice, the timberline, the 50°F isotherm, the modified 50°F isotherm, and a definition based on annual incident solar energy per unit area all result in similar boundaries. These boundaries include those areas that would be assumed to be Arctic by anyone casually glancing at an atlas — Greenland, Svalbard, the islands off the northern coasts of Russia and Canada — but exclude some areas that might surprise the atlas-examiner — Iceland, northern Scandinavia and much of Alaska. In this book a pragmatic approach has been adopted. The modified 50°F isotherm is assumed as a starting point. Adopting this definition rather than the timberline allows a limit to be placed on the number of essentially temperate, boreal species that can be defined as Arctic. In Europe, Iceland, which lies almost exclusively south of the Arctic Circle, but north of the timberline (though whether the island's present treeless state is a human-based or a natural phenomenon is debatable), is assumed to lie within the Arctic. By contrast, northern Scandinavia, which, like Iceland, is excluded from the modified 50°F isotherm boundary, is not included, though in the field guide sections reference is made to those species whose range includes the region. In North America, use of the modified 50°F isotherm includes the southern edge of Hudson Bay as Arctic, though not James Bay. However, James Bay can hardly be excluded because of its importance to Polar Bears. The modified 50°F isotherm also includes northern Quebec and Labrador.

In Alaska, the western and northern coasts are included in the definition of the Arctic adopted here, though much of the inland State is excluded. An exception is made for the Denali National Park, elevated sections of which are populated by an essentially Arctic fauna. In Asia, the northern coast of Russia is included. A specific problem exists in the Bering Sea, where the use of the modified 50°F isotherm omits much of what is usually considered Arctic. Here it is assumed that the Pribilof Islands, the Aleutian Islands chain, the Commander Islands, the

Kamchatka Peninsula and the northeastern coast of the Sea of Okhotsk lie within the Arctic. In defining this boundary, the Arctic is pushed farther north than has been agreed by CAFF, the program for the Conservation of Arctic Flora and Fauna, a report prepared for the Arctic Council, a joint initiative of the Scandinavian countries plus Iceland, Russia and Canada. Within its "Arctic," CAFF includes more of mainland Scandinavia and the hinterlands of Russia and Canada, and more of southwestern Alaska. However, it excludes the Kamchatka Peninsula and the Commander Islands, though it retains the Aleutian chain.

That said, any definition of the Arctic is subject to debate, and consequently any proposed faunal or avifaunal list will include or exclude species that are anomalous in some opinions. In practice, the apparently arbitrary definitions of what constitutes the Arctic do not greatly affect the species lists developed within this book and, it is hoped, such anomalies have been minimized. The boundary of the Arctic adopted in this book is shown below.

One other definition must be addressed before continuing. Many books and reports dealing with Arctic species use the terms "high" and "low" Arctic without necessarily defining what is meant by them. This is, in part, an absence which recognizes, again, that such definitions are somewhat arbitrary. In this book, high Arctic refers to polar desert or semi-desert, while low Arctic refers to tundra, though it has to be accepted that the change from one to the other is often gradual, a fact that can make the use of the terms occasionally unhelpful.

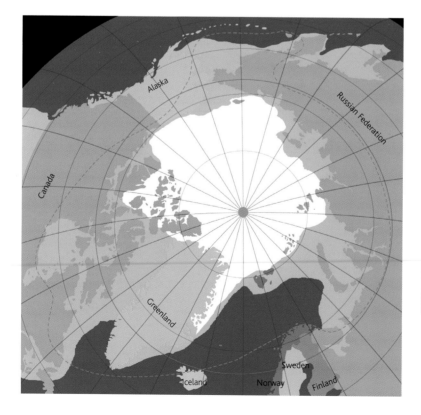

------ 50°F isotherm

——— Arctic Circle

Arctic geology

In 1906 and 1912 the German geophysicist Alfred Wegener took part in two Danish expeditions to Greenland. In 1915 he published a book entitled *The Origin of Continents and Oceans*, in which he presented his theory of continental drift. He had developed this as a result of watching the movement of ice floes during his time in the Arctic. Wegener's theory was that the continents had once been joined together in a single supercontinent, which he called Pangaea, that had broken up, the landmasses drifting apart to form the world we see today. Wegener's theory helped explain the distribution of fossils across the continents and the similarities of geology at continental edges, though it did not gain universal acceptance, as it was, in part, based on flawed data. However, by the time the flawed data came to light, Wegener had died of exposure in 1930 during another expedition to Greenland.

Wegener's book fueled further research and eventually led to the theory of plate tectonics, which describes Earth as a series of rigid plates floating on a "mantle," a layer of molten magma that surrounds the Earth's solid, iron-rich core. The plates are of two basic forms, continental and oceanic. The oceanic plates are denser and therefore float lower in the mantle. The world's oceans lie above the oceanic plates, lapping the edges of the continental plates.

The continents coalesced to form Pangaea about 250 million years ago; the supercontinent started to break up about 100 million years later when spreading ridges, created where the Earth's mantle rises through the crust, broke through, spilling out molten rock that forced the plates apart. One spreading ridge began to form the Atlantic Ocean. In the south Atlantic, Africa and South America were driven apart. In the North Atlantic, Laurentia, a combination of North America and Greenland, was driven northward away from Africa and westward away from Eurasia. About 50 million years ago a spreading ridge divided North America from Greenland. A major spreading ridge, the mid-Atlantic Ridge, continues to drive the Old and New Worlds apart and manifests itself, in the Arctic region, in the volcanic activity of Iceland and Jan Mayen.

Land of fire and ice

Iceland's volcanicity arises because of its position above a hot plume, which rises through the mantle to form a dome that has pushed the mid-Atlantic Ridge up to 1½ mi. (2.5 km) higher at that point than elsewhere. This is high enough to break the water's surface and so create an island. The plume has stayed stationary as the continents have been pushed apart.

On the Icelandic mainland, Hekla, the most famous of the island's volcanoes, dominates the country southeast of the famous tourist sites of Geysir and Gullfoss. Hekla's cone, now 4,892 ft. (1,491 m) high, has built up over the last 6,500 years, the last significant eruption being in 2000. Off Iceland's southern coast, a three-year eruption beginning in 1963 saw the creation of the island of Surtsey close to the Westmann Islands, while in January 1973 on Heimaey, another of the Westmann Islands, an eruption necessitated the evacuation of

the islanders. In September 1996 on the Icelandic mainland, the volcano Grímsvötn erupted through a 2½ mi. (4 km) fissure beneath the Vatnajökull ice cap. The meltwater produced threatened to create a huge wave of water, but fortunately this did not occur until November so no lives were lost. On November 5 an estimated 1 cu. mi. (4 km³) of water and one million tons of ice engulfed Iceland's southern coast. In addition to these intermittent, but highly explosive, indications of the mid-Atlantic Ridge's existence, Iceland also has related phenomena that have made it popular with tourists. Sulphur-rich hot water has been harnessed for swimming pools as well as geothermal power plants, bubbling mud pools abound and the geyser that gave its name to this geological phenomenon can be seen at Geysir, east of Reykjavik.

The spreading of the mid-Atlantic Ridge, and another that is moving Antarctica away from the other continents, causes the rigid oceanic and continental plates to interact. Where India is converging with Eurasia, the interaction has created the Himalayas, which are still being thrust upward as India heads north. Where plates slide relative to each other, fault lines are created, giving rise to earthquake zones. California's San Andreas Fault and the Fairweather Fault in south-eastern Alaska occur where the Pacific Plate is sliding beneath the North American Plate. When an oceanic plate converges with a continental plate, the denser oceanic plate dives beneath the lighter continental, a movement known as subduction.

▼ Geyser at Geysir, after which the phenomenon is named.

Eruptions and tsunami

Subduction creates an area of both earthquake and volcanic activity. The Aleutian Islands, where the Pacific Plate is subducted beneath North America, form part of such an area, as does Russia's Kamchatka Peninsula, formed where the Pacific Plate is subducted beneath the Eurasian Plate. In June 1912 the volcanoes of Katmai and Novarupta on the Alaska Peninsula ejected 5 cu. mi. (20 km³) of pyroclasts, one of the most productive eruptions of historical times. Mount Katmai had been a 7,497 ft. (2,285 m) glaciated, domeless, cratered peak before the eruption. The eruption reduced its height by some 2,625 ft. (800 m) and created a caldera 2½ mi. (4 km) across and up to 3,280 ft. (1,000 m) deep. On March 27, 1964, an earthquake measuring 8.6 on the Richter scale struck Alaska. The quake's epicenter was midway between Valdez and Portage, east of Anchorage. Earth movements and landslides onshore were accompanied by tsunamis up to 165 ft. (50 m) high that destroyed parts of the towns of Valdez and Seward. At Portage the ground subsided 7 ft. (2 m), causing the abandonment of the township and the death of local pine forests, which were inundated with saltwater. Surveying later revealed that the local area had not only subsided but expanded horizontally. By contrast, the town of Cordova, some 60 mi. (100 km) east of Portage, was raised by 7 ft. (2 m), with high tide no longer filling the harbor, leaving local fishing boats above the high-tide mark. On the island of Middleton, 90 mi. (150 km) south of Cordova, a wrecked ship that had been unreachable at the lowest tides was lifted clear of the sea — Middleton had been uplifted by 16 ft. (5 m).

The tsunami associated with the 1964 event was significant, but cannot compare with the wave created by an earthquake in 1958, which dropped an estimated 40 million tons of rock into Lituga Bay, part of the Glacier Bay National Park. This landslide caused a wave that travelled across the bay at 130 mph (210 km/h) and created a "tidemark" some 1,640 ft. (500 m) up the opposite cliff line. In terms of the impact on humans, both these tsunami events are, of course, trivial in comparison to the December 26, 2004, event in the eastern Indian Ocean.

Geological activity in Russia

On the Russian side of the Bering Strait, plate subduction has resulted in the volcanic arc of the Kamchatka Peninsula on which there are 28 active and 150 extinct volcanoes. In 1956 Bezymianny, at the northern end of the active range, erupted spectacularly; it is estimated that a jet of incandescent tephra was ejected at a velocity of more than 1,640 ft./s. (500 m/s) – equival to twice the speed of sound. The jet reached a height of 28 mi. (45 km), and dust reached Britain, almost exactly halfway around Earth, in just 72 hours. Bezymianny had been 10,121 ft. (3,085 m) high before the eruption; following it, the height had been reduced by some 655 ft. (200 m) and a huge caldera had been created. An eruption in October 1994 of nearby Klyuchevskoy, the peninsula's highest peak and the highest active volcano in Eurasia at 15,584 ft. (4,750 m), spewed out so much ash that international flights from North America to Asia were disrupted for days.

In addition to the volcanoes, many of which form textbook cones, Kamchatka has an array of huge geysers in the appropriately named Geyser Valley (a feature unknown until 1941), as well as the Uzon Caldera, where mud volcanoes, hot mud pots and crater lakes, sulphur-rich hot streams and associated thermophilic bacteria and plants can be seen.

The Arctic Basin

North of Iceland, the mid-Atlantic Ridge continues toward the North Pole, separating Svalbard and northeastern Greenland, then continuing as the Nansen-Gakkel Ridge, which is 932 mi. (1,500 km) long and rises 6,560 ft. (2,000 m) above the seabed. That ridge is one of several that make up the geologically complex Arctic Basin, the ridges separating deep oceanic basins. These deep basins are ringed by shallower seas that lie above the continental shelves. The continental shelves of Eurasia and Fennoscandia are extensive, reaching to and beyond Svalbard and the islands of Arctic Russia. The Siberian shelf, which forms part of the Eurasian shelf, is the world's widest, being up to 560 mi. (900 km) across. The seas that overlay the Eurasian shelves are very shallow; to the west, the Barents, Kara and Laptev Seas are only 33–65 ft. (10–20 m) deep; to the east, the East Siberian and Chukchi Seas are 98–130 ft. (30–40 m) deep. However, though similar in their depth and in the width of the underlying shelves, these seas differ markedly. The Barents Sea has the milder climate because of the influence of the northern arm of the Gulf Stream. The islands of Novaya Zemlya act as a barrier to the eastern transfer of these warmer waters, so the Kara Sea climate is much colder; while the mean January temperature above the Barents Sea is 14°F (-10°C), the mean temperature of the western Kara is 5°F (-15°C), falling to -22°F (-30°C) at the eastern side. The climate of the Laptev Sea is much more benign. The warm water outflow from the huge rivers that discharge into the sea cause the sea ice to melt; the enhanced heat pickup of the dark open water then ensures that in summer the sea can be ice-free to 77°N. Some areas remain ice-free throughout the winter. As a result, the Laptev population of Walruses is the most northerly in the world. Farther east, the minimal river flow into the East Siberian Sea means that it experiences the least summer ice melting and a harsher climate. The Chukchi Sea is colder in winter, but warm water passing through the Bering Straits promotes significant summer melting. West of the Barents Sea, the deeper Greenland Sea separates Svalbard and Greenland, with its continuation, the Norwegian Sea, extending as far south as the Faroe Islands. The continental shelf of North America is less extensive. Baffin Bay, between Greenland and Baffin Island, is a much deeper sea. So, too, is the Beaufort Sea, which lies off northern Alaska and Canada's Yukon and Northwest Territories. Here the continental shelf is much less extensive than that beneath the bordering Chukchi Sea.

Arctic rock types

The Arctic has a full range of igneous, sedimentary and metamorphic rocks, their distribution occasionally indicating the tectonic processes that created both the Arctic's oceanic basin and the ring of continental and island landmasses. Unfortunately these landmasses do not have simple geological boundaries. Consequently, the overall geological evolution of the Arctic can only be briefly sketched here. The oldest rocks on Earth lie within the Arctic, with ages of around 4,000 million years attributed by radioactive dating to volcanic rocks close to the Acasta River in Canada's Northwest Territories, and of 3,750 million years to sedimentary rocks in the Isua upland close to Nuuk, southwest Greenland. These, and younger rocks with ages to about 1,000 million years, form the shields that are the basis of the continental plates surrounding the Arctic Basin. The shield rocks are the metamorphic schists and gneisses that are visible in many areas, particularly in Canada and Greenland. During the period from about 1,000 million years ago, sedimentary rocks were laid down below a shallow sea. Later, tillites, a mix of material from clay to boulders, were laid down. Tillites can be seen in northeastern Greenland. They lend support to the "snowball Earth" hypothesis, which contends that Earth was wholly or largely ice-covered at about 650 million years ago, with the tillites created by glacial activity.

A time of mountain building and other geological upheaval, the Caledonian Orogeny took place in the Silurian and Devonian Periods, roughly 450–420 million years ago. Through folding of the rocks, it led to the creation of a mountain range against the stable Baltic Shield that extended from what is now western Scandinavia to the Appalachians by way of Scotland and eastern Greenland. The mountain-building was accompanied by metamorphosis and igneous intrusions. Newtontoppen, the highest peak in Svalbard at 5,633 ft. (1,717 m), is a granite intrusion from this period as are some of the granite formations in eastern Greenland. The most spectacular intrusions are the huge granite faces of the peaks of the Auyuittuq National Park on Baffin Island.

Between the Carboniferous and the Cretaceous, fossil-rich sedimentary rocks were laid down in extensive basins that covered much of the Canadian Arctic, Greenland and Svalbard. The basalt intrusions and extrusions of Franz Josef Land date from this long period of continent building. In the subsequent early Tertiary, the mid-Atlantic Ridge began the process of forming the Atlantic Ocean and moving the Old and New Worlds apart, laying the foundation for the present structure of the Arctic.

As well as some of the Earth's oldest rocks, evidence of some of the Earth's oldest life forms has been detected in the Arctic, in the banded ironstone formations associated with the ancient rocks of western Greenland. The existence of these organisms was inferred by measuring the ratio of two naturally occurring oxygen isotopes. Much younger, but among the earliest of visible fossils, are stromatolites, which are laminated, calcareous structures that indicate early microbial or algal forms. The earliest stromatolites date from the Archaean, but excellent later forms (perhaps 700 million years old) can be found on the coasts of east Greenland and north Spitsbergen. Fossils from later geological periods can be found all over the Arctic; the region is renowned for some stunning finds of early terrestrial vertebrates, including the seven-fingered *Ichthyostega* and eight-fingered *Acanthostega* from the Devonian of East Greenland. Perhaps the most important find to date was announced in 2006. This was the discovery in rocks on Ellesmere of *Tiktaalik*, a "missing link" between fish and tetrapods.

As the Atlantic Ocean was being formed, the developing continents were cloaked in vast areas of forest that were to form the basis of Svalbard's coal and Alaska's oil deposits, each of that has been a major incentive to the human development of the Arctic.

Snow and ice

Although water can exist in the three states common to almost all matter — solid, liquid and gas — it is curious in being able to change between solid and gaseous phases without having to go through a liquid phase. Generally, ice, when heated, melts to form water that, when heated further, boils to the gaseous form, steam. However, ice can form water vapor directly by a process known as sublimation. Water vapor can also solidify directly. Many Arctic travelers are familiar with this type of precipitation, which can occur from cloud-free skies; tiny ice crystals, usually no more than 0.007 in. (0.2 mm) across, fall gently and glitter in the sun (or, more rarely, in the light of the moon). This beautiful phenomenon is often and aptly referred to as diamond dust, though the more usual name for the gaseous-to-solid transformation is hoarfrost, well known to temperate-zone dwellers because of its deposition on roads and the frosting of windowpanes.

Despite the common notion that snow is frozen rain, this is not the case. The freezing of raindrops obviously does occur, but this falls as sleet. To complete the family of falling ice, hail is produced when snowflakes accumulate water as they fall through clouds, growing in size and losing the "softness" of snow. The production process for snowflakes involves water vapor turning to ice in clouds, where more and larger crystals can form than is the case for diamond dust. Snowflakes are usually 0.04–0.08 in. (1–2 mm) across and are formed when supercooled water vapour, of a temperature that is actually below the freezing point, is triggered to freeze by the presence of microscopic dust particles, which act as nuclei for the freezing. The beautiful shapes of snowflakes were first described after naked-eye observations by Johannes Kepler and René Descartes in the early 17th century. Both observed the hexagonal shape of the flakes, though their complexity and symmetry did not become apparent until the invention of the microscope. This sixfold (rarely twelvefold) symmetry is a product of the crystalline structure of ice and has its origin in the way that hydrogen and oxygen atoms interact to form chemical bonds. The extraordinary symmetry of snowflakes is a function of temperature and humidity. Because snowflakes are so small, these parameters are the same across the entire flake, so when growth occurs as a result of the condensation of more water vapor, it is the same at each identical point. It is always maintained that no two snowflakes are the same. This assertion clearly cannot be proved, but is likely to be the case. In a minute percentage of water molecules, the oxygen or hydrogen will not be the "standard" form, but of a different stable isotope. As each snowflake is composed of billions of water molecules, and the effect of these different molecules will be to alter the shape of the crystal in a random process, the likelihood of two crystals having the same structure is infinitesimally small.

On land, snow is the basis of ice formation, but the snow itself is important to certain Arctic species. The process of sublimation creates a form of snow that is important to Arctic rodents. Snow is an excellent insulator; 3 ft. (1 m) of snow is capable of maintaining soil temperature at around 32°F (0°C) in air temperatures of -40°F (-40°C), but the warmth of the soil stimulates sublimation in the basal snow layer. The loss of water molecules, which rise through the snow, is replaced by cooler, denser air, which encourages further sublimation as it warms. The net effect is to create a basal snow layer composed of needlelike crystals, with a specific gravity of 0.2–0.3. This layer is exploited by rodents, which are able to continue scavenging while benefiting from the insulating properties of the snow blanket. Mountaineers are less enamored of the condition as basal layer weakening by sublimation can result in avalanches on slopes.

Dry fresh snow has a specific gravity of 0.1, so 4 in. (10 cm) of fresh snow is the water equivalent of ½ in. (1 cm) of rain. This is only a generalization, though, as several factors influence the density of fresh snow. Snow is compacted both by its own weight and by the wind, aided by the fracturing of individual snow crystals, which allow a tighter packing, and by pressure-melting at lower depths, which allows water to fill the voids between the crystals before refreezing. At a specific gravity of about 0.5, the snow forms a compacted granular structure known as *firn* or *névé*. The top layer of wind-compacted snow, which may have a similar density, is known as wind slab. Wavelike ridges formed on the surface by wind action are known as *sastrugi*. Wind slab can be dangerous; on sloping ground it can avalanche, the crust sliding on a relatively unconsolidated base. As compaction increases due to continued snowfall and temperature variations that allow pressure-melting at lower levels as well as surface-melting, more water trickles down through the snow. This fills any gaps between the crystals, followed by refreezing, leading to an increase in the specific gravity of the ice. Deep within the snow, "sintering" also occurs. This is the transfer of water molecules by sublimation, leading to the creation of a complex, latticelike structure that squeezes air out.

At a specific gravity of about 0.8, the remaining air becomes trapped in bubbles within the firn. The trapped air is compressed as compaction increases. At a specific gravity of 0.9, the ice has become glacial; by comparison, the specific gravity of pure ice is 0.917. The trapped, compressed air has two aesthetically pleasing effects. One is that, when added to a drink, glacial ice fizzes as the air is released, a trivial diversion, but one that has given a moment of pleasure to many a polar traveler. The other is that the air, or lack of it, can affect the color of the ice. Blue ice, particularly blue icebergs, are among the most beautiful of polar sights. Ice absorbs light at the red end of the visible spectrum while transmitting blue light, but air bubbles and other impurities in the ice scatter light. In general ice is impure and so appears white, but highly pure ice allows light to travel a long way through it without scattering; the farther the light travels, the more red is absorbed and the deeper blue the ice appears. Blue-green ice is also possible if organic material such as algae has become trapped at some stage in the formation process.

Sea ice

The northern edges of the continental masses that surround the Arctic Ocean owe most of their landforms to the presence of land ice — glaciers and permafrost. Yet in the popular imagination the Arctic is defined by sea ice, the frozen Arctic Ocean, at the heart of which is the North Pole, and the expanding, contracting floe edge where ice and sea meet. The seawater of the Arctic Ocean has a salinity of about 33 parts per thousand, less than average because of the freshwater runoff from continental rivers, many of which are very large, and the lack of evaporation relative to more tropical seas.

The presence of salt reduces the temperatures at which water freezes to between 29°F (-1.8°C) and 28°F (-2.0°C). Salt also changes the way water freezes. The density of freshwater increases as its temperature decreases, reaching a maximum at 40°F (4°C), then decreasing again. This decrease in density explains why ice floats. As the surface of freshwater cools, cooler and less dense water forms a stable layer on top of the denser water column. Ice can therefore form in a thin layer on the surface. By contrast, seawater does not have this maximum density, which increases as the temperature falls. This means that as the surface layer of the sea cools, it becomes denser and sinks. Thus, the whole column of water at a uniform salinity must be cooled to its freezing point before ice can form. The depth of the water column depends on the extent of uniform salinity; in general, discontinuities in salinity occur at depths of 33–130 ft. (10–40 m), which means that in shallow seas the water column must be at the freezing temperature all the way to the seabed before freezing can occur. However, a further complicating effect is also at work; salts are lost from the surface layer as the water cools.

As the temperature of the surface layer falls, ice crystals begin to form in the water. This early stage is often referred to as frazil ice. The ice crystals rapidly multiply, forming a grayish surface layer that behaves like thick soup. This is grease ice, a form that most Arctic travelers will recognize even if they have not observed frazil. The ice crystals now combine, forming plates that are still flexible enough to move with the wind, or with wave action. The plates thicken and collide, increasing in size to create pancake ice, roughly circular plates with raised edges formed as the plates rub against each other. Eventually the plates coalesce, forming a continuous sheet that thickens as it ages. The thickening rate is temperature-dependent, but in very cold conditions it may be as much as 8 in. (20 cm) per day, though as thickness is added at the base of the ice, the ice above acts as an insulator, reducing the thickening rate so that this rate cannot be maintained for long periods. Growth of more than 16 in. (40 cm) in a week is uncommon and more than 3¼–6½ ft. (1–2 m) over an entire winter is rare.

Old ice, the name commonly given to sea ice more than two years old, can be up to 26 ft. (8 m) thick, the result of freezing on the lower surface and the accumulation of winter snow, which builds ice on the upper surface. It is strong enough to sustain substantial loads and to cause problems for the biggest ice-breakers; sea ice of about 8 in. (20 cm) will take the weight of a human. Old ice has a much lower salinity than the seawater from which it derived. For new ice, if the cooling of the surface water is fast, then its salinity can remain high, but in general it is about 5%, which means that around 85% of the salt has been lost. The salinity of old ice can be as low as two parts per thousand, allowing it to be used as a source of freshwater, at a pinch. Salts leach out of the ice into local pockets of brine within the ice matrix, which migrate downward to the underlying liquid.

Much of the central Arctic Ocean is covered by perennial ice, which is ice that does not melt from season to season. The existence of this perennial ice is one of many differences between the Arctic and the Antarctic: in the Antarctic, most of the sea ice forms annually, though there is some perennial sea ice in both the Weddell and Ross Seas. By contrast, about half the winter maximum cover of sea ice in the Arctic is perennial.

Heavy swells, the wind and currents can break up the sea ice sheet, particularly if it is thinning as a result of melting. The breakup creates ice floes. These may mass together to form larger areas of pack ice, but close to open water, they may also be smashed by continuing wind and wave erosion, forming a mass of small ice pieces called brash ice. Sea ice can anchor itself to the shore, where it is known as fast ice. Fast ice sticks to the coast so effectively that currents or wind can fracture the ice sheet, forming a lead of open water between the fast ice and the continuous, or pack, ice offshore.

Leads can also form between areas of pack ice, their existence an annoyance to ice travelers, as they can require long detours to places where the lead is narrow enough to negotiate. Leads can be hazardous to boats and even ships, and to Arctic cetaceans. They can form relatively quickly and can close just as fast, trapping and crushing boats, or marooning whales far from open water. Whales have often been seen desperately keeping a breathing hole open in a closing lead in the hope that an escape route will open.

Less dangerous are polynyas, areas of permanently open water, or water covered with thin ice. Polynyas can recur annually; the North Water in Smith Sound at the northern end of Baffin Bay and the Great Siberian Polynya in the Laptev Sea are classic examples. Their occurrence is due to reliable currents, such as inter-island currents, or reliable weather patterns, such as offshore winds. However, some polynyas exist away from such sources and are thought to result from upwellings of warm water, though the reasons for these are not fully understood. Polynyas are important ecologically. Not only does the open water allow the penetration of light and the dissolution of atmospheric oxygen, but their salinity differs from that under local floe ice. Differences in temperature and salinity set up convection currents that take oxygen to the depths while bringing nutrients to the surface. This supports a food chain that extends from plankton to large mammals such as Walruses and Polar Bears. The importance of North Water is reflected in the fact that the seabird population nesting within flying distance of it is measured in tens of millions. The existence of leads and polynyas can be inferred by observation of a "water" sky, the dark coloration of the clouds above pack ice due to less light being reflected from the open water.

The breakup of pack ice into floes also allows the formation of pressure ridges, where one floe is forced over another by current, wind or wave. Such ridges can be 50 ft. (15 m) high and, as with leads, are a nuisance to sea ice travelers. The ridge is caused by the overriding floe, the overridden floe creating an underwater ridge that, in shallow areas, can be driven into the seabed. Such downward ridges (occasionally given the tongue-in-cheek name of "bummocks," the opposite of "hummocks") can be a hazard to drilling rigs or underwater pipes and cables. Much more hazardous is the *ivu*, a potentially lethal event in which a jumble of floes are pushed at speed onto land. Ivu can kill, but fortunately they are rare. Scientists treated the existence of ivu with skepticism until 1982, when archaeologists uncovered the remains of a family of five at Utqiagvik, near Barrow, Alaska, who had clearly been overwhelmed by one.

As well as the local movements of sea ice that create leads, there are also macro-movements. The most famous of these is the Transpolar Drift, which flows from Russia's New Siberia Islands across the Pole to Svalbard and the Denmark Strait. This current deposited the relics of the *Jeanette*, lost near Wrangel Island, on Greenland's eastern coast, and prompted Fridtjof Nansen to attempt to reach the Pole in his ship, *Fram*. *Fram* took three years to drift from near the New Siberia Islands to a point west of Spitsbergen. The rate of ice drift depends on wind speed as well as ocean current, and the time taken for *Fram*'s journey was actually shorter than the average time, which is closer to five years for ice from a comparable starting point. The drift accelerates from the North Pole toward the Fram Strait, taking around one year. Drift rates are about $1/15$ mph (0.1 km/h) averaged over the entire Arctic Basin, but are closer to $3/10$ mph (0.5k km/h) as the ice approaches the Fram Strait. Rates as high as $1\frac{1}{4}$ mph (2 km/h) have been measured under storm conditions.

▶ A lead in the ice, Bylot. Note the fast ice anchored to the shore.

If the Transpolar Drift is the most famous ice current, the most infamous is the Beaufort Gyre, centred on the Arctic Ocean north of Alaska. This clockwise-circulating mass of ice about 745 mi (1,200 km) across played havoc with the American whaling vessels that used Herschel Island as a base; it still makes journeys difficult, even for powerful ice-breakers.

Icebergs

In the Arctic icebergs are chiefly formed from land ice, calved (created) by fracturing from the fronts of glaciers that reach the sea, or tidewater glaciers. They therefore differ from the majority of Antarctic icebergs, which form when the ice sheets of glacial snouts flowing above the waters of the Southern Ocean fracture. Such fracturing creates tabular icebergs, which are often vast. There are fewer of these ice shelves in the Arctic, and those that do exist are much smaller. Arctic ice shelves may also form in a different way to those in Antarctica. While some (e.g., the Milne ice shelf off Ellesmere Island's northern coast) are created by the flow of glacial ice across the ocean, others are formed when fast ice develops over many years and eventually creates an ice shelf rather than being just a form of sea ice. The most famous of the Arctic's ice shelves, that at Ward Hunt Island off the northern coast of Ellesmere Island, was formed from such a fast-ice accumulation. Once the ice shelf has been created, the accumulation of snow on the upper surface and sea ice on the lower surface tend to thicken the shelf, while the accretion of sea ice on the ocean edge tends to elongate it. The seaward edge of the shelf may also break off; however, in these cases the calved ice is not known as a tabular iceberg, but is instead called an ice island, a specifically Arctic name. Arctic ice islands comprise both freshwater and seawater ice, whereas the tabular icebergs of Antarctica are primarily of freshwater ice.

With the exception of ice islands, Arctic icebergs are smaller than the tabular icebergs of the Antarctic, and they are often pleasingly misshapen. But though smaller, they can be big enough to be a danger to shipping, as the *Titanic* discovered. The largest recorded Arctic iceberg was 8 mi. (13 km) long and 4 mi. (6 km) wide. Icebergs more than 490 ft. (150 m) high have been recorded, but such monsters are comparatively rare. As ice is less dense than water, icebergs float, with most of their mass beneath the surface, about 85%, as a general rule. One difference between icebergs and sea ice that has been important to Arctic travelers over the centuries depends on this mass distribution. As most of the mass lies below the surface, icebergs move with ocean currents. By contrast, sea ice, having only limited subsurface mass, moves with the wind. As a consequence, icebergs will occasionally plow a route through sea ice — this has enabled ships to escape entrapment.

Eroded by sun, wind and wave action above, and by water temperature and wave action below, icebergs disintegrate over time, occasionally rolling over, which can overwhelm boats unlucky enough to be too close. Fragments of a broken iceberg have the somewhat banal name of bergy bits. Bergy bits are sometimes classified as being within the size range of $6\frac{1}{2}$–$16\frac{1}{2}$ ft. (2–5 m) across. As with broken pack ice, smaller chunks of iceberg are known as brash ice. A more expressive name, growler, is given to another class of iceberg debris, or to

ice produced directly from glacial face collapse. Growlers are flat-topped masses that float low in the water, barely showing above the water line. Sizable growlers are a problem for shipping, as they do not readily show up on radar. Smaller growlers can be a problem for boats; if unseen they can be driven over, causing damage to propellers.

Changes in the ice

Though ice is the dominant feature of the Arctic in the minds of many, there is little or no permanent ice on much of the landmass surrounding the frozen Arctic Ocean, with the notable exception of Greenland, though winter brings significant snowfall. Ice represents about 2% of the water volume on Earth (the oceans represent 93.5% of the total, and rivers and lakes about 4.5%). Of the ice, about 90% is in the Antarctic ice cap and 8% is in the Greenlandic ice cap. Other smaller ice caps on Arctic islands and the world's glaciers account for the remainder. Though the frozen Arctic Ocean might appear to contribute significantly to the overall percentage of ice, it actually represents, even at the winter maximum, only about 0.05% of the total.

It is easy to imagine that features such as the Antarctic ice sheet and the frozen Arctic Ocean have always been present. In fact, the permanent ice of the Arctic has persisted for only about two million years. Large variations over time have resulted from movements of the Earth's continents, and from periodic changes in the Earth's climate as a consequence of the cyclical nature of the planet's orbital movement. These are called Milankovich cycles, having first been identified in the early 1900s by the Serbian mathematician Milutin Milankovich. These cycles are based on a variation of incident light energy on Earth over a period of approximately 96,000 years. The obliquity of the Earth's axis of spin (the angle between the spin axis and the plane of the ecliptic) also varies, from about 22.1° to 24.5°, with a period of approximately 41,000 years. Finally, with a periodicity of about 21,000 years, Earth precesses (wobbles) around its spin axis, which also moves the poles toward and away from the sun. These cycles may account for around 60% of the observed cyclical variation in Earth's climate. The remainder is accounted for by variations in the sun's output and changes in the atmospheric concentration of various gases, notably atmospheric carbon dioxide (CO_2), water vapor and methane. The overall interaction of these disparate effects is not well understood, as the rapid change of day to night as well as seasonal effects in air and sea currents, are complex and involve significant feedbacks and amplifications. However, although small-scale interactions are poorly understood, the large-scale effects are clear; the present-day level of CO_2 in the atmosphere is low and the mean temperature of Earth is correspondingly low relative to that of the past on a geological timescale. Although present values are low, that does little to allay the fears of climatologists, since the current rate of increase is high and is a cause of major concern.

Measurement of the ratio of two isotopes of oxygen (O^{16} and O^{18}) in ice cores from the Greenlandic and Antarctic ice caps, and of the ratio of alkenones (organic compounds produced by certain marine phytoplankton) in ocean sediments, indicate that the temperature of Earth began to fall some two million years ago. Before this, the tectonic drift of Antarctica had placed the continent over the South Pole and the first Antarctic ice sheet had began to form. Ice reflects up to 90% of incident radiation, so the existence of an Antarctic ice sheet led to a cooling of Earth. By about two million years ago permanent ice had begun to form in the Arctic. Ice cores from the Greenland ice cap indicate a sustained period of cold from about 250,000 years ago, though with temperature fluctuations, culminating in a glacial maximum about 18,000 years ago. Thereafter the Earth's climate has been more or less stable, though again there have been temperature fluctuations. For example, a warmer period in early medieval times saw Norse settlement in Iceland, Greenland and, for a brief time, North America, while the "Little Ice Age" of the 17th to early 19th centuries saw the River Thames freeze in almost all winters, with the ice thick enough for Frost Fairs to be held on it, attended by thousands of Londoners.

The core sample records also show the occurrence of two events that may indicate what the future holds for northern Europe if the present increases in the Earth's temperature continue. In the western North Atlantic, evaporation of seawater at a temperature close to freezing causes an increase in surface water salinity. This cold, salt-rich water is denser than the underlying ocean and sinks to the ocean bottom, where it flows south. The current creates a counter-current of warmer water flowing north. This thermohaline circulation is the basis of the Gulf Stream. Greenland ice cores show that about 13,000 years ago the climate warmed, but then abruptly cooled again. About 11,500 years ago the climate then warmed dramatically, by as much as 45°F (7°C) in only 50 years, implying an average temperature rise across Earth of 40°F (4°C), as temperature fluctuations are more pronounced in the polar regions. This cooling and rapid warming is thought to have resulted from a switching off and on of the thermohaline circulation. If the present increase in the Earth's temperature continues, the circulation could be switched off again, with disastrous climatic effects for northern Europe.

At the last glacial maximum, ice covered about 30% of the Earth's land surface. The ice sheets of the northern hemisphere covered most of North America south to latitude 39°N, a combination of the enormous Laurentide Ice Sheet, the smaller Cordilleran sheet on the Pacific coast and the much smaller Inuitian sheet on Ellesmere and Axel Heiberg Islands. In the Palearctic, much of northern Europe was covered. However, ice coverage of the Arctic was not complete. In the Nearctic much of Alaska was not covered, while in Eurasia, though there was ice coverage in Scandinavia, on the Kola Peninsula, and across much of European Russia, the coverage in northern Asian Russia was surprisingly limited. There were ice sheets on Franz Josef Land, the northern islands of Noyava Zemlya and Severnaya Zemlya (much of which is still glaciated), but there was little ice on the mainland and Wrangel Island was ice-free.

In North America the ice sheet was up to 13,125 ft. (4,000 m) thick near Hudson Bay. So heavy was the ice that it compressed the land beneath it, creating corresponding bulges in land at the sheet's periphery. When the ice retreated, the compressed land rebounded. This process, known as isostatic uplift, has raised the land beneath Hudson Bay, to the north of James Bay, by 395 ft. (120 m) since the ice retreat. The shorelines of Hudson Bay have risen by about 260 ft. (80 m); rebound can now be measured with great accuracy using GPS technology so the continuing effect of the uplift can be confirmed. By the time the rebound finally finishes, the shape of the Bay will be very different from that of today. James Bay will cease to exist, Southampton Island will become part of the mainland and the Bay's area will have been reduced to some 35% of its present extent. In addition to the rebound seen around Hudson Bay, there has also been a lowering of the peripheral bulges by up to 45 ft. (13 m) south of the Great Lakes.

In the Old World the glacial ice sheet reached a thickness of 9,845 ft. (3,000 m) at the head of the Gulf of Bothnia, where the rebound has been approximately 330 ft. (100 m) to date, with a peripheral lowering of about 30 ft. (10 m) in northern Germany. The present isostatic depression of Greenland by the overtopping ice cap has led to the creation a saucer-shaped landmass lying beneath the ice. On its eastern edge, Greenland rises to an average of more than 6,560 ft. (2,000 m) above sea level. On the west the average rise is lower, closer to 3,280 ft. (1,000 m) above sea level. But over most of central Greenland the landmass is at or below sea level. Occasionally elevated parts of the landmass, known as *nunataks*, protrude through the overlying ice.

Iceberg off Baffin Island.

Ice sheets and glaciers

Glacial ice, which is considered to be a mineral by geologists, is an elastic material that will flow under the influence of gravity. Ice caps therefore move outward in all directions from a mass center, and glaciers formed at their edges (or from snowfields at altitude in mountain areas) flow downhill to reach the sea, or a point where ablation, chiefly melting to form a meltwater river, causes the ice to disappear.

Glaciers accumulate mass in their upper regions, where the average temperature during the year tends to be sub-zero, so that accumulated snowfall outweighs ablation due to surface melting. The reverse is true for the glacier's ablation zone, where losses exceed gains. Ablation occurs due to energy input from solar and geothermal energy and, to a lesser extent, from friction due to sliding and, in tidewater glaciers, due to the calving of icebergs. If the mass balance of a glacier is positive, i.e., accumulation exceeds ablation, the glacier grows. If the mass balance is negative, the glacier retreats.

Glacier flow seems, at first glance, a straightforward process, but this is not the case. Glaciers are defined as cold- or warm-based. In simple terms a warm-based glacier is one not frozen to the bedrock beneath it, either as a result of geothermal heat or because the melt temperature of the basal ice is lower than the bedrock temperature. Because of the pressure of overlying ice on the basal layer, the melt temperature of the basal layer ice can be lowered (to about 14°F/-10°C at the base of 3,280 ft./1,000 m of ice). If the bedrock temperature is higher than this, the ice will melt and the glacier will slide, the meltwater acting as a lubricant. However, most Arctic glaciers are cold-based, as the bedrock temperature is below the basal ice layer melt temperature. The glacier is then frozen to the bedrock and basal sliding cannot occur. In this case, the glacier advances by ice creep, a deformation process unlike liquid flow, as it involves the elongation and displacement of individual ice crystals. Under certain circumstances, the bedrock may itself deform, contributing to glacial flow. At changes of slope beneath a moving glacier, the process of ice creep, which also occurs in the body ice of warm-based glaciers, cannot cause a quick enough adjustment to maintain the ice body, and faults develop in the ice, with ice masses moving relative to each other. Where faults reach the surface they form a series of parallel crevasses. Glaciers are essentially of two forms, valley or alpine and piedmont. Valley glaciers are confined within the valley they have carved, a tongue of ice culminating in a convex snout that is the precursor of a river. If the glacier reaches the sea, it becomes a tidewater glacier. Tidewater glaciers occasionally cut their valley floors below sea level. If that occurs the sea may flood the valley when the ice retreats. This is the origin of the fjords, some of which in the high Arctic retain their glaciers, though the famous fjords of Norway are now glacier-free. Cirque glaciers and hanging glaciers are specific forms of valley glaciers.

A piedmont (literally "mountain foot") glacier is one in which the ice has reached a plain at the base of the mountains that gave birth to it. On the plain, having escaped from the confines of its valley walls, the ice spreads to form a characteristic lobe. Piedmont glaciers are rare, with the global glacial retreat currently underway making them even rarer.

Glacial landforms

The continuous movement of a glacier is reflected in the geography of the country around it. The short-term and therefore most obvious effect is the collapse of the glacier front, which, though it can occur in land-based glaciers, is much more likely in tidewater glaciers. The ablation zone of land-based glaciers usually means that they end "quietly" with an outflowing river. By contrast, the ablation zone of a tidewater glacier may not have been reached before it encounters the sea, so the glacial front can be many feet high. Advancing because of the pressure of upstream ice, and undermined by the action of tides and waves, the glacier front routinely collapses, occasionally calving icebergs.

Glaciers have enormous power to alter the landscape over which they travel; glacial movement is both relentless and highly abrasive. The transformation of the terrain local to a glacier is by direct erosion and deposition by the glacier or outflowing water (glaciofluvial effects). Glaciers pluck boulders from their bedrock, entraining them in the ice to add to the erosional power of the ice itself. Glaciers are responsible for the carving of U-shaped valleys, and for the alpine scenery of arêtes and cirques, also known as corries, combes or cwms.

A glacier will often leave traces of its passing when it retreats. These traces include smoothed bedrock and bedrock striations caused by the "glass-paper" effect of ice with embedded rock fragments grinding across the bedrock surface, and roche moutonnée, isolated, asymmetric rock masses, with their upstream side shallow-angled and abraded smooth, their downstream side high-angled and roughed by ice-planing and frost erosion. The name, "rock sheep" in French, is usually said to derive from the sheeplike appearance of such rocks studding alpine meadows, but is more likely to be from the sheepskin wigs of the French court, which looked rather like these glacial boulders. Retreating glaciers also leave behind erratics, boulders of a specific rock type carried by the ice then dumped, stranded in an area of dissimilar rock.

Glacial erosion also creates moraine, the debris of rocks abraded by the ice. This debris accumulates within and at the edges of the glacier. At the edges it forms narrow dirty lines of lateral moraine. Occasionally such dirty lines are seen on the glacier away from its edges. This medial moraine is usually formed from two lines of lateral moraine where two glaciers have met, but may be from entrained debris reaching the surface. Terminal moraine is deposited at the glacial front. Behind this layer is often an area of hummocky moraine where rock debris covers mounds of unmelted ice.

Glacial debris is known generically as till. Retreating glaciers can leave behind drumlins, mounds of till fashioned into a distinctive shape, with a high-angled blunt end on the upstream side and a long, shallow, tapering end on the downstream side. Drumlins are normally found in groups known as swarms, which form a distinctive "basket of eggs" topography.

The most conspicuous glaciofluvial landform is the outwash fan, a lobe of till formed where numerous meltwater streams flow over a plain. Individual streams that flowed beneath the ice can form eskers, long sinuous ridges of debris exposed by the retreating ice. Streams on top of a glacier near its snout can create kames, mounds of debris. Kames are often steep cones, though at the edges of the glacier the streams can form extended kame terraces. Kettle holes can also form where large chunks of ice embedded in the till melt. Kettle lakes are water-filled kettle holes.

One glacial landform, still not completely understood, is the rock glacier. In cold, relatively dry, high-relief landscapes in which there is a good supply of talus (weathered rock fragments, often called scree), the talus may flow downhill, though the speed of movement is much slower than that of an ice glacier; speeds of only up to 3 ft. (1 m) per annum have been recorded. Most rock glaciers are small, less than 2,625 ft. (800 m) long and 328 ft. (100 m) wide, but one example in western Greenland is 3½ mi. (5.5 km) long, the longest rock glacier ever recorded. The exact structure and creep method of rock glaciers is not understood, but they are believed to consist of an upper layer of larger scree covering a layer of frozen rock that sits on a layer of smaller scree, which acts in a similar way to a layer of ball bearings.

Periglacial landforms

The term *periglacial* applies to cold but non-glacial landscapes. In general, periglacial landscapes occur near the margins of the ice sheets of the last Ice Age, where the intense cold of that period penetrated deep into the ground. This cold penetration often results in the development of permafrost, one of the major features of periglacial areas. Although popularly assumed to be ice-based, permafrost is actually frozen ground, and is defined as rock and soil in which temperatures do not rise above 32°F (0°C) during two consecutive summers.

Ironically, the ice that led to the development of permafrost also acted as an insulator, insulating the ground from the extreme cold of Ice Age winters. As an example, the permafrost layer beneath most glaciers in the high Arctic is considerably thinner than that below areas of Alaska and Siberia that are not glaciated. Despite the intuitive assumption that permafrost is a polar phenomenon, it is found well below the present timberline, for instance surprisingly far south in China and over a vast area of Asian Russia. Permafrost in these areas arises from their continental climates; in Europe at similar latitudes the influence of the Gulf Stream prevents permafrost creation, so Europeans only became aware of its existence when polar explorers attempted to bury their dead and encountered the unyielding, frozen ground beneath the shallow, seasonally thawed active layer.

In principle, permafrost requires groundwater in whatever form, in rock crevices, soil cavities or as lenses of water, to be frozen. In practice, the leaching of salts can increase the salinity of pockets of water, which can therefore remain liquid, even if the ground temperature remains permanently below 32°F (0°C). If the annual air temperature of a locality is below about 21°F (-6°C) then continuous permafrost will occur. At temperatures between 21°F (-6°C) and 30°F (-1°C) the permafrost is discontinuous, with fragmented frozen areas. The depth of permafrost depends upon the geothermal heat flow into the frozen ground and the net energy balance at the surface. In parts of Siberia, northern Alaska and Arctic Canada, the permafrost layer is 4,920 ft. (1,500 m) thick. Such depths are believed to be a relic of eras of extreme cold during the Earth's recent geological history rather than having been created by the present climate. In general, seasonal variations in the temperature of the permafrost do not occur at depths below about 65 ft. (20 m). One interesting aspect of the distribution of permafrost in North America is that it is much more northerly to the east of Hudson Bay than to the west. Westerly winds in northern Canada blow across Hudson Bay. As the Bay remains ice-free during the early winter, these winds pick up moisture, which is deposited as snow in northern Quebec and Labrador. Snowfall there is much higher than to the west of Hudson Bay, and the layer of snow acts as an insulating blanket over the ground, preventing cold penetration.

In summer the surface layer of permafrost thaws, creating an active layer, the depth of which depends on the local energy balance and may be as little as under an inch (a few millimetres) or as much as 10 ft. (3 m). Because the permafrost inhibits drainage, sections of the active layer may become saturated. These areas, called taliks, can remain in winter if downward freezing from the surface does not reach the permafrost layer. For the Arctic traveler, taliks can cause serious inconvenience. In summer they can form a gluey porridge that rapidly accumulates in the tread of boots, while in winter they represent hidden pockets, which, if they exist beneath a thin surface-ice crust, can pour over the top of the boot of anyone unlucky enough to break through the crust.

Cold also sculpts the landscape directly by the process of nivation, the frost erosion of rock that, over time, causes it to break down. As ice is less dense than water, water expands on freezing, levering chunks of rock from cliffs or bedrock. This is the same process that causes household pipes to fracture. The damage is done when the water freezes, but does not become apparent until a thaw sets in. Frost erosion occurs in both glacial and periglacial landscapes. In periglacial areas it is responsible for such distinctive features as scree slopes, created by the frost erosion of cliffs, the rock debris littering the slope below the cliff. If there is a snowfield on the slope, rocks can slide down it, piling up at the base. If the snowfield then disappears, the rocks form a distinctive rampart beneath the cliff from which they have been prised.

▶ Polygonal structures in frozen ground, Nunavut, Canada.

▲ A pingo, a characteristic feature of tundra, Ellesmere Island.

Frost action is also responsible for the creation of more exotic periglacial landforms. Frost wedging is the creation of V-shaped wedges of ice in frozen ground. In areas of frozen terrain, if the winter temperature falls significantly, the ground can contract, causing cracks to appear that form an irregular polygonal surface pattern. In summer, water seepage into the cracks causes an ice wedge to form, which then grows as each annual thaw-freeze cycle allows further seepage and a layering of the ice. Each winter's freeze causes an expansion of the ice, which pushes the rim of the wedge upward so that raised polygons are formed; this is the source of the patterned ground. One version of patterned ground that intrigued early Arctic travelers, because it appeared to be human in origin, was the sorting of material by size in the polygons. This natural process is now well understood; it relies not on human hand, but on the difference in thermal inertia of stones and finer material. Stones cool quicker than finer material, and so stick faster to overlying frozen material, pulled upward as the frozen material expands (frost pull). The underlying material also expands upward as it freezes (frost push). The effect is to bring stones to the surface. The stones form circles or polygons, but they may also form stripes on sloping ground, where the polygons extend downhill. In all cases, the stone lines are narrower than the intervening areas of finer material. One form of patterned ground that can be useful to nesting birds (though a nuisance to the traveler) is the hummock field, an array of roughly hemispherical mounds spread out across the landscape. Hummocks are of great interest to botanists because the hummock's surface usually supports a range of plants. Exactly how hummocks are created is not well understood, but it is assumed that they form in a similar fashion to other forms of patterned ground.

Pingos are another landform of the periglacial zone. The name means "conical hill" in the language of the Mackenzie Delta Inuit. It is estimated that about 25% of all the world's pingos are on the Tuktoyaktuk Peninsula to the northeast of the Mackenzie Delta. The Russian word for the form is *bulgunnyakh*, a Yakut term. Pingos are mounds of ice covered with a layer of sediment, usually circular and occasionally of extraordinary size, up to 245 ft. (75 m) high and more than 1,690 ft. (500 m) in diameter. There are made in one of two

ways. "Closed system" pingos form beneath a surface lake. As the lake acts as an insulator, the ground below does not freeze; this unfrozen ground in an area of permafrost is called talik. If the lake now drains, the talik volume freezes and the ice expands into the characteristic mound. Because they form from talik, pingos have a sediment cap that can produce an active layer capable of supporting considerable growth. In land beyond the timberline, pingos occasionally have trees growing on their southern slope, the effects of good drainage and shelter allowing growth that would be impossible on the flat ground nearby. "Open system" pingos are produced by artesian water feeding an expanding ice dome, and are usually found in discontinuous permafrost where groundwater movement is feasible. The time needed to create a large pingo is not known, but it may be many hundreds or even thousands of years. Pingos may also disappear, though again this process appears to occur on a long time scale. Exposure of a pingo's ice core can cause melting, and the tops of some pingos have collapsed to create volcaniclike craters. If the crater holds a pond, this may insulate the ice core, slowing further melting and extending the pingo's life.

As permafrost can form beneath the sea, or form and then be covered by the sea, pingos can also form underwater. This would be of concern if the opening of the Northwest or Northeast Passages allowed deep-draught vessels such as oil tankers to use routes currently off limits due to sea ice. Such vessels could collide with these submarine pingos. Submarine permafrost will also make any attempt at drilling very difficult in such areas.

Similar in appearance to pingos, though usually very much smaller, are palsas, mounds of frozen peat, occasionally with layers of pure ice as well. Found in areas of discontinuous permafrost, palsas can occasionally reach 20–26 ft. (6–8 m) in height in southerly regions of the Arctic, though they rarely attain heights above 3¼ ft. (1 m) in the high Arctic. In the high Arctic the peat forming the palsa may be 5,000 or 10,000 years old.

Two other periglacial landforms are worth noting. Thermokarst is the periglacial equivalent of a karst landscape, except that water is lost by melting rather than by the dissolving of bedrock and subsequent subsurface flow. Thermokarst landscapes are produced where drainage is poor because of the permafrost layer beneath essentially flat country. Surface-layer melting can then cause pools of water, which may coalesce to form thaw lakes. If the ground slopes gently, beaded drainage may occur, a linear series of lakes linked by small streams.

The final periglacial landform considered here is the gradual downhill drift of soil. This can occur as a consequence of frost heaving on sloping ground, when the stones brought to the surface are moved downhill by each freeze-thaw cycle in a process often called frost creep. Soil drift also results from gelifluction, the periglacial equivalent of solifluction, the downhill slumping of saturated material. When the active layer of the permafrost freezes, it expands perpendicular to the frozen underlayer, even if the ground is sloping. However, when the active layer thaws, it moves with gravity, i.e., downhill, rather than back toward the underlayer. Successive freeze-thaw episodes then cause distinctive gelifluction lobes to form.

The Arctic climate

The Arctic is cold. As a statement of fact this is both incontrovertible and a defining quality of the area in the popular imagination. Yet the answer to the question of why it is cold is much less obvious than might be imagined. During the Arctic summer, the sun is visible continuously; should that not compensate for the long period of winter darkness? Because of the low angle of the sun, the poles actually receive a yearly average of only 60% of the insolation (incident solar radiation) of a point on the equator. To this reduction must be added the effect of albedo, the reflection of the incident radiation by the Earth's surface or by cloud cover. Clouds can reflect as much as 80% of incident radiation. Darker surfaces absorb more of the incident radiation, as much as 90% for dark soils. By contrast, the Greenland ice cap and continuous sea ice reflect around 80% of the incident radiation. The albedo of pack ice, with its mix of ice and dark ocean, is 20%–40%.

The Earth's atmosphere also has an effect on insolation. Carbon dioxide and water vapor absorb some of the incident radiation, while air molecules and dust particles scatter a further fraction. Radiation that reaches the Earth's surface is absorbed and partially reradiated, but at longer wavelengths than the incident radiation. This emitted, long-wavelength radiation is more easily absorbed by the gases and water vapor in the atmosphere, warming it. But the atmosphere above the Arctic is famously clear, which allows details of features to be observed at much greater distances than is possible at lower latitudes. Cold air holds up to 10 times less water vapor than warm air, so much of the re-radiated energy from the Earth's surface is lost. In lower latitudes, the surface layer of air is also warmed by conduction, giving rise to convection currents that transfer heat vertically, producing thermals. As the surface of the Arctic is cold, this warming effect is also reduced. Overall, the Arctic suffers a net loss of radiation in all but the summer months. In the absence of any method of transferring heat to the region, the Arctic would become increasingly cold. In practice, heat is transferred to maintain the present balance. The transfer is through a combination of three methods: latent heat, air currents and ocean currents. Latent heat is gained each time water vapor is converted to snow. Movements of air and water currents create the weather patterns of the Arctic. They also tend to redistribute some of the extra solar energy reaching the tropics to the polar regions. But this does not compensate for the reduced energy input, so the Arctic remains cold.

Temperature

Temperatures in the Arctic are not as low as those of the Antarctic because of the moderating effect of the oceans. At Russia's Vostok research station in Antarctica, a temperature of -126°F (-88°C) has been recorded, making it the coldest place on Earth. In the Arctic the lowest temperatures are recorded at points away from the sea; at the North Ice station in Greenland (-8°F/-66.1°C) and at Oymyakon in the Verkhoyanskiy region of northeast Siberia (-108°F/-77.8°C).

Oymyakon lies south of the Arctic boundary as defined in this book. Its extreme temperature is due to its continental climate and the effect of temperature inversion; the temperature increases with height above the ground, over a limited height range, so a layer of cold air is trapped below a layer of warmer air. This is relatively common above ice and snow. Temperature inversions are more intense and longer-lived where cold, dense air is trapped in valleys. Where these are remote from the influence of the sea, such as in northeast Siberia, they create dramatic drops in temperature, perhaps by as much as 86°F (30°C).

One effect of temperature inversions with which regular Arctic travelers become familiar is ice fog, produced when water vapor, which may hail from vehicles or industrial processes, is added to air at a very low temperatures (below -22°F/-30°C) that is already saturated. The extra water vapor condenses to form the ice fog. Such fogs are not unknown in valleys with temperature inversions, but as they require a water vapor source, they are much more frequent in areas of settled population around northern towns. Fairbanks, Alaska, is an oft-cited source of such fogs, in which visibility is reduced to 10 ft. (3 m). The fog layer itself is often no more than 30–50 ft. (10–15 m) thick. The effect of the sea, and specifically the Gulf Stream, on northern temperatures can be seen by comparing Oymyakon and the Norwegian coast at the same latitude. In January the difference in mean temperature is around 120°F (50°C), about the same as the difference between the North Pole and the equator. The difference in mean temperature between inland and coastal Greenland, though less dramatic, is also, at about 86°F (30°C), very pronounced. Although the Gulf Stream is the most marked maritime effect, others are also at work. Northern Canada is cooled by air flowing south from the frozen Arctic Ocean and so experiences very low winter temperatures, while a warm current along the eastern edge of the Bering Sea keeps the Alaskan side warmer than the Russian side at the same latitude.

It is difficult to generalize about the variation of temperature through the Arctic year because so much depends on location. At a maritime location such as the island of Jan Mayen, which lies 373 mi. (600 km) north of Iceland, temperature varies from a January average of 23°F (-5°C) to a July average of 41°F (5°C). The variation at the North Pole for the same months is -26°F (-32°C) to 23°F (-0.5°C), and for the Arctic as a whole is -22°F (-30°C) to 48°F (9°C). These seasonal extremes are not matched by a daily differences. Because of the continuous daylight of the Arctic summer and the long sunless winter, the daily change in temperature is much less pronounced than it is for southern latitudes, with differences of only 37°F–41°F (3°C–5°C) usually being registered.

Precipitation

The central Arctic Basin is an arid area, with precipitation comparable to Antarctica, which is often referred to as a polar desert. Reduced solar energy at the North and South Poles compared to the equator causes hot air to rise at the Equator while cold air sinks at the poles; this sinking air inhibits precipitation. The northern Canadian Arctic archipelago and adjacent Arctic Ocean receive less than 4 in. (100 mm) of precipitation annually. The rest of the central Arctic receives double this amount, as does much of Siberia and the mainland Canadian Arctic. Precipitation is higher in eastern Canada and much higher, up to 47 in. (1,200 mm), at the southern tip of Greenland. Northern Greenland and eastern Siberia receive 8–12 in. (200–300 mm), though precipitation on the Pacific coast of eastern Siberia is higher at 19–23 in. (500–600 mm) and on Kamchatka it is as high as 35–39 in. (900–1000 mm). Svalbard and coastal western Siberia receive 12–16 in. (300–400 mm). Unsurprisingly, precipitation correlates with the proximity of the sea and the prevailing wind direction.

Though location in relation to the sea creates local distortions, the general rule is that precipitation decreases as one moves north. Precipitation is lowest in spring, with less than 2 in. (50 mm) over 70% of the Arctic. The frozen sea limits the take-up of moisture, but otherwise the seasonal variation of precipitation is muted. One effect of Arctic precipitation is snowfall, and it is instructive to look at the persistence of snow cover across the area. This peaks close to the North Pole, where snow cover is seen for about 350 days annually. Heading south this persistence inevitably falls. In Severnaya Zemlya it averages around 300 days, with about 240 days on the other islands of Russia's western Arctic and 250 days in Svalbard. The northern coast of Russia sees 260 days of snow cover. In the New World the northern areas of Canada's Arctic islands see 300 days, while Alaska's northern coast and the southern Canadian Arctic archipelago see 260 days.

Wind

The cold dense air of the Arctic draws warm air northward, the effect of the Earth's rotation creating an anti-clockwise vortex over the North Pole. In an ideal Earth, the westerly winds would flow evenly, but the existence of discontinuities between land and ocean and the landform patterns of the continents impose a local structure on the winds. Because of the effects of this local topography and of macro-climatic conditions, it is difficult to be specific about winds at particular Arctic locations. Some general comments are, however, possible. The Arctic wind pattern does not show a pronounced seasonal variation. Winds tend to blow from the central Arctic toward Arctic Canada, sweeping eastward across Hudson Bay; in winter they move toward the Atlantic. Winds are funnelled through the Denmark Strait, though in summer the wind heads toward the North Pole from northern Greenland. The prevailing wind is also northward from the Russian Arctic. The Barents and Norwegian Seas are infamous for the winter "polar easterlies" that sweep across them. The windiest part of the Arctic is the North Atlantic area.

In general, the areas with the lowest winter wind speeds are those with high atmospheric pressure and high anticyclonic activity — the central Arctic, and northern and western Canada. There the mean wind speed is 13–20 ft./s or 9–14 mph (4–6 m/s or 14–22 km/h). Areas of low atmospheric pressure and high cyclonic intensity, which include the North Atlantic Arctic, Baffin Bay and eastern Canada, and the Pacific Arctic, have a higher mean speed of 20–32 ft./s or 14–23 mph (6–10 m/s or 22–36 km/h). In the central Arctic, wind speeds above 82 ft. /s or 56 mph (25 m/s or 90 km/h) are rare: for comparison, speeds of up to 164 ft./s or 112 mph (50 m/s or 180 km/h) have been measured in the North Atlantic Arctic.

One type of wind that is restricted to the polar regions is the katabatic. The name of this wind derives from the Greek for "going downhill." Katabatic winds develop where cold, dense air drops off the Antarctic plateau or the Greenland ice cap and accelerates under gravity. Antarctic katabatics can reach phenomenal velocities of more than 186 mph (300 km/h) and are the more famous, but Nansen's team used them to sail their sledges down the western edge of the Greenland ice cap during the first traverse. Elsewhere the temperature inversions of the Arctic tend to reduce wind speed, insulating surface air from faster moving air at a higher level.

Wind speed causes windchill, the name given to the enhanced cooling of exposed flesh as a result of the speed of the wind. In still air, hot objects lose heat primarily by conduction. In moving air, convective losses dominate. In the same way, warm-blooded creatures lose heat more rapidly if skin is exposed to the wind. One way of considering this extra cooling is to evaluate the still-air temperature that produces equal cooling by chiefly conductive losses. This much lower temperature is the one often quoted in winter weather forecasts. The original equivalent temperatures were derived in Antarctica by observing the freezing rate of water. These rates were then converted into an empirical formula. More recent work has been less empirical, though most windchill tables are still based on the earlier work. The tables can be misleading, as they require the observer to be able to judge either temperature differences or wind speeds with some accuracy, not always a straightforward proposition in Arctic conditions. They do, however, draw attention to the need to cover flesh in the Arctic (if such advice was not obvious!). As wet flesh loses heat even faster than dry flesh, the lesson for Arctic survival is to keep dry and stay out of the wind, or to wear effective windproof clothes.

One further effect of wind is the creation of blizzard conditions. In general, blizzards are a combination of wind and falling snow, but that need not be so. In wind speeds above about 33 ft./s (10 m/s), lying snow will be picked up and sent scudding across the landscape, so long as it is not compacted. As wind speed rises, the height to which the snow is driven increases; above about 50 ft./s (15 m/s) the snow layer created is often dense enough to reduce visibility effectively to zero and prevent the traveler from moving.

Solar phenomena

To people living below the Arctic Circle, the sun rises in the east and sets in the west. This familiar pattern does not apply to the Arctic and can be a disorientating surprise to visitors. At the North Pole on Midsummer's Day, the sun circles the sky at an angle of 23.5°. At the Circle on that day, the sun is higher in the southern sky at noon and touches the northern horizon at midnight. Farther south, the familiar easterly rising, westerly setting becomes apparent, though the closer to the Circle the observer is, the more northeast and northwest are the risings and settings. At the Circle itself, the rising sun a day or two after Midsummer's Day still appears almost due north, as does the setting sun. As the midday sun is southerly, the effect is of a sun that goes across the sky rather than around it.

The Arctic night

Though all places above the Arctic Circle do not see the sun rise for a period varying from one day at the Circle to half the year at the Pole, there are extended periods of twilight. There are three types of twilight. Civil twilight is when the sun is less than 6° below the horizon, during which most operations requiring daylight can still be carried out. Nautical twilight occurs when the sun lies between 6° and 12° below the horizon; this is so-called because the brighter stars are then visible, allowing celestial navigation. The third category is astronomical twilight, when the sun is 12°–18° below the horizon. At this time the fainter stars become visible. When the sun is more than 18° below the horizon there is "total" darkness. With the sun continuously above the horizon, one might wonder whether a 24-hour period can be divided into "day" and "night." In practice the answer is yes, as only at the Pole (and then only for a relatively short time) is the sun at a constant elevation in the sky. Over much of the Arctic, and throughout the area in which wildlife is normally found, the sun's passage across the sky includes a dip toward and a rise away from Earth. The temperature therefore varies in a similar way to that of day–night in the temperate zone, though with a less well-defined range, and many Arctic animals maintain a discernible day–night activity pattern.

Though it is rarely mentioned in descriptions of the Midnight Sun and the long Arctic night, the moon is also worth considering. Because the moon's orbit around the Earth is about 5° from the plane of the ecliptic at places to the north of 72°N, there are periods each month when the moon does not set and other periods when it does not rise. During the winter it is the full moon, and periods close to the full moon when the moon does not set that counteract the otherwise bleak winter darkness. In summer it is the new moon, and periods close to the new moon, when the moon does not set. As these periods of minimal moonlight coincide with the time of continuous sun, the moon is rarely seen during the Arctic summer.

The aurora borealis

Earth has its own magnetic field. As with all such fields there are north and south magnetic poles, these aligned with the geographical poles as might be expected because of the Earth's rotation. There is not, however, perfect alignment; the Earth's north magnetic pole, to which compasses point, wanders around the Canadian Arctic. At the time it was first reached in 1831, the pole was on the western coast of the Boothia Peninsula. Since that time it has been migrating northward across Bathurst and Ellef Ringnes Islands into the Arctic Ocean northwest of Axel Heiberg Island.

Earth's magnetic field is responsible, in part, for the aurora borealis or northern lights, the most spectacular of all Arctic phenomena, intimately linked with the myths of Arctic dwellers. Early scientific theories of the aurora concentrated on the burning of gases. Not until the work of the Norwegian scientist Kristian Birkeland did it become apparent that the phenomenon was linked with electricity and magnetism. Even today, though the basic science behind auroras is now well understood, many aspects of them remain perplexing.

The aurora results from the interaction of the solar wind, charged atomic and subatomic particles emanating from the sun, with oxygen and nitrogen atoms in the Earth's upper atmosphere. The interaction results from the trapping of the particles by the Earth's magnetic field. In general the aurora is green, deriving from excitation of oxygen atoms. Oxygen can also emit red light, but this is rarer. Excited nitrogen emits a pale blue or violet light, which is usually overwhelmed by the green from oxygen. However, nitrogen also emits red light, mostly at low altitudes, so that green auroras sometimes have a red basal fringe.

Although auroras occasionally appear to touch Earth, the lower edge is rarely less than 37–50 mi. (60–80 km) from the surface. At lower altitudes the density of the air is such that oxygen atoms have no time to emit light before they collide with other atoms. At this level, the fast-emitting nitrogen red light can be seen. Auroras extend to about 250 mi. (400 km) above the Earth's surface. The conditions for auroras are present at all times, but the solar wind is not constant so displays are sometimes too faint to observe. Aurora visibility is also affected by the weather as well as by background lighting. Auroras primarily occur in a flattened oval belt. This is caused by distortion of the Earth's magnetic field; the flattened oval is fixed relative to the sun, while the earth rotates below it, with the bulge of the oval away from the sun. The aurora oval has a "diameter" of about 3,728 mi. (6,000 km) centered on the north magnetic pole and lying at about 60–65° north. At latitudes above and below this oval, the aurora is less likely to be observed. An equivalent auroral oval exists in the southern hemisphere, centered on the south magnetic pole. As expected, auroras occur symmetrically in the Arctic and Antarctic as the solar wind is equivalent at all points of the Earth's magnetosphere.

The particle flux of the solar wind varies with the 11-year sunspot cycle. At the peak of solar activity auroras are more intense and may then be visible a long way south: in Japan, the Caribbean and even North Africa and Indonesia. A good aurora is usually followed by a good one the next night, as the solar wind rises and falls in intensity rather than being switched on and off.

Although auroras are now reasonably well understood, aspects of them continue to intrigue scientists. Native peoples claimed to be able to hear the lights occasionally, a claim echoed by some European explorers and present-day Arctic travelers and inhabitants. Some scientists dismiss the idea as fanciful, but others wonder if it is due to ionization of the air close to the observer, to piezoelectricity in rocks or even that the observer somehow produces the sound. This latter need not be a metaphysical effect, but might be due to some unknown mechanism within the ear, or because of the leakage of electrical impulses from nerves within the eye. Normally the observer is in the wilderness, with the aurora observed in conditions of extreme quiet. In such conditions, electrical leakages might be picked up as sound in the brain. In support of this, many observers who claim to have heard the aurora notice that the noise stops if they cover their eyes.

Equally poorly understood is a phenomenon first described, but dismissed, in the early 20th century. At that time Australian scientists in Antarctica gathered evidence of what appeared to be an aurora crossing the oval. The center of the oval, known as the polar cap, should be light-free, but the observations suggested otherwise. Not until the early 1980s were these observations taken seriously when satellite photographs clearly showed a thin, linear aurora crossing the polar cap, linking with the oval on both sides. Later satellite photographs showed that this cap aurora was aligned with the sun, apparently sweeping across the sky as Earth rotated below it. The exact production method of this cap aurora is still debated. Also perplexing are the gaps that occasionally occur in the oval. Some gaps suggest that the oval is not complete, others that the oval has a curious notch in its otherwise smooth outline. These gaps are assumed to occur because of discontinuities in the magnetosphere, but what these are, and what mechanisms drive them, is not understood.

Parhelia

Parhelia is the general term given to the range of solar and lunar halos, arcs and sun dogs. These surround the sun, the effects created by light refraction in ice crystals suspended in the troposphere. At that height these crystals tend to be either hexagonal flat plates or hexagonal columns. The preferred angle of deflection for the sun's rays is about 22°, which occurs when the refraction angle of the light is the same at the entry to and exit from a hexagonal crystal, with the light path within the crystal parallel to the intervening crystal face. The most frequently seen parhelia phenomenon is therefore a 22° halo surrounding the sun. The actual minimum deflection angle is 21.7° for red light, so the inner edge of the halo often appears red, with the remaining spectral colors becoming fainter or being absent as the halo fades away.

One of the most famous examples of parhelia is that sketched by William Parry in 1819–19 at the Melville Island winter quarters of the *Hecla* and *Griper* during Parry's first voyage in search of the Northwest Passage. Some of Parry's parhelia were prismatic, with the rainbow of colors adding to the beauty and wonderment of the sighting. Parry's drawings included many of the parhelia phenomena, though some other, rarer forms of parhelia have been described subsequently.

As parhelia are produced by the interaction of light with ice crystals, they can occur at night as well as during the day. Full moons are best as they provide more light, a full moon behind thin cirrus cloud often producing a 22° halo. Moon dogs may also be seen. However, as moonlight is so faint, relative to sunlight, these more exotic halos are much rarer, although many have been observed.

Mirages

Mirages are created when the temperature of the air changes rapidly with distance from the Earth's surface. The temperature change can be a fall from a hot surface temperature, which is the cause of desert mirages, and also the frequently observed "water pools" observed by drivers above a hot road surface. Such mirages are called "inferior mirages" and are rarely encountered in the Arctic. If the temperature change is an increase from a cold surface, then the mirage is said to be a "superior mirage," though the name *fata morgana* is often given to such events. Mirages are caused by the distortions in the path of light from distant objects to the observer as a result of the light traveling through layers of air at different temperatures and, therefore, densities. Effectively the light is bent into a curved path, but the observer assumes it follows a straight line as is usually the case, and so is fooled into seeing distorted images of objects. Fata morgana mirages are relatively common in the Arctic where ice sheets and the cold sea set up the right conditions. Because in superior mirages the light follows a convex path, the observer sees a much taller object than is actually present. This explains the range of mountains that was seen by, and which stopped, John Ross during his first attempt to discover the Northwest Passage, and the non-existent lands such as Crocker Land famously "discovered" by Robert Peary. The shimmering quality of most mirages results from turbulence in the atmosphere.

Ice blink, water sky and whiteout

Ice blink is the name given to the very bright sections of clouds resulting from sunlight being reflected from sea ice or an ice sheet. The most spectacular blinks are when the ice is below the level of the horizon, the ice blink then being set just above the horizon. Ice blink can add an awesome element to sunsets viewed from eastern Greenland, when out-of-sight, sunlit sections of the inland ice act as a mirror of the out-of-sight setting sun.

Water skies are the opposite of ice blink, and occur when dark patches of open water cause dark streaks on the clouds. Early polar explorers, who spent relatively long periods exploring the pack ice because their sailing ships were slow and vulnerable, became experts at reading the base of the clouds, looking for the dark lines in the silver glare that indicated worthwhile leads.

One further effect that may affect Arctic travelers, though it is less an atmospheric effect than a climatic one, is the "whiteout," a condition usually assumed to occur in blizzard conditions but which may actually occur in more benign conditions. If the traveler is walking on snow beneath a heavy cloud that diffuses the sunlight, a whiteout may occur. If it is snowing and the wind is light, that enhances the effect. In a whiteout, orientation becomes difficult, one reason why the wind must be light; strong winds themselves aid orientation even if they create additional, unrelated hazards. Distance measurement becomes almost impossible in a whiteout, and such is the loss of orientation that nausea may result, as even "up" and "down" become difficult to register. In such events it is best to stop and wait, as the odds of walking over a cliff become frighteningly and dramatically shortened.

Humans in the Arctic

Peple have lived in the Arctic for thousands of years, for almost all of that time relying on a hunting lifestyle. European exploration began in the 15th century, driven by a search for a shortcut to the Orient. Following the explorers came settlers, who set about exploiting the Arctic and its wildlife.

History of the Arctic peoples

The earliest occupation of the Arctic mainland of Eurasia by paleolithic peoples had taken place by about 50,000 years BCE, but these people were subsequently forced south by the ice sheets. Occupation was, of course, impossible during the last glacial maximum, but by around 12,000 years BCE there is evidence of human habitation due south of the New Siberia Islands at 71°N. At around the same time people crossed the Bering land bridge from Asia to North America (though there is a growing band of skeptics that think the invasion of the Americas took place long before this). Asian settlers were the ancestors of the Sámi and northern Russian native peoples. In North America they were the ancestors of the Inuit and other northern native groups. In general the names given to these native peoples by explorers (e.g., Lapps and Eskimos) have been supplanted by names preferred by the peoples themselves. These names commonly derive from earlier times when the settlers were out of contact with southern dwellers. Sámi means "ourselves" or "the people," Inuit also meaning "the people." Inuit is a plural term; an individual is an Inuk. Sámi is both singular and plural. To the east of the Sámi of Fennoscandia are the Nenets, the most numerous native peoples of northern Russia, occupying the coast all the way to the Yenisey and including the southern half of Novaya Zemlya. East of them are the Nganasan, the most northerly of all Russia's indigenous peoples, whose range extended onto the Taimyr Peninsula. East again are the Yakut and Evenki, though among those major groups are smaller groups such as the Dolgan and Yukagir. Finally, in northeastern Siberia are the Chukchis, to the south of whom the Koryak and Eveni inhabit northern Kamchatka, while the Itelmen occupy the south of the peninsula. In Eurasia the Reindeer was domesticated only in the 16th century, though it had been used as a beast of burden for centuries. People on the Pacific coast of Chukotka and of North America hunted sea mammals.

In North America several stages in the evolution of Inuit culture have been identified; Independence, then Dorset, then the Thule people, who are the direct ancestors of modern Inuit. These earliest dwellers of the North American Arctic hunted sea mammals from kayaks, using harpoons. On land they used sleds drawn by dogs to hunt Polar Bears and other animals with bows and arrows. Although settlements arose on the rich hunting grounds of the Pacific rim, the people of the high North American Arctic were nomadic, occasionally using the umiak or women's boat to move whole families between hunting grounds. The development of polytheistic religions in the region may have been a response to the inherently unstable nature of the environment. These religions invested godlike qualities to natural forces over which people had no control and whose appearance (bad weather) or absence (prey animals) had a dramatic influence on their lives. From these beliefs a mythology of the creation of the world and a person's place in it arose, a religion known by the collective term shamanism. The word derives form the word *saman* "wise one," in the Tungusic language of the peoples of eastern Siberia. The shaman was the "priest" who, while in a trancelike state, was able to travel to the abode of the gods to influence them for the good of his people. In Sámi the priest was the *noaidi*; in Inuktitut, the language of the Inuit, he was the *angakok*.

The arrival of the Norsemen

The first Europeans to meet the Inuit were probably Norsemen from Iceland. Norse Vikings settled on Iceland in about 870 CE (though it was already inhabited by Celts). Greenland was first reached by Eirik the Red in 982, though it was not occupied until 986. The ruins of Eirik's own settlement of Brattahlid ("steep slope"), across the Tunulliarfik (or Eiriksfjord) from Narsarsuaq, can still be seen.

In 986 CD Bjarni Herjolfsson was blown off route while returning to Iceland from the Greenland settlements and saw land to the west. However, it was another 15 years before Liefur Eiriksson, son of Eirik the Red and the man who brought Christianity to Greenland, set out to explore this new land. A winter camp at L'Anse aux Meadows is the best-preserved Nearctic Viking site so far discovered, but other excavations appear to testify to Viking voyages as far west as Ellesmere Island. On Greenland, Norsemen certainly reached 73°N on the west coast, where three cairns discovered north of Upernavik suggest an overwintering during the 14th century.

▼ The remains of Eirik the Red's settlement of Brattahlid.

In the 15th century Greenland's western settlement, which had a maximum population of 1,000 living on 90 farms, and four churches, disappeared. The last bishop of Greenland died in 1377, and the last known ship to have sailed from Greenland left in 1410. Exactly what happened to the Greenland Norse is a mystery. The currently preferred theory is that a change in the climate ended the Norse occupation. The settlers were farmers, growing crops and keeping animals. When the climate cooled, agricultural yields dropped and winter fodder became scarce. There were at least 17 churches on Greenland, supported by tithes. With yields falling, the tithes were, perhaps, a final burden. Life became untenable: those who could probably returned to Scandinavia, but when the last ship had sailed, those that remained must have died of starvation.

European exploration

In 1497 European exploration and mapping of the Arctic began with the voyage of the Genoese voyager Giovanni Caboto, better known as John Cabot. Following him, many journeys were made in search of new trade routes to the east. The more important are listed below.

1553. Richard Chancellor sailed to Archangelsk, and then traveled overland to Moscow, meeting the Tsar, Ivan the Terrible, and forming the Muscovy Company. The company explored the Northeast Passage as far as the Kara Sea.

1576–78. Martin Frobisher looked for a Northwest Passage, finding Baffin Island.

1581. Ermak crossed the Urals and began the Russian conquest and occupation of Siberia.

▼ The anchor mast for Roald Amundsen's airship, Kongsfjorden, Svalbard.

1594–97. Two Dutch expeditions including Willem Barents sailed northeast. During the second, Barents reached Svalbard (naming Spitsbergen for the pointed mountains he found at the southern end of the island) and the northern tip of Novaya Zemlya, overwintering there. Barents and many others died of scurvy, but others reached Holland safely.

1607–10. On the last of three northern voyages, Henry Hudson discovered the vast bay that now bears his name, a sea so calm and immense that he was convinced it was the Pacific Ocean. His crew mutinied, putting Hudson and others adrift in an open boat. They were never seen again.

1609–16. Hudson mutineer Robert Bylot, spared the death penalty because of a claim to have discovered the Northwest Passage, along with William Baffin and others, made further discoveries in the Canadian Arctic.

1619–20. A Danish expedition under Jans Munk crossed Hudson Bay and wintered at the mouth of the Churchill River. Only Munk and two others of a crew of 65 survived.

1648. Semen Dezhnev followed the northern coast of Russia, rounding Chukotka's northeastern tip to reach Anadyr.

1670. Founding of the Hudson's Bay Company, whose officials continued the exploration of northern Canada, without discovering the Northwest Passage.

1735–42. Journeys of the Great Northern Expedition mapped the entire northern mainland coast of Russia. These journeys included that of Vitus Bering, who discovered Alaska and the Aleutian Islands. Bering and many of his men died of scurvy on Bering Island in 1741.

1818–45. British Royal Navy voyages in search of the Northwest Passage. The names Ross, Parry, Franklin and others became famous, and large areas of the Arctic Canada were mapped, but the explorers failed to find the Passage.

1831. James Clark Ross became the first man to reach the North magnetic pole during the voyage of his uncle John Ross.

1845. An expedition under the command of John Franklin sailed on what was to be one final attempt by the Royal Navy to find the Northwest Passage. Neither the expedition's ships nor the crews of 133 were ever seen again by Europeans.

1848. Franklin search expeditions completed the mapping of much of Arctic Canada and discovered the Northwest Passage.

1872. An Austrian expedition discovered Franz Josef Land. Novaya Zemlya had been known since earliest times, Wrangel Island had been seen as early as 1848 and the New Siberia Islands had also been seen. The final Russian Arctic island group, Severnaya Zemlya, was discovered in 1913.

1878–79. The Swede Adolf Erik Nordenskiöld took the *Vega*

from Karlskrona in southern Sweden along Eurasia's northern coast and through the Bering Strait, completing the first transit of the Northeast Passage.

1888. Fridtjof Nansen made the first crossing of Greenland's ice cap.

1893–96. Nansen's *Fram* expedition.

1898–1902. Norwegian Otto Sverdrup used Nansen's ship *Fram* to map Ellesmere Island's western coast and to discover Axel Heiberg and the Ringnes Islands. In 1913–18 Canadian Vilhjalmur Stefansson discovered the Parry islands after his ship, the *Karluk*, became trapped in the ice of the Beaufort Sea.

1903–05. Norwegian Roald Amundsen probably the greatest polar explorer of all time, made the first transit of the Northwest Passage in the *Gjøa*.

1908–09. Frederick Cook and Robert Peary claimed to have reached the North Pole. Most experts have dismissed Cook's claim, and many have also dismissed Peary's. Richard Byrd claimed to have reached the Pole by airplane in 1926, but this claim is also now dismissed. The Pole was definitely observed two days after Byrd's flight during an overflight in the airship *Norge*. The *Norge* crew included Roald Amundsen.

1948. First definite visit to the North Pole by a Russian team, which flew there.

1968. Team of Canadians and Americans led by Ralph Plaisted becomes the first to reach the Pole over ground.

The exploitation of Arctic wildlife
Fur trappers

Northern peoples used furs from the earliest times that those areas were settled, and it is known that in the ninth century the Sámi were trading furs with the Norsemen of southern Scandinavia, or supplying them as tribute. In medieval Europe furs were much sought after, not only to ward off winter's chills but for their status; the royalty of the European courts draped themselves in fur. These came from Scandinavia and European Russia, but by the mid-15th century the trade had reduced the numbers of animals north of Moscow to such an extent that the Tsar, Ivan the Terrible, was left facing economic ruin. Salvation was the apparently unlimited wealth in furs of Siberia. The numbers of European Beaver, Sable, Arctic Fox and many smaller species taken by the trappers is hard to estimate. As an example of the slaughter, in 1595, the Holy Roman Emperor asked Tsar Boris Godunov for soldiers to aid a crusade against the Turks, and the Tsar, fearing repercussions for his valuable trade with the Ottomans, instead sent a consignment of furs by way of compensation. The furs filled 20 rooms of the emperor's palace, with numerous wagons parked outside still loaded with less valuable squirrel furs. Throughout Russia the numbers of animals killed was limited only by difficulties

crossing the taiga, and by the numbers of trappers operating. Since the real prize was the white Arctic Fox, the white Ermine and the thicker winter coats of the other animals, these trappers needed to brave the Siberian winter, which imposed its own limit on trapper numbers. The invention of the snowmobile and the use of leg-hold traps made trapping easier, and the creation of the USSR pushed fur hunting to new extremes. By 1980 it is estimated that there was one Arctic Fox trap for every 4 sq. mi. (10 km^2) of tundra, with corresponding numbers of traps for other animals, particularly Sable and Muskrat. It is estimated that by this time the Russian population of Arctic Foxes had been reduced by about 99%. As well as the targeted animals, the effects on other wildlife was severe. The leg-hold traps for foxes were baited and often placed in relatively high positions. Gyrfalcons and Snowy Owls attempted to take the bait or, occasionally, perched on the traps and were captured. One estimate, based on capture records, gave a figure of one Gyrfalcon killed for every 50 traps, a highly significant contributor to net mortality in the population. There is no reason to suppose that the effects on Snowy Owls and other Arctic species were not equally devastating.

When Bering's ship, the *St. Peter*, reached what is now Bering Island (one of the Commander Islands), the crew found herds of Sea Otters in the surrounding waters. News of the find sent hunters eastward; within 20 years it is estimated that 70,000 Sea Otters and 1,250,000 Northern Fur Seals were taken. Destruction of the otters and fur seals continued when America purchased Alaska, but the Americans used rifles, shooting the otters at sea so that many died and sank before retrieval, while others escaped with injuries but died later. By 1911 the hunters were returning with fewer than 20 otter pelts per trip, and by 1925 it was assumed the animal had been hunted to extinction. Then, in 1931, a small remnant colony was discovered, and with full protection that colony has multiplied spectacularly so visitors can again enjoy the sight of this most remarkable animal.

Exploitation of the Northern Fur Seal population, both on land (principally on the Pribilof Islands) and at sea was such that, in the late 19th century, there were fears for the survival of the species. It is estimated that by the time of the purchase of Alaska in 1867, the Russians had taken almost two million seals. The Americans probably took another million by the early 20th century. Returns by then were diminishing markedly and an agreement was reached to limit the take. The seal population increased again, but it is once more in decline, falling by 30% over the last 30 years.

One other effect of fur trapping should not be ignored in terms of the overall health of Arctic species. To increase the Arctic Fox yields, and to ease the burden on the trappers, the animals were deliberately introduced to some Aleutian Islands on which they had not previously occurred. The introductions had a disastrous effect on local bird populations, which had never adapted to a terrestrial predator.

Though it never reached the capture rate, in terms of sheer numbers, of Siberia, the fur trade in North America also significantly affected numbers of fur-bearing animals. The history of fur trapping in Canada is largely the history of the Hudson's Bay Company, which set up a series of forts governed by "factors" (managers or governors) whose task was to trade with native peoples. In the hundred years following 1769, the company exported almost 5 million American Beaver furs, 1.5 million American Mink, more than 1 million Canadian Lynx, almost 900,000 Arctic Fox, about 500,000 Wolf, 288,000 Brown Bear and 275,000 American Badger pelts to England. Beaver was especially valuable, as the European fashion of the day was for beaver hats. When Queen Victoria's Consort, Prince Albert, appeared in public wearing a silk hat, the market in beaver fur dropped almost to zero overnight.

Modern heating systems reduced the need for furs in the west, while fur farming and the fur yielded by the import of Coypus (*Myocastor coypus*), the world's biggest rodent, reduced the need for wild capture. To these reductions were added the change to the fashion industry caused by the popular outcry over the use of fur. The collapse of the fur trade reduced the slaughter significantly in Russia, though the Russians themselves did not fully embrace the ethical issues of the west; fur remains the traditional way of combating the astonishing cold of the Russian winter. Trapping has continued there as well as in North America, where the annual kill is still around 40,000 Arctic Foxes, about half the number of those killed in the fashion-conscious 1980s. Trapping involves terrible suffering to the animal; the need to do as little damage as possible to the bulk of the pelt means that the leg trap is still favored. It must be hoped that the recent enthusiasm of the fashion industry for fur-trimmed accessories will be short-lived and a more responsible attitude will prevail. With modern, lightweight, warm materials now cheaply available, there is no need for people to wear furs.

▼ A welcome sign of the times, Myggbukta, northeast Greenland. An Arctic Fox cub beside an old trap with a trapping station nearby.

Whalers

While the numbers of animals involved in the fur trade were much higher than those killed by the whaling industry, the effect of whaling on the populations of individual species has been much more dramatic. Although whaling on a small scale had been carried on from at least the ninth century AD, it was not until the 16th century that exploitation of these mammals in Arctic waters began, when Basque whalers, who had hunted whales in the Bay of Biscay and were already active in cod fishing near Newfoundland, began to hunt them there.

During one of his early voyages, Henry Hudson discovered huge schools of Bowhead and Northern Right Whales in the sheltered bays of Svalbard, and soon after, the hunting techniques of the Basques were imported to slaughter them. The names of these species (the Bowhead was then known as the Greenland Right Whale) date from the time of these early hunts. These were the "right" whales to hunt; they were slow, did not put up much of a fight when harpooned and floated when they were dead, making them easy to tow to shore. The British and Dutch were at the forefront of Svalbard whaling, the Dutch building Smeerenberg (Blubber Town), whose remains can still be seen by visitors to Amsterdamøya, off Spitsbergen's northwestern shore. These include remnants of tri-pots, the three-legged pots in which blubber was rendered to oil. The Dutch also built another rendering station on Jan Mayen, which whales swam past on migration each year. The whales were killed from rowing boats that were either sent out from the shore or launched from larger ships already at sea. Eventually the whales became scarce in Svalbard's sheltered bays and they had to be pursued into the ice, which often entailed tying the dead whale to the side of the whaler and processing it on board. When whaling began, the North

Atlantic population of Bowhead Whales is estimated to have been about 20,000–25,000 animals. Within 50 years this number had been reduced so dramatically that the station on Jan Mayen had closed, with its maintenance no longer economically worthwhile. By the early 18th century, the Svalbard whale stocks had been worked out. With the stocks of the northeast Atlantic depleted, interest switched to the Davis Strait, where stocks were still high, and the Dutch and later the British took ships there. The depletion of that area took much longer, though by the early 20th century, whaling there was no longer worthwhile.

To the effect of whaling on the population must be added the effect of harpooning on an individual whale. Before the invention of the explosive harpoon, hand-thrown harpoons were used. Some whales took days to die; there are reports of Bowheads towing rowboats for several days before succumbing, while others died in agony. There are numerous tales of whaling men being covered in gore as dying whales spouted blood.

Whaling did not begin in earnest in the northern Pacific until 1835. The depletion of stocks there followed a similar pattern to that of the Atlantic, though much accelerated. Within 20 years American whalers had exterminated the Northern Right and Bowhead populations of the Sea of Okhotsk and the waters around Kamchatka, and had moved north to the Chukchi and Beaufort Seas. They also began hunting the Gray Whale near Baja, California. In Arctic waters, the catch of Bowheads remained high through the 1860s, but then dropped. Though high annual catches were occasionally made after that time, they never really recovered; by 1912 the annual catch had fallen to zero. At that time it is estimated that the total number of Bowheads killed in the Pacific was about 18,500. With the catches in the Atlantic, a population of 90,000 animals had therefore been reduced to less than 3,000. Today the population shows little sign of the hoped-for recovery, and the population of Northern Right Whales remains critically low.

Rowed boats were useless for catching larger rorquals, which occasionally reach speeds of 20 knots. Then, in the 1860s, the Norwegian Sven Foyn designed the steam-powered whaler and invented an explosive harpoon gun that could be fired from it. Now rorquals, much coveted for their size, could be hunted. In Antarctica the slaughter of these large whales was on an unprecedented scale; it is estimated that more than 350,000 Blue Whales were killed during the whaling period from Foyn's invention until a total ban was imposed, 90% of them in Antarctic waters. In the austral summer of 1930–31, more than 28,000 Blue Whales were killed. The slaughter of Fin Whales involved even larger numbers. During 1946–65, almost 420,000 Fin Whales were killed. The population of the other large whales, Sei and Humpback, were also decimated; some estimates suggest that the population of Humpbacks was reduced by 95%. Fortunately the populations of Humpback, Fin and Sei whales are now showing signs of recovery, but that of the Blue Whale remains static. There is concern that as with the Northern Right and perhaps the Bowhead, the population may never recover, and all of these species may be on a slow and inevitable road to extinction.

Ultimately the slaughter was stopped by the International Whaling Commission, though some nations, notably Japan and Russia, whose whalers had joined the whale harvest late but enthusiastically, both objected to zero quotas and continued to hunt for "scientific" purposes. With the Norwegians and Icelanders also wishing to take limited numbers of Minke Whales, and other species for which stock numbers are, they consider, adequate to allow harvesting without endangering numbers, the future for whales is unlikely to be peaceful.

Indigenous peoples in the modern world

In the Palearctic there are about 45,000 Sámi in Norway, about 20,000 in Sweden and about 7,000 in Finland. Each of these countries has a Samediggi, a Sami parliament, which is recognized by, and has an input to, the national government. With the economic expansion of these three countries, and particularly with the increases in forestry, hydroelectricity production, mining and tourism, the integration of the Sámi into mainstream society has been inevitable and has been largely successful. There have been more problems for the Kola Sami, who number around 2,000. Their historic territory has been exploited for its mineral wealth with some disastrous environmental consequences. Caribou herding was also collectivized. The collapse of the Soviet bloc meant that the Sámi were allowed to buy their herds, but they had almost no capital, there were few outlets for the sale of Caribou meat and land rights were open to dispute or, worse, available to rich outsiders. The shouts of freedom that accompanied the end of Soviet rule were not so much a clarion call for a new future as a death knell.

Farther east, the Russian invasion of Siberia had brought elements of Western civilization to the Caribou herders, but this was often after a culture clash that left many dead. The invasion also brought smallpox, influenza, measles and syphilis, which further decimated the populations. Shamanism was viewed with suspicion by Christian missionaries, who saw it as satanic. Massacres accompanied the forcible conversion to Christianity, and by the end of the 19th century the end appeared in sight for all the native communities. Communism saved them from extinction by offering tax concessions and exemptions from military service, but collectivization and education programs aimed at imposing Soviet ideology and lifestyle meant cultural upheaval and an insidious attempt at integration. So did the exploitation of Siberia's mineral wealth, which lured many local people into oil, gas and mining, and brought disproportionately large numbers of immigrant workers to the area. Land and livestock were confiscated to become state property, and the nomadic tribes were forced into settlements. Education was imposed on children, but that meant removing them from their families to places where there were schools. Away from their families, children were forbidden to speak their native languages, a further attempt at enforced integration. Under Khrushchev, many settlements were "closed," their populations forced to move to larger towns. When the Soviet Union collapsed, the loss of tradition meant that a cultural vacuum was created: left largely to fend for themselves, the peoples were now 70 years from the old way of life, too distant for many to find their way back. The poverty and hopelessness was appalling, the cultural vacuum too often filled by vodka. Life expectancy dropped dramatically, as did the birth rate as the northern societies disintegrated. The Association of Minority Peoples of the North, founded in 1989, seeks to address the problems left by years of exploitation and despondency. In 1989, a census estimated that the 26 indigenous native groups of Siberia and the Russian north numbered 180,000 in total. Yet these peoples occupied some 65% of Russia's total land area. Of these groups, the Nenets numbered about 34,000, the Evenki about 29,000, the Eveni about 17,000, the Chukchis about 15,000 and the Koryaks of the Kamchatka Peninsula about 9,000. Many of the remainder inhabited southern, non-Arctic Siberia, while some northern groups had populations only in the hundreds. The Kereks of southern Chukotka numbered just 50.

A particular problem was created by the richness of the Bering Sea, which allowed the development of fixed native villages sites along the Russian coast and, to a lesser extent, on the Alaskan coast. The peoples on each side were related, in both senses of the word, so that when Soviet authorities forcibly gathered the inhabitants of Big Diomede Island, the driving force for their decision was the possibility of collusion between family members, some Soviet and others American citizens. The separation of families was a tragedy that lasted right up to the end of the Cold War.

In the Aleutians, Russian otter and seal trappers aroused the anger of the native Aleuts, who resented not only the wholesale destruction but also the invasion of their lands; as the trappers denuded the animal population of one island they moved relentlessly on to the next. Fights occurred, but it was, of course, no real contest; the Russians had guns, the Aleuts only spears and bows and arrows. It is estimated that the Aleut population, which had numbered 10,000–20,000 before contact, declined by around 80% as a result of enforced

resettlement, disease, malnutrition, suicide and punishments.

The plight of the Aleuts did not stop when Alaska was bought by the Americans. Following the Japanese capture of Attu during World War II and its subsequent recapture a year later, the Americans evacuated the remaining Aleuts to inadequate housing on the Alaska Peninsula and fortified the island. Many of the evacuees died of malnutrition and disease. When the survivors returned, they found that the occupying American troops had burned many houses, used others and churches for target practice and had stolen their possessions. Final settlement for this abuse was not paid until 1988. Despite this unpleasant aspect to American history in the Aleutians, the native population has risen steadily. According to U.S. census estimates, the Aleut population is now around 24,000.

In the rest of the Nearctic, meaningful population statistics are more difficult to obtain because of the more widespread integration of native populations with incomers. According to U.S. census estimates, there are about 60,000 Inuit peoples in Alaska, which seems very high compared to an estimated first-contact population of less than 10,000, particularly as the first-contact figure dates only from the mid-19th century. The figure for indigenous peoples in Alaska is probably much smaller. In Canada the Inuit population is estimated at 30,000–35,000, which also implies an overestimate in Alaska. The Canada population is primarily in Nunavut, with smaller populations in the Yukon and Northwest Territories, northern Quebec and Labrador. Finally, the number of Inuit in Greenland is about 50,000.

Nearctic native peoples faced problems similar to those in the Palearctic. In Canada the southern native tribes were exploited by fur traders. Moreover, after the stories of the final agonies of Franklin's expedition reached Britain, the Inuit were portrayed as savages who were probably not above murder. These attitudes pervaded the early days of colonialism and have only been truly supplanted within living memory. Following the purchase of Alaska from Russia, the U.S. government all but ignored the state, selling fur-trading rights to outsiders and allowing a general lawlessness that did nothing to advance the condition of the native peoples. As a consequence, in both Alaska and Canada, the responsibility for the inhabitants of the north was only accepted when it became clear that a watching world would be singularly unimpressed if famines or epidemics were ignored. The problem was how to offer or distribute welfare to a nomadic or semi-nomadic people. This problem applied chiefly to Canada, where the indigenous population was spread over a vast area and was essentially nomadic, while the native population of western Alaska was essentially settled.

The only viable solution was to create settlements. In these the people could receive the services of a modern industrial society and be registered to prevent abuse of those services. But settlements created their own problems. Local wildlife was soon hunted to virtual extinction, and modern transport such as snow scooters and outboard motors allowed hunters to push back the boundaries of what could be called local.

◀ Whale Alley on Yttygran Island off the Chukchi coast. The local Inuit caught Bering Sea Bowheads and used this place as a butchery and meat storage site.

▲ Setting off on a Narwhal hunt, Thule, Greenland.

In a bid to overcome partially the problems caused by the concentration of Inuit families in fixed sites, in 1955 the government of Canada moved some families from Port Harrison in northern Quebec and Pond Inlet, on northern Baffin Island, to create new communities at Resolute on Cornwallis Island and Grise Fiord at the southern end of Ellesmere Island. In each case, the move, to an area where wildlife numbers were higher, has been reasonably successful, but such moves are not always guaranteed to succeed. Other, similar moves, carried out in almost all Arctic countries, have been less successful. Uprooted families find that traditional hunting methods are ill-suited to the local landscape, or that wildlife numbers are much lower than anticipated, or that homesickness is a major factor. In such cases, alcoholism in older people and drug abuse among disaffected youth is problematic.

Since the end of WWII, successive Canadian governments have also had to struggle to satisfy the desires of the indigenous peoples of the north regarding the claimed sovereignty over their lands. The creation of Nunavut in Canada in 1999 went some way to addressing this difficult problem. Nunavut was created by dividing the existing Northwest Territories into two. Nunavut, Canada's eastern Arctic, has a population that is around 80% Inuit. About half of the new, smaller Northwest Territories is Inuit. By controlling its natural resources and seeking renewable resources, of which tourism is the most obvious, Nunavut hopes to be able to tread the difficult line between tradition and modernity successfully. With global warming and the exploitation of mineral wealth threatening the entire Arctic, sensitive tourism is an important factor in encouraging governments to protect and sustain the Arctic environment. But here, too, there are problems. Too often the money derived from tourism heads south with the homeward-bound visitors. There is also the problem of perception of native peoples among visitors. Tourists come for a dog-sleding adventure or to see folk dressed in furs performing ancient dances and rituals. Few visitors make the long journey north hoping to catching a glimpse of an Inuit taxi driver or shop assistant. That expectation turns the peoples of the north into extras at a theme park. For many tourists, some parts of Inuit life are viewed with suspicion; it is only a short step from distaste at the clubbing to death of baby Harp Seals (usually by non-natives at places remote from Inuit hunting sites) to a more general distaste for seal-killing in general, even if, in reality, Inuit rarely kill Harp Seals and only take adults of the species they do kill. In time, the problem of who benefits from tourism will doubtless be resolved, but the bigger issue of the extent to which a hunting-based culture can continue to exist will remain. Quotas have had to be imposed for some hunted species, which created resentment, particularly when the native peoples concerned were not responsible for a population crash. A case in point was the Bowhead Whale. This species had been so overhunted by 19th and 20th century whalers, chiefly from the United States, that unrestricted native hunting could seriously endanger the species' ability to regenerate. In some settlements, the loss of a traditional way of life was and is a reason for sadness. On the other hand, some believe that allowing native peoples to live a life that included elements of both old and new is a deeply suspicious policy. Why was it acceptable for native peoples to continue a hunting tradition, sometimes hunting endangered species, when their settlements had supermarkets selling all the items that non-native citizens had to make do with, with no chance of supplementing their tables with free food while paying extra taxes for northern welfare programs? To what extent does the advent of rifles and snow scooters negate a hunting culture that traditionally had been based on harpoons and dog sleds? These and related questions warrant a wider discussion, but it is to be hoped that decisions over global warming and human exploitation of the Arctic mineral wealth will be made in time to make the discussion worthwhile.

Arctic habitats

The permanently frozen sea of the central Arctic Basin, where thick ice prevents the sunlight penetrating to the open water beneath, is an area of very low productivity. However, the shallow seas above the extensive continental shelves are, seasonally, highly productive. A reduction in ice coverage and the return of the sun in spring, together with the inflow of nutrients from thawing rivers, trigger a remarkable boom in marine life. The silt-rich beds of the Arctic seas are abundant with invertebrates; indeed, they are among the most productive seabeds on Earth.

Arctic seas

Before considering the waters beneath and around the sea ice, it is worth noting that the ice itself is not devoid of life. Not only do microalgae grow on the underside of the ice, where they are grazed by fish, but they also inhabit the body of the ice, utilizing the fact that, at a microscopic level, sea ice consists of ice crystals and brine channels, the latter providing a home for a range of algae, as well as to other organisms that feed on them.

Sunlight allows photosynthesis to take place. Red light is preferentially absorbed, being reduced to about 1% of the surface flux at about 33 ft. (10 m); blue light penetrates much farther (reducing to about 1% at about 490 ft., or 150 m). The

net effect of this graded absorption, which is the reason why water appears blue, is to create a euphotic zone; in other words, one in which photosynthesis is possible. This zone is around 490 ft. (150 m) deep. The dominant photosynthetic life of the marine Arctic is phytoplankton, principally diatoms and flagellates. The phytoplankton sustains other life-forms beneath the ice during the winter, and multiplies dramatically as light levels increase in the spring. Phytoplankton is eaten by herbivorous zooplankton, of which the most numerous are the *Calanus* copepods, the Arctic equivalent of Antarctica's krill. The most important of the copepods is *C. hyperboreus*. This crustacean takes three years to develop from egg to breeding adult. During the winter, the maturing copepods stay at depths below about 985 ft. (300 m), rising to < 330 ft. (< 100 m) during the summer when the phytoplankton blooms. At the Arctic fringe where there is darkness for a few hours during the summer, the copepods rise to the surface at night to escape predation.

Herbivorous zooplankton sustain the nekton, the generic name given to marine life-forms that can swim strongly and that are not, therefore, at the mercy of currents, as the phytoplankton and zooplankton generally are. Nektonic organisms comprise small fish, the larger fish that feed on them, and other marine forms up through the food chain. Of the marine fish, the most important as a food resource for larger animals are herring, cod, capelin, eels and salmonids. The salmonids are anadromous (they spend their adult life in the sea, but move to freshwater streams and rivers to mate and lay eggs), and the salmon runs of spawning fish are an important and famous feature of the Pacific Arctic fringe. Almost all Pacific salmon die after spawning, and the fish, both on their way upriver and after spawning, are a vital food resource for local wildlife, particularly Brown Bears and Bald Eagles. The Brown Bears of southern Alaska and those of the Kamchatka Peninsula are the largest of their kind, owing both their size and high population density to the salmon runs. The late (autumnal) spawning of Chum Salmon (*Oncorhychus keta*) in Alaska's Chilkat River is also responsible for the famous Bald Eagle concentrations that annually attract tourists and photographers.

During their spawning run, Pacific Salmon alter their appearance, occasionally in a bizarre manner. The Red or Sockeye salmon (*O. nerka*) changes from silver-blue to bright red, and the male Pink Salmon (*O. gorbuscha*) develops a humped back, hooked jaw and enlarged teeth. The purpose of these changes is not understood, and differ from anything seen in the Atlantic Salmon (*Salmo salar*). The Atlantic Salmon also often survives spawning and returns to the sea. These fish mainly spawn in rivers that are sub-Arctic and so they are not significant prey species for Arctic predators. However, the salmon are extensively fished in the coastal waters of southern

◀ An annual bounty of spawning salmon helps to sustain large Brown Bear populations in north-west North America and north-east Asia. Kodiak.

Greenland. Another Arctic salmonid is the Arctic Char (*Salvelinus alpinus*). Generally anadromous, there are freshwater Arctic Char in southern Canada (and also in England's Lake District) that descend from populations isolated in lakes cut off by glaciation. In cold northern waters the Char grows slowly; this has given rise to concerns over the survival of some populations as it is also a popular sport fish.

Of the wholly marine fish, Arctic Cod (*Boreogadus saida*), a smaller relative of the Atlantic Cod (*Gadus morhua*) and Pacific Cod (*G. macrocephalus*), are an important food resource for pinnipeds and whales. The lower jaw of the Arctic Cod is elongated beyond the upper so the fish can graze on the underside of the sea ice. The Capelin (*Mallotis villosus*), which has subspecies in both the north Atlantic and north Pacific, is also important for marine mammals, as are Herring and Pollock, particularly the Alaskan or Walleye Pollock (*Theragra chalcogramma*) in sub-Arctic waters. Herring are capable of survival in shallow estuarine waters that are brackish rather than truly saline; some may even be capable of surviving in freshwater. Arctic Cod and Capelin have not been extensively fished, due to the hostility of Arctic waters and the relatively small size of these fish, but the sub-Arctic cod species have been overfished to the point of both commercial and actual extinction. The range of these threatened species includes the formerly rich fishing grounds off the Labrador coast that lie within the 50°F (10°C) isotherm and, therefore, inside the Arctic boundary as assumed in this book. Walleye Pollock are now also fished in the Bering Strait, raising fears of overexploitation of another species important to the Arctic food chain.

Zooplankton is the staple diet of shearwaters and petrels, and of the Bowhead Whale, the only exclusively Arctic baleen whale. Nektonic species are eaten by Arctic seabirds, most Arctic pinnipeds and the exclusively Arctic toothed whales, the Beluga and Narwhal. Because of their silt burden, the shallow Arctic seas above the continental shelves support seaweeds and Eelgrass (*Zostera marina*), on which geese and other waterfowl feed, as well as a vast array of invertebrates and worms (food for shorebirds) and shellfish (food for walrus).

Occasionally seaweed is entrapped in the ice; its dark colors absorb sunlight in contrast to the high reflectivity of the surrounding ice mass, thus producing meltwater pools soon after the sun returns.

Avoiding the ice
The extent to which ice-free water controls Arctic marine productivity can be gauged by the influence of polynyas, which are consistent open-water areas. The cliffs close to the largest permanent polynya, North Water in Baffin Bay, hold some of the densest seabird colonies in the Arctic. North Water is also a significant wintering site for Bowhead Whales, and the local seal population has double the density of other sites. The concentration of whales in polynyas was exploited by the Arctic whaling fleets: it is claimed that some of the whaling captains understood the Arctic waters so well that they could also read the color of the sea (which depends on the plankton population) well enough to know where the whales would be abundant. By contrast, the polynya-free Beaufort Sea has

▲ A Polar Bear on the frozen sea ice, Peel Sound. The waters beneath support a rich diversity of life.

a much lower overall productivity, and many of the animals at the top of the food chain have fewer offspring that mature later. Later maturation is significant; for instance, it means that Beaufort female Polar Bears breed one year later on average (i.e., at five years rather than four) than their relatives to the east. The low productivity of the Beaufort Sea is in sharp contrast to that of the Bering Sea to the immediate south.

Tundra
The word *tundra* comes from the Finnish word *tunturia*, "treeless plain," which describes the circumpolar treeless belt that lies between the Arctic ice and the treeline. In North America the tundra area was previously called the Barren Lands or Grounds, a name that lives on in one subspecies of Caribou, but which has been superseded by the more common label. Tundra is characterized by low temperatures (in general, below 0°C for at least half the year), low precipitation and a short growing season. But although these characteristics apply to the entire land belt between timberline and ice, the tundra is not homogeneous: it has subdivisions based on latitude, geology and geography. As a consequence, the tundra does not have a unique vegetation type. However, throughout the tundra belt, vegetation is controlled by similar factors, so the total number of species is relatively small, and the species that are present tend to be similar.

Directly beneath the tundra lies permafrost. The annual thaw of the upper layers of this frozen ground may produce seasonal lakes and bogs; these provide water that compensates for the tundra's low precipitation. The annual thaw also produces an "active layer" in which plants may grow. These plants must, however, contend with a harsh environment created by the underlying unthawed permafrost. The active layer may have a negative thermocline (the temperature decreases through the layer), and may also be waterlogged since the permafrost inhibits drainage. The depth of the active layer defines the depth of the root structures of plants, as the permafrost is as impenetrable to roots as it is to water. However, the summer thaw of the active layer is actually slowed by plant growth, because leaf coverage prevents the soil from warming up. In areas where vegetation is stripped, the thaw depth is often two or three times that beneath vegetation cover.

The depth of the upper surface of the permafrost not only defines the root depth, it also regulates root (and therefore plant) growth: if it is close to the surface, the active layer is cooled and growth is retarded. At the surface, snow melt and local topography (such as shelter and aspect) control plant height. Tundra plants are generally low, and the farther north one travels the lower they become, though this generalization breaks down in the river valleys of the southern tundra, where shelter sometimes allows some of the willows (*Salix* spp.) and birches (*Betula* spp.) that form dwarf tundra forests to grow taller.

Much of the tundra supports cotton-grasses (*Eriophorum* spp.), other sedges, heathers such as *Erica* spp. and *Sphagnum* mosses. In general, these species form a sedge meadow. Harestail Cotton-grass (*Eriophorum vaginatu*), a multiheaded cotton-grass, and Hair-grass (*Deschampsia brevifolia*) are characteristic plants of tussock tundra (the former species dominating in the Nearctic, the latter in the Palearctic). To the Arctic traveler, tussock tundra is perhaps the least pleasant to cross, as closely knit tussocks make walking a trial, and the shallow, water-filled areas between the tussocks are an ideal place for the larvae of the mosquitoes that are the curse of the Arctic summer to develop. Tussock tundra is occasionally overwhelmed by fire, which allows regeneration: as elsewhere, fire is a good rejuvenator, though vegetation is too sparse for fire to spread over much of the tundra. Where the tundra is wet, *Eriophorum* species grow in abundance, particularly Arctic Cotton-grass (*E. scheuchzeri*), a single-headed sedge that produces characteristic areas of white fluffy seed heads; these wave in the breeze to create one of the Arctic's most aesthetically pleasing sights. The other common sedges of wet tundra are the true sedges (*Carex* spp.). Of these, the most widespread is Water Sedge (*C. aquatilis*).

The mesic tundra

Mesic tundra represents the best environment for plant growth in tundra areas. Better drained so as not to be too wet, yet adequately watered by springs, small streams or melting snow, it usually has varieties of grasses as well as many flowering plants. Such mesic areas often include curiosities, none more so than the 7 ft. (2 m) high Cow Parsnip (*Heracleum lanatum*), a member of the hogweed family, which grows in sheltered river valleys of the Aleutian Islands.

First-time visitors to the Arctic are often astounded by the profusion and variety of flowers on mesic tundra. Wrangel Island off the northeastern Siberian shore, which was not covered by an ice sheet during the last Ice Age, has around 400 species of plant, many of them flowering plants — more than in the whole of Arctic Canada. It is thought that this remarkable variety has developed as a consequence not only of the island having escaped glaciation and, therefore, maintaining an ancient flora, but from occasional periods of attachment to the mainland that allowed the spread of southern species. Subsequent periods of isolation allowed endemics to evolve. Wrangel's plants include *Pulsatilla nuttaliona*, a magnificent pasque flower. However, the apparent abundance of tundra plants must be seen in context; though species numbers run into the low hundreds in many Arctic areas (though many flower in the high Arctic), the species count would usually be expected to be in the thousands in temperate areas of similar size.

Crossing the continents

The intermittent presence of Beringia, the land linking northeast Russia with Alaska, has allowed some plant species to become truly circumpolar. Perhaps the best example is the buttercup (*Ranunculus sulphureus*), which occurs in Alaska and on the Aleutians, patchily on the northern Canadian mainland, on Canada's Arctic islands, on both northern coasts of Greenland, Svalbard, Franz Josef Land and the other islands of Arctic Russia, as well as on the northern Russian mainland and in places in Fennoscandia. Other species show a "Beringian" distribution, occurring in eastern Russia and western North America (Horsetail Cotton-grass is a good example). Some species occur in both the Nearctic and Palearctic around the North Atlantic, occurring, for instance, in western Russia, Fennoscandia, Svalbard, Iceland, Greenland and eastern North America. The Hairy Lousewort (*Pedicularis hirsuta*), which is familiar to visitors to Svalbard, Greenland and Baffin Island, provides a good example of this kind of distribution.

▼ Tundra on Cape Alexander, northern Canada.

The high Arctic also has the biodiversity equivalent of desert oases, areas where local topography allows a good, well-drained soil to develop and protects the plants that do take root from the wind. Such an area is the valley of Ellesmere Island's Lake Hazen, at about 82°N, where more than 100 flowering plant species have been identified. Similar oases may also occur on a "microhabitat" scale; small areas where there is protection from wind, or where an animal has died and so fertilized the soil, or beneath the lookout perch frequently used by a bird; these will all show greater productivity, either in terms of species diversity or with more abundant growth. In general, however, as the traveler moves north, vegetation becomes increasingly sparse and patches of bare ground grow more common. This thinning of vegetation cover is subject to a form of negative feedback that accentuates the onset of the "barren grounds"; fewer plants mean that an individual plant receives less protection against the elements and so finds it increasingly difficult to survive.

On the southern tundra, and also farther north if conditions are right, dwarf trees and shrubs grow. Chief among these are dwarf willows and birches, and a number of heathers. One of the prettiest is the Arctic Bell-heather (*Cassiope tetragona*), with its delightful evergreen stalks and white bell-shaped flowers. One important group of heathers is the *Vaccinium* spp. These produce berries that form an important food source for many tundra animals.

The fell fields

In all tundra areas there are isolated rocky areas, known collectively as fell fields from the Scandinavian *fjell* ("mountain"), which sustain less varied vegetation. These are dominated by Mountain Avens (*Dryas octopetala*), but also include such delights as Arctic Poppies (*Papaver* spp.); one of these, *P. dahlianum*, is the regional flower of Svalbard. The fell fields of the southern tundra have a similar appearance to the polar deserts farther north. The flowering plants differ, however, with hardier saxifrages (*Saxifraga* spp.) replacing more southerly varieties. The word *saxifrage* is from the Latin "stone-breaker", and has led to the occasional suggestion that these plants aid the production of soil in the rocky terrain they inhabit. This is incorrect; the name actually derives from the claimed similarity of its reproductive buds to kidney stones, a similarity that once led to the use of the plant as a remedy for this ailment.

Another plant of the fell fields is Moss Campion (*Silene acaulis*), which is often claimed to be the most northerly flowering plant in the world. Such a claim is difficult to prove, but this plant is certainly a contender. It produces a cushion comprising long shoots topped with small leaves, and can look like moss to the casual observer if its pink flowers are not visible. Mosses themselves are evident in damp areas throughout the tundra and are among the first species to colonize hostile environments. Jan Mayen, the volcanic Arctic island north of Iceland, is composed of lavas and basalts accreted over the half-million or so years that the island has been above water. The island has a limited and highly acidic soil formed by the weathering of these rocks, yet almost all low-lying land is covered by mosses. Around 75 species of vascular plants have also been identified on Jan Mayen, including at least five species of dandelion. Most of these plants are found beneath the extensive seabird nesting colonies.

Tundra lichens

Lichens occur across the tundra, but they are most noticeable in the plant-deficient northern regions. These offer splashes of color in otherwise uniform landscapes. Lichens are dual organisms, a symbiosis of fungus and alga, with the algae (usually unicellular green algae) lying a little below the surface of the fungal thallus. Lichens are an example of a mutualism; the fungus provides water and perhaps minerals to the algae in exchange for nutrients produced by photosynthesis.

Lichens are of three forms: crustose (crusty), foliose (leaflike) and fruticose (shrublike). The best known of the fructicose lichens is the inaccurately named Reindeer Moss (*Cladonia rangiferina*), which occasionally forms extensive and dense patches in open areas at the edge of the timberline. Other commonly seen lichens are the gray-and-orange crustose forms that colonize rocks throughout the tundra. These grow slowly, but at a quantifiable rate; *Rhizocarpon geographicum*, for example, may be used to measure the time since the retreat of ice from an area. Lichens produce acids that etch rock surfaces to allow them to gain a foothold; it was long thought that lichens were important in the creation of soil in barren areas, particularly as they are usually among the first organisms to invade a new area after glacial retreat, though this is no longer considered to be the case.

In general lichens are biochemically protected against freezing (usually by glycerols) and so provide a winter source of food for animals such as Reindeer, Musk Oxen, hares and, to a lesser extent, rodents. However, lichens are highly susceptible to airborne pollutants, especially sulphur compounds, and their presence is an indicator of the cleanliness of the local environment. Lichens also accumulate radioactive material, which has given cause for concern in recent times. Radioactive fallout from early nuclear weapon testing was concentrated in Reindeer Moss; though not a moss, this lichen is a favorite food of reindeer. The reindeer became contaminated, and when the Sámi and other reindeer-herding peoples ate the meat they

▼ Saxifrage in the Barren Lands, Northwest Territories. The saxifrages include some of the most northerly flowering plants.

also became irradiated. Something similar occurred after the Chernobyl reactor accident, when the prevailing winds at the time of the explosion carried radioactive contaminants into northern Scandinavia.

Waters of the tundra

Within the tundra there are areas of bog and numerous lakes, ponds created by glacial erosion or thermokarst processes, and rivers that flow through the tundra to Arctic seas. Lakes and ponds are usually limited in vegetation, with Horsetails (*Equisetum* spp.) and pondweeds dominating. This is because of the unpredictability of ice depth and duration. Vertebrate life is equally limited or even absent; if a water body freezes completely, then fish cannot survive. It is often said that the Blackfish (*Dallia pectoralis*), a form of mud-minnow, which is found in eastern Siberia and Alaska, can survive freezing, but this is not so. It can survive very low temperatures and short periods of freezing, during which it may be partially frozen, but a prolonged total freeze is fatal. Other freshwater fish in larger lakes and Arctic rivers include salmon, trout and char, and also grayling, minnow, carp and perch species, and even pike. From rivers the fish can, of course, "migrate" south during the Arctic winter.

Rivers emptying into the Arctic seas are among the largest in the world and form important habitats at their coastal boundaries. At more than 3,100 ft. (5,000 km) long, the Yenisey and Ob River systems of northern Russia are the fifth and sixth longest in the world. The catchment areas of both rivers exceed 193,050 sq. mi. (500,000 km²); the annual discharge of the Yenisey (whose name is from the Evenki *Ioanessi*, "great river") exceeds 144 cu. mi. (600 km³), while that of the Ob exceeds 95 cu. mi. (400 km³). The Lena, which also drains continental Russia into the Arctic, is more than 2,485 mi. (4,000 km) long, as is the Mackenzie in Canada. By way of a comparison, the annual discharge of the Lena is about 126 cu. mi. (525 km³), while that of the Mackenzie is about 77 cu. mi. (320 km³) (these numbers are enormous, but must be viewed in context; the total annual inflow of river water into the Arctic is estimated to be about 672 cu. mi. (2,800 km³), which is a little more than 1% of the annual water transfer (i.e., warm water in, cold water out) of the Fram Strait, between Greenland and Svalbard). These huge inflowing rivers, together with other smaller rivers such as the Yukon (annual discharge 48 cu. mi., or 200 km³), Pechora (36 cu. mi./140 km³), Kolyma (31 cu. mi., or 130 km³) and Nelson (18 cu. mi., or 75 km³), form large deltas. The deltas result from sediment build up; the Lena, for example, deposits over 11 million tons of sediment into the Laptev Sea annually, the silt creating a dark plume that extends for up to 65 mi. (100 km) offshore. The Lena Delta covers about 11,585 sq. mi. (30,000 km²) and comprises 6,000 channels and a collection of about 30,000 lakes. These water bodies may freeze to form ice dams. In spring, meltwater from farther south is blocked, causing a backup of water. This in turn results in periodic flooding by water and ice as the ice dams break under the burden, drastically changing the geometry of the deltas. It was the nightmare maze of the Lena Delta that doomed one group of sailors to death, following their escape from the sinking *Jeanette* in 1881.

Arctic forests

The boreal forest is the name usually given to the northern reaches of the forest belt that crosses North America immediately south of the tundra. The name derives from *Boreas*, the North Wind of Greek mythology. In Russia the forest is given the name taiga. There is no general consensus for the origin of the Russian word, which is now frequently seen in western literature; some authorities claim a derivation from an indigenous phrase for "swamp-forest", while others see a derivation from *tiy*, the local name for the Reindeer.

Based on a definition of the Arctic as lying within the 50°F (10°C) isotherm, little of the boreal forest is Arctic, but since this habitat encompasses the northern limit of trees and its associated peat bog land, it is important to a number of Arctic and sub-Arctic species. At the forest's northern limit is a zone often referred to as forest-tundra, an area with increasingly sparse tree cover and undergrowth. This zone is of variable extent, depending upon local topography, including altitude. On Russia's Taimyr Peninsula and inland Labrador in Canada, the forest-tundra zone is occasionally several hundred miles wide, but in eastern Labrador (and on mainland Scandinavia) it measures only a few miles across.

Even though some species of birds and mammals are circumpolar, the tree-dwelling species of the boreal forest often differ between the Old and New Worlds, though in each case the dominant tree species are coniferous. Conifers are able to photosynthesize at relatively low temperatures, they do not need to develop new leaves in the spring as they are evergreen (apart from the larches) and they can reduce growth if frozen ground limits water uptake. As most of the boreal forest lies in the permafrost region, the actual distribution of trees and of species depends on the thickness of the annual active layer. Spruces (*Picea* spp.) and larches (*Larix* spp.) dominate where the active layer is thinnest as they produce

shallow root systems. In both the Nearctic and the Palearctic larches are important at the northern limit of tree growth. Larches are unique trees; they can thrive in conditions of continuous permafrost, and are the only trees that grow in the colder areas of Siberia, including the Verkhoyanskiy region, the coldest place in the northern hemisphere. Larches shed their leaves in winter, and are therefore the only deciduous conifers. The ground cover of larch forest is dominated by lichens, while that of spruce forest is dominated by mosses, though there are exceptions to these general rules.

The North American forest is dominated by spruces; White Spruce (*Picea glauca*) favours well-drained land, while Black Spruce (*P. mariana*) prefers a damper environment. Other prominent species include the Jack Pine (*Pinus banksiana*) and the American Larch or Tamarack (*Larix laricina*). Firs (*Abies* spp.) are almost entirely absent except in the northern region of coastal Labrador, where the Balsam Fir (*Abies balsamea*) is a dominant species up to the timberline. Balsam Fir also occurs in the krummholz (from the German, "crooked wood"), an area in inland Labrador of gnarled, twisted, cold- and wind-deformed trees. This notoriously impenetrable scrub is known locally as tuckamoor. In general, krummholz forms from any tree species battered into a low, twisted shape by conditions at the northern extremity of its range.

The boreal forest of the Old World is vast, particularly that section extending across the old Soviet empire — the Siberian taiga, and its extension into European Russia. This covers more than 12 million acers (500 million ha) — about a fifth of the Earth's forested areas and more than half its total coniferous forest. The taiga covers a huge longitudinal range, and differences in composition occur as the traveler heads east from Scandinavia. In mainland Scandinavia, the forest is chiefly of Norway Spruce (*Picea abies*) and Scots Pine (*Pinus sylvestris*). In European Russia, Norway Spruce and Siberian Spruce (*Picea obovata*) dominate. Moving east again, the great forests of western Siberia are predominantly of Siberian Spruce, Siberian Fir (*A. sibirica*) and Siberian Stone Pine (*Pinus sibirica*). In central Siberia larches dominate, particularly Siberian Larch (*Larix sibirica*) and, to the east, Dahurian Larch (*Larix gmelini*). To the south of the larch forests there are further stands of Siberian Spruce and Siberian Pine, and also of Scots Pine at the edge of the steppe. An interesting characteristic of the central Siberian taiga is the alases: treeless areas with a meadow-type vegetation. Alases develop where thawing permafrost causes a lake to form. The soil around the lake collapses, tree growth halts and the area surrounding the lake changes to meadow. Alases may vary from 330 ft. (100 m) or so across to about 6 mi. (10 km), and can form as much as 50% of the taiga in some areas. East again, the severe Siberian climate limits the spread (and size) of larches; the forests of Dahurian Larch become more open and shrubby Dwarf Stone Pine (*Pinus pumila*) often dominates.

Of broad-leaved species, Cottonwood (*Populus balsamifera*), Aspen (*Populus tremuloides*) and birches (*Betula* spp.) occur in North America. Eurasian boreal broad-leaved trees include aspen and birches, together with willows (*Salix* spp.) and alders (*Alnus* spp.). In western and central Siberia broad-leaved forest (particularly of aspen and birch) forms a narrow band at the southern edge of the conifer forest, separating the conifers from the wooded steppe to the south. In eastern Siberia this narrow band disappears, with the conifers extending to the edge of the steppe.

As elsewhere in the Arctic, the number of vascular plants in the boreal forest north to the treeline is surprisingly high. Important Nearctic groups include asters (Asteraceae), willowherbs (Onagraceae), buttercups (Ranunculaceae) and roses (Rosaceae), as well as berry-producing shrubs. In the Palearctic taiga the main groups are similar, with the addition of crucifers (Brassicaceae). It is no surprise that shade- and cold-tolerant species dominate. One of the willowherb family, the Fireweed (*Epilobium angustifolium*), a colonizer of burned or otherwise disturbed areas, acts as a makeshift calendar for the inhabitants of Alaska. The flowers open progressively up the tall stem; when the last flowers, at the stem tip, open, then winter is just around the corner.

Forest bogs

One aspect of the boreal forest that has become infamous among travelers, but which nonetheless is ecologically important, is the peat bog (known in North America as the muskeg). One of the largest muskegs is close to James Bay, the southern extension of Hudson Bay. The James Bay bogs are dominated by Black Spruces and American Larches, and are rich in herbs and orchids, as well as grasses and sedges. Bogs are, in general, highly acidic and nutrients are scarce. Poor drainage produces a waterlogged environment; the decay of organic material is inhibited by a lack of oxygen and by leached acids, while the acidity also inhibits plant growth. The chief plants of bogs are the *Sphagnum* mosses. Some bog plants, such as sundews and pitcher plants, have evolved insectivory to boost nutrient uptake. For the traveler there are never enough of these insect-eating plants, or of insectivorous birds; northern bogs and muskegs are the breeding ground of mosquitoes and other biting insects, which add to the leg-devouring misery of a trip through such an area.

Birch Forest at Yellowknife, Northwest Territories.

Adaptations for Arctic life

For any organism, survival in the Arctic depends on dealing effectively with extremely low temperatures. Biological function depends on enzymes, biological catalysts that speed up biochemical reactions and allow the mechanisms of life to operate. Enzymes have an optimal temperature at which they work most effectively; the rate of enzyme function drops with decreasing temperature until a cutoff point is reached and the organism dies.

At first glance the problem of reduced enzyme rate might seem to apply solely to ectotherms (organisms whose temperature depends on the environment, such as insects and amphibians), as endotherms (organisms, mainly mammals and birds, that can regulate temperature internally) can, in principle, combat low temperatures by increasing insulation (blubber, fur or feathers) or by increasing metabolic rate (assuming an adequate food resource is available). However, the distinction between ectotherms and endotherms is not as clear as might be anticipated. Some endotherms control their temperatures only part of the time; small birds and rodents often "turn down" their metabolic rates, sometimes seasonally, occasionally at night. Many larger mammals and birds bask in the sun, allowing heat absorption to reduce the necessity for increased internal heat generation. By contrast, some ectotherms can "turn on" a form of endothermic heat production; bumblebees provide a classic example. They vibrate their wing muscles rapidly to generate body heat, while

hairs on the body help retain it. However, despite such strategies, ectotherms generally need specific, cell-based techniques to avoid death as temperatures fall.

There are two basic strategies used by ectotherms, freeze tolerance and freeze avoidance, each of which must combat the problem of ice formation within the cells — ice crystals do irreparable damage to cellular structures. In freeze-tolerant organisms, extracellular proteins trigger the formation of ice crystals. Water is then pumped from the cells to be replaced by sugars, leaving the cellular fluids ice-free. Freeze tolerance is a strategy used by many marine invertebrates and some insects.

The alternative strategy is freeze avoidance. Here organisms take advantage of the fact that very pure water can be supercooled to temperatures well below 32°F (0°C) (down to -40°F/-40°C in exceptional circumstances) Supercooling requires the use of "antifreeze" molecules in the cells, and the active removal of potential ice nuclei. Polar marine fish use this strategy, as do most insects and many spiders. Supercooling can be risky, since below -40°F (-40°C) freezing occurs very rapidly and death is almost certain. Endotherms do not have access to these methods; freezing for these animals means death. Most birds avoid the Arctic winter by migrating south; resident endotherms often must spend the winter in a state of torpor in a burrow or beneath an insulating layer of snow.

The following sections look at the ways different groups of organisms rise to the challenge of survival in the Arctic.

▼ Luxuriant plant growth on the slopes beneath a large seabird colony, Isfjorden, Svalbard.

Plants

Arctic plants use a combination of freeze tolerance and freeze avoidance to survive the winter, and they also have a variety of insulation adaptations to reduce the minimum tolerable temperature. Through these adaptations, broad-leaved evergreen trees can survive prolonged exposure at temperatures of around 5°F (-15°C). Deciduous broad-leaved trees can survive at temperatures approaching -40°F (-40°C), but only conifers can survive at lower temperatures .

Most Arctic plants are short and stunted. This is due to a variety of factors. Snow abrasion tends to kill off taller plants, as does desiccation, which is enhanced by the wind (wind strength increases with height above the ground due to absence of ground friction). Temperatures are higher closer to the ground, and can be significantly increased if the plant creates a mat of branches, if leaves are clustered close to the ground, or if the plant takes a "cushion" form. The trapping of air between the ground and the plant can raise the microhabitat temperature by as much as 59°F (15°C); the cushion form has evolved repeatedly in unrelated lineages as a result. Cushions have the additional advantage that dead leaves at the top of the plant add to its insulation, while those trapped at the base add nutrients to the soil. This is crucial; Arctic soil is generally very poor, and plants will take advantage of any available additional source of nutrients. Travelers will often see relatively luxuriant plant growth beneath the breeding sites of birds, or near an animal carcass.

Leaves and stems, and the branches of woodier forms, are dark to increase the absorption of sunlight, and many species have hairs on stems, leaves and flowers. The hairs trap air, reducing water loss and increasing local temperature. The reduction in water loss is critical, particularly in winter when the ground freezes and water uptake from the roots becomes impossible.

The life cycles of Arctic plants

Plants also benefit from shelter from the wind, favouring lee slopes where accumulating snow offers insulation during the winter. The snow may push back the onset of spring by taking longer to melt and so revealing the plant to the sun later, but for Arctic-adapted perennials this seems to be of limited importance. Most Arctic plants are perennial; this offers the most flexible approach to the short, and occasionally disrupted, polar summer. Annuals are almost entirely absent as the summer is too short for such plants to complete their entire life cycles. However, a small group of plants are both annual and biennial; annuals if the polar summer is long enough, but taking two years for their life cycle if not.

Many Arctic plants are "wintergreen," forming leaves late in the summer that survive through the winter. This has two advantages. Provided that snow cover can protect the leaves, they are ready to use available sunlight as soon as the snow melts, saving precious time otherwise required to grow new leaves. Also, old leaves provide a measure of protection for new leaves grown in the subsequent spring, ensuring that when they are finally exposed conditions are as benign as possible.

Though the polar day is long (and in all places where Arctic plants grow, up to about 82°N, there is a period of continuous sunlight), Arctic plants have evolved to photosynthesize at low light levels so as to take full advantage of all available light. Many flowers are also parabolic in shape, concentrating heat to increase metabolic rate. This has the important side effect

of creating a warm microclimate that attracts insects. Insects can often be seen basking in Arctic flowers; the plants sometimes exploit this basking by using these insects as pollinators. Many Arctic flowers are also phototropic, tracking the sun through the 24 hours of the polar summer day. The flower "moves" through continuous growth of the stem, though always at a slower rate on the side toward the sun, so the flower head tilts. Many Arctic plants overwinter with well-developed flower buds to avoid delays in flowering when spring finally arrives.

The Arctic is well-suited for the dispersal of plant seeds as winds are such a feature of the climate. As with plants from temperate and tropical regions, seeds, particularly those of berry-producing plants, are also dispersed by birds and mammals. But not all Arctic plants are seed-producers. Some spread by rhizomes (horizontal, underground stems that take root at intervals), others by stolons (above-surface creeping stems that produce new plants at their tips). Yet others produce bulbils, buds that form in place of some, or all, flowers. When detached, these are at the mercy of the wind, but will root if they land in a suitable spot. In some ways bulbil production has advantages over seed formation, as it is a form of asexual reproduction and so does not require either a pollinator or another plant, both of which may be scarce; a disadvantage is that the bulbils cannot survive for long periods if they do not implant, as seeds can.

▶ Arctic Willow, Moskusoksefjorden, north-east Greenland. Despite its dwarf form the willow still turns red in autumn.

Aquatic ectotherms

The vast majority of marine animals are ectothermic; exceptions include tetrapods such as cetaceans, sirenians, seals and sea lions, though some fast-swimming large fish (such as tuna) keep their body temperature relatively high through metabolic output, while large turtles retain high body temperatures due to their size. Most ectothermic marine animals, though, have body temperatures only marginally above that of the water, and they are stenothermic; they cannot tolerate anything other than minor deviations from normal body temperature. Most use freeze-tolerance or freeze-avoidance techniques, but they also rely to some extent on the fact that the freezing point of seawater declines as depth increases, so migration to greater depths protects against freezing in cold spells.

For intertidal animals, the situation is much more difficult, as they may be exposed to ambient temperatures that are much lower than the freezing point of seawater. Such animals are freeze-tolerant, surviving even though up to 90% of their body water freezes. These animals must, however, avoid being left above the ice when the sea freezes, as the prolonged low temperatures of the Arctic winter would be terminal. They must also avoid being in the region of freezing water as ice abrasion would be similarly deadly. Shellfish, which graze algae around the tide level, migrate downward as winter approaches to avoid being entombed by ice. In rock pools, the sea-ice cover, having leached its salt into the underlying water, lies above highly saline water in which the freezing point has been significantly depressed. Shellfish bury themselves in the sediment at the bottom of the pools to avoid freezing.

Large Arctic lakes do not generally freeze entirely; fish and freshwater invertebrates survive by using freeze-resistant techniques, and by avoiding contact with ice. Some river animals migrate into these large lakes. Invertebrates move to the depths to escape the advancing ice and may burrow into the lake bottom, though some insect larvae actually freeze into gravel beds close to pond edges, using freeze resistance to overwinter without ill effects.

Terrestrial invertebrates

A surprising number of invertebrates inhabit both the tundra and the taiga edge. Worms (especially nematodes and oligochaetes) and rotifers are the most numerous and form the major part of the animal biomass. The Arctic is also home to a diversity of freshwater copepods and, of course, insects, with spiders also important within the taiga.

All the major insect groups species are represented in the Arctic, though there are few beetles, and most are important either as food sources for birds or as plant pollinators. As a general rule, Arctic insects are smaller, darker and hairier then more southerly relatives, these being adaptations against the polar cold. Darker insects absorb heat faster, and it is particularly noticeable that most Arctic butterflies, which spend a good deal of time basking in the sun, are darker than southern species. A reduction in size may be a response to the reduced availability of food. The hairiness of Arctic insects

aids in creating an insulating air layer, and may also help in warming by redirecting reflected sunlight back on to the insect's body. Other adaptations are also noticeable; some species have reduced wing areas or have even dispensed with wings altogether to reduce the size of their flight muscles; some have even reduced the size of their eyes.

The most obvious insect adaptations to polar life concern reproductive and overwintering strategies. Many species have dispensed with males, with the females reproducing asexually. In the extreme case of the High Arctic Blackfly (*Simulium arcticum*), the insects do not always go through the full life cycle of egg, larva, pupa and adult; eggs develop inside the pupa and are released when the pupa dies, with no adult ever forming. Few insects overwinter as adults. The majority do so as pupae, which are freeze tolerant or freeze avoiders.

Arctic butterflies

Butterflies are one of the joys of the Arctic summer and can be seen as far north as flowers bloom. Despite their apparent fragility, which leads to the surprise with which many first-time Arctic travelers greet their presence, butterflies are adept at using their wings as sun collectors to raise their body temperatures, and are therefore better suited in some ways to the Arctic than wingless insects. Many Arctic butterfly species are dark to aid heat uptake. Dorsal basking involves flattening the wings so that the back and upperwings are exposed to the sun. In lateral basking the wings are raised so that the upper surfaces touch; the body is then turned sideways to the sun so that the flanks and lower wing surfaces are exposed to it. The wings may also be held in a V-shape, trapping sunlight. The wings act as a reflector; this is important for white butterflies, which concentrate the rays onto dark spots on the thorax. Butterflies (and other insects) also hold their thorax in contact with the ground rather than standing above it, as the surface of the bare soil is usually above ambient temperature.

All Arctic lepidopterans overwinter as larvae; some species require several years development before pupation to produce adult butterflies the following spring. Of these, the most astonishing is the Arctic Woolly Bear (*Gynaephora groenlandica*), a moth that can spend up to 14 years as a caterpillar before pupation. This caterpillar may be attacked by parasitoid wasps and flies, which similarly may take three or four years to develop.

Arctic flies

Like the butterflies, the true flies or dipterans of the Arctic tend to have elongated life cycles relative to their more southerly counterparts. Some flies remain as grubs for three years; some tipulids (or crane flies) take four years and some midges spend as long as seven years as larvae. However, insects are nothing if not adaptable, and most can shorten the wait for adulthood whenever conditions allow.

Flies with an aquatic larval stage are extremely important food sources for waders and diving ducks, while the adults are eaten by warblers at the edge of the boreal forest and by buntings and sandpipers on the tundra. Of particular interest to the Arctic traveler are mosquitoes and black flies, the females of which are facultative blood-suckers, i.e., they will feed on blood if the opportunity arises. Blood is preferred if available, as it allows more eggs to be laid than if the female feeds only on nectar, as male mosquitoes do. Female mosquitoes may consume up to five times their own body weight in a single blood meal and may feed, and subsequently lay eggs, more than once in their lifetime. The females inject saliva into the host's blood to prevent clotting, which causes swelling and irritation in the host. Female mosquitoes will feed on warm-blooded animals, driving the great herds of Caribou in the Nearctic, it sometimes seems, almost to the point of madness. Caribou will seek windy spots, walk into the wind, or rest on snow to avoid the insects, but some animals may lose 4 cups (1 L) of blood or more per week during the mosquito season. In rare cases Caribou have been known to die from blood loss. Birds also occasionally succumb; a team researching a Brünnich's Guillemot colony during a particularly warm spring noted the deaths of many birds from blood loss; mosquitoes attacked the feet of the birds, which, in warm weather, they expose and fill with blood to cool down. One gloomy calculation suggests that a naked, unprotected human would die from blood loss from mosquitoes within a day. But not all mosquitoes are lucky in finding a host, or even nectar; some females produce many fewer eggs autogenously, using food reserves built up during the larval stage. Arctic mosquitoes generally lay their eggs close to the water surface of their chosen pond or pool. Snow cover insulates the eggs during the winter, and meltwater triggers hatching and provides a pathway to the pool. Larval mosquitoes can develop in four weeks in water temperatures as low as 34°F (1°C). On emergence from the pupa, adult mosquitoes feed on nectar and are important plant pollinators before they become the misery that afflicts all Arctic animals and travelers.

Black flies can be even more of a menace to the Arctic traveler in and near the boreal forest, since their bloodsucking activities produce a more damaging wound. They are less of a problem in the high Arctic where the females cannot suck blood, as their mouthparts do not fully form. Instead, the eggs are produced solely on reserves built up during the larval stage.

Caribou suffer not only from myriad mosquitoes, but also from two specialized dipteran parasites. The Caribou Warble Fly (*Hypoderma tarandi*) lays sticky eggs on the legs or underside of the animal. When the larvae hatch, they burrow into the mammal, then migrate subcutaneously to the back close to the spine. There they excavate a breathing hole and begin to feed on the fluids of their host. Most Caribou are infested; some carry enormous parasite loads of up to 2,000 larvae, their skins becoming useless to native hunters as a result of the many breathing holes. The larvae overwinter in the animal, then emerge through their breathing holes in spring, tumbling to the ground to pupate. The breathing holes can subsequently become infected, adding to the suffering of the host.

A second important Caribou dipteran parasite is the Caribou Nose Bot (*Cephenomyia trompe*), which deposits live larvae (previously hatched inside the female) into the Caribou's nostrils. The larvae migrate to the opening of the throat, where the larval mass can be so large as to interfere with the host's breathing. The coughing heard in groups of Caribou represents the sound of the irritated deer attempting to dislodge the larval mass. The animal will, eventually, expel the larvae, but only when they are ready to pupate. Warble and Bot Flies are strong fliers and are difficult to shake off; Caribou lower and shake their heads when a Nose Bot Fly is seen, and the apparently random jump and run of an individual animal is usually a sign that one or other fly has been sighted.

Other Arctic insects

There are two species of bumblebee in the high Arctic. These are the largest of all the Arctic insects. Indeed, their size often surprises first-time Arctic travelers. Each species uses shivering to raise body temperature, and the muscle mass required for this process, together with a dense coating of insulating hair, explains the bees' large sizes. The queen of *Bombus polaris* is fertilized during the summer. After overwintering she founds a new colony, with her young including both workers and new reproductive queens and males (or drones). Interestingly, the second Arctic species, *B. hyperboreus*, is a social parasite of *B. polaris* (and presumably a close relative). A queen *B. hyperboreus* emerges some weeks after the queen *B. polaris*. She seeks out a *B. hyperboreus* nest, gains entry (probably by-passing the resident workers through chemical trickery) and stings the resident queen to death. Then she lays her own eggs, which are then tended, and the larvae raised, by the *B. polaris* workers — again chemical skulduggery is probably required to dupe the resident bees. All the *B. hyperboreus* larvae are queens or drones, nurtured to prepare for overwintering and for a new year of cuckoolike social parasitism.

Birds and mammals

The available strategies for surviving the Arctic cold are quite different for endotherms than for ectotherms. For birds there is the straightforward alternative of flying south to avoid the polar winter, a strategy adopted by virtually all species. Those that remain in the Arctic increase their feather density enormously. *Lagopus* grouse and the Snowy Owl, for example, have feathered feet; Snowy Owls also have modified foot pads to reduce heat loss, as does another resident, the Raven. The Snowy Owl is better insulated than *Lagopus*, but the grouse are able to lower their metabolic rate and avoid temperature extremes by digging into the snow to take advantage of the insulating snow layer. Arctic birds have down feathers below their contour feathers; these are fluffy to trap an insulating boundary layer of air. The insulating properties of the down of the Common Eider are so good that the down was formerly collected commercially in Iceland; females use their down to line their nests, and this was collected after the chicks had fledged. So famous are its insulating properties that the word "eiderdown" became the accepted term for the down-filled cover used on beds.

In terrestrial mammals migration is not generally an option (the migration of Reindeer is a search for food, not a true winter-avoidance strategy). One strategy used by several

◄ An Arctic Ground Squirrel must leave its dormant state from time to time during the winter to top up its food reserves.

sub-Arctic species is torpor, in which the heart rate and metabolic rate fall, though the body temperature stays within a few degrees of normal; the animal survives by metabolizing accumulated body fat. Prolonged, profound torpor in which body temperature falls significantly, or hibernation, is not feasible in high Arctic species; food supplies are inadequate to accumulate sufficient fat reserves, and the animal would probably succumb to hypothermia. However, female Polar Bears enter a dormant state in their birthing dens in the snow, though the female's state is not true hibernation since she remains capable of a relatively rapid response if danger threatens. South of the high Arctic, Black and Brown Bears and Arctic Ground Squirrels both enter states of winter sleep, often erroneously called hibernation. These animals tend to stay dormant for relatively brief periods, and occasionally wake to search for food. Periods of foraging are essential for Arctic Ground Squirrels as their body reserves are insufficient to last throughout the winter. Brown Bears approach a state that is closer to the true hibernation of boreal mammals such as the dormouse (*Glis glis*).

The other main mammalian survival strategy is to increase insulation, either internally by using layers of blubber (pinnipeds and whales) or externally by using dense pelts. Blubber is best for large marine mammals, while fur is preferable for terrestrial and smaller mammals. The Polar Bear uses a combination of both. Blubber is not as good an insulator as fur; about 2 ft. (65 cm) is required to produce the same insulting properties as ³/₄ in. (2 cm) of high-quality fur. However, blubber is best for marine mammals because fur is a high-maintenance material, particularly if it becomes matted or soiled. Sea Otters spend around 20% of their time grooming their fur to maintain its insulating properties, often blowing into the fur or creating water bubbles to enhance the air cushion at the fur base. Adult female otters frequently groom their young while they lie on their chests out of the water. Yet despite those efforts, a Sea Otter has to maintain a very high metabolic rate to stay warm, consuming up to a

third of its body weight each day.

In principle, making fur thicker increases its insulatory properties, but there is a limit depending on the size of the animal. The Polar Bear can grow fur up to 2 in. (6 cm) thick, which would not be feasible on a small rodent. Fur creates a layer of still air close to the animal's surface. Still air is a marvelous insulator (about seven times better than the natural rubber in a wetsuit). The winter fur of the Arctic Fox, which extends over both the top and bottom surfaces of the paws, is such a good insulator that the fox can maintain a constant metabolic rate even at ambient temperatures as low as -40°F (-40°C).

Size and shape

Size is an important determinant of insulation strategy. This is because as animals get larger, their surface area-to-volume ratio decreases, and therefore heat loss is relatively lower. For this reason a dead whale may take days to cool to the ambient temperature, while a dead shrew will take minutes. Insulation counters some of the thermoregulatory problems small mammals have to contend with due to their size, but not all; these animals compensate by increasing their metabolic rate to replace lost heat, and by burrowing beneath the snow in winter to take advantage of its insulating properties. Ironically, in view of the snow covering that epitomizes the Arctic winter, it is not the period of snowfall that is the most stressful for small mammals; autumn is far worse, since temperatures are low, but there is no snow to hide under.

The sizes and shapes of Arctic mammals are encapsulated by certain "rules"; Bergmann's Rule states that there is a within-species tendency for increasing body size with increasing latitude or decreasing temperature, due to the benefits of a decreased surface area-to-volume ratio. Allen's Rule states that endotherms such as mammals and birds tend to have smaller appendages in cold regions to reduce heat loss. A good example of this would be the ears of the Arctic Fox compared with those of the African Bat-eared Fox (*Otocyon megalotis*), for example. This "rule" does not seem to apply to the feet of Arctic mammals, since large feet allow easier travel over soft snow. Arctic Hares have much larger feet than their southern relatives (the Snowshoe Hare is named after this feature, of course), and Gray Wolves not only have large feet, but also have relatively long legs to help them bound through thick snow.

Heat production in young mammals

All northern seal pups have a thick first (or lanugo) coat that is white, although in some species this is molted within the womb. As most seal pups are born onto ice, this white coat also acts as camouflage. Young seals need powerful insulation; birth entails a temperature drop that might be as much as 140°F (60°C). They shiver muscles to generate heat, and also use a process unique to young mammals called non-shivering thermogenesis. This involves the metabolism of brown adipose tissue, which occurs in body cavities (especially on the shoulders) and around the major organs. The color of this uniquely mammalian tissue derives from the mass of capillaries it contains. Heat production by brown adipose tissue metabolism is around 10 times higher than that produced by normal shivering. As the young animal develops, its brown fat deposits diminish.

Exchanging heat

Blubber and fur do not provide the only means for retaining heat in Arctic animals. A feeding Gray Whale scoops in a giant mouthful of sediment from the ocean floor, forcing the water through its filamentous baleen with its tongue and thereby sieving out the organic material. The tongue of a Gray Whale has a very large surface, devoid of insulation and rich with blood vessels; heat loss through the tongue should, theoretically, be enormous, and fatal in cold seas. However, Gray Whale tongues contain some remarkable anatomical adaptations that minimize heat loss through this organ. Each artery that carries warm blood from the body is surrounded by a network of veins carrying blood back from the surface of the tongue. Heat is exchanged between warm and cold blood so it passes back into the body rather than being lost at the tongue surface. This arrangement of blood vessels is called a countercurrent heat exchanger, and it is an extremely efficient way of saving heat. Similar systems occur in a wide range of animals; countercurrent heat exchangers occur in the legs of waders and Caribou, in the horns of ungulates and in the tails of beavers.

Conversely, some Arctic mammals have the opposite problem; the efficiency of their insulation means that overheating may become a problem. For example, unlike most mammals, cetacean testicles lie inside the body cavity to aid streamlining. However, the body temperature is too high for successful sperm production. To cool the testes, blood is shuttled directly from the flukes and dorsal fin straight to the testes. A similar system in female cetaceans keeps the uterus cool — this is important for regulating the temperature of the developing foetus.

Color changes

Terrestrial northern mammals molt to a winter coat that is thicker and provides superior insulation than the summer version. The winter coat of many Arctic animals is white. This might appear to be counterproductive, as a black pelage or plumage would absorb more of the sun's radiation, while white is reflective. However, white is essential for these animals to camouflage them against winter snows. Some animals, such as Stoats and *Lagopus* grouse, become white to help them avoid predators; predators such as white-morph Gyrfalcons and Snowy Owls are white to escape detection by prey, both against the snow on the ground and the white of a cloudy sky. However, these predatory species do not molt out of their white plumages in summer; similarly, animals of the high Arctic, such as Gray Wolves and Arctic Hares, do not waste energy molting into a new coat for the short summer either. Given the shortness of the Arctic summer, the energetic input required for pigment production, hair growth and other physiological demands of molting may not be worth the energetic expenditure required. A handful of high Arctic species have no need of white plumage at all. The Raven, for example, is of course black. It is just about large and aggressive enough not to fall prey to falcons or owls, and it has little need for camouflage, being an opportunist feeder rather than a specialized hunter. So Ravens remain black all year-round, no doubt deriving some thermoregulatory benefit.

Hidden colors

Although they look white to us, some Arctic animals, such as the Polar Bear and Gyrfalcon, look very different at ultraviolet (UV) wavelengths. Polar Bear hair absorbs UV, so they are black in UV light. By contrast, Gyrfalcons are highly reflective of UV light. Unlike mammals, birds can see UV wavelengths; Gyrfalcons probably communicate with conspecifics using these UV signals, as has been shown to occur in some other bird species. The importance of UV adds complexity to the relationship between Arctic birds and color. If a white-morph Gyrfalcon glows brightly in UV light, how does it avoid being spotted by a *Lagopus* grouse, which can also see in UV? If camouflage is not so important for a Gyrfalcon after all, what is the true purpose of its white plumage?

The ability of birds to see UV light may have ramifications for Arctic mammals. For example, rodent urine is clearly visible in UV. As a response to this, some rodents, particularly lemmings, construct latrine chambers within their burrows. This means they do not betray their presence to avian predators by urinating above ground.

◀ The relatively long legs of a Gray Wolf help it bound through the snow, Barren Lands, Northwest Territories.

Speciation and biogeography

The formation of new species or speciation is generally thought by biologists to be a largely allopatric process in animals. One population becomes isolated, usually geographically, from the rest of a species, preventing the flow of genes from one group to the other. Once reproductively isolated, the populations can diverge. Processes such as natural selection and genetic drift then lead to the populations becoming genetically different. When reproduction between members of each population becomes impossible, speciation is complete.

In many cases, Arctic populations of animals have undergone reproductive isolation and speciation relatively recently, during late Pliocene and Pleistocene glacial periods. The advances and retreats of the ice had dramatic effects both on speciation and on the ranges of species, or biogeography. As the ice moved south the timberline retreated and forest areas became fragmented, with areas of open land between the remnant forests. It was not just the trees that retreated south at these times; a Snowy Owl is depicted in cave art in southern France, painted by a Palaeolithic artist living at the time of the last glaciation. As with the trees, the owl population was pushed south by the ice, and it expanded north again as the ice retreated.

Ice coverage during the last glacial maximum was greater in western Europe and European Russia than it was in Asian Russia, so larger areas of boreal forest remained in the east. This is reflected today in the greater biodiversity of the eastern Siberian taiga than the forests of western Europe; for example, there are five times as many bird species in the eastern forests than in those of the west. There is a similar though less pronounced disparity in species counts between eastern North America and western Europe.

The importance of refugia

There have been around 21 periods of glaciation over the last 2.5 million years, some of these lowering sea levels by as much as 100m. Drops of sea level exposed large areas of land that were under the sea during interglacial periods. One would assume that advancing ice would simply push species south along a vast front, as happened to the Snowy Owls seen by the Palaeolithic birder. However, ice coverage in the north was not complete. Ice-free areas became refugia in which organisms could survive the glaciation, although isolated from others of their kind — and therefore primed for speciation to take place.

Refugia formed in northwestern Siberia (the Angaron refuge), in northeastern Greenland (the Peary Land refuge) and on some Arctic Canadian islands (the Banksian refuge). The most important refuge, though, was Beringia. This included ice-free areas in Alaska and the Yukon, as well as in northwestern Siberia, and on a land bridge across what is now the Bering Strait, which became dry land as sea levels fell. These Ice Age refugia form the basis of the three most important Arctic tundra areas: Russia's Taimyr Peninsula (with 43 bird species), Canada's Arctic islands (with 42 bird species) and the remnant of Beringia — eastern Siberia and western Alaska (with 47 bird species). Each of these areas has some endemic species that evolved during glacial maxima, with Beringia having the most.

Refugia in time and space

Refugia formed during many of the Pliocene and Pleistocene glaciation events, with significant effects on Arctic populations. Evidence from studies of mitochondrial DNA, which mutates at a predictable rate and therefore adds a temporal aspect to assessing genetic change, allows biologists to unravel some of the story. The Dunlin (*Calidris alpina*) has a circumpolar distribution with a range of reasonably well-defined subspecies. Mitochondrial DNA sampling shows that the oldest form appears to be the one that now breeds in central Canada, *C. a. hudsonia*. This split from an ancestral form about 225,000 years ago, which coincides with the Holstein interglacial. Another split, between European and Siberian-Alaskan forms, occurred at about 120,000 years ago, an event that coincides with the Emian interglacial. The three remaining subspecies (central Siberian, eastern Siberian and Alaskan) split at about 70,000–80,000 years ago during a glacial period, when it seems that the tundra belt was fragmented by ice floes. Similar refuge-driven subspeciation occurred in other species, such as the Rock Ptarmigan.

Things are different in birds like the Ruddy Turnstone, in which subspecies are few and virtually identical. This suggests that glaciation saw the population "bottleneck," with offshoots not being isolated in refugia. Without barriers to gene flow, subspeciation did not take place and the marginal differences seen today between the races are due to other factors. In general, though, Arctic species are polytypic, an indication not only of the effect of refugia, but of the relatively species-scarce nature of the region. With few competitors, a species can diversify into ecological niches that would be closed to it in the more biodiverse ecosystems to the south.

Refuge speciation

The concept of refugia helps to explain speciation in a number of Arctic groups, with populations within them evolving into new species while the rest of the ancestral species is shuffled south by the ice sheets. Examples of probable refugia-generated species include the White-billed Diver and Great Northern Diver. The wax and wane of the taiga forests may have presented a similarly impenetrable barrier to gene flow for other species. For example, evolutionary biologists think that the division of an ancestral falcon into two populations, separated by the taiga, led to the evolution of the Saker Falcon (*Falco cherrug*) of the steppes and the Gyrfalcon (*F. rusticolus*) of the tundra. A similar process of isolation may have led to the evolution of the Polar Bear when a population of Brown Bears was isolated to the north of the Pleistocene ice. A study of the mitochondrial DNA of the two species suggests a divergence within the last few hundred thousand of years, perhaps even less; the Polar Bear is a comparatively recent addition to the

Arctic fauna. Polar Bear x Brown Bear crosses and Saker Falcon x Gyrfalcon crosses are viable (the first wild bear hybrid to be found was discovered — shot dead — in 2006), supporting the suggestion that the species diverged recently. However, as with the dating of the divergences of the Dunlin subspecies, times are dependent on the estimated time scales of mutation in mitochondrial DNA and are therefore subject to alteration as our understanding of this rate improves.

The speciation of Arctic Gulls provides a particularly intriguing field of study for taxonomists and biogeographers because of the clear similarities between many of the larger northern species, and in particular the problem of determining whether Thayer's and Kumlien's Gulls are separate species or simply subspecies of Iceland Gull. Similar questions arise over the taxonomy of the Herring Gull, American Herring Gull and Vega Gull, and of the Lesser Black-backed and Heuglin's Gulls. It is assumed that glaciation separated ancestral forms. With the retreat of the ice, populations expanded their ranges, perhaps contacting groups from which they had long been isolated.

This process of long-separate populations coming together is still going on. Perhaps the most interesting is the current merging of formerly distinct populations of the Snow Goose. Before the early years of the 20th century, the western (white-morph) and eastern (blue-morph) forms of the goose were allopatric in both their breeding and wintering ranges. It is assumed that changes to intensive food production in the southern United States led to an expansion of the ranges of both forms. Interbreeding occurred, and the offspring were viable, so population merging has continued. As the blue morph is genetically dominant, the merged population is trending toward the blue, but in a flock a complete range of forms (white, blue and intermediate) may be seen. The trend is likely to be slow, as the birds exhibit partial assortative mating, i.e., white birds prefer white mates, blue birds prefer blue mates. The Snow Goose story is further complicated by the existence of a "greater" form of Snow Goose, which is larger but represents only 20% of the total population. This form is almost exclusively white and is found in the east of the species' range where the blue form formerly resided exclusively. Also, the majority (lesser) form is known to hybridize with Ross's Goose.

As well as indirectly aiding the spread of the Snow Goose, humans have also assisted an extension of the range of several other bird species. The spread of the Northern Fulmar and the Great Skua are attributed to the growth of the fishing industry, as ship-processing produces a great deal of waste. Changes in land use have also assisted some species; a growth in population forces a subsequent expansion of range. Classic examples are the northward spread of two non-Arctic species. The Eurasian Collared Dove (*Streptopelia decaocto*) was confined to southern Asia and Turkey at the end of the 19th century, but the species had reached Britain by 1955 and has continued to expand northward through Scandinavia. It has been calculated that the species has spread at a rate of up to 25 mi. (40 km) per year. In April 1890, 80 European Starlings (*Sturnus vulgaris*) were

released in New York's Central Park. They had spread into a semicircle of about 250 mi. (400 km) radius by 1910, but the spread then accelerated; by 1970 they had reached the borders of the Arctic throughout North America. Climate then acted to limit the species' expansion. Almost as dramatic has been its colonization of Iceland, whose position in the middle of the North Atlantic would not make it an obvious candidate for the regular acquisition of new species. However, Iceland has gained 10 species since the early 20th century. These range expansions are probably due in part to climatic changes, as there has been little change of land usage in the Arctic, and what change there has been has been at the southern fringe. Climatic change is also a likely reason why some northern species, such as the Atlantic Puffin and Glaucous Gull, have withdrawn from the southern parts of their ranges. If there is a climatic dimension to the range extension of southern species, this is likely to be enhanced by global warming, with a possible reduction in the range of current Arctic species.

As well as aiding in the expansion of certain species, humans have caused or hastened the extinction of some, and drastically reduced the population size of others. It is believed that humans caused the extinction of most of the sub-Arctic megafauna around 10,000 years ago — Mammoths, Wooly Rhinoceros and other large animals of northern Eurasia and North America. Arctic cetaceans have suffered from over-hunting, fur-bearing mammals have been threatened and some bird species have been drastically reduced by egg- and adult-collecting for food. The Great Auk was hunted to extinction by the mid-19th century, and the Eskimo Curlew, once abundant, was relentlessly hunted during migration; if not now actually extinct, it is on the verge of disappearance, since no confirmed sighting has been recorded since 1989. The Spectacled Cormorant (*Phalacrocorax perspicillatus*), discovered during the Bering expedition, was extinct by the 1850s. Entire colonies of other species have also been wiped out.

▼ Snowy Owl, north Norway. These owls ranged as far south as southern France during the last glacial maximum.

▲ Dunlin, North Norway. The evolutionary history of this species has been unraveled by biologists studying mitochondrial DNA.

For mammals, the most obvious example of adverse human influence is Steller's Sea Cow, hunted to extinction within 27 years of its discovery. For other Arctic mammals bar the megafauna and cetaceans, hunting for fur or food and habitat loss have had a limited impact; humans have yet to exploit the region in the ruthless fashion that they have elsewhere, though both the Sea Otter and the Northern Fur Seal can be classified as "near misses." The major exception to the rule of negligible human impact is the importation of the Brown Rat (*Rattus norvegicus*), which has wrought havoc on ground-nesting birds. The Wood Mouse (*Apodemus sylvaticus*) has also been added to the very short list of Icelandic mammal species. However, it is perhaps true that the domestication of the Reindeer saved that species from going the way of the rest of the megafauna.

Joining the Old and New Worlds

Beringia was important not only as a refuge, but also because of the land bridge it provided, linking the Old and New Worlds for animals, including humans, to cross. Beringia may have been useful for birds, but even today the Bering Sea is little impediment to avian species, and several are believed to have extended their ranges, east or west, since the last disappearance of Beringia beneath the waves around 10,000 years ago. The Northern Wheatear and the Arctic Warbler have spread east from Siberia to Alaska, while the Gray-cheeked Thrush has expanded the other way.

Although the intermittent appearances of the Beringia land bridge assisted the expansion of Asian species into North America, it may also have led to speciation in some groups by providing a geographical barrier to gene flow. In auks, for example, Beringia may have prevented the Pacific and Atlantic populations of ancestral auks from interbreeding, leading to allopatric speciation. The distribution of auks is highly asymmetric, with far more species in the north Pacific than in the north Atlantic. It is assumed that the only circumpolar species, three species of *Uria* guillemots, crossed from the Pacific to the Atlantic via the Arctic, a route that was subsequently closed off by Beringia. The present distributions of

other bird groups can prove enlightening in helping us understand how Arctic species have evolved and expanded their ranges. The number of bird species shared by Eurasia and North America increases to the north, as does the similarity of species present. This reaches a maximum in the Arctic, where many birds are circumpolar. This is also true of mammals; the Polar Bear, Brown Bear, Arctic Fox, Reindeer, Musk Ox and many other mammals are either circumpolar in distribution or show marked similarities between the Palearctic and the Nearctic. In Greenland, about two-thirds of bird species are circumpolar, the remainder equally divided between Nearctic species (primarily on the west coast) and Palearctic species (primarily on the east coast). Despite the proximity of the western coast to North America, there are 50% more non-circumpolar species on the eastern side of the island. Greenland was completely ice covered until around 6,000 years ago, so most if not all of the birds there are relatively recent colonists.

Stepping stones

European species have used both Iceland and Greenland as a stepping stone en route to colonization of the Nearctic. Some of these birds offer further indications of their origins by migrating back to or through Europe in winter, though some have found wintering sites in North America to become truly Holarctic species. An example of the latter is the Shore Lark, which seems to have been wintering in North America only since as recently as the 19th century.

The same is also true of some Siberian species, some of which breed in Alaska but migrate back to Eurasia in winter. One species, the Northern Wheatear, is unusual in having reached North America from both directions, so it is now found in Alaska and Canada's Yukon Territory, and in the eastern Canadian Arctic (Labrador, Baffin Island), but not in the Arctic regions between.

Range differences

In general, the ranges of northern species are larger than those of more southerly species. This is called Rapoport's Rule. There are a variety of possible explanations for this. Some biologists have suggested that repeated glaciations may have wiped out organisms with smaller ranges. Alternatively, the range of climatic extremes that organisms need to tolerate to survive at high latitudes may have led these animals and plants to be "pre-adapted" for a greater climatic range overall. Also, habitat diversity, and hence niche availability, is more limited at higher latitudes. Whatever the reason, the tendency for species to be circumpolar in distribution increases as the circumference of Earth shrinks toward the North Pole, a tendency aided by the almost unbroken chain of land circling the Arctic. However, mention must be made of the numerous exceptions to Rapoport's Rule. It does not apply to groups such as freshwater fish or marine invertebrates, for example, and there are avian exceptions. One of the most pronounced is the Bristle-thighed Curlew, which has a breeding range in Alaska that is much smaller than the available habitat. In this case the population is limited by the species' wintering quarters on small Pacific islands. They cannot support a population large enough to exploit the vast potential breeding habitat in Alaska.

fleet is nothing more than a cover for the harvesting of whales for the table. Japanese enthusiasm for funding projects in, for instance, small Caribbean islands with no history of, or apparent interest in, whaling, are also viewed with suspicion when those same countries join the IWC and then vote with the Japanese. The reason for such voting is officially denied by both sides, but seems to occur more frequently than coincidence suggests.

The Japanese position on Bowhead Whales was particularly problematic, as the whole issue of Bowhead take divides people into opposing camps with little common ground. In 1977, Bowhead hunting was banned because of fears over the stock of the whales in the north Pacific (the north Atlantic stock was even lower, as a consequence of European rather than American whaling). The IWC population estimate was 600–1,500 animals, which the IWC and the U.S. government considered to be so low that any take was unsustainable. In response, the native population set up the Alaska Eskimo Whaling Commission (AEWC), which used hydrophones to show that the population was both higher and increasing, so that limited harvesting was acceptable.

Fur trapping

The story of fur trapping, and in particular its devastating effects on Sea Otters, Northern Fur Seals, Arctic Fox and Sable, is discussed on pages 25–26. One aspect of fur trapping that has significantly affected wildlife was the introduction of foxes to almost all the islands of the Aleutian chain. They prey on native bird populations that had developed in the absence of terrestrial predators.

Conservation of Polar Bears

Because of its iconic status as an Arctic animal, the Polar Bear is considered here even though hunting no longer represents a threat to the species' survival. In 1973, an Agreement on the Conservation of Polar Bears and their Habitat was signed by Canada, Denmark (Greenland), Norway, the USSR and the United States. The agreement was finally ratified in 1978, and has been adhered to by the signatories, even though it is not actually binding. The bear population in1973 was declining, and the agreement meant that the take of bears should be restricted. The effect of the agreement was the introduction of

▼ A former sealing vessel has a close encounter with a berg off Svalbard.

a blanket ban on bear-killing in Norway, which, on Svalbard, had no indigenous population with a bear-taking tradition. The USSR had already banned hunting, so that situation prevailed, though there was and still is a poaching problem in that country. Canada, the United States and Greenland allowed for a continuation of traditional hunting by native peoples, with quotas. Canada also allowed hunting, with quotas, by non-Inuit if they were led by Inuit. The Agreement has worked well, but although it led to excellent research on many aspects of bear biology, the accumulation of population data has been less impressive, so harvest quotas are yet to be set in terms of sustainable yield. However, with hunting forbidden in Russia and Svalbard, and with access difficulties reducing outside hunting interest in Greenland, hunting is no longer a threat to Polar Bear populations.

Other birds and mammals

In general the take of animals by native peoples has not yet contributed to population reductions on a par with the destruction of whale and fur-bearing mammal stocks by European hunters in earlier times. An exception is Greenland, where a program of subsidies for fishing and hunting paid by the Danish government to Greenlanders has led to significant population decreases in some species and a scandalous waste of resources, with takes far exceeding both the needs of the population and any possibility of export. Whole colonies of guillemots have been exterminated by overhunting, as modern transport and hunting techniques allow slaughter on a massive scale, and no tradition exists among indigenous Greenlanders of limiting the take; as with other subsistence hunters, they took what was available. It is to be hoped that future policies will stop the slaughter and allow these sensitive populations to increase.

Logging

The boreal forest at the Arctic fringe is affected by airborne pollution and over exploitation, each of which leads to habitat destruction. It is well known that human hardwood demand has led to the drastic over exploitation of the rain forests. Similar demand for softwoods is putting pressure on the boreal forests, and these will become significant if climatic changes lead to large-scale alterations in the forest's make up.

Climate Change

By far the worst threat to the Arctic and its wildlife is that from climate change, specifically global warming. The major concern for the area is less the prospect of increased storminess, though that is clearly not trivial for Arctic inhabitants, than the potential loss of sea-ice cover. In the popular press, certain evidence, such as ice thinning and sea-ice cover shrinkage, is put forward as proof of global warming, and proof by association of human involvement. While few credible scientists now doubt that Earth is indeed warming, and even fewer doubt that there is an anthropogenic input to that change, I have tried here to separate evidence from supposition.

From analysis of ice cores, from the Greenland ice cap for example, it is possible to determine the level of greenhouse gases, specifically carbon dioxide (CO_2) and methane, in the Earth's atmosphere in pre-industrial times. This calculated level of CO_2 is 290 parts per million (ppm). The present level is about 375 ppm. The methane concentration has doubled over the same period. The levels of other greenhouse gases (nitrogen dioxide and CFCs) have also risen. The current rate of increase of CO_2 is around 2 ppm per year.

Visible and ultraviolet radiation from the sun is absorbed at the Earth's surface and then partially reradiated at infra-red (IR) wavelengths. While they are transparent to visible and UV radiation, greenhouse gases absorb or back-reflect IR, leading to an increase in the temperature of the atmosphere, in an analogous way to the increase in temperature of a greenhouse because of the similar transmission/reflectance properties of glass. Without the levels of greenhouses gases that existed in pre-industrial times, life, in the forms that now exist, would not be possible. The greenhouse effect raises the surface temperature of Earth by about 95°F (35°C). Without the pre-industrial levels of these gases, the Earth's mean temperature of about 59°F (15°C) would be -4°F (-20°C). Greenhouse gases are, therefore, essential to life on Earth. However, an increase in the temperature of Earth will have some very undesirable consequences, and if the observed increase in the concentration of gases is responsible, then there are reasons for grave concern.

The probable cause of the increase in CO_2 is anthropogenic use of fossil fuels; 80% of the world's energy is derived from burning fossil fuels. Whether that is the true cause or not, what cannot be disputed is that the temperature of Earth is increasing, and that this will have consequences not only for Arctic species, but for all species, including humans. The temperature of the Arctic is increasing faster than that of Earth as a whole due to a variety of factors, such as declines in albedo (reflectance of incoming light energy) due to loss of ice cover. Current measurements indicate that, while the average temperature of Earth has risen by 34°F (0.8°C) over the last 25 years, that of the Arctic as a whole has risen by around 34°F (1°C). The average winter temperature in the Arctic has risen by around 36°F (2°C) over the same period. That temperatures have risen is beyond dispute; data suggests that 2005 was the warmest globally since records began. Not only are recorded temperatures rising, but some of the effects of a warming Earth are equally indisputable; Arctic sea-ice cover has reduced, and in Africa, Mount Kenya's glaciers have lost 75% of their area since 1899, with 40% of that loss occurring since 1967.

Computer models of the Earth's climate indicate a likely further rise in Arctic temperature of 37–41°F (3–5°C) on land and up to 45°F (7°C) in the ocean by 2100 if anthropogenic production of greenhouse gases continues at present rates. Winter temperatures are calculated to be even higher, 39–45°F (4–7°C) on land and up to 50°F (10°C) in the ocean. Temperatures in parts of Alaska have shown a winter average increase of 37–39°F (3–4°C) over the last 25 years. The consequences of a warming Arctic are detailed below.

Reduction in sea ice

Although sea ice, including that of the Antarctic, represents around 70% of the Earth's surface area of ice coverage, it represents only 0.05% of the Earth's ice volume. Small changes in global climate can therefore dramatically affect the sea-ice volume with consequential changes in albedo and hence increased polar temperatures relative to those of the temperate zone. It is clear that the extent of the sea ice in the Arctic has declined over the last 50 years. The extent during the summer of 2005 was the smallest measured in the last 100 years. The average minimum since 1979, when accurate extents became available from satellite photography, has been about 3 million sq. mi. (7 million km²). The 2005 value was 20% below this figure. The 2005 figure was the latest in a series of extreme minima measured since 1980. The present reduction in extent is about 2.9% ±0.2% per decade. However, with the temperature in the Arctic predicted to rise, this rate will increase. Present computer estimates of the reduction suggest an annual average loss of 50% by the end of the century. The models predict higher summer losses than in winter, with some models predicting that within this time frame the Arctic Ocean could become ice-free in summer.

An ice-free ocean would mean the extinction of the Polar Bear, but some populations of bear will be under threat and perhaps extinct well before that time. Male Polar Bears coming ashore in southern Hudson Bay and moving to Churchill may lose up to 30% of their body weight before the sea freezes again. Pregnant females may lose 55%. The condition of the bears has declined over the past two decades, with a 15% reduction in average weight, and a reduction in the number of cubs reaching adulthood. The number of cubs that become independent in their first year has also decreased. In contrast to northern bears, achieving early independence used to be fairly common, up to 40% of cubs. Now it is much less common (0%–5%).

The reduction in the extent of sea ice will allow sea travel on the Arctic Ocean. While this will be advantageous in terms of cutting journey times, easier access will also allow easier exploitation of Arctic resources, which may increase the stress on declining Arctic species.

Thawing of permafrost

As well as a reduction in the extent of sea-ice cover, snow cover has reduced on adjacent lands. Snow cover influences the behavior of permafrost, because, as well as insulating the ground, snow has a higher albedo than bare ground. With a shorter period of cover, the permafrost active layer will penetrate deeper. Borehole data from northern Alaska indicate that the temperature of the permafrost has risen by 36–39°F (2–4°C) over the last 80–100 years. As the active layer enlarges, there will be changes in local hydrology. The process is complex, as differing thicknesses of the active layer lead to differences in water runoff, with corresponding changes in water chemistry and distribution. However, hydrological changes might mean that lakes shrink or disappear, with a consequent loss of habitat. Thawing of the permafrost may also disrupt Arctic settlements and infrastructure, as some of these are built directly onto the inactive permafrost layer.

Higher precipitation

Warming of the Arctic will lead to more evaporation from the exposed ocean, more cloud formation and more precipitation. Increased cloud cover means warmer winters (because of the back-reflection of IR radiation) but cooler summers because of increased albedo from the clouds. Warmer winters mean a potential further decrease in winter sea-ice cover, while the cooler summers cannot compensate for increased air temperatures due to the greenhouse effect.

While computer models predict a global increase of up to 5% in precipitation by the end of the century, the increase in the Arctic is likely to be two or three times higher. Snow falling on glaciers will increase their thickness, but if much of the precipitation falls as rain, glacial melting will be enhanced.

Autumnal rains that freeze reduce the ability of Reindeer, in particular, to feed, as they are unable to break through the ice to reach forage below. The reduction in the population of Peary Caribou in Canada from 26,000 in 1961, to 1,000 in 1997 has been largely attributed to this situation. Similar problems have affected domestic Reindeer herds in Norway. Any increase in winter snowfall exacerbates the problem.

In addition to increased precipitation, there is likely to be an increase in storminess. Such an increase has already been seen: 2005 had one of the highest hurricane counts ever recorded, including Hurricane Katrina, which devastated New Orleans. This, and other incidents of extreme weather, does not prove the existence of global warming, but it is consistent with that hypothesis.

Positive feedback

Each of the effects mentioned above will lead to an increase in global warming due to positive feedback; as the temperature of the Arctic increases, the rate of increase may itself accelerate. As sea ice is replaced by open water, albedo decreases so that more heat is absorbed, adding further to the warming of the air above the ocean during the winter. The thaw of sea ice is also not a sudden event; pools of meltwater form on the ice surface and the numbers of leads increase. The albedo of meltwater is also less than that of ice. Enhanced precipitation, if it falls as rain, dramatically increases thawing. This phenomenon is well known to southern dwellers; sunny days will cause lying snow to thaw slowly, but a much shorter period of rain will remove it completely. Even if the precipitation falls as snow, the albedo reduces, particularly if the snow is wet, as the albedo of wet snow is much lower than that of dry snow. As the temperature of the active layer in permafrost increases, so does microbial activity. This activity releases CO_2 into the atmosphere. It is estimated that that the uppermost and more vulnerable layer of the northern hemisphere's permafrost holds around 30% of all the carbon stored in the world's soils. In addition to the potential release of this, the warming of permafrost releases methane gas trapped within it. It is estimated that the permafrost of Siberia contains 25% of the world's methane, in a frozen form. In August 2005, Siberian scientists reported a record thaw in the world's largest peat bog. Thawing the permafrost releases the methane, which is around 20 times more efficient as a greenhouse gas than CO_2. A survey in 2005 suggested that, at the present rate of loss of permafrost, some 75% of it will be gone, to a depth of 10 ft. (3 m), by 2050. Even on the most optimistic models, the reduction will be of 60% by 2100. As the world's forests are also being denuded, the uptake of CO_2 has declined. At one time it was considered that an increased uptake of CO_2 by the world's oceans would alleviate the problem of increased CO_2 production. However, it is now clear that this uptake is limited. The oceans do absorb CO_2 from the atmosphere and transfer it to deep water. But increased rainfall reduces the density of the surface layer of water, creating a stratification that decreases the movement of absorbed gases to the deep ocean, and as the water temperature rises, the solubility of both CO_2 and methane decreases, so that rather than being a sink the oceans eventually become an extra source of greenhouse gases.

Ice-cap thawing and sea-level rises

Although thawing of the Arctic's sea ice will not cause sea levels to rise, thawing of ice caps and glaciers will, as freshwater locked onto landmasses is released into the sea. It is estimated that the thaw area of the Greenland ice cap, the second largest on Earth after that on Antarctica, has increased by 16% since 1980. As noted above, global warming will increase precipitation at the poles. On Antarctica, snowfall on the central ice cap is calculated to add more water volume than is lost due to thawing of the ice cap at its edge, so that overall the impact on sea-level rise would be negative. The situation is different for the Greenland ice cap, where thawing will outweigh snowfall. Thawing of the Greenland ice cap is a net contributor to sea level rise.

In addition to a rise due to ice cap thawing, sea levels will also rise if sea temperatures increase as a result of the thermal expansion of the water. In practice, thermal expansion is the most significant contributor to sea level rise. Using the thermal model that is considered to offer the best estimate of the overall effect of sea temperature rise and glacial and ice cap thaw, the thermal effect contributes 56% of the expected rise in sea level, the Greenland ice cap contributes 32%, while Antarctica's contribution is -2%. The remainder derives from the thaw of glaciers and other ice caps. If the Greenland ice cap thaws completely, the expected rise in sea level is around 20 ft. (6 m).

The end of the North Atlantic Drift

Although the rise in sea levels is the most critical effect of global warming on a worldwide basis, a more significant effect for northern Europe, with the potential to occur much sooner, would be the termination of the North Atlantic Drift, the northern arm of the Gulf Stream, which keeps winters in the area mild and wet. The Gulf Stream is a thermohaline current that would be affected by an influx of fresh water to the North Atlantic, from the Greenland ice cap thaw, increased precipitation and an increase in the flow volume of the rivers that discharge into the Arctic Ocean, all of which are occurring There is already evidence that the salinity of these northern waters is falling, and in late 2005 measurements detected a 30% decrease in bottom flow, representing a weakening of the Gulf Stream, and a 30% increase in the Azores Current, the latter suggesting a reduction in the North Atlantic Drift. The Drift is part of a stable ocean configuration, and any change to the configuration might mean a shift to a different stable position, which could happen over a very short period, perhaps measured in decades. However, scientific opinion is divided on the likelihood of such a scenario. While some think that the probability is now greater than 50% and that the "point of no return" may already have been passed, others are more cautious, believing that the volume of fresh water required to turn the Drift off completely is more than that available from the increased flow in northern rivers and ice-cap thaw. But even those scientists believe that the Drift is slowing in terms of volume flow, and that northern Europe can expect to see colder winters in future. It is ironic that global warming may raise the area's summer temperatures at the same time that it reduces winter temperatures. However, the extent of winter cooling is unclear. In principle, without the benefit of the warm waters of the Drift, winter temperatures in the British Isles, for example, would compare to those of Newfoundland, with a 4°C–6°C decrease in mean January temperature. This might mean regular periods with temperatures of 5°F (-15°C) and even sea-ice blockage of some ports. But global warming will counteract some or most of this temperature reduction, so the full effect is unlikely to be seen. The best estimate is that, on average, winters in northern Europe are likely to be colder in future as the Drift reduces, though exactly how cold is open to conjecture.

Northern movement of species

As the Earth's temperature increases, the boreal forest will spread north and the area of tundra will shrink. The spread of trees will be matched by a northward spread of southern species, squeezing northern species, whose northward movement is restricted by the availability of land. Adaptation through natural selection does not work as swiftly as the extrapolated temperature increase, so some northern species may be squeezed out of existence. Humans will also move north, adding further stress to northern ecosystems and their animals and plants.

The Arctic Ocean limits not only the spread of northern wildlife, but also of the trees, and this may present a further problem. The White Spruce is the most widespread boreal species in North America and a very valuable timber tree. As temperature increases, the trees' growth rate decreases and ultimately ceases. The trees then die off. In addition, increasing temperature means that infestations of the Spruce Bark Beetle (*Dendroctonus rufipennis*) and Spruce Budworm (*Choristoneura fumiferana*) will increase, damaging the dwindling resource further. The risk of forest fires will also increase.

Rise in sea temperature

The world's oceans are a vast heat sink, and therefore moderate an increasing trend in atmospheric temperature. However, once the sea temperature has risen, the thermal inertia of the system acts against any attempt to reduce atmospheric temperature. The effects of thawing sea ice and rising sea temperatures are complex, and the only thing that can be said with certainty is that changes will alter food chains and the distribution of species. Examples of the effect of temperature rise have already occurred. The rise in sea temperature around Antarctica has caused an alarming reduction in the population of krill; of 80% since the 1970s, with a consequent effect on penguin and seals. In Britain, populations of Fulmars, Black-legged Kittiwakes and Common Guillemots are all falling, as warmer seas mean reduced plankton yields, and consequently fewer organisms in all parts of the food chain. In response to warming seas, fish move to deeper waters or migrate northward, either event being catastrophic for birds, which may not be able reach them as the fish are too deep or too far from traditional breeding areas. As smaller fish tend to change their breeding areas more quickly than larger predatory ones, stocks of the latter, already stressed by overfishing, become even more vulnerable.

Absorption of CO_2 by the sea, which acts against the build-up of this gas in the upper atmosphere and therefore serves to counteract the greenhouse effect to a limited extent, also increases the acidity of the water to damaging effect for a range of marine organisms. One further effect, which has caused temperature rises in the Bering Sea, is the frequency of El Niño events. Though associated with the tropical western Pacific, El Niño events also affect the North Pacific and are seen in the Bering Sea. The effect of an event is a rise in water temperature that can last for up to two years. El Niño events appear to be occurring more frequently.

Conclusions

Some scientists believe that global warming is a myth and are willing to quote spurious data in support of the view, for example pointing to percentages of glaciers that are advancing, which, when the quoted references are explored, do not exist. Recently in the United States it was discovered that official documents had been altered to present a less definite picture of the problems. There are, of course, scientists who genuinely believe that global warming is a short-term, reversible phenomenon, driven by the sun's output, and detectable by the number and size of sunspots. They note that the sun will soon enter a low output phase and that temperatures will decrease. The majority of other scientists in the field, however, believe that the effect of increased greenhouse gases in the atmosphere is the dominant cause, and point to the positive feedback mechanisms mentioned above, as well as others. For example, they note that tropical forests are dying out and being replaced by grassland; the albedo of grasslands is higher that that of the forests but cannot compensate for the lack of CO_2 uptake by the trees. This scientific majority accept that there are unknowns because of the complex nature of feedback mechanisms, but agree that global warming represents a grave threat to life as presently seen. Some scientists conjecture that there may be a turning point in the increase in the Earth's temperature at which the thaw of the Arctic will become self-perpetuating and irreversible. At that stage, changes might affect all life on Earth at a rate so rapid that adaptation might be difficult and, for many species, impossible.

The Kyoto Protocol was an attempt to persuade world governments of the importance of global warming. The plan was for industrialized nations to reduce aggregate emissions by 5.2% from 1990 levels by 2008-12. The United States, which is responsible for about 23% of the world's CO_2 emissions, did not ratify the treaty. Other major producers are China (13%), Russia (6%), Japan (5%), India (4%), Germany (3%), the United Kingdom, Canada, South Korea and Italy (all about 2%); these 10 countries account for 66% of emissions. The situation improved in December 2005 when, at Montreal, the signatories of Kyoto agreed an extension of the protocol beyond 2012 and the United States was persuaded, apparently by the shock of negative world reaction after their negotiators had initially walked out, to agree to future negotiations though not, as yet, to a binding series of commitments.

Shortly after the meeting, it was announced that U.S. emissions of greenhouse gases were at their highest level ever in 2004 and had doubled since 1990; not only was the level of emissions increasing, but the rate of increase was also increasing. It is anticipated that figures for 2005 will show another significant rise. It is difficult to understand the American point of view, as ultimately the prosperity of the United States depends on that of the rest of the world. The problem is that altruism is not a notable behavior pattern in any species, and humans are no exception. Many believe that the vested interest of oil companies is a major obstacle to serious consideration of the problems, leading some to wonder whether Earth can endure long enough for the oil to run out so that their influence will wane. This observation takes on extra significance with the news in late 2005 that lobbyists for the U.S. oil industry were attempting to persuade European business and political leaders to abandon their support for the Kyoto agreement.

But there is a problem with individuals as well as corporations. The American enthusiasm for gas-guzzling SUVs at a time of increased hurricane activity is a case in point. Similar personal enthusiasms to those of SUV drivers can be detected in politicians, as correct but unpopular decisions can affect their careers. When Tony Blair, the British prime minister, was asked what he intended to do about the proliferation of low-cost airlines in the UK, given that airlines are far "dirtier," in terms of CO_2 emissions than other mass transport systems such as railways, he replied that political reality meant that the subject was difficult to tackle. In this context, political reality translates as there being no votes in tackling the subject.

In his authoritative book, *Collapse*, on the survival and failure of civilizations, Jared Diamond wonders what was going through the minds of Easter Islanders as they felled the island's last tree and so doomed themselves to a collapsing economy and civilization. Was it "jobs not trees"? Was it the Micawberesque hope that something would turn up? Or the apparently sensible, though ultimately foolish, idea that what was needed was more research and that concern about a lack of trees was scaremongering? Diamond could perhaps have added that one tribe dared not have stopped because another might not. The situation has a close analogy with the present situation, with Western countries declining to initiate meaningful reductions in greenhouse gas emissions, as it would harm their economies, and developing countries declining to do so as they seek Western-style materialism. Everyone is waiting for someone else to make the first move; meanwhile, the last tree falls.

Montreal 2005 was an encouraging step forward, but the scale of what may be required in terms of emission reductions to contain the problem is such that the nations of the world may recoil from it or talk for so long that irreversible change may become inevitable. Even if politicians were to act decisively tomorrow, the Earth's temperature is still likely to rise by at least 33°F (0.6°C) over the next 30 years. That alone will bring the majestic Polar Bear and many other charismatic Arctic animals to the brink of extinction.

▼ Melting of the Greenland ice cap will have a major effect on the world's sea levels. Inglefield Fjord, Thule, north-west Greenland.

How to use the field guides

The field guide sections of this book are divided into two sections: birds and mammals. Species entries are generally in phylogenetic order, divided into major taxonomic groupings. There is at least one photograph of every species of Arctic bird and most of the mammals, with the Arctic region considered to lie broadly within the modified 50°F (10°C) isotherm as discussed on pages 6–8. Some other species that occur in sub-Arctic regions or that occasionally stray into the Arctic are discussed in the introduction to each group. Groups such as shrikes and starlings that contain sub-Arctic species but no truly Arctic species are discussed in brief.

The species accounts

Common names follow ITIS and USDA guidelines. Scientific names of birds follow the *"British Birds" List of Western Palearctic Birds*, which incorporates revisions up to the end of 2005. Alternative names are also included.

The accounts contain detailed information subdivided into the following sections:

Identification

In the field guide to Arctic birds, this section concentrates on features of plumages seen mainly in the Arctic; for example, breeding plumages of waders are discussed in detail, but less prominence is given to winter plumages that are more likely to occur extralimitally. Identification features of the chicks and juveniles are also noted. Mammal identification features are discussed in relation to pelage in winter and summer, including that of the young; note that some of the shrews and microtines are virtually impossible to identify to species level in the field, so general notes only are given for these groups.

Confusion species

This section details species that may possibly cause identification problems within the Arctic region, and how best to separate them.

Size

A variety of dimensions are given. In the bird accounts, these are abbreviated as follows:

L   = length
WS = wingspan
W   = approximate weight

In the mammal accounts, additional abbreviations relate to:

HB = head and body length
T   = tail length
TL = total length, including head, body and tail
SH = shoulder height

Voice

This section discusses the song and calls of birds in the region;

in the field guide to Arctic mammals this section is referred to as Communication, and it includes non-auditory inter- and intraspecific signals.

Distribution

The breeding range of each species within the Arctic is discussed, presenting the summer range, followed by summer habitat. The winter distribution and habitat then follow.

This section is accompanied by a detailed color map, showing the breeding range (for migrants) or the range year-round (for residents). The maps are based on a globe, and three main projections have been used, depending on the faunal zone(s) occupied by the species in question: Circumpolar, Nearctic and Palearctic. Each of the Arctic countries is filled with a contrasting shade. The range illustrated on the map is a "mask" so the underlying sea conditions or landmass can still be observed. Ranges of animals that are probably extinct (e.g., Eskimo Curlew) are shown in yellow.

Key to the species maps:

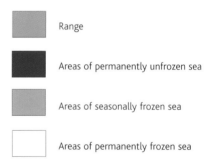

Range

Areas of permanently unfrozen sea

Areas of seasonally frozen sea

Areas of permanently frozen sea

Note that a standard transcription of Russian names has been used in the distribution section, except where features have well-known English versions of their names. A good example is the use of Commander Islands for the island group close to Kamchatka's southwestern shore. The English name is now known well enough to be used instead of the Komandorskiye Islands. Similarly, New Siberia Islands is preferred to Novosibirskiye Ostrova.

Diet

A discussion of the predominant foods taken in summer and winter is presented.

Breeding

A full description of breeding biology is given. Accounts in the field guide to Arctic birds include information on sociobiology, courtship behavior, nest location and structure, number and color of eggs, incubation time, chick status on hatching, brooding and rearing, fledging time and time to sexual

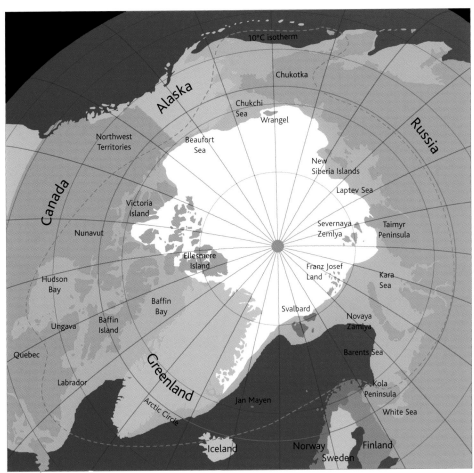

▲ Large-scale map of the region. This shows the Arctic countries and their territories (such as Jan Mayen, Svalbard and Franz Josef Land). The modified 50°F (10°C) isotherm appears as a dotted red line; the traditional Arctic Circle at 66° 33′ N, the point at which the sun can be seen for 24 hours on the summer solstice, is shown in green.

maturity. Accounts in the field guide to Arctic mammals include additional information on gestation period, the size of the young at birth, the duration of lactation and time to sexual maturity, with probable life-span information given where appropriate.

Taxonomy and geographical variation

This section discusses the taxonomy and racial variation seen in the species of interest. For birds, both Howard and Moore (3rd edition) and Clements (6th edition) have been used as major authorities, though a number of other important works have been referred to. Mammalian taxonomy has been gleaned from a variety of sources; since subspecific variation is usually very difficult or impossible to determine in the field, this is generally not discussed in detail.

Plates

Accompanying the species entries for each major taxonomic group are a series of color plates. Annotation on these has been kept as simple as possible; all illustrations are of the nominate race unless otherwise indicated. For birds, the plates generally show the male bird in breeding plumage.

The following abbreviations are used to describe plumage:

ad(s)	=	adults
br	=	breeding
imm	=	immature
juv	=	juvenile
sum	=	summer
1st-sum	=	first-summer
win	=	winter
1st-win	=	first-winter

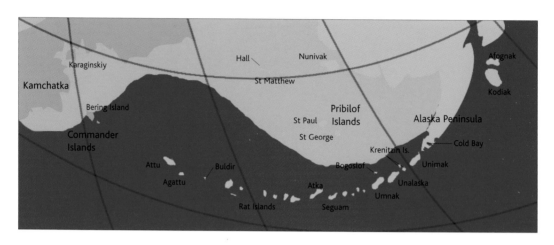

▲ Map of the larger Aleutian and southern Bering Sea Islands.

▲ Map showing the larger islands and peninsulas of the Canadian Arctic.
Note that the word *Island* has been omitted for clarity on the smaller islands.

Field guide to
Arctic Birds

Loons

The five species of loon are all Arctic specialists. Highly specialized swimmers, they have considerable difficulty walking. This is believed to be the basis for the birds' name, which is derived from the Norse word *lømr*, meaning lame or clumsy.

The difficulties of loons on land stem from the legs being placed far back on a long body. Auks partially overcome this problem by adopting an upright stance, but loons do not and instead walk with a shuffling gait with the body held at an angle. Because of this angle, loons walk uphill more easily than they do on flat ground, though they dislike both and walk as infrequently as possible, nesting close to the edges of their breeding lakes and ponds. Loons have very high wing loadings, which in combination with their poor walking ability means that they struggle to take off from land and take off from water is protracted, requiring a long stretch of water. They therefore generally nest only on large bodies of water. On tree-surrounded lakes, loons occasionally have to circle the lake after takeoff, as they gain height so slowly that they are unable to clear the trees in a straight line. Once airborne, the birds are powerful fliers, often traveling 35 mi. (60 km) or more to feed in the sea. Due to the positioning of the feet, loons must land on their bellies.

While their foot and leg morphology causes loons problems on land, these features mean the birds are supreme in water, hence their British name, divers. In diving, the feet operate together as highly efficient paddles and are the only part of the bird to break the streamlined profile of the head and body. Between paddle strokes the bird holds its head stationary relative to its surroundings to search for prey. The wings are not used for propulsion during the dive, but occasionally aid in turning. Before diving the birds often "snorkel," dipping their heads below water for long periods to scan for prey. The feet extend beyond the tail, helping to distinguish all loons from cormorants in flight.

The voice and diving ability of loons led them to become part of many ancient myths and legends. The bird's haunting cry, an evocative sound of the wilderness, seemed almost to be an echo, a memory of the dead, and in Siberia and North America it was believed that loons aided the dead in their journey to the spirit world. Some cultures would bury the skull of a loon with the dead, with carved ivory eyes replacing the bird's originals to allow it to "see" the right way. The bird's long dives suggested an ability to see in the dark, and from this grew a legend that loons could restore the sight of the blind by transporting them to the black depths of lakes. The white spots on the backs of the birds were said to be a shell necklace given by one grateful recipient of this healing power. However, the respect in which many native peoples held loons was not universal; the birds were also coveted for their good eating and for the beauty of their feathers.

Common Loon (Great Northern Diver)
Gavia immer

Identification See p. 69

Breeding adults are large, attractive birds with stunning plumage. The head is black, occasionally with a greenish sheen. The neck is black with small throat and larger lower neck patches of black-and-white vertical striping. The iris is red. The bill is dark gray and is usually held horizontally. The forehead is steep and ends in a distinct bump if the bird's small crest is raised. Behind this the crown is flat. The back is beautifully checkered in black and white, predominantly white on the coverts. The underparts are white. In flight the large feet extending beyond the tail are prominent, particularly if the webs are spread. The neck curves down in flight. Winter adults lose the prominent red eye and gain a white eye-ring. The bill becomes gray-white, but with a distinct black culmen and tip. The chin and front of the neck are white. There is sometimes a partial white collar. The head and back of the neck are dark grayish-brown. The upperparts lose the checkerboard pattern, becoming dark with a pattern of still darker bands; the underparts remain white. Juvenile birds are similar to the winter adults, but the dark bands on the upperparts are

◄ Adult Common Loon in breeding plumage, Barren Lands, Northwest Territories.

replaced with a scale pattern picked out by paler fringing. first-summer birds are as juveniles; second-winter birds similar to winter adults but slightly darker. Downy young are dark brown or black. Adults molt into breeding plumage early in the year and are flightless for about one month at this time.

Confusion species

Adult in summer plumage is easily confused with Yellow-billed Loon, which is comparable in size and in the patterning of the head and upperparts. The ranges of the two adjoin but do not really overlap. The pale bill of the Yellow-billed Loon is distinctive, as is its upward-tilt. Bill color and orientation are the best identification features in winter, though the Yellow-billed Loon's head and neck are both much paler and browner. The paler head and neck of Yellow-billed is the best identification clue for juvenile birds.

Size

L: 30–36 in. (75–90 cm). WS: 4–4½ ft. (120–140 cm). W: 8¾–9¾ lb. (3.8–4.4 kg), but to 13 lb. (6 kg). Heavy bird for its size — some bones are solid rather than hollow, to assist diving.

Voice

Usually silent outside the breeding season. Four calls have been noted. The most appealing is the beautiful wailing call, often heard at night. Male loons also have a yodel, a long, rising call used only by the male when defending his territory. A higher-pitched laughing call is occasionally heard from an anxious or startled bird; this is also used occasionally between a pair. There is also a short, one-note call used between the pair if they are out of sight of each other.

Distribution

Essentially Nearctic, but breeds on Iceland, Jan Mayen, Greenland (on southwest, northwest and east coasts) and Bear Island. In North America breeds from Alaska to Labrador,

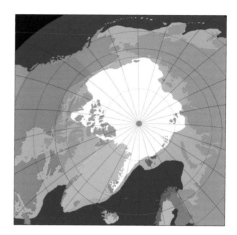

including southern Baffin Island. Found in larger bodies of water within the tundra and also in shallow bays. Migratory; in North America, birds winter offshore along the whole of the Pacific and Atlantic coasts and into the Gulf of Mexico. In Europe, the birds winter around Iceland and off the coasts of the northern British Isles and Norway. Adults migrate south first, with juveniles following a few days later.

Diet

Fish in summer (trout are favored in Iceland, perch in North America) supplemented by frogs, salamanders, crayfish and snails. In winter hunts marine fish as well as shellfish. Can dive to more than 260 ft. (80 m) in search of prey (a Common Loon has been found trapped in a net set at 266 ft./81 m).

Breeding

Gregarious in winter, but pairs are solitary and highly territorial at breeding site. Birds arrive in pairs from their wintering grounds, each pair staking claim to a single lake or to a well-defined territory of a larger lake. Courtship includes mutual bill-dipping and diving with significant splashing. Pair-bond

▼ Common Loons with a young chick, northern Ontario.

probably monogamous, and long-lasting or lifelong. Pairs are highly territorial with threat displays that include adopting an upright stance on water with bill thrust forward. Preferred nest site is a small islet or floating vegetation mass, but if these are not available, a shore site close to the water will be used. Nest made by both birds of vegetation, sometimes with clumps of mud. Two dark buff eggs (occasionally one), speckled brown; these may be laid directly on the substrate if little nest material is available. Incubation is by both birds for 25–28 days (incubating bird invariably facing the water); the second hatchling often perishes. Chicks nidifugous and precocial; can swim almost immediately, but spend time on their parent's backs to conserve heat and avoid predators. The normally shy adults become aggressive when they have young, rearing up from the water on their legs and flapping their wings vigorously, even making mock runs at a potential predators. Chicks do not return to nest from one to two days after hatching. Adults care for chicks for about eight weeks. Fledge at 70–77 days and are independent at that time. Breed at 2–3 years.

Taxonomy and geographical variation
Monotypic.

Yellow-billed Loon
(While-billed Diver)
Gavia adamsii

Identification See p. 69
The largest of the five loons. The adult bill is pale yellow or ivory (the variability allowing both British and North American names to seem correct!). The bill is slightly upturned and invariably held pointing slightly upward, which is accentuated by the upward angle of the gonys. Because of its pale color, the bill can seem large against dark backgrounds but is in fact no larger than that of the Common Loon. The head and neck are black, but without the green sheen of the Common (the sheen is usually not discernible, but occasionally looks purplish). The iris is red. The neck is marked in similar positions to the Common, but with fewer and much broader white stripes. Checkerboard pattern on upperparts has fewer but larger white spots. The forehead lacks the steepness and the head the flat crown of the Common so the head appears rounded, though it also has a forehead bump. In winter the bill is paler and less yellow and often has a dark base. The culmen is also dark along half its length. Rest of the plumage mirrors that of the Common Loon, but the Yellow-billed is brown rather than gray and usually has a few white spots ("sugar lumps") on the wing-coverts. The eye-ring is also larger, often forming an eyepatch rather than a ring. The neck is also more extensively white. Juveniles are browner than those of Common, though both have scalelike fringing. As in Common Loons, juveniles retain their appearance during their first summer, becoming darker during their second winter. Downy young are dark brown or black.

Confusion species
See Common Loon. As well as bill color, the greater proportion of white to black on the upperparts can also aid identification, particularly in flight.

Size
L: 32–36 in. (80–90 cm). WS: 4½–5 ft. (135–150 cm). W: 10–12 lb. (4.5–5.5 kg), exceptionally to 14 lb. (6.5 kg).

▼ A Yellow-billed Loon on the nest. The shape and color of the bill are the strongest identification features, Lena Delta.

Voice

Very similar to that of the Common Loon, but lower and harsher and tending to have a slower delivery.

Distribution

Circumpolar. Breeds along the Arctic coast of Russia, from the Urals to the Pacific and on the southern island of Novaya Zemlya, with densest populations on the Taimyr and Chukotka Peninsulas. In North America, Yellow-billed Loons breed in northern Alaska and the central Canadian Arctic, including Banks and Victoria Islands. Found in larger bodies of water on the tundra, and occasionally on rivers and in shallow bays. Russian birds head either east or west for winter; they can be seen in the Bering Sea as far south as Kamchatka and northern Japan, along the north Norwegian coast, and very occasionally in the Baltic Sea. Nearctic birds move to the eastern Bering Sea and the Great Slave Lake. Adults migrate first, with juveniles following on a few weeks later.

Diet

As for Common Loon.

Breeding

Gregarious in winter, but solitary at breeding sites. Birds arrive in pairs from their wintering grounds. Displays similar to Common Loon. Pair-bond monogamous and apparently lifelong, but evidence is scarce. As in other species of loons nest sites close to the water are chosen, though Yellow-billed Loon will choose river as well as lake sites and is less eager to choose islets. Nest made of vegetation. Two dark buff eggs speckled dark brown; incubated by both birds for around 28 days. The eggs hatch a day or two apart, with the younger chick often perishing. Chicks nidifugous and precocial. Cared for by each parent in turn; chicks spend only one day at the nest before taking to the water. Sometimes brooded on the shore. Fledge at about 70 days. Breed at 2–3 years.

Taxonomy and geographical variation

Monotypic.

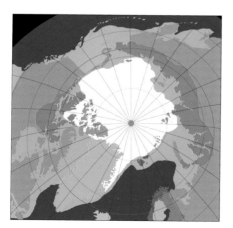

Arctic Loon (Black-throated Diver)
Gavia arctica

Identification   See p. 69

Smaller than the Common Loon but with equally stunning plumage. The adult has a pale gray head, the color extending down the back of the neck. The throat and lower front of the neck are black, and the sides of the neck are striped white and pale gray. At the top edge of the black throat patch is a half collar of white and gray stripes. The head and neck are the same thickness, the head rounded or with a slight bump at the top of the forehead. The iris is red. The bill is dark gray. The chest is bulbous at the waterline. The breast and underparts are white. The mantle and flanks are black-and-white striped, and the coverts are white with gray barring. The outer wings are dark gray with some white spotting. There is a white patch on the belly and lower flanks, which is very distinct in the swimming bird.

In winter adults the gray head is retained, though the color is darker and the sides of the head below the eye are white. The black throat patch is lost, with that and the lower neck becoming white. There is a darker band where the gray and white areas of the neck merge. The striping of the flanks is more muted, and the upperparts are entirely dark gray with some white spotting. The white belly and lower flank patches are retained. In juveniles the white flank patch is even more pronounced. Their head/neck coloration is as adult winter plumage but the gray is paler. The upperparts are browner and

▼ Arctic Loon in breeding plumage, Finland.

have the white fringing of the larger loons, though the "scaling" is less pronounced. The bill of winter adults and juveniles is pale gray with a black tip. Downy young are dark brown, but molt into a second down, which is paler brown above, cream beneath.

Confusion species
Summer adults are distinct from the larger loons. In winter, smaller size and white flank patch aid identification from larger loons. White flank patch distinguishes winter Arctic from winter Red-throated. Red-throated Loon is also much flatter-chested at the waterline. In their limited areas of overlap, Arctic Loon can be distinguished from Pacific Loon by the white flank patch and the more pronounced striping on sides of neck in summer.

Size
L: 24–30 in. (60–75 cm). WS: 3½–4 in. (110–125 cm). W: 4–5½ lb. (1.8–2.5 kg), occasionally to 7½ lb. (3.4 kg).

Voice
Usually silent in flight and in winter. Has a distinctive gull-like wail which is often heard at night, and an evocative, low-pitched whistling song. Also has a sharp *kraat* that can remind the listener of a goose or raven.

Distribution
Essentially Palearctic, but small population breeds in western Alaska. Breeds in Eurasia from northern Scotland and northern Scandinavia across northern Russia and in Kamchatka. Absent from Iceland and Greenland. Found on open water in tundra or taiga. Requires less extensive water area than Common Loon. Also found on rivers. Russian birds migrate east then south, wintering in northwestern Pacific around Japan south to the Chinese coast. European Russian birds head west to join Scandinavian birds in the north Atlantic and North Sea. Adult birds usually migrate first, but some families are known to depart together.

Diet
Freshwater fish and lake invertebrates such as dragonfly nymphs in summer. Some vegetation is also taken. Feeds on marine fish in the winter. Capable of staying submerged for up to two minutes and able to travel several hundred yards in that time.

Breeding
Gregarious in winter. Occasionally migrates in small, loose flocks. Solitary at breeding sites. The males are highly territorial and if several pairs nest on the same large lake will vigorously defend an area of at least 120 acres (50 ha). The resident male makes loud wails and croaks and may hold his neck in an S-shaped threat posture. Courtship display is more elaborate than for the larger loons, the pair dipping their bills and splashing water during short runs, during which the bird is vertical with neck arched and bill thrust forward. Pair also makes quick dives. Pair-bond is monogamous and lifelong or very enduring. The nest is at the water's edge, with islets preferred to the main shore. Arctic Loons also nest in bays with minimal tidal reach; if the nest is threatened by rising water, the pair will rapidly add material to raise it. One, usually two dark olive or brown eggs with dark brown spots; incubated, chiefly by female, for 28–30 days. Chicks nidifugous and precocial. Leave nest on day of hatching. Fed and brooded by both parents. Fledge in 60–65 days and are independent at that time. Breed at 2–3 years.

Taxonomy and geographical variation
Polytypic. The nominate race breeds in the Western Palearctic, east to the Lena Delta. Some authorities also recognize *G. a. viridigularis*, which breeds in eastern Siberia. It is a little larger and has a green sheen to the black throat patch.

Pacific Loon (Pacific Diver)
Gavia pacifica

Identification See p. 69
Very similar to Arctic Loon; the difference in the summer adult is a slightly paler gray nape of the neck and the absence of the Arctic's white flank patch. The Pacific Loon's black throat patch also has a purple sheen. There is also slightly less white on the upperparts, and the black-and-white striping on the sides of the neck tends to be less pronounced. The winter adult is darker on the upperparts, with few or no or white spots, and usually has a dark "necklace" of an incomplete collar. In juvenile birds, only the absence of the white flank patch distinguishes Pacific from Arctic Loon. At all ages the Pacific Loon is slightly smaller than the Arctic, though this is hardly discernible in the field. Downy young are dark brown.

Confusion species
Notable confusion with Arctic Loon occurs where both birds are present. The Pacific Loon shows little or no white on the flanks and has a much less distinct pattern on the upperparts and throat than the Arctic Loon.

Size
L: 22½–28 in. (57–70 cm). WS: 3½–4 ft. (105–120 cm). W: 4–4¾ lb. (1.8–2.2 kg).

Voice
Very similar to Arctic Loon but higher-pitched. The song tends to be harsher and there are more short, guttural calls, though

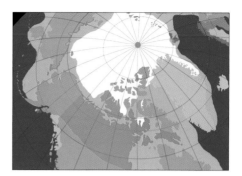

▲ Pacific Loon in breeding plumage, Chukotka.

these are equally goose- or ravenlike. Noisy at the breeding site but silent during the winter.

Distribution

Nearctic, but also breeds on the Russian Arctic coast from the Yana Delta to Chukotka. Overlaps with the Arctic Loon throughout this range. In North America breeds in Alaska, from the Yukon to Hudson Bay, and in the lower Canadian Arctic islands (Banks, Victoria, Southampton and southern Baffin). In North America there is a limited overlap with Arctic Loon in northwestern Alaska. Found on open water in tundra and also on slow-flowing rivers and coastal lagoons. The Russian population migrates south to waters off southern Kamchatka, while the North American population moves to the Pacific coast, where it occurs as far south as California.

Diet

As for Arctic Loon.

Breeding

Gregarious in winter. Also migrates in flocks, unlike the other loons. Solitary at the breeding sites. As with Arcitc Loon, the courtship display is more elaborate than in the larger loons, with bill-dipping, short, splashing runs and quick dives. Nest site as Arctic Loon but tends to choose nest sites closer to the coast. One to three (usually two) dark buff or olive eggs with dark brown spots, incubated chiefly by female for 23–25 days. Chicks nidifugous and precocial. Cared for mainly by female. Fledge in 60–65 days and are independent at that time. Breed at 2–3 years.

Taxonomy and geographical variation

Monotypic. Until fairly recently, the Pacific Loon and eastern Siberian Arctc Loon were thought to form a single race of Arctic Loon, classified as *Gavia arctica pacifica*. It was then noted that the two forms were sympatric, and that the Pacific Loon formed a separate species. Despite the similarity of the two, hybridization with Arctic Loon is not known (though the zone of range overlap is far from observers and hybrids might be virtually impossible to spot).

▼ Pair of Pacific Loons, Barrow.

Red-throated Loon
(Red-throated Diver)
Gavia stellata

The smallest of the loons (though only slightly smaller than the Arctic and Pacific Loons), and the only one capable of standing upright. As a consequence, Red-throated Loons occasionally take off and land on land rather than on water. Red-throated Loons are also more tolerant of close approach by the Arctic traveler than other loons.

Identification

See p. 69

Unmistakable in summer, when the red throat patch is visible. The patch extends from the throat to the chest. The sides of the neck and head are steel gray, with a hint of blue. Unlike the larger loons, the neck is thinner than the head. The top of the head and back of the neck is striped in black and white, the striping continuing to the back and upper flanks. The forehead slopes to a rounded crown. The iris is red. The gray bill is slightly upcurved and is held pointing slightly upward. The upperparts are dark gray-brown with small white spots and with white fringing on some feathers. The breast is white and flat, unlike the bulbous chest of the Arctic Loon. The flanks are striped black and white, but the striping is uneven.

In winter neck is mostly white, and crown of head is dark gray, which continues as a stripe down nape of neck. Breast remains white, flanks white with some gray mottling. Upperparts are dark gray with white speckling. Juveniles are similar to the winter adult but browner and with more gray-brown on the neck and crown. Downy young are dark gray-brown.

▼ Red-throated Loon in breeding plumage, Kamchatka.

Confusion species
At a distance, the darker red patches of some birds can look black. In winter there is more room for confusion, but the white neck and head and the lack of a white flank patch distinguish Red-throated. In flight the Red-throated Loon has a habit of looking around, which can help identification.

Size
L: 21½–28 in. (55–70 cm). WS: 3½–3¾ ft. (105–115 cm). W: 2½–4 lb. (1.1–1.8 kg).

Voice
In flight the bird has a curious gooselike cackling *kar kar kar*. The song is a moaning wail, often heard as a duet between a breeding pair. The bird also has a sharp, foxlike bark.

Distribution
Circumpolar. Breeds further north than any other loon, with the range including Russia's Arctic islands (except, as far as is known, the New Siberia Islands) and the northern islands of Arctic Canada. Occurs on both coasts of Greenland, on Iceland and on Svalbard. Found on open water in tundra and also on surprisingly small pools in marshland. Often found in coastal bays. North American birds migrate as far south as California and Florida. European birds move to the Atlantic off southern Iceland and western Ireland, the North Sea, and as far south as the Bay of Biscay and even the Adriatic. Asian birds move south of Kamchatka and to seas around Japan.

Diet
Feeds on freshwater fish and invertebrates during the summer, but will often fly to the coast from the breeding site to feed on

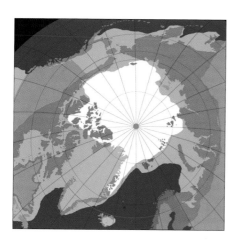

▲ Typical lakeside Red-throated Loon nest site, Adventdalen, Svalbard.

marine fish. In winter feeds on herring, sand eels and other small fish.

Breeding

The most gregarious of the loons, though more solitary at breeding sites. Has an elaborate pair ritual that is also used if their territory is invaded, the invading bird(s) occasionally joining in. At first the pair will swim side by side, moving very fast with their necks extended and their heads and bills pointing downward, this often becoming a delightful dance in which the birds submerge their rear ends, raise their front ends, arch their necks, open their bills and make wailing calls, then dip their bills; the whole display is closely synchronized. This dance can develop further, the pair rising vertically, pointing their bills straight up and running across the water. However sometimes rituals consist of nothing more elaborate than bill-dipping and water-splashing. Pair-bond is monogamous and lifelong. Pairs can nest on smaller lakes and ponds as the birds require less room for takeoff. As with the other loons, nest is located at water's edge to minimize the need to walk. The nest is made of vegetation. Two (rarely one) pale olive or brown eggs spotted dark brown, incubated for 26–28 days by both birds. Chicks are nidifugous and precocial. The chicks leave the nest after one day but stay close to it, occasionally riding on the back of the guarding adult. Chicks molt to a dark gray down after about one week. Fledge at 38–48 days and are independent at that time. Breed at 2–3 years.

Taxonomy and geographical variation

Monotypic, but Russian birds are usually heavier while Svalbard birds are often paler.

▼ Red-throated Loon on the nest, Badlanddalen, northeast Greenland.

Grebes

Though grebes are visually similar to the divers and normally placed after them in field guides, DNA sequencing indicates that divers are closer to penguins and petrels and are actually distant from grebes. Grebes have lobed toes rather than the webbed feet of divers and waterfowl, but, as with the divers, the feet are so far back on the body that the birds have difficulty walking on land. Indeed, so difficult do grebes find walking that when forced to walk, if falling water levels strand their nest for example, the birds often fall over. Because of the position of the feet, grebes need a long run across water to take off. They fly with rapid wingbeats, feet trailing. They have small tails with little more than a tuft of downlike feathers (often called a "powder puff") and maneuver poorly. Despite this they can migrate over considerable distances. At wintering sites grebes are more gregarious than divers. Some species are also gregarious at breeding sites, forming small colonies, though most are aggressively territorial. Grebes molt their flight feathers simultaneously, as waterfowl do, so they cannot fly for part of the year. The combination of difficult takeoff and poor maneuverability means that the birds rarely fly except during migration. Migration flights are mostly at night, which may be why grebes are occasionally stranded on roads: poor morning light and wet roads combine to make tired birds mistake the roads for rivers, and once landed they are unable to take off again.

When diving, grebes use the lobed toes as both rudders and paddles. The ankle and toe joints are extremely flexible, giving grebes superb maneuverability underwater. Diving is assisted by the birds' ability to squeeze out air from between the feathers (though this, of course, also results in a loss of insulation) and from their air sacs; they can also absorb water in the flank feathers. These adaptations allow silent diving that aids hunting (and hiding if threatened).

Grebes habitually eat their own feathers, usually during preening; the ingested feathers form a marshmallowlike ball that is fed to their chicks from first feeding. The significance of this behavior is still not understood.

Members of the grebe family are found in both hemispheres and include flightless species, but they are not true Arctic birds. Of the northern species, only the Slavonian and Red-necked Grebes breed beyond the Arctic boundary as defined in this book.

Horned Grebe (Slavonian Grebe)
Podiceps auritus

Identification See p. 69

A beautiful and unmistakable bird in breeding plumage. The head is black, sometimes with a greenish sheen. The forehead is angled and the crown is flat but peaked at the rear, though this peak is not readily discernible as it is hidden by the horns, which give this bird its common name. These are bright yellow feather tufts, occasionally with reddish lower and rear borders. The iris is pink or light red, and there is a red stripe between the eye and the bill. The bill is black with a pale tip: it is short and usually held horizontal or pointing very slightly downward. There are prominent black cheek patches that accentuate the black head. The neck and flanks are a rich chestnut brown. The back is gray and looks scaled because of the white fringing of the coverts. In winter the tufts are lost, and the head is black above the eye and white below but with a prominent dark cheek patch. The throat and neck are white, and the neck shows a pale gray collar and a dark gray line on the back. The upperparts are also dark gray, while the flanks are white and flecked with gray. Juvenile birds are similar to the winter adult, but the prominent white

▼ Adult female Horned Grebe on the nest, Churchill.

cheek patch is replaced by a dark band. Downy young are light gray with a distinctive black-and-white head pattern.

Confusion species

In areas where they overlap, all of which lie south of the Arctic (central Europe, southern Russia and central United States), there may be confusion with the Eared (or Black-necked) Grebe (*P. nigricollis*). Within the Arctic, only the Red-necked Grebe overlaps with Slavonian (in western Alaska and the Aleutians). The Slavonian is smaller, more compact and has a short, stubby bill. In summer the yellow ear tufts are distinctive. In winter the Slavonian is much paler, white/gray rather than gray/brown.

Size

L: 7–10 in. (18–25 cm). WS: 18–24 in. (45–60 cm). W: 12–16 oz. (350–450 g).

Voice

Usual call is a nasal *ja-arrr*, descending in pitch and ending with a throaty rattle. This can be used as a territorial call and also in alarm (when it tends to be more shrill). Breeding pairs often perform a duet trill with rising and falling pulses, sometimes called a giggle, usually ending in a long nasal whine. Usually silent in winter.

Distribution

Circumpolar. Breeds throughout Iceland, though chiefly near Lake Myvatn. Breeds in northern Scandinavia (but occurs in Svalbard only as a vagrant), southern Russia, Kamchatka and southern Chukotka. Also found across the Bering Sea in Alaska and western Canada, and near the southern end of Hudson Bay. Found in both eutrophic and oligotrophic waters, often in more upland areas than Red-necked Grebe. Slavonian may be displaced by Red-necked in sites that both find suitable, which may explain why Slavonian has a wider range of acceptable habitats. In winter European birds migrate to waters around western Ireland, southern England, and the Irish, North and Baltic Seas. North American birds are found on the Pacific coast from the Aleutians to California, and on the Atlantic coast from Newfoundland to the Gulf of Mexico.

Diet

Chiefly feeds on arthropods taken from the water surface and by diving, supplemented by small fish and fish eggs. Also takes some vegetation. In winter the diet is almost exclusively fish and crustaceans. The birds are expert at disappearing beneath the water without a splash, diving for 30–35 seconds using the feet as paddles, with the wings folded against the body.

Breeding

Not gregarious, though small groups (occasionally up to 50 birds) form in winter. Breeding

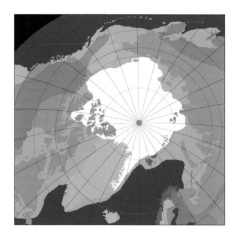

territory is a small lake or the secluded bay of a larger lake. Although small colonies have been noted, in general the birds are highly territorial with several threat postures (head held low against water, neck held straight up with ear tufts raised, or neck held straight up with ear tufts flattened and small crest at back of head raised). Slavonian Grebes also have an elaborate courtship display. This involves a "penguin dance" in which the pair stand upright in the water (looking not unlike penguins) facing each other, turning their heads from side to side quickly, occasionally pausing to preen. This dance may end with the pair swimming side-by-side or with mutual diving. If diving, this may lead to a "weed ceremony" in which the two birds each gather a beakful of weed and surface face to face. They then turn and, maintaining an upright posture, move quickly, side by side, for 30 ft. (10 m) or so, before turning and repeating the action. This "weed rush" can be repeated up to 15 times.

The pair-bond is monogamous and probably seasonal. The nest is built at the water's edge, often as an anchored, floating mass of vegetation. Four to five white eggs, often red- or brown-stained; incubated for 22–25 days by both birds. The eggs are covered with vegetation if the sitting bird is disturbed. Chicks semi-nidifugous and precocial. Chicks leave the nest soon after hatching, often traveling on backs of adults. Brood occasionally split between adults, which separate to feed. In southern part of range, Horned Grebes occasionally have a second brood, with young of the first helping to raise new hatchlings; however, second broods are unlikely in short Arctic summer. Fledge at 55–60 days, but are independent around 10–15 days earlier. Breed at 2 years.

▶ Horned Grebe egg. The nest is a depression made in a floating mat of aquatic vegetation.

Taxonomy and geographical variation

Atlantic birds tend to be longer and North American birds grayer, which once suggested two subspecies, but species is now considered monotypic.

Red-necked Grebe
Podiceps grisegena

Identification See p. 69

The boldly colored adult birds are unmistakable. The crown and head to the level of the eye is black, the cheeks and throat pale gray with white border and the neck chestnut (i.e., brown rather than the red of the Horned Grebe). The iris is dark brown. The bill is yellow at the base, with a black culmen and tip, and is held pointing downward. The upperparts are brown/gray, the underparts are pale gray/white except for the flanks, which are mottled brown. In winter the black of the head is replaced by dark brown, the gray/white by darker gray with a paler, occasionally yellow/gray, outline. The upper- and underparts are as in summer, but duller. Juvenile birds are as winter adult, but with darker body color, redder neck and a stronger pattern on the head; the cheeks being striped in gray/brown and pale gray. Downy young are gray with similar head pattern to Horned Grebe.

Confusion species

Unlikely with the Horned Grebe (the only other grebe to overlap in the Arctic): Red-necked is larger and has a longer, more pointed bill and distinctive head color pattern. Wintering birds are much darker.

Size

L: 9½–12 in. (24–30 cm). WS: 30–34 in. (75–85 cm). W: 25–32 oz. (700–900 g), with North American birds to 2½ lb. (1,100 g).

Voice

Noisy in the breeding season, quiet in winter. Much less musical than Horned Grebe. The main call is a loud, nasal bray, reminiscent of a pig's squeal. It is the loudest call of any grebe. There is also a shortened version, sounding more ducklike. The pair "song" is a harsh *ga-ga-ga* ... repeated up to 10 times.

Distribution

Circumpolar. Found in southern Finland and east-central Europe. In Arctic, occurs on Kamchatka Peninsula and southern Chukotka, in the Aleutian Islands and western Alaska. Found in central Canada (e.g., the Great Slave Lake in Northwest Territories), but rarely in the Canadian Arctic. Found chiefly on lowland ponds and lakes, favoring shallow water. European birds winter in North and Baltic seas, Asian and American birds along Pacific coasts.

Diet

Invertebrates, especially insects and their larvae. Will also take fish.

▲ Red-necked Grebe in summer plumage, Northwest Territories.

Breeding

Less gregarious than other grebes. Courtship displays are noisier, but otherwise similar to Horned Grebe, even including a "weed ceremony." There is a similar "penguin dance," but with more pronounced head-shaking, much of this being slower. Head-turning also occurs without the full dance. The "weed rush" is less often seen than in Horned Grebe, being replaced by a slower parallel swim, although this can develop into a "parallel rush." Pair-bond monogamous and perhaps enduring. Nesting habits similar to Horned Grebe. Four to five white (though often stained) eggs; incubated for 20–23 days by both parents. Chicks are semi-nidifugous and precocial. Chicks are carried on back of parent; occasionally one bird incubates while the other cares for early hatchlings. Sometimes adults abandon unhatched eggs if they can cope only with early hatchlings. Fledging assumed to be 60–70 days, but probably independent before this time. Thought to breed at 2 years.

Taxonomy and geographical variation

Polytypic. Nominate is found in western Palearctic; race *holboellii* occurs in the eastern Palearctic and Nearctic. It is larger and longer-billed but otherwise similar.

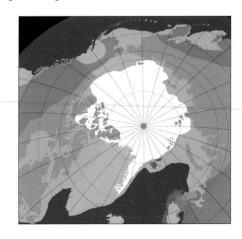

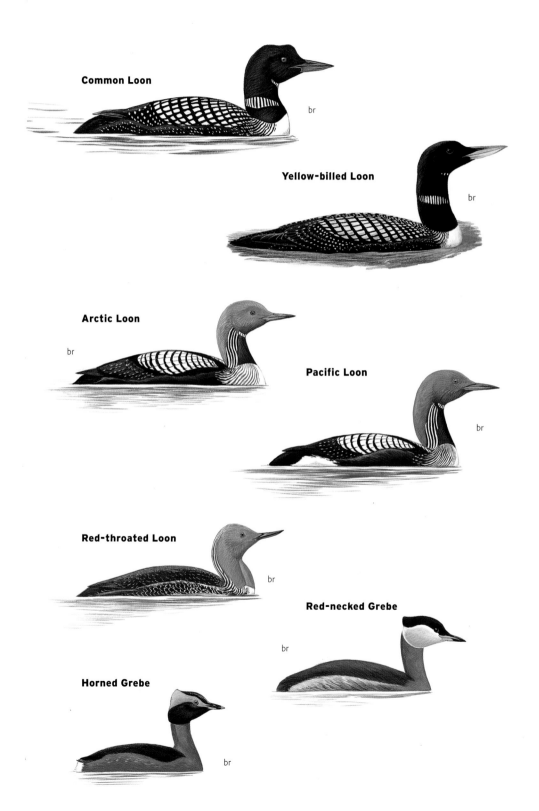

Common Loon br

Yellow-billed Loon br

Arctic Loon br

Pacific Loon br

Red-throated Loon br

Red-necked Grebe br

Horned Grebe br

PLATE 2: CORMORANTS, SHEARWATERS AND PETRELS

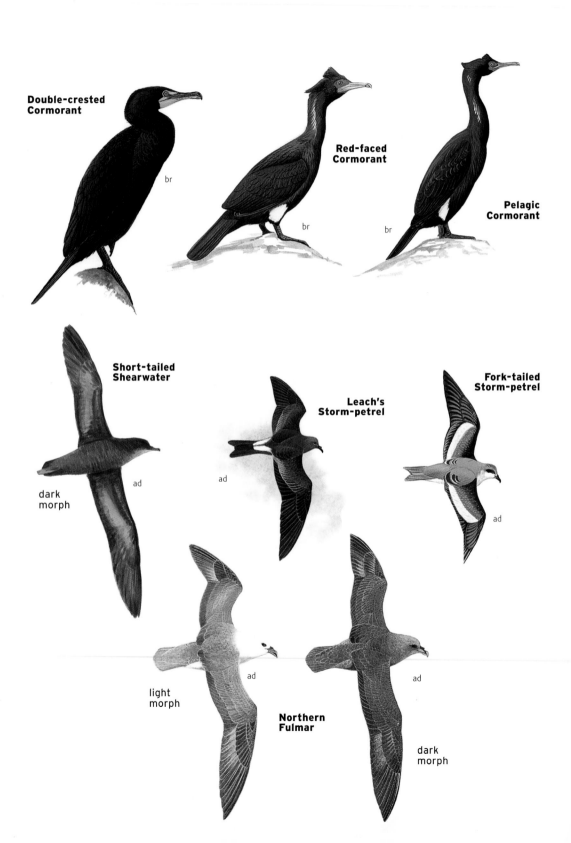

Double-crested Cormorant

br

Red-faced Cormorant

br

Pelagic Cormorant

br

Short-tailed Shearwater

dark morph

ad

Leach's Storm-petrel

ad

Fork-tailed Storm-petrel

ad

light morph

ad

Northern Fulmar

ad

dark morph

Albatrosses, petrels and allies

Albatrosses

In Arabic the pelican is *alcadous*, which was transformed by early Portuguese sailors into *alcatraz* (hence the association with the infamous prison island) and transferred to any large seabird. Subsequently *alcatraz* was transformed again, becoming *albatross*. The vernacular name *mollymawk* is still occasionally applied to smaller albatrosses. The name derives from the Old Dutch *molle mok*, meaning "strange gull," which was once applied to the Northern Fulmar. Although albatrosses are rightly considered birds of the Southern Ocean, where continuous winds over the land-free, circumpolar waters aid their flight (and, in particular, their takeoff), there are four "northern" species (though in this context "north" is relative only to the equator). Of the four, the Waved Albatross (*Phoebastria irrorata*) breeds on the Galapagos Islands and disperses to the local Pacific. The other three species may be seen off the Aleutian Islands, the Kamchatka Peninsula and Commander Islands. One, the Short-tailed Albatross (*P. albatrus*), which breeds on a few remote islands off Japan's southern coast, is a very rare visitor. The species was believed extinct (due to plume hunters and volcanic eruptions) but was rediscovered in 1953. The other two species are more common.

The Black-footed Albatross (*P. nigripes*) is a large, dark brown bird with white tail-coverts. Its dark feet extend beyond a very dark, wedge-shaped tail. Pale-morph adults have light underparts. All forms have a pale face and dark pink bill, though juveniles tend to be uniform dark brown. Breeds on Hawaiian Islands. Noisy in flocks with squawking calls and frequent bill-snapping. Unlikely to be confused with other species, though juvenile Short-tailed Albatrosses are similar.

The Laysan Albatross (*P. immutabilis*) is the most numerous of the four "northern" albatrosses. The head, rump and underparts are white, the wings dark brown with white fringing on the primaries. The underwings are white with dark brown patches, but distinct dark brown leading and trailing edges and tips. The tail is dark brown. There is a dark eyepatch. The bill and feet are pale pink. Juveniles are similar but tend to have more brown on the underwing. May be confused with the Short-tailed Albatross at a distance, but the white back and covert patch of the latter is distinctive. Breeds on Hawaiian Islands. Quieter than Black-footed Albatross, but calls similar, tending to be higher pitched.

Shearwaters and petrels

The Procellariidae, which includes fulmars, shearwaters, gadfly-petrels, and storm-petrels, has one of the widest distributions of any family of birds, covering the northern and southern oceans (and including species that migrate between the two), though with a preponderance of species in the south. These birds are often called tubenoses because of the tubular canals, housing the nostrils, that are set on top of the bill. In most birds the plates that form the bill are fused and their structure

▲ This Northern Fulmar shows clearly why the group are often referred to as the "tubenoses."

is, therefore, invisible. In a few species (e.g., skuas), the plate structure is indistinct, but in the Procellariidae the plates are separate and highly visible. The combination of the dorsal tubes (of varying lengths in the various species), the plated bill and the pronounced hook at the end of the upper mandible gives the birds an ugly (and some say malign) appearance, which is countered by the birds' elegance as they work the air above the waves.

The significance of the tubenose is not well understood. The structure may allow the birds to find food by smell, but it may also help them detect differences in air pressure or wind speed. These allow the birds to make use of varying conditions; they use changes in wind speed as the wind interacts with the waves, riding up on headwinds and gliding down on tail-winds, so that distance is made with virtually no effort. The maneuver — shearing or shearwatering — is spectacular, particularly the occasional changes of angle of the stiffly held wings relative to the horizontal. Remarkably, the birds exhibit a negative dihedral, i.e., a downward tilt of the wingtips. Soaring birds (e.g., raptors) use a positive dihedral as it is a much more stable configuration. A negative dihedral offers better maneuverability, but it requires much greater control.

Northern Fulmar
Fulmarus glacialis

The Northern Fulmar is the only petrel with a range that extends into the Arctic. These birds are pelagic. In the north of their range they are often seen among pack ice or at the floe edge. In flight they are among the most inspiring of all true Arctic birds, effortlessly gliding above the waves. If the observer is ship-based, watching a Fulmar using the ship's slipstream near the stern is a joy. The birds occasionally come close enough for the dark eye to be seen clearly (and for the realization that the observer is also being observed). Any sudden movement will cause the bird to move away, the change of direction accomplished with no discernible movement of wings or tail. The astonishing fluidity and grace of the Northern Fulmar over the sea is not, however, matched by its ability in tight maneuvers. Northern Fulmars often share nesting cliffs with Kittiwakes, and while they are almost double the weight of Kittiwakes, their wing area is only about 20% larger. The increase is due to a longer humerus that supports more secondary feathers, while the primary wing lengths are approximately the same. The Northern Fulmar's primary feathers also have a much stiffer shaft. In gliding and soaring, the Kittiwake is almost the equal of the Northern Fulmar, but in maneuvering it is far superior. Observers at a cliff that is home to both birds will note Kittiwakes landing effortlessly, while the fulmars frequently have to make many passing glides before wind conditions allow them to reach their nest sites.

◀ Dark-morph Fulmar. Note the dark upperwing and back but pale head and tail. North Norway.

Identification See p. 70

Superficially gull-like in appearance, the Northern Fulmar has both a different shape and a markedly different flight pattern, riding the wind on straight, stiff wings, with occasional bursts of rapid wingbeats during which the wings remain stiff. Fulmars have two distinct morphs as well as intermediate forms. From the distribution of the forms, it is conjectured that the dark morph evolved in the north Pacific and the pale form in the north Atlantic when an ice maximum separated the population. During a later interglacial period, mixing occurred when the now ice-free Arctic Ocean allowed circumpolar travel. However, while it is true that Norhtern Fulmars in colonies in southern Alaska, the Aleutians, Kamchatka and the western Sea of Okhotsk are predominantly dark, so too are those in the colonies of southeast Baffin Island, northeast Greenland, Svalbard and Franz Josef. Similarly while the west and southeast Greenlandic, Labrador, Icelandic, Scandi-navian, British and Novaya Zemlya colonies contain predominantly pale birds, so too do the Bering Sea island, Chukotka and eastern Sea of Okhotsk colonies. In general, more dark birds are found farther north. Dark-morph birds have dark gray upperwings and back, but white/pale gray head, underparts and tail. In an even darker form (double dark, dark-dark or D2), the head and tail are also dark gray, though usually not as dark as the wings. The underparts are steel gray, and this form is occasionally called the Blue Fulmar. Pale-morph birds have pale gray upperwings with paler gray or white heads and tails and generally white underparts. An even paler form (double light, light-light or L2) is virtually all white with pale/medium gray wing edges and tail. All forms have a pale primary patch, white in pale morphs, light gray in darker forms. There is no seasonal variation in the plumage of all morphs, and juveniles are indistinguishable from adults.

The head is large and round and set on a short, thick neck. These characteristics, together with the short but heavy bill, hooked at the tip and with prominent nasal tubes, give the bird a robust appearance. The iris is dark brown. The bill is yellow but can occasionally be grayish. The legs and feet vary from pink/yellow to blue/gray. Young acquire two down covers

▲ Northern Fulmar, Norway. Note the distinct mandibular plates.

before juvenile plumage. Pale-morph young have pale gray down, and dark-morph young are dark gray.

Confusion species

As noted above, pale-morph birds are superficially similar to gulls, but the robust head, stubby bill and flight action are different from all gulls. Dark-morph birds may be confused with shearwaters, particularly at a distance or in poor light. In good conditions the head shape is distinctive.

Size

L: 18–20 in. (45–50 cm). WS: 3¼–3¾ ft. (100–115 cm). W: 21–30 oz. (600–850 g).

Voice

Usually silent in flight if alone, but flocks can be noisy. Main call is a loud cackle. In duets between a breeding pair, this cackle can increase in both frequency and volume.

Distribution

Circumpolar, breeding in almost all suitable locations below the pack-ice limit. The population of Fulmars has increased exponentially in the last 150 years or so as a result of the increase in commercial fishing. The fishing industry has historically discharged vast amounts of offal and unwanted

▼ Dark-morph Northern Fulmar over the sea at Hornsund, Svalbard.

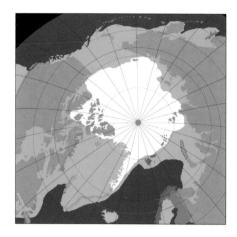

fish into the sea, a food source that was bound to lead to a population explosion in a scavenging species (and benefiting other species as well). The population increase led to larger colonies of Northern Fulmars and, when sites were saturated, to a southward expansion of the species (northern expansion being limited by pack ice). The reduction in European fishing fleets as a result of the drastic overfishing in the North Sea and north Atlantic may have a significant impact on the southern colonies of Atlantic Fulmars. In winter, Northern Fulmars move south ahead of the ice, reaching California and Japan in the Pacific, southern coasts of Britain and New England in the Atlantic.

Diet

They are surface feeders, though they dive to about 13 ft. (4 m) in pursuit of food, using their feet as paddles with wings half open as stabilizers. They feed on crustaceans, cephalopods and fish. They are also scavengers, feeding not only on the by-catch and offal from trawlers, but also on dead whales and seals.

Breeding

Fulmars nest colonially on cliffs, though *nest* is a misnomer as eggs are laid on what is little more than a scrape (and not even that on bare rock) or occasionally on dunes or earth banks. Pair-bond monogamous and long-lasting, but birds do not necessarily overwinter together, instead meeting again at the nest site, where they reinforce the bond with a head-waving display, by mutual nibbling, in which one bird pecks at the other's bill, and by mutual billing, in which the pair jab at each other with open bills. One white egg (rarely two) incubated by both adults, often with very long sittings (up to seven days) for 48–52 days. Chick altricial and nidicolous, one parent always present for first 10–14 days of life. Chick is fed regurgitated food, placing its bill inside the adult's. The name *fulmar* derives from the Scandinavian for "foul gull," referring to the habit of defensive adults and developed chicks vomiting foul-smelling fish oil over intruders, remembered ruefully by rock climbers of Scottish (and other) cliffs who accidentally haul themselves onto a fulmar-inhabited ledge. The viscous oil, about 7 oz. (200 cc) in volume, is produced in the bird's proventriculus. Fortunately, the bird's aim is often poor. It is said that fulmar oil was once used to light lamps on the Scottish island of St. Kilda; in view of the oil's pungency, this practice seems unbelievable. Chicks fledge at 45–50 days and are independent at the same time. Breed at 6 years or even later.

Taxonomy and geographical variation

Somewhat confused and debatable. Pacific Fulmars, which have a narrower bill, sometimes classified as *F. g. rodgersii*. Nominate usually classified as the northern, darker, Atlantic form, with *F. g. auduboni* a southern, lighter form. But natural variation in bill size probably eclipses that considered to define *rodgersii*, and the gradation in coloration from lightest to darkest birds, often seen within colonies, negates any attempt to use color as a definition of subspecies.

Short-tailed Shearwater
Puffinus tenuirostris

The Manx Shearwater (*Puffinus puffinus*) breeds on Iceland but is not considered an Arctic species. In winter Great Shearwater (*P. gravis*) and Sooty Shearwater (*P. griseus*) are occasionally seen in the Denmark Straits and Norwegian Sea, while Sooty is more frequent in the Aleutians, the Commander Islands and off eastern Kamchatka. However, the commonest Shearwater in Arctic waters by far is the Short-tailed Shearwater.

Identification See p. 70

A medium-sized shearwater. Essentially dark brown plumage but with a light panel on the underwing. Adult birds have a

limited range of coloration: the panel is light brown in darker birds and gray in lighter birds. The bird has a rounded head with a high-angle forehead and a short, stubby bill. Feet and legs dark gray/brown. Males, females and juveniles essentially identical.

Confusion species

Similar in coloration to dark-morph Northern Fulmars, but slender wings and narrower neck and head are distinctive. Short-tailed Shearwater is virtually identical to Sooty Shearwater, though observers spotting a dark shearwater from a ship in the

▲ Part of a spectacular "mega-flock" of Short-tailed Shearwaters at sea west of the Pribilofs.

northern Bering Straits area are almost certainly watching the former. Sooty is slightly larger than Short-tailed, has a less rounded head, a less high-angled forehead and a longer bill. Most distinctive is the underwing panel, which in Sooty is very pale, often silver/white.

Size
L: 16–18 in. (40–45 cm). WS: 3–3½ ft. (95-105 cm). W: 18–28 oz. (500–800 g).

Voice
Usually silent at sea. Screeches and squeals at nest sites.

Distribution
Bering Sea. A bird of the Southern Ocean that migrates north away from the austral winter, occasionally as far north as Cape Dezhnev and the Seward Peninsula. Huge flocks, numbering tens of thousands, are often seen off St. Lawrence Island in autumn.

Diet
Cephalopods and fish. Also krill in the Southern Ocean. Feeds

by plunge-diving and underwater pursuit. May occur in flocks at abundant food sources. Sometimes found in association with cetaceans.

Breeding
Breeds on Tasmania and southern shore of Australia. Nests in burrows. Single egg laid. Incubation 50–55 days. Fledging at 80–105 days. Historically, Short-tailed and Sooty Shearwaters were known collectively as "muttonbirds" as they were good eating. The chicks of both species are still harvested in regulated fashion canned, and sold as Tasmanian squab.

Taxonomy and geographical variation
Monotypic.

Storm-petrels
A contrast to the elegant flight actions of the shearwaters and petrels is provided by their close relatives, the storm-petrels. The wing loading of the former is among the lowest of any bird (around 0.7g/cm² or ⅙ oz./sq. in.) whereas that of storm-petrels is among the highest (around 6 g/cm² or 1⅜ oz./sq. in.). Storm-petrels are renowned for their fluttering flight; the birds hover above the water to feed, occasionally patting the surface with their feet. It is thought that part of the species' name originated from this behavior: the birds often use ships to shelter from the weather (hence *storm*) and look as though they walk on water, as St. Peter did (hence *petrel*).

No species of storm-petrel is considered to be Arctic, though several species are Antarctic birds and one, Wilson's Storm-petrel (*Oceanites oceanicus*), actually breeds on that continent. However, by the definition of the Arctic boundary used here, three species are Arctic breeders. Of these, the European Storm-Petrel (*Hydrobates pelagicus*), that breeds on Iceland's Westmann Islands, is a southerly species that tolerates the north Atlantic because of the Gulf Stream. Leach's Storm-petrel (*Oceanodroma leucorhoa*) breeds on the Westmann Islands and on Iceland's southern coast but can also be found on Newfoundland and, in the north Pacific, on the Aleutians and other southwestern Alaskan islands, and on Russia's Commander Islands. This Nearctic range of Leach's is shared by the Fork-tailed Storm-petrel (*O. furcata*). Consequently, the latter two species are considered briefly below.

Storm-petrels are rarely seen from shore, though observers at the breeding burrows may see the nocturnal return of flocks, and the birds can often be heard in their burrows (adults/chicks at night, chicks during the day). From a ship, storm-petrels are often seen off the stern searching for food churned up by the propellers. They also follow cetaceans and seals for the same reason. The feeding method, a hovering flight with the feet padding the water, is characteristic and a sure identification feature; no other seabird does this. However, storm-petrels will also feed from the surface after a brief landing. Perhaps the most remarkable feature of Leach's Storm-petrel is its legendary use as a lamp. It is said that a wick thrust down a dead bird's throat would create a candle that would give an effective light for many hours, due to the bird's high oil content, an adaptation to help it survive the chill of Arctic weather.

Leach's Storm-petrel
Oceanodroma leucorhoa

Identification
See p. 70

A small, dark brown pelagic bird with a long notched tail. Two color morphs exist: a white-rumped form predominating in the Atlantic and northern Pacific and a dark-rumped form in the southern Pacific. Intermediate forms also exist. The dark form is uniformly dark brown, with darker, almost black, primaries and distinctive pale brown carpal bands that cross the wing from rear to leading edge. The white-rumped form has a distinctive V-shaped white patch on the rump, occasionally with a dark central streak. On both forms the head is rounded, but with a flat crown and almost vertical forehead. The iris is brown. The short, slightly downcurved bill is black, as are the legs and feet. Winter and juvenile plumage as in adults. Young have two gray/brown down plumages.

Confusion species
None in area covered by this book. Small size, dark brown plumage and feeding habits are distinctive.

Size
L: 7–8 in. (18–21 cm). WS: 17½–19 in. (44–48 cm). W: 1½–1¾ oz. (40–50 g).

Voice
Usually silent at sea. As a flock returns to the breeding site, the birds chatter loudly. In the burrow the adults have a curious *purr*, rising in pitch and ending with an in-breath *whee*. The young have a plaintive *peep*.

Distribution
Circumpolar, but limited in extent. As noted, colonies occur in Iceland, Newfoundland, southwestern Alaskan Island and on the Commander Islands. Leach's is the only storm-petrel that breeds in both the north Atlantic and north Pacific. Spends winter at sea off the Atlantic and Pacific coasts.

Diet
Crustaceans, small fish and detritus, including the feces of whales and seals. Feeds by hovering, rarely alighting on the sea and never diving.

Breeding
Solitary in the winter, but gregarious at breeding sites. Display flight is fast, erratic circling above nesting burrow or slow, hovering flight with wings vibrating quickly. Usually performed at night so difficult to observe. Pair-bond monogamous and lifelong. Colonial breeder, nesting in self-excavated burrows or suitable hollows beneath boulders. Single white egg, occasionally with pale lilac spotting, incubated by both sexes for 40–42 days (a very long period — see also Fork-tailed Storm-petrel). Nidicolous, semi-altricial chick brooded continuously for five days, then fed by both parents by regurgitation. Fledges in 60–70 days and is independent at same time. Breeds at 4–5 years.

Taxonomy and geographical variation
Monotypic.

◄ Leach's Storm-petrel in flight.

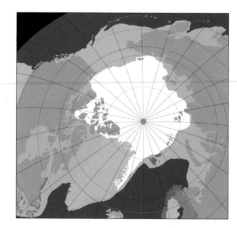

Fork-tailed Storm-petrel
Oceanodroma furcata

Identification See p. 70

Unique among storm-petrels in being pale gray rather than dark brown. Head, back and underparts are beautiful soft pearl gray. Head shape as Leach's Storm-petrel. Has distinctive black elongated patch around eye. The iris is dark brown. The bill is black and slightly downcurved. Underwing has dark gray coverts contrasting with pale gray of other feathers. Upperwing primaries are dark gray, becoming darker toward leading edge of wing that is very dark. Shows carpal bar (as in Leach's and other storm-petrels), which is very pale gray/white. Rump has V-shaped white patch with no central streak. Tail distinctly forked, with feathers darker toward the tips. Legs and feet black. Winter and juvenile plumage as adult. Downy chicks are gray.

Confusion species

None. Smaller than any gull and feeding flight is very different from any tern.

Size

L: 7½–9 in. (20–23 cm). WS: 16½–18 in. (42–46 cm). W: 1¾–2 oz. (50–55 g).

Voice

Usually silent at sea. At breeding site flocks chatter quietly, as do adults in burrow, although there is also a harsher *skee, skee* call.

Distribution

Aleutians, and islands off southwestern Alaska, and Commander and Kuril Islands. Winters in southern Pacific, particularly along the Japanese coast.

Diet

Crustaceans and small fish. Regularly follows fishing boats, feeding on offal.

Breeding

Solitary or in small groups in winter, but highly gregarious at breeding sites with colonies of up to 100,000 birds recorded. Nocturnal and burrowing habits make behavior difficult to study. Male defends a burrow and calls to attract female. Pair will mutually preen. Pair-bond is monogamous and occasionally renewed, depending on success of previous year's breeding. Burrow usually about 24 in. (60 cm) long. Single white egg, often with ring of purplish spots at blunt end, incubated for about 50 days (an unusually long period, around two or three times that for similarly sized eggs of birds from other groups). Chick is nidicolous and semi-altricial, and is brooded and fed by both parents through regurgitation. Chick grows very quickly, but does not fledge until about 60 days. Thought to breed at 3–4 years.

Taxonomy and geographical variation

Polytypic. Nominate race breeds in northeast Asia, including Kuril and Commander Islands and perhaps southern Kamchatka. *O. f. plumbea* breeds from southeastern Alaska to northern California. It is smaller and darker.

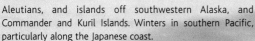

◀ This *plumbea* Fork-tailed Storm-petrel is exhibiting classic storm-petrel feeding behaviour, with the bird "paddling" on the water.

Cormorants

The habitat and morphology of these large birds is underlined by their English name, which derives from *corvus marinus*, or "sea raven." Cormorants are dark, aquatic, usually marine birds, adapted for the underwater pursuit of prey. Their feet are large, webbed and set far back, but cormorants have an upright stance and can move relatively easily on land. In fact, many perch and even nest in trees. The feet are used as paddles when diving, the wings held close to the body. Steering is done with the feet and tail. Cormorants are excellent divers, reaching depths of 330 ft (100 m). As well as the streamlined body shape and webbed feet, cormorants have other adaptations for aquatic hunting, e.g., the lens of the eye can be modified to improve underwater vision. To aid diving and allow the birds to stay submerged longer, the bones are heavy (cormorants often swim semi-submerged), there is limited body fat (fat being buoyant) and the blood weight is high relative to body weight. However, feeding excursions are limited because the plumage is not waterproof, which, along with low body fat, means that the birds quickly become chilled. The familiar pose of cormorants perched with outstretched wings aids the drying of the wing feathers, though Arctic-breeding cormorants adopt this pose less often as it exposes poorly insulated areas of the body to the cold, increasing heat loss. As a consequence, cormorants are extremely vulnerable to oil spillages, because the clogged feathers force the birds to extend the wings for long periods, causing rapid heat loss.

Because of the lack of waterproofing, cormorants are not truly pelagic, and they lack the large flight muscles of other marine birds. They are, nonetheless, strong fliers (though with a generally limited range) and look gooselike in flight, though attempts at close formation are erratic. Above water they fly close to the surface.

A sister taxon of the Phalacrocoracidae, the Sulidae (or gannets and boobies), are plunge-diving colonial birds that breed across a broad band of the world's oceans, centered, more or less, on the equator. In the northern hemisphere, relatively small colonies of Northern Gannets (*Morus bassanus*) occur on the coast of Fennoscandia and fish the Barents Sea, but the species is essentially sub-Arctic. Similarly, the North Atlantic phalacrocoracid species Great Cormorant (*Phalacrocorax carbo*) and European Shag (*P. aristotelis*) breed in northern Fennoscandia and on Iceland. The Great Cormorant also breeds in Greenland. However, neither species can be truly considered Arctic. Three North Pacific cormorants occur north of the Arctic boundary as defined here.

Double-crested Cormorant
Phalacrocorax auritus

Identification   See p. 70

The largest of the North Pacific cormorants. Adults are black with a subdued green sheen (except for the face), the black extending to the legs and feet. The iris is green. The chin and lores are orange, sometimes yellow-orange, the bill dark, occasionally with a dark yellow section to the lower mandible. The double crests of the name (ear tufts) can be black, gray or even pale gray. In general, Alaskan birds have lighter tufts. The winter plumage is similar, but it lacks the ear tufts and the chin patch is less bright. Juveniles have pale orange lores, chin patch and bill. They are also much lighter than the adults, with a pale pink/brown breast and darker belly. The wings and rump are also dark gray rather than black. Downy young are black.

▼ Great Cormorants breed as far north as Disko Bay on Greenland's west coast, but they are not considered true Arctic birds.

Confusion species

Can be confused with Pelagic and Red-faced Cormorants at a distance or in poor light. In adults the lack of a colored chin and green sheen distinguishes Pelagic. The bright red face patches of Red-faced are also distinctive when viewing conditions are good. In flight the Double-crested Cormorant flies with its neck kinked. This can also be a feature of the other two cormorants, but they tend to maintain a straight neck.

Size

L: 32–36 in. (80–90 cm). WS: 4¹/₂–5 ft. (140–150 cm). W: 3¹/₄–3³/₄ lb. (1.5–1.7 kg).

Voice

Usually silent when flying. At breeding site has a hoarse *croak* and a curious *ya ya*.

Distribution

Nearctic. The coasts of North America, on the eastern coast as far north as Newfoundland and on the western coast up to and including the Aleutians. Rare on Alaska's western coast north of the Alaska Peninsula. Also seen on James Bay and some inland lakes in the continental U.S. it is the only North American cormorant to nest inland. Alaskan birds stay close to their breeding range in winter or migrate to northwest Pacific coasts.

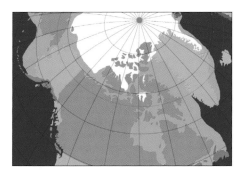

Diet

Feeds almost exclusively on fish, but also takes small mammals and probably other marine animals opportunistically. Feeds in the sea in shallow waters (< 25 ft./8 m) close to the shore (usually < 3 mi./5 km). Sometimes forages in coordinated flocks, forming a line and driving fish into shallow waters.

Breeding

Gregarious at all times and a colonial nester. Monogamous, long-lasting pair-bond and high fidelity to nest site. The male arrives first at nest site and defends it by jabbing with his bill. Male displays by raising and fanning tail, half-extending wings, pointing bill vertically upward, and calling loudly. Fidelity to nest site means that nests may become very large, up to 6¹/₂ ft. (2 m) high. Both birds contribute to building (e.g., with seaweed and driftwood) and also to nest defense, as material theft is common. One to seven (usually four) pale blue eggs, unmarked but usually with calcareous deposit, incubated for 25–30 days by both birds. Chicks are nidicolous and altricial,

▲ Adult non-breeding Double-crested Cormorant, Alaska.

brooded and fed by both birds by regurgitation, chick putting bill inside adult's. Fledge at 20–30 days and fly 15–20 days later. Young form crèches but return to the nest site for feeding. Independent at about 10 weeks. Breed at 2–3 years.

Taxonomy and geographical variation

Polytypic with four subspecies. Nominate race breeds over much of the range. *P. a. cincinatus* breeds in Alaska. It is larger, with white, straight crests.

Pelagic Cormorant
Phalacrocorax pelagicus

Identification   See p. 70

The smallest of the North Pacific cormorants. Adults are black with a distinct metallic-green sheen. The thin neck, which has a blue sheen, is flecked with white. Breeding adults have a large white patch on each flank, prominent when the bird is in flight, but not always visible in resting birds as it is hidden if the bird is upright. The throat pouch is bright red or orange, and the bare skin at the base of the bill is very dark or black. The iris is dark green/brown. The bill is noticeably thin, which accentuates the length. The head is smaller than that of the other cormorants and has two tufts, on the crown and on the nape. The legs and feet are black. Winter birds lack tufts, have a less intensely orange/red chin and lack the white neck streaks and flank patches. Juveniles are uniformly dark brown and lack face and chin coloration. Downy young are dark gray.

Confusion species

Can be confused with other cormorants at a distance or in poor light. Breeding adults can be confused with Red-faced Cormorants as both have white thigh patches (which both

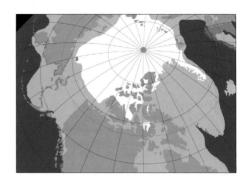

▲ Pelagic Cormorant in flight above coastal Kamchatka. The relatively straight neck is diagnostic of this species.

lose in non-breeding plumage). However, Red-faced has much more red on the throat and a much paler bill. In flight Pelagic's neck is kept straight rather than kinked as in Double-crested, and its wingbeats are much faster. Juvenile Pelagic is much darker than juvenile Double-crested and has a much darker bill than juvenile Red-faced.

Size
L: 24–28 in. (60-70 cm). WS: 36–40 in. (90–100 cm). W: 3½–4 lb. (1.6–1.8 kg).

Voice
Silent away from the nest site. At the nest a variety of hoarse grunts and occasional loud hisses.

Distribution
West coast of North America from California to the Aleutians and along the west coast of Alaska. Also coastal east Russia from Sakhalin and the Kuril Islands, along the coast of the Sea of Okhotsk and the coasts of Kamchatka and the Commander Islands to Chukotka. Rare on the north coast of Chukotka and on Wrangel. The Pelagic's presence on Wrangel makes it the world's most northerly breeding cormorant. In winter some birds remain within the breeding range (e.g., on the Aleutians), but northern birds migrate south as far as Baja California and Taiwan.

Diet
Fish, marine invertebrates, crustaceans and marine worms. Although the birds are rarely seen more than 1 mi. (2 km) from shore, they forage in deep water, to about 330 ft. (100 m), and are assumed to dive deep in search of prey.

Breeding
More solitary than other cormorant species, though usually breeds in small colonies, often with auks. The pair-bond is apparently monogamous and long-lasting. Limited display; usually the male merely opens his bill to show the red throat lining when the female approaches. Nest is on an inaccessible ledge or crevice of cliff, built by both birds from seaweed and grasses, occasionally reinforced with mud and lined with dry grass. Three to five pale green/white or pale blue eggs, usually with calcareous deposits, incubated by both birds for 28–32 days. Chicks nidicolous and altricial, brooded and fed by both

▼ Adult Pelagic Cormorant displaying its white flank patch at a coastal nesting site on an island off western Kamchatka. The patch is characteristic of the breeding plumage in this species.

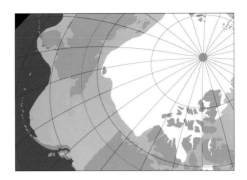

birds. Fed by regurgitation, the chick putting bill inside that of the adult. Fledge at 35–45 days, but not independent for a further 20–30 days. Breeding begins at 2 years.

Taxonomy and geographical variation

Polytypic. Nominate breeds north of British Columbia; *P. p. resplendens* breeds to the south; it is smaller with a more slender bill. There are slight mDNA differences between Alaskan and Siberian birds.

Red-faced Cormorant
Phalacrocorax urile

Identification See p. 70

Adults are glossy black with a green, sometimes violet, sheen. The neck, which is thicker than that of the Pelagic Cormorant, has a similar blue tinge and white streaking. The iris is dark green/brown. The face around the eye and behind the bill is bright ruby red. The bill is long and yellow, but sometimes can appear bluish. The chin/throat pouch is blue with red wrinkles at the edges. The head has two tufts of dark bronze feathers, on the crown and nape. As in Pelagic Cormorant, breeding adults have a white flank patch, more noticeable in flight than in standing birds. The legs and feet are black.

The flight pattern is similar to the Pelagic, with fast wingbeats and a straight neck. Winter adults are as breeding adults except that they lose the head tufts, the white streaks on the neck, and the white flank patch. Juvenile birds are uniformly dark brown, lack the red face patch, and have a paler bill. Downy young are gray or gray-brown.

Confusion species

Similar to Pelagic Cormorant, but in good viewing conditions the red face is diagnostic.

Size

L: 26–30 in. (65–75 cm). WS: 3½–4 ft. (110–120 cm). W: 4¼–4¾ lb. (1.9–2.2 kg).

Voice

Usually silent away from the nest site. A hoarse, guttural croak at the nest site.

Distribution

In North America, occurs on the Aleutian and Pribilof Islands and southern Alaskan Peninsula. In eastern Russia, on the Commander Islands and eastern Kamchatka. Small numbers also breed on the Nemuro Peninsula in Hokkaido, Japan. The North American birds tend to winter within their breeding range or to move south. By contrast, Russian birds migrate as far south as Taiwan.

Diet

Demersal fish (e.g., smolt, flounder) and crustaceans obtained by diving and pursuit.

Breeding

Gregarious (though the least gregarious of the Nearctic cormorants) but defends a nesting area. Male birds stare at potential rivals, call loudly and may jab with the bill. The male waves his wings at females to expose his white breeding patch. The pair may indulge in mutual wing-waving. Pair-bond is apparently monogamous and long-lived. Nests colonially (usually with about 50 pairs), often with auks. Nests are made of seaweed, usually cemented with guano and placed on inaccessible cliff ledge. Two to four blue or blue-green eggs with a white chalky deposit, incubated for 34–38 days by both birds, sometimes with the egg between the feet and breast. Both parents brood nidicolous and altricial chicks and feed them by regurgitation. Fledge at 40–50 days, but generally the biology of chicks is poorly known. Breed at 3 years.

Taxonomy and geographical variation

Monotypic.

▼ Adult Red-faced Cormorant in breeding plumage, St. Paul, Pribilofs.

Wildfowl

For many northern travelers, the highly visible flocks of geese epitomize both Arctic wildlife and the Arctic summer, the birds arriving as winter's snow thaws and leaving as the autumn snows begin. Wildfowl have been associated with human occupation of the far north for millennia. They are large and offer good eating, which has been the downfall of several other bird species. Some studies suggest that throughout the ranges of swan and goose populations, hunting has, on average, reduced the natural lifespan from 20 to 10 years. Because of the diversity and wide range of wildfowl, generalities are limited, but some comments on the group are worthwhile.

In general, wildfowl nest on or near freshwater, even species that make their living in the sea. They are aquatic, with broad bodies and webbed feet that are often set so far back that walking is awkward. Swans have short legs, are not very mobile on land and are essentially aquatic. Geese are more terrestrial than swans and other wildfowl, have more centrally set and longer legs and are much more adept walkers. Indeed, some can run remarkably quickly, as observers approaching too close to nests can discover to their cost.

Most wildfowl are vegetarian. In general they have broad bills, the sides of the mandibles having comblike lamellae that sever plant stalks and aid in straining food. The tongue is rasplike for gripping food items and has basal lamellae, which, together with those of the bill, form the filter for food straining. A few wildfowl eat fish. In these the lamellae have evolved into sawlike teeth. Swans and geese dip their heads to feed, but some ducks dive, the Red-breasted Merganser using its wings as well as its feet in pursuit of fish. Geese are gregarious in both winter and summer, the latter because, as ground-nesters, colonial nesting offers the best defence for an individual against mammalian predators. Swans nest at less accessible sites and are gregarious only in winter. Ducks also form winter flocks but do not, in general, nest colonially, many of them instead nesting in holes or burrows for protection against predation.

Swans

Swans are the largest and heaviest of the wildfowl. There are seven species, of which four are northern (breeding in the sub-Arctic or at higher latitudes). The northern species are predominantly white with male and female similar. They have very long necks and are strong fliers, though takeoff is laborious, as might be expected for so heavy a bird. Swans are largely vegetarian but opportunistic, and birds have been seen to swallow surprisingly large fish. They are gregarious in winter, less so in summer. They pair for life.

Geese

The *Anser* and *Branta* geese are northern groups. They vary in color, though apart from the Red-breasted Goose are not brightly colored, and again the sexes are similar. Geese are vegetarian, usually feeding on land (whereas swans usually feed in shallow water). However, both swans and geese will feed below the water's surface by up-ending (thrusting their heads below the surface and raising their rear ends).

Dabbling ducks

These ducks, which comprise the genus *Anas*, either feed on the surface or up-end. They eat vegetation and small aquatic insects. They are short-legged and waddle on land, but a handful of species can perch on branches or other structures. In many species the male is brightly colored during the breeding season, when it invariably shows an iridescent wing speculum. By contrast, females and juveniles are drably cryptic, and are usually predominantly brown.

▼ A family of Red-breasted Geese. Taimyr.

▲ Ross's Goose coming in to land.

Males lose their bright plumage during the summer molt. Wildfowl molt their flight feathers simultaneously, so they are flightless for a period that varies from three weeks for small ducks to six weeks for large geese. When flightless, male dabbling ducks adopt an "eclipse" plumage similar to that of the breeding female. In some species of dabbling ducks, the male birds guard their mates, but in most the male deserts his mate after egg-laying.

Diving ducks and sawbills

Diving ducks are freshwater and maritime species of several genera that dive for food rather than up-ending, and include pochards, scaups and eiders among their number. These ducks have legs set farther back on their bodies to assist in diving, and are consequently only rarely seen on land. Diving ducks are vegetarian or omnivorous, the marine diving ducks taking mollusks. In other respects they are similar to dabbling ducks, though the males lack a colored speculum.

Sawbills are wildfowl with toothlike lamellae that feed on fish. They are good divers, hunting in both freshwater and in the sea, occasionally communally.

Vegetarian wildfowl do not have bacteria in their gut to allow the digestion of cellulose. Instead, plant cell walls are broken down in the gizzard, and the cell nutrients are then absorbed. This explains why geese and swans prefer to eat the newest parts of plants, which have the most nutrients (ducks, though, are less selective). To extract enough nourishment to maintain good health and to lay down reserves in the form of subcutaneous and abdominal fat for their long migration flights, swans and geese must feed almost continuously. The spring migration coincides with the first growth of plants along the migratory route, with arrival at the breeding range synchronous with both the spring thaw and the rapid plant growth that greets the short Arctic summer. Some species even practice an altitudinal as well as a latitudinal migration, ascending hillsides to keep feeding on the new year's growth.

At the breeding sites, swans and geese feed continuously during the 24 hours of the midnight sun. But timing is crucial. At first the birds feed for a week or so to replenish reserves lost in the northward flight. Those that time it correctly will be in prime position to breed and will raise their entire clutch of eggs to fledging. However, if spring is late and new plant growth is unavailable, some birds may not breed at all, while some may die of starvation while incubating their eggs.

Young wildfowl

Goslings and ducklings are nidifugous, and they can swim, dive and feed themselves soon after leaving the nest. Many have patterned down, including an eye-stripe, which is thought to be an adaptation to protect them from curious siblings pecking at their eyes. The chicks are protected by one or both parents, and are also brooded if the weather threatens their survival. In some species crèches of young from several nests are formed and protected by one or more of the adults. Most wildfowl parents do not feed their young, though swans and geese may churn up the water to bring food to the surface for their chicks.

Despite the guarding of the chicks, predation rates are high and the list of potential predators long. When attacked from the air, chicks dive to avoid capture, but wily predators can confound this by repeated attacks that tire the young. For example, on Ellesmere Island a Glaucous Gull was watched systematically attacking a Long-tailed Duck family, consuming the entire brood as each chick in turn became exhausted and unable to dive, with the mother unable to do anything except watch, distraught and helpless. Some geese deliberately nest within the territories of Snowy Owls to gain some protection from other predators, which the owls will not tolerate near their nest. The strategy seems to work well, perhaps less so in years of low lemming numbers when the owls will turn their attention to wildfowl.

Wildfowl in flight

Flying wildfowl are renowned for flying in a V-formation, formed so that the following birds take advantage of the updraft of air from the bird ahead (leading to decreased drag and reduced energetic output). The lead bird, which works hardest, is periodically replaced by a trailing bird. Geese claim the record for the highest recorded flight, more than 32,000 ft. (10,000 m), the benefits of the jet stream at high altitude compensating for oxygen debt. However, they usually fly much lower; ice on the wings can lead to disaster.

Swans

The grace and beauty of swans has inspired humans for at least 2,000 years. A few examples include the Greek legends of Phaeton and Cygnus (from whom the genus received its name), and Leda and the Swan, and the later Scandinavian tale that was the basis for the ballet *Swan Lake*. For sheer elegance a swimming swan is hard to beat, and the bird's power on takeoff and during migratory flights is awesome. Migrating swans have been known to fly at 26,000 ft. (8,000 m), though generally they fly at 6,500–10,000 ft. (2,000–3,000 m). Yet the affection people have for swans has not always protected the birds. In medieval England, swans were royal birds, owned by the Crown — woe betide anyone who killed one — but royal protection was only offered to ensure that the king ate the birds and no one else. Canadian Inuit still often hunt Whistling Swans, with one adult swan providing enough flesh to feed a family of seven.

Several swans are named after their voice, which is often loud and distinctive. Indeed, the name "swan" may derive from an Old English word for noise. The Trumpeter Swan (*Cygnus buccinator*) has a long, twisted windpipe; its voice is the loudest of all wildfowl and ranks among the loudest of all birds. Trumpeters occur in southeastern Alaska; though occasionally seen in western Alaska, they are not a true Arctic species.

Whooper Swan
Cygnus cygnus

Identification   See p. 134
Adults entirely white, but occasionally with yellowish tinge to head and neck, and often with red-brown staining of same

areas during the summer as a result of iron in the breeding lake. The bill is black with a yellow base; the extent of yellow is variable but extends to and usually beyond the nostril. Whoopers have the most yellow on the bill of any northern swan. The bill is also large, both longer and less slender than that of the Bewick's. The iris is brown. The legs and feet are black. Winter plumage as in summer. Juvenile birds are gray-brown overall, usually darker on the head and neck. The bill is pink with a pale yellow base and, often, black at the extreme tip. First-winter birds are white, and Icelandic birds are noticeably whiter than those from Scandinavia and Russia. Downy cygnets are pale gray/white.

Whooper Swans are surprisingly good walkers. They are elegant swimmers, holding the long neck upright stiffly, and in flight they are magnificent, flying with slow wingbeats that create a gentle swishing noise. Getting into the air and landing are somewhat less elegant, the former achieved by a high-speed rush across the water with feet and wings in hectic action, the latter by extending the feet and skiing to a halt. If the landing site is frozen, the slide is even more impressive.

Confusion species
There is little overlap in the breeding ranges of Whooper and Bewick's Swans, and so little opportunity for confusion in summer. There is, however, some overlap in the wintering ranges of the two. The main distinguishing characteristic is the bill: the Whooper has a wedge-shaped bill with a greater area of yellow and, specifically, yellow beyond the nostril. Whooper Swan is also larger and heavier, with a longer neck.

Size
L: 4½–5½ ft. (140–160 cm), of which the body represents about half. WS: 6¾–8 ft. (210–245 cm). W: 16½–22 lb. (7.5–10 kg).

Voice
The *whoop* of the name, often heard in flight as a double

▼ Mixed flock of adult and 1st-year Whooper Swans, north Norway.

whoop, a powerful, trumpetlike call. There is also a threat call, a *honk* rather than a *whoop*, repeated several times. If a pair succeeds in driving off rivals, they will often honk in duet.

Distribution
Palearctic. Breeds from Iceland to Kamchatka, but with fewer birds than might be imagined in Fennoscandia. Instances of breeding in Alaska are known. Found in marshy and swampy areas of the tundra and taiga. Whoopers prefer breeding sites south of the timberline but also breed in Iceland and in Russia's southern tundra. In winter, Whoopers migrate along the coast or along chains of lakes and rivers to northern Europe, the Mediterranean, Black and Caspian Seas, Sea of Okhotsk, China and the Aleutians. Winters are spent on lakes or coastal lagoons and bays. Most Icelandic birds migrate to the British Isles (chiefly Ireland), but some (about 25%) overwinter on their breeding ranges in the south of Iceland and near Lake Myvatn, moving to the coast if lakes freeze. The flight from Iceland to Ireland is, at more than 650 mi. (1,100 km), the longest over-water crossing for any swan.

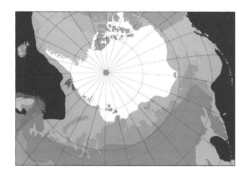

Diet
Aquatic vegetation in both fresh and sea waters. Feeds both by dipping the head below the surface and also by up-ending. On cultivated land and at reserves (e.g., Caerlaverock in Scotland) will feed on grain.

Breeding
Gregarious in winter, but pairs are highly intolerant of others when breeding. Pairs arrive as ice on breeding lake is thawing. Mating display is limited to mutual head-turning and head-bobbing, but if pair drive off intruders they perform a triumphant display, facing each other with wings and necks outstretched and honking in duet. Monogamous, but not necessarily enduring, with divorces being recorded. Nest is a large mound (sometimes 6½ ft./2 m) or more across and over 20 in./50 cm high) of vegetation constructed by both adults, but with female making final decisions. Built at water's edge. Three to five white or pale cream eggs (becoming brown-stained) are incubated, mainly by female, for 35–40 days. Cygnets nidifugous and precocial. Cared for by both adults and brooded by female at night and in poor weather. The cygnets are not carried by the adults. They are capable of self-feeding, but the adults often break off vegetation and sometimes feed them. Fledge at 75–95 days, migrating with parents to

▲ Adults and a young Whooper Swan. Note the extent of yellow on the bill compared to other northern swans.

overwinter as a family group, with the young becoming independent in following spring. Breed at 3–4 years.

Taxonomy and geographical variation
Monotypic. At one time Icelandic birds, which tend to be smaller, were considered a separate subspecies (*islandicus*).

Whistling Swan
Cygnus columbianus columbianus

The species *Cygnus columbianus* is usually referred to as the Tundra Swan. This species has two distinctive subspecies. *C. c. columbianus*, the Whistling Swan of the Nearctic, and *C. c. bewickii*, Bewick's Swan of the Palearctic (confusingly, both races are sometimes called Tundra Swan in various parts of the range). Although a few authorities consider these to be separate species, most retain them as subspecies. They are treated separately here, however, to reflect the significant morphological and biogeographical differences between the two taxa.

Identification See p. 134
Adults entirely white with black legs and feet. The bill is mostly black (sometimes but uncommonly all black) with yellow patches at the base. The iris is brown. At its maximum extent, the yellow patches reach about halfway to the nostril but do not meet on top of the bill. Juvenile birds are gray-brown overall with a pink bill, which becomes black during the first summer. Downy cygnets are pale gray/white.

Confusion species
Little overlap with other swans in the breeding season. On eastern edge of Chukotka, Whistling and eastern population of

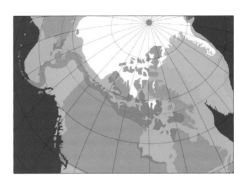

◄ Adult Whistling Swan. The amount of yellow on the bill is a key ID feature for distinguishing them from Bewick's Swan in areas of potential vagrancy.

Bewick's Swans may overlap. Whistling Swans are larger and have longer necks; Bewick's have much more yellow on the bill. In south-central and southeast Alaska, there is overlap with Trumpeter Swans, which are considerably bigger and have entirely black bills, as well as a much lower voice.

Size
L: 4–4½ ft. (120–135 cm), of which the body represents about half. WS: 5¼–6¼ ft. (160–190 cm). W: 13¼–15½ lb. (6–7 kg).

Voice
Higher and more melodic than the Trumpeter Swan. The flight call is a *kwoop kwoop*, much more gooselike than the whistle suggested by the name. On the water the birds are usually silent, but a gentle murmur can often be heard from a flock or a pair.

Distribution
Nearctic. Breeds across Arctic North America, including western and northern Alaska (more than 50% of the population breeds in the state), mainland Canada (including southern shore of Hudson Bay) and the southern Canadian Arctic islands, including southern Baffin. Does not occur on the northern islands. Whistling Swans also nest in eastern Chukotka, where hybridization with eastern Bewick's Swans is believed to have

▼ Pair of Whistling Swans. Both birds were shot by an Inuit hunter moments after this photograph was taken. Southampton Island.

occurred. Found on tundra pools and lakes, in marshy areas and at coastal delta sites. Whistling Swans are the last of the geese and swans to migrate south from the Arctic (and the first to return), wintering in large flocks along both coasts of the United States and on inland lakes. Interestingly, many Alaskan birds fly across America to the east coast rather than heading south along the Pacific coast. A small flock also overwinters on Unimak Island in the eastern Aleutian, where warm water springs maintain a tolerable habitat. Overwintering birds have also been seen on other Aleutian Islands.

Diet
Aquatic vegetation, but known to take shellfish. Feeds at the surface, by dipping and up-ending. When a flock is up-ending, some birds remain on guard. Wintering birds also search cultivated fields for grain.

Breeding
Gregarious in winter, but intolerant of others at breeding sites. Pairs arrive early, preferring islets in lakes, but accepting shore sites and even sites at some distance from water. Displays are similar to those of Whooper Swan. Nest is a vast mound of usually aquatic vegetation. Three to five pale cream (but quickly brown-stained) eggs incubated for 30–33 days, chiefly by the female, the male sitting only occasionally while his mate feeds.

Cygnets nidifugous and precocial. Cared by both adults, but self-feeding. The aggressiveness of adults in defence of chicks means that chicks are not especially vulnerable to predators such as the Arctic Fox, though if the nest is far from water the cygnets may be picked off as they make their first journey

there. Cygnets fledge and fly in 65–75 days, migrating with the adults. Breed at 2–3 years.

Taxonomy and geographical variation
This form is a subspecies of Tundra Swan (*C. columbianus*).

Bewick's Swan
Cygnus columbianus bewickii

Identification See p. 134
Bewick's Swan is named after the 18th-century English bird artist Thomas Bewick. Bewick's Swan is similar to its Nearctic counterpart, the Whistling Swan, but smaller, and with more yellow on the bill. Adults are entirely white, though occasionally with head, neck and underparts red-stained. The legs and feet are black. The bill is black but with yellow base extending about halfway to nostril. The yellow pattern is so irregular that it can be used to identify individual birds. The iris is brown. Juveniles are pale gray, usually much paler than juvenile Whooper Swans. Juvenile bill has pale yellow base, otherwise pink, occasionally dark gray. Bill approaches adult form by December of first year. Downy cygnets are pale gray/white.

▲ Adult Bewick's Swan.

Confusion species
Bewick's Swan is smaller and shorter-necked than the Whooper and has much less yellow on the bill. Where these characteristics are not obvious (e.g., in flight), identification can be difficult. Bewick's is generally seen much farther north in the breeding season.

Size
L: 3¾–4 ft. (115–125 cm), of which the body is about half. WS: 6–7 ft. (180–215 cm). W: 10–14 lb. (4.5–6.5 kg), exceptionally to 17 lb. (7.5 kg).

Voice
Similar to Whooper Swan, but higher and with a more distinct *honk* rather than a *whoop*. The threat call is similar but sharper and repeated more quickly. Pairs also murmur quietly to each other and to cygnets.

Distribution
Palearctic. Breeds along the northern coast of Russia from the White Sea to Chukotka, including the southern island of

Novaya Zemlya, but does not occur on other Russian Arctic islands. Found on northern tundra marshland, or areas with open water or slow-moving rivers. Western birds winter in coastal Denmark and Germany and in the British Isles. Eastern birds winter on Kamchatka, Kuril Islands and Japan.

Diet
Aquatic vegetation and roots, obtained by surface feeding, dipping and up-ending. Studies in Russia have shown that the swans also graze tundra vegetation. At some English wintering sites, Bewick's are fed on grain; in Ireland wintering birds feed on potatoes and carrots.

Breeding
Gregarious in winter, forming large flocks. Solitary in the breeding season, though occasionally nests in loose colonies. Pairs seek a dry spot close to water, occasionally in shallow water, but hummocks or other raised sites are preferred, allowing observation of surrounding area. Displays similar to Whooper Swan. Monogamous, with apparently lifelong pairing. Nest is vast mound of vegetation. Three to five white or pale cream (but soon stained) eggs incubated for 28–32 days, the shortest period of any swan. Incubation by female only, though male may sometimes sit when female is feeding. Cygnets nidifugous and precocial. Cared for by both parents, but self-feeding. Adults are aggressive in defence of young. Fledge in 40–45 days, an astonishingly short time for so large a bird, and accompany adults on migration flight. Breed at 2–3 years.

Taxonomy and geographical variation
This form is a subspecies of Tundra Swan (*C. columbianus*). Birds of the population east of the Lena Delta are sometimes claimed to be larger, to have more yellow on the bill and to form a separate race, Jankowski's Swan (*C. jankowskii*). However, perceived size and bill-pattern differences do not exceed those encountered in western populations of Bewick's Swan.

Geese

▲ White-fronted Geese and Bean Goose (bottom) in flight, Norway.

Twelve of the 15 species of northern geese are Arctic breeders, and watching skeins of geese crossing the Arctic sky is one of the great joys of northern travel. By contrast to the highly visible flocks in flight, geese on the ground are frequently elusive, being understandably wary of humans, who have hunted them throughout history. Flocks always have at least one vigilant guard, and geese are rarely taken unawares. Observers approaching nesting birds will discover how aggressive they can be, with both sexes leaping to the defence of their eggs. Those thinking it easier to approach moulting flightless geese will find that, although the birds might look heavy and ungainly, they can easily outrun the standard Arctic traveler. Geese are gregarious in winter, forming large, sometimes huge, flocks. The birds are less tolerant of one another on breeding sites, though loose colonies are common. Although associated with water, most geese do not feed there. Adult geese feed on grass, and some species dig for roots and tubers. Young geese also take invertebrates. One notable feature of a feeding goose is the speed with which it snips the plants it is grazing.

Geese generally mate for life; this is perhaps an advantage for Arctic breeding, where time is short, since it dispenses with time-consuming pairing and displaying. The whole time can instead be devoted to raising young from egg to large bird in readiness for the autumn migration. Goose nests are built close to water, and the eggs require a remarkably short incubation. Goslings are brooded and guarded diligently, with colonies occasionally forming crèches. Juveniles migrate with their parents, returning with them the following spring, although first-year birds do not breed but form colonies with other yearlings. Before each of their annual migrations, geese feed almost continuously, putting on weight to sustain them during long flights. This is especially important for

females before spring migration, as the energetic requirements of egg-laying are significant. Geese often leave eggshells in the nest and may consume them the following year, as nests are reused and the demand for calcium to produce eggshells is high.

Northern geese are divided into two genera: "gray geese" (*Anser*) and black geese (*Branta*). Each is something of a misnomer, but they provide a good way to group the species.

Gray Geese

Gray geese are distinguished from black geese not only by their general color but also by having serrated mandibles and vertical furrowing of the neck feathers. The neck feathers are vibrated when the bird shows aggression.

Bean Goose
Anser fabalis

Identification   See p. 134

A large, elegant goose, less heavily built than the slightly larger Graylag and with a longer, more slender neck. Head and upper neck are dark gray-brown, the neck color fading to paler brown. The bill is long and yellow/orange with a black tip. Some birds show a white basal ring. The iris is dark brown. The chest and underparts are pale brown, becoming darker from the belly to the flanks and showing darker strips, sometimes indistinct. The upper flank feathers are edged white, the white forming a continuous line. The wings and back are dark gray-brown (similar to the head); the feathers have paler tips so that the bird appears to be thinly striped, with stripes varying from pale brown close to the neck to white on the tertials and upperwing-coverts. Vent and undertail-coverts are white, a feature characteristic of all gray geese. Legs and feet yellow-orange. In flight from below, Beans have uniform dark wings. Very noticeable from above are the white feather edging, dark back and the alternately white-and dark-banded tail with its narrow white edge. Juveniles are similar to adults but duller, with less distinct dark barring on flanks. Downy goslings are olive/dark brown.

Confusion species
Several. Bean Geese with white basal bill ring can resemble White-fronted Geese. Look for the distinct black barring on the adult White-fronted's belly. Large Beans are very similar to Graylag geese, but the latter have pink feet and white bill nail. Pink feet also distinguish Pink-footed Geese. In all cases the distinguishing colorations can vary in individuals.

Size
L: 26–34 in. (65–85 cm), body 16–20 in. (40–50 cm). WS: 4¹/₂–5³/₄ ft. (140–175 cm). W: 6–8³/₄ lb. (2.7–4 kg).

Voice
A nasal *ung-unk* or *ow-ow* (occasionally *ow-ow-ow*). The least vocal of the gray geese.

Distribution
Palearctic. Breeds in northern Fennoscandia and in Russia east to Chukotka, including southern island of Novaya Zemlya. In Russia the range extends south to Mongolian/Chinese border. Found on marshy tundra and wetlands. Western birds migrate to southern Scandinavia/Germany/Belgium (and a few in British Isles). Eastern birds move to China and Japan. Wetland habitats preferred in winter.

Diet
Grass and other tundra vegetation, roots and tubers. Wintering birds graze on cereals and other crops. The common name derives from the goose's fondness for beans.

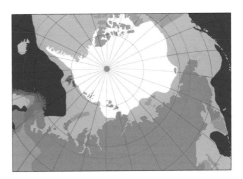

▼ Taiga Bean Goose.

Breeding
Gregarious in winter, though less so than other gray geese. Flocks of mixed species occasionally form. Solitary at breeding sites. Pair-bond apparently monogamous and lifelong. Nest is set close to water, though occasionally at distances up to ¹/₂ mi. (1 km) away. Southernmost breeders may nest, uniquely for geese, among dense conifers. Previous year's nest frequently used with new lining. Displays limited to "triumph ceremony," which male performs after driving off rival and which pair perform after driving off a predator. The geese raise their heads, spread their wings and cackle noisily. Nest is of vegetation lined with down. Four to six (three to five at northern edge of range) very pale yellow eggs. Eggs incubated for 27–29 days, but as few as 25 days for northern pairs. Goslings nidifugous and precocial. Cared for and vigorously protected by both adults, but self-feeding. Brooded at night by female. Chicks fledge in about 40 days. Migrate with adults. Breed at 2–3 years.

Taxonomy and geographical variation
Polytypic. Five races are usually cited, with nominate (Western Bean or Taiga Bean) the most westerly, breeding on the taiga of Fennoscandia and Russia east to the Urals. Nominate has a long yellow-orange bill with a black nail. *A. f. johanseni* breeds on the taiga from the Urals to the Yenisey River. It is smaller and darker-billed. *A. f. middendorffii* breeds on the taiga east of the Yenisey. It has a long, slender black bill, the yellow-orange forming a band close to the tip. The Tundra Bean Goose (*A. f. rossicus*) breeds on the tundra from the White Sea to the Taimyr Peninsula. It has less distinct edging to the wing-coverts and a shorter, thicker black bill with a yellow-orange band close to the nail. East of the Taimyr, the Thick-billed Bean (*A. f. serrirostris*) replaces *rossicus*. It is larger, with a similar bill.

Several authorities split Bean Goose into two species: Taiga Bean (*A. fabalis*, with three subspecies: *fabalis*, *johanseni* and *middendorffi*) and Tundra Bean (*A. rossicus*, with subspecies *rossicus* and *serrirostris*).

Graylag Goose
Anser anser

Identification   See p. 134
The largest of the gray geese; only the largest Beans equal the Graylag, though Graylags look heavier. The head and upper neck are pale gray-brown, the bill heavy and dull orange with

a pale nail. A few birds show a thin white basal bill ring. The iris is dark brown. The furrowing of the neck is usually very marked. The lower neck and underparts are paler gray-brown with a pattern of both lighter and darker stripes, sometimes indistinct. The vent and undertail-coverts are white. The upperparts are gray-brown, darker on the primaries and secondaries. The coverts are tipped with dark gray-brown and then cream-brown, which gives the appearance of darker and paler striping across the back. By contrast the darker flight feathers are edged with white. The tail is gray, edged with white. The legs and feet are dull pink. Viewed from below in flight, the Graylag has a two-toned wing with pale gray coverts

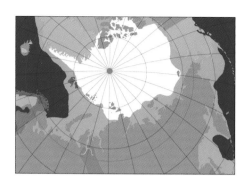

▲ Comparing the heads of grey geese: a) White-fronted Goose; b) Greylag Goose; c) Bean Goose; d) Pink-footed Goose.

and dark gray primaries and secondaries. From above, the wings are pale gray with dark gray trailing edges. Juveniles are similar to adults but lack the bill's pale nail, and underparts are more mottled than striped. Downy goslings are olive.

Confusion species
Bean Goose (pp. 88–89) and Pink-footed Goose. The darker head, smaller size and blue-gray wings of Pink-footed are diagnostic. In flight, the silvery-gray panel on the upperwing and pale underwing-coverts are diagnostic.

Size
L: 30–26 in. (75–90 cm). WS: 5–5³/₄ ft. (150–175 cm). W: 6¹/₂–10 lb. (3–4.5 kg).

Voice
The honking of the Graylag leaves the observer in no doubt

▼ Greylag Geese, North Norway.

that this is the ancestor of the domestic goose. The honk is a loud, raucous, delightful *ung-ung-ung*. There are also several other shorter, nasal honks.

Distribution
Palearctic. Breeds in southern Eurasia; only the breeding birds of Iceland fall within the Arctic. Also breeds in north Norway. Found on wetlands and near lakes and streams, though often seen on grasslands, particularly in the winter. Some populations partially migratory, others fully migratory, reaching northern India and southern China.

Diet
Grasses and marsh plants. Feeds in water as well as on land. In winter the geese feed on grasslands and cereal fields, but will also eat root crops such as potatoes and carrots.

Breeding
Gregarious in winter, more solitary at breeding sites. Pair-bond monogamous and lifelong. Breeding display is similar to triumph ceremony of Bean Goose, with male often initiating the performance by driving off an imaginary rival. Huge nest constructed of vegetation set close to water, sometimes in reed beds or even on a floating raft. Lining mostly of grass, with little down. Four to six pale cream (soon brown-stained) eggs (though clutches of up to 12 recorded). Incubated by female only for 27–30 days. Goslings nidifugous and precocial. Cared for by both adults, but self-feeding. Female broods chicks at night (sometimes on the nest), the male maintaining guard. Fledge in 50–60 days, migrating with adults and staying with them until spring migration. Breed at 2–3 years.

Taxonomy and geographical variation
The nominate race is found in west and northwest Europe. To the east, *A. a. rubrirostris* occupies central Eurasia. The latter has a pink or pinkish-orange bill, is generally paler and has much broader pale edgings on the wing feathers.

Pink-footed Goose
Anser brachyrhynchus

Identification See p. 134
Smaller than both the Graylag and Bean but with characteristics of each. The head and upper neck are dark gray-

▲ Pink-footed Geese. Note their small size and darker colours.

brown, the bill short and dark with a pink band behind the nail. Some birds show a ragged white basal ring. The iris is dark brown. The neck is short but slender. The lower neck is pinkish-brown, blending into gray-buff underparts with some dark striping, particularly toward the vent. The vent and undertail-coverts are white. The upperparts are blue-gray, most noticeable if the observer is lucky enough to see the bird from above. The feathers are edged in paler blue-gray, which gives the appearance of blue stripes on the gray. Some birds are gray-brown rather than blue-gray. The legs and feet are pink. In flight from below, the wing is uniformly dark gray-brown. Juveniles are duller than adults, with bill and legs a duller pink. Downy goslings are yellow/brown.

Confusion species
Gray-brown birds are similar to Bean Geese. Beans are larger, with longer bills and have orange legs and feet. Gray-brown birds are also similar to Graylags, which are bigger and have paler heads and orange bills. White-fronted Geese have darker upperparts with less pronounced banding, distinct black patches on the underparts, and a white basal bill ring.

Size
L: 24–30 in. (60–75 cm). WS: 4½–5½ ft. (135–165 cm). W: 4¼–7 lb. (1.9–3.2 kg).

Voice
Very similar to Bean and Graylag, but higher. Usually a double *honk*, but occasionally triple. A softer, nasal *king-king* and a single sharp note of alarm also heard.

Distribution
North Atlantic. Breeds in east Greenland mainly north from Scoresby Sound, Iceland and Svalbard. Has attempted to breed on Franz Josef Land but not established. Found chiefly on low wetlands. Greenland/Iceland birds winter in northern England and Scotland (with a few in Ireland). Svalbard birds winter on Norwegian coast, Denmark and Holland. Wintering birds found on coastal wetlands, inland grassland or stubble fields.

Diet
Tundra and marsh vegetation, including roots and tubers. In Iceland feeds mainly on sedges/cottongrass. Wintering birds feed on grassland or cereal fields, brassicas and root crops.

Breeding
Gregarious at all times; less so at breeding sites though occasionally nests are surprisingly closely packed. Pair-bond monogamous and lifelong. Displays similar to Bean and Graylag. In all parts of the bird's range either lowland or cliff ledges nest sites are chosen, depending on the extent of predation by the Arctic Fox. The nest is of vegetation lined copiously with down. Three to five white/pale yellow eggs are laid that are soon brown-stained. Eggs incubated by female only, with male on guard close by. Incubation 25–28 days. Goslings nidifugous and precocial. Brooded by female broods, but self-feeding. Fledge in 55–60 days and migrate with adults spending winter with them. Breed at 2–3 years.

Taxonomy and geographical variation
Monotypic. Pink-footed Goose was once considered a form of Bean Goose.

▼ Pink-footed Goose nest. Note the use of down. Iceland.

Greater White-fronted Goose
Anser albifrons

Identification See p. 134

Similar in size to Pink-footed but with a longer neck. The head and upper neck are pale gray-brown. The long, slender bill is pink or orange-pink with white nail and prominent white basal ring extending over forehead. The iris is dark brown. Lower neck is light brown, blending to buff on the chest. Flanks are darker with dark gray-brown striping. Belly is pale, boldly marked with black patches. Vent and undertail-coverts white. Upperparts are gray-brown with pale striping from feather edges. The legs and feet are orange. Viewed in flight from below, the wing is uniformly dark. From above wing is very similar to Bean Goose, but with striping much less distinct. Juveniles have pale pink bills and no basal ring. Belly is pale and unmarked. Flanks mottled rather than striped. Downy goslings are olive/brown.

▲ Nominate White-fronted Goose in flight, Finland.

Confusion species

White facial ring and dark patches on belly are distinctive in adults, but juvenile birds are very similar to juvenile Pink-footed and Bean Goose. Bill is best distinguishing feature, if close inspection is possible.

Size

L: 26–32 in. (65–80 cm). WS: 4¼–5¼ ft. (130–160 cm). W: 3¾–7 lb. (1.7–3.2 kg).

Voice

Most vocal of the gray geese. Higher and less raucous than Bean and Graylag. Occasionally called musical, which stretches the definition. Usually *kling-kling*, but sometimes three syllables. Wintering flocks occasionally murmur gently.

Distribution

Circumpolar. Russia from the White Sea to Chukotka including southern island of Novaya Zemlya, west Greenland from Disko Bay to Narsaq, north, west and central Alaska, and isolated sites in Yukon, Northwest Territories and Nunavut. Found on low-lying scrubby tundra with many pools or lakes, or on marshy land. North American birds winter in California, Mexico

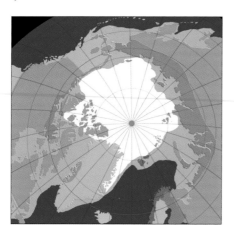

and Gulf of Mexico. Birds from eastern Russia winter in China and Japan, birds from western Russia in Balkans and Turkey, British Isles, France and the Low Countries. Greenland birds migrate through Iceland to Ireland and Scotland. Wintering birds occur in a variety of habitats, including inland fields and marshes and coastal flats.

Diet

Tundra vegetation and tubers. Favors cereal and grass fields in winter.

Breeding

Gregarious in winter, much less so at breeding sites. Pair-bond apparently monogamous and lifelong. Displays very similar to Bean Goose. Nests close to water on dry mounds, often reusing old nest. Four to six white/pale yellow (soon brown-stained) eggs, incubated by female for 26–28 days. Goslings nidifugous and precocial. Cared for by both adults, but self-feeding. Brooded by female only. Fledge in 40–44 days and migrate with adults. Breed at 3 years.

Taxonomy and geographical variation

Polytypic. Five races are generally recognized. Nominate is the European White-fronted Goose, which breeds in Russia east to the Kolyma River. The Pacific White-fronted (*A. a. frontalis*) has a longer bill, is darker overall and occupies the rest of Russia and northern North America. Intermediate forms occur at the Kolyma boundary. The Greenland White-fronted Goose (*A. a. flavirostris*) is larger, has a yellow-orange bill and a more heavily blotched belly. Gambel's White-fronted (*A. a. gambeli*) is a larger, darker Pacific race with a longer neck and bill. It breeds in the Mackenzie Delta in the Northwest Territories and over the border in nearby Alaska. The Tule White-fronted or (more usually) Tule Goose (*A. a. elgasi*) is the largest of the five races. Most Tule Geese have a distinctive narrow yellow orbital ring. The name derives from the tules (bullrushes) that they favor in their central California wintering grounds. Tule Geese breed on the Cook Inlet, southwest of Anchorage and in Denali National Park.

Lesser White-fronted Goose
Anser erythropus

Identification   See p. 135

Smaller than but very similar to White-fronted Goose. The neck is shorter and thicker, the head paler and more rounded. The bill is much smaller and pinker, with a white nail. The basal bill ring extends onto the crown. There is a yellow orbital ring, much more prominent than in those White-fronted Geese that show one. The iris is dark brown. The color of the underparts is as for White-fronted, but there are many fewer black patches on the belly. The wings are browner than those of White-fronted and, when the bird is on the ground, extend beyond the tail (those of White-fronted do not). Legs and feet are orange. Juveniles are similar to juvenile White-fronted but usually darker; yellow orbital ring is less prominent than in adult, but still discernible. Downy goslings are olive/brown.

Confusion species

White-fronted Goose. Lesser's smaller bill, more extensive white forehead and yellow eye-ring are the best features in adults. In mixed feeding flocks note the faster feeding action.

Size

L: 21½–26 in. (55–65 cm). WS: 3¾– 4½ ft. (115–135 cm). W: 3½–5 lb. (1.6–2.3 kg).

Voice

Higher and more rapid than in White-fronted. Two or three syllables, *kow-kow*, more a squeak than a honk.

Distribution

Palearctic. Breeds in north Fennoscandia (where it has been partly re-introduced following overhunting) and northern Russia to Chukotka. Overlaps with White-fronted Goose for most of its Russian range but is much less abundant. Found on both inland wetlands and coastal sites, particularly estuaries. Wintering birds from west of range migrate to southern Sweden, coastal Denmark, Germany, Holland and eastern England (rare). From center of range the geese migrate to the Balkans, Turkey and Caspian Sea. Eastern birds migrate to China. Wintering birds are the least maritime of geese.

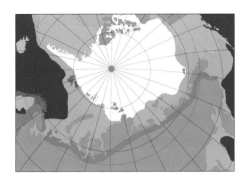

▼ Lesser White-fronted Goose.

Diet

Tundra vegetation, but taiga-breeding birds eat Least Willow (*Salix herbacca*).

Breeding

Gregarious in winter, solitary at breeding sites. Pair-bond apparently monogamous and lifelong. Displays as in White-fronted Goose, but performed much more rapidly. Nests both on tundra and in taiga. Tundra breeders choose rocky outcrops or mounds, usually close to water and rarely more than 490 ft. (150 m) from it. Taiga breeders can nest in dense scrub, but prefer sites with easier access. Nests are smaller and less well built than those of other geese. Old nests are often reused after relining with grass and, after egg-laying, with down. Four to six pale yellow (soon brown-stained) eggs, incubated by female only for 25–28 days, the female covering the eggs with down when she vacates. Goslings nidifugous and precocial. Cared for by both parents, but self-feeding. Brooded by female only. Fledge at 35–40 days, migrating with the adults and overwintering with them. Breed at 2–3 years.

Taxonomy and geographical variation

Monotypic.

Snow Goose
Anser caerulescens

Identification   See p. 135

Unmistakable, the black wingtips ensuring no confusion with swans (which are also much bigger). Flocks of Snow Geese are redolent of the Arctic and are an inspiring sight.

Snow Geese occur in two morphs. Adult white morphs are entirely white with pale gray primary coverts and black primaries. There is occasionally a yellowish tinge to the head and upper neck, and these areas may also be stained a rusty red. The bill is short, stubby and red or red-pink with a white nail. The bill has prominent dark cutting edges on both mandibles, which give the goose an appearance that is often termed *grinning*, though *grimacing* may be more apt. The iris is dark brown. Dark-morph birds are often termed Blue Geese (and were thought to be a different species until the early 1960s). In the darkest form, the lower neck, chest, belly, flanks and mantle are blue-gray, sometimes with a brownish tinge. As the two morphs hybridize, birds with varying amounts of blue-

▲ White- (bottom bird) and blue-morph Snow Geese in flight over Southampton Island.

gray and white are seen. The bill of the Blue Goose is as the white morph. Both forms have reddish-pink legs and feet. Juvenile white-morph birds are pale gray with brown speckling on the head, mantle and wings. Juvenile Blue Geese are as adults, but with more distinct brownish tinge to plumage. Juvenile hybrids take an intermediate form. All juveniles have gray-pink bills, legs and feet. Downy goslings are gray, but color varies with morph; blue-morph young are much darker.

Confusion species
None. White head of Blue Goose is distinctive even in brownish birds.

Size
L: 26–32 in. (65–80 cm). WS: 4¼–5¼ ft. (130–160 cm). W: 4¾–7½ lb. (2.2–3.4 kg).

▼ Blue- and white-morph Snow Geese, Southampton Island.

Voice
A distinctive high, doglike yelp rather than a true honk. There is also a deeper cackle, particularly from alarmed birds.

Distribution
Nearctic, plus small population in northeast Siberia (though still in significant numbers on Wrangel). Breeds across North America to northwest Greenland. Snow Geese are found to 82°N on Ellesmere Island and occur on many of Canada's Arctic islands, sometimes in great numbers. Found on wetlands, particularly in low-lying areas, near freshwater or saltwater. Also occasionally found in rocky environments. In winter some Russian birds move south to China and Japan, but many migrate across the Bering Sea to join Arctic American birds heading south to Mexico and the southern States, from California to Florida. Greenland birds head south along the eastern seaboard to the south. Wintering birds occur on wetlands or grassland. Snow Goose numbers have increased dramatically in recent years. This has been attributed to changes in agricultural practice. The increase has not been without a downside: not only have areas of saltmarsh been overgrazed, but the birds' droppings, once a fertilizer, are now so numerous that they have altered water chemistry and reduced plant growth.

Diet
Tundra vegetation, including roots and tubers. Also eats seaweed during late summer. Canadian Inuit still hunt Snow Geese regularly, but stop hunting in late summer as seaweed-

▼ Snow Goose showing the distinctive "grin."

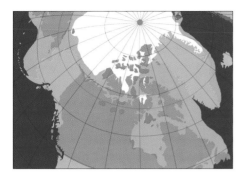

▲ Ross's Goose. The blue caruncles are visible at the base of the bill.

eating ruins the flavor of the meat. In winter the geese search cereal fields for grain and also feed on grassland.

Breeding
Gregarious in winter and still relatively tolerant of others in breeding range, forming loose colonies. Pair-bond monogamous and lifelong. Displays as in other gray geese. Nests of vegetation in dry areas close to water. Four to six white (soon brown-stained) eggs, incubated by female only for 22–25 days. Goslings nidifugous, precocial and self-feeding. The chicks feed on vegetation as well as mosquitoes (another reason for the Arctic observer to be enthralled by the birds). They fledge in 33–37 days and migrate with parents. Breed at 2–3 years.

Taxonomy and geographical variation
Polytypic. Nominate race is often called the Lesser Snow Goose. Race *atlanticus*, sometimes called the Greater Snow Goose, is restricted to eastern North America (coastal regions of Baffin Bay, including Baffin, Bylot and Ellesmere Islands) and northwest Greenland. Race *atlanticus* is larger and heavier, with a heavier bill; dark-morph *atlanticus* are rare.

Ross's Goose
Anser rossii

Identification   See p. 135
As with Snow Goose, Ross's Goose has two color morphs, though the dark (blue) morph is rare (and may result either from direct hybridization with Blue Goose [blue-morph Snow Goose] or from egg-dumping in mixed breeding colonies, leading to imprinting, then hybridization, of Blue Goose chicks). White-morph Ross's have almost identical plumage to white Snow Geese, but are only 50–60% of the size by weight (and only one-third the size, by weight, of Greater Snow Geese). Ross's rarely show the rusty head and neck-staining of Snow Geese, and the bill grimace is much less pronounced or non-existent. The base of the bill is bluish and males have distinct dark gray, warty protuberances (caruncles) at the base, which increase with age. The iris is dark brown. Blue-morph Ross's is similar to Blue Goose but with much darker mantles and white coverts, which create a distinct white stripe along the flank. The flight feathers are also much lighter than those of Blue Goose. As in Snow Geese, juvenile Ross's are grayer in

the white morph and browner in the dark morph. Downy goslings vary from pale yellow-gray to much darker.

Confusion species
Smaller than Snow Goose, with shorter neck and bill and more rounded head.

Size
L: 20–24 in. (50–60 cm). WS: 3½–4 ft. (110–120 cm). W: 2–3¼ lb. (1–1.5 kg).

Voice
Much less vocal than Snow Goose. Most frequent call is a rapid, high squeaking *keek-keek*. There is also a lower *honk*.

Distribution
Nearctic. Limited to a few places in the Canadian Arctic: western Banks Island, the mainland around Bathurst Inlet, Southampton Island and western Hudson Bay. Found in low-lying wetlands, occasionally near coasts. Migrates to the southern United States and the Gulf of Mexico.

Diet
As for Snow Goose.

Breeding
Gregarious at all times. The most colonial nester of all the gray geese, though colonies are still loose and nesting sites are aggressively defended. Ross's breeding sites were not discovered until 1940. Pair-bond probably monogamous and

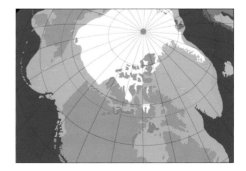

lifelong. Displays as in other gray geese. Nest is made of vegetation in dry areas of tundra close to water. Four to six very pale pink (soon brown-stained) eggs, incubated by female only for 21–23 days. Goslings nidifugous, precocial and self-feeding. Crèches formed within the colony may contain several hundred goslings. Fledge at 33–38 days and migrate with adults. Breed at 2–3 years.

Taxonomy and geographical variation
Monotypic. Hybridization with Snow Geese has occurred.

Emperor Goose
Anser canagicus

The curious name of the Emperor Goose reputedly descends from Russian émigrés to the Aleutian Islands, who called the goose *sasarka* because of its resemblance to the Helmeted Guineafowl of East Africa, which had been called the same name by early Russian travelers to that area. The Aleuts, not familiar with Russian but understanding that the Czar was the Russian ruler, assumed that the goose was, somehow, the emperor's bird.

Identification   See p. 135
A small goose intermediate in size between Ross's and Snow Geese, and beautifully marked. Adult Emperors are unmistakable. The head is small, round and white, occasionally gray forward of the eye. The iris is dark brown. The bill is very short and dull pink with a white nail. The neck is short and slender, white at the rear and dark gray at the front. The white of head and neck is occasionally stained rusty red. The rest of the plumage is a delightful blue-gray, almost silver-gray, with flecks and bars of darker gray and white from feather edging that give a scaly appearance. The tail is white. The legs and feet are orange. Viewed in flight from below, the wings are uniformly dark gray. Wings are also relatively short and broad, consistent with the limited migratory range of the goose. Juveniles have a white tail, but lack the white on the head and neck, the overall plumage being patterned as the adult, but being both grayer and duller. The bill is dull pink, the legs and feet dull yellow. Downy goslings are pale gray.

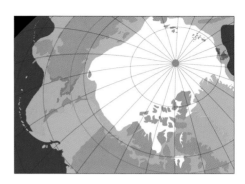

▼ Swimming Emperor Goose.

Confusion species
Unlikely, but resembles Blue Goose at a distance or in poor light. The red bill and grimace of the Blue Goose is quite different from the short, pink bill of the Emperor.

Size
L: 24–28 in. (60–70 cm). WS: 3¾–4 ft. (115–125 cm). W: 5¼–6¼ lb. (2.4–2.8 kg).

Voice
High and (relatively) musical. Usual call is a rapid *kla-kla*, occasionally with three syllables. There is also a single trumpetlike cry and a lower grunt.

Distribution
Bering Sea. The most restricted of the gray geese. Emperors breed at sites on the western coast of Alaska and in limited numbers on the eastern coast of the Chukotka. The geese are maritime, rarely seen more than a few miles inland. They are essentially non-migratory, though western Alaska birds tend to overwinter on the Aleutians or Kodiak Island. Occasionally seen on the Pacific coast of the continental United States, but it is conjectured that these may be birds that imprinted on White-fronted Geese after egg-dumping by female Emperors.

Diet
Seaweed and salt-tolerant plants found on beaches and brackish lagoons and mudflats. Also take mollusks. Flocks also feed on kelp washed ashore by storms. Because of this diet, feeding Emperor Geese follow the tides.

Breeding
Gregarious in winter, less so at breeding sites. Nests in loose colonies but vigorously defends a small territory around the nest. Pair-bond apparently monogamous and lifelong. Displays similar to Ross's and Snow Goose. Beach locations beyond the high-water mark favored for nest site. The nest is poorly lined. That and position mean that losses are high as chicks become wet and cold. Four to six cream eggs incubated for 23–26 days by female only. Goslings nidifugous and precocial. Cared for by both parents, crèches sometimes forming. Fledge at 50–55 days and migrate with parents if they do. Breed at 3 years.

Taxonomy and geographical variation
Monotypic.

Black Geese

Of the five species of northern black geese, only the Hawaiian Goose or Nene (*Branta sandvicensis*) shows any furrowing of the neck feathers; it is also the only one of the five that is non-Arctic. Black geese lack the prominent mandible serrations of gray geese and are more boldly marked, with only the Emperor Goose approaching the patterning of black species.

Barnacle Goose
Branta leucopsis

The name of this species derives from the medieval belief that the geese, which seemed to appear from nowhere in northern Europe each autumn, emerged from the barnacles that drifted ashore on Atlantic currents. An early 17th-century English writer suggested that the barnacles were themselves the fruit of a tree that grew in north Scotland and the Orkneys, and one early alternative name for the bird was Tree Goose. The barnacles, which with a good dose of imagination look like legless geese, were therefore christened Goose Barnacles. Both names have stuck. In reality, of course, the appearance of the geese was due to nothing more magical than the existence of the poorly known lands of the north, though the same English writer who set down the tale of the barnacle tree also reported rumours that Dutch explorers had seen the geese sitting on nests in the Arctic. It has been claimed that the persistence of the legend of the birds' birth from the barnacle was aided because such origins meant the goose was considered "fish" rather than "meat," meaning that Christians (particularly Catholics) could eat the birds on Fridays.

Identification See p. 135

A black-and-white goose. The small, round head is white (some birds show a distinct yellow tinge) with a black cap and a black patch forward of the eye, reaching the bill. The iris is dark brown. The bill is short and black. Below the white chin the short neck is black, the black extending on to the mantle and chest. The underparts are white/pale gray with delicate gray barring on the flanks. The wing-coverts are gray with thick black and thin white barring. The flight feathers are pale gray

▲ Barnacle Geese in flight; an unmistakable Arctic species.

with darker tips. The tail is black, the vent and rump white. The legs and feet are black. Viewed in flight from below, the wings are pale gray with dark trailing edges. Juveniles are as the adults, but with speckled rather than barred flanks, and the wing-coverts are barred with brown and black. Downy goslings are gray-brown.

Confusion species
None.

Size
L: 21¹/₂–28 in. (55–70 cm). WS: 4¹/₄–4³/₄ ft. (130–145 cm). W: 3–4³/₄ lb. (1.4–2.2 kg).

Voice
The single call is a curious doglike *yap*. The birds are noisy in both winter flocks and at the breeding colonies.

Distribution
North Atlantic. There are four populations, in northeastern

▼ A distant skein of Barnacle Geese fly in towards their breeding grounds. Myggbukta, northeast Greenland.

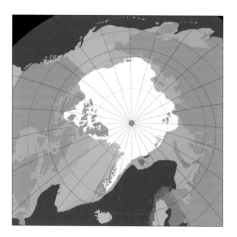

Greenland, Svalbard, the southern island of Novaya Zemlya and the nearby Russian mainland (including Kolguyev Island), and Gotland and nearby Swedish Baltic islands. Pairs have also nested in Franz Josef Land. The Gotland group is believed to have arisen from some birds on migration to Russia that stayed on at what had been a staging post. Found on both wet and dry tundra. All populations are migratory. The Greenland birds migrate through Iceland to northern Ireland and the Inner Hebrides (particularly Islay). Svalbard birds migrate to the Solway Firth in southern Scotland. Russian and Gotland birds move to coastal Netherlands and Germany. Interestingly, although the Greenland and Svalbard birds winter only 60 mi. (100 km) apart, mixing of the populations is extremely limited. Wintering birds are frequently seen on inland grasslands.

Diet
Tundra vegetation, which is clipped at a rate of more than 200 snips per minute, the highest rate recorded for a goose. In winter the geese eat grass (which causes conflict with farmers, as the geese preferentially take younger shoots and so inhibit spring growth) and vegetation in coastal dunes and marshes.

Breeding
Gregarious at all times, but the most quarrelsome of all geese. Although Barnacle Geese have staging posts on migration, these are limited for the Greenland and Svalbard birds so that the migration to the breeding sites cannot be timed to the "spring" at stopping points along the route as it is in North American and Russian goose species. Arrival at the breeding sites can therefore be early or late, depending on the timing of the year's spring. Pair-bond is monogamous and lifelong. Barnacle Geese have limited displays, showing the triumph ceremony of other geese when rivals are dispatched from a pair's territory. This happens often as Barnacle Geese are colonial breeders. Nest, constructed by the female only, is little more than a scrape in a sheltered spot, copiously lined with down. In Greenland, Svalbard and Novaya Zemlya, the geese nest on cliff ledges to avoid the Arctic Fox. In Greenland, cliff-nesting Barnacle Geese often choose sites close to Gyrfalcons for protection from other predators. Three to five pale gray eggs, becoming yellow-stained, incubated for 24–25 days by the female with the male standing guard. The trials of incubation for the female and guarding for the male are significant, with the birds losing 30–40% of their body weight before the eggs hatch. Goslings nidifugous and precocial, the brood leaving the nest for the tundra. Cliff-hatched goslings tumble to the ground below to join their parents, a hazardous start to life made more so by patroling foxes and gulls. Cared for by both parents, but self-feeding. Fledge in 40–45 days and migrate with the adults. Breed at 2–3 years.

Taxonomy and geographical variation
Monotypic.

Brant Goose (Brent)
Branta bernicla

Identification   See p. 135
A very dark goose, slightly smaller and less heavy in the body than the Barnacle Goose. The small, round head, neck, mantle and chest are black, but there is a triangular white/black speckled patch on each side of the neck. The iris is dark brown. The short bill is dark gray. The underparts are mid-gray, with paler striping on the flanks. The upperparts are uniformly mid-gray, though the flight feathers are black, as is the tail. The vent is white. The legs and feet are dark gray or black. In flight from below or above the wing is uniformly mid-gray, the flight feathers forming a black trailing edge. Juveniles very similar to

Brant Geese of the dark-bellied nominate race, Norway.

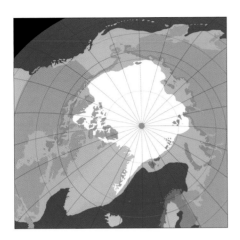

▲ Brant Goose of the race *nigricans*, the Black Brant, Alaska.

adults, but with white barring on the upperparts and little or no white on the neck. Downy goslings are pale gray.

Confusion species
None. The completely black head is diagnostic.

Size
L: 21½–24 in. (55–60 cm). WS: 3½–4 ft. (105–120 cm). W: 3–3½ lb. (1.2–1.6 kg).

Voice
Usual calls are a nasal *ong-ong-ong* or a monosyllabic *ronk*. Flocks can be very noisy, though in general Brants are silent.

Distribution
Circumpolar. Breeds in northeast and northwest Greenland (once common, but now rare), Svalbard, northern Russia and the Russian Arctic islands, western and northern Alaska, the northern Canadian mainland west of Hudson Bay and some Canadian Arctic islands including Ellesmere Island, where they are probably the most northerly nesting goose. Prefers wet tundra with numerous pools. Northeast Greenland birds winter in Ireland. Svalbard and Russian birds migrate in flocks heading southwest to the coast of mainland Europe, from Denmark to France, and in eastern England, or southeast to Japan and China. Northwest Greenland and North American birds head south, as far south as Baja California and Florida. Brants from the Canadian Arctic fly across Greenland and Iceland to Ireland, the longest migration of any Arctic goose.

Diet
Vegetation, either on land or in shallow water. Occasionally feed by up-ending in deeper water. In winter, feed on mudflats and salt marshes, consuming eelgrass and marine algae, as well as on grasslands and in cereal fields. Brants are maritime geese, able to drink saltwater as they have efficient salt glands.

Breeding
Gregarious at all times, nesting in colonies, though within these territories are established and guarded aggressively. Pair-bond monogamous and lifelong. Displays as for other geese, particularly for triumph ceremony. Nests, sited on dry mounds in wet areas or close to the high-water mark in coastal sites, are little more than a shallow depression lined with moss and, after eggs are laid, with down. Three to five cream or pale yellow (soon brown-stained) eggs, incubated by female only for 24–26 days. Goslings nidifugous and precocial. Cared for by both parents, but self-feeding. Fledge at 40–45 days and migrate with adults. Breed at 2–3 years.

Taxonomy and geographical variation
Polytypic. Nominate *bernicla*, or Dark-bellied Brant Goose, breeds in Russia from Taimyr to Chukotka, including Russia's Arctic islands except Franz Josef Land. The Pale-bellied Brant Goose (*B. b. hrota*) breeds in eastern Canadian Arctic (from Melville Island), northwestern and northeastern Greenland, Svalbard and Franz Josef Land. It has lighter upper- and underparts, the upperparts pale gray (though still with black flight feathers), the underparts pale gray/buff with less distinct barring. The lower belly is also white (that of nominate is dark gray, like the belly and chest) so that up-ending *hrota* show all-white rather than a dark gray area near the waterline as nominate does. Juvenile *hrota* are also much paler, particularly the underparts. The Black Brant (*B. b. nigricans*) occupies Alaska, (where most breed on the Yukon Delta) and the western Canadian Arctic. Black Brant differs from the nominate in having a much larger white neck patch, sometimes forming a collar, and being much darker. The upperparts are almost uniformly black, the underparts dark gray with whiter flanks. However *nigricans* has several forms, including a pale form (which is lighter than the nominate) and an intermediate form (which is very similar to nominate).

Canada Goose
Branta canadensis

Native to North America, this species is now widespread in northwest Europe as a result of introductions, and has become a familiar species.

Identification   See p. 135
The largest of the black geese; indeed, the largest of all Arctic geese. The head and neck are attractively marked, a white chinstrap separating a black crown and black neck. The back of

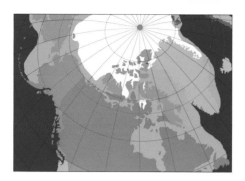

▲ Canada Goose of the Hudson Bay race *interior* protecting the nest.

the head is black so the chinstrap is not continuous. The iris is dark brown. The bill, longer than in other black geese, is dark gray. Chest is light buff/cream, flanks buff with darker buffish gray striping. Upperparts pale gray/brown with paler barring. Tail black, vent white. Legs and feet dark gray or black. In flight from below, the wings are gray/brown with dark leading edge and much darker trailing edge. Juveniles paler and browner and have speckled (not barred) flanks. Downy goslings olive/gold.

Confusion species
None. Barnacle Geese have a similar (but not identical) facial pattern, but are much smaller with a black-and-white body.

Size
Variable because of different races. L: 21½–43½ in. (55–110 cm). WS: 4–6 ft. (120–185 cm). W: 3½–11 lb. (1.6–5 kg).

Voice
Distinctive loud, two-syllable honk *ur-honk*. Flocks often grunt softly. There is also a sharp, guttural cry.

Distribution
Nearctic (wild birds). Breeds from Alaska to Newfoundland, including southern Canadian Arctic islands. Mainly in marsh or wet tundra, but also in drier areas and cultivated land in southern part of range. Breeding flocks of introduced birds now occur in Europe, particularly British Isles and Scandinavia. In winter American birds migrate to southern U.S., from California to Florida, and to Mexico. European birds do not migrate.

Diet
Vegetation, including roots and tubers. Wintering birds in U.S. eat grass and water plants, plus cereals, peanuts and soybeans.

Breeding
Gregarious, though less so at breeding sites, nests being solitary or in loose colonies. Pair-bond monogamous and lifelong. Triumph ceremony as in other geese. Has head-dipping display between mated pair, which is also used aggressively against intruders, accompanied by hissing. Nest sited on dry mound, usually close to water but occasionally at some distance (up to 2 mi./3 km). Nests are frequently reused. Nest is more elaborate than in other black geese, with a large mound of twigs and vegetation lined with down. Five to seven white/cream (soon brown-stained) eggs incubated for 28–30 days by female only with male on guard

close by. Goslings nidifugous and precocial. Cared for by both adults, but self-feeding. Brooded by female only. Fledge at 40–48 days and migrate with adults. Breed at 2–4 years.

Taxonomy and geographical variation
Polytypic. Eleven extant races are recognized. Nominate breeds on southeast Baffin Island and east Labrador. Richardson's Canada Goose (*B. c. hutchinsii*) breeds on southwest Baffin Island, Ellesmere and Southampton Islands, and on the Boothia Peninsula. It is much smaller and paler, usually with a white neck ring. Hudson Bay Canada Goose (*B. c. interior*), which breeds around Hudson Bay, is larger and darker. Lesser Canada Goose (*B. c. parvipes*) breeds in Northwest Territories and eastern Alaska. It is variable in terms of plumage, but about half the size of the nominate. To the south of *interior* and *parvipes* breed the Giant (*B. c. maxima*) and Western (*B. c. moffitti*) Canada Geese. The Giant is the largest of the races, up to 35% larger than the nominate (with the largest ganders to 19 lb./8.5 kg). Giant has a longer neck than the nominate, as well as white forehead spots or, in some cases, completely white faces. Western breeds near the Great Lakes. It is larger than the nominate and has a thin neck.

Vancouver Canada Geese (*B. c. fulva*) are larger and darker than the nominate. They breed on Vancouver Island and in southeast Alaska. Darker still are Dusky Canada Geese (*B. c. occidentalis*), which breed in southwest Alaska; these have the smallest chinstraps and are uniformly dark apart from a white vent. Taverner's Canada Geese (*B. c. taverneri*) breed north across Alaska from the Alaskan Peninsula east to the Mackenzie Delta. They are about half the size of the nominate, with shorter necks and bills. Smaller still is the Cackling Canada Goose (*B. c.*

▼ A family of Dusky Canada Geese, Cook Inlet, Alaska.

minima), which weighs only 3–4 lb. (1.3–1.8 kg) and is almost as dark as the Dusky. Aleutian Canada Geese (*B. c. leucopareia*) breed on Aleutian Islands, though their range has been reduced since the introduction of foxes (for fur) in the 19th century. Slightly larger than the Cackling, the Aleutian has a conspicuous white neck ring. The geese once bred on most Aleutian Islands and the Commander Islands. Reduction in fox numbers by trapping, protection of the birds and reintroduction programs have increased both numbers and range. An extinct race, Bering Island Canada Goose (*B. c. asiatica*), bred on the Commander and Kuril Islands but has not been seen since 1914. It was a pale form of the Aleutian with a larger neck ring.

It is likely that more than one species is involved, and several authorities now recognize two species groups: Greater Canada Goose (*B. canadensis*), (seven races) and Lesser Canada Goose (*B. hutchinsii*), (four races).

Red-breasted Goose
Branta ruficollis

Identification
See p. 135

The smallest of the geese and the most flamboyant, with its jigsaw plumage of red, black and white. The head is small and set on a short, thick neck. Adults have a black face with a white spot between the eye and the small black bill. The iris is dark chestnut-brown. Behind the eye, the head is white with a prominent chestnut cheek patch. The crown and back of the neck is black. The throat, lower neck and chest are chestnut, and the belly is black with broad white stripes along the flanks and black-and-white stripes between belly and vent. Upperparts are black with two white bars across the coverts. Rump is white, tail black. Legs and feet black. In flight from below, the wings are black. Juveniles are as adults, but lack the two white covert bars. Downy goslings are chestnut/dark brown.

Confusion species
None.

Size
L: 20–21½ in. (50–55 cm). WS: 3½–4¼ ft. (110–130 cm). W: 2¼–2¾ lb. (1–1.3 kg).

Voice
A shrill, staccato *kee-kee*.

Distribution
Breeds in southern parts of Russia's Taimyr, Gydan and Yamal Peninsulas, though this assumed range seems to have resulted in part from a lack of research. In recent years nesting geese have been found west toward the White Sea (apparently a recent range expansion, the geese having reached islands in Pechorskaya Bay) and east in Yakutia. Occurs in wet tundra and scrubby areas. Traditionally wintered near Caspian Sea, but now favors shores of Black and Azov Seas, including Romania, where the Red-breasted Goose is the national bird.

Diet
Grasses and sedges. Wintering birds eat grass, shoots of winter wheat and barley, and grain in cereal stubble.

Breeding
Gregarious at all times. Displays as for other geese. Red-breasted Geese actively seek avian predator territories in which to nest, sometimes placing nests within 16½ ft. (5 m) of the predator's. Snowy Owls, Rough-legged Buzzards and Peregrines are all used, with colonies of several dozen geese occasionally nesting close by. The relationship is a mutualism; the alert geese give early warning of the approach of a potential enemy, while the owl or raptor offers protection for the geese against terrestrial predators. However, the nest site is not without its dangers. Although falcons rarely hunt close to their eyries, Snowy Owls have no such scruples; when a female owl is released from brood duties to hunt, goslings and even adult geese may fall victim. Red-breasted Geese also occasionally nest near gull colonies, a strategy that is more difficult to understand. The females sit tight in these circumstances, but the predation of goslings by gulls must be considerable.

The nest is set in a dry place, occasionally on a cliff ledge, the latter requiring the chicks to tumble down the cliff to join the parents. Three to eight cream or pale green eggs incubated by the female only for 24–26 days. Female covers eggs with down when she leaves to feed. Goslings nidifugous and precocial. Cared for by both parents, but self-feeding. Fledge at 28–32 days, migrating with their parents. Breed at 2–3 years.

Taxonomy and geographical variation
Monotypic.

▼ Female Red-breasted Goose on the nest, Taimyr.

Ducks

Shelducks

Most of the shelducks are birds of warmer climates (and mostly in the southern hemisphere). Only the Common Shelduck (*Tadorna tadorna*) breeds in northerly latitudes, a small number breeding in northern and western Iceland.

Dabbling ducks

Dabbling ducks, named for the continuous, rapid way in which they work the surface of the water with their bills for food, are a large and successful group. They favor shallow freshwater but frequent saltwater as well. They have long, broad wings allowing an almost vertical takeoff and relatively fast flight. On land, the short legs of dabbling ducks, which are set at each side of a rounded body, give walking birds the waddle that so typifies the group. Northern species are invariably dimorphic, males (drakes) having striking plumage for display purposes, while females (ducks) are drab, a protective measure against predators when incubating. After the breeding season, drakes molt to an eclipse plumage similar to that of the females. In most species drakes are in eclipse for about nine months, though in some species eclipse can be as short as three months. The drake and duck do not pair for life, changing mates each season. Ducks return to the area where they were reared, drakes following their chosen mate.

In addition to the species detailed below, the Gadwall (*Anas streper*) breeds in Iceland and in southern Alaska, though this species is essentially sub-Arctic throughout its range.

American Black Duck
Anas rubripes

Formerly, numerous overhunting of this species has taken its toll, but a more serious threat is posed by the expanding range of the Mallard and the reduction in the American Black Duck's

◀ American Black Duck.

favored habitat, hardwood wetlands. Hybridization between American Black Ducks and Mallards also occurs so that the number of pure Black Ducks is decreasing. Black Ducks are less susceptible to cold than Mallards, but as Earth warms and the adaptable Mallard edges north, this is likely to offer less of a selective advantage.

Identification See p. 136

Something of a misnomer as the birds are not black, though they are very dark. Large and heavily built. Drakes are uniformly dark brown, apart from the neck and head, which are paler. The body/wing color is broken by paler, U-shaped feather edging, giving a subdued mottled appearance. The head has a darker crown and a dark eye-line extending from the base of the bill to the back of the head. The iris is dark brown, the bill yellow-green and the throat is streaked with gray. The legs and feet are red (in the United States, the duck is occasionally called the Redfoot). Females are as the males, but with a dark olive-green bill and paler legs and feet. The speculum of both male and female is purple/blue edged with darker brown bands. Eclipse drakes are as breeding, though the head and neck tend to be grayer and less streaked. Viewed in flight from below the wings are silver, darker on the flight feathers. Juveniles are similar to females, but with less distinct pale U-shapes. Downy ducklings are yellow-brown.

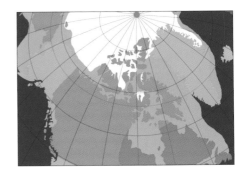

Confusion species

Female Mallards, though Mallards are paler, particularly on the belly. Female Mallards also have cream rather than silver underwings, and the Mallard speculum is bluer and edged with white bands. American Black Ducks on the sea may be confused with female Black Scoters. The latter have a much paler face below a dark crown and a slightly longer tail, which tends to be inclined at a greater angle.

Size

L: 20½–24½ in. (52–62 cm). WS: 34–38 in. (85–95 cm). W: 2¼–2¾ lb. (1–1.3 kg).

Voice

Drake's quack is very similar to that of a drake Mallard. There is also whistle from displaying drakes. Female voice is similar to female Mallard but lower in pitch.

Distribution
Nearctic. Breeds from northern Manitoba to Newfoundland, including northern Quebec and Labrador and the shores of Hudson Bay. Also south to Great Lakes. Partially migratory, some birds flying south to Mississippi, Alabama and Georgia. Essentially a boreal duck, favoring wooded wetlands, but also found at the coast. Being cold-hardy, some American Black Ducks do not migrate or move only a small distance, but this is only possible if adequate unfrozen water remains during the winter.

Diet
Aquatic vegetation and invertebrates. Occasionally the ducks will dive to 10 ft. (3 m) to retrieve plants or roots. Consume more invertebrates than Mallards do, and more inclined to feed in saltwater, occasionally braving rough seas.

Breeding
Gregarious at all times, though drakes are aggressive to others in competition for females. Pair-bond apparently long-lasting. Courtship includes a variety of head- and tail-flicks, usually on water and occasionally communal, with several males displaying to one female. There are also air displays, though these are little more than short, close-formation flights. Nests set in tall vegetation, sometimes beneath old tree stumps, and can be up to 2 mi. (3 km) from water. Also occasionally use old crows' nests, sometimes up to 50 ft. (15 m) above the ground. Nests are of vegetation lined with down. Nine to 12 cream or pale green eggs incubated by female for 26–30 days. Ducklings nidifugous and precocial. Cared for and brooded by female, but self-feeding. Fledge in 50–60 days and are independent at this time. Breed at 1 year.

Taxonomy and geographcial variation
Monotypic.

Mallard
Anas platyrhynchos

The most widespread, numerous and widely recognized of all ducks.

Identification See p. 136
Breeding drakes are unmistakable, with glossy, metallic bottle-green head and neck and a yellow or orange-yellow bill. The iris is dark brown. At the base of the neck is a narrow white collar separating the green from the purple/chestnut chest. The remaining underparts are pale gray. The upperparts are darker gray. The speculum is blue, bordered with thin black and wide, distinct white bands. The tail is pale gray/white, with two central black feathers that curl upward and black coverts. The feet and legs are dull orange. Females show the same speculum, but are otherwise pale brown with darker mottling from feather edging and dark crown and eye-line. The bill is much paler, sometimes yellow-brown. In flight from below, wings are cream with pale gray flight feathers edged darker gray. Eclipse drakes are similar to females, but darker. They also retain the yellow bill (though usually duller) and the black-and-white tail.

▲ Drake Mallard in breeding plumage.

Juveniles are similar to females, but less mottled and with browner bills. Downy ducklings are yellow-brown.

Confusion species
Female Mallards are best told from other dabbling females by the speculum.

Size
L: 20–26 in. (50–65 cm). WS: 32–40 in. (80–100 cm). W: $1^{7}/_{8}$–3 lb. (850–1,400 g).

Voice
The archetypal duck's *quack*, though this is really only heard from the female. The drake's call is a staccato *quelp*, sometimes repeated. Drakes also have a loud, high whistling *phu*, used during display, and a deep grunt. The female call is either a series of rapid quacks that decrescendo to silence, a single *quack* or a monotonous series of quacks repeated for up to a minute.

Distribution
Circumpolar, but never reaching the high Arctic. In the Palearctic, Mallards breed in Iceland, Scandinavia and north-west Russia, but in Eurasian Russia they are rarely found above the Arctic Circle. They breed throughout Kamchatka.

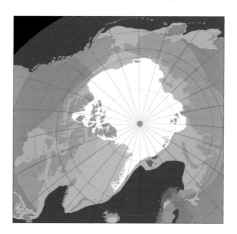

In Greenland, Mallards occur around the island's southeastern and southwestern coasts. In North America, Mallards breed in western and southwest Alaska, and in Yukon and the Northwest Territories, but the northern limit drifts south toward the east. Mallards are found on the southwestern shores of Hudson Bay. Mallards are adaptable and occur in a variety of habitats — rivers, standing freshwater, brackish lagoons and sheltered coastal sites. Though essentially a sub-Arctic bird, also found on tundra ponds. Birds are non-migratory where food sources allow (e.g., British Isles) but will head south to avoid harsh winters. Eurasian birds go south to the Black, Mediterranean and Caspian Seas, China and Japan. Nearctic birds head for the southern United States. Greenlandic and Icelandic Mallards stay on the islands, though some Iceland birds migrate to the British Isles.

Diet
Feed by surface-dabbling, submerging head and up-ending. Also feed on land in a gooselike manner. Rarely dive. Feed on vegetation, but also on invertebrates, mollusks, crustaceans, amphibians and fish. Also feed opportunistically on small mammals and even chicks and small birds. Wintering birds feed in stubble fields.

Breeding
Gregarious in both summer and winter, but drakes are aggressive in pursuit of females. Pair-bond is monogamous and may be renewed annually. Courtship displays begin communally in mixed flocks, the drakes performing a number of tail-wagging, head-flicking and water-flicking displays. Once pairs have formed, the establishment of territories include a display similar to the triumph ceremony of geese, but also more intimate drinking and preening ceremonies and head-pumping. After copulation and egg-laying, the drake abandons the incubating female. Many ducks, Mallards included, have penises, and drake Mallards are given to pursuing and forcibly inseminating females. Occasionally groups of drakes attack a female, which may drown in the process. Nest in ground cover close to water, though occasionally up to 2 mi. (3 km) distant. Will also nest at the base of tree stumps or in hollow trees, in the forks of trees of heights to 30 ft. (10 m), or in nest boxes where provided. Nine to 13 or more greenish or bluish buff eggs incubated by the female only for 26–28 days. Ducklings nidifugous, precocial and self-feeding. Brooded and cared for diligently by the female, who makes distraught runs to retrieve straying chicks. Fledge in 50–60 days, becoming independent at the same time. Breed at 1 year.

Taxonomy and geographical variation
Polytypic, with at least five subspecies. Of these, the nominate race breeds in Iceland, Eurasia and North America (North American birds tend to be larger). Race *conboschas* breeds in Greenland. It is larger by about 10%, has a smaller bill and is adapted to overwinter on saltwaters, having larger salt glands. Its winter diet includes algae, seaweed, mollusks and crustaceans. Greenland Mallards live a precarious life, as sea-ice formation can eliminate their food sources. The ducks tend to breed in their second year. Other races are extralimital.

Northern Pintail
Anas acuta

Identification See p. 136
The elegant, beautifully marked drake is the same size as the Mallard, but less heavily built. The head and upper neck are chocolate brown, the lower neck is white, the white extending upward as a curved line ending backward of the eye. The iris is yellow-brown. The bill is gray-blue and deep at the (black) base so that it appears to be upcurved. The chest and belly are white, the flanks pale gray with darker speckling. The vent is cream/pale brown, the undertail-coverts black. The back and wings are streaked in pale brown, gray and black. The speculum is metallic dark green, with a buff band at the front and a white band at the rear. Among most notable features are the elongated tail feathers. The legs and feet are gray with black webs. Females are similar to other *Anas* ducks (pale brown with darker mottling) but also have elongated tail feathers, though not strikingly so. The head is pale brown with no eye-line, the bill is gray. The female speculum is dark brown, bordered at the front by a narrow white band and at the rear by a broad white band that is highly visible in flight. Eclipse drakes are similar to females, but paler and with slightly longer tail feathers. Viewed in flight from below, the wing is pale gray, darker gray on flight feathers, with white barring. Juveniles are as females but darker and more heavily marked. Downy ducklings are buff/gray.

Confusion species
None for the drake. The female may be confused with other *Anas* females, but the speculum and elongated tail feathers are diagnostic.

Size
L: 20–26 in. (50–65 cm), with the drake's tail feathers adding a further 4–6 in. (10–15 cm). WS: 32–38 in. (80–95 cm). W: 1½–2¾ lb. (700–1,200 g).

Voice
Relatively silent. Drakes have a long, low *geeee* and a gentle whistle during the breeding season. Females have a decrescendo quacking, similar to the Mallard but quieter, and a crowlike *kak-kak-kak* during breeding season.

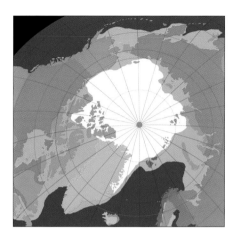

▲ Drake Pintail in breeding plumage is unmistakable.

Distribution

Circumpolar but not found on Greenland, Svalbard or the Russian Arctic islands. Russian Pintails breed almost to the northern coast in most of the range, and on the Bering Sea coast of Chukotka. North American birds breed in west and north Alaska, the north Canadian mainland and the southern parts of some Canadian Arctic islands. Occurs in a variety of habitats, wooded or open land, always favoring shallow, often eutrophic water. Nearctic birds migrate to the coast of California, the Gulf of Mexico and Florida. Some Nearctic birds fly 6,200 mi. (10,000 km) to winter on the Hawaiian Islands. Some Icelandic Pintails overwinter on the island, but most migrate to the British Isles. European birds move to the Mediterranean coast, Asian Russian birds to southern Asia. Wintering birds favor sheltered coastal sites, particularly estuaries, brackish lagoons or coastal wetlands, but also feed on arable land.

Diet

Vegetation, invertebrates, mollusks, crustaceans and small amphibians. Feeds at surface and by head-ducking, but chiefly by up-ending in shallow water to scour the bottom

▼ Male (right) and female Pintail, Hudson Bay.

mud. Wintering birds feed in stubble fields, but usually on vegetation and animal matter. In France's Camargue, snails are a favorite winter food.

Breeding

Gregarious at all times, but drakes aggressive in breeding season. Pair-bond is monogamous and seasonal. Communal and pair displays similar to Mallard. Drakes also abandon incubating female and forcibly inseminate other females as in Mallard. Nests in scrub or on bare tundra, usually 100–200 yds. (100-200 m) from water, but occasionally closer or up to a mile (2 km) away. Nest usually of vegetation, but sometimes little more than a scrape. Always lined with down. Six to nine pale yellow or yellow-green eggs incubated by female only for 22–24 days. Ducklings nidifugous and precocial. Defended and brooded by female, but self-feeding. Fledge in 40–45 days and are independent at about the same time. Breed at 1 year, occasionally at 2 years.

Taxonomy and geographical variation

Monotypic.

Baikal Teal
Anas formosa

Identification   See p. 136

Breeding drakes are exquisitely marked, the head especially so. The crown is dark gray/black separated from the facial pattern by a wide white band. There is a green crescent extending from the eye around the back of the neck and to its base. Forward of this are two buff-yellow patches separated by a black stripe that descends from the eye, then curls to the lower bill to give a black throat. The iris is brown. The bill is mid-gray. At the base of the neck, a thin white collar separates breast and underparts of mid-gray speckled with white. There is another white stripe near the black vent. The back and wings resemble Pintail, but are more deliberately streaked black, white and pale brown. The speculum is green, bordered at the front by red-brown and at the rear by a broader white band. The legs and feet are dull yellow. Females are as other *Anas*, but with cream breast, belly and vent. The mottling is also more regular, giving a spotted appearance, small dark gray-brown spots on the breast and larger dark gray-brown on the flanks. Females also have a prominent dark-bordered white lore spot and a black line backward of eye. The female speculum is dark green/dark gray with banding as drake. Female legs and feet are gray. Eclipse drakes are similar to females, but overall more chestnut brown. The underwing is banded dark, then pale, then mid-gray from front to rear. Juveniles are as females, but duller and more gray-brown. Downy ducklings are yellow-brown.

Confusion species
None for the drake. The female may be confused with other *Anas* species, but the speculum is diagnostic.

Size
L: 15½–18 in. (39–45 cm). WS: 24–28 in. (60–70 cm). W: 8¾–16 oz. (250–450 g).

Voice
Drakes have an often heard *klo-klo* call, while females have a very Mallardlike *quack*.

Distribution
Russia. Once one of the most widely distributed and numerous Asian ducks, the Baikal Teal has suffered a drastic reduction in both numbers and distribution due to hunting and loss of habitat. The species is now officially "vulnerable"; breeds in central and eastern Russia from the Taimyr Peninsula to central Chukotka and from Lake Baikal north to Lena, Indirka and Kolyma Basins. Also on Kamchatka Peninsula. Found in ponds and lakes of the taiga, forest edge and open tundra, and also on tundra shorelines. Migrates to

Japan and China, where it occurs in marshes, at sheltered coastal sites and inland in flooded paddy fields, where flocks of thousands may sometimes be seen.

Diet
Feeds mostly at night on vegetation and invertebrates. Wintering birds feed in stubble and paddy fields.

Breeding
Gregarious at all times, but drakes aggressive in breeding season. Pair-bond apparently monogamous and seasonal. Displays as other *Anas* species, but drakes also have a head-lifting display that allows the black throat to be seen. Nests on riverbanks, on islands or on marshy tundra, rarely far from water, preferring dry hummocks, sedge thickets or birch scrub. Nest is of vegetation lined with down. Six to 10 pale gray-green eggs incubated by female only for 21–24 days. Ducklings nidifugous and precocial. Cared for and brooded by female only, but self-feeding. Fledge in 25–30 days and are independent at that time. Breed at 1 year.

Taxonomy and geographical variation
Monotypic.

Green-winged Teal (Eurasian Teal)
Anas crecca

Identification See p. 136
The smallest of the Arctic dabblers. Breeding drakes have chestnut heads and necks with horizontal, upside-down iridescent green "commas" stretching back from the eye to the nape of the neck, the green edged with a thin buff or pale yellow band that extends to the dark gray bill. The iris is dark brown. The breast is buff speckled with gray, the remaining underparts gray with an indistinct pattern of waving darker gray lines. The upperparts are gray with polar striping. There is a prominent horizontal white stripe along the scapulars below which is an equally prominent, but narrower, black stripe. The undertail is bright buff bordered with black. The speculum is metallic green and black with a broad pale buff band at the front and a narrow pale buff band at the rear. The legs are

◀ Drake Baikal Teal. These birds are often kept in wildfowl collections due to the male's remarkable summer plumage.

▲ Drake of the endemic Aleutian race *nimia*. Unlike other races, the Aleutian Green-winged Teal does not migrate, shifting from ponds to the unfrozen sea in winter. Unalaska.

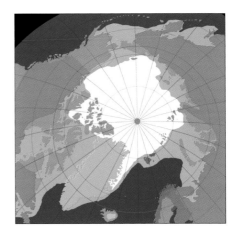

gray/green with darker webs. Females are pale buff-brown with distinct markings (U-shapes and crescents) of gray/brown. The head has a darker brown crown and eye-line. The speculum is as the drake, but the borders are narrower. The bill is paler gray. Eclipse male is as female, but darker and with much more distinct eye-line. Viewed in flight from below, wing is mid-gray with distinct paler patch at center, extending from body. Downy ducklings are yellow-brown.

Confusion species
None for the drake. The female may be confused with other *Anas*, particularly Garganey, but the base color is paler and the speculum is diagnostic.

Size
L: 13¾–16 in. (35–40 cm). WS: 21½–26 in. (55–65 cm). W: 7–16 oz. (200–450 g).

Voice
Drake has a high, whistling *krick-krick* often used as a sign of approaching predators. Female has several Mallardlike quacks, all of them high, rapid but growing quieter, *skee-ki-ki-ki*.

Distribution
Circumpolar. Breeds in Iceland, Scandinavia, Russia from Kola to Chukotka and Kamchatka and north to Arctic shores (but absent from the Arctic islands). North America from Alaska to Newfoundland (but absent from the Arctic islands). Absent from Greenland. Favors small (often eutrophic) ponds but also found near slow-flowing streams, in forest, at forest edge or on tundra. Also occasionally found at coastal sites, especially brackish lagoons and salt marshes. Icelandic birds migrate to British Isles. European Russian birds migrate to southern Europe and Mediterranean, Asian Russian birds to southern Asia. Nearctic birds migrate to southern U.S. and Central America (but Aleutian birds resident). Favored winter habitats include brackish estuaries and intertidal waters.

Diet
Vegetation, invertebrates, mollusks and crustaceans. Feeds by dabbling in shallow water, by head-dipping and up-ending, and by limited diving. Wintering birds feed mainly on small seeds of sedges and bullrushes but omnivorous.

Breeding
Gregarious at all times, but drakes aggressive in breeding season. Pair-bond monogamous and seasonal. Communal courtship displays and head-flick, tail-wagging as in other *Anas* species. Ceremonial drinking, mock preening and triumph ceremony as in other *Anas*. Drake abandons female after mating and may pursue other females. Forcible insemination known. Nests in thick scrub or tussock close to water, often very close to conspecifics. Female forms cup from nearby vegetation, shaping it with body. Lined with down.

▼ Drake *A. C. carolinensis*, the Green-winged Teal, Churchill.

▲ Adult drake Green-winged Teal of nominate race, Karelia, Finland.

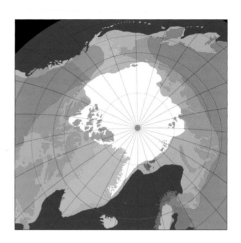

Eight to 12 pale yellow eggs incubated by female only for 21–23 days. Disturbed females frequently perform a distraction display. Ducklings nidifugous, precocial and self-feeding. Fledge at 25–30 days, independent at that time. Breed at 1 year.

Taxonomy and geographical variation

Polytypic. Nominate breeds throughout Eurasia. *A. c. carolinensis*, a Green-winged Teal subspecies, breeds in the Nearctic. It is very similar to the nominate, but drake lacks the defining thin stripes around the green patch on the head, and has a prominent vertical white bar separating the breast from the remaining underparts. *Carolinensis* is now often treated as a separate species. Nominate birds reach both coasts of North America (although rarely), and *carolinensis* strays to the Palearctic. *A. c. nimia*, the Aleutian Green-winged Teal, was recognized as a subspecies in 1948. Drakes are identical to nominate apart from being 10–15% larger. The females of all three races are essentially indistinguishable.

Northern Shoveler
Anas clypeata

Identification   See p. 136

The extraordinary large spatulate bill of the Northern Shoveler distinguishes it from all other Arctic (in this case sub-Arctic) dabblers, though even if the dark gray bill is not seen (unlikely given its size) the drake is unmistakable. He has an iridescent dark green head and neck and piercing yellow eyes. The breast is white, the flanks and belly chestnut brown. There is a broad white stripe behind the belly, contrasting with the black undertail. The speculum is green, bordered with a white band at

the front. The forewing is pale blue; the remaining wing is dark gray, black and white. The legs and feet are orange. Females are the typical mottled light/dark brown of *Anas* species, though usually with an overall cream (even pale pink) appearance. The female speculum is duller green, with no white band at the front. The pale blue, so vivid in the drake, is also duller and more gray-blue. Eclipse males are as females, but the body color is more cinnamon overall, and the head and neck are mid-gray, at first maintaining a hint of the breeding green and with a white crescent forward of the eye. The latter features are lost by midwinter. Eclipse drakes maintain the pale blue forewing. Viewed in flight from below, drakes show white forewings and black rear wings. Females show the same pattern, but with pale gray/dark gray. Juveniles are as females, but darker, particularly on the head and back. Downy ducklings are yellow-brown.

Confusion species

None for the drake. The female may be confused with other *Anas*, but the speculum is distinctive, as is the forewing gray-blue panel, plus of course the bill.

Size

L: 18–21½ in. (45–55 cm). WS: 28–34 in. (70–85 cm). W: 14–26½ oz. (400–750 g).

Voice

Calls of both sexes rather quiet. Drake has a *thock-thock* call, similar to two pieces of wood knocked together, usually when

▼ Drake Northern Shoveler (foreground), Hudson Bay.

alarmed, and a nasal *paay*. The female quack is a hoarse *gack-gack*. There is also a deeper, guttural *kworsh*.

Distribution
Circumpolar. Eurasian birds breed in Iceland (where it is rare), but not northern Scandinavia, and in Russia from the White Sea to central Siberia, but rarely north of the Arctic Circle except on the Kolyma Delta. Breeds throughout Kamchatka. In North America, breeds in central Alaska, northern Yukon, northwest Northwest Territories and on the southwest Hudson Bay shore. Absent from Greenland. Northern Shovelers are ducks of the taiga, but also breed on tundra, preferring shallow, productive ponds because of their the feeding methods. In winter Icelandic birds migrate to the British Isles. Russian birds move south, some reaching the Mediterranean. North American birds move to the southern United States and Mexico. Birds winter on tidal mudflats, estuaries and lagoons.

Diet
Omnivorous, but preferentially takes planktonic invertebrates. Feeds from the surface, by up-ending and by diving. The Norhtern Shoveler is the most frequent diver among dabbling ducks, though even then it does not dive often. The spatulate bill is an efficient filter, the duck "vacuuming" the water surface with sweeping motions as it moves forward, sucking in water. This is then pumped out through the lamellae of the mandibles in a similar way to the feeding mechanism of baleen whales.

Breeding
Gregarious, but not in breeding season. Pair-bond is monogamous, but probably seasonal. Displays similar to other *Anas* species. Nests close to water, usually well concealed in low scrub, reeds or sedge, but sometimes in more open areas. Nest lined with grass and down. Seven to 11 buff or pale green eggs incubated by female only for 21–24 days. Ducklings nidifugous and precocial. Cared for and brooded by female, but self-feeding. Fledge in 40–45 days and are independent at that time. Breed at 1 year.

Taxonomy and geographical variation
Monotypic.

Eurasian Wigeon
Anas penelope

Identification See p. 136
An elegant duck. The drake has a dark chestnut head with prominent buff forehead and a thin dark green/black crescent backward of the eye. The iris is dark yellow-brown. The bill is pale bluish-gray with a black tip. The breast is pinkish-buff. The belly is white, extending to a white band behind the pale gray flanks. Behind the white band the undertail is black, and the tail itself is gray. The speculum is dark gray with broad black bands in front and behind. Forward of the speculum is a large white patch. The remainder of wing is gray with darker gray-brown primaries. In the sitting bird, the large white wing-patch is seen as a white patch between flank and upperparts. The legs and feet are gray, sometimes brownish. Females have upperparts much as other *Anas* females, though the primaries are dark gray with light edges. The speculum is much darker, almost black, with an indistinct green sheen. The head and neck are more uniform pink-brown than other *Anas*, while the white belly and pale red-brown flanks are distinctively different. Eclipse males are as females, but darker and distinctly more rufous. The white patch at the top of the flank, seen on the sitting bird, is still visible. In flight the underwing is gray with a paler gray center, but the white belly is distinct in both male and female, and the black tail of the male contrasts sharply with the paler underparts and pink breast. Juveniles are as females, but young males have rufous heads and are brighter overall. Downy ducklings are buff/brown.

Confusion species
None apart from vagrant American Wigeon.

Size
L: 17–20 in. (43–50 cm). WS: 28–35 in. (70–85 cm). W: 18–28 oz. (550–800 g).

Voice
Drake has a distinctive high, descending whistle *weee-co*, either singly or in a series, when it may end with a trill. Female voice is different, a growling *karr* dropping to decrescendo.

Distribution
Palearctic. Breeds in Iceland, northern Fennoscandia and the

Female Eurasian Wigeon flanked by two males, north Norway.

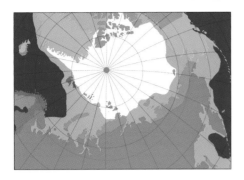

Russian mainland to Chukotka, though only the northern coast in Kola/White Sea. In Chukotka the birds are found to the Bering Sea coast; they breed throughout Kamchatka. Eurasian Wigeon from eastern Russia migrate to eastern U.S. states and have also bred on Alaskan Bering Sea islands. Hybridization with American Wigeon has also occurred. Icelandic Wigeon migrate to the British Isles, western European birds migrate to the Mediterranean and Black Seas. Central and Eastern Russian birds migrate to Caspian and Azov Seas and to southern Asia, but as mentioned above some eastern birds cross the Bering Sea. Essentially forest and forest-edge birds rather than tundra dwellers, they prefer large bodies of water in which a variety of water-edge and submerged plants can grow.

Diet
Vegetation, but little animal matter. Nocturnal feeders. Food obtained by surface-feeding and occasional head-submerging, and also by grazing on land. In winter Eurasian Wigeons are primarily maritime feeders in the intertidal region, though they also feed on arable land. Wintering ducks in the British Isles are known to be fond of potatoes. Often seen feeding with other ducks, geese and waders.

Breeding
Gregarious except during breeding season. Pair-bond monogamous and probably seasonal. Displays as other *Anas* species. Nests close to water, rarely more than 200 yds. (200 m)

distant, choosing dry, sheltered sites. Nest is shallow depression lined with grass and large quantities of down. Six to 12 cream or pale brown eggs incubated by female only for 23–25 days. Ducklings nidifugous and precocial. Cared for and brooded by female, but self-feeding. Fledge at 40–45 days and are independent at that time. Breed at 1 year.

Taxonomy and geographical variation
Monotypic. Hybrids with American Wigeon occur.

American Wigeon
Anas americana

Identification   See p. 136
Larger than Eurasian Wigeon but just as elegant. The drake has a buff head with black stippling and two prominent color areas. The first is a cream forehead and crown, the second a large green crescent that covers and extends backward from the eye to the nape. The iris is dark yellow-brown. The bill is pale blue/gray with a black tip. The breast and flanks are salmon pink, sometimes darker and more rufous. The belly is white. On the lower abdomen is a broad white stripe and a white patch on the upper flank of the sitting bird as in the Eurasian Wigeon. The speculum is black with a narrow central band of dark green. The tail and wings are as the Eurasian Wigeon, though the back is the pink or rufous of the breast. The legs are gray, sometimes gray/brown. Females are as the Eurasian Wigeon, but more rufous and brighter. Eclipse males are as Eurasian Wigeon, but with lighter breast and flanks, and the head gray rather than rufous. In flight the underwing is as the Eurasian Wigeon, but the central area is white instead of the pale gray center of the Eurasian, and again the white belly is distinctive. Juveniles are as females, but with more streaking on the head. Downy ducklings are buff-brown.

Confusion species
None, apart from vagrant Eurasian Wigeon.

Size
L: 18–21½ in. (45–55 cm). WS: 30–36 in. (75–90 cm). W: 21–30 oz. (600–850 g).

Voice
Drake has a similar whistle to Eurasian Wigeon, but lower and

Male (right) and female American Wigeon in breeding plumage. Churchill.

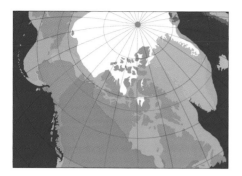

with two or three syllables, *wee-wee-wee.* Female voice is also as Eurasian Wigeon, a low growling *drr* or *wrr.*

Distribution
Nearctic. Breeds in western, southwestern and central Alaska and northern Yukon, but farther south across the rest of the continent. Breeds on southwestern and southern Hudson Bay shores. As with the Eurasian Wigeon, large boreal or forest-edge ponds are favored, but also occurs at estuaries and deltas. Alaskan birds migrate south along Pacific coast. Others migrate to southern United States and Gulf of Mexico, and the Atlantic coast south of Cape Cod. Wintering birds found in shallow coastal bays as well as inland.

Diet
As Eurasian Wigeon, but more of a terrestrial grazer. Wintering birds often frequent arable fields where they may damage winter crops.

Breeding
Gregarious except in breeding season. Pair-bond as Eurasian Wigeon. Displays as other *Anas* species. Nests in dry, sheltered sites as Eurasian Wigeon, but will use sites much farther from water. Nest is shallow depression lined with grasses, leaves and down. Six to 12 cream eggs incubated by female only for 24–26 days. Ducklings nidifugous and precocial. Cared for and brooded by female, but self-feeding. Fledge at 40–45 days and are independent at that time. Breed at 1 year.

Taxonomy ang geographical variation
Monotypic. Hybrids with Eurasian Wigeon and Gadwall occur.

Pochards
Pochards, members of the genus *Aythya*, are heavy diving ducks with long necks and relatively large feet set far back on the body. These features aid diving, which is the chief feeding method of these ducks, but make walking awkward. Unlike dabbling ducks, pochards need a paddling run across the water to become airborne. Most *Aythya* drakes exhibit the dabbler drake strategy of abandoning incubating females to form moulting flocks. Pochards interbreed more readily than do other ducks and geese (which, as a group, are more prone to interbreeding than other birds), often causing confusion for the observer. The tendency of pochards to sieve the mud at

the bottom of lakes and ponds for food means that they are more likely than other species to ingest lead shot in wildfowling areas. As a consequence, pochards are vulnerable to early mortality from lead poisoning. Most species overwinter at maritime locations, where they may be parasitized by gulls when they surface after a feeding dive.

Canvasback
Aythya valisineria

A sub-Arctic species found in central (and occasionally northern) Alaska and central Northwest Territories, it is included because the ducks follow the Mackenzie River to the north Canadian coast and so can be considered Arctic.

▲ Drake Canvasback in breeding plumage.

Identification See p. 136
Drakes are handsome birds, with rufous heads and necks, a brown iris and black bill. The breast is glossy black, body and wings white and pale gray (giving the species its name). Undertail-coverts black, tail dark gray/black. Legs and feet dark gray. Females have light brown head, neck and breast, pale gray-brown body, while undertail-coverts and tail are light brown. Eclipse male very similar to breeding male, but body pale gray-brown (as female) and breast dark brown. In flight the underwing is white with gray primaries. Juveniles similar to females. Downy ducklings are yellow-brown.

Confusion species
None.

Size
L: 20–24 in. (50–60 cm). WS: 28–32 in. (70–80 cm). W: 2–2³/₄ lb. (900–1,300 g), but up to 3³/₄ lb. (1.7 kg).

Voice
Drakes have curious moaning squeak *go-woo-oo-oo.* Females have low, guttural growl *grritt.*

Distribution
Nearctic. Prefers marshes and lakes with vegetated edges, usually

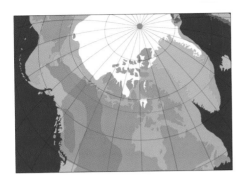

in forest or at forest edge. Northern birds migrate to Atlantic/Pacific coasts of southern United States, where they prefer sheltered bays and estuaries. Males winter at more northerly latitude than females.

Diet

Vegetation, especially wild celery (both duck and plant are named after naturalist A. de Vallisnera), aquatic roots and seeds filtered from mud. Feed by diving up to 30 ft. (10 m), but prefer water up to 10 ft. (3 m) deep.

Breeding

Gregarious in winter, more solitary at breeding sites. Pair-bond monogamous and seasonal. Communal and head-flicking displays very similar to those of *Anas* species. Nests in waterside vegetation, often building nest up to avoid flooding. Nest lined with down. Eight to 11 gray-green eggs, incubated by female only for 26–28 days. Nests parasitized by Redheads (*A. americana*) and Ruddy Ducks (*Oxyura jamaicensis*), which reduces productivity. Ducklings nidifugous and precocial. Cared for and brooded by female, but self-feeding. Fledge in 40–45 days and are independent at same time. Breed at 1 year.

▼ Drake Greater Scaup on the nest, Cook Inlet, Alaska.

Taxonomy and geographical variation

Monotypic, but all *Aythya* species hybridize with others occasionally.

Greater Scaup
Aythya marila

Identification   See p. 136

The drake is a handsome bird with a rounded black head, neck and breast. The head plumage has a green gloss (in some lights appears purple, which can confuse the observer). The iris is yellow/orange and prominent against the black plumage. The bill is long, broad, flattened; it is pale blue-gray with a black nail. The belly and flanks are white, the mantle and scapulars white and vermiculated dark gray/black. The upper forewing is gray, the rearwing being white with a black trailing edge. The upper and undertail-coverts are black. The legs and feet are dark gray/olive. Females have dark brown heads, necks and breasts, with a pale crescent on the cheek. In winter females lose this cheek patch, but have a prominent white ring around the base of the bill. In summer this ring is less prominent and may even be absent. The female upper and flank color is brown with white vermiculation that gives an overall gray-brown appearance. The belly is white, the undertail white, mottled with dark brown. The upperwing is as the drake, but the forewing is brown rather than gray. Eclipse males are not as female, being much paler. The head and neck are gray-brown (the head still tinged green), the breast gray-brown streaked with white. The flanks are vermiculated brown, the belly pale brown. The under-forewing is pale gray, the rear wing white with a gray trailing edge. Juveniles are as female, with a narrow white ring at the base of the bill, and a similar cheek patch, but the mantle and scapulars are dark brown with much less vermiculation, and the breast and flanks are pale yellow-brown. Downy ducklings are yellow/olive-brown.

Confusion species

In the Palearctic, confusion arises with the Tufted Duck and with vagrant Lesser Scaup. Male and female Tufted, in both summer and winter, have a distinct head tuft and much darker backs. Juvenile Tufted have an indistinct tuft and lack the pale cheek patch. In the Nearctic, the main confusion is with the Lesser Scaup. In general the Greater Scaup has a green gloss to the head plumage, while that of the Lesser Scaup is purple. But in certain light these glosses may be reversed and are not, therefore, reliable. Head shape is a better ID feature. Viewed face on, the Lesser Scaup has a tall, narrow head; the Greater a wider, more oval head. Viewed side on, the Greater Scaup's head is more rounded, particularly the back, the head contour falling from a peak at the top of the forehead. The Lesser Scaup's head is more square, the nape and crown flatter. However, these shapes are only distinguishable in resting birds as the head shape of both species "change" when they are active. The Lesser Scaup has a darker

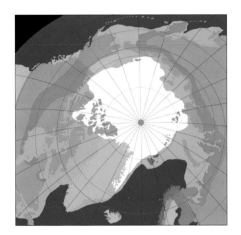

back, shorter, more spatulate bill and a thinner neck. In flight the white bar on the Greater Scaup's upperwing extends farther toward the wingtip, while the Lesser Scaup's bar is on the secondaries only. Lesser Scaup's voice is higher and thinner.

Size
L: 16–20 in. (40–50 cm). WS: 28–34 in. (70–85 cm). W: $1^7/_8$–$2^1/_2$ lb. (850 g–1.15 kg).

Voice
Drakes are mostly silent, and what calls they do make are quiet. There are two calls: one a dovelike burble, the other a soft whistle, *wek-wek*. Females are louder; one call is a harsh *karr-karr*, another a softer *chup-chup*.

Distribution
Circumpolar. Large numbers breed in Iceland, particularly at Myvatn. The lake is named after (and renowned for) its vast

▼ Male (top) and female Greater Scaup, breeding plumage.

numbers of midges and mosquitoes. The Scaup (and Tufted Duck) resident there do their best to reduce this population. Breeds across Eurasia from Scandinavia to Chukotka and Kamchatka but does not reach the northern coast of Asiatic Russia. In the Nearctic, Greater Scaup breed in the Aleutians, across Alaska and the Yukon (but not in the far north). The range is increasingly southerly toward Hudson Bay. Small numbers only are found east of the bay. A bird of the taiga, forest edge and tundra, favoring freshwater lakes and ponds. Greater Scaup are the most maritime of the pochards, particularly in winter. Migratory; Icelandic birds fly to Britain and the Netherlands, though a few stay on the southwest Iceland coast. Western European birds travel as far south as the Adriatic, with Russian birds reaching the Black and Azov Seas. East Russian birds winter on the Kuril Islands. North American birds migrate to the Pacific (southeastern Alaska to California) and Atlantic (New England to Florida) coasts. Shallow bays are favored, but the birds can occur far from the coast.

Diet
Omnivorous. In summer vegetation, aquatic larvae and fish eggs are taken in freshwater, mollusks and crustaceans in saltwater. Greater Scaup also eat rotting fish. Shellfish are the major constituent of winter diet. Food is obtained by diving, using the feet as paddles, and also by up-ending and dabbling.

Breeding
Gregarious in winter, aggressive at breeding grounds, the birds nest in solitude or loose colonies. Pair-bond is monogamous and seasonal. Displays similar to those of *Anas* ducks. Nests close to water in sedges or reeds. Dry, concealed sites in tussock or low scrub preferred. Nest is little more than a depression lined with grass and down. Six to 10 gray-green eggs incubated by females only for 26–28 days. Ducklings nidifugous and precocial. Cared for by female, though some drakes do not abandon female at incubation and may assist in early stages of rearing. Ducklings are self-feeding. Broods may merge to form crèches of several dozen chicks. Fledge in 40–45 days and are independent at that time. Breed at 1, sometimes 2 years.

Taxonomy and geographical variation
Polytypic. Nominate breeds in western Europe and Russia to Lena Delta. Pacific Greater Scaup (*A. m. mariloides*) breeds in eastern Russia and North America. Drakes tend to be smaller and darker than nominate, with bolder vermiculations on the back. However, the differences are subtle and some authorities believe they lie within the normal range of the nominate and question the validity of this subspecies. Greater Scaup hybridize with other *Aythya* species occasionally.

Lesser Scaup
Aythya affinis

Identification See p. 136
In all forms very similar to Greater Scaup. The drake tends to have a purple gloss to its head and its back tends to be darker

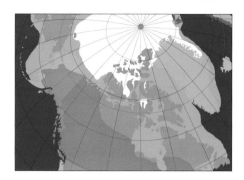

with coarser vermiculation. The pale cheek patch of the breeding female is less pronounced.

Confusion species
Greater Scaup. See Identification for that species.

Size
L: 13³/₄–18 in. (35–45 cm). WS: 24–30 in. (60–75 cm). W: 26¹/₂–33¹/₂ oz. (750–950 g).

Voice
Similar to Greater Scaup but higher and thinner. Drake whistle is a piping *peet-peet*, harsh female call is a more guttural *garff*.

Distribution
Nearctic. Chiefly sub-Arctic but to the northern coast of Canada at the Mackenzie Delta, and on south-astern shore of Hudson Bay. Otherwise western United States where it can be very numerous. Forest-edge freshwater lakes and ponds preferred. Less maritime than Greater Scaup even in winter, when the birds migrate to southern United States.

Diet
As for Greater Scaup. Lesser Scaup are more likely than Greater to sieve bottom mud, and are prone to feeding around sewage outfalls, making the birds vulnerable to lead poisoning and disease.

Breeding
Gregarious in winter when vast flocks form. In summer loose colonies aggregate, particularly on islands, and also close to

▼ Pair of Lesser Scaup in breeding plumage, Churchill.

gull or tern colonies, the ducks presumably gaining benefit from the aggressiveness of gulls and terns to intruders. Pair-bond monogamous and seasonal. Displays similar to those of *Anas* species. Lesser Scaup tend to nest later than other ducks (a limiting factor on their spread northward). Incubation and fledge times as for Greater Scaup. Ducklings nidifugous and precocial. Broods may merge to create huge crèches of up to 100 chicks guarded by several females. Some females then make no effort to retrieve their young, with the chicks self-feeding and cared for communally. Breed at 1 year.

Taxonomy and geographical variation
Monotypic. May hybridize with other *Aythya* ducks.

Tufted Duck
Aythya fuligula

Identification
See p. 136

Drakes are mostly black, the head with a purple gloss. The white belly and flanks contrast sharply with remaining black plumage. From the crown of the head, the tuft of the name is long and drooping. It is highly conspicuous when visible, but as it is black it can merge into the head from certain angles. The iris is gold, the bill blue-gray with a black nail. The upperwing is black with a broad white stripe from body to tip, the white becoming more gray toward the tip. The legs and feet are dark blue-gray. Females have chocolate brown heads with a shorter tuft. In winter females have a white ring at the base of the bill, as do Scaup, but in summer this ring is much narrower or absent. The upperparts are dark brown, sometimes almost black. The breast is rich dark brown, the flanks lighter. The belly is cream or white. The overwing shows the same white stripe as the drake. Eclipse drakes are as breeding, but the black is much duller and the belly and flanks are heavily flecked with light brown. The tuft is shorter, similar to the female tuft. In flight the underwing is white/pale gray. Juveniles are as the females, but lighter and much duller, and with only the hint of a tuft. Downy ducklings are light/dark brown.

Confusion species
None. Tuft and dark back distinguish Tufted from either scaup.

Size
L: 16–20 in. (40–50 cm). WS: 26–30 in. (65–75 cm). W: 23–34¹/₄ oz. (650–1,000 g).

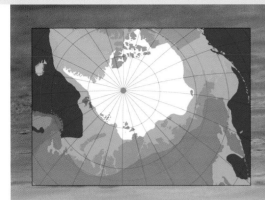

Voice
Drakes have a bubbling, falling pitch whistle *waa-waa-weew*. Occasionally this becomes a single, hoarser note. There is also a higher peeping. Females have a harsher *karr-karr* typical of pochards.

Distribution
Palearctic. Breeds on Iceland, in northern Fennoscandia and in Russia from the White Sea to the Kolyma Delta (but not to the northern coast) and throughout Kamchatka. Found at the forest edge and on the tundra on shallow, eutrophic lakes and ponds; also seen on tidal estuaries. Some Icelandic birds overwinter on the island in shallow bays to the south. Most migrate to British Isles and French coast. Western European birds migrate to the Black and Mediterranean Seas. Russian Tufted Duck overwinter on Azov and Caspian Seas, and some on the Aleutian Islands (some birds stay year-long on the islands, though breeding is unconfirmed). Although birds are found in sheltered coastal bays, Tufted Ducks do not tolerate rough seas and favor inland sites such as lakes and reservoirs.

Diet
Omnivorous, taking vegetation (particularly seeds), aquatic insects and crustaceans. At coastal sites, mollusks and crustaceans are taken. Up-ends and dabbles, but chiefly obtains food by diving, reaching depths of up to 50 ft. (15 m).

▼ Female Tufted Duck. Note the white on the face. This is variable, but never as extensive as in female Greater Scaup.

▲ Drake Tufted Duck, Iceland. Note the tuft at the back of the head.

Breeding
Gregarious at all times, but drakes aggressive in breeding season. Pair-bond monogamous and seasonal. Displays similar to those of *Anas* species. Prefers island sites for nest, though nests rarely more than 80 ft. (25 m) from water, occasionally up to 490 ft. (150 m) away. Nests usually in concealed sites, but occasionally in the open close to gull or tern colonies. Nest is shallow grass- and down-lined depression. Eight to 11 gray-green eggs incubated by female only for 23–27 days. Because of egg-dumping some nests hold up to 20 eggs. Tufted Ducks also lay in the nests of Common Pochard (*A. ferina*). Ducklings nidifugous and precocial. Cared for by female only, but self-feeding. Fledge in 45–50 days and are independent at that time. Breed at 1–2 years.

Taxonomy and geographical variation
Monotypic.

Eiders
With the increased use of goose down in bed coverings and mountaineering wear, few people may realize that, in the recent past, "eiderdown" was synonymous with the warmest, most luxurious bedding. Fewer would have known the origin of the feathers that filled their eiderdowns, and fewer still would have seen the bird itself. The warmth of eiderdown has been renowned for centuries, leading to the generic name for the three large eiders, *Somateria*, from the Greek for "down body." Of the three large eiders, the finest down comes from the Common Eider, its specific name *mollissima* deriving from the Latin for "softest." Weight for weight and thickness for thickness, Common Eider down has the best insulating properties of any natural substance. As early as the seventh century, St. Cuthbert, the first Bishop of Lindisfarne, set up a sanctuary for Common Eiders at his hermitage on one of the Farne Islands, where, eiders are still known by locals as Cuddy Ducks. Commercial farming was begun by the Norse two centuries or so later, and continued until the 20th century. Until the mid-20th century, down farming was a major export industry on Iceland. Each nest produced about 1/2 oz. (15 g) of raw down. This was reduced to about 1/20 oz. (1.5 g) of usable down by the cleaning process; almost 700 nests were needed to yield 2 lb. (1 kg) of usable down. In some years Iceland exported 3 tons of raw down, obtained from more than 250,000 nests.

Eiders are the most maritime of all wildfowl; non-breeding birds are entirely marine and have highly developed suborbital salt glands. They feed by diving, making the deepest dives of any duck, using their feet as paddles with the occasional wingstroke. All eiders are heavy, requiring a run across the water surface for takeoff. Though strong fliers, they are not maneuverable. Landings have little of the grace seen in smaller ducks, more akin to crash-landings with an accompanying large splash. Drake eiders are among the most attractive of birds, with wonderful head patterning. Females are drab; this is necessary for camouflage during incubation, since drakes abandon their mates as egg-laying starts. Females may sit throughout incubation, vacating only if startled or in mortal danger. If forced to leave the nest, they frequently eject foul-smelling feces over the eggs, presumably as a disincentive to egg-stealing predators. This strategy may well work on the Arctic Fox, but it is unlikely to deter avian thieves; gulls do not have a good sense of smell.

Technically, only Steller's Eider has a true speculum, though several other species have color patches on the secondaries, which, to the non-specialist, appear as a speculum and are referred to as such in the descriptions below.

Common Eider
Somateria mollissima

Identification   See p. 137

Large and heavily built. Drakes are handsome birds with strikingly patterned heads. The face is white, the crown black and the nape pale green, the color patch divided into three by thin white stripes. The iris is brown. The bill is olive-gray with a pale, hooked nail. The breast is cream, tinged with pink or cinnamon. The remaining underparts are black, apart from a round white patch on the rump. The mantle and scapulars are white. The under- and upperwings are white with black flight feathers. The legs and feet are yellow/green. Females are light brown overall with black barring, which is heavier on the flanks and black. The upperwing shows a dark brown speculum with white bands at front and rear. The underwing is brown with a lighter (white or pale gray) center patch. Eclipse males are gray-brown with white splashes on the upperparts, due mainly to the retained white wing-coverts. Juveniles are as females, but darker and much duller, with an indistinct white crescent from the eye. First-summer adults are paler versions of the adult eclipse. Downy ducklings are gray-brown.

▲ Female Common Eider on the nest, northern Iceland.

Confusion species

Drake has none. Female is similar to other ducks, but heavier build, large head and long, wedge-shaped bill are distinctive.

Size

L: 20–28 in. (50–70 cm). WS: 2¾–3½ ft. (85–110 cm). W: 4–6¼ lb. (1.8–2.8 kg).

Voice

Drakes have a ghostly, drawn-out *oh-oooo*, very evocative when heard from an impenetrable sea mist. Females have a guttural version of the same call, as well as a croaky call, either a single *krok* or a rapid *kow-kow-kow*.

Distribution

Circumpolar, though absent from much of the Russian mainland. Breed on Iceland, Jan Mayen, Svalbard, Franz Josef Land, the Kola Peninsula, Novaya Zemlya, the New Siberia Islands, Wrangel Island and the Russian mainland east of the Lena Delta, including the Bering Sea coast of Chukotka and the Sea of Okhotsk coast. In North America, Common Eiders breed on the western and northern Alaskan coasts, along much of the north Canadian mainland (including the coasts of Hudson Bay) and on Canada's Arctic islands south of Ellesmere Island. Also found on both coasts of Greenland up to the ice edge. Prefers islands or offshore rocks but also found in bays. Only partially migratory, moving south away from the ice. Eastern Greenland birds winter with non-migratory Icelandic birds. Svalbard and Franz Josef birds winter on northern Scandinavian coasts. Eastern Russian birds move to the Bering Sea. North American birds move south along Pacific and Atlantic coasts.

Common Eiders at sunset, Churchill.

Diet

Almost exclusively carnivorous, feeding mostly on benthic animals — mollusks (mainly), crustaceans and echinoderms. These are obtained by diving (up to 65 ft./20 m) but also by head-dipping and up-ending in shallow water. The birds also paddle the sand or silt at the bottom of shallow water to reveal prey. No change of diet with season.

Breeding

Highly gregarious at all times, though drakes are aggressive in breeding season. Pair-bond monogamous and seasonal, though some drakes apparently promiscuous. Communal and pair-courtship displays are very similar to those in other duck species, with a variety of head-flicks, pseudo-preening, bill-dipping and water-flicking activities. Nests are sometimes in sheltered places by rocks or vegetation but are more usually in the open, and then usually in large colonies and often with Arctic Terns, which are particularly belligerent to intruders. Nest is usually a shallow depression made from seaweed or moss lined with available vegetation and always with down. Four to six gray-green or green eggs incubated by female only, though drake will sometimes stay close by during the early stages before departing. Incubation period 25–28 days. Ducklings nidifugous and precocial. Cared for by female only, but self-feeding. Brooded at night at first. Crèches of up to 100 or more ducklings, protected by several females. Females make little or no effort to retrieve young. Some crèches may include Snow Geese as well as Eiders. Juveniles independent at 55–60 days, fledged at 65–75 days. Breed at 2–3 years.

▲ A party of King Eiders in flight, Baffin Bay.

Taxonomy and geographical variation

Polytypic. Nominate race occupies northern European coast to Novaya Zemlya. *S. m. faroeensis* occupies the Faroe Islands. It is non-migratory, and the smallest form with the smallest bill. The females are very much darker than those of the nominate. *S. m. borealis* occupies the high Arctic from Baffin Island to Franz Josef Land, including Greenland and Iceland. These are slightly smaller than nominate and have short, narrow frontal processes. Drake's bill is orange-yellow at the base, tending to gray-green. *S. m. dresseri* occupies the east mainland coast of Canada. The head has a forehead dome and the green extends to the eye. The frontal processes are large and rounded and the bill is orange-yellow. *S. m. v-nigra* occurs from the New Siberia Islands eastward to Baffin Island. Drakes have an orange-red bill and (usually) a distinctive black V on the throat. *S. m. sedentaria* is non-migratory, wintering in patches of open water. It is very similar to *dresseri* Eiders but smaller, and the females are much paler and grayer.

King Eider
Somateria spectabilis

Identification See p. 137

Well named, with the drake's head being magnificently regal. The bill is orange-red (with a pale nail) and merges with an orange forehead shield edged with thin black lines. The shield

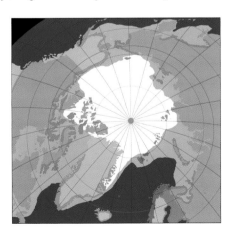

▼ Drake King Eider in breeding plumage with drake Common Eider.

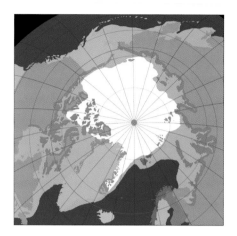

is a delicacy for Inuit, who often bite it off immediately after killing a drake. The crown and nape are pale blue/pearl gray, and below the eye is a pale green patch merging to white. The patch is separated from the nape by a thin black stripe from the eye. The iris is yellow. The breast is buff-pink. The upper mantle is white, the rest of the upperparts black with two "shark fin" plumes rising from the tertials. The underparts and tail are black, apart from white patches on each side of the tail base. The upperwings are black with large white patches on the coverts. The underwing is white, the flight feathers dark gray/black. The legs and feet are dull orange. Females are rufous-brown with dark brown U-shaped patterning on both the upper- and underparts. Some females show small "shark fins" from the tertials. The bill is gray with a dark nail. Eclipse males retain the bill and shield colors, but the head and breast are mottled gray-brown and the remaining plumage is browner and duller. First-summer males are as eclipse males, but with less mottling on the breast and grayer heads. The forehead shield is buff, the bill pink. Downy ducklings are buff-brown.

Confusion species
Females and juveniles resemble those of Common Eider, but Kings are more compact, have dark bills and are more rufous.

Size
L: 20–26 in. (50–65 cm). WS: 34–40 in. (85–100 cm). W: 3–4½ lb. (1.4–2 kg).

Voice
Similar to Common Eider for both sexes; the drake's call is more quavering, and the duck's is lower and clucking rather than croaking.

Distribution
Circumpolar. Breeds on Svalbard, Novaya Zemlya, the northern Russian coast from the White Sea to Chukotka, the New Siberia Islands, the Alaska coast, the northern Canadian mainland coast from Yukon to northern Quebec (including the northwest coast of Hudson Bay), Canada's Arctic islands as far north as northern Ellesmere (where the birds are, with Long-tailed Ducks, the most northerly breeding waterfowl) and northern coasts of Greenland. More likely to be seen on tundra pools than Common Eider. On the sea Kings are less inclined to inhabit rocky islets and shores than Common Eider, instead occupying shallow bays and estuaries. Partially migratory. Tends to winter farther out to sea than Common Eider. American birds move to Aleutians and the Labrador coast. Svalbard birds move into Barents Sea, western Russian birds to Kara Sea and eastern Russian birds to Bering Sea.

Diet
On tundra takes plant material, aquatic insects and crustaceans using head-dipping and up-ending as well as diving. Lemmings and other rodents have also been found in the stomachs of King Eiders. Maritime birds take benthic animals. Known to dive to 40–50 ft. (12–15 m) and probably deeper, but tales of dives beyond 165 ft. (50 m) are unconfirmed.

Breeding
Gregarious except at breeding sites. Drakes aggressive in breeding season. Pair-bond and displays as Common Eider (i. e., similar to *Anas* ducks). Nests close to water (both fresh and salt) with marked preference for island sites. Colonial nesting occurs but is uncommon. Nest is on dry site, with cover if available, but often on open tundra. Little nest material, a small, down-filled hollow. Four to five pale olive eggs incubated by female only, but with drake often on guard in early stages. Incubation period 22–24 days. Ducklings nidifugous, precocial and self-feeding. Brooded by female when small. Cared for by female, but crèches often form. Juveniles fledge in 50–60 days and are independent at that time or shortly after. Because the high Arctic summer is so short, some juveniles are not fledged before they must head to sea, so they spend the early days of "migration" in a flightless state. Breed at 3 years.

Taxonomy and geographical variation
Monotypic.

Spectacled Eider
Somateria fischeri

The Spectacled Eider is the smallest and least known of the four eiders. It is also the most elusive; most birders would be amazed to learn that the Spectacled Eider was once sufficiently numerous on the northeastern coast of Siberia for

▼ Drake Spectacled Eider, Barrow.

the local Chukchi people to use the heads of 40–50 drakes at a time as trimming for the collars and cuffs of fur clothing.

Identification

See p. 137

The drakes have the most curious of eider head markings. Large white eye-patches are bordered by thin black lines, which give the impression that the birds are wearing goggles and after which the species is named. In front of and behind the goggles are patches of pale green, the rear patch extending over the nape of the neck. The forward green patch merges with white feathering to the nostril of the orange bill (the only duck to be so feathered). The iris is white, ringed in blue. The breast, underparts and tail are dark gray. The mantle, scapulars and tertials are white and there are white patches on the rump. The upper- and underwings are white with dark gray flight feathers. The legs and feet are yellow-brown. Females show the same "goggles" on the head, the inner pale brown and black-edged. The rest of the head is gray-brown, darker forward of the "goggles." The bill is gray. The body is brown with bold dark brown barring. The upperwing is barred brown with dark gray flight feathers. The underwing is dark gray, with pale gray axillaries. Eclipse males are similar to females, but darker and more gray-brown. Juveniles are as females, but with less distinct barring. They also have goggles, as do newly hatched ducklings. Adult plumage assumed after three years; young summer drakes are paler gray and "dirtier" white than adults. Ducklings have buff-brown down.

Confusion species

Both drake and duck are superficially similar to Common Eider, but the goggles are highly visible and distinctive.

Size

L: 20–24 in. (50–60 cm). WS: 34–38 in. (85–95 cm). W: 3¼–4¼ lb. (1.5–1.9 kg).

Voice

Relatively quiet. Drake call very similar to Common Eider, but not as loud. Female call is a throaty *go-go-go*, similar to Common Eider.

Distribution

Bering, Chukchi and Beaufort Seas. Very localized, breeding on northern Russian coast from the Lena to Chukotka, on Wrangel and the New Siberia Islands and on northern coast of Alaska. The Alaskan population crashed catastrophically around 1990 for unknown reasons and has continued to decline. Frequents tundra pools, coastal lagoons and muddy estuaries. Until the mid-1990s the Spectacled Eider wintering range was unknown. At that time radio-tagged birds led researchers to huge flocks of birds (perhaps as many as 150,000 in 30 or so flocks) at open leads in the Bering Sea. It is now known that the birds winter in large numbers at leads, chiefly near St. Lawrence and St. Matthew Islands. Arial photography suggests that the birds help to keep the leads free of ice by diving and swimming.

Diet

In tundra pools, Spectacled Eiders feed on a range of aquatic invertebrates. At sea in both summer and winter they dive for

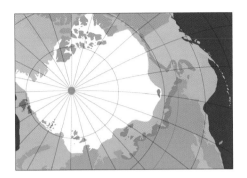

benthic animals, as do other large eiders. The Spectacled Eider is believed to dive deeper than other sea ducks.

Breeding

Gregarious, highly so in winter. Tends to nest solitarily, but may nest in small colonies on isolated islets. Pairs then attempt to maximize nest separation. Pair-bond and displays as other eiders. Nests close to water, near sheltering hummocks or in the open. Nest is a shallow depression lined with down. Five to seven olive eggs, incubated by female only for 22–24 days. Ducklings nidifugous, precocial and self-feeding. Ducklings are reared in tundra pools rather than on sea, the favored method of the other large eiders. Fledge at about 50 days. Breed at 2–3 years.

Taxonomy and geographical variation

Monotypic.

Steller's Eider
Polysticta stelleri

Named after the famous naturalist on Bering's expedition, Georg Steller, who collected the first specimen of this duck in Kamchatka. Steller's Eider is the smallest and least spectacular of the eiders.

▼ Pair of Steller's Eider in breeding plumage, Barrow.

Birds migrate to Bering Sea and Aleutian Islands. Occasionally seen near Kodiak Island in winter. Birds also reach the Baltic Sea and north Fennoscandia coast, probably from migratory flocks off the Kola Peninsula, where they may nest.

Diet
In freshwater, Steller's feed on aquatic insects. At sea consume mollusks, aquatic worms, isopods, amphipods and some small fish. Head-dipping and up-ending used when feeding in shallow water, but diving preferred in salt water, to depths of about 25 ft. (8 m). The birds also dabble on mudflats, and paddle mud and silt to uncover prey.

Breeding
Highly gregarious, except during breeding. Pair-bond and displays as other eiders. Nests close to water, preferring concealed sites, but often nests on open tundra. Nest is shallow depression lined with grass, moss and down. Five to seven pale olive eggs, incubated by female only for 25–27 days. Ducklings nidifugous, precocial and self-feeding. Cared for by female on freshwater, crèches sometimes forming. Is thought to fledge in about 50 days, but chicks are abandoned by females while still flightless. Thought to breed at 2–3 years.

Taxonomy and geographical variation
Monotypic.

Identification
See p. 137
The drake has a pale gray head with a black eye-ring, a pale green forehead and curious green tufts emerging from black spots on either side of the rear crown. It is sometimes suggested that the birds appear to have been madeup as clowns. The iris is red-brown, the bill blue-gray. The throat and neck collar are black. The breast and lower flanks are orange-buff, the upper flanks white. The belly is darker brown with a very dark center. The breast-side has a prominent black spot visible just above the waterline. The mantle, back and stern are black. The scapulars and tertials are black and white, giving the upperparts a striped appearance. The upperwing is white with black primaries and a black speculum (with purple gloss), which has a white band at the rear. The underwing is white with black flight feathers. The legs and feet are blue gray. Females are uniformly brown, mottled with dark brown with a purple-black speculum bordered front and rear with white. Long tertials create a drooping crest on the sitting bird. The upperwing is dark gray-brown apart from the speculum. The underwing is white, with gray flight feathers. Eclipse males are very similar to females, but the flanks are white and the head paler. Juveniles are as females, but the white speculum borders are much thinner and the tertials much shorter. First-summer drakes show the beginning of the neck color, buff breast and head tufts. Downy ducklings are dark brown.

Confusion species
None.

Size
L: 16–20 in. (42–50 cm). WS: 28–32 in. (70–80 cm). W: 26¹/₂–34¹/₄ lb (750–1,000 g).

Voice
Relatively silent, particularly the drake, which has a quiet, low *croon* during courtship. Females have a rapid, guttural *gaa-gaa*.

Distribution
Bering, Chukchi and Beaufort seas. Breed on the New Siberia Islands and northern Russia coast eastward from Khatenga Bay, and western and northern coasts of Alaska. It is speculated that some birds nest on the coast of the Russian mainland south of Novaya Zemlya. Prefer clear water, so seen off rocky coasts and at small river mouths. However, they also visit intertidal mudflats and estuaries. Also seen among sea ice.

Sea ducks
Sea ducks is the collective name for a highly maritime group of waterfowl. Though this group should, technically, also include eiders, their plumage is so different from other sea ducks (with the exception of the Harlequin Duck) that eiders are grouped separately here. In general sea ducks are small, black and white, and similar both anatomically and in lifestyle. Arctic sea ducks have short legs set far back on the body, efficient for paddling but awkward for walking, so they rarely travel far from water. They are therefore vulnerable to oil spills: the *Exxon Valdez* disaster in 1989 virtually annihilated the Harlequin Duck population of Alaska's Prince William Sound.

Sea ducks feed on benthic animals (apart from the mergansers, which are quick enough to catch fish). They swallow their prey whole, grinding up hard parts such as shells in the gizzard (as do eiders). Sea ducks can dive to remarkable depths and stay submerged for up to two minutes. They are only partially migratory, preferring to stay in the north and so moving ahead of the ice edge as winter deepens. In other

respects they are as the dabbling and diving ducks: drakes abandon their incubating mates, and chicks are precocial, diving soon after hatching, protected from the freezing Arctic waters by thick down and a layer of subcutaneous fat.

In addition to the species below, Bufflehead (*Bucephala albeola*) breeds in southern and central Alaska (but is rare in the west and rarer in northern Alaska), and also breeds on the southern shores of Hudson Bay.

Common Goldeneye
Bucephala clangula

Identification
See p. 136

The drake has a large black head with an iridescent green gloss and a prominent white spot between the yellow eye of the name and the dark gray bill. The rest of the plumage is black and white. The neck, breast, belly and flanks are white. The back is black, the tail dark gray. The inner scapulars, primaries and primary coverts are black, the rest of the wing white, though the outer scapulars have black edges that add black lines to the white flanks of the sitting birds. The underwing is dark gray with a white speculum. Females have chocolate brown heads and dark gray bills with a prominent orange band behind the dark nail. There is a sometimes an indistinct white collar. The rest of the body is mottled pale gray on the breast, belly and flanks and darker gray on the tail and back, a pattern broken only by the white speculum. The upperwing is dark gray with a white speculum, which has no rear border, but a thin black band followed by a thicker white band at the front. The

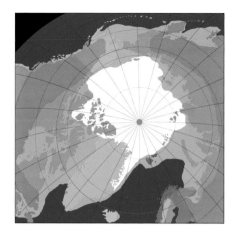

▼ Pair of Goldeneye of the race *americana*.

underwing is as the drake. The legs and feet are yellow-orange with black webs. Eclipse males are as females, but show more white on the scapulars and wing-coverts. The head is also darker, but may retain a fleeting green gloss. Some males also retain the white spot. Juveniles are as females, but darker overall and without the orange bill ring. The juvenile iris is brown. Downy ducklings are mottled dark brown and white.

Confusion species
Drakes are similar to Barrow's Goldeneye, but the head gloss is different and Barrow's show much less white plumage. Common Goldeneye males have a round white loral spot; Barrow's Goldeneyes have a white loral crescent. Females of the two species are virtually indistinguishable. Barrow's has a more rounded head and more orange on the bill.

Size
L: 16–20 in. (40–50 cm). WS: 26–32 in. (65–80 cm). W: 1³/₄–2³/₄ lb. (800–1,200 g).

Voice
Drakes have a loud *zee-zee*, emphasizing the second syllable, and a quieter rattling *drurrt*. Females have a hoarse *arr-arr*, very similar to *Aythya* species. As notable as the call is the whistling of the wings in flight.

Distribution
Essentially circumpolar, but largely sub-Arctic. Found near the Kolyma Delta and on Kamchatka in Russia, and near the

Common Goldeneyes on Hudson Bay.

Mackenzie Delta, southern Hudson Bay and Labrador in Canada. Prefers slow-flowing rivers and lakes close to forest edge. European birds migrate to North, Black, and Caspian Sea coasts, eastern Russian birds to coasts of Kuril and Commander Islands, Japan, China and Korea. Wintering birds favor estuaries and sheltered bays, but also feed on freshwater lakes.

Diet
Mollusks, crustaceans and aquatic insects, usually obtained by diving, infrequently by up-ending and dabbling. Flocks of Common Goldeneyes occasionally dive synchronously. Excellent diver to depths of 26 ft. (8 m), patrolling the bottom and overturning stones in search of prey.

Breeding
Much less gregarious than other waterfowl, though small flocks are still seen frequently. Drakes very aggressive during breeding season. Pair-bond monogamous and seasonal. Communal courtship as other waterfowl and courtship displays also similar to others, but the drake also has some specific and delightful displays. He may raise his head and neck vertically (masthead display) or at an angle (bowsprit display), or throw his head back onto his body, with the bill vertical, and call; he may also thrust his breast forward and raise neck and head vertically while kicking rapidly with his feet. Females also perform the bowsprit display. Once pairs have formed, the displays are less intense, usually little more than synchronous head-turning. Goldeneyes are extraordinary in that they nest in tree hollows; occasionally these are too deep for the birds to escape, so females sometimes become trapped and die of starvation. For so non-terrestrial a bird, the choice of nest site seems bizarre, particularly when females are observed perched on branches, but this preference is so specific that artificial nest boxes are willingly accepted. The nest (at heights to 16 ft./ 5 m) is merely a depression lined with peat and down. Eight to 11 blue-green eggs, incubated by female only for 27–30 days. Ducklings nidifugous and precocial. Cared for and brooded by female only, but self-feeding. Fledge at 55–65 days, but are usually independent before that time. Breed at 2 years.

Taxonomy and geographical variation
Polytypic. Nominate race breeds in Eurasia. Race *americana* breeds in North America. It is larger and has a larger, broader bill, but some authorities believe that size difference lies within the range of the nominate. Common and Barrow's Goldeneyes hybridize where species overlap.

Barrow's Goldeneye
Bucephala islandica

The bird is named after Sir John Barrow, the main instigator of expeditions in search of the Northwest Passage mounted by the Royal Navy in the 19th century.

Identification   See p. 136
The drake has a black, purple-glossed head and a white, crescent-shaped spot between the eye and the dark gray bill.

▲ Drake Barrow's Goldeneye, Myvatn, Iceland.

The iris is golden-yellow. The neck and underparts are white. The back is black, shading to dark gray tail. A prominent series of white blobs lies on the black scapulars, and the white speculum is also prominent in sitting bird. The upperwing is dark gray, the speculum separated by a thin black band at the front from further areas of white, so the innerwing appears as three broad white bands separated by two thin black bands. The underwing is dark gray apart from the white speculum. Females have chocolate-brown heads and dark gray bills, with an orange ring as in Common Goldeneye but much broader. The upper- and underwing patterns are as for the drakes. Other plumage as Common Goldeneye. Eclipse males are as females, but with more white on the upperparts. Juveniles are as females but darker overall. Downy ducklings are black and white.

Confusion species
Common Goldeneye, see pages 121–122.

Size
L: 16–21 in. (40–55 cm). WS: 26–34 in. (65–85 cm). W: 2–2 3/4 lb. (900–1,300 g) .

Voice
Silent except during courtship. Drakes have a grunting *ka-kaa*, with the second syllable louder, plus a nasal clicking. Females have a high croaking *arr-arr*, similar to Common Goldeneye. The birds' wings whistle in flight as Common Goldeneye.

Distribution
Essentially Nearctic. The breeding colony in Iceland is the only

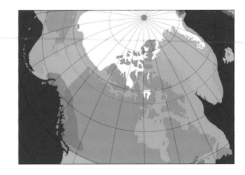

one in Eurasia. Breeds in southern Labrador and northern Pacific North America, including central and southwestern Alaska. Favors boreal and tundra pools and lakes, and rivers (including much faster-flowing waters than for Common Goldeneye). Many birds are partially or non-migratory, moving only as far as necessary to avoid frozen water. Icelandic birds do not migrate. Non-migratory birds winter in coastal regions of New England, along the Pacific coast and on some inland waters of the continental United States. Coastal birds favor sheltered bays and inlets.

Diet
Mollusks, crustaceans, aquatic insects and fish eggs, with feeding methods as in Common Goldeneye.

Breeding
Gregarious, but not highly so. Drakes aggressive in breeding season. Pair-bond monogamous and seasonal. Displays similar to Common Goldeneye. Also as with Common Goldeneye, the female nests in tree holes, at heights to 53 ft. (16 m). In Iceland, Barrow's nest in crevices in lava fields and cliffs, but also in nest boxes, sometimes on the sides of houses (the bird's Icelandic name is "houseduck"). In North America some birds nest in thick scrub. Nest is a depression lined with grass, leaves and down. Eight to 11 blue-green eggs incubated by female only for 28–30 days. Ducklings nidifugous and precocial. Brooded by female at first, but self-feeding. Fledge at 55–65 days and usually independent before that time. Breed at 2 years.

Taxonomy and geographical variation
Monotypic. Hybridizes with Common Goldeneye.

Harlequin Duck
Histrionicus histrionicus

Identification See p. 137
A beautiful small duck. Drakes have a dark blue-gray head with a prominent white face-patch extending to the crown and merging with a V-shaped rufous streak, which ends at the nape. There is also a white ear-spot and a white streak on the thick neck. The iris is dark brown, the bill blue-gray. A black-bordered white collar separates the neck from the dark blue-gray breast, on which there is another black-bordered white streak. The body is dark blue-gray, except for a large rufous patch on the flanks. The back is blue-gray with symmetrical white streaks, the stern black with a small white spot. The tail is black and pointed. The upperwing is dark blue-gray with a blue speculum fronted by a white bar. The fore-underwing is blue-gray, the rear-underwing paler. The legs and feet are blue-gray. Females have a dark brown head with a pale patch around the eye and

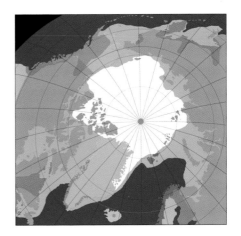

a distinctive white ear-spot. The underbody is light mottled brown, the belly white/pale brown. The upperparts are dark brown. The tail is pointed, as in the drake. The upperwing is uniformly dark brown (with slightly paler flight feathers), the fore-underwing dark brown, the rear-underwing paler. Eclipse males are as females but darker, the flanks more rufous, the head markings whiter. There are also white streaks on the upperparts. Juveniles are as females but lighter and more olive than dark brown. Downy ducklings are dark brown/white.

Confusion species
Drakes are unmistakable. Females are similar to female Velvet Scoters. The latter are much larger, tend to be darker overall and have less conspicuous white ear-patches.

Size
L: 15–18 in. (38–45 cm). WS: 24–28 in. (60–70 cm). W: 19½–26½ oz. (550–750 g).

Voice
Relatively silent. Drakes have a high, piercing, whistling trill (the high, piercing components carry over the noise of tumbling streams). Females have a high, harsh *ek-ek-ek*.

Distribution
Essentially circumpolar, but patchy. European birds are confined to Iceland. Breeds in eastern Russia, Commander Islands, Kamchatka and southern Chukotka. North America has two populations. Western birds are confined to western, southwestern and southeastern Alaska, the Aleutians and the

▼ A pair of Harlequin Ducks in typical habitat — a powerful, fast-moving torrent rich with eddies, Starichkov Island, Russia.

Group of Long-tailed Ducks in breeding plumage, Mackenzie Bay, northeast Greenland.

Pacific seaboard south to the Mexican border. Eastern birds breed in southern Baffin Island and Labrador. Also breeds in southwestern and east-central Greenland. Prefers fast-flowing rivers, even torrents and waterfalls. Partially migratory. Icelandic and Greenlandic birds winter on the islands, but may move to southern coasts. Russian birds migrate to Kuril and Commander Islands, Japan and Korea. North American birds move south along Pacific and Atlantic coasts. Wintering birds invariably coastal, seeking headlands and other exposed areas rather than sheltered bays.

Diet
Mollusks, crustaceans and aquatic insects, almost exclusively obtained by diving. Harlequins are also adept at catching small fish. Dives of wintering birds are highly synchronous. The Harlequin is the only sea duck that frequently dives from the air instead of the surface. It can also emerge from the sea into the air in one movement, a spectacular sight.

Breeding
Gregarious except in breeding season when drakes are very aggressive. Pair-bond monogamous and seasonal, though may be renewed. Displays very similar to *Anas* species. Nests very close to water on the ground in low scrub or beneath rock. Nest is little more than a depression lined with grass and down. Five to eight pale yellow eggs, incubated by female only for 27–29 days. Ducklings nidifugous and precocial. Brooded by female when small, but self-feeding. Cared for by female only, occasionally transported on her back. Fledge at 60–70 days. Icelandic juveniles migrate with female before independence, but elsewhere are abandoned before fledging. Breed at 2 years.

Taxonomy and geographical variation
Polytypic. Nominate race breeds in eastern North America, Greenland and Iceland. Pacific race *pacificus* breeds in eastern Russian and western North America. Pacific birds are duller, with smaller chestnut V-stripe, but differences are slight.

Long-tailed Duck (Oldsquaw)
Clangula hyemalis

Historically called the Oldsquaw, a pejorative reference to the perceived talkativeness of elderly Inuit women. However, it is the drake that is the most talkative, which says much about the originator of the name. The scientific name continues the theme, translating as "noisy winter bird."

Identification See p. 137
With its long central tail feathers, the drake is unmistakable in all plumages. In summer the drake has a chocolate brown head, neck and breast, a white patch from eye to ear and a larger grayer patch forward of the eye. The iris is variable, from yellow to red-brown. The bill is short and broad, with a black base and nail and a wide salmon-pink band between the two. The underparts and stern are white. The back has a broad black Y extending from the shoulders, bordered with white toward the tail, and with dark, yellow-brown edge scapulars. The upperwing is dark brown, with grayer primaries and an unbordered paler brown speculum. The underwing is uniformly dark gray-brown. Females resemble summer drakes more than in other ducks. The back and upperwing are similar but much duller, the breast gray mottled with brown, but the remaining underparts are similarly white. The head is also similar, though the white patch extends to the nape and becomes an almost complete white collar. The upperwing is more uniformly gray-brown and lacks a speculum. The underwing is paler. The female's tail feathers are much shorter than the drake's. In autumn drakes are very white. The head is white apart from a gray-pink eye patch that blends into a darker brown, sometimes gray-pink edged, lower cheek patch. The neck is white. The breast is very dark brown or black, the flanks gray, the stern white. The upper mantle and scapulars are white, but the lower back and long central tail feathers remain dark brown. In winter the head patches are lost, replaced by a fuzzy-edged dark cheek patch, and the breast also becomes mottled.

Females also change to a winter plumage, the head becoming whiter but retaining a dark crown cap and cheek patch as winter drake. Legs and feet are blue-gray. Juveniles are as summer females but with less white on the head and with flanks flecked rufous brown. Downy ducklings are dark brown.

Confusion species
None.

Size
L: 16–20 in. (40–50 cm), with an additional 4–6 in. (10–15 cm) of tail feather in the male. WS: 26–32 in. (65–80 cm). W: 23–33½ oz. (650–950 g).

Voice
The drake's call is arguably the most delightful of all waterfowl. It is a melodious, long-carrying yodel, *ow-owlee-owlee,* which is sometimes heard faintly and is, in early morning, redolent of the north. By contrast the female voice is a much more duck-like quack, *kak-kak-kak.* Alarm call is a staccato, barking *ark.*

Distribution
Circumpolar. Breeds in Iceland, Svalbard, northern Russia including Franz Josef Land, Novaya Zemlya, Severnaya Zemlya New Siberia Islands and Wrangel Island, and in North America from Alaska to Newfoundland, including the Canadian Arctic islands as far north as Ellesmere. Breeds on both coasts of Greenland to the extreme north of the island. Long-tailed Ducks may be the world's most northerly breeding waterfowl, though King Eiders also breed in the extreme north. Found on all available open water, including tundra pools and pack-ice leads, but much less common in flowing water. Partially migratory, wintering at sea. Some Icelandic birds migrate to northern Britain, European Arctic birds seen along northern and western Norway coast and in the Baltic (often in large numbers). Asian birds move to the Bering Sea, Sea of Okhotsk, and Kuril and Commander Islands. North American birds move to the Aleutians and north Pacific or north Atlantic coasts, occasionally surprisingly far south.

Diet
Benthic animals, but also eats plant material and, in freshwater, insect larvae. Chiefly obtained by diving, usually to depths of 30 ft. (10 m), but if tales are true of Long-taileds being trapped in fishing nets at depths of 165–230 ft. (50–70 m), then this is almost certainly the deepest-diving waterfowl.

Breeding
Gregarious except at breeding sites, where drakes are highly aggressive. Pair-bond is monogamous and seasonal. Courtship displays include head-throws

▶ Female Long-tailed Duck, Badlanddalen, northeast Greenland.

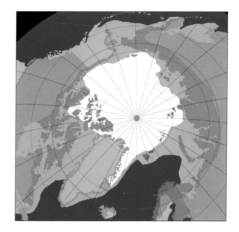

that resemble those of Goldeneye, but also include a drake masthead display. The drake raises his head, then throws it forward as he raises his rear end, pushing the tail vertically upward, a position maintained by vigoros foot-kicking. Pair displays include synchronous chin-lifting and neck-stretching. Nest site is usually close to water, in low scrub or a rock crevice, but often in the open when on tundra. Nest is a small depression lined with vegetation and down. Six to nine pale olive eggs, incubated by female only for 24–28 days. Ducklings nidifugous and precocial. Brooded when small, cared for by female only. Crèches of up to 40 chicks may form. Fledge in 30–40 days (the short period a necessity at extremes of range) and are independent at that time. Breed at 2 years.

Taxonomy and geographical variation
Monotypic.

Scoters

Melanitta, "black duck," is the generic name for the four appropriately named scoters, all of which are northern birds. All are large with bills enlarged at the base.

Common Scoter
Melanitta nigra

Identification See p. 137

The plumage of drake is entirely glossy black, apart from paler primaries and belly. The bill is black with a prominent knob at the base of the upper mandible. At the front of this and on the upper mandible to beyond the nostril, there is a yellow-orange patch, the only splash of color on the male. The iris is dark brown. The tail is long and pointed. The upper- and underwings are black apart from the paler primaries. Females have chocolate brown crown and nape, but paler brown/cream cheeks and neck. The bill is green-gray, but without a nasal knob. The body color is also dark brown, but with paler barring from feather edging. Upper- and underwings patterned as the drake, but primaries dark and pale brown. Legs and feet are dark olive brown. Non-breeding drakes are as breeding males but brown-black and duller overall. Juveniles as females but with more uniform dark brown bodies. First-winter males more mottled than breeding males, bill knob less pronounced, yellow-orange patch muted. Ducklings dark brownish buff.

Confusion species

At a distance or in poor light, it can be difficult to differentiate the Common and Velvet Scoters. The white secondaries and "half-moon" of the Velvet drake are diagnostic. Female Velvet Scoter also has white secondaries, and this and the darker neck and head aid identification. Common and Black Scoters' tails are more pointed than those of the other scoters. See also Black Scoter, following.

Size

L: 18–21½ in. (45–55 cm). WS: 28–34 in. (70–85 cm). W: 1⅞–2¾ lb. (850–1,300 g).

Voice

The most vocal scoter. Drakes have a piping *peew*, usually in flight, and a mournful, whistling *cree*. In flight the drake's wings produce a shrill whistle. Females have calls that resemble the males, but also a hoarse, grating *kra-kra*.

Distribution

Iceland and northern Eurasia from Fennoscandia to the Lena Delta and the southern island of Novaya Zemlya only. Occurs in a wide range of habitats including forest, forest edge and tundra, in lakes and ponds, slow-flowing rivers and marshland. Migratory. Icelandic birds winter around coasts of the British Isles and western Europe; Scandinavian and European Russian birds move to the southern Norwegian coast, Baltic and Black Seas. Wintering birds are mainly maritime, chiefly in shallow bays and other inshore waters.

Diet

Mollusks and, to a much lesser extent, crustaceans and echinoderms. In freshwater the birds take aquatic larvae and fish eggs. Prey is obtained almost exclusively by diving, using partially opened wings for stability in turbulent water.

Breeding

Highly gregarious except during breeding season, when males are aggressive (but not as much as some other waterfowl). Pair

Common Scoter taking off from the sea, Iceland.

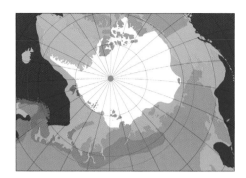

bond is monogamous and seasonal, but drakes are occasionally promiscuous and may even attempt to forcibly inseminate females other than mate. Communal courtship displays include head-shaking and wing-flapping, and a rushing display in which a drake lowers his head and neck and rushes across the water with much splashing from the feet, before stopping and shaking his head. The drake also snaps his pointed tail vertically upward vigorously. Breeding pairs show mock preening and mutual head-shaking. Nests are set close to water, usually in thick scrub or tall sedge. Nest is a hollow, lined with grasses, lichens and down. Six to 10 cream or buff eggs incubated by female only for 27–28 days. Ducklings nidifugous and precocial. Brooded when small but self-feeding. Cared for by female with small crèches sometimes forming. Fledge in 45–50 days; independent at that time. Breed at 2–3 years.

Taxonomy and geographical variation
Monotypic. Until recently Black Scoter was considered a subspecies of Common Scoter.

Black Scoter
Melanitta americana

Identification
See p. 137

Very similar to the Common Scoter, but there are differences in the bill. In drake Black Scoters the knob on the upper mandible is completely yellow-orange and less prominent, so the profile of the front of the head is much smoother. The Black Scoter mandibular knob is also wider and longer, reaching the nostrils, which are closer to bill tip than for in Common Scoter. Female Black Scoters are very similar to their Common cousins, but have nostrils closer to bill tip.

Confusion species
As noted for Common Scoter, it can be difficult to differentiate scoters at a distance or in poor light. Again, the white secondaries and "half-moon" of drake Velvet Scoter are diagnostic, as are the white secondaries, darker neck and head of female Velvet. The white nape and forehead together with the spectacular bill distinguishes drake Surf Scoter, while the overall dark plumage but pale cheek patch of female Surf Scoter is a good identification feature. Common and Black

Scoters' tails are more pointed than those of the other scoters. In flight, Common and Black Scoters hold the bill horizontal or pointed slightly upward while Velvet and Surf normally point the bill downwards.

Size
L: 18–21½ in. (45–55 cm). WS: 28–34 in. (70–85 cm). W: 1⁷/₈–2³/₄ lb. (850–1,300 g).

Voice
As the Common Scoter.

Distribution
There is an abrupt demarcation between the ranges of Common and Black Scoters in Asian Russia, the former breeding to the Lena, the latter breeding east of the Yana to the Bering Sea coast (though not to the northern coast in any part of that range) and throughout Kamchatka. In North America, Black Scoters breed on both the west coast of Alaska and in Labrador, but despite this extent they are extremely local, breeding only in a handful of areas — western Alaska and the Alaska Peninsula, Ungava and southern Quebec and Labrador. Populations have also recently been identified around James Bay and central west Hudson Bay. Habitat as Common Scoter. Asian Russian birds move to the Aleutians and the Korean, Japanese and Chinese coasts in winter; Alaskan birds occupy the Aleutians and the Pacific coast of North America; Labrador birds move south along the Atlantic coast. Wintering habitat is also as Common Scoter.

Diet
As Common Scoter.

Breeding
As Common Scoter.

Taxonomy and geographical variation
Monotypic, but see Common Scoter.

▶ Pair of Black Scoter, Alaska Peninsula.

Surf Scoter
Melanitta perspicillata

Identification See p. 137
Apart from the head, the drake's plumage is black but less glossy than the other scoters. The head is black apart from white patches on the forehead and nape. The nape patch abrades during the summer, revealing underlying black feathers. The iris is gray-blue. The bill is spectacular, prominently swollen on the top and sides of the upper mandible. The culmen is black-feathered almost to the nostril. Forward of this the bill is orange-red, while below the feathering there is a black square bordered by orange-red above and toward the bill base, and by pale orange or white below and toward the bill tip. The tail is pointed but shorter than in Common or Black Scoters. The upper- and underwings are dull black. The legs and feet are bright orange. Females are dark brown above, paler brown below. The head is dark brown with whitish patches on the ears and lores and often a whitish nape patch. The bill is large but not swollen as for the drake, and is gray-black. Wings as drake. The legs and feet are duller orange. Non-breeding males are as breeding drake but duller and usually lack the white nape patch. Juveniles are as females, but the heads have darker crowns and paler cheeks, and lack the whitish nape patches. First-winter drakes are very dark brown and have a developing white nape patch, but no forehead patch; the bill shape, size and color is forming and will develop by the spring. Ducklings are dark gray-brown.

Confusion species
See Common and Black Scoters, pages 126–127.

Size
L: 18–21½ in. (45–55 cm). WS: 30–38 in. (75–95 cm). W: 1¾–2½ lb. (800–1,100 g).

Voice
Usually silent. The drake has a low whistle and a gurgling *puk-puk*. The wings whistle in flight. The female has a croaking *kraak-kraak* similar to the Common Scoter.

Distribution
Nearctic. Breeds in central and western Alaska, in the Aleutians, in Yukon and Northwest Territories west of the Amundsen Gulf and in Labrador. Occurs at forest edge but also in open tundra, lakes and pools, and marshland. Migratory, with western birds moving to the Pacific coast from the Aleutians to Baja California, eastern birds moving to Atlantic coast south to the Carolinas. Wintering birds are almost entirely maritime, favoring sheltered, shallow bays and inlets, but may also be seen on freshwater lagoons.

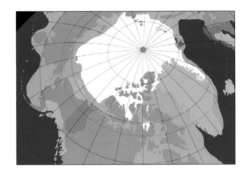

Diet
Mainly mollusks, also crustaceans, and aquatic insects in freshwater. Food obtained almost exclusively by diving.

Breeding
Gregarious except when breeding. Pair-bond and displays as Common Scoter. Details of nesting, incubation and fledging of the species were virtually unknown until recently, and are still poorly understood. The nest is well concealed in scrub, preferably forested scrub. Six to 10 cream eggs, incubated by female, probably for only 26–28 days (as Common Scoter). Ducklings nidifugous and precocial. Brooded by female when small. Cared for by female only, but self-feeding. Crèches known, but apparently rare. Assumed to fledge at 45–50 days (as Common Scoter). Breed at 2–3 years.

Taxonomy and geographical variation
Monotypic.

Velvet Scoter
Melanitta fusca

Identification See p. 137
Despite their respective common names, it is the Surf Scoter that appears to have velvet plumage, that of the Velvet Scoter drake being much glossier. Drakes are black apart from the secondaries, which are white and often show as a white "speculum" on the swimming bird. There is also a white horizontal "half-moon" under the eye. The iris is blue-gray. The bill has a small black basal knob on the upper mandible. The lower mandible is black at its base. The remaining bill is yellow-orange with a red tip. The upperwing is black, with paler primaries and the white secondaries. The front of the

▲ Adult Surf Scoter — note the amazing bill.

underwing is black, the remaining feathering mid-gray apart from the secondaries. The legs and feet are orange-red. Females are uniformly dark brown, slightly paler below, with paler barring. The head shows a white ear-patch and a pale patch between the eye and the bill extending to the forehead. The bill is dark olive. The wings are as the drake. The eye is much darker. The legs and feet are dull orange-red. Non-breeding males are as breeding drakes, but duller and brown rather than black. Juveniles are as the female, but paler and duller, and with paler, mottled breasts and bellies. First-year males are paler and more mottled, and lack the facial half-moon and the developed bill. Adult plumage is acquired in second year. Downy ducklings are very dark brown/buff.

Confusion species
See Common and Black Scoters.

Size
L: 20–24 in. (50–60 cm). WS: 36–40 in. (90–100 cm). W: 3¹/₄–4¹/₂ lb. (1.5–2 kg).

Voice
Relatively silent. Males have a double whistle *whick-err* and a growling croak *karr*. Females have a vibrating *braaa-braaa* and a harsh *karr-karr*.

Distribution
Circumpolar. Breeds from Fennoscandia to Chukotka, but not to the northern Russian coast (except on the White Sea and, patchily, near and on Vaigach Island) or on Russia's Arctic islands. Breeds throughout Kamchatka. In North America breeds in the Aleutians, central Alaska, around the Mackenzie Delta and then at decreasing latitudes to southwestern Hudson Bay. Found in forests and at the forest edge, rarely on tundra and on slow rivers. Also seen on brackish lagoons. Migratory; European birds move to northern Scotland, western European coasts; central Russian birds move to the Black and Caspian Seas. Asian birds migrate to Commander and Kuril Islands and the coasts of Japan and China. Frequents more exposed maritime habitats than

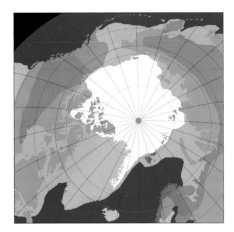

other Scoters, but also estuaries and inlets. Also found on inland waters, but then generally as single birds rather than in flocks.

Diet
Mainly mollusks (chiefly mussels), also crustaceans and echinoderms. Diet more varied than other Scoters as it feeds in summer on brackish lagoons and has wider range of winter habitats. Food obtained by diving.

Breeding
Gregarious, but less so than other Scoters. Males aggressive in breeding season. Pair-bond and displays as other Scoters. Nests are concealed in tall grass or sedge or in low scrub, though usually close to water. Nest is minimal, mostly of twigs and lined with grass and copious down. Six to 10 cream/buff eggs, incubated by female only for 26–28 days. Ducklings nidifugous and precocial. Brooded by female when small, but self-feeding. Cared for by female only, crèches occasionally forming. Fledge in 50–55 days, but independent much earlier. Breed at 2–3 years.

Taxonomy and geographical variation
Polytypic. The nominate race breeds in Eurasia east to Yenisey River. *M. f. stejnegeri* breeds in eastern Russia. Drakes have much larger bill knob and more black at the bill base, and the

▼ Adult Velvet Scoter, Kodiak Island, Alaska. This bird is of the Nearctic race *deglandi*. (Dave Menke).

▲ Two male Goosanders, north Norway.

remaining bill is purple-red. *M. f. deglandi* breeds in North America. The drake is dark olive-brown rather than black and the bill knob is larger. Both *stejnegeri* and *deglandi* are now often treated as two subspecies of a separate species, the White-winged Scoter (*M. deglandi*).

Sawbills

These sea ducks are named after their elongated, thin bills, which have hooked tips and serrations on the mandibles to help them grasp their prey. Though quick enough when diving to catch fish (the only waterfowl able to do so), sawbills are not capable of sustained chasing and so tend to swim at the surface with the head submerged searching for prey, which can be taken with a quick dive and dash. Of the four northern species, three are Arctic or sub-Arctic, while the fourth, the Hooded Merganser (*Lophodytes cucullatus*) seems to be expanding its range northward; there have even been reports from as far north as Southampton Island.

Goosander
Mergus merganser

Identification See p. 137
Large, long-bodied and very attractive birds, which are much more freshwater than saltwater ducks. The drake has a dark green head and upper neck with a green gloss. There is a crest, which is tight to the nape, like a well-greased haircut. The iris is dark brown. The bill is red with a black culmen and nail. The lower neck, belly and flanks are creamy white, occasionally pink-tinged. The mantle and back are black tending to gray. The tail is gray. The outer feathers of the upperwing are black, the inner feathers are white with dark gray on the coverts and tertials. The outer underwing is black, the inner feathers white. The legs and feet are red. Females have red-brown heads with a full crest and a white chin. The upper neck is also red-brown. The lower neck and breast is white or pale gray. The upperparts are blue-gray flecked with dark gray, the lower parts pale blue-gray flecked with white. The

outer upperwing has the black of the drake, but the inner wing is more complex, with pale gray coverts separated from white secondaries by a black band, the secondaries also half-crossed by another black bar. The legs and feet are orange. Eclipse males are as females, but they retain the large white upperwing patch, which is visible on the sitting bird. Juveniles are as females, but the abrupt boundary between the red-brown neck and white breast in the female is much more diffuse. As well as the white chin patch, a white stripe runs from just below the eye to the bill, the bill being much paler. Downy chicks are brown-white.

Confusion species
Females are very similar to female Red-breasted Mergansers. The lack of an abrupt boundary between neck and breast colors on the Red-breasted is diagnostic. The drake is more easily distinguished from the Red-breasted drake, being much whiter.

Size
L: 21½–28 in. (55–70 cm). WS: 32–40 in. (80–100 cm). W: 2½–3½ lb. (1.1–1.6 kg).

Voice
Relatively silent. The drake has a strange, twanging *kroo-kroo* and a clear, bell-like single note. Females have a rapid, harsh *ak-ak-ak* and a croaking *korr*.

Distribution
Circumpolar. Breeds in Iceland, and from Fennoscandia to the Bering Sea coast, but rarely north of the Arctic Circle east of the Kola Peninsula. Breeds throughout Kamchatka. In North America breeds in southwestern and central Alaska, but then at decreasing latitudes, except in eastern Canada, where they occur in southern Quebec and Labrador. Essentially a boreal and mountain species, found in lakes and on fast rivers. Avoids ice in all locations. Partially migratory. Icelandic birds stay on the island, moving to the coast if inland waters freeze. European and central Russian birds move to western Europe and to the Black and Caspian Seas. Eastern Russian birds move to Kuril Islands and southern Asia, though some stay on Kamchatka. North American birds move to southern states on

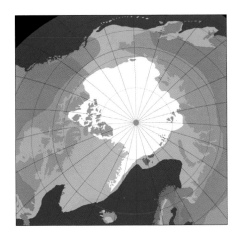

both Pacific and Atlantic coasts. Wintering birds prefer fresh to saltwater, choosing inland lakes and rivers where available, but they may also occur in sheltered bays.

Diet

Primarily fish obtained by diving, using the feet as paddles. Also takes amphibians, small mammals, mollusks and crustaceans.

Breeding

Gregarious at most times. Drakes are rarely aggressive even in breeding season. Pair-bond essentially monogamous and seasonal, but polygyny has been observed. Communal courtship is followed by pair displays. Displays include head-throwing and feet-splashing, and also a masthead-type display. Pair behavior includes synchronous preening and drinking. Nest in a tree hole or rock crevice, though they occasionally nest in scrub. They readily use nest boxes and have nested in the roof spaces of houses. Nest is little more than a depression lined with down. Seven to 12 creamy-white eggs, incubated by female only for 30–32 days. Chicks nidifugous and precocial. Brooded by female when small, but self-feeding. Cared for by female, but crèches often form. Fledge in 60–70 days and are independent at that time. Breed at 2 years.

Taxonomy and geographical variation

Polytypic. The nominate race breeds in Eurasia. *M. m. americanus* breeds in North America. Drakes of this race have brighter red bills and a prominent broad black wing-bar on the wing, appearing almost as a band above white speculum. Another subspecies, *M. m. comatus*, is extralimital, occupying the Pamirs and Tibet. It has a shorter, narrower bill and larger wings.

Red-breasted Merganser
Mergus serrator

Identification See p. 137

Large (though smaller than Goosander), long-bodied and elegant birds. The drake has a dark green, glossy head and upper neck, with a prominent red iris and a long, thin, slightly upturned red bill with a black culmen and tip. There is a prominent crest at the nape. The dark green on the upper neck terminates abruptly in a white collar, which diffuses into a buff breast speckled with black. The shoulders are black with large and small white spots. The belly is white, the flanks, rump and tail-coverts vermiculated black and white. The tail is dark gray-brown. The mantle and inner scapulars are black, the outer scapulars white. The outer upperwing is dark gray. The inner upperwing is white with two prominent black bars and a black leading edge. The outer underwing is gray, the inner white. The legs and feet are orange-red. Female head and upper neck are pale rufous-brown, diffusing into a brownish-gray lower neck and breast. The crest is short but prominent. The throat has a white patch and, usually, a thin black stripe between the red eye and the red bill. The rest of the bird is also brownish-gray with pale gray barring from feather edging. The outer upperwing is gray, the inner upperwing has a broad gray leading edge, separated from the white secondaries by a black band. The secondaries have a speculum formed by another, thinner black band. Eclipse males are as female, but with the large white wing-patch visible on the sitting bird. Juveniles are as females but generally darker and with less prominent crests. Downy chicks are a creamy rufous-brown.

Pair of Red-breasted Mergansers, Hudson Bay.

Confusion species
See Goosander, pages 130–131.

Size
L: 20–24 in. (50–60 cm). WS: 28–34 in. (70–85 cm). W: 2–2³/₄ lb. (950–1,200 g).

Voice
Relatively silent. The drake has a disyllabic coughlike call *chita ... pittee*. The female call is a single harsh *krrrr*, which sometimes develops into a cackle.

Distribution
Circumpolar. Breeds in Iceland, Fennoscandia and Russia to the Bering Sea coast, but not to the northern coast except at the White Sea and near Vaigach Island. Also breeds on the southern island of Novaya Zemlya and throughout Kamchatka. In North America, breeds throughout southern Alaska and the northern Canadian mainland (except Boothia and Melville Peninsulas) and on southern Baffin Island. Breeds on southwestern Greenland coast and around Scoresby Sound and Ammassalik. Eclectic in habitat; boreal, mountain and tundra pools, rivers and a variety of maritime sites — shallow, sheltered bays, inlets and estuaries, favoring clear rather than muddy waters. Partially migratory; Icelandic and eastern Greenland birds may stay at local sea coasts, but some migrate to the British Isles. Western Greenland birds stay locally. Northern European birds move to North Sea coasts, central Russian birds to the Black and Caspian Seas, eastern Russian birds to Kamchatka and the Kuril and Commander Islands. North American birds move to the Great Lakes and the Atlantic and Pacific coasts, as well as to inland waters of the southern states. Wintering birds predominantly maritime.

Diet
Mainly small fish, but also mollusks, aquatic insects and some vegetation. When diving uses feet as paddles, as Goosander, but will also readily use half-spread wings. Feed cooperatively if shoals of fish are encountered, with the birds forming arcs to drive the fish into shallow waters.

▼ Red-breasted Mergansers. The long bill is a fish-catching adaptation.

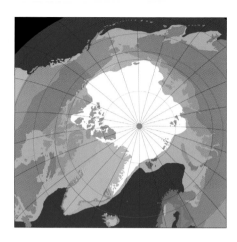

Breeding
Gregarious at all times. Pair-bond monogamous and seasonal. Polygyny rarely observed. Displays as Goosander, but drake also has a display in which he lays his neck and head on the water and raises his rear end, dipping the tail toward the water. He opens his bill and moves toward the female, calling. He then closes the bill, withdraws the neck and back-paddles from her with tail still lowered. Nests in low scrub or crevices of riverbank or rocks, sometimes on a floating mat of reed or sedge, and even in burrows. Red-breasted Mergansers are the most proficient walkers of the sawbills, but usually nest close to water. Nest is a shallow depression lined with grass and down. Seven to 10 pale olive eggs, incubated by female only for 29–32 days. Chicks nidifugous and precocial. Brooded by female when small, but self-feeding. Cared for by female, but crèches often form. Fledge at 60–65 days, but independent at about 50 days. Breed at 2 years.

Taxonomy and geographical variation
Monotypic. Some authorities suggest that Greenland birds form a separate subspecies, *M. s. schioleri*, which have longer bills and the females are paler; however these differences lie within normal range of variation and the subspecies is generally not accepted.

Smew
Mergellus albellus

Identification   See p. 137
Beautiful birds, unmistakable in all plumages. Smew are the smallest Arctic sawbills, and are different enough from the *Mergus* ducks to merit their own genus. Drakes are white with black eye patches extending to the bill base, which gives them the look of masked robbers. The crest is white and on top of the head. Behind it a black V extends down the nape. The iris is red-brown. The blue-gray bill is shorter and stubbier than in *Mergus* spp. The breast and underparts are white. On each side of the breast is a thin black line, a V with the point at the base of the neck. The flanks are vermiculated gray, the rump and tail darker gray. The mantle and back are black. The outer

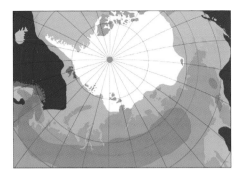

upperwing is black, the inner upperwing white with a black leading edge and two broad black bars at the rear. The outer underwing is dark gray, the rest white. The legs and feet are dark gray. The female has a red-brown head and back of the neck, with a white throat and front neck. The rest of the body is mid-gray with white and darker gray mottling. The mantle and back are dark gray. The wing patterns are as the drake, but dark gray rather than black. The legs and feet are greenish-gray. Eclipse males are as females, but the white crest is retained; the breast is pale gray and the back and upper wings are darker. Juveniles are as females. Downy chicks are black/gray-brown.

Confusion species
None.

Size
L: 14½–18 in. (37–45 cm). WS: 21½–28 in. (55–70 cm). W: 19½–26½ oz. (550–750 g).

Voice
Relatively silent. Drakes have a rattling, hissing call, like a finger drawn along a comb. Females have a harsh *krrrr* and a rapid *wok-wok*.

Distribution
Palearctic. Breeds in Sweden, Finland and the Russian sub-Arctic to the Yenisey River, but also in central Chukotka and northern Kamchatka. Occurs in taiga and at the forest edge, on lakes, pools and slow-flowing rivers. Also in marshland with trees. Migratory; European birds move to coasts of North and southern Baltic Sea. Central Russian birds to Azov, Black and Caspian Seas. Eastern Russian birds move to China and Japan. The birds are often reluctant to migrate and will fish below the ice of semi-frozen lakes. Wintering birds occur on inland waters, occasionally on sheltered, shallow bays and estuaries.

Diet
Mainly small fish, mollusks, crustaceans and significant numbers of insects and their larvae. Food obtained by diving, though rarely deeper than 13 ft. (4 m).

Breeding
Gregarious at all times. Drakes rarely aggressive, though will defend mate. Pair-bond monogamous and seasonal. Drakes have head-shakes as other ducks, but two specific displays. In one the head and neck are drawn back on to the mantle. In the other the drake rises out the water and throws the bill and neck vertically upward. Nest sites are usually tree holes, but the birds will use nest boxes. Smew nesting at the forest edge sometimes set the nest in well-concealed locations on the tundra. Nest is little more than hollow, sometimes lined only with down. Seven to nine cream eggs, incubated by female only for 26–28 days. Chicks nidifugous and precocial. Cared for by female only, but self-feeding. Fledging time thought to be at 50–60 days. Probably breed at 2 years.

Taxonomy and geographical variation
Monotypic.

Smew in spring, north Norway. A female (often called a redhead) is on the right.

PLATE 3: SWANS AND GEESE

Whistling Swan
(*C. c. columbianus*)

ad

Whooper Swan

ads

Bewick's Swan
(*C. c. bewickii*)

ads

Pink-footed Goose

ads

Graylag Goose

ad

Tundra Bean Goose
(*A. f. rossicus*)

ad

Taiga Bean Goose
(*A. fabalis*)

ad

Bean Goose

ad

Greater White-fronted Goose

ad

juv

Emperor Goose
ad

Lesser White-fronted Goose
ad

Red-breasted Goose
ad

Barnacle Goose
ad

Canada Goose
ad
ad

Lesser
Canada Goose
(*B. c. parvipes*)

Greater
Canada Goose
(*B. canadensis*)

Dark-bellied
Brant Goose
(*B. bernicla*)
ad

Brant Goose
ad

Black Brant
(*B. b. nigricans*)

Pale-bellied
Black Goose
(*B. b. hrota*)
ad

white morph

Snow Goose

ads

Blue Goose
(dark morph)

white morph

Ross's Goose
ad

dark
morph

PLATE 5: DABBLING DUCKS AND DIVING DUCKS

♂ eclipse
Mallard
♂ br

♂
American Black Duck

Northern Shoveler
♂

Northern Pintail
♀
♂

Green-winged Teal
♂
♀ win
♀ sum

Eurasian Wigeon
♂
♀

American Wigeon
♂
♀

Baikal Teal
♂ ad

♂ br
Canvasback
♂ eclipse

Greater Scaup
♂

Lesser Scaup
♂

Tufted Duck
♂

Common Goldeneye
♂ 1st-win
♂

♂
Barrow's Goldeneye

PLATE 6: SEA DUCKS AND SAWBILLS

Spectacled Eider

♂

Common Eider

♂

♀ win

♂ eclipse

Steller's Eider

♂

King Eider

♂

Velvet Scoter

♂

Surf Scoter

♂

Black Scoter

♂

Common Scoter

♂

Harlequin Duck

♂

♂ fall

♂ br

Long-tailed Duck

Goosander

♂

♀

♂ 1st-sum

♂ 1st-sum

Red-breasted Merganser

♂

Smew

ad ♂ in molt

♂

♀

Raptors

▲ Osprey in flight, Great Slave Lake, Canada.

The word *raptor* derives from the Latin *rapere*, to ravish, so in the broadest sense, the term could be applied to owls and other birds that take live prey (e.g., large Arctic gulls) as well as to eagles, falcons and hawks. However, the term is more strictly applied to diurnal birds of prey, defining those with hooked beaks, a basal cere and sharp talons that are strong fliers and that exclusively or predominantly feed on animal prey. Raptors feed mainly on prey that they catch and kill. Vultures are an exception; they are absent from the Arctic, where other scavengers such as foxes, gulls and crows fulfil their role. Given the extent of coastal waters and inland lakes in the Arctic, it is not surprising that fish eagles form a significant fraction of Arctic raptor species; three of the world's 10 species breed there.

Non-Arctic species not discussed here that may sometimes be seen at higher latitudes include the Red-tailed Hawk (*Buteo jamaicensis*) in central Alaska and around southern James Bay, and the Eurasian Sparrowhawk (*Accipiter nisus*), which breeds toward the Kolyma Delta and in southern Kamchatka.

Osprey
Pandion haliaetus

A borderline Arctic species, though found at the timberline in many northern locations. The position of the Osprey within the order Accipitriformes has long been debated. Ospreys share many characteristics with accipiters but have a smaller supra-orbital process (and so lack the aquiline look of accipiters) and display other distinct differences, including a lack of sexual dimorphism. This is otherwise marked in most raptors, the size difference generally increasing with increased body size. Ospreys are large raptors but the dimorphism is marginal, females being the same size or only slightly larger (about 2%) than males. Ospreys also share some characteristics with Cathartiformes (New World vultures).

Identification   See p. 158

Large, elegant birds with long legs, large feet and a narrow head. The wings are long and narrow. Ospreys exhibit classic countershading: the throat, breast and belly are white and the undertail and underwing are pale to mid-gray, so the bird is hard to spot from below against the sky, helping it to catch fish. The back and upperwing are darker, making the bird hard to see against the water. This helps thwart kleptoparasites and predators (in areas where their ranges overlap, Ospreys endure piratical attacks from larger fish eagles). The adult head is

▲ Ospreys exhibit countershading, a light/dark color scheme common in animals that live or feed at the water's surface.

white, usually with some dark speckling, and has a distinct black stripe from eye to nape. The bill is black, gray at the base. The cere is blue-gray, the iris yellow. The white underbody is interrupted by a broad necklace of brown streaks. The upper body, wings and tail are uniformly dark brown but with lighter brown bands on the tail. If seen from above, the white head is distinctive. The undertail has narrow bars of dark brown/gray, while the underwing shows white coverts, a distinct dark wrist and primary tips and heavy dark barring on the remaining feathers. The feet are blue-gray. The soles are covered in spicules, and the outer toe can be moved back, both adaptations for gripping fish. Juveniles have lighter tips on the upper body and wing feathers, giving a somewhat indistinct pale barring. The head is more heavily streaked and the breast necklace is light brown. Downy chicks have a buff head, light brown upperparts with buff dorsal streak and initially cream underparts, molting to browner overall, but still with buff dorsal streak. Ospreys are long-lived, with reported ages of more than 30 years.

Confusion species

Viewed from beneath, as is usual, the Osprey is superficially similar to a juvenile Bald Eagle, but the narrower wings, overall whiter color, and dark feet are distinctive.

Size

L: 20–24 in. (50–60 cm). WS: 5–5¾ ft. (150–170 cm). W: 2¾–3¾ lb. (1.2–1.7 kg).

Voice

A series of short, high-pitched, whistles (*whee, whee* or *eep-eep*) or yelps (*che-up, che-up*), mostly heard during the breeding season. They are uttered by the male during courtship, or by either bird when alarmed near the nest.

Distribution

Circumpolar, but not found in Greenland, Iceland, or Svalbard. Occurs in northern Scandinavia, but south of the Arctic Circle in European and Asian Russia, though throughout Kamchatka.

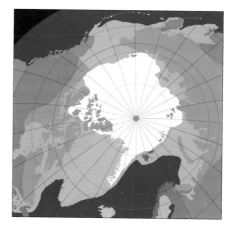

Rare throughout Alaska. Found in Yukon and at the treeline of the Northwest Territories, Hudson Bay, Quebec and Labrador. Outside the Arctic region, the Osprey has a curious distribution: in northern North America, northern Europe and central Russia but also in parts of southern Asia, Indonesia and Australia. Migratory, with Eurasian birds wintering chiefly in Africa and southern Asia and North American birds in the southern U.S., Mexico and South America. The Osprey's distribution is one of the largest of any diurnal raptor, and is probably only exceeded by that of the Peregrine Falcon. Ospreys favor freshwater lakes, but are also found in coastal areas, feeding from brackish water and from the sea.

Diet

Primarily fish of all species. Has been seen to take birds (chiefly waterfowl), amphibians and reptiles. Ospreys use a variety of fishing techniques. The bird flaps or glides across the water, occasionally hovering, while searching for prey. Dives can be from as high as 230 ft. (70 m) or as low as 16½ ft. (5 m), and can be high-angle (almost vertical on occasions) or very shallow, snatching fish from the surface. In dives the bird usually half-folds its wings before striking the water, and

▶ Female Osprey on the nest, Sirdalsvannet, Norway.

extends the legs and feet to catch its prey. Capture is often subsurface, the bird emerging with the fish and shaking vigorously to remove water as it rises with heavy wingbeats. The Osprey success rate is impressive, frequently as high as two captures from three dives. The fish is repositioned headfirst in flight to improve aerodynamic efficiency. The usual size of prey is about 11 oz. (300 g), but fish of up to 7 lb. (3¼ kg) are claimed. After feeding Ospreys wipe their bills to remove fish particles and scales, and may fly with their feet dangling in the water to clean them.

Breeding

Chiefly solitary, but loosely gregarious during winter, and occasionally nests in loose colonies. During courtship the male performs a "hover-flight"; he rises steeply to the point of stall, displaying the feet, in which he holds a fish or, occasionally, nest material. Males also perform a "sky-dance," a series of closed-wing dives followed by upswings, occasionally interspersed with flapping or gliding flight. Males also perform the sky dance to warn off rivals. Both male and female perform "high-circling" in which they glide above the nest site. All displays are usually very noisy. Pair-bond is monogamous and seasonal but perhaps renewed, as fidelity to nest site is high. Nest is of sticks, usually quite shallow and lined with moss, bark or grass, but can be very deep if refurbished over successive years. Construction is by both male and female. Nest is usually on top of a dead tree, but live trees and rocks (and even tall cacti in Mexico) can be used, as can artificial structures. May nest on the ground where predators are absent. Two to three cream/red-brown eggs are incubated by both birds (but female more frequently) for 35–40 days. Chicks nidicolous and semi-altricial, brooded by female. Fed by female, bill to bill at first, as male hunts. Fledge at 45–55 days, but are cared for over another 50 days. Breed at 3 years.

Taxonomy and geographical variation

Polytypic. The nominate subspecies breeds across the Palearctic; *P. h. carolinensis* breeds in the Nearctic. Other races are extralimital.

White-tailed (Sea) Eagle
Haliaeetus albicilla

Identification   See p. 158

Large and heavy-bodied, with a long neck and huge bill. The wings are long and broad, the tail short and wedge-shaped. Adults are mid-brown with paler head, neck and breast. The iris is yellow. The bill and cere are pale yellow. The flight feathers are dark brown. The tail is distinctively white, though with occasional brown mottling at tip and base. The upperbody feathers are pale-tipped, giving a scaly appearance. This scaling is almost entirely absent on the underwing. The legs and feet are yellow and the tarsi unfeathered, as for all northern fish eagles. Juveniles are darker, though they can also show gray/pale brown in a lighter form. The juvenile tail is longer and brown, though the feathers have pale centers (though these

are often difficult to see, even in flight). Body and wing feathers have dark tips and edges so that from above and below juveniles appear both darker and barred, particularly on the forewing. Immature birds may take five years to assume adult plumage, gradually acquiring the more uniform adult brown plumage and paler head, neck and breast, the tail whitening and losing the dark band of feather tips only at the final molt. Downy chicks are gray at first, molting to gray-brown.

Confusion species

Adult is unmistakable, but juvenile Golden Eagles have a white tail-base. Juveniles are similar to both adult and juvenile Golden Eagles. In general the White-tailed is bulkier, has a shorter, wedge-shaped tail (but the juvenile tail is longer), longer neck and larger bill, but confusion is possible, especially at a distance.

Size

L: 30–36 in. (75–90 cm). WS: 6¼–7¾ ft. (190–240 cm). W: 7¾–12 lb. (3.5–5.5 kg). The White-tailed Eagle is one of Europe's largest raptors, equaling the Lammergeier *Gypaetus barbatus* in weight.

Voice

A loud and shrill *kee-kee-kee*, the male's call higher than the female's. The alarm call is very similar, though sharper and lower in both male and female. Usually silent outside the breeding season.

Distribution

Palearctic. Breeds in west Greenland, western Iceland, northern Scandinavia (but not Svalbard) and across Russia as far as Chukotka and Kamchatka, though in general only on the Arctic coast east of the Kolyma Delta. Resident in the southern parts of the range, but migratory in the northernmost parts: eastern Russian birds head to Japan, China and Korea, and Scandinavian

▲ Adult White-tailed Eagle in flight, north Norway.

▶ Adult White-tailed Eagle, Karelia, Finland.

birds move south along the Norwegian coast of the North Sea and into the Baltic Sea. Greenland and Iceland birds are non-migratory. Although primarily considered to be a bird of the sea coast (and formerly known as the Sea Eagle in Europe), White-tailed Eagles are found not only at coastal sites, but also on lakes and rivers and even in wetlands with abundant prey.

Diet

Primarily fish, chiefly taken close to the surface as the bird glides over the water but also occasionally by diving. Also takes waterfowl, often by forcing them to dive repeatedly until exhausted and then taking them from the surface. Rarely takes birds in flight. Raids gull colonies for eggs and chicks, and will feed on carrion (e.g., dead sheep in Iceland and dead reindeer in Scandinavia). Also parasitizes birds such as gulls, Ospreys and other raptors. Will also take small mammals, amphibians and reptiles.

Breeding

Solitary, but may roost communally in winter. Pairs tend to stay together throughout the year. Show high-circling and sky dance similar to Osprey. High-circling may develop into mutual cartwheeling, as in other *Haliaeetus* species. Some

▼ Adult White-tailed Eagle, Karelia, Finland.

observers claim talon-grasping, but others do not. Talon-touching does seem to occur. Pair-bond monogamous and probably lifelong. Nests on cliff ledges and occasionally in tall trees. Nest built of sticks and driftwood, and lined with grass, moss and seaweed. The nest is a huge structure, particularly as it may be added to in successive years. One Icelandic nest, known to have been used for at least 150 years, was more than 10 ft. (3 m) deep and 8¼ ft. (2.5 m) across. Construction chiefly by the female, though male brings her material. Two to three cream/white eggs, incubated chiefly by female for 35-40 days. Chicks nidicolous and semi-altricial, brooded by female for up to 14 days. Chicks fed by female, bill-to-bill, though male provides majority of food. Fledge at 45–60 days, but cared for over a further 30–50 days. Breed at 3 years.

Taxonomy and geographical variation

Monotypic. Some authorities consider Greenlandic birds a subspecies, *H. a. groenlandicus*, but this view is not generally accepted.

Bald Eagle
Haliaeetus leucocephalus

The New World fish eagle and the emblem of the United States, where numbers are increasing after the sharp decline occasioned by the widespread use of organochlorines and subsidized slaughter. Until 1940, the shooting of eagles in the continental United States almost exterminated the species, and despite a protection act in that year, DDT continued to decimate the population. Since the banning of DDT in 1972, the population has begun a slow recovery. In Alaska, which remained a stronghold of the eagles and where the use of pesticides was minimal, a bounty on eagles was enacted in 1917 as a consequence of pressure from fishermen, fox farmers and trappers, who considered the birds a threat to their livelihood. The bounty act was not repealed until 1953.

▲ Adult Bald Eagle with chicks on the nest, Great Slave Lake, Canada.

Identification
See p. 158

See p. 158

Adult birds are unmistakable, having white heads and necks and fan-shaped white tails. The bird is named after its white head, as from a distance it appears "hairless." The bill, cere and iris are yellow, as are the legs and feet. There are sharp demarcations between both the neck and tail and the rest of the body, which is dark brown, as are the upper and lower wings. The uniform brown is interrupted only by pale feather tips on the upper wing, which give a scalloped appearance, and on the underwing by a pale gray patch at the base of the outer three or four primaries. Juveniles lack the white head and tail and have dark gray bills with a paler base (though the feet and legs are yellow). The overall color is mid-brown, generally with a reddish tinge. The back and upperwing are paler, with darker primaries and both leading and trailing edges. The tail edge is also darker. The underwing and undertail show significant white/pale gray areas with heavy streaking of dark brown. Second-year birds are heavily streaked dark brown and white. By the third year the bill color is changing, as is the head, which shows a distinct dark eye-stripe. Adult plumage is acquired in the fifth year. Downy chicks are pale gray-brown molting to darker gray-brown.

A unique feature of Bald Eagles is the "flare-up" display in which a bird will bank upward at a near vertical angle, wings flapping, to signal danger to nearby conspecifics.

Confusion species
Adult: none. Immature is similar to immature Golden Eagle, but usually whiter overall.

Size
L: 28–38 in. (70–95 cm). WS: 6–7¾ ft. (180–240 cm). W: 7¾–12 lb. (3.5–5.5 kg).

Voice
A wailing *yaah*, not unlike a gull, and a sharp *whee-whee*. The alarm call is a high-pitched *kah*. Male voice is higher

◀ This Bald Eagle has chosen the tip of an iceberg as a lofty (if chilly) perch to scan for food. Alaska.

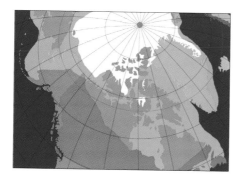

than female's. Vocal in all seasons, but especially so during breeding.

Distribution

Nearctic. Breeds across North America; the majority of the population lies north of the Great Lakes, though populations have now been re-established in the southern states. Particularly numerous in Alaska (perhaps 80% of the U.S. population). Occurs at coastal and inland water sites. Resident or migratory, though rarely travels far. The Alaskan population moves to the Aleutians and southern Alaskan coast in winter.

Diet

Primarily fish, but will take waterfowl, gulls and mammals as large as muskrats and rabbits. Also scavenges at garbage dumps. Famously fishes for salmon during the annual spawnings, often walking into shallow water to collect prey rather than diving. During the late salmon run in Alaska's Chilkat River, Bald Eagles congregate in huge numbers, and when perched look a little like candles on Christmas trees. There is an annual photographic competition for the number spotted in an individual tree, the winner often including almost 100 birds.

Breeding

Solitary during the breeding season but gregarious in winter. Pairs remain together throughout the year. Pairs perform a mutual soaring flight, and males occasionally chase females as well as performing a sky-dance. Males also have a "fly-around," where they patrol their territory. Pair flight often ends with talon-grasping and a cartwheeling fall. Pair-bond monogamous and lifelong. Nests are built in trees, sometimes on cliffs and other structures. Nests are used in successive years and may become vast, up to 13 ft. (4 m) deep and 10 ft. (3 m) across, constructed of sticks by both birds, and lined with grass and similar material. Two, occasionally three cream/buff eggs, incubated chiefly by female for 34–36 days. Fratricide is common, so often only a single chick is raised. Nidiculous, semi-altricial chick fed by female bill-to-bill while male hunts. Fledge at 70–80 days, but cared for another 50 days. Occasionally breed at 3 years, more commonly at 4–5 years.

▲ The symbol of the United States — the majestic Bald Eagle. This one is perching close to its nest.

Taxonomy and geographical variation

Generally considered polytypic, with two subspecies separated by size alone. *H. l. washingtoniensis* breeds north of 40°N, with the nominate race breeding to the south of this population.

◀ Juvenile Bald Eagle, Unalaska, Aleutian Islands.

Steller's Sea Eagle
Haliaeetus pelagicus

Identification See p. 158
The largest fish eagle. Indeed, apart from the Harpy (*Harpia harpyja*) and Philippine (*Pithecophaga jefferyi*) Eagles, Steller's is the largest of all eagles, and even then some Steller's are larger. Adult Steller's are magnificent, mostly dark brown/black, but with contrasting white tail, legs and forewing, the latter revealed as a white shoulder on the perched bird. There is also usually a white forehead patch. The massive bill (the largest of any raptor) is yellow, as are the legs and feet. The iris and cere are pale yellow. The tail is wedge-shaped. Juveniles are uniformly dark brown, though occasionally with paler mottling, particularly on the legs. The juvenile bill is dark brown. As the bird ages, the extent of mottling increases on the body and wings but decreases on the tail as it becomes white. Before adult plumage is assumed, usually in the sixth or seventh year, the overall plumage takes on a golden sheen. Downy chicks are gray, moulting to gray-brown.

Confusion species
Adults: none. Immature birds are very similar to White-tailed Eagles, but significantly larger.

▼ Adult Steller's Sea Eagle, the world's largest fish eagle, Zhupanova River, Kamchatka. Note the truly massive beak.

▲ Recently hatched Steller's Sea Eagle chick, southeast Kamchatka. In the background are the remnants of a salmon.

Size
L: 32–40 in. (80–100 cm). WS: 7 1/4–8 1/4 ft. (220–250 cm). W: 10–14 1/4 lb. (4.5–6.5 kg), but exceptionally females to 20 lb. (9kg).

Voice
Similar to the White-tailed Eagle, but lower and hoarser. There is also a deep, barking *rau-rau*.

Distribution
Breeds throughout Kamchatka, on northern Sakhalin and the northern Kuril Islands, along the coasts of the Sea of Okhotsk and the southern coast of Chukotka. Found on sea coasts and in river valleys. Resident where waters remain unfrozen. Winters on the coast south to Korea and Japan or, on Kamchatka, near lakes kept unfrozen by volcanic activity. Overlaps with White-tailed Eagle throughout its range.

Diet
Primarily fish, principally salmon. Feeds almost exclusively on salmon when the fish is available, changing diet only in times of scarcity. Fishes from a perch, but may also circle low over the water or by standing in shallow water. Adults parasitize immatures and other adults for food. When fish are not available, Steller's take waterfowl, gulls and game birds, and mammals including Arctic Fox and seal pups. They also scavenge on carrion at the tideline.

▼ Adult Rough-legged Buzzard of nominate race in flight.

and less streaking on breast. Juveniles also have a light patch at the base of the upperwing primaries, and a much lighter underwing, lacking the dark trailing edge. The undertail also lacks a distinct dark band. Downy chicks are gray-white, browner on the head initially, molting to a similar color but with a darker head.

Confusion species
None.

Size
L: 20–24 in. (50–60 cm). WS: 4–5 ft. (120–150 cm). W: 25–35¼ oz. (700–1,000 g).

Voice
Nominate race has a catlike mewing, but the voice of North American race *sanctijohannis* is less plaintive, more a whistling *keeah*. Quiet outside the breeding season.

Distribution
Circumpolar, but absent from Greenland and Iceland, and an irregular visitor only to Svalbard. Breeds across Eurasia, from Scandinavia to Kamchatka to the northern coast, but absent from Russia's Arctic islands. In North America, breeds across Alaska and the northern Canadian mainland, and on southern Canadian Arctic islands to northern Baffin, Banks, Victoria and Somerset Islands. European birds migrate to central and eastern Europe. Russian birds head south to the Ukraine, the Caucasus and Transbaikalia. North American birds winter across the United States but not the extreme south. The Rough-legged Buzzard prefers tundra and treeless mountains, but alsooccurs in the taiga if prey conditions are favorable. Winters in open country.

Diet
Feeds on small mammals, chiefly rodents, killed after a quartering flight or hovering, or occasionally by dive from a perch. Takes small birds in poor rodent years. Opportunistically takes fish, amphibians and reptiles and also scavenges carrion. Dependency on rodents not as marked as for, say, Snowy Owl: Rough-legged Buzzards will change diet if rodent numbers are low, with little apparent effect on breeding success.

Breeding
Solitary or in pairs at all times, but often gregarious during migration. Males sky-dance and pair engages in high-circling. Pair-bond monogamous and probably lifelong. Large nest of branches lined with grasses and fur or feathers from prey, on ground or cliff, less frequently on trees. Nest constructed by female, but male brings material. Two to five red-brown blotched white eggs, incubated almost entirely by female for 28–31 days. Chicks are nidicolous and semi-altricial, brooded continuously by female when newly hatched. Fed bill-to-bill by female at first, but by both parents when capable of tearing prey. Fratricide by strongest chick often occurs. Fledge in 35–45 days, but stay with parents for a further 15–20 days. Probably breed at 2–3 years.

Taxonomy and geographical variation
Polytypic. Nominate breeds in Eurasia as far east as the Yenisey River. *B. l. menzbieri* breeds from Yenisey to Pacific coast and is paler and larger. However, interbreeding takes place around Yenisey and some nominate birds are as pale and large as *menzbieri*, so some consider the distinction to be artificial. *B. l. kamtschatkensis* breeds in Kamchatka. It, too, is larger and paler than the nominate race. Subspecies *B. l. sanctijohannis* breeds in North America. These North American birds are generally darker than the nominate (though pale morphs exist) and have dark morphs in significant numbers (about 10% in Alaska to 40% in Labrador). Dark morphs are extremely rare or nonexistent in Eurasia; records of such birds may well refer to accidental *sanctijohannis*.

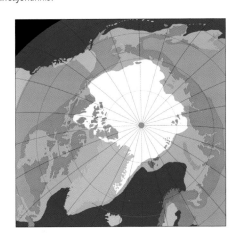

Northern Goshawk
Accipiter gentilis

Identification See p. 159

Adult has mid-gray, occasionally brownish-gray upperparts, the uppertail with four or five dark bands and a white tip, the upperwing having darker tips. The head is the same color, but with a distinct white supercilium. The iris is yellow, becoming orange with age. The cere is yellow-green. The bill is black, with a blue-gray base. The throat is white streaked with gray. The underparts are white with narrow gray bars, except at the vent, which is white, and the undertail, which is pale gray but shows the uppertail bars. Underwing similarly white with close, narrow barring. Females as males but much larger, paler and with more distinct supercilium. Legs and feet are yellow. Juveniles have mid-brown upper body and head, and gray-brown upperwing with distinct dark barring. Uppertail is grayer, with dark gray bands. Underparts are cream or buff with a droplike pattern of dark spots. Downy chicks are pale grayish white, molting to buff upperparts, pale grayish white underparts.

Confusion species

Adult may be confused with Gyrfalcon, particularly in north-eastern Siberia where Northern Goshawks are almost white, but the falcon shape and flight of a Gyr is distinctive. Goshawks have short, broad wings and fairly long, rounded tails. Northern Harrier has larger dark area on wingtips and lacks barring below.

▼ Adult female Northern Goshawk, Orre, Norway.

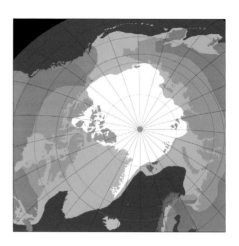

Size

L: 20–24 in. (50–60 cm). WS: 3–4 ft. (95–125 cm). W: 1½–2¾ lb. (650–1,250 g).

Voice

Loud, low, harsh *kak-kak*, most often heard at dawn. Quiet outside breeding season.

Distribution

Circumpolar and boreal, but absent from Greenland, Iceland, and Svalbard. Breeds from Scandinavia to Chukotka and Kamchatka, but only to the timberline. Uncommon in Alaska, but breeds to the timberline there and across Canada. Much of population is resident, but some birds migrate south.

◀ Adult male Northern Goshawk.

and in mutual calling, and females also call for food. Pair-bond monogamous and probably seasonal. Nest is of sticks high in a tree; also uses unoccupied nests of Ravens. In general, females build new nests, males refurbish old ones. Three to four blue-white eggs, incubated chiefly by female for 35–38 days. Chicks nidicolous and semi-altricial, brooded and fed bill-to-bill by female while male hunts. Fledge at 35–40 days, but cared for about 30–35 days longer. Breed at 2–3 years of age.

Taxonomy and geographical variation
Polytypic. The nominate race breeds in central and southern Palearctic. A. g. buteoides breeds from northern Scandinavia to the Kolyma Delta. It is larger, paler and less heavily barred. A. g. albidus breeds east of the Kolyma and on Kamchatka. This subspecies is increasingly pale to the east, and in Chukotka is essentially white, a magnificent bird. The North American race is A. g. atricapillus. It has blue-gray upperparts, indistinct, fine gray or no barring on the underparts and a much more distinct supercilium. Some authorities recognize another subspecies in northern North America. This is A. g. laingi, the "Queen Charlotte" Goshawk, which is much darker, and breeds on Queen Charlotte and Vancouver Islands. There are other, extralimital subspecies.

Diet
Birds and small mammals, hunted by rapid, agile flight through trees. The Northern Goshawk is astonishingly quick at maneuvering between trees in pursuit of prey, yet mostly kills on the ground. Birds to the size of Western Capercaillie (T. urogallus) and mammals to the size of hares are taken. Northern Goshawk numbers fluctuate with rodent numbers. Also takes insects and will occasionally feed on carrion.

Merlin
Falco columbarius

Identification
See p. 159
The smallest of the three Arctic falcons. Adult males have blue-gray upperparts with conspicuous black shaft-streaking. The head is blue-gray, but with an orange-buff nape, cream cheek patches and pale forehead (occasionally indistinct), all black-streaked. The iris is dark brown, the eye-ring and cere yellow. The bill is blue-black with a dark tip. The throat is cream, blending to buff-orange underparts with dark brown streaks and drops, heavy on the flanks. The upperwing shows dark primaries (dark gray or gray-brown). The uppertail has a broad dark terminal band and several less distinct narrow bands. This coloration is repeated on the undertail. The underwing shows buff-orange coverts blending to grayish-cream flight feathers, all with conspicuous dark barring. Adult females show the same color pattern, but dark brown above and cream-buff below. However, the head is more distinctly marked, with clearer mustachial stripes, and the tail-barring (broad dark brown/narrow buff) is also more distinct. Juveniles as female, but darker above and below, with much more distinct barring on the upperwing and back. Downy chicks are cream/white, molting darker.

Breeding
Generally solitary. Males sky-dance and perform perch-and-call, choosing a perch within territory and calling loudly, especially at dawn (see Voice). A pair will engage in high-circling

▲ Juvenile Northern Goshawk.

Confusion species
None.

Size
L: 10–12½ in. (25–32 cm). WS: 21½–26 in. (55–65cm). W: 5¼–8¾ oz. (150–250 g).

▲ Adult male Merlin, northern Norway.

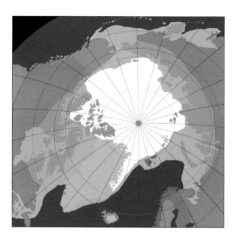

Voice

A rapid *kikiki* alarm call, usually only heard in the vicinity of the nest. Also a short *peek*, most often made by juveniles seeking food. Usually silent outside breeding season.

Distribution

Circumpolar. Absent from Greenland, Svalbard and Kamchatka. Breeds in Iceland and across Eurasia, though not to northern coast except near the Barents Sea. Rare throughout Alaska, but found in northern Yukon and Northwest Territories, around southern Hudson Bay and in Quebec and Labrador. Found in open areas, avoiding heavily forested country. Resident and migratory. Some Icelandic birds remain on the island, others migrate to western Europe. Eurasian birds move to central and southern Europe and southern central Russia. North American birds move to the southern United States, Central America and northern South America.

Diet

Feeds on small birds (e.g., thrushes, pipits, small waders), usually caught on the wing after being flushed by low flight. Also takes insects and small rodents. Will occasionally pursue prey for some distance, but usually spots prey, rises, then descends at speed to flush and capture. Combined hunting by a pair or even several birds has been observed.

▼ Adult female Merlin, northern Norway.

Breeding

Solitary, but seen in pairs and occasionally hunts and roosts communally. Males have a short, fluttering display flight and feed the female at proposed nest site (rarely in the air). Pair-bond monogamous and perhaps long-lived. Nest is on ground in thick cover or on cliff ledge, occasionally uses old nests of other birds. Nest is little more than a scrape, usually with minimal lining of vegetation. Three to five heavily red-blotched buff eggs, incubated by both parents (female predominantly) for 28–32 days. Chicks nidicolous and semi-altricial, brooded and fed bill-to-bill by female while male hunts. Fledge in 25–30 days and are independent after a further 25–30 days. Breed at 1 year.

Taxonomy and geographical variation

Polytypic. The plumage described above is race *aesalon*, which breeds in northern Europe and eastward to central Siberia. The nominate is the North American Merlin, which breeds at the timberline. Nominate race differs in lacking rufous nape, having a more heavily barred tail and more uniformly blue-gray upperwing. *F. c. subaesalon* breeds in Iceland. It is larger and darker than *aesalon*. *F. c. insignis* breeds in central eastern Siberia. It is paler overall than *aesalon*, has a much paler forehead and less streaking on the underparts. *F. c. pacificus* breeds on the Pacific margin of east Siberia. It is darker than both *aesalon* and the nominate and similar to *F. c. suckleyi*, a North American subspecies of the Pacific Northwest. Other extralimital subspecies are also recognized.

Peregrine Falcon
Falco peregrinus

One of the world's best-known birds. Following a drastic decline in the 1950s and 1960s as a result of the widespread use of organochlorine pesticides (specifically DDT), it has benefited from a series of reintroduction/conservation programs, together with protection laws. These have been successful in raising numbers and public awareness. Peregrine populations are now much healthier in western Europe and North America, though the situation is not as good in all parts of the range.

Identification   See p. 159

A compact, powerful falcon. Adult birds have dark blue-gray upperparts, including the crown of the head and nape. The throat and cheeks are white. There is a highly distinctive broad, blue-gray mustache. The iris is dark brown, the eye-ring and cere yellow. The bill is blue-gray, yellowish at the base, with a black nail. The uppertail is heavily dark-barred, the upperwings also barred but more distally; barring is most visible on the rump, which is paler than the rest of the upperparts. The underparts are cream, sometimes pale buff, with a pattern of black markings: drops on the breast and heart-shaped spots on the belly and thighs that merge to form bars. The underwing is cream with black barring on the coverts and dark gray barring on the flight feathers. In general females are more heavily marked than males. The legs and feet are yellow. Juveniles

▼ Adult male Peregrine Falcon of the northern race *tundrius*, Nunavut, Canada.

are patterned as adults, but the basic upperpart color is dark brown (with barring from paler feather fringes), and the underpart color is cream/buff with dark brown markings. Downy chicks are white, molting to pale gray.

Confusion species
Gray-morph Gyrfalcons are similar, particularly when viewed in the air from below. The heavier build and longer tail of the Gyr is distinctive. On perched birds, the more uniform upperpart coloration and broad mustache of the Peregrine aid identification.

Size
L: 13³/₄–18 in. (35–45cm). WS: 3–3¹/₂ ft. (90–110cm). W: 21–35¹/₄ oz. (600–1,000 g).

Voice
Display call is sharp, two-syllable *ee-chup*. Normal call is a harsh *rek-rek-rek*, often repeated at length.

Distribution
Cosmopolitan species breeding on every continent bar Antarctica; circumpolar in the Arctic. Breeds on Greenland (particularly on the western coast), but absent from Iceland and Svalbard. Breeds across Eurasia, including southern island of Novaya Zemlya, but excluding the other Russian Arctic islands. In North America, breeds in Alaska (though only commonly in southwest) on parts of northern Canadian

▼ Adult female Peregrine Falcon of race *tundrius* on nest, Nunavut, Canada. Note the variation in appearance of the eggs.

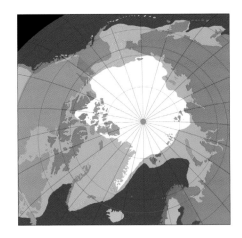

mainland, and southern Arctic islands (Banks, Victoria, Southampton and Baffin). Found in open terrain, including tundra, and also on the coast. Resident and migratory. Some Greenland birds apparently remain throughout winter, but others move to the southern United States. North American and Eurasian populations move south to the tropics.

Diet
Primarily other birds, often specializing on single local prey. Famous for its fast stoop onto prey after spotting it from high observation flight. Popular idea that Peregrines hit prey at full speed is untrue, as this would also cause extensive damage to falcon, but observations suggest that occasionally prey is "raked" by clenched foot at high speed, causing sufficient injury to drop

prey to the ground or stun it for easy capture. Some observations suggest that a talon is left unfurled, which would explain instances where the struck bird was lacerated along the back. The speed of stoop is hotly debated, with claims of up to 200 mph (400 km/h). In reality the highest measured speed is around 90 mph (140 km/h), lower than that measured for the Gyrfalcon. Theoretical speeds to 160 mph (260 km/h) have been calculated for "ideal" falcons and it is, of course, possible that speeds above 85 mph (140 km/h) are achieved. Peregrines also catch prey in pursuit flight, dispatching the prey with a bite to the nape. Such prey may even be partially plucked and eaten in flight: Peregrines have been observed catching and eating several bats without landing. Coastal Peregrines will feed on auks and gulls. Mountain Peregrines also feed on rodents.

Breeding

Solitary or in pairs. Flight displays include high-circling and food transfer, and the male has a variation of sky-dance with rolls and other maneuvers. There are also a number of ledge displays, with the birds calling *ee-chupp* while lowering the head, either singly or together. Pair-bond monogamous and often lifelong. Nesting can be in an old nest of a different species or on an inaccessible cliff ledge. On cliffs there is no nest as such, merely a scrape. Three to four cream eggs

▲ Adult male *tundrius* Peregrine Falcon in flight, Nunavut, Canada.

▼ Juvenile Peregrine Falcon of the nominate subspecies in flight, northern Norway.

heavily blotched red-brown; incubated by both parents, but chiefly the female, for 29–32 days. Chicks nidicolous and semi-altricial, brooded and fed bill-to-bill by female while male hunts. Fledge in 35–42 days and are independent after a further 50–60 days. Breed at 2 years.

Taxonomy and geographical variation

Polytypic. The nominate race breeds in central Europe from Great Britain to the Yenisey River. *F. p. calidus* breeds north of the nominate to the shores of the Arctic Ocean and in Novaya Zemlya, and east to the Lena Delta. It is larger than the nominate (by up to 15%) and has longer wings and much less barring on the underparts. *F. p. japonensis* breeds in Chukotka, on Kamchatka, around the Sea of Okhotsk and in northern Japan. It is darker than the nominate race (and on islands in the Sea of Okhotsk birds are so dark that some claim a separate subspecies, *F. c. pleskei*). In North America, *F. p. anatum* breeds from Alaska to Labrador. It is darker above and paler below than the nominate race; juvenile *anatum* is very dark. To the north, *F. p. tundrius* (the Nearctic equivalent of *calidus*) is smaller than *anatum* and paler on the breast; indeed, some birds have almost no barring. There are at least 13 extralimital subspecies.

Gyrfalcon
Falco rusticolus

Together with Snowy Owl, Ross's Gull and Ivory Gull, the ultimate find for the Arctic birder, particularly the white morph. Recently the scientific name has been questioned, with the suggestion that *F. gyrfalco* has precedence.

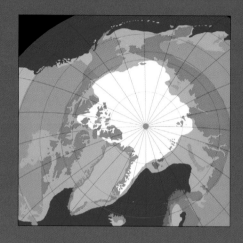

Identification
See p. 159

The world's largest falcon. A large, heavy bird with morphs ranging from very dark to almost pure white, with white birds the most sought-after. White adults are almost entirely white, usually with black wingtips and some black spotting or barring on the wings and breast. There is a distinct gray eye-stripe and mustache. The iris is dark brown, the eye-ring yellow. The cere and feet are yellow (though young birds have blue feet). The bill is blue-gray with a darker tip. In "gray" birds, the upperparts are slate-gray with irregular barring from dark feather edgings, and the underparts are white with gray barring. The extent of barring varies from very light to very heavy. In the former the barring is replaced by dark spots, which may form lines on the breast, and discontinuous bars on the belly, while in the latter the bird appears to have alternate dark gray and white bars. In Icelandic birds, the slate-gray upperparts show irregular white, rather than dark, barring. In extreme cases, the adult can be overall dark brown above and very heavily barred and spotted dark brown below. To complicate matters further, adults of different morphs mate, and broods can be of several morphs. Downy chicks are cream/white, molting darker.

Confusion species
White birds: none. Gray birds: possible confusion with Peregrine Falcon.

Size
L: 20–24 in. (50–60 cm). WS: 4¼–5¼ ft. (130–160 cm). W: 1¾–3½ lb. (800–1,600 g).

Voice
Most often heard is the hoarse *kwa-kwa* alarm call. Displaying pair make a *chup* call.

Distribution
Circumpolar. Breeds in Greenland (west, northwest and northeast) and Iceland, but absent from Svalbard. Breeds across Eurasia, but not on Russian Arctic islands. Breeds across North America including high Arctic Canadian islands (e.g., Ellesmere). Found on tundra and on coasts. Eastern Greenland birds move to Iceland. Russian birds move south, as do North American birds, but all remain within the tundra. Though the Gyr is widely assumed to be the world's most northerly breeding raptor, the northernmost nesting record is held by a Peregrine.

Diet
Almost exclusively grouse, which winter in the high Arctic, explaining the limited migration of the Gyr. Also takes other birds and small mammals. Gyrs hunt chiefly by quartering low across the ground in a harrierlike fashion, but also fly high and stoop, as Peregrines

◀ Adult male white morph Gyrfalcon, Nunavut, Canada. An unmistakable and stunning member of the Arctic avifauna.

do. Stoop speeds of 105–126 mph (170–203 km/hr) make the Gyr the fastest bird in measured flight. The switch from quartering to stooping is adaptive for hunting their primary prey: grouse are fast in short flights and can often outfly a pursuing Gyrfalcon, reaching cover before being overtaken. The Gyr's best strategies, therefore, are to flush the grouse and catch it before it has time to accelerate, or to use stoop speed to catch a bird in full flight.

▲ Adult female gray-morph Gyrfalcon coming in to land, Norway.

Breeding
Solitary or in pairs. Aerial and ledge displays as Peregrine. Pair-bond monogamous and probably long-lived. The Gyrfalcon is the earliest breeder of any northern bird (with the possible exception of the Raven), preparing the nest (such as it is) in early March in Iceland and laying eggs in early May, even in the high Arctic. Does not build a nest, using nests of other birds (chiefly Raven) on cliff or in tree, or laying in scrape on cliff ledge. Sites are used in successive years; some have been used for decades, perhaps centuries. Three to four creamy buff eggs blotched with red; incubated by both birds, but predominantly female, for 34–37 days. Chicks nidicolous and semi-altricial, brooded and fed bill-to-bill by female while male hunts. Fledge in 45–50 days and are independent in a further 30–40 days. Breed at 2 years.

Taxonomy and geographical variation
Monotypic, but numerous subspecies have been suggested historically to account for color variation. In general, white birds are found in northeastern Siberia, northern Canada and northern Greenland, with gray and dark birds in southern parts of the range.

▲ An adult female gray-morph Gyrfalcon on the nest, Nunavut, Canada. She feeds her young by passing flesh from bill to bill.

PLATE 7: OSPREY AND EAGLES

Osprey

ad

juv

White-tailed Eagle

ad

ad

Steller's Sea Eagle

ad

imm

Bald Eagle

Golden Eagle

ad

ad

PLATE 8: HAWKS AND FALCONS

Northern Goshawk

♂

Merlin

♂

♀

Northern Harrier

♂

Rough-legged
Buzzard

♂

ad

white morph

ad

Peregrine
Falcon

Gyrfalcon

juv

dark
morph

ad

dark morph

ad

white morph

Grouse

Grouse are, in many ways, the characteristic birds of the Arctic. They are resident, surviving the cold, dark winter beneath insulating snow blankets, eating whatever vegetation they can find and changing color to avoid predation. Wintering grouse are white, apart from their black tails, which, presumably, are a signaling device, as the birds are gregarious in winter. Further adaptations include feathered feet (which some authorities suggest are as much for gripping the snow as for insulation) and feathered nostrils; strong, clawed toes that allow burrowing into the snow; large crops and gizzards to accommodate the vast quantities of poor-quality food they must consume; and long intestinal tracts, in which symbiotic microbes assist in the digestion of cellulose, and oils and resins in pine needles, which would otherwise be both indigestible and poisonous. Grouse are abundant in virtually all vegetated areas of the Arctic, and so are a major constituent of the area's biomass. Consequently, they are also an important food source for terrestrial and avian predators.

Willow Grouse (Willow Ptarmigan)
Lagopus lagopus

Identification
See p. 168

Adults have three plumages each year: the breeding plumage of spring/early summer molts to non-breeding, which molts to winter, which molts to breeding. Breeding males have rich red-brown upperparts, throat and upper chest with darker barring. The iris is dark brown, the eye-ring white. The bill is dark brown, as is the feathering at its base. There is a conspicuous red "eyebrow." The underbody is white, the wings white with brown scalloping. The legs are white. The tail has central white feathers (which are actually elongated tail-coverts), with black on either side. Breeding females are overall tawny-brown with darker barring. Some white winter feathers are retained, particularly on the underparts; the red eyebrow is much less conspicuous. Wings as male, but upperwing-coverts are as upper body to maintain camouflage when perched. Similarly, upperside of central tail feathers is as upper body. Non-breeding adults are darker, vermiculated tawny, with some white on belly, wings and tail as in breeding birds. Adult winter birds are white apart from black tail feathers. Claws are dark brown. Juveniles undergo rapid plumage changes, but are essentially gray-brown with primaries 9 and 10 white. Downy chicks are buff/rich brown.

▲ Adult female Willow Grouse, tundra scrub, Churchill.

Confusion species
(Rock) Ptarmigan (*Lagopus muta*). Breeding females of this species are duller, the males dark brown rather than rich red-brown. In winter only the stouter bill of Willow Grouse distinguishes females, but the male Ptarmigan has black lores.

Size
L: 13³/₄–16 in. (35–40 cm). WS: 21¹/₂–26 in. (55–65 cm). W: 18–25 oz. (500–700 g).

Voice
A rapid, pulsating *ka-ka-ka* when flushed and in flight. When the bird lands, the call is terminated with *ko-ah, ko-ah,* often repeated many times. There is also a single *cluck.*

Distribution
Circumpolar, but absent from Greenland, Iceland, and Svalbard. Breeds across Eurasia as far as northern shore and also on the New Siberian Islands. Breeds across North America to northern coast of Alaska and Canada and on southern Canadian Arctic islands (Banks, Victoria, southern Baffin). Found wherever there is an adequate food supply. All populations resident except in Russia, where birds are partially migratory.

Diet
Almost exclusively vegetarian, but chicks feed on insects. Adults eat buds and catkins chiefly of Arctic Willow, though birch may also be taken as well as any available berries. In winter eats twigs, primarily of willow, and pine needles at the timberline.

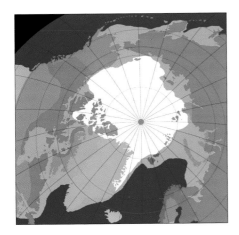

the variations in color, pattern, size and molt are often within the degree of variability seen in the nominate (which breeds in Scandinavia and northern European Russia). The following currently recognized subspecies are Arctic breeders:

L. l. alascensis	mainland Alaska
L. l. alba	mainland Canada from Yukon to the Gulf of St. Lawrence
L. l. birulai	New Siberian Islands
L. l. kamtschatkensis	Kamchatka
L. l. koreni	northern Eurasia
L. l. leucoptera	Baffin, Banks, Southampton and Victoria Islands
L. l. muriei	Aleutian Islands and Kodiak Island
L. l. ungavus	northern Quebec and Labrador

Breeding

Solitary or gregarious, depending on season and on other factors not entirely understood. Where *Lagopus lagopus* and *L. muta* are both found (as is frequently the case), the species coexist in winter but do not mingle. In the breeding season, males of the two species compete for territories, leading to a clear territorial demarcation. Male displays include a complex series of wing-drooping, tail-fanning, strutting, bowing and stamping behaviors. The pair-bond is monogamous and often relatively long-lasting. The nest is placed in the thickest available cover. It is a shallow scrape lined with available vegetation. Six to nine pale-yellow eggs blotched dark brown, incubated for 20–25 days by female only; female covers eggs when absent. Chicks nidifugous and precocial. Cared for by both parents, but brooded when first hatched by female alone. Fledge in 30–35 days, but may fly at 12 days, and independent after further 40–55 days. Breed at 1 year.

▲ Adult male Willow Grouse molting to summer plumage.

Taxonomy and geographical variation

Polytypic. At least 15 subspecies have been documented, but

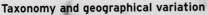

◀ A party of Willow Grouse in winter plumage in southern Alaska.

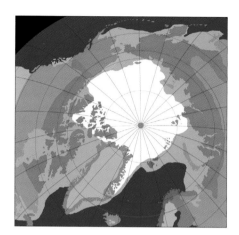

▲ Adult female Ptarmigan, late summer. NE Greenland.

Rock Ptarmigan
Lagopus muta

Identification See p. 168

Breeding males have head, neck, upper breast and back/upper-central tail dark gray-brown, heavily vermiculated dark gray and with thin, discontinuous white barring. The iris is dark brown, the eye-ring white. The bill is black. There is a prominent red eyebrow. The lores are black. The tail feathers are black. The wings and remaining underbody are white, occasionally with the upper-body coloration on the inner coverts. Breeding females are patterned as the male, but the base color is brown rather than gray-brown, and the vermiculation tawny rather than black. Non-breeding males are grayer, the wing-coverts are also gray so that less white is visible. Non-breeding females are similar but darker. Winter adults are white apart from black tails, though the males retain black lores. The claws are dark blue. Juveniles are as non-breeding females, but the tail is as body color rather than black. The wings are also similar, occasionally showing some white on the outer primaries. Downy chicks are cream-gray/dark brown.

Confusion species
Willow Grouse. See above.

Size
L: 12–13¾ in. (30–35 cm). WS: 20–24 in. (50–60 cm). W: 11–21 oz. (300–600 g).

Voice
Almost identical to the Willow Grouse, but has a larger repertoire of clucks, and males have a curious hissing, unlike any part of male Willow Grouse vocabulary; this is used as a defensive/threat call.

Distribution
Circumpolar. Breeds throughout Greenland, Iceland, and Svalbard. Breeds across Eurasia, probably (but not definitely) including Franz Josef Land. Breeds across North America, including Canadian Arctic islands as far north as northern central Ellesmere. Found wherever there is an adequate food supply. All populations are resident, though northern dwellers may move south if food is unavailable.

Diet
Almost exclusively vegetarian, feeding on catkins, buds, seeds and twigs, chiefly of birch. Since *L. muta* tends to occupy higher and/or more northerly areas than *L. lagopus*, its diet is often much more restricted. For example, birds on Amchitka, one of the Aleutian Islands, exist almost exclusively on Crowberry, while for some Spitsbergen birds, Alpine Bistort constitutes more than 80% of their diet. As with *L. lagopus*, chicks feed largely on insects, particularly during their first few days of life.

Breeding
More gregarious than *L. lagopus*, though still usually found singly or in pairs. See *L. lagopus* for comments on intermingling. Bond and male displays as *L. lagopus*. The nest is a scrape with no or minimal lining (available vegetation and

▲ Pair of Ptarmigan in winter plumage, north Norway.

female breast feathers), formed by both male and female. Five to eight buff eggs, botched dark brown; incubated by female for 20–24 days. Chicks nidifugous and precocial. Cared for by both parents. Can fly at 10–15 days. Fledge at 30–35 days and are independent after further 40–50 days. Breed at 1 year.

Taxonomy and geographical variation
Polytypic. Status even less clear than the taxonomy of Willow Grouse with some 30 subspecies documented (26 in North America/Greenland alone). As with the Willow Grouse, the differences are often within the range of variations of the nominate (which breeds in Scandinavia and on the Kola Peninsula). Within the Arctic the following are recognized:

L. m. hyperborea	Svalbard and Franz Josef Land
L. m. islandorum	Iceland
L. m. pleskei	northern Russian Asia
L. m. krascheninnikovi	Kamchatka Peninsula
L. m. ridgwayi	Commander Islands
L. m. rupestris	northern Canada including Arctic islands to southern Greenland
L. m. saturata	west Greenland
L. m. capta	northeast Greenland
L. m. nelsoni	Yukon, Alaska, Unimak, Unalaska

Up to seven endemic subspecies are recognized in the Aleutians. From west to east, these are *evermanni* (Attu), *townsendi* (Kiska), *gabrielsoni* (Amchitka, Little Sitkin and Rat Islands), *sanfordi* (Tanaga), *chamberlaini* (Adak), *atkhensis* (Atka) and *yunaskensis* (Yunaska).

Two other grouse species occur to the edge of the timberline and so may be observed in the Arctic.

Spruce Grouse
Falcipennis canadensis

Identification See p. 168
Males have dark-brown upperparts vermiculated black. The head is dark brown/black with a prominent red eyebrow, and white stripes around the eye and on the cheeks. The iris is dark brown, the bill black. The underparts are black with white barring on the upper breast and white spotting on the lower chest, belly and flanks. The tail is dark brown with a distinct orange-brown tip. Females are as males in color pattern, but two color morphs occur, with basic color either red-brown or gray. In each case the barring of the underparts differs: white and black in gray birds, black and dark brown in red-brown birds. The tail has an orange-brown tip, as on the male. Juveniles are as red-brown females, but with white spotting on the wing-coverts. Downy chicks are dark/light brown.

Confusion species
None.

Size
L: 15–18 in. (38-45 cm). WS: 20–24 in. (50-60 cm). W: 1–1½ lb. (450-650 g).

Voice
Displaying males have a low hoot. Male and female have several clucks, but in general the Spruce is the quietest of the grouse.

Distribution
Nearctic and boreal. Breeds in central Alaska (rare in west and north), across Yukon and central Canada, including southern Hudson Bay, and northwards in Quebec and Labrador. Resident but many move short distances south in winter.

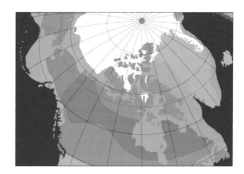

Diet
Primarily seeds and buds of northern conifers. Often seen climbing among the branches of conifers.

Breeding
Solitary or in pairs, but occasionally gregarious in winter. Males display as other grouse, but are promiscuous, establishing

▼ Adult male Spruce Grouse, southern Hudson Bay.

territories that encompass several females. Nest is a scrape among dead needles, placed on the ground at the base of a conifer. Five to six brown-blotched olive eggs incubated by female only for 21–24 days. Chicks nidifugous and precocial. Fledge at 30–35 days and are independent in another 45–50 days. Breed at 1 year.

Taxonomy and geographical variation
Polytypic. Nominate race, the Taiga Grouse, breeds from central Alaska to Labrador. Other subspecies are extralimital.

Black-billed Capercaillie
Tetrao parvirostris

Identification
See p. 169
Similar to but smaller than the Western Capercaillie (*T. urogallus*), with which it is sympatric in central Siberia. Males have black heads with purple or blue-purple sheen. The bill is black, the iris dark brown and eyebrows a distinctive red. The breast is black with a green sheen, the lower underparts brown/black with white spotting. The upperparts are dark brown with some white flecking and distinctive white spotting on the upper tail. The wings are dark brown with large white spots, particularly on the coverts. The underwings are dark brown, but with white coverts that show as white shoulders. Females have red-buff head and neck, with black-and-white streaking from feather edges. The underparts are red-buff with black barring and white flecking. The back and upperwings are dark brown with buff barring and white flecking, the coverts have terminal white spots. The rump is paler. The underwings are red-buff with black

barring. The tail is dark brown with black barring and a white edge. The feet are dark brown. Juveniles are poorly documented but are, apparently, as female. Downy chicks are red-buff.

Confusion species
Western Capercaillie, though this is larger. Male Western has a throat "beard," a much paler bill and much less white spotting. There is little overlap of the two in the Arctic.

Size
L: 28–38 in. (70–95 cm). WS: 2½–3¾ ft. (75–115 cm). W: 3¼–4¾ lb. (1.5–2.2 kg).

Voice
A very loud, rippling *tak-tak* and a series of clicks.

Distribution
Palearctic. Confined to Siberia, east of about 100°E. Does not extend north of the taiga, so has a limited range in Chukotka. Found throughout Kamchatka. Found in taiga, particularly birch and mixed forests. Non-migratory.

Diet
Buds, pine needles and berries, with seasonal variation much as other grouse.

Breeding
Solitary, though females are gregarious toward the end of the breeding season. Males form leks, but aggregations are smaller and looser than for Black Grouse (*T. tetrix*). Males are polygamous, forming small harems if they can. Nests are chiefly placed in deciduous areas. They consist of little more than a scrape with minimal lining. Six or seven spotted ochre-brown eggs incubated by female only for 20–25 days. Chicks nidifugous and precocial, cared for by female only. Fledge at 50–70 days (but are capable of flight much earlier, about 15–25 days) and are independent at that time. Males probably breed at 3 years, females at 2.

Taxonomy and geographical variation
Polytypic. The nominate subspecies breeds in central Siberia. *T. p. kamschaticus* breeds in Kamchatka. It is smaller and paler, and has more white markings. Males are also gray rather than black. There is a further subspecies found south of Lake Baikal.

▲ Female Black-billed Capercaillie. Like Spruce Grouse, these birds are taiga specialists.

Cranes

A flock of migrating Sandhill Cranes approach their breeding grounds at Churchill.

Cranes are among the most elegant of birds, tall and graceful, both in flight and on the ground. They are one of the oldest bird groups and the tallest of flying birds. Though usually thought of as birds of tropical or temperate wetlands, two species are Arctic breeders. In common with other cranes, the Arctic species do not have webbed feet. Cranes are famous for their dancing displays. They pair for life and rarely breed before four or five years of age. Many species raise only a single chick, so their productivity is low. This makes them particularly vulnerable to habitat destruction and hunting, and many cranes are endangered.

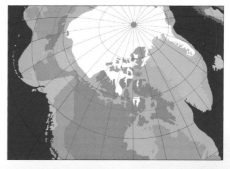

Sandhill Crane
Grus canadensis

Identification See p. 169
Adult breeding Sandhill Cranes are unmistakable, with bare red lores, red forehead to eye level and red crown. The rest of the face is white, blending to pale gray on the long neck. The iris is orange or brown-orange, the bill is gray. The upper body is red-buff with gray flecking, the upperwing similar, but often with greater areas of gray and a dark-gray trailing edge. The underparts and wing are pale gray. The legs and feet are dark gray. In winter adults are overall pale gray, but with indistinct dark gray barring and red-buff on the outer feathers of the upperwing. Juveniles are similar to adults, but the red-buff is both paler and less red, and the red head coloring is absent. Sandhills fly with extended neck and feet (though the feet are tucked into body feathers in cold weather). Downy chicks have brown upperparts, with pale tawny/buff underparts.

Confusion species
None.

Size
L: 3–3½ ft. (90–110 cm), body length 16–20 in. (40–50 cm). WS: 6–6¾ ft. (180–210 cm). W: 6¼–8½ lb. (2.8–3.8 kg).

▶ Displaying male Sandhill Crane — an amazing spectacle. Churchill.

Voice
An unmistakable, rippling *gar-oo-oo*, once memorably described as being a cross between a French horn and a squeaky barn door. Once heard, never forgotten, the call is why the Sandhill is occasionally called the garoo in the United States. The call carries great distances and often the birds, which are nervous and elusive, are heard but not seen.

▲ Sandhill Crane nest, Chukotka.

Distribution
Eastern Russia/western North America. Breeds in North America from Alaska to Hudson Bay, extending north to Banks, Victoria and Baffin Islands, and in eastern Siberia from the Kolyma Delta to northeastern Chukotka. Migratory, with Siberian birds crossing the Bering Sea to join American birds in migratory flight to southern United States. Found in forested areas and on open tundra, in wetland and on tidal flats.

Diet
Wetland vegetation including seeds, buds and berries, but also insects and larvae, snails, reptiles, amphibians and young birds. Migrants feed on stubble, but also in cereal and potato fields.

Breeding
Gregarious at all times. As many as eight male displays have been recorded, including an upright wing stretch, horizontal head pump, vertical leaps (some to 8¼ ft./2.5 m, usually with wings half-open and calling) and head-tosses. In conjunction these amount to a "crane dance." Pair-bond is monogamous and long-lived. Breeds in dry, concealed place close to wetlands (in south of the range nests are built over water). Nests often made from twigs, usually with minimal or no lining. One to three (usually two) pale brown or pale olive eggs blotched gray-brown or red-brown, incubated by both birds for 29–32 days. Chicks are nidifugous and precocial. Leave nest within 24 hours. Chicks are brooded by the female, but fed by both birds. Fledge at 50–56 days, but fly at about 70 days. Breed at 3–4 years.

Taxonomy and geographical variation
Polytypic. The nominate race is the northern breeder (and is occasionally known in North America as the Lesser Sandhill Crane). Five extralimital (southern) subspecies are larger and are usually much less brown in breeding plumage.

Siberian White Crane
Grus leucogeranus

Identification See p. 169
Standing adults are pure white (though the black wing feathers are occasionally visible), with red lores, forehead and crown. The iris is pale yellow. The bill is red or red-brown. The head and neck are occasionally stained rusty from local iron-rich waters. In flight adults show black primaries, primary coverts and alula. The legs and feet are pink, deepening to red during the breeding season. Juveniles are red-buff with no red on the head, but significant white flecking and spotting overall. The extent of

red-buff decreases over four years, with the white adult plumage obtained at that time, though the red head is visible at two years. Downy chicks have cinnamon and buff upperparts, white underparts with rufous patches.

Confusion species
None.

Size
L: 4–4½ ft. (120–140 cm), body 24–26 in. (60–65 cm). WS: 7½–8½ ft. (230–260cm). W: 10¾–15¼ lb. (4.9–6.9 kg).

Voice
Quiet for a crane. Usual call is a rolling *turr-turr*, but in flight there is also a musical rippling *tooya*.

Distribution
Russia. Rare and critically endangered, with a population estimated at no more than a few hundred. There are two breeding populations, one in northern Yakutia between the Indigirka and Yana Rivers, the other (a much smaller population) on the Ob River. The Ob birds migrate to northern India and Iran, the Yakutia birds to China. Migrating birds from the critically endangered western population cross the Himalayas and have been seen at heights to 18,000 ft. (5,500 m). The cranes are found in wetlands and on riverbanks, frequently wading in pools and shallow river waters. The destruction of wintering sites, along with hunting, has led to a dramatic reduction in numbers.

Diet
Chiefly the roots and tubers of water plants, but also takes insects, reptiles, amphibians and small rodents. Often feeds by probing in the mud at the bottom of the water in which it wades. Does not feed on cultivated fields.

Breeding
Pairs solitary during the breeding season, but gregarious at wintering sites. In the display dance, the male's wings are half-extended and flutter noisily, the head lowered, the neck and

▲ Siberian White Crane chick, Kolyma Delta.

bill parallel to the ground, then raised, the bird calling loudly as it circles its intended mate. Pair-bond is monogamous and probably long-lasting. The nest is large, made of vegetation and placed on a dry rise near a lake or wetland area, often on a raised island in the water. Two (rarely one) violet- or red-brown spotted pale olive eggs are incubated for 28–30 days, by the female, while the male stands guard. The male is very hostile to potential predators and will see off an Arctic Fox. Usually only one chick survives. The cranes are exceptionally nervous of humans, so any approach causes incubating birds to move away, which may result in loss of either eggs or chicks, further reducing breeding success. Chicks are nidifugous and precocial, brooded by female and fed by both birds. Fledge at 40–50 days. Probably breed at 6–7 years.

Taxonomy and geographical variation
Monotypic.

▼ Pair of Siberian White Cranes, Kolyma Delta.

PLATE 9: GROUSE

Willow Grouse

♂ win

♂ sum

♂ win

♀ win

♂ spring

♂ sum

Rock Ptarmigan

♂ sum

♀ sum

♂ win

♀ win

♂ sum

♂ fall

♀ fall

♂ win

♂

♀

♂

Spruce Grouse

Black-billed Capercaillie

♂

♂

♀

Siberian White Crane

ad

ad

ad

juv

juv

Sandhill Crane

ad

ad

juv

juv

Waders

Waders (or shorebirds) form the largest group of Arctic breeding birds. They are among the most difficult to identify, as the plumage of adult birds changes during the year and many species are superficially (and sometimes profoundly) similar. Furthermore, the profile of an individual bird changes with activity. Resting birds draw their heads toward their shoulders and may crouch, making them appear smaller, but if cold may also fluff their feathers and so appear fatter. Bill size and shape can be helpful; plovers have short bills, as they are peck-feeders, while sandpipers have longer bills for probing, which, depending on the species, may be straight, upturned or downturned. All species feed on insects, worms and crustaceans, and occasionally vegetation, amphibians and fish. In general their nests are merely a scrape in open ground, the incubating bird relying on camouflage. Wader chicks are nidifugous and precocial, and are cared for by the parents, though in some species the female may leave before the young are fledged. All Arctic species are migratory, with some covering huge distances to their wintering grounds.

In this book, waders are dealt with in conventional groupings and in the following sequence: oystercatchers; plovers; *Calidris* and allies; dowitchers and snipes; godwits, curlews and allies; turnstones; and phalaropes.

Oystercatchers

Though essentially sub-Arctic, two species of oystercatcher breed in the Arctic as defined in this book. The Eurasian Oystercatcher (*Haematopus ostralegus*) breeds in Iceland, northern Fennoscandia and throughout Kamchatka. The nominate form breeds in northern Europe, while race *osculans* occurs in eastern Asia. Icelandic birds are occasionally considered a separate race, *H. malacophaga*, though differences in bill shape and size are slight. The American Black Oyster-catcher (*H. bachmani*) breeds in southern and southeastern Alaska and on the Aleutian Islands. This species is monotypic.

▼ Nesting Dotterel, Jotunheimen, Norway.

Plovers

Plovers are compact and relatively long-legged waders, with short bills and large eyes. Typically they are peck-feeders, characterized by "look-run-peck, look-run-peck" behavior. Breeding birds have complex displays and are usually monogamous. Seven species are Arctic breeders.

Eurasian Dotterel
Charadrius morinellus

Identification   See p. 227
Breeding adults have black crowns, gray foreheads speckled with white, white cheeks and throat and dark gray eye-stripes. The bill is dark olive or black, the iris brown. The back and upper breast are pale gray, often with a pink tinge. The upper breasts of males are usually white-streaked, though not heavily so. A white bar, with a thin black line above, separates the upper breast from a rufous belly, which becomes black before ending with a white vent. Females are usually more brightly rufous than males. The upperwing is uniform pale gray, but buff feather ends can give the appearance of fine scalloping if the bird is viewed at close range. The wing also has a thin white leading edge (from the white shaft of the longest primary) and trailing edge. The uppertail is gray, becoming black and with a white terminal band. The legs and feet are yellow or yellow-brown. Non-breeding adults are much less bright, maintaining the white breast-band but losing the thin black line, and becoming white/cream on the lower body with gray flanks. The strong colors of the head are also lost, becoming mottled light/dark brown, with a distinct buff tinge to the rear of the eye-stripe. The upper color is more buff-gray. Juveniles are similar to non-breeding adults but with more heavily patterned upperparts, and buff rather than cream underparts. Downy chicks are dark brown/rufous above, white below.

Confusion species
Lesser Sand Plover in eastern Chukotka. Lesser Sand Plover has black eye-stripe and lacks the white breast bar.

◄ Eurasian Dotterel. The pale breast indicates a breeding male.

Size
L: 8–9½ in. (20–24 cm). WS: 21½–26 in. (55–65 cm). W: 3–4¼ oz. (85–120 g).

Voice
Usually silent, but has a soft *peet, peet* and rippling *purr* on takeoff.

Distribution
Palearctic, though small numbers of birds breed in the upland tundras of western Alaska. Absent from Greenland, Iceland and Svalbard. Breeds in Scandinavia and across Russia from the Kola Peninsula to Chukotka, to the northern shore and including the southern island of Novaya Zemlya. Found on shorelines and on tundra. Migratory, wintering in the Middle East and North Africa. Eastern Siberian birds may travel 6,200 mi. (10,000 km) on migration.

Diet
Chiefly insects, but also worms and mollusks and occasionally buds, berries and flowers.

Breeding
Gregarious, especially in winter, but also in summer when loose breeding colonies form. Female often initiates breeding with display that includes raising and folding the wings and spreading the tail. Females attempt to lure or isolate a male from a group. Females are polyandrous, laying multiple clutches. Males are occasionally polygamous. The bigamous partner may not always share brood responsibilities. Nest is a shallow scrape on open ground, occasionally lined with vegetation. Two to four (usually three) heavily dark brown blotched, light brown eggs incubated for 24–28 days by either parent. Birds, even incubating ones, can be remarkably tame, but will use distraction if faced with a predator. In polyandrous couples, males do most of incubating and are usually on eggs at hatching. Chicks nidifugous and precocial, often cared for by the male, but self-feeding. Fledge in 25–30 days and are independent soon after. Breed at 1–2 years.

Taxonomy and geographical variation
Monotypic.

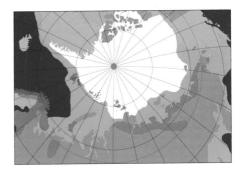

Common Ringed Plover
Charadrius hiaticula

Identification See p. 227
Breeding adults have a black ring encircling a white forehead, including the lores and eyes, passing above bill and extending back to the ear-coverts. A distinct white crescent is above the black ear-covert. The crown and upper nape are gray-brown. The bill is orange with a black tip, the iris dark brown with thin yellow eye-ring. In females, the black facial ring is more broken, the ear-coverts gray-brown and the eye-ring usually gray. Both adults have a white collar covering the throat and nape, below which is a black collar, broad at the upper chest. The remaining underparts are white, though the underwing shows pale gray on the lesser coverts and darker gray on the trailing edge. The upperparts are gray-brown, but the upperwing has a distinct white bar across the primary and secondary bases and very dark trailing edge. The uppertail is dark brown, darker toward the terminal edge, and with white side-bars that continue to the rump. The legs and feet are orange-red. There is partial webbing between middle and outer toes. Non-breeding adults are duller overall, the bill losing its orange base, the head losing the facial black ring and the chest collar becoming gray-brown. Juveniles are similar to non-breeding adults, but with buff scalloping from feather fringes on the upperparts. Downy chicks are buff/black above, cream below.

Confusion species
Little Ringed Plover (*C. dubius*) at the southern part of the range, though the range of *C. dubius* does not extend into the Arctic. Virtually indistinguishable from Semipalmated Plover unless the birds are generous enough to show foot webbing. The calls, however, are different and represent best chance of avoiding confusion, though Semipalmated also lacks the distinct white patch behind the eye.

▼ Adult male of race *tundrae*, Finnish Lapland.

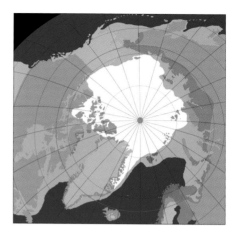

Size
L: 7–7¾ in. (18–20 cm). WS: 18–21½ in. (45–55 cm). W: 2–2½ oz. (55–75 g).

Voice
Distinctive disyllabic, rising *too-ee*, sharper when alarmed. Display flight call is a simpler *twee-oo*.

Distribution
Mainly Palearctic, but breeds on eastern Canadian Arctic islands. Breeds in Greenland, Iceland, Svalbard, Scandinavia and along the northern coast of Eurasia, including the southern island of Novaya Zemlya and the New Siberia Islands. Favors sandy or pebbled shorelines of coasts, lakes and rivers. Migratory; Greenlandic and Icelandic birds move through the British Isles to southern Europe and northern Africa. Scandinavian birds use similar wintering areas, and Russian birds head for the Caspian Sea and the Middle East.

Diet
Invertebrates. Favors insects and their larvae in breeding season, mollusks at wintering sites.

Breeding
Gregarious at all times, though less so in the breeding season. Pair-bond monogamous and seasonal. Males take lead in pairing ceremonies, chiefly with a crouched run at the female. Nest is a shallow scrape lined with local vegetation. Three to four cream or pale buff eggs lightly blotched dark brown. Incubated for 23–26 days by both parents. Breeding bird sits tight if approached, but then shows sophisticated distraction behavior by realistically feigning injury, moving away with fanned, depressed tail and half-open, drooping wings, often dragging itself or tumbling. Chicks nidifugous and precocial. Cared for by both parents, but self-feeding. Fledge at 22–26 days and are independent soon after. Breed at 1 year.

Taxonomy and geographical variation
Polytypic. Nominate race occurs in northern Canada, Greenland, Iceland and Svalbard. Race *tundrae* occurs in

▼ Adult Semipalmated Plover, Alaska Peninsula.

northern Europe, Scandinavia and across much of northern Russia.

Semipalmated Plover
Charadrius semipalmatus

Identification
Virtually indistinguishable from the Ringed Plover, particularly from the *tundrae* subspecies. Semipalmated Plover has webs between inner and middle, and middle and outer toes. It also lacks the Ringed Plover's prominent white patch behind the eye, having an indistinct crescent and sometimes no white at all.

Confusion species
Ringed Plover and its confusion species.

◄ This Semipalmated Plover is exhibiting classic plover distraction behavior. It is feigning a broken wing to lure an enemy away from the nest. Cold Bay, Alaska Peninsula.

Size
L: 6½–7½ in. (17–19 cm). WS: 17–20½ in. (43–52 cm). W: 1½–2¼ oz. (45–65 g).

Voice
Differs from Ringed Plover and is often the only way of distinguishing the two. Semipalmated Plover has a clear, rising whistle, *chee-wee*, much sharper than Ringed Plover.

Distribution
Nearctic. Breeds across North America, including whole of Alaska, Yukon and the Northwest Territories, and much of southern Nunavut, including Banks, Victoria, Southampton and southern Baffin Islands. Found on tundra and at the coast. Migratory, moving to southern Pacific and Atlantic coasts of the United States, the Caribbean islands and the coasts of Central and South America, where it favors mudflats and shorelines, but also occurs on inland river and lake margins.

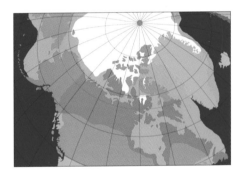

Diet
As Ringed Plover.

Breeding
As Ringed Plover.

Taxonomy and geographical variation
Monotypic.

Lesser Sand Plover
Charadrius mongolus

Identification See p. 227
The following refers to race *stegmanni*. Breeding adult has white forehead divided by a thin black vertical stripe reaching the bill. There is also a thin black line above the white forehead. The lores and ear-coverts are linked by a broad black stripe below the eye. The crown is gray surrounded by a buff-rufous ring, which extends down the sides of the neck to link with the breast. The

▲ Adult male Lesser Sand Plover of the race *stegmanni* in breeding plumage, Chukotka.

iris is dark brown, the bill dark gray-brown. The throat is white, separated by a thin black line from a rufous-chestnut chest, sometimes with buff scalloping from feather edges. The rufous coloration continues a little onto flanks, but the remaining underbody and undertail are white. The back is gray-brown, merging with the gray rump. The upperwing has gray-brown inner coverts, but dark gray primary coverts and flight feather tips, separated by a broad white band. The underwing is pale gray along the front edge, trending to dark gray at the tip and dark gray on the trailing edge, the two separated by a broad white stripe. The legs are olive-gray, the toes dark gray. Non-breeding adults lose the facial pattern and rufous breast, becoming overall gray-brown above and white below, with a white supercilium and a darker gray stripe below the eye. Juveniles are as non-breeding adults, but buff-gray on the head and neck, with a buff supercilium. Downy chicks are gray-white.

Confusion species
None in the region.

Size
L: 6½–7¾ in. (17–20 cm). WS: 18–21½ in. (45–55 cm). W: 1¾–2½ oz. (50–75 g).

Voice
A short, harsh *drik* and a softer, rippling *trrrip*.

Distribution
Eastern Russia. Breeds on Chukotka, Kamchatka and the Commander Islands. Has bred on western Alaskan coast. Though often seen on St. Lawrence Island and the Aleutian Islands is not an established species there. A mountain species, but found on tundra and shorelines. Occurs among sand dunes on the Commander Islands. Migratory, with birds moving to Philippines, Indonesia and Australia.

Diet
Insects and their larvae, crustaceans and mollusks, but data are limited.

Breeding
Gregarious at all times. Pair-bond and displays similar to other plovers, with main display a parallel flight. Nest is a scrape in gravel or bare ground lined with lichen. Two or three (occasionally four) cinnamon or olive-green eggs with heavy dark red-brown blotches incubated for about 21 days. The male usually incubates, the female often deserting soon after laying. However, there are reports of incubation by pairs (infrequent) and females only (rare). Chicks nidifugous and

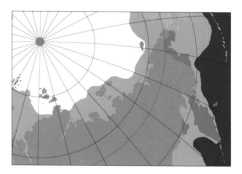

precocial. Cared for by both parents, but self-feeding. Fledge at 25–30 days and are independent soon after. Breed at 1 year.

Taxonomy and geographical variation
Polytypic. Nominate race (which lacks the thin black line bisecting the forehead, is paler overall and is smaller) breeds in inland eastern Siberia. Race *stegmanni* breeds in Chukotka, Kamchatka Peninsula and Commander Islands.

American Golden Plover
Pluvialis dominica

The three golden plovers and the Black-bellied Plover, collectively referred to as the tundra plovers, are extremely attractive black, white (and gold) birds, which often seem relatively at ease around humans, allowing a close approach.

Identification See p. 227
Breeding adults have crown, nape and upperparts mottled dark gray and gold. The lores and cheeks below the eye are black, separated from the crown/nape by a broad white band, which

extends to but does not completely cover the chest. The bill is black, the iris dark brown. The black facial patch extends to the chest (as a narrow vertical strip, linking it to the black belly and flanks). The patterning on the upper body is very bold, with gold and white triangles (mainly gold on back, white toward the tail) on dark gray/black. The pattern covers the upperwing, with mainly gold at the leading edge, white at the rear. The legs and feet are black but dark gray in non-breeding birds. Adult females show some white streaking on flanks. Non-breeding adults lose the black and white of the head and lower body, becoming pale gray or gray/brown with brown markings. The broad white band fades to a white supercilium. The underwing is uniform gray-brown, with occasionally an indistinct, paler-gray bar on greater primary coverts. Juvenile birds are as non-breeding adults. but have indistinct gray barring on the lower body. Downy chicks are gold/dark brown above, white below.

Confusion species

The Eurasian and Pacific Golden Plovers and Black-bellied Plover. American Plovers are darker overall and lack the white flank stripe. American Plovers are also smaller, lack the white underwing and have wings that extend beyond the tail-tip. Pacific Golden Plovers have proportionally longer legs and a uniform gray-brown underwing. The wings also extend beyond the tail (but usually by less than those of the American Golden). The Black-bellied Plover lacks the golden mottling of the golden plovers and has a distinctive white vent.

Size

L: 9–10½ in. (23–27 cm). WS: 24–28 in. (60–70 cm). W: 4½–5½ oz. (125–155 g).

Voice

Usual call is a high-pitched urgent *quee* or *twee*, occasionally as two syllables, the first with more stress *QUE-ee* or *TWE-ee*. There are also peeps and a flight call, *wit-wit-wit*.

▼ Adult male American Golden Plover in breeding plumage, Southampton Island. Note the diagnostic absence of the white flank streak.

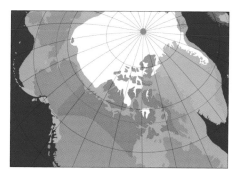

Distribution

Nearctic. Breeds in western North America from Alaska to Hudson Bay; also on Banks, Victoria and Southampton Islands and on western Baffin Island. Seen rarely on Chukotka and has bred on Wrangel Island. Found on tundra, preferring drier habitats, but occasionally occurs on sandy shorelines. Migratory, with birds flying as far south as Argentina.

Diet

Insects and their larvae, crustaceans and marine invertebrates. Also takes seeds and berries, and worms at wintering sites.

Breeding

Gregarious at all times. Pair-bond monogamous and lifelong. The main male display is the "butterfly flight," with slow, deliberate, stiff-wing beats, the male singing as he flies. There is also a "torpedo" run, in which the male extends his head and neck so that the whole body is horizontal and pursues the female with his tail twitching. Nest is a scrape lined with lichen. Four cream-yellow eggs with heavy, dark brown blotching incubated by both parents for 27–32 days. Chicks nidifugous and precocial. Cared for by both parents, but self-feeding. Fledge in 25–33 days and are independent soon after. Breed at 1 year.

Taxonomy and geographical variation

Monotypic.

Eurasian Golden Plover
Pluvialis apricaria

Identification See p. 227

Breeding adults have dark gray crown, nape and upperparts with a bold pattern of gold flecks and arrowheads. The bill is black, the iris dark brown. The cheeks below the eye are dark grayish-black, separated from the crown by a broad white band that extends across the supercilium, then down the neck and along the flanks. The remaining underparts are a dark grayish-black continuation of the facial mask, merging with a white vent and undertail. The flank white stripe is ragged on the chest and belly. The underwing is white, merging to pale gray on the leading edge and darker gray on the trailing edge. The upperwing-coverts are as upperparts, but with a distinct white bar between the covert patterning and the more uniformly dark gray flight feathers. Females tend to have a duller facial disk and underparts than the male, but males in the southern part of the range are similar. The legs and feet are gray. Non-breeding adults lose the dark facial disk and underparts, which become gray with yellow spotting, and upperparts are duller. Juveniles are as non-breeding adults. Downy chicks are dark golden above, white below, and indistinguishable from chicks of other golden plovers and Black-bellied Plover.

Confusion species

See American Golden Plover pages 174–175.

Size

L: 10¼–12 in. (26–30 cm). WS: 26–30 in. (65–75 cm). W: 6¼–8½ oz. (180–240 g).

▼ Adult Eurasian Golden Plover, Norway.

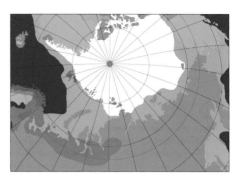

Voice

A plaintive, whistling *puree*. There is also a shorter, sharper *teep* and a flight song, which begins as a repeated fluting *per-pee-oo*, with the stress on the middle syllable, and becomes a more rapid repetition.

Distribution

Palearctic. Breeds in northeastern Greenland (though not in large numbers), Iceland, Scandinavia and northern Russia as far east as the southern part of the Taimyr Peninsula. Absent from Svalbard (though breeding records do exist) and the western Arctic islands of Russia. Found on open tundra near shores and lakes. Although generally preferring drier areas, the birds are also found in very wet areas, even in blanket bogs, in the southern parts of their range. Migratory, with Greenlandic and Icelandic birds moving to Iberia; Scandinavian and Russian birds moving to Iberia and North Africa.

Diet

Insects, particularly beetles, and berries. Wintering birds also feed on earthworms, and on crustaceans and mollusks at coastal sites.

Breeding

Gregarious at all times, but especially so outside breeding season. Male display as American Golden Plover. Pair-bond monogamous and lifelong. Nest is a shallow scrape lined with local vegetation; old nests are occasionally reused. Four cream/pale-buff eggs, heavily blotched red or dark brown, incubated for 28–31 days by both sexes. Breeding bird may sit tight until approaching human or predator is close, but may also depart nest early, taking to the air at a distance. Will attempt to lure predators away by feigning injury, usually a broken wing or exhaustion, the latter by lying on the ground and calling plaintively. In colonial breeding sites other birds may join in this behavior, confusing the predator.

Chicks nidifugous and precocial. Cared for by both parents, but self-feeding. Fledge at 25–33 days and are independent soon after. Breed at 1 year.

Taxonomy and geographical variation

Polytypic; northern birds, which average more black below when breeding, form a separate subspecies, *P. a. altifrons*. The nominate race occurs to the south of this form.

Pacific Golden Plover
Pluvialis fulva

Until recent times, the American Golden Plover was considered the nominate form of the Lesser Golden Plover; another subspecies, *P. d. fulva*, was regarded as the Eurasian version of this species. However, the absence of interbreeding where the two birds occasionally overlap in western Alaska and, more rarely, in eastern Chukotka has led to the promotion of these former subspecies to full specific status. Since acceptance of this split, the name Lesser Golden Plover has been abandoned in favor of American and Pacific Golden Plovers.

Identification   See p. 227
Very similar to the Eurasian Golden Plover, but with longer, darker gray legs and a uniform gray-brown underwing. The upperparts are darker and less heavily mottled with gold. Juvenile birds are very difficult to distinguish from juvenile European birds.

Confusion species
See American Golden Plover, pages 174–175.

Size
L: 7¾–10 in. (20–25 cm). WS: 24–28 in. (60–70 cm). W: 4¼–5 oz. (120–140 g).

Voice
A rapid *ku-wit* with stress on the second syllable. The flight song is as the American Golden Plover, but notes are not as well separated. Overall, however, the differences between Pacific and American birds are slight.

Distribution
Russian Asia and western Alaska, where it is uncommon. Breeds east of the Yamal Peninsula, north to the northern shore, but absent from the Arctic islands. Prefers dry tundra. Migratory, moving as far south as Australia and New Zealand. Wintering birds occur on mudflats and shorelines, but also on grassland where growth is not tall enough to interfere with feeding.

Diet
Adult and larval insects and berries. Wintering birds also concentrate on insects, but also take worms and crustaceans.

Breeding
Gregarious at all times. Display, nesting habits, incubation and fledging as American Golden Plover.

Taxonomy and geographical variation
Monotypic.

Black-bellied Plover (Gray Plover)
Pluvialis squatarola

Identification   See p. 227
Breeding adults are patterned as American Golden Plover, but with no gold markings. Thus crown, nape and upperparts are white/pale gray with heavy scallop markings in black. Black facial disk separated from crown by white bar above the eye, which descends sides of neck to form white patches on sides of the breast. The bill is black, the iris dark brown. The breast and belly are black, the vent is white. The undertail, rump and uppertail are white with gray barring toward the end of the tail. The underwing is pale gray with contrasting black axilliaries and a dark gray trailing edge on the primaries. The upperwing is mottled black

▶ Adult Pacific Golden Plover in breeding plumage.

▶ Adult female Black-bellied Plover on the nest, Alaska.

and white on the inner coverts, but the primary coverts and trailing edges of the flight feathers are dark gray/black, separated from the inner converts by a distinct white stripe. Breeding females are as males, but usually with some white streaking on the flanks. The legs and feet are black, but dark gray on wintering birds. Non-breeding adults lose the black and white head and underbody pattern, becoming white/buff with brown barring. The upperbody is much duller. Juveniles are as non-breeding adults, but the upperbody is yellow/buff rather than white. Downy chicks are golden dark brown above, white below, as other tundra plovers.

Confusion species
See American Golden Plover, pages 174–175.

Size
L: 10¼–12½ in. (26–32 cm). WS: 28–34 in. (70–85 cm). W: 7–9½ oz. (200–270 g).

Voice
A mournful *pee-oo-wee*, usually with stress on second syllable, though during the butterfly-display flight the first and third syllables are more usually stressed.

Distribution
Circumpolar, but only occasional breeder in Greenland and absent from Iceland, Scandinavia and Svalbard. Breeds in Russia from the White Sea to Chukotka, to the northern coast and perhaps on the New Siberia Islands, as well as on Wrangel Island. In the United States, breeds on the western and south-western coasts of Alaska, but rare on the north coast. Breeds on southern Canadian Arctic islands and on the northern mainland. Found on tundra, especially near lakes and rivers. Prefers drier areas, but also found in wetter country. Migratory; Eurasian birds move to southwestern Europe, but also to Southeast Asia and Australia. North American birds move to the Atlantic and Pacific coasts of the southern U.S., and into Central and South America. Wintering birds prefer mudflats and shorelines but may also be found on grasslands.

Diet
Almost exclusively insects and their larvae, though wintering birds take worms on grasslands and crustaceans on mudflats.

Breeding
Gregarious, but less so than the golden plovers and often found in pairs or solitary. Male has the torpedo run as other tundra plovers, but usually stops before female and bends forward with bill almost on the ground. Also performs a butterfly flight, but this includes periods of gliding rarely seen in other tundra plovers. Pair-bond monogamous and probably lifelong. Nest is shallow scrape lined with local vegetation or stones. Four light brown/buff eggs, heavily blotted with dark or red-brown, incubated by both birds for 25–27 days. Chicks nidifugous and precocial. Cared for by both parents, but self-feeding. Fledge at 35–45 days and are independent soon after. Breed at 1 year.

Taxonomy and geographical variation
Monotypic.

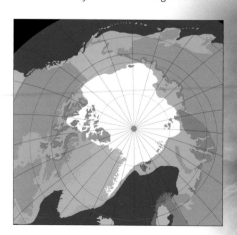

▼ Male Black-bellied Plover calling at breeding grounds, Alaska.

Stints and sandpipers

The true sandpipers of the genus *Calidris*, and related species, have relatively long wings and legs and short tails. Their bills show a range of adaptations; there are the short, thin bills of the stints, the curious broad, flattened bill-tip of the Spoon-billed Sandpiper and the long, downcurved bill of the Curlew Sandpiper. These species are similarly variable in breeding strategy. They are highly migratory and many have extraordinarily long migration flights, taking advantage of the highly productive but short Arctic summer for breeding, then migrating to spend long periods in southern "winter" sites that are less productive. Chicks hatch nidifugous and precocial, which necessitates large eggs. In all *Calidris* species, the clutch weight is a remarkably large fraction of the female's body weight, up to 90% in the case of the stints.

▲ Adult Baird's Sandpiper, Chukotka.

Baird's Sandpiper
Calidris bairdii

Identification
See p. 228

Breeding adults have a dark brown crown, nape and mantle, all streaked with buff from feather edging. The supercilium is pale buff (not always distinct). The cheeks are white, heavily buff-streaked. The throat is white. The bill is thin, straight and black, the iris dark brown. The breast is buff, streaked with brown or occasionally chestnut, blending into a white belly and undertail. The feathers of the mantle, scapulars and tertials have dark brown centers and buff fringing, which give the bird distinctive triangular-/crescent-spotted upperparts. The rump and uppertail are dark brown with buff fringes, and the tail has gray sides. The upper wing is dark brown and the coverts have buff scalloping. The flight feathers are more uniform. Some birds have silver/brown coverts with darker spotting. A thin white bar becomes indistinct as the feathers wear. The legs and feet are black, occasionally greenish-black. Non-breeding birds are paler overall with gray-brown upperparts. Juveniles are intermediate between breeding and non-breeding adults, with buff heads and breasts, but more heavily streaked breasts and less prominent supercilia. The upperparts are closer in base color to breeding adults, but the buff-edged feathers give a "scaly" appearance. Downy chicks are mottled gray and dark brown with pronounced malar stripe.

Confusion species
The wings of Baird's Sandpiper project well beyond the tail and describe an oval as the bird walks and pecks. This is diagnostic, but the wings of the White-rumped Sandpiper also extend significantly. White-rumped is more heavily streaked on the underparts and looks heavier. Semipalmated Sandpipers are also very similar, but smaller.

Size
L: 5½–6½ in. (14–17 cm). WS: 16–18 in. (40–45 cm). W: 1¼–1½ oz. (35–40 g).

Voice
A high-pitched, hoarse *tr-r-reet*. There are also a trilling flight call and a sharp *krip*.

Distribution
Eastern Russia to western Greenland. Breeds in Chukotka, on Wrangel Island and across North America from northern Alaska to Baffin Island (but limited to the west of Hudson Bay on the Canadian mainland) and northwestern Greenland. Prefers drier tundra and rarely wades, but is found on shorelines and on the margins of lakes and marshland. Migratory, wintering in South America south of the equator in similar habitats.

▶ Baird's Sandpiper chicks, Chukotka.

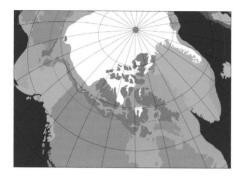

Diet

Invertebrates. Feeds mostly by pecking with busy walk, often through shallow water. Occasionally probes.

Breeding

Gregarious in winter, though much less so than other calidrids. Flocks of up to 100 are known but rarely exceed 20–30. Solitary at breeding sites. Several males compete to establish territories on the breeding grounds. When territory established, the male circles above his area, calling loudly. He threatens rivals with lowered head, bill horizontal and feathers ruffled. Males run at females much as against rival males. Pair-bond monogamous and seasonal. Nest is a shallow depression among pebbles or in clump of vegetation, sparsely lined with moss and lichen. Sitting bird will decorate nest with vegetation within bill reach. Four eggs of variable color, base from pale gray or cream-buff to deep olive or red-brown, splotched dark or red-brown. Eggs incubated by both parents for 19–22 days. Chicks nidifugous and precocial. Leave nest at about three days. Cared for by both parents (though female occasionally abandons nest area), but self-feeding. Fledge at 15–20 days and are independent soon after. Breed at 1–2 years.

Taxonomy and geographical variation

Monotypic.

Curlew Sandpiper
Calidris ferruginea

Identification See p. 229

Breeding adults have a black-and-chestnut streaked crown. The rest of the head is chestnut, occasionally with a whitish supercilium and chin. The iris is dark brown. The bill is black, long and distinctly downcurved. The underparts are chestnut becoming white, streaked dark chestnut on the undertail. Females are paler than males and have white streaking. The upperparts are chestnut with some dark gray barring. The rump is white, the uppertail gray, often with darker gray or chestnut barring. The upperwing has gray lesser coverts and darker gray primary coverts, separated by a white bar from dark gray/black flight feathers. The underwing is white with a dark gray trailing edge. The legs and feet are black. Non-breeding adults lose the chestnut coloration, the underparts becoming white with occasional gray speckling, the upperparts mid-gray. The head is mid-gray, with a white supercilium and chin. Juveniles are as non-breeding adults, but with a pale chestnut or buff breast and scaly, dark brown/gray upperparts. Downy chicks are rust-colored with dark brown bands, speckled paler.

Confusion species

Similar to Red Knot and Gray Phalarope, but the bill is distinctly different. Wintering birds similar to Dunlin, but distinguished by the white rump and white supercilium.

Size

L: 7–8 in. (18–21 cm). WS: 16½–18½ in. (42–47 cm). W: 2–3 oz. (55–85 g).

Voice

A rippling *chirrup*. There is also a series of chatters and trills.

Distribution

Northern Russia. Breeds from the Taimyr Peninsula to Chukotka, and perhaps on the New Siberia Islands. Found in both dry and damp tundra. Migratory, wintering in Africa, southern Asia, Indonesia and Australia, where it prefers mudflats and silty shorelines.

Diet

Larval and adult invertebrates obtained by pecking and probing. Also takes some vegetable matter, and mollusks and worms at wintering sites.

Breeding

Gregarious at all times, sometimes forming flocks with other calidrids. Displays as other calidrids. Pair-bond unclear. Some observations suggest that males chase females throughout their shared time at the breeding site and will mate with any willing bird. Others suggest that the pair-bond is chiefly monogamous and seasonal, and that the bond may be renewed, as nests are often reused. The uncertainty extends to

▼ Adult Curlew Sandpiper in breeding plumage, Chukotka.

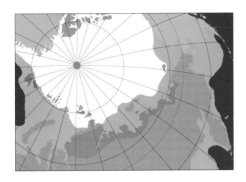

incubation. In general only one bird incubates; this is often the female, since the male departs the area, but incubation by both birds has also been observed, as has incubation by the male only, though rarely. Nest is a depression in dry tundra lined with lichen and local vegetation. Four brown-mottled, olive-green eggs incubated for 18–20 days. Chicks nidifugous and precocial. Parental care is again uncertain; there are reports of care by both parents as well as by a single bird of either sex. Chicks are self-feeding. Fledging time unknown, but probably as other calidrids. Breeding age also unknown but probably 1–2 years.

Taxonomy and geographical variation
Monotypic.

Dunlin
Calidris alpina

Identification

See p. 229

Breeding adults have a brown crown streaked with black, with the remainder of the head white with fine black streaks. There is a white, often indistinct, supercilium. The iris is dark brown. The bill is black and droops at the tip. The breast is white, heavily streaked with black. There is a large black patch on the belly, contrasting with the white flanks, vent and undertail. The

nape is gray with black streaks, and the mantle is black with chestnut or pale gray fringing, as are the scapulars and tertials. The upperwing shows gray/brown coverts with dark gray flight feathers, the two areas separated by a distinct white bar. The rump and central tail are dark brown/black, the side of the rump and uppertail white, the tail sides gray. The underwing is white with a dark gray trailing edge. Breeding males are brighter overall than females, and females have a brownish rather than gray nape. The legs and feet are black. Non-breeding adults lose the black belly patch, the underparts becoming white/gray with some black streaking on the breast. The head becomes gray, with a white supercilium and throat. The upperparts are uniformly dull gray, sometimes dull gray/brown. Juveniles have buff/pale chestnut heads with an indistinct white supercilium and chestnut streaking. The breast is similar, trending toward a white belly with black spots. The upperparts are pale chestnut with dark brown and white scalloping, but flight feathers are dark gray. There is a thin, often indistinct white bar. The underwing is as adult birds. Downy chicks are dark brown/chestnut.

▲ Male *pacifica* Dunlin in breeding plumage, St. Lawrence Island.

Confusion species
Breeding adults are unmistakable because of the black belly patch. Indeed, the numerous Dunlin can be used as a yardstick for identifying other waders. If the patch is not visible, Dunlin are similar to Baird's Sandpipers.

Size
L: 6¼–8 in. (16–21 cm). WS: 11–18 in. (28–45 cm). W: 1¼–2 oz. (35–55 g).

Voice
The flight call is a thin, buzzing *treep*. Flocks have a continuous low twitter. The frequently heard alarm call is a sharp, high *chree*. Display song is a wheezy, rolling, descending *chru-ri-ri*.

Distribution
Circumpolar. Breeds in east Greenland (but rarely on the west coast), Iceland, Jan Mayen, Svalbard, Scandinavia, Russia from the Kola Peninsula to Chukotka, including Novaya Zemlya

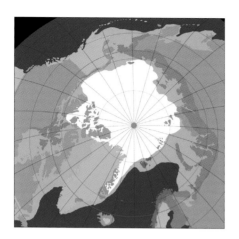

only loose breeding colonies. Displaying males perform arched-wing or V-wing flights, in which wings are held in position during a glide. In arched-wing flight, the wings may also be quivered. On the ground males hold one wing aloft. The displays are territorial against other males and also serve as advertisements to potential mates. Pair-bond monogamous and usually long-lived. Nest is a scrape or depression, formed by both birds (chiefly female) on the ground, but concealed by vegetation if possible. Nest lined with some vegetation. Four red-brown blotched, cream/pale-buff eggs incubated by both birds for 21–22 days. Sitting bird will creep off nest if predator approaches, but may also perform rodentlike run or feign injury as distraction. Chicks nidifugous and precocial. Cared for by both parents, but self-feeding. Fledge in 19–21 days and are independent at that time. Breed at one or two years.

Taxonomy and geographical variation

Polytypic. Nominate race described above breeds in Scandinavia and Russia east to Kolyma Delta. *C. a. arctica* breeds in northeastern Greenland. It has duller, red-brown upperparts with more dark markings and is smaller than the nominate. Race *schinzii* breeds in southeastern Greenland and Iceland, as well as in southern Scandinavia and Great Britain. It resembles *arctica*, but with fewer dark markings; the belly patch is more ragged at the edges and dark gray rather than black. Race *sakhalina* breeds in northeastern Siberia. It has cinnamon, even orange, upperparts with few dark markings. Race *pacifica* breeds in western Alaska. It has deep red-brown upperparts with few black markings. Race *hudsonia* breeds in northern Alaska and Canada. It has upperparts as *pacifica*, but the streaking on the breast extends to the black patch — there is no intervening white band. Some authorities also recognize race *arcticola* in northern Alaska and northwestern Canada, and two other races in the northwest Pacific.

(both islands), the New Siberia Islands and Wrangel Island, western and northern Alaska, and the northern Canadian mainland west of Hudson Bay, including Southampton Island (though not common in Canada except on the northwestern shore of Hudson Bay and Southampton Island). Prefers damper habitats such as the margins of standing water and marshland. Migratory, though some Icelandic birds stay on the south coast. Wintering Palearctic birds are found in western Europe, northern Africa and southern Asia. Nearctic birds winter on the east and west coasts of North America and in central America. Wintering birds prefer beaches and mudflats.

Diet

Invertebrates, located both by pecking and probing. Wintering birds take crustaceans, mollusks and worms.

Breeding

Highly gregarious, forming vast flocks at wintering sites but

▼ A flock of Dunlin of the nominate race, Finland.

Red Knot
Calidris canutus

Identification
See p. 229

A bulky sandpiper. Breeding adults are red on the head and underparts, varying from rich chestnut red to deep salmon pink. There are darker streaks on the crown and below the eye. The base of the bill has a paler, almost white ring around it. The bill is black, the iris dark brown. Some birds have occasional white spotting to the breast and belly, and all have a white vent with black markings. The mantle and scapulars are black, fringed rufous-brown with gray tips. The wing-coverts are gray and the flight feathers dark gray, the two areas separated by a thin white bar. The rump is pale gray with dark gray scalloping extending to the tail. The tail tip is pale gray. The underwing is pale gray, darker at the leading and trailing edges and at the tip. The legs and feet are dark olive-gray. Non-breeding adults have pale gray heads, with some dark gray streaking. The breast is also pale gray, streaked darker. The belly and vent are white with some dark streaks on the flanks. The upperparts are uniformly pale gray, with limited white scalloping. Juveniles are as non-breeding adults, but with much more white scalloping, giving a scaly appearance and a buff tinge to the breast. Downy chicks range from cinnamon to dark brown speckled white.

▼ Red Knot molting into breeding plumage, Finland.

Confusion species
Breeding adults are similar to Curlew Sandpipers, but Red Knots are larger and much stockier, have shorter, straighter bills and have dark olive rather than black feet.

Size
L: 9–10¼ in. (23–26 cm). WS: 22½–24½ in. (57–62 cm). W: 4–5¾ oz. (115–165 g).

Voice
Usually silent, especially if alone. Display call is a whistling *kivie-wee*. Otherwise, a low-pitched, harsh *quee-quee*.

Distribution
Circumpolar, but very local. Breeds in northern and north-eastern Greenland, in Russia on the Taimyr Peninsula, New Siberia Islands, Wrangel Island and inland Chukotka, in northern Alaska (but not consistently), on Canada's Melville Peninsula and on Southampton, Victoria, Ellesmere and Bylot Islands (and probably the Parry Islands). Prefers well-drained tundra with patches of vegetation but also occurs on freshwater margins where it will wade to feed. Less often on seashores. Migratory; Greenlandic and some eastern Canadian birds move through Iceland to western Europe. North American birds move to the coasts of southern U.S., Central Russian birds to Africa and eastern Russian birds to Australia. Wintering sites include tidal margins and mudflats.

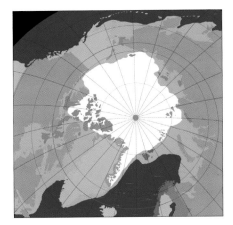

Diet
Insects and some plant material, obtained by pecking and probing. Wintering birds also take mollusks and other invertebrates in the intertidal zone.

Breeding
Gregarious, forming huge flocks at wintering sites, but solitary at breeding grounds. Males have a V-wing glide, and pair will also perform circling flight around the nest site. Pair-bond monogamous and perhaps renewed seasonally. Nest is shallow scrape, often among lichens, with minimal lining of lichens. Four brown-blotched olive eggs, incubated by both parents for 21–22 days. Distraction display as Dunlin. Chicks nidifugous and precocial. Cared for by both parents, but self-feeding. Female usually leaves before young fledge at 18–20 days. Young independent at fledging. Breed at 2–3 years.

Taxonomy and geographical variation
Polytypic. Nominate race breeds on Taimyr Peninsula and the New Siberia Islands; race *rogersi* breeds in Chukotka and on Wrangel. It has a shorter bill, mid-chestnut underparts and a red-brown speckled mantle. Race *rufa* breeds in the western Nearctic. It is pale chestnut and has an extensive white patch on the lower belly. Race *islandica* breeds in the eastern Nearctic and on Greenland. It has mid-chestnut underparts and a yellow-flecked mantle.

Great Knot
Calidris tenuirostris

Identification See p. 229

The largest calidrid. In breeding adults, head, mantle and breast are white, heavily spotted dark brown and black, the black forming lines on the head but less coherent on the breast. The long, straight bill is dark gray or black, the iris dark brown. The heavy spotting of the breast becomes discrete black arrows on flanks, thinning in number so that lower belly, vent and under-tail are almost entirely white. Scapulars have large chestnut ovals that create chestnut bands on the sitting bird. Mantle and upperwing are mid-brown, occasionally fringed rufous. Feather edges are white, though the greater primary coverts are solid dark brown with white tips. The white covert tips form a thin white bar. Rump is white with some dark brown flecking. Central tail is dark brown/black, tail sides gray-brown. Underwing is white with a pale gray-brown bar and trailing edge. Legs and feet are dark gray or dark olive-gray. Non-breeding birds are less heavily spotted on the head and underparts and have no rufous flecking on the upperparts. Juveniles similar to non-breeding adults, but breast is pale buff with dark brown spotting, and upperparts are darker brown with pronounced buff feather edging, giving a scaly appearance. Downy chicks are mottled gray/pale rufous/dark brown above, pale gray below. Upperparts are speckled white due to white feather tips.

▼ Great Knot chick, Chukotka. The stunning camouflage allows the chick to vanish among the lichens of the tundra floor.

Confusion species

The range may overlap with the similar Western Sandpiper, but the latter is much smaller. No other confusion species, though wintering birds are similar (apart from size) to Red Knot.

Size

L: 10–11 in. (25–28 cm). WS: 24–28 in. (60–67 cm). W: 5–7 oz. (140–200 g).

Voice

Usually silent, but has a call similar to Red Knot though longer and lower, *nyut-nyut*.

Distribution

Northeastern Siberia. Rare and little studied. Breeds close to the Kolyma and Anadyr Rivers. Prefers mountain tundra. Migratory, moving to southern Asia and Australasia, preferring estuaries and coastal intertidal areas.

Diet

Presumably invertebrates, though data lacking. Wintering birds take crustaceans and mollusks.

Breeding

Gregarious in winter. Little data on breeding habits, as few nests have been discovered. Male display involves circling flight while calling loudly. Pair-bond apparently monogamous. Prefers nesting in rocky areas with lichens or sparse vegetation; these are used to line simple scrape nest. Four red-brown spotted, yellow-gray eggs, incubated by both birds for about 20 days. Chicks nidifugous and precocial. Cared for by male only, but self-feeding. Thought to fledge at 20–25 days. Breeding age unknown, probably 1–2 years.

Taxonomy and geographical variation

Monotypic.

▲ Adult male Great Knot in breeding plumage, Chukotka Peninsula.

Least Sandpiper
Calidris minutilla

Identification
See p. 228

The smallest calidrid, though only just. Breeding adults have pale chestnut crowns streaked dark brown and white. The cheeks are pale chestnut. The facial ring around the bill and the supercilium are white with fine streaks of dark brown. The bill is black, slightly drooped at the tip, the iris dark brown. The breast is pale chestnut or cream with streaking formed from dark brown diamonds. The belly and remaining underparts are white. The mantle and scapulars are dark brown/black, fringed dark chestnut or pale yellow. The upperwings are similar, with white feather edging on the coverts, showing as a thin white bar delineating the dark brown flight feathers. The rump is dark brown leading to a black central tail. The tail sides are gray, merging with white rump sides. The underwing-coverts are white, apart from the gray greater primaries and a gray leading edge on the lesser primaries. The underwing flight feathers are dark gray. The feet and legs are yellow-green, sometimes dark olive. Non-breeding adults have brown-gray head and upperparts and white underparts, though the breast is brown-gray streaked with darker brown. Juveniles are similar to breeding adults but much brighter, with rich chestnut and black upperparts and distinct white supercilia that usually merge to form a white forehead. Downy chicks have mottled black and orange-buff upperparts with white underparts.

Confusion species
Semipalmated Sandpiper is very similar but has black legs. Palearctic Long-toed and Little Stints are almost identical; some authorities consider Long-toed Stint and Least Sandpiper to be conspecific.

Size
L: 4–4³/₄ in. (10–12 cm). WS: 12¹/₂–13³/₄ in. (32–35 cm). W: ¹/₂–⁷/₈ oz. (16–25 g).

Voice
Usual call is a high-pitched, trilling *preee*. There is also a sharp *dididi*. Flocking birds have a rapid twitter.

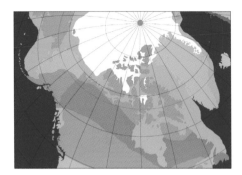

Distribution
Nearctic. Breeds from western Alaska to Labrador but excludes the Canadian Arctic islands. Variable in habitat, found within forests, at the timberline and on open tundra, usually in marshland or at water margins, but also on beaches and coastal mudflats. Migratory, wintering in southern United States, on Caribbean Islands, in Central America and in northern South America, on both inland and coastal sites.

Diet
Benthic and terrestrial invertebrates collected by pecking and probing.

Breeding
Gregarious in winter, but solitary at breeding grounds. Male display flight involves a rapid ascent with alternating bursts of rapid wing-fluttering and gliding. On the ground the male approaches the female with one or both wings either partly or fully lifted. Pair-bond monogamous and apparently long-lived. The nest is set in a damp area close to water. The male forms a scrape, which the female lines with sparse grass. Four (rarely three) brown-spotted and blotched pale-buff eggs, incubated by both birds for 19–23 days. Sitting birds will attempt to distract

▼ Least Sandpiper, Churchill.

a predator with spread wings, fanned tail and back feathers raised. Chicks nidifugous and precocial, becoming mobile within hours. Brooded and cared for by both birds when young. Fledge at 12–15 days and are independent soon after. Breed at 1 year.

Taxonomy and geographical variation
Monotypic.

Little Stint
Calidris minuta

Identification See p. 228
Breeding adults have rufous-brown heads with fine black streaking, occasionally with a pale patch on the forehead. The straight bill is black or dark brown/black, the iris dark brown. The chin and throat are white, blending to a buff breast with regular dark brown spots and then to white underparts. The mantle and scapulars are black, fringed with chestnut, this coloration carried on to the upperwing-coverts, with a thin but distinct white bar separating the coverts from dark brown and black flight feathers. The rump is black and chestnut becoming black, this continuing to the central tail feathers. The side tail feathers are gray, the lateral coverts white. The legs and feet are black, occasionally dark green. Non-breeding adults have gray-brown crowns and upper cheeks, separated by white supercilia that meet at a white forehead patch. The chin, throat and underparts are white, the upperparts uniform a gray-brown. Juveniles have similar color patterning to non-breeding adults but are chestnut and black, almost as bright on the back and wings as breeding adults. They also have pale buff breasts with dark brown streaking. Downy chicks are mottled chestnut, black and white.

▼ Little Stint, north Norway.

Confusion species
Long-toed Stint is similar, but Little Stints are redder when breeding and have black legs. Red-necked Stint has brick-red throat and upper breast when breeding.

Size
L: 5–5½ in. (12–14 cm). W: 1 ft. (33–37 cm). W: ¾–1¼ oz. (20–35 g).

Voice
Usual call is a sharp *chit*. Display song is weak *svee-svee-svee*. There is also a short, buzzing trill.

Distribution
Palearctic. Breeds in northern Scandinavia and Russia from Cheshskaya Guba to the Lena Delta, including the southern island of Novaya Zemlya and the New Siberia Islands. Prefers coastal tundra, but also found at the fringe of the taiga. Occurs mostly in dry areas, but also on marshland. Migratory, wintering in northern Africa, the Middle East and southern Asia, where it occurs on coasts and near inland rivers and lakes.

Diet
Invertebrates, obtained by pecking and, rarely, by probing. Wintering birds also feed on invertebrates, especially mollusks at the coasts.

Breeding
Highly gregarious in winter, much less so in breeding areas, though loose colonies form. Male display flight includes phases with slow wingbeats, feet-dangling, a V-wing glide with wings quivering and a glide with wings held below horizontal. Pair-bond is polygamous for both sexes, with female laying two clutches by two mates, one brooded by a male, the other by herself; male behavior mirrors this. Nest concealed in vegetation, often close to water. Nest is shallow depression lined with vegetation. Three to four heavily red-brown blotched buff or cream eggs, incubated by either bird. Incubation period 20–21 days. Chicks nidifugous and precocial. Cared for by incubating parent. Thought to fledge in 15–18 days and are independent at that time. Breed at 2–3 years.

Taxonomy and geographical variation
Monotypic.

▲ Long-toed Stint. The long middle toes after which the bird is named are clearly visible in this photograph.

Long-toed Stint
Calidris subminuta

Identification   See p. 228
Breeding adults are very similar to Least Sandpipers in overall color and patterning, but upperparts show more chestnut-brown, breast is yellow-buff rather than pale chestnut and streaking is in the form of thin lines rather than diamonds. Long-toed Stint also has a thin, distinct white stripe running along the inner edge of the scapulars. Non-breeding adults resemble Least Sandpipers, but upperparts darker brown and breast has buffish tinge. Juveniles also as Least Sandpipers, but overall brighter above and with buff tinge to breast. Downy chicks are rufous-brown with darker spots.

Confusion species
The long middle toe that gives the bird its name is at best a limited diagnostic tool in the field. Range separation avoids confusion with Least Sandpiper, though Long-toed Stint also has longer neck. Within range, Long-toed may be confused with Little and Red-necked Stints, but its yellow-olive legs are diagnostic.

Size
L: 5–5½ in. (13–14 cm). WS: 12–13¾ in. (33–35 cm). W: ⅞–1¼ oz. (25–35 g).

Voice
A short, rippling *chirrup* and a sharp *tik-tik-tik*.

Distribution
Palearctic. A rare species, breeding in isolated pockets in central Siberia eastward from the Ob, specifically near Magadan, southern Chukotka, northern Kamchatka and on the Commander Islands. Prefers mountain tundra but also occurs in marshland. Migratory, moving to southeastern Asia, Indonesia and Australia, where frequently forms flocks with Temminck's, Little and Red-necked Stints. Wintering birds usually found on inland marshes, but occasionally on coastal mudflats and among sand dunes.

Diet
Invertebrates, usually collected from shoreline vegetation. Feeds by walking quickly and pecking; also more methodically.

Breeding
Gregarious at all times, often nesting colonially. Male display is a circling flight. Pair-bond unclear. Nest is a depression concealed in vegetation hummock in dry spot close to water. Two to four brown-blotched, gray-green eggs incubated for 18–22 days by both parents. Chicks nidifugous and precocial. Usually cared for by male only, as female leaves breeding area after the eggs hatch, but self-feeding. Fledge at 17–22 days and are independent soon after. Thought to breed at 1 year.

Taxonomy and geographical variation
Monotypic.

Pectoral Sandpiper
Calidris melanotos

Identification   See p. 228
Breeding adults have a dark brown crown streaked with black and lighter brown, a vague white supercilium, dark brown lores and red-brown ear-coverts contrasting with paler, finely streaked cheeks. The brown/black-tipped bill is long and slightly downcurved at the tip. The iris is dark brown. The throat is white, the neck and breast buff with dark brown streaking, the coloration ceasing abruptly to form a pectoral band (hence the name). The underparts beyond the band are white and unmarked apart from minimal streaking on the flanks. The mantle and scapulars are dark brown with chestnut or buff fringing, giving a warm dark brown or chestnut mottling to the sitting bird. The upperwing-coverts are dark gray or gray-brown with buff

fringing. A thin, often indistinct white bar separates the coverts from the dark gray flight feathers. The underwing is white, but with pale gray greater primary coverts and leading and trailing edges to primaries. The central rump and uppertail are dark brown/black, the sides of the rump white, the outer tail feathers gray. The central tail feathers are elongated; this is usually visible in flight and is a good identification feature. The legs and feet are greenish yellow. Adult males tend to have darker chests. They are also significantly larger than females. Non-breeding adults are as breeding, but duller and browner overall. Juveniles are as breeding adults, but with white fringing on the mantle and scapulars that forms distinctive V-shapes. Downy chicks have black and brown mottled upperparts, white underparts.

Confusion species
Very similar to Sharp-tailed Sandpiper, but the sharp cutoff of pectoral band is diagnostic. The legs also tend to be lighter.

Size
L: 7½–9 in. (19–23 cm). WS: 16½–20 in. (42–50 cm). W: 2–4¼ oz. (55–120 g).

Voice
A hoarse but thin *krik*, repeated often but irregularly. Male also has a hooting song *do-do-do*, usually given in flight but also on ground. The hoot is aided by the expansion of an air-filled sac that causes the neck or upper breast to puff out.

Distribution
Eastern Russia and western North America. Breeds in Asian Russia from the Taimyr Peninsula to Chukotka, usually to the north coast, but absent from all islands except Wrangel. In North America, breeds from northwestern Alaska along the mainland coast to Hudson Bay, and on Banks, Victoria and Southampton Islands, Prince of Wales Island, the southern Parry islands and southern Ellesmere. Prefers dry, hummocky tundra close to pools; also found in marshy areas. Migratory, with both Russian and North American birds moving to South America, though small numbers also migrate to Japan and Korea. Wintering sites are usually grassy plains, though also found on coastal mudflats.

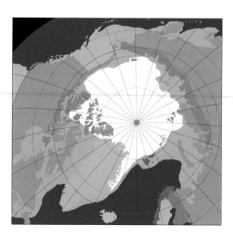

▲ A singing male Pectoral Sandpiper, Barrow. The bird amplifies its *hoot* by use of a throat pouch, which is expanded here.

Diet
Freshwater, marine and terrestrial invertebrates, particularly insects and insect larvae. Wintering birds also take crustaceans and mollusks.

Breeding
Gregarious in winter, more solitary at breeding grounds. The male has territorial displays that involve the expansion of the air sac (see Voice above) or taking up a position on a high mound where they may drop their wings. Males also pursue females with the throat sac expanded. Males are polygamous and females also visit other male territories. Nest is deep depression concealed under vegetation. Four heavily red-brown spotted, cream/pale-green eggs, incubated chiefly by female, as males often leave breeding grounds before eggs hatch to pursue other females. Incubation period 21-22 days. Chicks nidifugous and precocial. Brooded and cared for by female for several days. Fledge at about 30 days, but deserted by parent earlier, usually about 20 days. Thought to breed at 1 year.

Taxonomy and geographical variation
Monotypic.

Purple Sandpiper
Calidris maritima

Identification See p. 229
Breeding adults are dark overall, which can aid identification, as no other calidrid is as dark. The crown is dark brown with buff fringing. The supercilium is pale, distinct only in contrast to blackish lores and red-brown ear-coverts. The rest of the head is buff, heavily dark brown streaked. The iris is dark brown. The bill is dark brown or dark olive with an olive-yellow base, offering strongest contrast in spring (though all-dark bills are seen). The

bill is long and slightly downcurved at the tip. The underparts are white/pale gray, heavily spotted with dark brown, the spots thinning toward the vent and occasionally forming a dark patch on the belly. The mantle and scapulars are dark brown, fringed chestnut or white. The rump, uppertail-coverts and central tail are black, the rump sides white, the remaining tail gray-brown. The upperwing is dark overall, dark gray towards body, black toward the tip. There is a thin white bar, very noticeable because of the dark wing. The inner underwing is white, the outer underwing gray, the pale underwing a strong contrast to the dark underbody. The legs and feet are yellow-orange in winter/early spring, becoming olive green. Non-breeding adults are overall slate-gray with a purplish gloss on the upperparts (hence the name). The throat is paler, the belly and vent white with slate gray spots. The upperparts are darker than the lower. Juveniles are as breeding adults, but the mantle and scapulars are fringed white and are less heavy spotted on the breast. Downy chicks are mottled chestnut, black and white.

Confusion species
Rock Sandpiper, particularly the Aleutian form with which the Purple Sandpiper is virtually identical (and some authorities consider conspecific). The difference in range (i.e., the unlikelihood of a Purple Sandpiper in the Aleutians) is the only reliable distinction, though the Rock tends to be a paler and richer chestnut.

Size
L: 7¾–8½ in. (20–22 cm). WS: 15–17½ in. (38–44 cm). W: 2–2¾ oz. (60–80 g).

Voice
Usually silent in winter. Usual call on breeding grounds is a short, sharp *kwit*, the display song a wheezing trill.

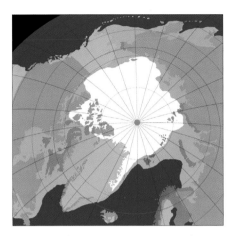

▼ Purple Sandpiper, Badlanddalen, northeast Greenland.

Distribution
Circumpolar, but very limited in the Nearctic. Breeds in southwestern and southeastern Greenland, and rarely in the north. Also breeds throughout Iceland, on Jan Mayen, in northern Fennoscandia, Svalbard, Franz Josef Land, Novaya Zemlya, the Taimyr Peninsula, the southern island of Severnaya Zemlya and northeast Chukotka. In the Nearctic, breeds on Baffin, Southampton and southern Ellesmere Islands. Almost always found at the coast, particularly rocky coasts, though also on coastal tundra. Migratory, though many Icelandic birds are resident. Greenland birds move to Iceland and the British Isles, birds from Svalbard and Russia move to the Norwegian coast or western Europe. Canadian birds move to the northeastern coast of the U.S. Wintering habitat is rocky coasts.

Diet
Chiefly invertebrates, especially crustaceans, often obtained by following a retreating wave to explore seaweed and rocks. Dodges waves with great agility, but will wade in shallow water and is occasionally (presumably deliberately) submerged.

Breeding
Gregarious at all times. Male has limited display repertoire: may fly with exaggerated slow, stiff wingbeats, and also has V-wing glide (these displays are chiefly territorial, and female may also perform the same). Pair will also lift one or both wings when on the ground. Pair-bond monogamous and probably seasonal. Female usually deserts male at hatching. Nest is placed among pebbles or on hummocky tundra. Nest is shallow depression with minimal lining of vegetation. Three to four red-brown blotched buff or light brown eggs, incubated by both birds (female has brood patch but since she often deserts, the male usually does most of the incubation) for 21–22 days. Sitting bird will perform rodent-run to distract potential predators, a strategy more typical of Purple Sandpipers than of any other calidrids. Chicks nidifugous and precocial. Cared for by male, but self-feeding. Fledge in *c.* 20 days and are independent at that time. Breed at 1–2 years.

Taxonomy and geographical variation
Monotypic.

Rock Sandpiper
Calidris ptilocnemis

Identification See p. 229

Breeding adults have dark brown crown and indistinct white/pale buff supercilia that occasionally meet to form a forehead patch. Cheeks are chestnut, rest of head is pale buff streaked chestnut, but throat is unmarked. There is a dark spot forward of the eye. The bill and iris are as Purple Sandpiper. The breast is buff, heavily streaked with dark brown. Streaking becomes heavier and darker toward belly, occasionally forming dark patch. The remaining underparts are white with minimal streaking. The mantle and scapulars are dark brown, fringed chestnut and buff. The rump and uppertail are dark brown with white sides. The central tail is dark gray-brown, the tail sides paler gray. The upperwing-coverts are gray, fringed white, the flight feathers black, the two areas separated by a broad white band. The underwing is white with dark gray leading and trailing edges to the flight feathers. Legs and feet as Purple Sandpiper.

Non-breeding adults resemble Purple Sandpipers but are paler overall, particularly on the underparts. Juvenile is as breeding adult but much less richly brown, and mantle and scapulars more broadly fringed buff. The underparts are also less heavily streaked, showing no hint of a dark belly patch. Downy chicks have marbled chestnut and black upperparts and white underparts.

Confusion species

See Purple Sandpiper. Few other waders favor rocky shorelines.

Size

L: 7³/₄–8¹/₂ in. (20–22 cm). WS: 15–17¹/₂ in. (38–44 cm). W: 2–2³/₄ oz. (60–80 g).

Voice

As Purple Sandpiper, though often claimed to be of higher pitch.

Distribution

Bering Sea. Breeds in western Alaska, Pribilof and Aleutian Islands, east Chukotka and the Commander and Kuril Islands. Habitat is as Purple Sandpiper. Migratory, moving to the west coast of the United States as far south as northern California. Habitat as in summer.

▲ Adult Rock Sandpiper of race *couesi*, Cold Bay.

Diet

Marine mollusks, crustaceans, larval flies and other terrestrial invertebrates, particularly beetles and spiders.

Breeding

Gregarious in winter, arriving at breeding sites in flocks, but then dispersing. Breeding is semi-colonial and birds gather to feed. Males defend and patrol territories to attract females. They are more vicious than Purple Sandpipers in their defense of territory, jumping at rivals with feet and bill. There is also a display flight in which the male flies close to the ground, then rises and hovers before gliding to the ground with wings in a V. Male also has a single wing-lift, and makes scrapes in the ground. Nest is one such scrape, improved a little by female. Nest is of vegetation and is lined with finer grasses. Two to four (usually four) eggs, variably colored pale green, pale gray, olive or buff olive, and heavily spotted or blotched dark brown. Incubation 22–24 days, sometimes by both birds, but often mainly by one or the other. Chicks nidifugous and precocial. Leave nest after about12 hours. Brooded at first, but self-feeding. Usually only the male stays with the chicks. Breed at 1–2 years.

Taxonomy and geographical variation

Polytypic. Nominate (described above) breeds on Pribilof Islands; occasionally referred to as the Pribilof Sandpiper. Three other races are recognized. *C. p. tschuktschorum*, the Northern Rock Sandpiper, breeds in Chukotka and western Alaska. It is smaller and redder than the nominate. *C. p. couesi*, the Aleutian Sandpiper, breeds on the Aleutians and in southern Alaska. It is smaller than the nominate and has cinnamon-washed upperparts with white feather tips, which give a scaly appearance. The Commander Sandpiper (*C. p. quarta*) breeds on the Commander and Kuril Islands. It is the smallest race and has the most uniform color. Despite the differences noted here, the three are almost indistinguishable from one another and from the Purple Sandpiper.

Red-necked Stint
Calidris ruficollis

Identification   See p. 228
Breeding adults have head, neck and upper breast solidly rufous or chestnut. The crown is streaked dark brown, the lores are darker, the supercilium paler behind the eye (but usually indistinct). There is a white ring around the base of the bill. The short, straight bill is black, the iris dark brown. The underparts are white, the lower breast with some dark brown streaking. The mantle and scapulars are dark brown, fringed chestnut and (sparse) pale gray. The rump, uppertail and central tail are dark brown, the tail and uppertail sides white/pale gray. The upperwing-coverts are gray-brown, becoming darker toward the tips, and separated from dark gray-brown flight feathers by a thin but distinct white bar. The underwing is white with mid-gray leading and trailing edges. The legs and feet are black. Non-breeding adults lose the chestnut coloration, the crown, nape and upperparts becoming uniformly gray-brown. The white supercilium is clear between the crown and the gray-brown upper cheeks. The underparts are white with some streaking to the sides of the breast. Juveniles have upperparts much as breeding adults but are brighter, with rufous and white fringing. The head is as non-breeding adults but chestnut-gray. Underparts are white with a buff tinge to the upper breast, which is also streaked dark brown. Downy chicks are mottled chestnut, black and white.

Confusion species
Within range, Little Stint is similar but smaller (though there is a size overlap so this is not always useful). Red-necked Stint has longer wings and shorter legs, and the upper breast color is always more solid. Red-necked Stint is also similar to the Spoon-billed Sandpiper, although the extraordinary spatulate bill of the latter is, of course, diagnostic if visible. Non-breeding birds in western Alaska may be confused with Semipalmated and Western Sandpipers.

Size
L: 5–6¼ in. (13–16 cm). WS: 13¾–15 in. (35–38 cm). W: ¾–1¼ oz. (20–35 g).

Voice
Very similar to Little Stint but a little lower, a sharp *chit*. Also a squeaking *week*. Display song is usually a repetitive *yek-yek*, also a curious whistling *oo-ea*.

Distribution
Eastern Russia, but also breeds sporadically in western Alaska. Breeding range extends from the Taimyr Peninsula to eastern Chukotka but not continuously. Prefers coastal locations, also found in damper areas of the tundra. Migratory, moving to southern China, Indonesia, Australia and New Zealand, where it occurs on coastal mudflats and salt marshes.

Diet
Invertebrates obtained by pecking and occasional probing. Wintering Red-necked Stints tend to focus on crustaceans and mollusks.

Breeding
Highly gregarious, particularly in winter. Male displays are apparently similar to those of Little Stints. Pair-bond unknown, perhaps monogamous. Nest is a depression concealed in vegetation in hummocky areas of the tundra, lined with available vegetation. Three to four cream or pale yellow eggs speckled red. Incubated by both adult birds for 21–23 days. Chicks are nidifugous and precocial. Cared for by the male only but self-feeding. Fledge at 15–20 days and become independent soon after. Breeding age unknown, but probably 1–2 years.

Taxonomy and geographical variation
Monotypic.

◀ Adult male Red-necked Stint in summer plumage with a chick, Chukotka. Compare the adult bird with Spoon-billed Sandpiper, which is very similar apart from the bill.

◄ Adult Sanderling in breeding plumage foraging for food on the shoreline. Victoria Island.

darker lores and ear-converts. Mantle and scapulars are dark gray, fringed buff. The upperwing is patterned as adult but browner. The underparts are white but with buff on sides of breast. Downy chicks are mottled black, buff and white.

Confusion species
Habits and habitat of breeding adults make confusion unlikely. Sanderling is much paler than Purple Sandpiper and does not overlap with the similar Spoon-billed Sandpiper. The pale wintering birds are unmistakable.

Size
L: 7³/₄–8¹/₂ in. (20–22 cm). WS: 16–18 in. (40–45 cm). W: 1¹/₂–2¹/₄ oz. (45–65 g).

Voice
Usual call is a short *klir*. There is also a high-pitched, thin *twee-twee-twee*. The flight song is a complex series of rippling churrs, trilling and curious froglike croaks.

Sanderling
Calidris alba

Identification   See p. 228
Breeding adults have brown-streaked chestnut head, neck and upper breast. There is a white ring around the base of the bill but no supercilium. The short, straight bill is black, the iris dark brown. The underparts below the breast are white. The mantle and scapulars are dark brown with pale gray and some chestnut fringing. The rump, uppertail and central tail feathers are dark brown, the sides of the rump and uppertail are white, the outer tail pale gray. The median and greater coverts are gray fringed by paler gray, the remaining coverts are darker, the flight feathers gray becoming almost black. The coverts and flight feathers are separated by a broad white band. The underwing is white, with a thin gray leading edge and broader gray trailing edge. The legs and feet are dark gray/black. Non-breeding adults are pale gray above, white underneath, with occasional gray shading on the breast. The wing pattern and colors are similar to breeding adults. Juveniles have a dark gray-brown crown, the rest of the head being white apart from

Distribution
Eastern Russia and North Atlantic. Probably the most northerly breeding wader. Breeds northern Greenland (on both coasts), Svalbard, Asian Russia (the Taimyr, Severnaya Zemlya and the New Siberia Islands) and the eastern Canadian Arctic islands north to Ellesmere Island. Prefers sandy shores, but will breed on dry, rocky tundra. Migratory; Asian birds move to Australia and southern Africa, Greenlandic and west Siberian birds to Europe and west Africa, and Canadian birds to both coasts of the U.S. and to Central and South America (as far as south as Tierra del Fuego), where sandy beaches are again preferred.

Diet
Invertebrates, usually obtained by probing as waves retreat, Also plant buds in spring. Wintering birds generally take mollusks and worms.

Breeding
Gregarious, except during breeding. Male display flight involves wing-fluttering followed by glides with the wings decurved, and occasional periods of hovering. Male also chases female on ground and performs jerking walk with female following, both birds calling. Pair-bond apparently varies from one breeding area to another; can be monogamous or polygamous, and probably seasonal. Nest is shallow scrape in open ground, sometimes even on a raised site. Minimal lining of available vegetation. Four buff/light-brown eggs with red-brown spots, incubated by both birds. Occasionally female will lay two clutches, with each parent incubating one. Incubation period 24–27 days. Chicks nidifugous and precocial. Incubating parent(s) cares for young, though chicks are self-feeding. Fledge in about 18 days and are independent at that time. Thought to breed at 2 years.

Taxonomy and geographical variation
Monotypic.

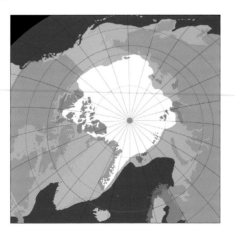

▲ Semipalmated Sandpiper in summer plumage, Seward Peninsula.

Semipalmated Sandpiper
Calidris pusilla

Identification   See p. 228
Breeding adults have pale gray/white heads, the crown and nape heavily streaked dark brown and gray. The lores are dark brown, the ear-coverts pale chestnut. The supercilium is white. The cheeks, throat and neck are streaked dark brown. The bill is black, the iris dark drown. The underparts are white with brown streaking on the breast and upper flanks. The mantle and scapulars are black, fringed pale gray and chestnut. The rump, uppertail and central tail are dark brown. The rump and tail have white sides. The upperwing-coverts are gray-brown, with buff fringing, and separated from the gray flight feathers by a thin white bar. The underwing is white, with gray leading and trailing edges. The legs and feet are dark brown/black, occasionally dark olive.

Non-breeding adults have white underparts with gray streaking to the sides of the breast. The upperparts are uniform gray-brown. Juveniles have head as breeding adults, but with darker crown and cheeks. The underparts are white, apart from the buff breast, which is indistinctly streaked brown. The mantle and scapulars are dark brown, fringed pale buff to give a scaly appearance. The upperwing-coverts are browner than the breeding adult. Downy chicks have buff/dark brown upperparts flecked white by feather tips and pale gray underparts.

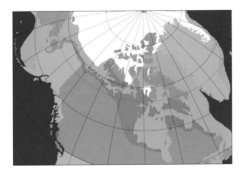

Confusion species
Baird's Sandpiper is larger. Western Sandpiper is almost identical, especially in non-breeding plumage, but breeding birds are more chestnut-colored, particularly on the head.

Size
L: 5–6 in. (13–15 cm). WS: 13½–15 in. (34–38 cm). W: ¾–1 oz. (20–30 g).

Voice
Usual call is a low, harsh *chrup* or *cheet*. Feeding flocks have a continuous rapid chattering. The flight call is a trilling *dree-dree*.

Distribution
Nearctic. Breeds across northern Alaska, the northern Canadian mainland and southerly Canadian Arctic islands (Banks, Victoria, Southampton and southern Baffin). Found in many habitats, ranging from coast, margins of inland pools and lakes to bare, even upland tundra. Migratory, moving to the Caribbean Islands and South America as far south as Uruguay. Wintering birds occur on mudflats and salt marshes, also on lake and river margins.

Diet
Benthic freshwater and marine invertebrates, found by pecking and probing. Also terrestrial insects and larvae.

Breeding
Gregarious in winter, forming flocks and even breeding colonies with Western Sandpipers. However, breeding pairs are territorial and less social. Displays poorly known, but probably as in related species. Males establish a breeding territory and attract females. Pair-bond apparently monogamous and probably seasonal. Female creates several nest scrapes in open ground, then lines one with available vegetation. Four brown-mottled, pale olive-buff eggs, incubated by both birds for 20–22 days. Chicks nidifugous and precocial. Self feeding. Fledge at 14–15 days but often abandoned at 10 days. Breed at 1–2 years, though some females apparently first breed at 4 years.

Taxonomy and geographical variation
Monotypic, but three distinct populations are recognized (Alaskan, central Canadian, and eastern Canadian) by their different migration routes and through their faithfulness to different breeding areas.

Western Sandpiper
Calidris mauri

Identification   See p. 228
Breeding adults have dark-brown, chestnut-fringed crown and nape. The supercilium is white with fine brown streaks. The lores are dark brown, the ear-coverts chestnut, the rest of the head white with fine brown steaks. The long, downcurved bill is dark brown/black, the iris dark brown. The underparts are white, heavily streaked with brown on the breast and with

brown arrowheads on the flanks. The belly has fewer, paler arrowheads, the vent is unmarked. The mantle is dark brown, fringed chestnut and gray, the scapulars are black and chestnut, fringed gray. The rump, uppertail and central tail are dark brown, the rump sides white, the tail sides gray. The upperwing-coverts are gray-brown, separated from the gray-brown flight feathers by a thin white bar. The legs and feet are dark brown/black. Non-breeding adults are as non-breeding Semipalmated Sandpipers, but paler on the breast. Juveniles are as juvenile Semipalmated Sandpipers, but upper scapulars are richly patterned with chestnut. Lower scapulars also differ, being gray/black. As in other calidrids, downy chicks are cryptic, being mottled black and brown with white flecks.

Confusion species
Breeding adults are very similar to Semipalmated Sandpipers but are more chestnut, particularly on the head, and have a longer bill, downcurved at the tip. Winter birds and juveniles are virtually indistinguishable from Semipalmated Sandpipers. In Chukotka, Western Sandpiper may be confused with Long-toed Stint (which has yellow legs) and Spoon-billed Sandpiper (the bill of which is diagnostic).

Size
L: 5½–6½ in. (14–17 cm). WS: 13¾–15 in. (35–38 cm). W: ¾–1½ oz. (20–35 g).

Voice
Usual call is a thin, harsh *cheet* distinguishable from the Semipalmated Sandpiper with experience. Feeding flocks chatter as Semipalmated. Display flight call is a weak, trilling *twee-twee*.

Distribution
Bering Sea. Breeds in Chukotka and western Alaska. Rare in northern Alaska. Prefers drier habitat than Semipalmated Sandpiper, though mixed flocks are seen. Migratory, with Russian birds crossing the Bering Sea to join Alaskan birds on flights south to California and the Caribbean, where birds prefer sandy beaches and mudflats.

▼ Western Sandpiper in breeding plumage, St. Lawrence Island.

Diet
Chiefly freshwater insects and other arthropods, also mollusks and worms. Pecks and probes. Distinctive feeding pattern, often feeding with head beneath the water.

Breeding
Highly gregarious, both in winter and at breeding-site feeding grounds, where Western Sandpipers occasionally form colonies with Semipalmated Sandpipers (though they are also sometimes antagonistic to them). Nesting density at colonies can exceed 500 nests per hectare. Males are highly territorial, lifting wings against rivals and occasionally rushing at them with head lowered. Pair-bond monogamous and seasonal. Male makes several nest scrapes (usually in marshy areas, but also in concealed places on drier tundra), the female choosing one and lining it with leaves and lichen. Three to four (usually four) pale brown or cream eggs, heavily spotted red. Incubated for 18–21 days by both parents. Chicks nidifugous and precocial. Usually cared for by male as female leaves nesting area, but self-feeding. Fledge at 17–21 days and are independent soon after. Breed at 1–2 years.

Taxonomy and geographical variation
Monotypic.

Sharp-tailed Sandpiper
Calidris acuminata

Identification
See p. 228

Breeding adults have a chestnut crown streaked black, a white supercilium with fine brown streaking and mid-brown lores and ear-coverts. The remainder of the head and the neck are cream/buff finely streaked with brown. The slightly downturned bill is dark brown, yellow-brown toward the base. The iris is dark brown and there is a white eye-ring. The upper breast is buff, heavily marked with dark brown spots. The remaining underparts are white, the spots becoming arrowheads on the lower breast, belly and flanks but with fewer markings on the vent and undertail. The rump and uppertail are dark brown, the central tail darker. The sides of the rump and uppertail are white, mottled with dark brown, the tail sides are brown. The mantle and scapulars are dark brown, fringed chestnut and pale buff. The upperwing is uniformly gray-brown (the flight feathers darker), the coverts fringed cinnamon. There is a very thin white wing-bar. The underwing-coverts are white, but pale gray toward the leading edge. The underwing flight feathers are gray. The legs and feet are yellow-green, sometimes gray-green.

Non-breeding adults are as breeding adults, but paler overall and without the heavy marking of the underparts, and with no chestnut fringing of the upperparts. Juveniles have a chestnut/rufous crown, a more distinct white supercilium and less streaking on the head and neck. The upper breast is pale chestnut and lacks the heavy marking of breeding adults. The upperparts are more richly fringed chestnut. Downy chicks are rufous-brown, spotted with black.

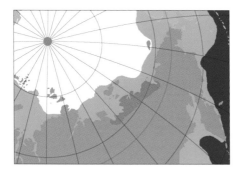

Confusion species
The range of the Sharp-tailed Sandpiper lies wholly within that of the Pectoral Sandpiper and confusion may occur, particularly with wintering birds. Breeding Sharp-tailed Sandpipers are more chestnut, and heavily streaked below, without the pectoral band.

Size
L: 6½–8 in. (17–21 cm). WS: 16½–19 in. (42–48 cm). W: 2–3 oz. (55–85 g).

Voice
Higher, more metallic and more musical than Pectoral Sandpiper, often a twittering *weep-weep-weep*. Flight song includes a soft trill and a curious low *hoot*.

Distribution
Eastern Russia. Breeds only in northern Yakutia between the Yena and Kolyma Rivers, where it is found on both wet and dry tundra, though preferring hummocky peat. Migratory, moving to New Guinea, Australia and New Zealand, where it prefers mudflats, estuaries and coastal lagoons.

Diet
Probes for insect larvae (chiefly tipulids) in spring, but pecks for adult insects in summer.

Breeding
Gregarious in winter, often forming flocks with other calidrids, but more solitary at breeding sites, though as in Western Sandpipers breeding-site nest density can be high. Display not well documented, but male has short, rising flight followed by a glide with raised wings. Males are polygynous, mating with several females, each of which will raise a brood. Nest is placed in a damp area concealed by vegetation, particularly willow. Nest is a shallow depression lined with willow leaves or other plant material. Four brown-speckled olive-brown eggs, incubated for 19–23 days by female only. Chicks nidifugous and precocial. Cared for by female, but self-feeding. Fledge at about 20 days and are independent soon after. Breeding age unknown, but probably 1–2 years.

Taxonomy and geographical variation
Monotypic.

Temminck's Stint
Calidris temminckii

Identification
See p. 228

Breeding adults have a chestnut crown streaked dark brown, the remaining head and neck pale brown with darker streaking. The lores are dark brown, the ear-coverts gray-brown. The

▼ A foraging group of Sharp-tailed Sandpipers.

supercilium is indistinct. The short, straight bill is dark brown/black, the iris is dark brown. The throat is white, the upper breast buff with brown and gray-brown streaking. The cutoff to the rest of the white underparts can be abrupt. The mantle and scapulars are dark brown, fringed chestnut and gray-tipped. In some birds the dark brown on the scapulars dominates, giving the sitting bird a dark-spotted look, but in others the overall appearance can be gray-brown. The rump, uppertail-coverts and central tail are gray-brown, the central tail dark brown at the tip. The sides of the tail are pale gray, then white. The long tail and the outer white feathers, together with the white sides of the uppertail, are diagnostic. The upperwing is gray-brown, the coverts fringed buff, with a thin white bar. The underwing-coverts are white with gray on the primary coverts. The underwing flight feathers are gray. The legs and feet are green, gray-green or yellow-brown.

Non-breeding adults are duller overall, the head and upper breast gray-brown, the upperparts gray-brown, mottled dull brown on the sitting bird. Juveniles are as non-breeding adults, but with upper feathers buff fringed, and upper breast brown rather than gray-brown. Downy chicks are mottled buff, pale chestnut and dark brown.

Confusion species
Little Stint, but greenish yellow legs are diagnostic.

Size
L: 5–6 in. (13–15 cm). WS: 13½–15 in. (34–38 cm). W: ½–1 oz. (18–30 g).

Voice
A distinctive, loud trilling *tirr-tirr-tirr*. Display song, which is heard on the ground as well as in flight, is a rhythmic reel, recalling a cricket.

Distribution
Palearctic. Absent from Greenland and Iceland, but breeds from Scandinavia to Chukotka along the north coast of Russia, though absent from Russia's Arctic islands apart from the New Siberia Islands. Found in all types of tundra, though prefers the sheltered margins of rivers and lakes to exposed coastal shores. Migratory; European birds move south to sub-Saharan Africa, Asian birds travel to southern Asia and Japan. Wintering birds prefer inland waters or sheltered inlets.

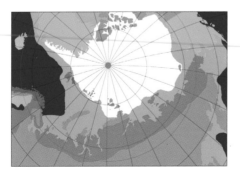

▲ Adult Temminck's Stint.

Diet
Invertebrates, particularly insects and especially beetles. Coastal birds take crustaceans and mollusks. Prey found by pecking, rarely if ever by probing.

Breeding
Gregarious, but not highly so. Male display flight is a slow round of its territory, occasionally with fluttering V-wings, but also a hover with fluttering wings. On the ground the male adopts V-wings and flutters them vigorously while rising on tiptoe. Pair-bond often bigamous. Female mates with one male who incubates first clutch, then mates with second male and incubates that clutch herself. First male mates with second female during breaks from incubation. Nest is shallow depression in open ground or low vegetation, lined with available vegetation. Four heavily red-brown blotched, cream/buff eggs, incubated by both sexes, but if polygamy occurs each bird may incubate one clutch, as above. Incubation period 21–22 days. Chicks nidifugous and precocial. Cared for by incubating adult, but self-feeding. Fledge in 15–18 days and are independent at that time. Breed at 1 year (up to 3 years for male).

Taxonomy and geographical variation
Monotypic.

White-rumped Sandpiper
Calidris fuscicollis

Identification See p. 228
Breeding adults have crown and ear-coverts pale chestnut, finely streaked with dark brown, and a white supercilium also finely streaked dark brown. The lores are dark brown. The remainder of the head and neck is whitish with fine dark brown

streaking. The bill is black, usually with a dark-olive base to the lower mandible. The base of the lower mandible also has a dull red spot, seen in all plumages, but this is hard to observe at a distance. The bill tip droops slightly. The iris is dark brown. The underparts are white, the breast and flanks heavily streaked dark brown, with spots on the breast, arrowheads on the flanks. The mantle and scapulars are dark brown, fringed chestnut, gray and buff. The rump is as the mantle, despite the bird's name: it is the uppertail that is white. The tail is gray. The upperwing-coverts are gray-brown, fringed white or cream, the flight feathers dark gray-brown. There is a thin white bar. The underwing is white with a narrow gray leading edge and a broader gray trailing edge. The legs and feet are dark gray/black. Non-breeding adults are gray-brown overall, the breast more buff-gray with faint darker streaking. The white supercilium, somewhat indistinct in breeding adults, is more prominent. Juveniles are as breeding adults, but much more boldly patterned on the upperparts of the mantle and scapulars; these are fringed chestnut, white and buff. The breast is buff, finely streaked dark brown, but there is no heavy marking to the flanks. Downy chicks have mottled black and brown upperparts and pale gray or buff underparts.

Confusion species
White-rumped Sandpiper has long wings that extend beyond the tail, the tips describing ovals as the bird walks and pecks. This is also characteristic of Baird's Sandpiper, the range of which it overlaps, so it does not help to distinguish these two similar species. However, White-rumped is more heavily marked on the underparts, brighter above and the white uppertail is diagnostic in flight. The reddish spot at the base of the lower mandible is diagnostic if visible.

Size
L: 6–7 in. (15–18 cm). WS: 16–18 in. (40–45 cm). W: 1¼–1½ oz. (35–45 g).

Voice
The flight call is very distinctive, a high, rodentlike, squeaking *zeet*. There are also a rattling *tik-tik-tik*, occasionally as a single note, and a more musical twitter.

▼ Female White-rumped Sandpiper on the nest, Alaska.

Distribution
Breeds in northern Alaska where rare, also Arctic Canada from Yukon to western Hudson Bay and the southern Arctic islands (Banks, Victoria, Southampton and western Baffin). Very rare east of Hudson Bay. Feeds on coastal shorelines and near tundra pools, also found on drier tundra. Migratory, moving to southern South America as far as Tierra del Fuego and the Falkland Islands, where it is found at the coast and by inland waters.

Diet
Invertebrates, particularly insects, aquatic worms and mollusks. Also takes some seeds.

Breeding
Gregarious, occasionally forming flocks with other calidrids, but males are aggressively territorial at breeding sites. Male flies to 10–25 m, then hovers and makes its rattling call before gliding to the ground. Female occasionally joins in. On the ground, males raise one wing and may also expand the highly inflatable throat. Males are polygynous and take no part in incubating or chick-rearing, departing the breeding grounds before egg-laying is completed. Nest is usually on a dry hummock in wet tundra. Female constructs a cup of twigs and grass and lines it with vegetation. Four dark red-brown spotted and blotched eggs, incubated by female only for about 22 days. Chicks nidifugous and precocial. Brooded and cared for by female. Fledge at 16–17 days and are independent at that time. Probably breed at 1 year.

Taxonomy and geographical variation
Monotypic.

Broad-billed Sandpiper
Limicola falcinellus

Identification See p. 228
Breeding adult has a dark brown and black crown, delineated by a thin white stripe that meets the white supercilium in front of the eye. The lores are dark brown, the ear-coverts dark chestnut. The remaining head and neck are white with dark brown streaks. The bill is overall black, but sometimes dark brown or dark green and usually yellowish at base. It is broad at the base (as viewed from above), tapering toward the tip,

which curves downward. The iris is dark brown. The underparts are white, though the breast is occasionally gray-buff with heavy, dark brown streaking on it, the upper belly and the flanks. The mantle and scapulars are dark brown, fringed pale chestnut and white, the white fringing producing white lines on the sitting bird that form a V if seen from above in flight. The rump, uppertail and central pair of tail feathers are dark brown, the sides of the rump and uppertail are white, the remaining tail mid-gray. The wing-coverts are dark brown, fringed lighter brown. The flight feathers are dark brown. There is a narrow, often indistinct, white bar. The relatively short legs and feet are dark gray or dark olive.

Non-breeding adults have white heads, dark gray streaked crown, distinct supercilium and dark lores and ear-coverts forming a dark eye-stripe. The face and neck are finely streaked dark gray. The underparts are white, with mid-gray streaking on the breast. The upperparts are gray, with dark gray streaking from feather shafts. Juveniles are as breeding adults, but the crown is more boldly streaked, the breast less heavily streaked and the upperparts fringed chestnut and buff. Downy chicks are mottled dark brown, chestnut and white.

Confusion species
None. The bill shape is diagnostic in all plumages.

Size
L: 6–7 in. (15–18 cm), of which the bill is 1 in. (3 cm). WS: 14–16 in. (36–40 cm). W: 1–1½ oz. (30–45 g).

Voice
Usual flight call is a buzzing *krreeet*. There is also a short, sharp *chet*. Display song is a more rhythmic buzz, occasionally more a trill.

Distribution
Palearctic. Breeds in northern Fennoscandia and in isolated areas of Asian Russia (e.g., the Taimyr Peninsula and near the Indigirka and Kolyma Rivers). Rare and elusive, preferring wet areas, but also occurs on more accessible margins of marshland, ponds and coast. Migratory, moving to southern Africa, southern Arabia, southern India, Indonesia and northern Australia, where it winters on tidal mudflats and beaches.

▼ Broad-billed Sandpiper on the nest, Norway.

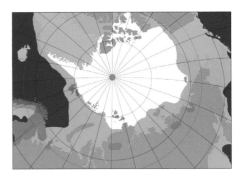

Diet
Insects and seeds. Wintering birds also take mollusks and worms. Feeds by both pecking and probing.

Breeding
Gregarious, but not highly so, though forms loose colonies at breeding sites. Little data on display flight but pair apparently indulge in chasing flights. Pair-bond monogamous and apparently long-lived. Nest is placed in dry tussock or sedge clump in marshland. Nest is depression lined with vegetation. Three to four buff or light-brown eggs very heavily blotched red-brown, incubated by both birds for 20–22 days. Chicks nidifugous and precocial. Cared for by both parents initially, finally by male only, but self-feeding. Thought to fledge in around 20 days and to breed at 1 year.

Taxonomy and geographical variation
Polytypic. The nominate race breeds in Scandinavia and on the Kola Peninsula. Race *sibirica* breeds in Siberia. It has brighter and more chestnut upperparts, a less distinct white stripe on the crown and a buffish cinnamon breast.

Buff-breasted Sandpiper
Tryngites subruficollis

Identification See p. 229
Breeding adult has buff head, neck and breast, with paler buff belly and vent and very pale undertail. Crown and forehead are streaked brown. Distinctive short bill is dark brown, with a yellowish-brown base to the lower mandible. Iris is brown. There is some brown spotting to the sides of the breast. Pale fringing to the breast feathers gives a vague mottling effect. Mantle, scapulars, rump and uppertail are dark brown with wide buff fringes. Tail is dark brown with a narrow white tip. Upperwing-coverts are dark brown with buff fringes, the pale tips of the greater coverts forming a thin wing-bar. Flight feathers are vermiculated dark brown and buff. Underwing is silver-white with a buff leading edge, and flight feathers have black tips and black spotting on subterminal zones. Legs and feet are yellow, sometimes olive-yellow.

Non-breeding adults are as breeding adults, though the buff fringing of the upperparts tends to be broader. Juveniles are as non-breeding adults, but the upper feathers have buff/white fringing, which gives scaly appearance. Downy chicks have gray-brown upperparts and cream underparts.

▶ Buff-breasted Sandpiper.

Confusion species
Ruff is similar but larger, grayer and longer-billed. Ranges of the two species do not overlap (except rarely in north Chukotka).

Size
L: 7–7³/₄ in. (18–20 cm). WS: 17–19 in. (43–48 cm). W: 2–2¹/₂ oz. (55–75 g).

Voice
Usually silent, but has a rattling flight call *grr-r-eet*. Also a quiet *tik* and short *chut*. Displaying birds make a rapid clicking.

Distribution
Eastern Russia and western Nearctic. Breeds on Wrangel Island and northeastern Chukotka, in northern Alaska and Yukon, southern Banks Island and on Victoria, Prince of Wales, Somerset and Devon Islands. Though once numerous, hunting in the 19th century caused a dramatic decline in numbers, and the species is now rare. Prefers dry tundra; also seen in damper areas, but is one of least aquatic waders. Migratory, with both Russian and American birds moving to Argentina and Paraguay, where they prefer dry, usually upland, grasslands.

Diet
Insects and their larvae, other terrestrial arthropods, and occasionally seeds. Usually feeds in dry areas away from water. Walks and pecks, very rarely probes.

Breeding
Gregarious, but not highly so, at all times. Winter flocks of 10–50 birds. Males engage in a form of lekking, defending territories of up to 10 a. (4 ha) and displaying by standing with one or both wings raised to show the silver underwing. Males also jump with fluttering wings. However, solitary displays are also seen. Males mate with any approaching female, but that is their sole contribution to chick-raising. Females will also mate with several males. Nest set on the ground, usually on a tussock in a damp area, but also concealed by vegetation in drier area. Nest is depression lined with grass and moss. Three to four white, pale buff or pale olive-buff eggs, spotted or blotched darker. Incubated for 19–25 days by female only. Chicks nidifugous and precocial, leaving nest on day of hatching. Cared for by female, but self-feeding. Fledge at 16–20 days and are independent soon after. Thought to breed at 1 year.

Taxonomy and geographical variation
Monotypic.

Ruff
Philomachus pugnax

Identification   See p. 229
Breeding males (ruffs) have bare red or orange-red faces with many warts, either of the same color or yellowish or greenish. Ear-tufts cover the sides of the nape and a circular ruff extends to breast; these have highly variable shades of chestnut, white or black with purple gloss. The ruff may have complete rings of black, incomplete rings or no rings at all. The bill is dark brown, reddish toward the base, but may also be orange-yellow to red-pink and may have a black tip. The iris is dark brown. The underparts are white, but there may be some or extensive black or chestnut on the breast and flanks. The mantle and scapular colors are also variable, being black with purple gloss, chestnut with heavy black barring or white with gray or black barring. Rump is dark brown, uppertail brown with white sides and tail gray. Upperwing-coverts gray-brown with paler fringing, flight feathers dark brown, with a narrow white wing-bar. The underwing is white, with pale gray shading toward the tips of the flight feathers. The legs and feet are orange-yellow or orange-pink, though some males have yellow legs.

Breeding females (reeves) are much duller, and generally smaller than the males. They lack the bare face, ear-coverts and ruff, having a gray head with a chestnut tinge and dark streaking. The upperparts are gray-brown, fringed white and the tertials show a bold pattern of cinnamon, dark gray and white. The underparts are white with heavy buff and black streaking on the breast and flanks. Non-breeding adults are similar to breeding females, but have white heads with gray-brown crown and nape, much duller upperparts and much whiter underparts, with gray-brown mottling on the breast. Some males have white breasts and collars, and some even have white heads and mantles, and white on the scapulars, appearing almost as white birds with gray-brown wings. Juveniles are similar to breeding females but overall brighter, as the upperparts are dark brown, fringed pale chestnut and

▲ Adult female Ruff (known as a reeve), north Norway.

white, with breasts that are buff with gray mottling. Juvenile males have pale, less mottled breasts and lighter upperparts. Downy chicks are mottled chestnut, black and white.

Confusion species
Breeding males are unmistakable. Females are less distinctive, but Ruff does not share range with possible confusion species.

Size
Male L: 10–12 in. (25–30 cm). WS: 21½–24 in. (55–60 cm). W: 5½–7¾ oz. (160–220 g). Female L: 7¾–10 in. (20–25 cm). WS: 18½–20½ in. (47–52 cm). W: 2¾–5¼ oz. (80–150 g).

Voice
Almost silent. Feeding birds have a series of hoarse grunts and croaks. In flight, there is an occasional shrill, rising *oo-ee*.

Distribution
Palearctic, but absent from Iceland. Breeds in Scandinavia and eastern Russia to central Chukotka, but absent from all Russian Arctic islands. Prefers deltas and the margins of shallow lakes, but avoids barren tundra. Migratory, moving to western Europe, the Mediterranean, the Indian subcontinent and much of Africa, where water margins are preferred.

Diet
Invertebrates obtained by pecking and probing, occasionally in shallow water, sometimes with the head submerged. Swims to reach emerging insects at surface. Similar diet in winter.

Breeding
Gregarious, usually highly so, with flocks of tens of thousands recorded in Africa. Ruffs have elaborate lek behavior. Lek arenas are traditional sites, sometimes 100 years old or more. Ruffs at these sites form three distinct groups: residents (that hold territories at the arena), migrants (that attempt to obtain territories, and may hold territories at other arenas) and opportunistic satellites. Color variability of ear-coverts and ruff are associated with these groups. Residents invariably have black ear-coverts. Satellites invariably have white ear-coverts and ruffs and are tolerated by residents because this coloration is attractive to females. Satellites will hold territory in the absence of residents, but resume their satellite role when a resident returns. Satellites may display a behavioral dimorphism; this and their white coloration are probably heritable. A displaying Ruff flutters his wings and jumps in the air, with ruff in full-circle position and ear-coverts raised. Birds also threaten one another in horizontal posture and may fight. A Ruff will mate with any interested reeve. Polygamy is common, but monogamy has been suggested by some studies. Nesting reeves are solitary, though often there will be several nests near the lek. Nests are often in wet areas, in concealed places. Nest is a shallow scrape lined with local vegetation. Three to four heavily creamy buff eggs with red-brown blotches. Incubated by reeve only for 20–23 days. Chicks nidifugous and precocial. Cared for by reeve but self-feeding. Reeve has rodent-run and injury-feigning anti-predator strategies. Young fledge in 25–28 days but usually independent earlier as reeve leaves breeding area. Reeves probably breed at 2 years, ruffs at 3 years.

Taxonomy and geographical variation
Monotypic.

◀ Adult male Ruff in breeding plumage, Finland.

Spoon-billed Sandpiper
Eurynorhynchus pygmaeus

Identification See p. 228

Breeding adults have chestnut head and neck, with forehead, crown and nape streaked dark brown. The lores are mid-brown, the coloration continuing as an eye-stripe. Occasionally there is a vague brown collar. At the base of the bill is a ring of paler, sometimes whitish, feathers, this coloration continuing on the chin. The bill is black. It is broad at the base then tapers, before becoming flattened into a diamond shape. The iris is dark brown. The upper breast is chestnut, the lower breast paler, then merging into white underparts. The breast is finely streaked dark brown. The belly and vent are unmarked, the flanks have few marks. The mantle and scapulars are dark brown, fringed chestnut and white. The rump and central uppertail are dark gray-brown, the sides white. The tail is dark gray. The upperwing-coverts are dark brown, fringed buff and separated by a distinct white bar from dark brown flight feathers. The underwing is white, with gray-brown leading and trailing edges. The legs and feet are black. Non-breeding adults replace the chestnut of the head and breast with white. The crown and forehead are streaked gray-brown, but there is little or no streaking on the underparts. The upperparts are gray, fringed white. Juveniles are as breeding adults but without the chestnut head and breast. The crown is dark brown, streaked darker, the ear-coverts dark brown. The sides of the lower breast are buff, the buff occasionally forming a complete band. Some fine, dark brown streaking is on the sides of the lower

▼ Spoon-billed Sandpiper with chicks, Chukotka.

breast and on the flanks. The upperparts are dark brown, fringed buff or white. Downy chicks have mottled chestnut and dark brown upperparts, with creamy buff underparts.

Confusion species

As the name suggests, the bill is diagnostic if visible. However, feeding birds often show only the bill profile so the spatulate tip is not apparent. Spoon-billed Sandpiper is then difficult to separate from Red-necked Stint; the latter has grayer upperparts.

Size

L: 5½–6¼ in. (14–16 cm). WS: 14–16 in. (36–40 cm). W: ¾–1¼ oz. (20–35 g).

Voice

Usually a soft *teep* or a shriller *wheep*. Display song is a rippling trill.

Distribution

Eastern Russia. Breeds in far eastern Chukotka and (very rarely) northern Kamchatka. Prefers coastal lagoons and estuaries in summer. Migratory, moving to southeastern Asia where it winters on sandy beaches. Rare, with a population estimated at around 2,500.

Diet

Chiefly aquatic invertebrates, usually obtained by sweeping the water surface with the bill, hence this species' preference for shallow saline waters. The feeding method is reminiscent of a flamingo, though the head is not inverted.

Breeding

Gregarious, but as the limited population is spread thinly over a considerable length of coastline this can mean only a few dozen pairs in any one area. Male display involves a circling flight at 50–66 ft. (15–20 m) with occasional hovering and plunging, usually calling throughout. Apparently monogamous. Nests in dry place close to water. Nest is shallow scrape, usually lined with willow leaves.

Three to four pale yellow-brown or olive-buff eggs with brown spots and blotches. Incubated by both birds, but often chiefly or solely the male, for 19–23 days. Chicks nidifugous and precocial. Usually cared for by male only but self-feeding. Fledge at 15–18 days. Probably breed at 1 year.

Taxonomy and geographical variation
Monotypic.

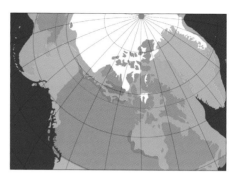

Stilt Sandpiper
Micropalama himantopus

Identification
See p. 229

Breeding adults have white heads with several distinctive features: the crown is streaked brown, fringed chestnut and white; the supercilium is white and very distinct: the lores are dark chestnut; the ear-coverts are bright chestnut. The remainder of the face and the white neck are streaked brown. The black bill is long and downcurved. It is laterally flattened at the base, which may be dark gray. The iris is dark brown. The underparts are white, the breast heavily streaked and barred with dark brown, the belly and vent barred with dark brown. The mantle and scapulars are dark brown, fringed white, giving the appearance of white with dark blotches on the sitting bird. The mantle is also fringed chestnut. The upperwing-coverts are gray-brown, fringed white, the flight feathers gray-brown, the primaries darker. The rump and upper tail are white. The central tail is dark gray, the sides paler. The underwing-coverts are white, the flight feathers gray-brown. The long legs and feet are greenish-yellow. Non-breeding adults are as breeding adults, but more "restrained"; they lack the chestnut patches on the head and the upperparts are much duller, a uniform pale gray-brown. Juveniles have pale buff head, neck and breast, with darker crown, lores and ear-coverts. The supercilium is white and distinct. The head, neck and breast are finely streaked brown. The remaining underparts are white. The mantle and scapulars are dark brown with wide white fringes, giving a scaly appearance. The upperwing-coverts are gray-brown, fringed pale buff. The underwing is gray or gray-brown with a white center. Downy chicks have mottled brown and black upperparts flecked white by feather tips, and buff or pale buffish white underparts.

Confusion species
None, though care is needed when Stilt Sandpipers are feeding with dowitchers.

Size
L: 7–8½ in. (18–22 cm), bill 1½ in. (4 cm). WS: 17–19 in. (43–48 cm). W: 1¾–2½ oz. (50–70 g).

Voice
Usual call is either a rolling *gr-uhr* or a sharper *whuu*. Display song is a series of guttural trills and buzzes.

▶ Stilt Sandpiper in breeding plumage, Hudson Bay.

Distribution
Nearctic. Breeds from northern Alaska (where rare) to Bathurst Inlet, and on southern Victoria Island. Also breeds around southwestern Hudson Bay. Chiefly found in wet tundra, but also found on drier tundra of Victoria Island. Migratory, moving to central South America, where it occurs in shallow or coastal pools, rarely on beaches.

Diet
Terrestrial and aquatic invertebrates, occasionally obtained by pecking but usually by probing, with bill thrust vertically downward (as in dowitchers). Also takes seeds.

Breeding
Gregarious in winter, less so at breeding sites. Males establish territory with flight display, hovering at 65–195 ft. (20–60 m) above chosen site then circling it while calling. Male then glides to ground with wings held in a V. On the ground the male pursues the female, still holding wings in a V. Pair-bond monogamous and probably seasonal. Nest is set in an open, dry place or on hummock in damp area. Male makes one or two scrapes and female chooses. Nest lined with vegetation. Four olive eggs, heavily marked brown; incubated by both birds for about 20 days. Chicks nidifugous and precocial. Brooded and cared for by both birds but self-feeding, and parents leave before fledging. Fledge at about 18 days. Breed at 2 years.

Taxonomy and geographical variation
Monotypic.

Snipes and dowitchers

Snipes and dowitchers are usually grouped together in the subfamily Gallinagininae as they share characteristics in shape and feeding behavior, though less so in plumage. In addition to the species below, the Jack Snipe (*Lymnocryptes minimus*) breeds in northern Russia, though not to the coast except near the White Sea.

Long-billed Dowitcher
Limnodromus scolopaceus

Identification See p. 230

Breeding adults have chestnut heads apart from a dark brown crown, which is finely streaked paler. The supercilium is pale chestnut, the lores dark brown, this coloration continuing as a narrow eye-stripe. The bill is dark brown tinged greenish at the base. The iris is dark brown. The underparts are chestnut or pale chestnut, the neck and upper breast finely streaked dark brown, the lower breast, flanks and undertail finely barred dark brown at the sides. The mantle and scapulars are dark brown and black, fringed chestnut or buff. The back, rump and uppertail are white, the lower rump and uppertail barred with dark brown. The tail is barred dark brown/black and white, the dark bars being broader than the white so the tail looks dark in flight. The upperwing-coverts are gray-brown, fringed paler, the flight feathers dark gray-brown, but with pale or white tips to the secondaries. The underwing-coverts are white with fine brown barring. The legs and feet are pale olive or yellow-olive. Non-breeding adults are pale gray-brown above, the white supercilium distinct. The neck and upper breast are mottled gray-brown, the coloration ending abruptly: the rest of the underparts are white. Juveniles have gray-brown head and neck, the crown and eye-line darker, the supercilium white. The breast is gray-cinnamon with fine brown streaking. The flanks are similar, the belly white, the vent and undertail white with dark brown spots. The mantle and scapulars are dark brown with narrow chestnut fringes. The tertials are dark gray-brown with pale rufous or buff fringes. Downy chicks are mottled chestnut and tawny flecked gray.

Confusion species

The Long-billed and Short-billed Dowitchers were only recognized as separate species in 1950. Their similarity may cause confusion, though the range differences mean the two rarely overlap. The tail pattern and golden, rather than chestnut, upperparts of the Short-billed are diagnostic (though may be difficult to discern at a distance). If the two species are adjacent, the longer bill and legs of Long-billed are usually apparent. Calls are also diagnostic.

▼ Long-billed Dowitcher foraging at the water's edge, Barrow.

Size
L: 10¼–12 in. (26–30 cm), bill 2–3 in. (6–8 cm). WS: 1½–2 ft. (48–55 cm). W: 3–4½ oz. (90–130 g).

Voice
Usual call is a high-pitched, sharp *keek*, sometimes repeated four to six times. Feeding flocks have soft chatter (whereas Short-billed flocks are invariably silent). Display song is sharp, buzzing *pee-tee-wee*.

Distribution
Eastern Russia and western North America. Breeds in western and northern Alaska and the northern coast of Canada around the Mackenzie Delta, and occasionally on Herschel Island. In Asian Russia, the bird breeds on the northern coast from the Yana Delta to Chukotka and south to the Anadyr River, and on Wrangel Island. Prefers shallow freshwater, but also found in coastal locations. Migratory, moving to southwestern United States and Mexico, where it favors the same habitat.

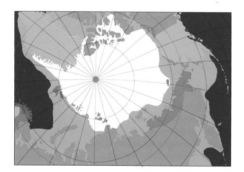

Diet
Burrowing crustaceans, aquatic worms and mollusks obtained by probing the substrate rapidly, the bill moving almost vertically in a "sewing machine" action. Nocturnal feeder in winter.

Breeding
Gregarious in winter, less so at breeding sites, though small colonies form. Male has hovering display flight, calling throughout. Not highly territorial or aggressive, often feeding with neighboring birds, though defending nest area. Pair-bond apparently monogamous and seasonal. Nests on a dry mound within a swampy area or near water. Nest is a depression lined with local vegetation. Three to four variably brown eggs; base colour is green, olive or blue, always heavily spotted with shades of brown. Eggs incubated for 21–22 days by both birds at first, but finally by male only. Chicks nidifugous and precocial, leaving nest on day of hatching, being led through long grass by male bird hovering ahead of them. Brooded and cared for by male bird only but self-feeding. Fledge at 20–30 days. Probably breed at 1–2 years.

Taxonomy and geographical variation
Monotypic.

Short-billed Dowitcher
Limnodromus griseus

Identification
See p. 230
Breeding adults as Long-billed Dowitcher, but mantle and scapular fringing is golden-buff rather than chestnut. Underparts more solidly chestnut with no streaking on throat or neck, and spotting rather than barring on the sides of the breast. Non-breeding adults are paler overall than Long-billed Dowitcher. Juveniles have buff rather than gray-brown breasts and flanks, and less abrupt cessation of color on breast. As with breeding adults, the perched bird looks more golden than chestnut. Downy chicks are mottled black and red-brown, flecked white by feather tips.

Confusion species
See Long-billed Dowitcher.

Size
L: 9–11 in. (23–28 cm), bill 2–2¼ in. (5–6 cm). WS: 18–20 in. (45–50 cm). W: 3–4¼ oz. (85–120 g).

Voice
Usual call is a rippling *tu-tu-tu*. Feeding flocks are usually silent, but single sharp *tu* occasionally heard. Display song similar to Long-billed.

▼ Short-billed Dowitcher, Churchill.

◀ Bar-tailed Godwit in summer plumage, north Norway.

Pair-bond monogamous, probably long-lived. Nests on dry, high ground in marshland. Nest is a shallow scrape lined with vegetation. Three to four light-brown eggs, heavily blotched red-brown; incubated by both birds (chiefly male) for 20–21 days. Chicks nidifugous and precocial. Cared for by both parents. Thought to fledge in 25–30 days. Breed at 2 years.

Taxonomy and geographical variation
Polytypic. The nominate race breeds in Scandinavia and western Russia. *L. l. baueri* breeds in eastern Russia and Alaska; *baueri* has dark gray-brown back and upper rump, and white lower rump and uppertail, heavily barred dark brown. The underwing-coverts are also heavily barred dark brown. Central Russian birds are intermediate and sometimes separated as a third subspecies, *menzbieri*.

Hudsonian Godwit
Limosa haemastica

Identification
See p. 230

Breeding males have pale gray heads and necks, finely streaked dark brown. The crown is dark-brown streaked pale chestnut. The white supercilium is broader in front of the eye. A dark line through the lores continues as an eye-stripe. The long bill has a slightly upcurved tip. The distal third of the bill is dark brown, the remainder orange. The iris is dark brown. The underparts are dark chestnut, becoming whitish on the vent and undertail. The sides of the breast and flanks are streaked dark brown, the vent barred dark brown. The mantle and scapulars are dark brown, fringed chestnut and buff. The rump is gray-brown, the uppertail-coverts white, which, with the outer tail feathers, forms a distinctive white band that contrasts with the dark brown tail. The tail has a thin white terminal bar. The upperwing-coverts are gray-brown, the flight feathers dark brown. A distinct white bar is formed from the bases of the

▼ Hudsonian Godwit in summer plumage, Churchill.

Voice
Usual call is a harsh *kirrik*. Display song is soft, melodic, rapid *a-wik-a-wik*.

Distribution
Palearctic (but not in Iceland or Svalbard) and western Alaska. Breeds in northern Scandinavia (chiefly Finland) and in pockets of western Russia (Kola Peninsula, southeastern White Sea, Ob and Yenisey Rivers) but more continuously across eastern Russia from the Taimyr Peninsula to the western edge of Chukotka, and on the Anadyr River. In North America, breeds on the western Alaskan coast. Prefers coastal tundra but occasionally found inland. Migratory; European birds move to western Europe and western Africa. Western Asian birds move

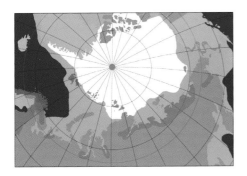

to the Arabian Peninsula, Pakistan and eastern India; eastern Asian and Alaskan birds move to Indonesia, Australia and New Zealand. Some birds are believed to fly from Alaska to New Zealand nonstop. If so, this journey of about 7,500 mi. (12,000 km) is the longest single flight of any bird. Wintering birds occur chiefly on sandy beaches of sheltered bays and estuaries.

Diet
Invertebrates, especially insects, but also crustaceans, molluscs and worms. Will peck at surface prey, but mainly feeds by probing, often in shallow water when head may be submerged.

Breeding
Gregarious except at breeding sites. Male display flight involves slow beat of stiff, decurved wings interspersed with short glides.

outer secondaries and inner five primaries. The underwing is dark brown, the silvery white bases of the flight feathers creating a distinctive central bar. Breeding females are as males, but with much less or no chestnut on the underparts; these are whitish with heavy chestnut or brown barring. The upperparts are usually duller. Some males can be similar. The legs and feet are dark gray. Non-breeding adults have pale gray head, neck and breast and a white supercilium and chin, the lore maintaining the dark line. The remaining underparts are white. The upperparts are uniformly dark gray or gray-brown, the upperwing-coverts fringed white. The bill is dark brown apart from the basal third of the lower mandible, which is dull orange. Juveniles have gray-brown neck and head with darker crown, white supercilium and dark lores. Breast is buff, blending to white underparts. The upperparts are dark brown, fringed buff. Downy chicks are colored variably, even within a brood, downranging from white through pale gray to dark gray.

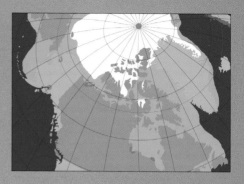

Confusion species
None.

Size
L: 14½–16½ in. (37–42 cm), bill 2¾–4 in. (7–10 cm). WS: 28–32 in. (70–80 cm). W: 8¾–16 oz. (250–450 g)

Voice
Silent except at breeding sites. Usual call is a high *twee*, sometimes *twee-ta*. Display song is a variation of a repeated *twee-ta*.

Distribution
Nearctic. Breeds near southern coast of Hudson Bay, near the Mackenzie Delta, and rarely in Alaska, mostly on the western and southern coasts. Prefers sedge marshland near coast or river. Migratory, moving to southern Argentina, where the same habitat is occupied.

Diet
Invertebrates, crustaceans, molluscs and worms, obtained by rapid probing. Wades in shallow water and occasionally probes with head below surface. Occasionally pecks.

Breeding
Gregarious in winter, but not highly so (flocks of *c.* 30 birds), solitary at breeding sites. Males chase and fight to establish a territory. Duel starts with male pointing bill down, depressing tail, and walking at rival. Male pursues female in flight, flying below and behind. Male also has display flight in which he starts low down, then rises in curved flight with fast wingbeats, calling throughout. Male then lands, raises his wings and fans his tail. Male may also hover with wings in a high V. Pair also have quivering flight, the wings arched and held below the body. Pair-bond apparently monogamous and seasonal. Nest set in dry spot in marshy ground. Nest is depression minimally lined with local vegetation. Two to four pale olive eggs, sparingly brown-spotted; incubated by female during the day, male at night, for 22–25 days. Chicks nidifugous and precocial. Leave nest on day of hatching. Cared for by both parents and aggressively defended, but self-feeding. Chicks fledge at about 17 days. Breed at 1–2 years.

Taxonomy and geographical variation
Monotypic.

Hudsonian Godwit perching awkwardly on a tree at the timberline. Churchill.

Bristle-thighed Curlew
Numenius tahitiensis

One of the rarest, strangest (in terms of feeding habits) and least-known of all Arctic waders.

Identification   See p. 230

Adults show no variation between breeding and non-breeding plumage. The head is pale cream or buff, with a darker crown split by a buff stripe. The distinct supercilium is pale buffish cream with a dark eye-stripe below, running from bill to nape. The bill is long and downcurved, dark brown and pink-tinged at the base. The neck and underparts are pale buffish cinnamon, the neck, breast and flanks heavily streaked brown. The breast streaking stops abruptly, and the belly is unmarked. The mantle, scapulars and tertials are dark brown, spotted pale buffish cinnamon. The lower rump is unmarked buff, the tail buff, broadly barred brown. The upperwing-coverts are dark-brown spotted buff, apart from the greater primary coverts that are dark brown with pale buff tips. The flight feathers are dark brown with buff or white tips and spots. The underwing-coverts are cinnamon, barred brown. The legs and feet are steel gray. There are, uniquely, long bristlelike feathers on the thighs. Juveniles are as adults, but the head is lighter overall, and the streaking on the neck and breast is much lighter, occasionally almost absent. The upperparts are lighter, due to more extensive buffish white feather tips. Downy chicks are pale buff or pink-buff, the upperparts marked with dark brown.

Confusion species

Very similar to Whimbrel. The "bristled" thighs after which the bird is named are diagnostic but are of no value in the field unless the bird is in the hand. In flight, the Whimbrel's white rump patch would appear useful, but that feature is absent from Nearctic birds. However, the Bristle-thighed Curlew's buff rump and barred tail are diagnostic and, overall, the species tends to be brighter and more buff-colored than the darker Whimbrel. The voices of the two are also distinctively different.

◀ Adult Bristle-thighed Curlew.

Size

L: 1–1½ ft. (40–44 cm), bill 2¾–3½ in. (7–9 cm). WS: 32–36 in. (80–90 cm). W: 12–19½ oz. (350–550 g).

Voice

Usual call is a long, humanlike whistle. Display song is a more rippling whistle.

Distribution

Western Alaska. Breeds only in western Alaska, where it occurs on mountain tundra and, more uncommonly, on lowland sites. Very rare. Migratory, moving to Polynesia, where it is often found in seabird colonies.

Diet

Breeding birds eat insects, spiders, fruits and flowers. Also takes eggs, lizards, small rodents and carrion. Mostly feeds by walking and pecking, but also chases mobile prey. Wintering birds probe for invertebrates and take crabs, snails and rodents, but most remarkably feed on seabird eggs, even snatching them from beneath incubating birds. The eggs are pierced with the bill or simply broken. Although birds usually break eggs by dropping them onto the ground, birds have been observed picking up pieces of coral or rock and deliberately dropping them onto eggs — one of the few observations of tool use by birds.

Breeding

Gregarious on migration and in winter, with flocks of between 75 and 100 birds. Solitary at breeding sites. Male has a territorial flight display, rising to around 7,500 ft. (150 m) then gliding above territory while calling. Male will hover above the courted female. Pair-bond monogamous and often renewed, but male attempts to mate with any available female until he has paired. Nest set on the ground, concealed by vegetation. Nest is a depression lined with moss and lichen. Four brown-spotted olive-buff eggs, incubated by both parents for 22–26 days. Chicks nidifugous and precocial. Cared for by both parents (though female leaves breeding site before chicks fledge), but self-feeding. Fledge at 22–27 days. Breed at 3 years.

Taxonomy and geographical variation

Monotypic.

Whimbrel
Numenius phaeopus

Identification See p. 230

Breeding and non-breeding adults are identical. The head is gray, the crown dark brown with a gray central stripe. There is a dark brown eye-stripe; the supercilium above is faintly streaked and the face below more heavily streaked. The long, downcurved bill is dark brown. The iris is dark brown. The neck and underparts are grayish buff with heavy brown streaking on the neck, breast and flanks. The undertail is barred brown. The mantle, scapulars, tertials and upperwing-coverts are dark brown with white or pale buff fringing and spotting, though the greater primary coverts are more uniformly dark brown. The back, rump and uppertail are white, the uppertail also having some dark barring on the edges. The tail is gray-brown, barred dark brown. The underwing-coverts are white, with some fine dark barring, usually only on the greater primary coverts. The legs and feet are steel gray. Juveniles are as adults, but the underparts more buff and the upperparts more buff-spotted. Downy chicks are black and buff.

Confusion species

Bristle-thighed Curlew. There may be some overlap of Whimbrel and Far-eastern Curlew in eastern Siberia. Far-eastern is much larger and has a much longer bill.

Size

L: 16–17½ in. (40–44 cm), bill 2¼–4 in. (6–10 cm). WS: 30–36 in. (75–90 cm). W: 10½–21 oz. (300–600 g).

Voice

Usual call is distinctive rippling *kikikiki*. Display song is a low whistle followed by a bubbling trill. In general Eurasian birds whistle as they climb but Nearctic birds do not.

Distribution

Circumpolar but patchy. Absent from Greenland, but breeds in Iceland. Breeds in Scandinavia and western Russia, then in isolated patches with no clear pattern across Siberia. In North America breeds in western, central and (less commonly) northern Alaska, around the Mackenzie River and on south-western and southern shores of Hudson Bay. Usually found close to the shore, but Russian Whimbrels breed far inland on tundra close to the timberline and even within the taiga. Migratory; North American birds move to coasts of southern U.S., Central America and South America. Eurasian birds winter sub-Saharan Africa, southern Asia and Australasia. Wintering birds chiefly coastal, but also occur on inland pools.

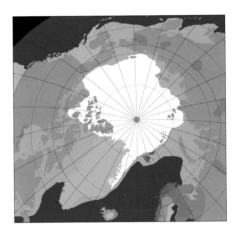

Diet

Invertebrates and plant material. Despite the bill, Whimbrel is chiefly a peck-feeder, taking insects from plants and following retreating waves to collect crabs and other invertebrates. Probing, if carried out, is never deep.

Breeding

Gregarious, except at breeding sites, then solitary or forms loose colonies. Male display flight involves steep ascent with vigorous flapping, followed by a glide or parachute-descent. On the ground the pair indulges in tail-fanning (especially the male, exposing his white rump) and wing-raising, the wings occasionally fluttered. Pair-bond monogamous, lasting over several seasons. Nests in the open or in short vegetation. Nest is shallow depression minimally lined with vegetation. Four pale olive or light-brown eggs heavily blotched red-brown, incubated by both parents for 27–28 days. Chicks nidifugous and precocial. Cared for by both parents, but self-feeding. Fledge in 35–40 days and are independent then or soon after. Breed at 2 years.

Taxonomy and geographical variation

Polytypic. The nominate race breeds from Iceland to western Russia. Race *variegatus* breeds from the Taimyr Peninsula to Anadyr. This subspecies and race *hudsonicus*, which breeds in North America, have buff or gray-buff rumps rather than the white of the nominate. Race *hudsonicus* differs from *variegatus* in being more buff both on upper- and underparts. An Icelandic subspecies, *N. p. islandicus*, has been proposed, but is not generally accepted. A further subspecies, *N. p. alboaxillaris*, breeds in the southern Urals.

▼ Adult Whimbrel at the coast.

▲ A famous image of an almost certainly extinct species, the Eskimo Curlew. This photograph was taken in 1962.

Eskimo Curlew
Numenius borealis See p. 230

The present status of this species is unclear. Once abundant, breeding around the Mackenzie Delta and perhaps in Alaska, the bird migrated in huge flocks to Paraguay, southern Brazil and Argentina. The migration route took the flocks through the Mississippi and Missouri Valleys and across Texas, a route along which the birds were relentlessly hunted. Hunting as well as habitat destruction in South America reduced numbers to such an extent that the species was believed extinct by the early 20th century. Since then sporadic sightings have been reported. Apparently reliable sightings were made as late as the early 1980s, but the present situation is perhaps best described as hope tinged with pessimism. However, it seems extremely unlikely that a bird that migrates across such a region as well-watched as the U.S. could avoid detection for so long, and the likelihood is that the species is indeed extinct.

The Eskimo Curlew has (had?) a buff head with dark brown crown stripes and an indistinct dark eye-stripe. The throat is white, the underparts buff (paler or white on the belly and vent), streaked on the breast and flanks with dark Y- or V-shapes. The upperparts are dark brown with paler or buff spotting. The upper wing is dark brown, the coverts buff or white fringed. The underwing-coverts are cinnamon,

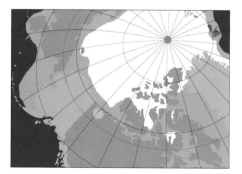

barred dark brown. The short, downcurved bill has a black tip and pink-brown base. The legs and feet are blue-gray. The bird's usual call is a soft, whistled *tee-dee-dee*.

The Eskimo Curlew's breeding habits are unknown, but are probably similar to those of the Little Curlew (*Numenius minutus*), which breeds in isolated patches of central Siberia. This slightly smaller species winters in Australasia. Its diet is invertebrates, chiefly beetles. The male bird has a display flight in which he flies high while singing, then dives steeply, producing a non-vocal whistle from both wings and tail. The Little Curlew nests on the ground, the nest a shallow depression lined with grass in which four pale green, brown-spotted eggs are laid. Incubation and fledging times are poorly known, but are probably similar to other *Numenius* species.

Lesser Yellowlegs
Tringa flavipes

Identification See p. 231
An elegant and attractive wader. Breeding adults have white or pale gray heads finely streaked dark brown. There is an indistinct white supercilium, a more distinct white eye-ring and a white chin. The thin, straight bill is black, often tinged yellow-brown at the base. The iris is dark brown. The neck and underparts are white or pale gray, the breast streaked and spotted dark brown. The mantle, scapulars and tertials are dark brown spotted with white or pale gray. The back is dark brown,

▼ Lesser Yellowlegs, near Great Slave Lake, Northwest Territories.

the rump and uppertail white. The tail is white or pale gray barred with brown. The upperwing is gray-brown, the coverts fringed white. The underwing-coverts are white barred brown. The long legs and the feet are bright yellow. Non-breeding adults are as breeding birds, but the head and upperparts are more uniformly gray-brown, the breast is also gray-brown but only finely streaked brown. Juveniles are as non-breeding adults, but the throat is lighter, often white, the upperparts browner and the breast grayer, though still streaked brown. Downy chicks have pinkish buff and black mottled upperparts, pale gray underparts.

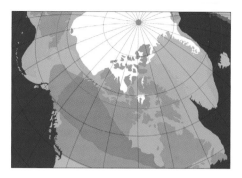

Confusion species
None except in southern Alaska and southern Hudson Bay, where Greater Yellowlegs may also be present. The plumage of the two is essentially the same, the species distinguished by size and call.

Size
L: 9–10 in. (23–25 cm), bill 1¼–1½ in. (3–4 cm), legs 2–2¾ in. (5–7 cm). WS: 22¼–25 in. (58–64 cm). W: 2–3½ oz. (60–100 g).

Voice
Usual call is a whistled *too* or *too-too*, flatter and softer than call of the Greater Yellowlegs. Breeding birds often issue a sharp *klip* alarm call. Display song is a rapid musical *pill-e-ya-wee*.

Distribution
Nearctic. Breeds in central Alaska (but rare on western and northern coasts), around the Mackenzie Delta, then south to southern shore of Hudson Bay. Prefers marshland close to the timberline (e.g., muskegs). Migratory, moving to the coasts of southern United States, Central America and the Caribbean, and South America to Tierra del Fuego; occurs on coastal lagoons, mudflats and inland marshes in winter.

Diet
Terrestrial and aquatic invertebrates, obtained by pecking.

Also takes small fish and seeds. Lesser Yellowlegs are active birds. They are elegant feeders, moving through the marsh with a high-stepping action, jabbing at prey; they will also occasionally run through the water.

Breeding
Gregarious in winter, less so in breeding areas, though does form loose colonies. The male has an undulating flight over his territory, alternating flapping with gliding, and usually calling throughout. Some observers claim that females also perform this flight. Males are extremely protective of females after pair is successfully established. Bond is monogamous and seasonal, but the enthusiasm of the male for guarding his mate suggests that extra-pair copulations are attempted, though females have been seen to resist such advances. Nest is scrape lined with dry grass, usually well concealed on a dry ridge or hummock. Two to six (usually four) brown-blotched, gray or pale olive eggs, incubated by both birds for 22–23 days. Chicks nidifugous and precocial. Brooded by both birds, but self-feeding. Fledge at 22–23 days and are independent soon after. Breed at 2 years.

Taxonomy and geographical variation
Monotypic.

▼ Pair of Lesser Yellowlegs, Churchill.

Solitary Sandpiper
Tringa solitaria

Often referred to as the Nearctic equivalent of the Green Sandpiper *T. ochropus*, which it closely resembles. However, the Green Sandpiper is a more southerly bird, though it does breed into northern Scandinavia.

Identification See p. 231
Breeding adults have olive-brown heads, finely streaked white. The white supercilium is distinct only in front of the eye, as is a dark eye-stripe. The iris is dark brown. There is a white eye-ring. The thin bill is black, dull green at the base. The chin, throat and underparts are pale grayish white, the breast heavily streaked dark brown. The upperparts and upperwings are dark brown, with some pale buff spotting. The rump and central tail are dark brown, the outer tail feathers white with broad dark brown bars. The underwing is dark brown, contrasting sharply with white underparts. The legs and feet are olive or gray-green. Non-breeding adults are as breeding, but gray-brown on the head and breast, with little streaking, and gray-brown on the upperparts. Juveniles are as non-breeding adults but the head and breast are darker, there is more white spotting on the upperparts and the legs are much greener. Downy chicks are mottled brown, gray and black.

Confusion species
Resembles Spotted Sandpiper, but leg and bill color are diagnostic. Solitary Sandpiper also has darker upperparts, while the Spotted lives up to its name with a clearly spotted, not streaked, breast when breeding.

Size
L: 7–8 in. (18–21 cm). WS: 21½–24 in. (55–60 cm). W: 1¼–2 oz. (35–60 g).

Voice
Usual call is a high, rising whistle *peet-weet*. There is also a sharp *pit*.

Distribution
Nearctic. Breeds in central Alaska (but rare on the western and northern coasts), Mackenzie Delta, then more southerly, breeding around southern Hudson Bay, James Bay and into Quebec and Labrador. Prefers woodland rivers and bogs.

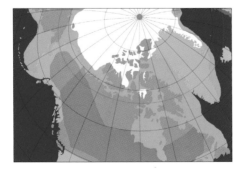

▲ Adult Solitary Sandpiper in summer plumage.

Migratory, moving to eastern Central America, the Caribbean and South America, where it occupies similar habitat.

Diet
Invertebrates, amphibians and small fish. Feeds by stirring the water with its feet and pecking prey from the surface. Also, probes in shallow water and mud, though rarely.

Breeding
As the name implies, not gregarious either with conspecifics or with other waders. More than three birds rarely seen together. Often aggressive toward other species sharing feeding area. However, does migrate in small groups. Male defends territory by standing upright, raising his wings, and chasing rival. Defeated bird crouches to stop the attack, then retreats. Male displays to female by flying about 3 ft. (1 m) above ground with fluttering wings, calling loudly. Pair-bond monogamous and seasonal. Nests in old nests of other species, particularly thrushes, at heights of up to 43 ft. (13 m). The Green Sandpiper is the only other wader to do this regularly (Wood Sandpiper will also do it occasionally). Female will refurbish nest if necessary. Three to five (usually four) red-brown or purple-brown splotched eggs, incubated by both birds (but usually female) for 22–24 days. Chicks nidifugous and precocial. Chicks leave the nest soon after hatching, though it is not clear exactly how this is accomplished, particularly from high nests. Chicks are cared for by the female, but self-feeding. Fledge at 18–21 days and are independent soon after. Breed at 1–2 years.

Taxonomy and geographical variation
Polytypic. Nominate race breeds east of Hudson Bay. *T. s. cinnamomea* breeds to the west. It is slightly larger, paler overall and cinnamon-washed, and has a spotted rather than solid loral streak. However, the ranges of the two overlap and the differences are marginal.

◀ Adult Spotted Sandpiper.

dots on the inner primaries. The underwing is white, with dark brown barring on the coverts, and broad dark bars on the leading edge of the primaries and on the entire trailing edge. The legs and feet are pink or pink-brown. Non-breeding adults have dark brown bills. The underparts lose the dark spotting, being white apart from gray-brown patches at the sides of the breast. The upperparts are uniform, unmarked brown. Juveniles are as non-breeding adults, but with upperwing-coverts barred buff. Downy chicks are pale gray above, white below.

Confusion species
See Solitary Sandpiper.

Size
L: 7–7³/₄ in. (18–20 cm). WS: 14¹/₂–16 in. (37–40 cm). W: ⁷/₈–2 oz. (25–60 g).

Voice
Usual call is a thin, high piping *twee-twee* or a descending *peet-weet-weet*. Display song is a rolling whistle.

Distribution
Nearctic. Breeds from central Alaska (but rare on west and north coasts). Mackenzie Delta, then south to southern Hudson Bay and James Bay and north to the Labrador coast. Found on the margins of rivers and lakes and on coastal beaches. Migratory, moving to coastal southwestern United States, Central America and the Caribbean, and South America, where it occurs in the same habitats.

Diet
Chiefly terrestrial invertebrates, which it obtains by pecking. When stalking prey, the birds use the same technique as herons (and look rather like small herons), adopting a crouched stance and then suddenly lunging at the prey. At beach sites, the birds walk along the water's edge, pecking at prey and other food items washed ashore. Wintering birds will take fish and crabs.

Spotted Sandpiper
Actitis macularius

The Spotted Sandpiper is the Nearctic equivalent of the very similar Common Sandpiper, which is sub-Arctic apart from breeding in northern Scandinavia, throughout Kamchatka and to the north around the Kolyma and Indigirka Rivers.

Identification   See p. 231
The breeding adult's head, nape and rear neck is green-brown, the white supercilium thin and much less distinct than the dark brown eye-stripe, which extends beyond the ear-coverts. The bill is bright orange with a black tip. The iris is dark brown. The throat, front neck and underparts are white, the throat, front neck and breast heavily spotted black, the remaining underparts with fewer spots. The undertail is white, barred dark brown. The upperparts, including the tail and upper wings, are greenish-brown. The outer tail is white with dark brown barring. There is a partial wingbar formed from white

Breeding
Mainly solitary, but small groups may form in winter. Pair-bond monogamous or polyandrous, with bond usually lasting only until chicks hatch, or for a few days after that time. Limited display repertoire, usually females soliciting males by gliding toward them and calling from a perch. Nests on the ground in a well-concealed site. Nest is a shallow cup lined with local vegetation. The male fashions several cups, the female chooses. Three to five buff eggs, speckled red-brown; incubated by both birds in monogamous pair, otherwise male only for 21–22 days. Chicks nidifugous and precocial. Cared for by both birds or male depending on bond but self-feeding. Fledge at 18–21 days and are independent at that time or soon after. Breed at 1–2 years.

Taxonomy and geographical variation
Monotypic.

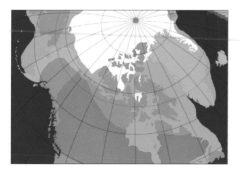

Wood Sandpiper
Tringa glareola

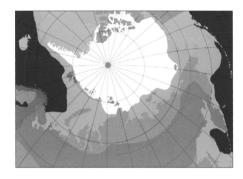

Identification See p. 231

Breeding adult has a pale grayish buff head with a dark brown crown, streaked pale gray. The prominent white supercilium is finely streaked dark brown behind the eye, where it extends almost to the nape. There is a dark eye-stripe and a white eye-ring. The short bill is black, the iris dark brown. The neck and underparts are pale grayish buff, the neck, throat, breast and flanks heavily streaked dark brown. The mantle, scapulars and tertials are dark brown, heavily barred and spotted pale gray-brown or white. The rump and uppertail are white, the tail light brown, barred white. The greater upperwing-coverts are as the mantle, the lesser coverts are dark brown, fringed white. The flight feathers are dark brown. The underwing is white with delicate gray-brown barring. The long legs are pale yellow-green or yellow-brown.

Non-breeding adults are as breeding adults, but the underparts are more subtly streaked and the upperparts are gray-brown. Juveniles are as breeding adults, but the upperparts are cinnamon-brown, mottled buff. The streaking on the underparts is also cinnamon-brown. Downy chicks are dark brown and buff.

Confusion species

The Green Sandpiper can be confused in the southern (i.e., non-Arctic) part of the range.; it is much darker, with a blackish underwing The Wood Sandpiper bobs when alarmed, and all toes project beyond the tail in flight.

Size

L: 7½–8 in. (19–21 cm). WS: 21½–22¼ in. (55–58 cm). W: 1¾–2¾ oz. (50–80 g).

▼ Adult Wood Sandpiper, northeast Finland.

Voice

The flight call is a whistling *chiff-it*. The alarm call is a sharp, repetitive *gip-gip-gip*. The display song is a high yodel.

Distribution

Palearctic. Breeding in Scandinavia and across Russia to central Chukotka and throughout Kamchatka. Range does not extend as far as the north coast except at the Kolyma Delta. Essentially boreal, rarely found on tundra north of the timberline. Migratory, moving to southern Africa, India and Australasia, where it occupies inland wetlands, coastal lagoons and mangrove swamps.

Diet

Invertebrates, especially insects. Takes insects by leaping to catch them in flight or from the water surface. Also probes, and if in water will immerse head to do so. Wintering birds have similar diet but also take mollusks.

Breeding

Gregarious, but not highly so, forming small groups rather than large flocks. Pair-bond monogamous, probably seasonal. Display flight (usually by male, but female also) is a mix of ordinary flight, then rapid wingbeats to ascend followed by a downward glide. Nests on the ground in dense vegetation, occasionally in old nests of tree-nesting species. Self-built nest is shallow depression lined with vegetation. Four cream or buff eggs lightly or heavily speckled red-brown. Incubated by both birds for 22–23 days. Chicks nidifugous and precocial. Cared for by both birds at first, then male only as female departs, but self-feeding. Fledge in about 30 days. Thought to breed at 1–2 years.

Taxonomy and geographical variation
Monotypic.

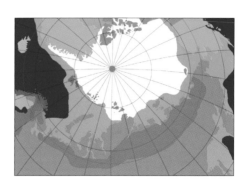

Spotted Redshank
Tringa erythropus

Identification See p. 231
Breeding adults have black head, neck and underparts. The long, thin bill has a slight droop at the tip. The bill is black, apart from the base of the lower mandible, which is red. The iris is dark brown. The upperparts are black with white spotting and fringing, apart from the white back and upper rump, the barred white and gray lower rump and uppertail and the tail that is dark gray with narrow white bars. The long legs are red. Non-breeding adults could hardly be more different.

The head, neck and breast are pale gray or gray-brown (apart from a white chin and throat). The supercilium is white and very distinct. A dark stripe crosses the lores, continuing more vaguely behind the eye. The bill is orange-red. The underparts are pale gray or white, with some gray barring on the flanks and vent. The upperparts are gray-brown with light, white spotting. The back, rump and tail are as breeding adults. The legs are orange-red. Juveniles

▼ Adult male Spotted Redshank in breeding plumage, one of the more stunning Arctic waders.

▲ Spotted Redshank chick among the lichens of the taiga floor, Yamalo-Nenetsky, northern Russia.

are as non-breeding adults, but head and underparts (apart from white chin) are pale gray, barred gray-brown, and the upperparts are gray-brown. Downy chicks are dark brown and gray-buff.

Confusion species
None.

Size
L: 10¹/₂–12¹/₂ in. (29–32 cm), bill 2–2¹/₄ in. (5–6 cm). WS: 24–26³/₄ in. (60–68 cm.) W: 5¹/₄–6³/₄ oz. (150–190 g).

Voice
Usual call is a whistling *chu-wit*. Alarm call is a short *chip*. Feeding flocks have a murmuring *uck*. Display song is a series of shrill, grinding whistles.

Distribution
Palearctic. Breeds in northern Fennoscandia, on the eastern shores of the White Sea, and from the Ob River east to Chukotka and north toward the coast, except on the Taimyr Peninsula where it breeds only in the south. Essentially boreal, but also on taiga fringe and in open tundra. Not usually found on the coast. Migratory, moving to the Mediterranean coast, central Africa and the coasts of India and Southeast Asia. Wintering birds more often seen at the coast, in sheltered

▶ Adult Spotted Redshank in flight. Note the distinctive white back and upper rump. Utsjoki, Finnish Lapland.

littoral sites such as mudflats and salt marshes, as well as inland sites.

Diet
Invertebrates, especially insects, usually taken by pecking but also by probing. Birds at coastal sites take fish.

Breeding
Gregarious, but not highly so, with wintering birds forming small groups. Male has a circular display flight over territory. This consists of a steady flight interrupted by a series of dipping glides. Pair-bond is seasonal, with the females being polyandrous. The nest is made on open ground or, for boreal birds, close to a tree. Nest is a shallow depression with a minimal lining of vegetation and some feathers. Three or four buffish eggs, heavily blotched and red-brown. Incubated chiefly by the male (exclusively so in pairs in which the female deserts for another male) for around 20 days. Chicks nidifugous and precocial. Cared for by both parents at first (though male only where female has deserted), then male only as female departs, but self-feeding. Fledge in around 30 days. Breed at 1–2 years.

Taxonomy and geographical variation
Monotypic.

Wandering Tattler
Heteroscelus incanus

Identification See p. 231
Breeding adults have crown, nape and all upperparts, including tail and upperwings, uniform slate gray with some white tips on the coverts. The greater primary coverts and outer five primaries are darker gray, forming distinct dark patches on the upperwings. The supercilium is narrow and white, broader in

front of eye. There is a white eye-ring. The bill is dark gray, yellowish-gray at the base. The nasal groove is very long, around 75 percent of bill length. The iris is dark brown. The cheeks, chin, throat and underparts are white, heavily barred dark gray, though usually with a plain white patch on the central belly. The underwing shows dark gray coverts and paler gray flight feathers. The relatively thick legs and the feet are bright yellow or bright yellow-green. Non-breeding adults are as breeding, but the barring of the underparts is replaced by slate gray on the breast and flanks, pale gray elsewhere. Juveniles are as non-breeding adults, but with subtle barring on the breast and flanks and white tips on the upper coverts, creating an indistinct scaly appearance. Downy chicks have black-marked blue-gray upperparts and cream underparts.

Confusion species

None, though wintering birds overlap in range with the very similar Gray-tailed Tattler. The calls of the two are diagnostic.

Size

L: 10¼–12 in. (26–30 cm). WS: 21½–28 in. (55–70 cm). W: 3-4½ oz. (90–125 g).

Voice

Usual call is a somewhat plaintive, piping trill *du-du-du*. There is also a sharp *klee-ik*. Display song is a ringing whistle.

Distribution

Western North America. Breeds in Alaska and the Yukon, but it is uncommon and the range is patchy. Not found in north or in central Alaska. Prefers gravelly river margins or rocky coasts. Migratory, moving to the southwestern coast of mainland United States, as well as Hawaii and other remote Pacific Islands; occurs on rocky shores in winter.

Diet

Invertebrates, particularly insects and their larvae (especially Caddisfly larvae), mollusks and marine worms. Feeds by pecking from water surface or by probing, often with head below water. Seeks out Caddisfly larvae by wading in fast-flowing mountain streams.

Breeding

Gregarious, though not highly so, in winter, but solitary at breeding sites. Male establishes territory by song, and by chasing rivals. Male display is a fluttering flight alternating with glides and steep dives. There is also an undulating flight. Pair-bond monogamous and seasonal. Nests on bare ground, or gravel close to water in depression sparsely lined with local vegetation. Three to four olive or pale green eggs spotted or blotched brown, incubated for 23–25 days by both parents. Chicks nidifugous and precocial, leaving nest soon after hatching. Cared for by both parents, but self-feeding. Fledge at 18–21 days and are independent soon after. Thought to breed at two to three years, perhaps earlier.

Taxonomy and geographical variation
Monotypic, but once considered conspecific with Gray-tailed Tattler.

Gray-tailed Tattler
Heteroscelus brevipes

Identification
See p. 231
Breeding adults are as Wandering Tattler apart from the following subtle differences: upperparts are paler slate gray, and there is more white on the tips of the greater converts so the upperwing has a very thin white bar; the supercilium is more distinct, particularly behind the eye; the eye-stripe is more distinct behind the eye; the underparts are less heavily marked (cheeks, neck and breast are lightly streaked rather than barred); and there is little or no marking on the belly and vent. Non-breeding adults are as Wandering Tattler, but paler overall, particularly on the underparts. Juveniles are as Wandering Tattler, but with paler underparts and with distinct white spotting and fringing on the upperparts. Downy chicks are gray and white.

Confusion species
Wandering Tattler, but call is distinctive.

Size
L: 9½–10½ in. (24–27 cm). WS: 20–26 in. (50–65 cm). W: 3–4 oz. (85–115 g).

Voice
Usual call is a two syllable whistle *tu-whip*, distinctly different from Wandering Tattler. However, the alarm call is similar, though monosyllabic.

Distribution
Palearctic. Breeds on the northern Yenisey River, patchily from Lena River to western Chukotka, and throughout Kamchatka. Prefers rocky riverbeds in mountainous areas. Migratory, moving to coastal areas of Indonesia and Australasia, though some birds remain around Kamchatka's hot springs. Wintering birds occur on coastal mudflats.

Diet
Invertebrates, chiefly insect larvae pecked from the surface of water or the streambed or collected at the water margin.

Breeding
Gregarious in winter, but solitary at breeding sites. Breeding biology poorly known, but probably much as Wandering Tattler. Pair-bond mono-gamous. Nests on ground on shores of fast-flowing streams, or on islands within them, but as with the Wandering Tattler will use old tree nests. Four pale blue eggs, speckled with black; incubated by both birds for an assumed period of around 23 days. Chicks nidifugous and precocial, leaving nest soon after hatching. Cared for by both parents, but self-feeding. Probably fledge at about 20 days. Probably breed at 2–3 years, perhaps earlier.

Taxonomy and variation
Monotypic, but see Wandering Tattler.

◄ Gray-tailed Tattler in breeding plumage, Chukotka. Compare the length of the nasal groove with that of the Wandering Tattler — the difference is diagnostic.

Turnstones

Both species of turnstone breed within the Arctic region. Ruddy Turnstone is usually called simply the Turnstone in Europe, but the full name is required here to avoid confusion with the Black Turnstone, a Nearctic species.

Ruddy Turnstone
Arenaria interpres

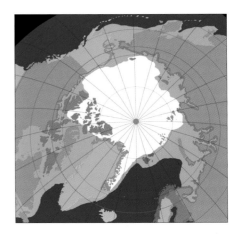

Identification

See p. 231

Breeding males have variable head patterns but generally white with crown streaked black, and black line from forehead to eye then down across cheek to reach black line from base of bill. The two then form a collar, usually incomplete, there being a small white patch on the nape. There is also a band across the upper breast to the mantle, this linked to the collar by a vertical black stripe. The bill is black, the iris dark brown. The mantle, scapulars and tertials are dark brown with broad chestnut (even orange-chestnut) fringes, which give the bird a tortoiseshell appearance. Back, rump and uppertail are white, the uppertail banded black. The tail is white with a broad black band at the end, beyond which is a thin white terminal band. The median and inner upperwing-coverts are chestnut with darker centers, the outer coverts black. The flight feathers are black, separated from the coverts by a broad white bar. The underwing is white with a narrow black leading edge and a broader black trailing edge. The legs and feet are orange-red. Breeding females are as males, but have a buff crown streaked black, a buff nape, and the black pattern is less sharply defined.

The upperparts are duller. Non-breeding males and females are similar; as breeding birds, but head is mid-brown, some black patterning is lost, and the rest of the pattern is duller. The upperparts are mottled gray-brown and black. Legs and feet are dull orange-red. Juveniles are as non-breeding adults, but the head has paler patches, and the upperparts are dull brown with buff fringing, giving a scaly appearance. Downy chicks are chestnut buff above, white below.

Confusion species
None

Size
L: 8½–10 in. (22–25 cm). WS: 20–22¼ in. (50–58 cm). W: 3–5 oz. (90–140 g).

Voice
Usual call is a rolling *tuk-tuk-tuk*. Alarm call is a sharp *kew*. Display song is a long rattle.

Distribution
Circumpolar. Breeds in northwestern and northeastern Greenland, western Spitsbergen, Scandinavia, Russia (all along the northern coast and on southern island of Novaya Zemlya, the New Siberia Islands and Wrangel), western and northwest Alaska (including the Pribilofs), the northern coast of western Canada, and most of the Arctic islands (though only southern Baffin). Found on coasts, preferring rocky shores to beaches or mudflats. Migratory, though Icelandic birds remain on southwestern coast. Eurasian birds move to the coasts of western Europe, Africa, the Middle East, India, Southeast Asia and Australasia. American birds move to the coasts of the southern U.S., Central America, the Caribbean and South America to northern Chile and Argentina. Same habitats preferred.

Diet
Breeding birds take range of arthropods and some plant material, wintering birds crustaceans and mollusks. As name implies, birds use the bill to flip pebbles to search for prey

◀ Ruddy Turnstone in summer plumage, north Norway.

beneath. Also turns seaweed, searches in crevices and occasionally probes in sand or mud. However, this is not probing as in other waders, but rather digging; the bill is used as a shovel, pushed into the substrate then moved up to excavate a pit.

Breeding
Gregarious in winter (flocks usually <100 birds), solitary or forming loose colonies at breeding sites. Male display flight is a slow circle of his territory followed by prolonged calling from a prominent perch. On the ground male has head-up, tail-up, and tail-down displays. Monogamous pair-bond, which may be renewed. Nest is shallow depression in the open lined with minimal vegetation. Three to four cream or buff eggs, heavily red-brown speckled; incubated by both birds (but chiefly female) for 22–24 days. Chicks nidifugous and precocial. Brooded by both birds at first, then male only as female departs, but self-feeding. Fledge in 19–21 days. Breed at 2 years.

Taxonomy and geographical variation
Polytypic. The nominate race breeds in Eurasia, including Novaya Zemlya and the New Siberia Islands, in western and northwestern Alaska, the Canadian high Arctic islands, and northern and northeastern Greenland. *A. i. morinella* breeds in northeastern Alaska and Canada south of 74°N. It is smaller and redder, with less black streaking on the head and upperparts, and longer bill and legs.

Black Turnstone
Arenaria melanocephala

Identification   See p. 231
Breeding adult has black head with delicate white streaking on crown and nape, and prominent white spot at the base of the bill. The bill is black, the iris dark brown. Throat is black, breast black, fringed white so that it looks speckled white. Breast coloration spreads to upper flanks, but rest of underparts are white. Mantle, scapulars and tertials are black, some scapulars white-tipped. Back, rump and uppertail are white, the tail black. Upperwing is black with a broad white bar. Underwing is white with a thin black leading edge and a broader black trailing edge. Legs and feet are dark red-brown, sometimes orange-brown. Non-breeding adults as breeding, but head is dark brown with less streaking and no white bill spot. Breast and upperparts are dark brown. Juveniles are as non-breeding adults, but breast is gray-brown and upperparts dark brown, fringed pale buff. Downy chicks are mottled black and cream.

Confusion species
None.

Size
L: 8½–10 in. (22–25) cm. WS: 20–22¾ in. (50–55 cm). W: 3½–5 oz. (100–140 g).

Voice
Usual call is a high, chattering *skeet*. Display song is similar to Ruddy, but more rattling and changing pitch frequently.

▲ Black Turnstone in breeding plumage, Alaska.

Distribution
Limited to western and southern Alaska. Prefers rocky coasts as Ruddy Turnstone. Migratory, moving to the western coast of the continental United States and Baja California, where it is found on rocky shores as well as beaches and mudflats.

Diet
Aquatic and terrestrial invertebrates, and occasionally the eggs of small birds. Winter diet mainly invertebrates.

Breeding
Gregarious in winter, solitary at breeding sites. Males establish territory using aerial and ground pursuit of rivals. Mating display flight often follows such chases, the male circling over the territory, rising with fluttering wings. Male also has a fast zigzagging flight, but occasionally climbs high and dives to produce a non-vocal drumming from vibrating feathers, similar to (but not as loud as) snipe. Male often secures same territory annually. He makes several scrapes, the female choosing one. Nest is usually near water. Three to four (usually four) pale olive or pale green eggs with gray or olive-brown splotches. Incubated by both parents for 20–22 days. Chicks nidifugous and precocial. Brooded and cared for by both birds, but self-feeding. Fledge at 25–30 days. Breed at 1–2 years.

Taxonomy and geographical variation
Monotypic.

Phalaropes

The two Arctic-breeding phalaropes are delicate and extremely attractive birds, especially the females in their bright breeding plumage. The two species share many traits; in both, the female is larger than the male (around 10% for Red-necked Phalarope, about 20% for Red) and polyandrous, mating with several males and providing clutches for two of them. Males incubate the eggs and brood the chicks. The feeding habits of the two are also the same, including a technique known as "spinning," in which the bird swims in tight circles to stir up the water and bring prey to the surface.

The phalaropes are highly gregarious during migration; as many as two million Red-necked Phalaropes congregate in Newfoundland's Bay of Fundy before heading south. Though the migration flights are long, the bird is a poor flier, frequently carried along by strong winds, which explains the frequency with which these species appear as vagrants. Phalaropes are invariably tame, allowing close approach.

Red Phalarope (Gray Phalarope)
Phalaropus fulicarius

North American ornithologists call this species the Red Phalarope after its stunning summer colors; the British and European name derives from the gray winter plumage.

Identification   See p. 231
Breeding females have dark brown and black crowns and nape, the color extending to the forehead, forming a ring around the bill base and continuing to the chin. The upper cheeks are a sharply contrasting white. The bill is yellow with a black tip, the iris dark brown. The lower cheeks, neck (apart from the nape) and underparts are chestnut-red or rufous-red. The lower nape, mantle, scapulars and tertials are dark brown, fringed chestnut and buff. The rump and uppertail are chestnut-red, the central feathers much darker, almost black. The central tail is also dark brownish-black, the outer feathers gray. The upperwing is pale gray, the greater primary coverts and flight feathers darker. There is a white bar, broad toward the body. The underwing is white, pale gray toward the leading and trailing edges. Breeding males are as females, but paler chestnut-red, and with less abrupt delineation of red and white on the face and a more heavily streaked crown. The short legs and feet are gray-brown.

Non-breeding adults are gray. The nape and upperparts are uniformly pale gray, the upper flight feathers darker. The remaining head is white with a black smudge through the eye. The bill is black, paler at the base (this sometimes with yellowish tinge). The underparts are white, with pale gray areas on the sides of the breast and flanks. Juveniles are patterned as non-breeding adult, but the head and underparts are cinnamon-buff, with white patches on the belly and vent. The upperparts are dark brown with broad buff fringes. Downy chicks are cinnamon-buff and white above, white and buff below.

Confusion species
None for breeding adults. Non-breeding birds are very similar to non-breeding Red-necked Phalaropes but are paler, with a distinctive white stripe along the outer edges of the mantle and scapulars, and their bills are shorter and stouter.

Size
L: 7³/₄–8¹/₂ in. (20–22 cm). WS: 16–17¹/₂ (40–44 cm). W: 1¹/₂–2¹/₂ oz. (40–70 g).

▼ Adult female Red Phalarope in breeding plumage, Southampton Island.

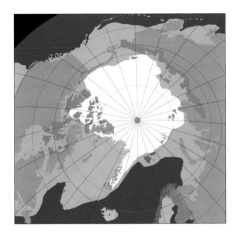

Note: dots on Iceland and Spitsbergen do not indicate breeding location.

Voice
Usual call is a high, piping *pik*. There is also a softer *preep*, and breeding birds have a buzzing twitter.

Distribution
Circumpolar. Breed in western and, more rarely, northeastern Greenland, Iceland (where it is among the rarest breeding birds, with a population of a few dozen pairs), Svalbard (population probably similar to Iceland), Asian Russia along the north coast from the Yenisey to the Bering Strait and on New Siberia and Wrangel Islands; also around the Anadyr River, northern Alaska, northern Yukon and the Mackenzie Delta, Canada's Boothia Peninsula, northwestern Hudson Bay, the Parry Islands, northern and southwestern Baffin, and Banks, Victoria and Southampton Islands (the Southampton population has declined drastically in the last few years). Prefers coastal sites, but also found on inland marshland close to the sea. Migratory; European birds move to the Atlantic Ocean off central and southern Africa, American and Asian-Russian birds move to the Pacific off southern South America.

Diet
Invertebrates and some plant material during the breeding season, prey being obtained by pecking, up-ending and spinning. Wintering birds feed on crustaceans and other invertebrates on seaweed mats, and even on whale lice and other parasites on the backs of whales.

Breeding
Gregarious at all times. Breeding roles reversed, so female exhibits mating display with circling flight, usually with slow wingbeats and several ground displays, with the male usually joining in. Swimming pair will cross bills and touch breasts. On land there is synchronized head-lowering, often with pecking, and a head-up display, the neck extended at a high angle and the bill pointing upward. Females are polyandrous. Nest is shallow depression lined with local vegetation, placed on the ground, sometimes in vegetation. Breeding colonies often found near Arctic Tern colonies — the terns provide protection

▲ Male Red Phalarope in breeding plumage, with a female in the background, Badlanddalen, northeast Greenland.

against predators. Four buff eggs, heavily blotched red-brown, incubated by male only for 18–20 days. Chicks nidifugous and precocial. Brooded by male, but self-feeding. Fledge in 16–18 days and are independent at that time. Breed at 1 year.

Taxonomy and geographical variation
Monotypic.

Red-necked Phalarope
Phalaropus lobatus

Identification See p. 231
Breeding females have dark gray crown and nape. A white spot lies above and to the front of the eye. The chin is also white, usually thinly outlined in gray. A broad black strip runs through the eye. The needle-thin bill is black, the iris dark brown. The neck is bright chestnut-red, starting behind the eye and expanding downward around a white chin patch. The breast and upper flanks are dark gray, the remaining underparts white with gray patches on the lower flanks, but these are usually absent from the belly and vent. The mantle, scapulars and tertials are dark gray, fringed pale chestnut-buff. The rump and tail are gray, the sides of the rump white, the central tail darker than the outer. The upperwing is dark gray, the coverts tipped buff. There is a broad white bar. The underwing is white, though the flight feathers are gray, and there are gray patches on the

▲ Red-necked Phalarope in breeding plumage exhibiting typical spinning feeding behavior, St. Lawrence Island.

medium and primary coverts. Breeding males are patterned as the female, but the crown and neck are dull gray-brown, the neck is dull chestnut-brown, and the white eye-spot is less distinct, forming a ragged supercilium. The fringing of the upperparts is brown rather than buff. The short legs and the feet are dark blue-gray.

Non-breeding adults have white heads with pale gray crown and distinct black stripe behind the eye. The underparts are white with irregular gray patches on the flanks, the upperparts gray (darker than the Red Phalarope), white edging creating white lines on the mantle and scapulars. Juveniles have white or pale buff heads with dark brown crown and stripe behind the eye. The chin is white. The supercilium is buffy white, blending into buff neck and upper breast. The remaining underparts are white with buff patches on the flanks. The upperparts are dark brown, with buffish pale chestnut fringing that creates bold stripes. Downy chicks are boldly marked, chestnut, black and buff above, white below.

Confusion species
None for breeding adults. For winter birds see Red Phalarope.

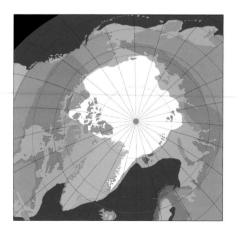

Size
L: 7–7½ in. (18–19 cm). WS: 12½–16 in. (32–40 cm). W: 1–1½ oz. (30–40 g).

Voice
Usual call is a sharp *chek*. Breeding birds have a repertoire of buzzing calls.

Distribution
Circumpolar. Breeds in southwestern and southeastern Greenland (rare in the north), Iceland, Svalbard, Scandinavia, northern Russia from the Kola Peninsula to Chukotka (but absent from the Arctic islands), Kamchatka, Commander and Aleutian Islands, and across North America from Alaska to Labrador (coastal and inland to the west, coastal only to the east), and on the southern Arctic islands from Banks to Baffin. More eclectic in habitat than Red Phalarope, found both at coastal sites and on inland waters far from the sea. Migratory; details of movements not fully known. Known wintering sites include Pacific Ocean off central South America and north of Indonesia, and Arabian Sea; also inland East Africa.

Diet
Invertebrates, taken as Red Phalarope, but rarely up-ends. Wintering birds presumed to feed as Red Phalaropes.

Breeding
Gregarious at all times. Breeding roles reversed as in Red Phalarope, female displays as that species, but circling flight path more zigzag. Nests on ground, usually in the open, but occasionally concealed in vegetation. Nest is shallow depression lined with vegetation. Four buff eggs, heavily blotched red-brown; incubated by male only for 17–21 days. Chicks nidifugous and precocial. Brooded by male, but self-feeding. Fledge in about 20 days, but usually independent earlier. Breed at 1 year.

Taxonomy and geographical variation
Monotypic.

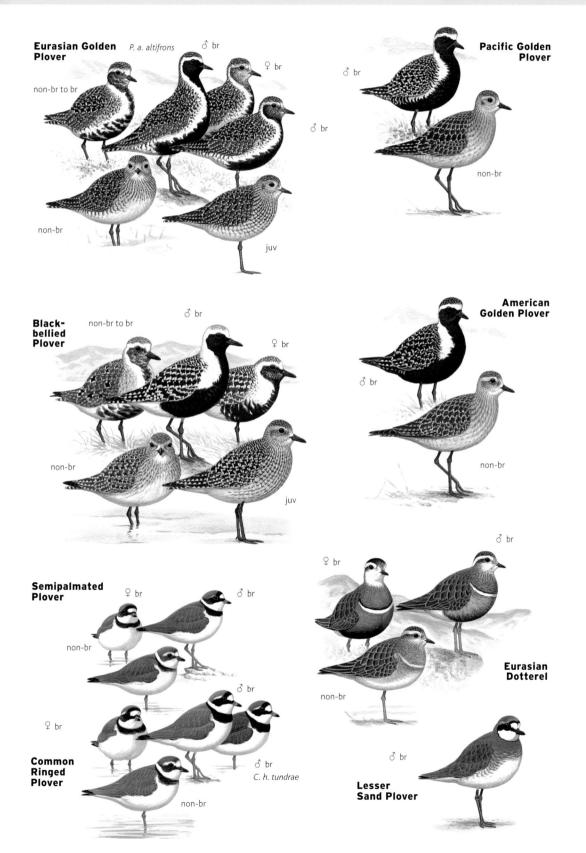

Eurasian Golden Plover

P. a. altifrons

♂ br

♀ br

non-br to br

♂ br

non-br

juv

Pacific Golden Plover

♂ br

non-br

Black-bellied Plover

non-br to br

♂ br

♀ br

non-br

juv

American Golden Plover

♂ br

non-br

Semipalmated Plover

♀ br

♂ br

non-br

♂ br

♀ br

Common Ringed Plover

♂ br

C. h. tundrae

non-br

♀ br

♂ br

non-br

Eurasian Dotterel

♂ br

Lesser Sand Plover

PLATE 12: STINTS AND SANDPIPERS

Spoon-billed
Sandpiper

br

Little Stint

Red-necked
Stint

br

Temminck's Stint

br

br

Least Sandpiper

Long-toed Stint

br

White-rumped
Sandpiper

br

♂ br

Pectoral Sandpiper

♀ br

Baird's Sandpiper

br

Western Sandpiper

br

br

Sharp-tailed Sandpiper

"worn" br

Semipalmated
Sandpiper

br

br

Broad-billed
Sandpiper

"fresh" br

Sanderling

♂ br

Dunlin

♀ br

♂ br
C. a. arctica

♂ br
C. a. pacifica

♂ br
C.a. schinzii

non-br to br

"fresh" br

**Stilt
Sandpiper**

br

br

Curlew Sandpiper

♂ br
C. c. islandica

Great Knot

♂ br
C. c. rufa

Red Knot

br

♂ br

juv

br
C. p. couesi

Rock Sandpiper

br

br
C. p. tschuktschorum

**Purple
Sandpiper**

♂ ♂ br at lek

Ruff

**Buff-breasted
Sandpiper**

br

♀ br

PLATE 14: SNIPES, DOWITCHERS, GODWITS AND CURLEWS

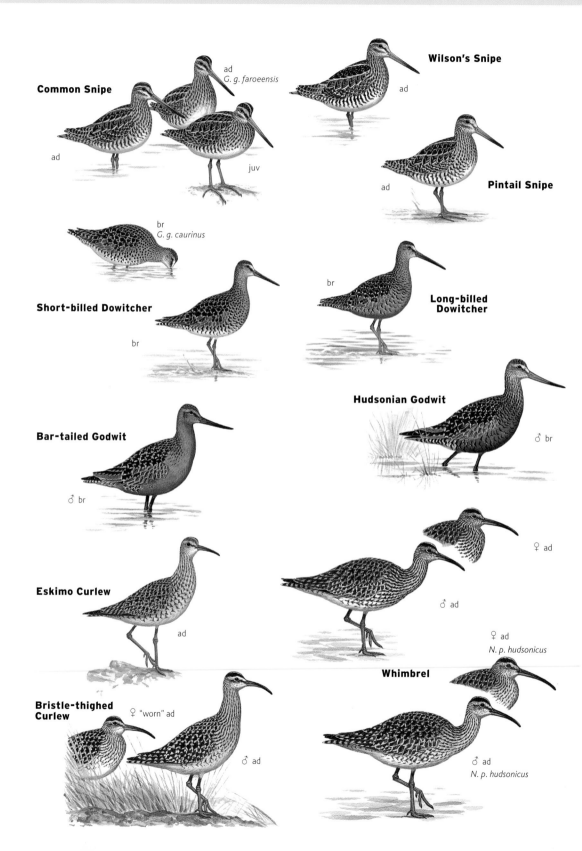

Common Snipe

ad
G. g. faroeensis

ad

juv

Wilson's Snipe

ad

ad

Pintail Snipe

br
G. g. caurinus

Short-billed Dowitcher

br

br

Long-billed Dowitcher

Hudsonian Godwit

♂ br

Bar-tailed Godwit

♂ br

♀ ad

Eskimo Curlew

ad

♂ ad

♀ ad
N. p. hudsonicus

Bristle-thighed Curlew

♀ "worn" ad

Whimbrel

♂ ad

♂ ad
N. p. hudsonicus

PLATE 15: SANDPIPERS, TATTLERS, TURNSTONES AND PHALAROPES

Lesser Yellowlegs

br

non-br to br

Spotted Redshank

♂ br

Wandering Tattler

non-br

br

non-br

Gray-tailed Tattler

br

Solitary Sandpiper

Wood Sandpiper

br

br

br

Spotted Sandpiper

Ruddy Turnstone

♀ br

♂ br

Black Turnstone

♂ br

♀ br

Red Phalarope

♂ br

♀ br

♂ br

Red-necked
Phalarope

♀ br

Skuas

The Stercorariidae or skuas comprises seven species. The Great Skua, and three other large species of the Southern Ocean, are sometimes placed in the genus *Catharacta*, though recent evidence does not support this separation; the skuas are today generally placed together in the genus *Stercorarius*. The three smaller species are known in North America and some other places as jaegers (from the German, "hunter"). Skuas evolved from gulls; early forms bred in the northern hemisphere, with one group that moved south being ancestral to the large southern skuas. After evolving separately from the other skuas for a time, one of those southern species moved back north to become the ancestor of the Great Skua.

Skuas differ from gulls in having a complex bill structure (somewhat akin to that of the petrels), supraorbital salt glands that allow them to drink saltwater (while preferring fresh) and prominent claws (though gull-like feet). Although the diets of the various skuas differ, all practice some degree of kleptoparasitism — the harassing of gulls, terns and other smaller seabirds until they drop or disgorge their catch, which the skua then retrieves, often in mid-air. Kleptoparasitism occasionally develops into predatory attacks on the pirated bird.

Polymorphism occurs in some species, its extent being latitude-dependent, with paler birds more common in the north. Female skuas are larger than males by 10–18%; the smallest difference between sexes is in the South Polar Skua (*Stercorarius maccormicki*), the largest in the Long-tailed Jaeger.

Skuas are not only aggressive predators, they are aggressive toward potential predators at nest sites, diving at anything, including birders, who

venture too close. Nor are such attacks mere bluffs; I have been knocked down by a Great Skua and had blood drawn by a Long-tailed Jaeger. The usual skua clutch is two eggs, one hatching several days before the other. In years of scarcity, the older chick invariably kills and eats its sibling. Skuas mature relatively slowly, taking four years to achieve adult plumage. Apart from the Long-tailed Jaeger, juveniles are more chestnut or rufous-brown than adults, pale feather fringing giving the upperparts a scaly appearance. Juvenile Long-tailed Jaegers are grayer than adults. First-summer birds are, in general, as the juveniles, but gray-brown overall. Second-summer birds are, in general, as adult winter, but retain the juvenile barring. Third-summer birds are as the breeding adults, but retain some juvenile barring and the color pattern is more ragged. In the sections below, only adult and juvenile plumages are discussed. However, these generalizations do not always match the subtle variation shown by certain birds.

Great Skua
Stercorarius skua

Identification

See p. 238

Breeding adults have cinnamon-brown upperparts. The crown is darker and there are paler streaks on the sides of the head, nape and scapulars. The bill is black, occasionally dark olive at the base. The iris is dark brown. The underparts are also cinnamon-brown, but more gray-brown on the flanks and vent. The primary coverts, distal section of the flight feathers and the tail are darker than the remaining plumage. The upperwing lesser- and median-coverts are dark brown but with a central cinnamon streak, giving the inner wing a mottled appearance. The underwing is more uniformly dark brown. There is a broad white stripe at the base of the primaries. The legs and feet are black. Some adults are much paler (though retaining the dark crown), the upper- and underparts (but much less so on the wings) are overall buffish or gray-brown with dark brown mottling. There are also intermediate forms. Juveniles are as adults but darker and more rufous-brown and spotted rather than streaked. Some show a distinctly bicolored bill, with a black tip and a dark blue-gray base. The similarity of juveniles and adults makes the age of immature birds difficult to assess. Downy chicks are cinnamon.

Adult Great Skua, Runde, Norway.

▲ Great Skua eggs in the nest, southern Iceland.

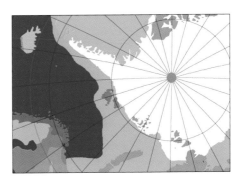

Confusion species
None. Size and uniform color are distinctive.

Size
L: 20¾–22¼ in. (53–58 cm). WS: 4¼–4½ ft. (132–140 cm). W: 2¾–3½ lb. (1.2–1.6 kg).

Voice
Silent except during breeding. Skuas have short and long calls used, sometimes in combination, against congeners when establishing territories and against intruders. The Great Skua's short call is a sharp *kek*. The long call, used aggressively, is a harsh *piah-piah-piah*.

Distribution
Palearctic. Breeds in southern Iceland, Jan Mayen, Svalbard, the northern North Sea coast of Norway and the Kola Peninsula, as well as the Faroes, Hebrides, Orkneys and Shetlands, and Bear Island. The "original" breeding range only included Iceland, the Faroes and the Shetlands, but the Great Skua expanded its range in the 1960s, reaching Svalbard in the mid-1970s. Some of the expansion has been at the expense of the Parasitic Jaeger. The Great Skua breeds earlier and does not tolerate the smaller bird, killing both adults and fledglings. Migratory, moving to the Atlantic from Ireland to central Africa and the Mediterranean, though some Icelandic birds head for waters off Newfoundland. Breeding birds are coastal, wintering birds pelagic.

Diet
Chiefly fish, either hunted by surface-seizure, scavenging or piracy. However, predation on both adult and young seabirds is important during the breeding season. On St. Kilda Island, off western Scotland, Great Skuas feed nocturnally on storm-petrels. Great Skuas may take birds as large as Graylag Geese (though it is likely that such large prey are sick or injured) and have been seen taking Mountain Hares (*Lepus timidus*).

Breeding
Solitary, occasionally in small groups, but loose colonies form at breeding sites. Pair-bonds are monogamous and apparently lifelong. Pairs form initially at "clubs" of immature birds that have yet to breed. Male approaches female, adopting an upright posture to discourage potential rivals. Female may beg for food, courtship-feeding a prelude to bonding even if the pair does not breed that year. Nest is a shallow scrape on open ground. Two brown eggs blotched red-brown; incubated by both birds but mainly by female for 26–32 days. Birds are highly aggressive to intruders. Chicks semi-nidifugous and semi-altricial. Guarded by female, fed by both birds (but male is chief source) by regurgitation until self-feeding. Fledge at 40–50 days, but not independent for up to 20 days. Breed at 7–8 years.

Taxonomy and geographical variation
Monotypic.

▼ Adult Great Skua on the nest, Runde, Norway.

Dark- and pale-morph Parasitic Jaegers, Runde, Norway.

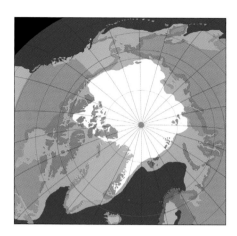

Parasitic Jaeger
(Arctic Skua)
Stercorarius parasiticus

Identification
See p. 238

Breeding adults have three distinct forms: dark morph birds are more common in the south of the range, light morphs are more common in the north, and an intermediate form occurs between. Pale morph adults have a dark brown crown, the color extending forward to the lores and bill, and backward to the upper nape. The sides of the head and lower nape are yellow, the chin white. The bill is dark brown or black, the iris dark brown. The underparts are white, the undertail-coverts dark slate-gray. The sides of the breast are gray, occasionally extending to form a complete breast band. There may also be gray patches on the upper flanks. The upperparts are dark slate-gray or gray-brown, apart from the flight feathers and greater coverts, which are dark brown. The tail is as the upperparts, the central feathers are longer and pointed. The underwing-coverts are dark brown, the flight feathers paler with a white bar on the base of the primaries. Some adults are paler, lacking any gray on the underparts.

Dark morph adults are overall dark or sooty brown, but with a black crown and paler cheeks (though on the darkest birds these are absent). There is little difference in color between the tail and flight feathers and the rest of the plumage, though the white wing-bar remains (though often reduced). Intermediate morph birds are close to dark morph but much paler, even tinged yellow, on the cheeks and nape. The underparts are pale gray-brown, occasionally barred darker. The legs and feet are black. Pale morph adults lose the distinct pattern in winter: the underparts show dark brown streaking, and the upperparts

have pale fringing on the mantle and pale barring on the tail. Dark morph adults in winter show varying amounts of pale streaking and barring.

Juveniles and immatures have variable plumage because of the pale and dark morphs, but in general show significant dark barring on the underwing and buff barring on the upperwing lesser and median coverts. Downy chicks are cinnamon.

Confusion species
The central tail feathers of the three smaller *Stercorarius* skuas are distinctive: the Parasitic Jaeger has long, pointed feathers, the Long-tailed Jaeger has very long pointed feathers, the Pomarine Jaeger twisted and club-ended feathers. In flight the smallest of the three, Long-tailed, is ternlike, Parasitic is falconlike, and Pomarine is more ponderous.

Size
L: 16¼–18 in. (41–46 cm). WS: 3½–4 ft. (110–125 cm). W: 10½ –18 oz. (300–500 g).

▼ Parasitic Jaeger in flight near the timberline, Churchill.

Voice
Usual call is a mewing *gee-oo*. The short call is a sharp *tuk*, the long call a whining, nasal *fee-err*.

Distribution
Circumpolar. Breeds on southern, western and northeastern coasts of Greenland, on Iceland, Svalbard, Scandinavia, northern Russia including Franz Josef Land and Novaya Zemlya, Kamchatka, and across North America from western and northern Alaska and along the north Canadian mainland and the Arctic islands north to southern Ellesmere. Migratory, mainly moving to the coasts of South America, the western and southern coasts of Africa, but also the Arabian Sea and the coasts of Australasia. Parasitic Jaegers tend to migrate with Arctic Terns, pirating their catches along the way. Coastal in summer, pelagic in winter.

Diet
Chiefly fish obtained by piracy, but also rodents, small seabirds, eggs, insects and berries. In some locations predation on seabirds is a major food source. Wintering birds feed almost exclusively by piracy.

Breeding
Solitary or in small groups in winter, but forms loose colonies at breeding sites. Males are very aggressive to other males when establishing territories. Pair-bonds are monogamous and lifelong. Pair-bond is formed initially at a "club" as in Great Skua. Although there are spectacular display flights when the birds first arrive at the breeding grounds, with several birds zigzagging around the sky, only limited displays occur before bonding, though the bond is reinforced by courtship-feeding. Nest is on open ground, often on a dry spot in marshland. It is a shallow depression with minimal vegetation lining. Two olive or light brown eggs, blotched red-brown; incubated by both birds for 25–28 days. Birds aggressive to intruders. Chicks semi-nidifugous and semi-altricial. Fed by both birds by regurgitation until self-feeding. Fledge at 25–30 days, but not independent for up to further 30 days. Breed at 4–5 years.

Taxonomy and geographical variation
Monotypic.

Long-tailed Jaeger
(Long-tailed Skua)
Stercorarius longicaudus

Identification
See p. 238

The smallest and lightest of the skuas. Adults are not thought to exhibit polymorphism, though some reports exist from Greenland. Breeding adults have black cap extending to upper nape and below the eye to the bill. The cheeks and lower nape are yellow, the throat white. The bill is black, the iris dark brown. The breast is white, merging into pale gray belly, flanks and undertail-coverts. The mantle, rump and upperwing-coverts are uniformly slate-gray, occasionally with a paler bar on the foremantle and striping on the scapulars. The greater primary

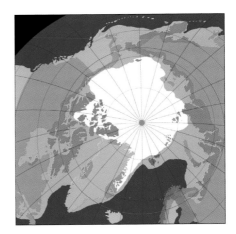

coverts and flight feathers are black, the outer primaries with pale shafts appearing as a thin, broken white leading edge. The tail is black, with the central feathers very long (though often broken by the end of summer). The underwing is uniformly dark gray apart from the outer primary shafts. Wintering adults lose the yellow on the head, the crown becoming more ragged. The underparts have gray-brown barring, often producing a dark breast band and distinct barring on the lower belly and vent. The upperparts are as in summer, but the mantle, scapulars, rump and uppertail-coverts barred paler. The legs are dark blue-gray, the feet black.

Juveniles have pale and dark morphs. Pale morph birds show heavy light/dark gray-brown barring on the underwing, and dark barring on the flanks and vent, with pale barring on the upperparts (apart from the flight feathers) and a

▼ This nominate-race Long-tailed Jaeger has caught and killed a Siberian Brown Lemming, Pyasina Delta, western Taimyr.

◀ Long-tailed Jaeger of race *pallescens* in flight, Ellesmere Island.

eastern and western coasts of southern South America and the western coast of southern Africa, where, as with the Parasitic Jaeger, it exploits the food-rich Benguela Current. Wintering birds are pelagic.

Diet
In summer, chiefly feeds on rodents, primarily lemmings, which comprise up to 99% of diet; Long-tailed Jaegers do not occur where lemmings are absent. Also eats insects, berries, small birds and eggs. Wintering birds are almost exclusively piratical.

Breeding
Solitary, or in small groups at all times. Males aggressive during establishment of territories. There are courtship flights with spectacular aerobatics, and courtship-feeding before bonding. Bonds are monogamous and apparently long-lasting. The nest is a shallow depression on dry, open ground, sometimes minimally lined. Two olive or light brown eggs blotched red-brown, incubated by both birds (with eggs held on foot webs) for 23–25 days. Parents highly aggressive against intruders. Chicks semi-nidifugous and semi-altricial. Fed by both parents by regurgitation until self-feeding. Fledge at 24–26 days, but are not independent for further 15–20 days. Probably breeds at 4 years.

white/dark gray barred rump and uppertail. Dark morph birds have uniformly sooty black upperparts with indistinct pale barring on the mantle and wing coverts and distinct white barring on the uppertail. The underparts are uniformly sooty black, but with white spotting on the coverts and a white wing-bar at the base of the primaries. Downy chicks are pale brown above, pale gray below.

Confusion species
See Parasitic Jaeger, pages 234–235.

Size
L: 19–21½ in. (48–55 cm), tail streamer length about 7 in. (18 cm). WS: 3½–3¾ ft. (105–115 cm). W: 7¾–15½ oz. (220–440 g).

Voice
The short call is a sharp *krip*, distinctively different from that of the Parasitic Jaeger. The long call, most often heard in breeding birds, is a rattling series of *krips* ending with a plaintive *feee-oo*.

Distribution
Circumpolar. Breeds in northwestern, northeastern and western Greenland. Absent from Iceland, but breeds on Jan Mayen and Svalbard, in mountainous parts of Scandinavia, sand across Russia to Kamchatka, including the southern island of Novaya Zemlya and Wrangel. In North America, breeds across Alaska and the northern Canadian mainland east to Hudson Bay. Absent from eastern Canada apart from east-central Hudson Bay. Breeds on all Canadian Arctic islands to northern Ellesmere. Essentially a tundra dweller (and known as the Mountain Skua in Scandinavia), but also found at the coast. Migratory, moving as far as the Southern Ocean in winter, but chiefly migrating to waters off the

Taxonomy and geographical variation
Polytypic. The nominate race breeds in Scandinavia and Russia to the Lena Delta. *S. l. pallescens* breeds in eastern Asian Russia, North America and Greenland. It has paler underparts, occasionally white to the vent.

Pomarine Jaeger
(Pomarine Skua)
Stercorarius pomarinus

A large, deep-chested, bulky skua. As with the Parasitic Jaeger, the Pomarine has two forms, with pale morphs representing about 90% of the population.

Identification See p. 238
Pale morph adults are patterned as Long-tailed Jaegers. The crown cap is dark brown or black, extending below the eye and bill, but not to the nape. The cheeks and nape are yellow, the chin white. The bill has a black tip, but is otherwise dark brown or dark gray. The iris is dark brown. The breast and upper belly are white (some birds have a dusky partial breast band), often strongly delineated from the gray-brown lower belly, vent and undertail-coverts. The upperparts are dark brown or gray-brown, relieved only by the white bases of the primary webs. The tail is dark gray-brown, the central pair of feathers elongated, twisted

at the base and ending in "clubs." The underwing shows dark brown or gray-brown lesser coverts, paler median and greater coverts, and flight feathers with a more distinct white patch at the base of the primaries. Dark morphs are overall dark brown or gray-brown, relieved only by the white basal patches on the primaries. The head is occasionally bronze-glossed. Wintering pale adults lose the yellow on the head, becoming white with brown barring or streaking, and have extensive brown barring on the underside, particularly across the breast, and on the vent and undertail. Wintering dark adults show little change. The legs and feet are black.

Pale juveniles have creamy buff heads, the underparts and underwing buff with heavy dark streaking and barring, apart from the white patch at the base of the primaries and a broad, gray underwing trailing edge. The upperparts are rich-brown fringed buff, apart from the solid dark brown greater primary coverts and flight feathers. The uppertail-coverts are barred dark brown and buff. Dark juvenile birds are as adults, but lightly speckled white or buff on the underparts, the undertail-coverts barred dark brown and buff. The upperparts are narrowly fringed buff, the uppertail-coverts barred dark brown and buff. There are also intermediate juvenile forms. Downy chicks are mid-brown above, gray below.

Confusion species
See Parasitic Jaeger, pages 234–235.

Size
L: 18–20½ in. (46–52 cm), tail streamer length about 4 in. (11 cm). WS: 4–4½ ft. (125–140 cm). W: 19½–29¼ oz. (550–830 g).

Voice
Usually silent except at breeding sites. The short call is a sharp barking *gek*, though there is also a gull-like *veek-veek*. The long call is a series of nasal yelps.

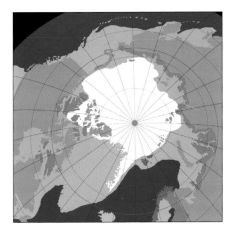

Distribution
Circumpolar. Breeding not proven in western Greenland or Svalbard, but unlikely due to the absence of lemmings. Breeds on Russia's northern coast from the White Sea to the Bering Sea. Probably breeds on all Arctic islands, but this not proven. In North America, breeds on the western and northern coasts of Alaska, on the Canadian mainland around Bathurst Inlet, on northeastern Hudson Bay, on Banks and Victoria Islands and on southern and northern Baffin Island. May also breed on remote sites of other islands. Migratory, moving to the Caribbean, the Atlantic off northern Africa, the Arabian Sea, and the Pacific Ocean off eastern Australia, northern New Zealand, Hawaii and northwestern South America. Summer birds occupy tundra and coastal sites. Wintering birds are pelagic.

Diet
Chiefly rodents (particularly lemmings) in summer, also small birds and eggs. Wintering birds take fish, occasionally by piracy; rather than simply settling for crop contents, they also regularly catch and kill smaller seabirds.

Breeding
Solitary or in small groups in winter. May breed colonially, the nest density depending on lemming numbers. Displays are more similar to that of Great Skua than to other *Stercorarius* skuas. Pair-bond is monogamous, but of unknown duration. Courtship-feeding reinforces the bond. Nest is shallow depression on dry, open ground, with minimal vegetative lining. Two brown eggs blotched red-brown; incubated by both birds for 25–27 days. Parents much less aggressive to intruders than Great Skua or smaller skuas. Chicks semi-nidifugous and semi-altricial. Fed by both birds by regurgitation until self-feeding. Fledge at 32–37 days, but not independent for a further 14 days. Probably breed at 5–6 years.

Taxonomy and geographical variation
Monotypic.

◄ Pomarine Jaeger in flight, high above the ice floes, Beaufort Sea.

PLATE 16: SKUAS

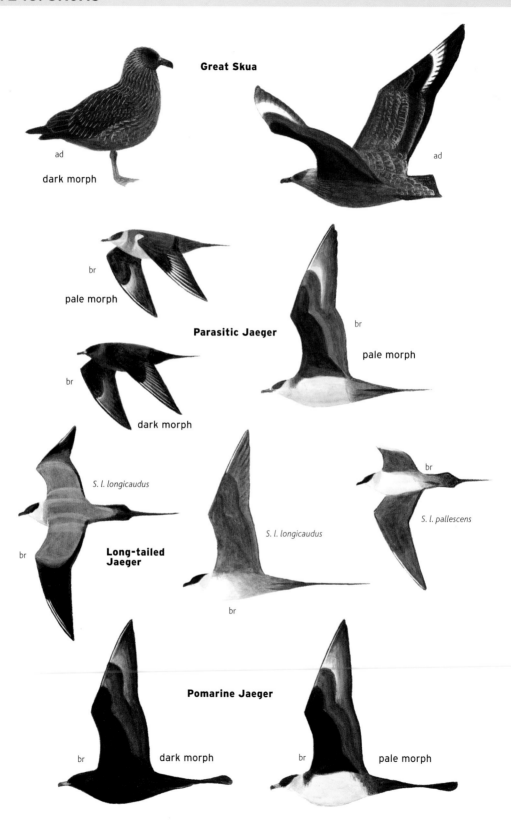

Great Skua

ad

dark morph

ad

Parasitic Jaeger

br

pale morph

br

pale morph

br

dark morph

S. l. longicaudus

S. l. longicaudus

br

S. l. pallescens

br

**Long-tailed
Jaeger**

br

Pomarine Jaeger

br dark morph

br pale morph

Great Black-backed Gull

br

Herring Gull

br

L. a. argenteus

ad win

L. a. argenteus

Glaucous Gull

br

1st-win

ad win

Lesser Black-backed Gull

br

1st-sum

L. fuscus

br

Glaucous-winged Gull

1st-win

ad win

br

L. f. heuglini

L. f. heuglini

L. f. taimyrensis

Gulls

For ship-borne visitors — and many of the most interesting Arctic locations are really only accessible by sea — gulls are the most visible of northern birds. But that visibility does not automatically translate into identification, as apart from Ross's Gull, which has a rosy-pink tinge during the breeding season, breeding Arctic gull plumages are all black, white and shades of gray, with juvenile and immature forms adding brown to the mix.

Gulls are generally gregarious at all times. As it is neither possible nor profitable to stake out a territory on the open sea (too much energy is required, and prey is too randomly distributed in both time and space), gulls congregate wherever the feeding is good. Territories are, however, held by predatory gulls on prey-nesting cliffs, the territorial gull chasing off any conspecifics that enter the territory with the apparent intention of taking prey species' chicks or eggs. Opportunistic feeding on these requires a slow pass of the cliff, and this, in turn, requires flying upwind, so conspecifics moving downwind are ignored and those moving upwind chased. Colonial nesting pays dividends as it reduces an individual's risk of being taken by a predator. In addition, of course, cliffs and islands are close to the sea. Gulls are not well adapted to terrestrial life, and fewer good nesting sites are near good feeding grounds than might be expected.

The identification of gulls is not at all straightforward. Newly hatched gulls will not attain full adult breeding plumage until their third, fourth or even fifth summer (see box). Identification is made more difficult by the similarity of many juvenile/immature forms, the timing of molts (which differs both between and within species) and variations in plumage, and bill and leg color. The problem is compounded by hybridization, which often results in "problem" individuals. The taxonomy of several gull species is also confused and controversial. For example, it is debatable whether the following are different species or simply subspecies; Mew Gulls; Iceland and Kumlien's Gulls; Herring, American Herring and Vega Gulls. Here, such similar birds are described as single species, but with notes on the variation and taxonomy of types. The adult form of the species is described in detail, with only brief notes on the juvenile and immature forms.

The Black-headed Gull (*Larus ridibundus*) is a Palearctic species, breeding in southern and southeastern Greenland, Iceland, northern Fennoscandia and Kamchatka, but is essentially sub-Arctic. The Little Gull (*L. minutus*) is also essentially sub-Arctic, but breeds around Russia's White Sea and in recent years has begun to breed in small numbers on the southern shores of Hudson Bay.

▼ Black-headed Gull, a sub-Arctic species that can occur north of the Arctic Circle, Kamchatka.

The molt and age sequence of Arctic gulls:

Two-year gulls

Juvenile	June–September
First-winter	August–March
First-summer	February–September
Adult winter	from August

Three-year gulls

Juvenile	June–September
First-winter	August–March
First-summer	February–September
Second-winter	August–March
Second-summer	February–September
Adult winter	from August

Four-year gulls

Juvenile	June–September
First-winter	August–March
First-summer	February–September
Second-winter	August–March
Second-summer	February–September
Third-winter	August–March
Third-summer	February–September
Adult winter	from August

Bonaparte's Gull
Larus philadelphia

Bonaparte's Gull is a smaller, Nearctic version of the Black-headed Gull. The bird is named after French zoologist Charles Lucien Bonaparte, a nephew of Napoleon Bonaparte.

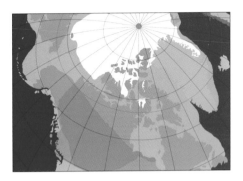

Identification See p. 257
A two-year gull. Breeding adults have a dark gray or black hood extending from the upper nape to the chin. The bill is black, the gape bright orange-red, the orbital ring dark red, the iris dark brown. White crescents are above and below the eye. The underparts and tail are white, with an occasional pink tinge to the breast and belly. The upperparts, including the inner wing and inner primaries, are blue-gray. The outer primaries are pale gray with black tips to P4–P10, giving a black trailing edge. The inner underwing is gray, the primaries and primary coverts white. The legs are red. Winter adults lose the dark cap apart from a dark ear spot, a small dark spot in front of the eye, and a dark smudge on the crown. The legs become pink. Juveniles have a dark ear spot and pale ginger-brown crown and nape. The upper body is gray-brow, fringed paler. The upperwing has a dark brown carpal bar and black leading and trailing edges, the remaining wing gray with some dark buff fringing. The tail has a broad, black subterminal band and a thin white terminal band. First-winter birds lose the brown wash and have a black stripe at the rear of the head. Downy chicks are mottled black and brown.

Confusion species
Sabine's Gull has a forked tail and a broad black leading edge on the wing.

Size
L: 11–12 in. (28–30 cm). WS: 3–3¼ ft. (90–100 cm). W:6¼–8 oz. (180–230 g).

Voice
Usual call is a harsh, rasping *reeek*. Flocking birds have a sharp *kew*.

Distribution
Nearctic. Breeds in southern Alaska (but rare on the western and northern coasts), in northern Yukon (but not on north Canadian Mainland), and on southern Hudson Bay. Prefers ponds and lakes within the timber belt, or close to the timber-line. Migratory, moving to the east and west coasts of the United States and to the Great Lakes. Habitat as in summer.

Diet
Breeding birds chiefly consume insects, catching them in flight as well as on the ground and water surface, but fish and crustaceans are also taken. Bonaparte's Gulls peck and dip from the surface, but also plunge-dive occasionally. Wintering birds take fish by wading and diving, and also crustaceans.

Breeding
Highly gregarious in winter, less so at breeding sites, though small colonies do form. Male has a swooping and soaring display flight, also a head-flagging display. Pair-bond apparently monogamous and seasonal. The species' habit of nesting in trees is unusual among gulls. The nest is of sticks, lined with mosses and grass. Abandoned nests are sometimes refurbished and reused. Usually three (rarely two or four) pale buff-olive or gray-buff eggs blotched brown; incubated for 22–25 days by both birds. Chicks are nidifugous and semi-precocial. Brooded and fed by both parents. Fledge in about 35 days and are independent at that time. Breed at 2–3 years.

Taxonomy and geographical variation
Monotypic.

Mew Gull (Common Gull)
Larus canus

Identification See p. 257
A compact three-year gull. Breeding adults have a white head. The bill is yellow, usually with a brighter tip and greenish tinge to the base. The gape is orange-pink, the orbital ring red, the iris dark brown. The underparts, underwing (apart from the primaries) and tail are white. The upperparts and upperwing are mid-gray. The secondaries and inner primaries are white-tipped, forming a white trailing edge. The outer primaries (P5–P10) have an increasing fraction of black, becoming all black; P9 and P10 have large white mirrors and small black tips, P5–P8 have white tips. The overall impression is of a black wingtip with a terminal white spot. Perched birds shows clear white crescents dividing the gray upperparts and white-spotted wingtips. The legs and feet are yellow or greenish-yellow. Wintering adults have gray-brown smudges above and behind the eye and (more extensively) on the neck. Juveniles

◀ Bonaparte's Gull in summer plumage, Churchill.

are overall gray-brown with a scaly appearance from paler fringing. The tail is paler or white, with indistinct and incomplete dark gray-brown barring and a broad black terminal band. The bill is dull pink with a black tip. The legs are dull pink. First-winter birds are similar to juvenile, second-winter birds similar to adult. Downy chicks are dark brown, buff and white above, white below.

Confusion species
Mew Gull's size, yellow feet and lack of a bill spot are diagnostic.

Size
L: 16–16½ in. (40–42 cm). WS: 3½–4¼ ft. (110–130 cm). W: 10½–19½ oz. (300–550 g).

Voice
Usual call is long mewing *miieeww*. Long call is a high series of mews.

▲ Mew Gull (race *brachyrhynchus*) incubating a chick, Cook Inlet.

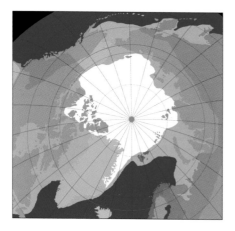

Distribution
Circumpolar. Absent from Greenland, but breeds in limited numbers on Iceland (where it first bred as recently as 1936; the range is now extending). Breeds in northern Fennoscandia and across Russia, but always sub-Arctic except on the southeastern Chukotka coast. Breeds throughout Kamchatka. In North America, breeds throughout Alaska (but rare in the north) and in Yukon and Northwest Territories (again rare in the north). Found on coasts and inland waters. Migratory European birds move to the North, Mediterranean and Black Seas, though some Icelandic birds are resident. Asiatic birds move to the Black and Caspian Seas, and to coastal Southeast Asia. Wintering birds more often seen on coasts.

Diet
Invertebrates and fish, but opportunistic and will take amphibians, rodents, chicks, eggs and berries where available. Will also scavenge (much less so than Black-headed Gulls) and occasionally pirates other seabirds. Inland wintering birds will take grain from stubble fields.

Breeding
Gregarious, but not highly so. Males have a long call as other gulls. The head is first held horizontal, then tipped down slightly before being flung back vertically. Females approach males in crouched position. Head-flagging can occur and there is courtship-feeding. Pair-bond is monogamous (though polygyny observed), renewed annually. Usually nests on ground, but occasionally on a cliff ledge or in a tree on a tree-surrounded inland lake. Nest is of vegetation, usually seaweed at coastal sites, built by both birds. Two to five very variable eggs ranging from white to dark brown; usually blotched or streaked olive-brown. Incubated for 23–28 days by both birds. Chicks semi-nidifugous and precocial. Fed by both birds bill to bill with regurgitated food initially. Fledge in about 35 days and are independent soon after. Breed at 2–4 years.

Taxonomy and geographical variation
Polytypic. The nominate race breeds in Europe and Russia east to the White Sea. *L. c. heinei* breeds eastward to Lena River. It has darker upperparts than the nominate (increasingly dark eastward), smaller mirrors on P9 and P10 and darker yellow legs. *L. c. kamtschatschensis* breeds on Kamchatka, around the Sea of Okhotsk and in Chukotka. It is darker than the

◄ Mew Gull of the nominate race, north Norway.

nominate, but lighter than *heinei*; *kamtschatschensis* is also larger than the nominate with a larger, heavier bill. Juveniles are darker than those of either nominate or *heinei*. This subspecies is often called the Kamchatka Gull (though not by the ornithologists of Kamchatka). Interbreeding between *heinei* and *kamtschatschensis* occurs at their range boundary.

The status of the Nearctic version of the Gull Mew (*L. c. brachyrhynchus,*) is still debated. Most authorities consider it a subspecies; it has more white and less black on the wingtips than the nominate, and a shorter bill. Some consider brachyrhynchus to be a separate species because of the differences in plumage in all forms (particularly juveniles, which are gray-brown overall, with gray-brown and white barred uppertail and broader black subterminal tail). This potential split seems to be supported by mitochondrial DNA evidence. Mew and Black-headed Gulls have hybridized.

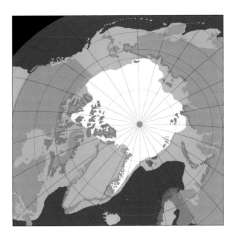

Glaucous Gull
Larus hyperboreus

Identification
See p. 239
A very large, very pale four-year gull. Breeding adults have a white head. The bill is yellow with a red gonys spot, the gape is yellow. The iris is yellow, the orbital ring bright lemon. The underparts including the underwing are white. The upperwing is pale gray with a white trailing edge. The remaining upperparts are white. Winter adults have gray-brown streaking to the head and upper breast, occasionally limited but sometimes heavy. The legs and feet are pink. Juveniles can be very pale, almost white, with buff-brown streaking above, but they can also be much darker; overall they are gray-brown with pale fringing giving a scaly appearance. Immature birds are as juvenile, acquiring partial gray upperparts in the second winter. The bill of the juvenile/immature is yellow-pink with a dark subterminal band and pale tip. The iris is dark brown. Downy chicks are cream, lightly spotted dark and light brown.

Confusion species
Some Iceland Gulls show no dark markings on the primaries and so are virtually identical to Glaucous Gull. However Iceland's iris is usually yellow-brown and orbital ring purple. Size is usually a good guide, but female Glaucous can be same size as large Iceland Gulls. The situation is not helped by Glaucous x Iceland hybrids. Glaucous-winged Gulls are also very similar to Glaucous, but have patterned outer primaries. Glaucous x Glaucous-winged hybrids add to the confusion.

Size
L: 24½–26¾ in. (62–68 cm). WS: 5–5½ ft. (150–165 cm). W: 2¼–4¾ lb. (1–2.2 kg).

▶ Glaucous Gull with chicks, Bear Island.

Voice
Long call as Herring Gull, but hoarser, also a higher *ke-lee*.

Distribution
Circumpolar. Breeds on all coasts of Greenland, on Iceland, Jan Mayan, Svalbard, northern Scandinavia, across Russia (including all Arctic islands) and across the northern mainland of North America and the Canadian Arctic islands to northern Ellesmere. Found on coastal sites and on inland waterways. Migratory, moving south mainly in response to sea ice. Winters in the north Atlantic and in the Pacific to northern California and the Kuril Islands. Winter birds are both pelagic and coastal.

Diet
Omnivorous; chiefly feeds on fish, marine invertebrates, chicks and eggs, rodents and the afterbirth and feces of seals. Food obtained by scavenging and piracy, but will also plunge-dive. Can also be a ruthless predator; I have seen it consume an entire brood of Long-tailed Ducks on Ellesmere. The gull forced the ducklings to dive by low traverses of the pond until one became exhausted. The duckling was then picked off as it lay helpless on surface. The gull then resumed its harrying.

Breeding
Gregarious, but in relatively small flocks. Displays include long-calling, mutual head-tossing and courtship-feeding. Pair-bond monogamous and apparently long-lived. Nests on open ground, but more often on rock pinnacles or cliff ledges. The nest is a mound of seaweed gathered by both birds. Two to

three creamish-buff eggs, blotched red-brown; incubated by both birds for 27–28 days. Chicks semi-nidifugous and precocial. Fed by both parents. Fledge in 45–50 days and are independent soon after. Breed at 4–7 years.

Taxonomy and geographical variation

Polytypic. The nominate race breeds from Jan Mayen and Spitsbergen to the Taimyr Peninsula. *L. h. barrovianus* breeds in Alaska and Canada to the Mackenzie Delta. It has longer legs and wings than the nominate, but a smaller bill. Upperparts may be darker and the orbital ring may be red. *L. h. pallidissimus* breeds in Asiatic Russia from the Taimyr Peninsula to Chukotka. It is larger and paler than the nominate. *L. h leucertes* breeds from northern Canada to Greenland and Iceland; it is very similar to the nominate.

Glaucous-winged Gull
Larus glaucescens

Identification   See p. 239

A large, broad-winged four-year gull. Breeding adults have a white head. The bill is yellow with a red-orange gonys spot. The gape is pink or purple-pink. The small, dark eyes are distinctive. The iris is dark or tawny brown, occasionally dirty yellow, the orbital ring pink to reddish-purple. The back and mantle are mid-gray with a blue tinge. Rump and tail are white. The upperwing is mid-gray (again blue-tinged) with a white trailing edge. The outer primaries, P6–P10, are usually darker with white tips; P10 usually has a white mirror, and there are occasionally white spots on P6–P8. The underparts are white, the underwing is as the upperwing. Winter adults have brown streaking or barring to the head, neck and upper breast. The bill is duller yellow, the gonys spot often replaced by a subterminal dark brown band. The legs and feet are pink, sometimes pink-purple. Juveniles are overall gray-brown, the rump and both upper- and undertail-coverts paler and barred brown, the mantle and scapulars fringed paler to give a scaly appearance. The bill is black. Immature birds become paler. Second-winter bird shows some gray on the upperparts. Thrid-winter bird has a dull yellow bill with a black tip. Downy chicks have black-spotted pink-buff upperparts, buff underparts.

Confusion species

Glaucous-winged Gulls hybridize with Western Gull (*L. occidentalis*), Glaucous Gull, *smithsonianus* Herring Gull and Slaty-backed Gull, which adds to confusions already existing with these species. Gray wingtip is diagnostic from other large Arctic gulls.

Size

L: 22³/4–24³/4 in. (58–63 cm). WS: 4¹/2–5¹/4 ft. (140–160 cm). W: 2–3³/4 lb. (850–1,700 g).

Voice

Usual call is low, slow *oow-oow*, very repetitive and often heard outside the breeding season. Long call is as Herring Gull, but lower and slower.

▲ Glaucous-winged Gull in adult breeding plumage, Seward.

Distribution

Bering Sea. Breeds in southern and western Alaska, southern Chukotka, and on Kamchatka and the Commander Islands. Found in coastal locations, rarely inland. Partially migratory, moving to southern waters as far as Baja California and Japan. Still essentially coastal in winter, but also found on garbage dumps.

Diet

Marine invertebrates, fish, and chicks and eggs. Also scavenges for carrion. In Siberia, the gull is well known for following walrus hunters to feed on discarded offal.

Breeding

Not highly gregarious; breeding colonial, but often found alone away from breeding sites. Displays as other large gulls, but during long call head is not thrown vertically but is instead moved horizontally after forward-bend. The pair-bond is monogamous, but extra-pair copulations occur, and occasionally forcible insemination. Nests on bare ground or on

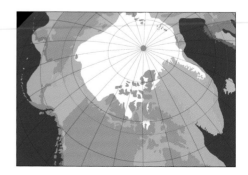

rock pinnacles, cliff ledges and similar structures (e.g. piers and even flat roofs). Nest is of seaweed, usually lined with grass or feathers. One to four (usually two or three) pale green or olive eggs spotted dark brown; incubated for 26–29 days by both birds. Chicks semi-nidifugous and semi-precocial. Fed by both parents by regurgitation at first. Fledge at 37–53 days and are independent soon after. Breed at 4–7 years.

Taxonomy and geographical variation
Monotypic. Siberian birds generally have darker upperparts and longer wings.

Herring Gull
Larus argentatus

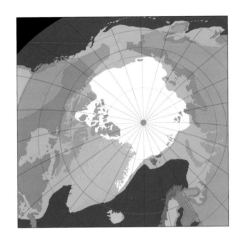

Identification
See p. 239

A four-year gull. Breeding adults have a white head. The stout bill is yellow with large red spot at the gonys. The gape is orange-yellow, the iris pale yellow, the orbital ring orange-yellow. The underparts and tail are white. The back, mantle and upperwing are mid-gray, usually with a bluish tinge. The trailing edge of the wing is white. The primaries show considerable variation, but in general P10 is black with a white tip, P9 is black with white tip and a white mirror, P5–P8 black with white tips. In general, northern birds show less black. The underwing is white, the primary pattern visible. The legs and feet are pink. Winter adults have extreme gray-brown streaking on the head and neck. Juveniles are overall gray-brown, mottled darker on upperparts. The tail has a broad dark brown subterminal band and a thin white terminal band. Immature birds are increasingly paler; second-winter birds acquire a gray mantle; third-winter birds look similar to adult winter birds. Downy chicks are black, buff and pale buff.

Confusion species
Juveniles and immatures resemble young nominate Mew Gulls but are larger, less round-headed and longer-billed. Red gonys spot and pink legs of adults are shared by Iceland and Thayer's Gulls, but wingtip pattern easily distinguishes them.

Size
L: 21½–26½ in. (55–67 cm). WS: 4½–5 ft. (138–155 cm). W: 1½–2¾ lb. (700–1,300 g).

Voice
The familiar seagull cackle. All calls are based on a buglelike *keeyow*.

Distribution
Circumpolar. Absent from Greenland, but breeds in Iceland (where it became established in the 1920s) and northern Fennoscandia. The rest of the range through Russia is unclear. Herring Gulls probably breed in small numbers on the White Sea coast and Taimyr Peninsula, and certainly east from the Lena River to Chukotka. Breed to the northern coast, but absent from the Arctic islands, including Svalbard. In North America, breeds in central Alaska (but rare on the western and northern coasts) and across Canada, but only to the northern coast around and east of Hudson Bay. Breeds on Southampton and southern Baffin Islands. Being opportunistic feeders, Herring Gulls are found at the coast, on freshwater lakes and pools or inland far from water. Migratory, with northern birds moving south, but destinations depend on food supply. In general, stays close to the coast, but often found at sea in winter.

Herring Gulls of the North American race *smithsonianus*, Barren Lands, Northwest Territories.

▲ Nominate-race Herring Gull in flight, north Norway.

Diet
Essentially omnivorous; feeds opportunistically by hunting fish, crustaceans and mollusks, also predatory on amphibians, small mammals, birds, chicks and eggs. Will eat unguarded chicks of its own species (about 25% of Herring Gull chicks at one breeding site were cannibalized); also scavenges and engages in piracy. Has readily adapted to feeding on refuse dumps, including those at Inuit settlements in Canada.

Breeding
Gregarious, forming huge flocks, but also encountered alone. Displays as nominate Mew Gull, with a more flamboyant long call; head is thrust down with bill pointing toward feet, then head is thrown back, bill pointing skyward. Mutual displays include head-tossing (rather than head-flagging) and courtship-feeding. Pair-bond is monogamous and often lifelong. Nests on open ground or cliff ledges. The nest is usually a mass of vegetation built by both birds. Two to four cream, olive or light brown eggs, often blotched red-brown; incubated by both birds (but chiefly female) for 28–30 days. Chicks semi-nidifugous and precocial. Fed by both parents, with feeding stimulated by the chick pecking at the gonys spot. Fledge at 35–40 days and are independent soon after. Breed at 3–7 years.

Taxonomy and geographical variation
Polytypic. The nominate race breeds in Fennoscandia. *L. a. argenteus* breeds on Iceland, the Faroes and in western Europe. It is smaller and paler gray. The Vega Gull (*L. a. vegae*) breeds in eastern Asian Russia. Some authorities consider *vegae* to be a separate species, based on its isolation from western Palearctic birds; *vegae* is larger and darker than the nominate, with a longer bill. In the western part of its range (northwestern Yakutia), *vegae* may have yellow (or pink) legs, leading some to refer to a separate race here, *birulai*. The American Herring Gull (*L. a. smithsonianus*) breeds in North America and is considered by many to be a separate species. Adult birds are virtually indistinguishable from the nominate, though juveniles are much darker. There are also several extralimital subspecies.

The confusing taxonomy of several of the races of Herring Gull is not helped by hybridization. Nominate Herring Gulls hybridize with Glaucous and Lesser Black-backed Gulls; American Herring Gull with Glaucous Gull; Vega Gull with Slaty-backed, Glaucous-winged and Heuglin's Gulls.

Lesser Black-backed Gull
Larus fuscus

Herring and Lesser Black-backed Gulls are sympatric, but share a common ancestor. The Pleistocene ice separated groups of ancestral gulls, the two forms evolving separately but meeting when the ice retreated. Although the two species do not normally interbreed, if one species' eggs are replaced by the other's, the chicks will successfully interbreed when adults.

Identification See p. 239
A four-year gull. Essentially a dark-backed and more slender version of the Herring Gull. Breeding adults have a white head, underparts and tail. The bill is yellow with a red gonys spot, the gape orange. The iris is pale yellow, the orbital ring red. The

▼ Lesser Black-backed Gull, Kjorholmane, Norway.

rump is white. The back, mantle and upperwing are very dark gray or black with little discernible color difference on the wingtips. The upperwing has thin white leading and trailing edges, on all but the outer primaries. Feather P10 has a white mirror, P5–P9 show white tips. The underwing is white, with a dark trailing edge and primaries. The legs and feet are yellow. Winter adults have gray-brown streaking to the head. Juveniles are dark gray overall, but with contrasting white rump and uppertail-coverts (with some dark streaking) and a broad, black subterminal tail band. Juveniles are mottled brown and white and have a black bill. First-winter birds have paler underparts, second-winter show gray on the upperwing, third-winter has mid-gray upperwing apart from dark wingtips, and bill that is dull yellow with a dark subterminal band. Downy chicks are dark-brownish buff.

Confusion species

Greater Black-backed Gull is much larger and has more white on the wingtips and pink legs. Significantly darker than the Herring Gulls.

Size

L: 20½–26½ in. (52–67 cm). WS: 4½–5 ft. (135–155 cm). W: 1½–2 lb. (450–1100 g).

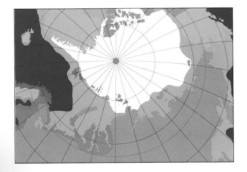

Voice

As Herring Gull, but lower and hoarser.

Distribution

Palearctic. Breeds in increasing numbers in southern Greenland, but not yet fully established. Breeds in Iceland (where it arrived in the 1920s and is now widespread), northern Fennoscandia and Russia east to the Taimyr Peninsula. Increasing numbers are seen in North America, but not yet an established breeding species. Essentially maritime, but also seen inland. Migratory. Icelandic birds move to Iberia and northwestern Africa; Scandinavian and European Russian birds to the eastern Mediterranean, the Arabian Sea and eastern Africa. Some birds now winter on the eastern coast of the United States. Asian Russian birds winter off the western Indian coast and the coasts of southern Japan and South Korea. Winter habitats similar to those of summer.

Diet

Omnivorous; much as Herring Gull, with birds in developed areas increasingly feeding on garbage dumps.

Breeding

Gregarious, but isolated pairs occur. Displays as Herring Gull. Pair-bond monogamous and long-lived. Nest on open ground, though usually concealed by vegetation, or on cliff ledges. Nest is large mound of seaweed and vegetation built by both sexes. Three (rarely two or four) highly variable eggs (base color white to red-brown, markings from none to gray-brown or red-brown streaks or blotches), incubated by both birds for 24–27 days. Chicks semi-nidifugous and precocial. Fed by both parents. Fledge at 30–40 days and are independent soon after. Breed at 4 years.

Taxonomy and geographical variation

Polytypic. Nominate race (occasionally referred to as the Baltic Gull) breeds in northern Scandinavia east to the White Sea. Race *graellsii* breeds in Iceland, the Faroes, British Isles and western Europe. It is larger, with paler upperparts so the darker wingtips are more obvious. In general, there is also more white on the tips of the outer primaries. Race *intermedius* breeds in southern Norway, Denmark and Holland. As the name implies, it is darker than *graellsii*, but paler than the nominate.

Heuglin's Gull (*L. f. heuglini*) breeds from the White Sea to the Taimyr Peninsula. Several authorities consider this a separate species; there is no evidence of interbreeding with the nominate, molt and plumage are different, and migration is substantially different. Heuglin's Gull is larger than the nominate, with upper color as *graellsii*, i.e., dark gray with black wingtips, the white markings as nominate. Heuglin's Gull is less gregarious than the nominate and is also less coastal, favoring tundra habitats near rivers and lakes. Those who consider Heuglin's to be a separate species consider the nominate *L. h. heuglini* to occupy the western part of the range, with a paler race *taimyrensis* to the east.

Iceland Gull
Larus glaucoides

Identification See p. 257

A four-year gull. Breeding adults have a white head. The bill is yellow (often tinged green) with a red gonys spot. The gape is pink. The iris is yellow or yellow brown, the orbital ring purple-red. The underparts, rump and tail are white. The upper and lower wings are pale gray or blue-gray, with distinct white trailing edge. The outer primaries are often unmarked, but race *kumlieni*, Kumlien's Gull, has some darker gray on the outermost five. In Kumlien's Gull, the primaries can be half dark gray and half pale gray or white around the shaft. Birds with marked primaries always have white tips, so the trailing edge is all white. Legs and feet are pink. Winter adults have limited streaking on the head (sometimes so limited that they appear as breeding plumage). Juveniles have two forms. The paler form is almost entirely white, with pale brown barring on the upperparts. The darker form is pale gray-brown overall, but with distinct darker barring on the upper- and underparts. The juvenile bill is black, becoming dull pink with a black tip by first-summer, dull yellow with a dark gonys marking by thrid-winter. Immatures show gray on the upperparts by the second

Adult Iceland Gull in flight, east Greenland.

winter. Third-winter birds are as winter adult, but with heavier streaking on the head. Downy chicks are buff with dark brown markings.

Confusion species

Glaucous Gull has similar plumage but is much larger, flatter-crowned and larger-billed. Iceland Gull looks less menacing than Glaucous Gull. On adult birds, any dark markings on wingtips indicates an Iceland (but may then cause confusion with Thayer's Gull).

Size

L: 20½–24 in. (52–60 cm). WS: 4½–5 ft. (140–150 cm). W: 1–2 lb. (500–1,000 g).

Voice

As Herring Gull, but much shriller.

Distribution

Eastern Nearctic. Despite its name, the bird is only seen in winter in Iceland. Apparently once bred on Jan Mayen, but now absent. Breeds in western and southern Greenland, more rarely on the southeastern coast. Breeds on eastern and southern Baffin Island, southeastern Ellesmere and, more rarely, on

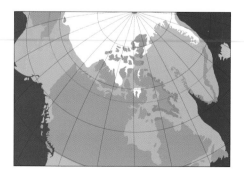

eastern Southampton Island and the extreme northern tip of Quebec. Occurs at coastal sites, rarely inland. Often feeds in open water between ice floes or bergs. Moves south in winter, seen across the north Atlantic from Newfoundland to Iceland (and, rarely, east to Scandinavia and Svalbard). Winter birds are both coastal and pelagic.

Diet

Chiefly fish, also feeds on crustaceans and mollusks. Will also take chicks and eggs, and scavenges carrion. Takes food from the water surface, but also plunge-dives. Inland birds may feed on berries and seeds.

Breeding

Gregarious at all times, nesting colonially, frequently with other gulls. Males defend nest site against other males, pulling grass as a threat before attacking intruder. Also makes choking call. Attracted female may beg for food. Little information on pair-bond, but probably monogamous and long-lived. Nests on cliff ledges; the nest is a crude mass of vegetation and detritus. One to three pale gray eggs blotched dark brown, apparently incubated by both parents for 24–27 days. Chicks nidifugous and semi-precocial. Fed and cared for by both parents. Fledge at 25–30 days. Thought to breed at 4 years.

Taxonomy and geographical variation

Polytypic. Nominate breeds in Greenland, northern Baffin and southern Ellesmere Islands. Race *kumlieni* breeds in southern Baffin and around northern Hudson Bay. Kumlien's Gulls have darker gray wingtips, the pattern variable, but invariably with a white trailing edge.

It is thought that the Laurentide ice sheet that covered North America during the last glaciation isolated populations of an ancestral gull that evolved into Iceland Gulls (to the east) and Thayer's Gulls (to the west). However, differences between these two are much less marked than between the Herring and Lesser Black-backed Gulls, questioning the validity

▶ Thayer's Gull in adult summer plumage.

of Thayer's Gull as a separate species. Kumlien's Gull (sometimes suggested to be a full species in its own right) is thought by some authorities to have developed through hybridization between Iceland and Thayer's Gulls.

Thayer's Gull
Larus thayeri

Identification

See p. 257

A four-year gull. Breeding adults are patterned as Herring Gulls of the race *smithsonianus* (American Herring Gulls) and Iceland Gulls; Thayer's is darker gray than Iceland Gull, being the same color (sometimes even darker) than American Herring Gull.

Bill of breeding adult is yellow with a red gonys spot. The gape is pink. The iris is dark yellow-brown (about 10% of birds have a yellow iris), the orbital ring red-purple. The upperwing is uniformly gray, with a white trailing edge. Feather P10 is black with a large white mirror and tiny black tip (the black tip absent in a few birds); P7–P9 are streaked black, the white mirrors blending to the feather's rear edge. Again there are white tips. Feathers P5 and P6 show some black. The overall effect is of a streaked black-and-white wingtip, rather than the solid black with a white tip of the American Herring. The streaking is black and white, rather than the gray and white of Kumlien's Gull. The legs and feet are pink. Winter adults have heavy gray-brown streaking on the head, always heavier than that of the Iceland, usually more smudged than the American Herring. Juvenile birds have two forms: the paler form is very similar to dark Iceland juveniles, the darker form is paler (but still very similar to) juvenile American Herring. Second-winter immatures show some gray upperparts, third-winter are as winter adult, but head is washed, rather than streaked, gray-brown. Downy chicks are as Iceland Gull.

Confusion species

American Herring Gull shows much bolder black wingtip and has yellow rather than dark iris. Differentiating Thayer's and *kumlieni* Iceland Gulls is much more difficult, but Thayer's Gulls have darker wingtips.

Size

L: 21½–24¾ in. (55–63 cm). WS: 4⅝–5 ft. (142–152 cm). W: 1½–2½ lb. (700–1,100 g).

Voice

Usually silent except at breeding sites. Calls as Iceland Gull.

Distribution

Nearctic. Breeds on the western shore of Hudson Bay and the Canadian Arctic islands from Banks to northern Baffin, and north to Ellesmere Island, though apparently absent from the Parry Islands. Coastal, but occasionally seen inland. Migratory, moving to the western coast of North America, from British Columbia to California. Winter birds are coastal, but more often seen on inland lakes. Also frequents garbage dumps.

Diet

As Iceland Gull.

Breeding

As Iceland Gull, though eggs tend to be more variable in base color, from pale gray to buff-brown and often heavily marked with purple-brown and gray splotches.

▼ Gulls dispute carrion from a Polar Bear kill on the sea ice, Baffin Bay, east of Bylot. An Ivory Gull (left) and Glaucous Gull are in the foreground, while a Thayer's Gull waits in the background. The gull in flight is very dark; probably a Thayer's, definitely mysterious.

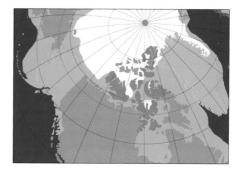

Taxonomy and geographical variation
Monotypic. The taxonomic position of Thayer's Gull is still debated, with some authorities considering it a subspecies of Iceland Gull. Thayer's x Kumlien's Gull hybrids are known from Southampton Island and southern Baffin Island, which adds to the confusion.

Great Black-backed Gull
Larus marinus

Identification See p. 239
The largest of the gulls. A four-year gull; breeding adults have white heads. The heavy bill is yellow with a red gonys spot. The gape is bright red. The iris varies from yellow to gray-yellow to dirty yellow. The orbital ring is red. The underparts, rump and tail are white. The back and upperwing are dark gray, with a white trailing edge and black primaries. Some birds have a clearly dark wingtip, but with others the upperwing is so dark that the wingtip is not distinctly darker. Feather P10 has an extensive white tip, P9 has a white mirror and white tip and P6–P8 have limited white tips, but these may wear. Rest of the primaries are white-tipped, seen as a trailing edge. Underwing is white with a white trailing edge, then a broad gray band extending to the black primary pattern. Legs and feet are pale pink. Winter adults show gray-brown streaking on crown and, occasionally, neck, but many are as breeding adults. Juveniles are as other large gulls, particularly Herring Gull, i.e., uniformly gray-brown with streaking and barring from the pale fringing. The tail is pale with a dark terminal bar, the underwing showing paler flight feathers. Juvenile bill is black, becoming dull yellow with black tip by the second winter. The bills of third-winter birds have a black subterminal band and small red gonys spot. The darker upperwing develops in third-winter birds. Chicks are dark brown, spotted cream or buff.

Confusion species
None. Lesser Black-backed Gull is significantly smaller and less powerfully built.

Size
L: 26–32 in. (65–80 cm). WS: 5–5½ ft. (150–165 cm). W: 2–4¾ lb. (1–2.2 kg).

▼ Greater Black-backed Gulls in breeding plumage, north Norway.

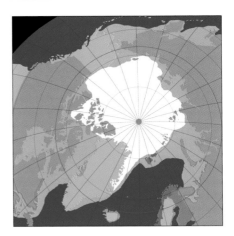

Voice
As Herring Gull, but lower and slower. The long call is also shorter and slower. In flight the gull often utters a deep, hoarse *ack*.

Distribution
North Atlantic. Breeds on Canada's Labrador coast, on the central western coast of Greenland, Iceland, Jan Mayen, northern Fennoscandia and on Svalbard (where it arrived in the 1930s). Now also established on the southern island of Novaya Zemlya and the nearby mainland coast of Russia. Coastal, more rarely inland. Partially migratory, moving south in winter but rarely seen beyond the limit of the continental shelf. Seen on garbage dumps and sewage outfalls.

Diet
Omnivorous. Predator of birds such as Puffins, which are caught in mid-air or taken on the ground. Puffins captured in mid-air may be swallowed whole in flight. Also preys on mammals, including animals as large as sheep if they are sick or injured. Also takes eggs and mollusks (which are broken by being dropped to the ground). Will obtain food by piracy and scavenging, and hunts for fish and crustaceans. Wintering birds tend to be marine surface feeders.

Breeding
Solitary or in small groups at all times. Displays as Herring Gull, but long call ends with head and bill horizontal rather than vertical. Male also has a territorial flight, using slow, deliberate wingbeats with head thrust forward. Pair-bond monogamous and may be renewed. Bond cemented by courtship-feeding and mutual head-tossing. Nest set on a rock outcrop or pinnacle. The nest is a mound of seaweed, vegetation and tidal debris. Two to three cream or light brown eggs speckled red-brown, incubated by both birds for 27–28 days. Chicks semi-nidifugous and precocial. Fed by both parents. Fledge at 50–55 days and are independent soon after. Breed at 4–5 years.

Taxonomy and geographical variation
Monotypic. May hybridize with Glaucous Gull, *smithsonianus* Herring Gull and (probably) nominate Herring Gull.

Slaty-backed Gull
Larus schistisagus

Identification   See p. 257
A large, stocky, large-billed four-year gull. Breeding adults have white heads. The bill is yellow with a red gonys spot. The gape is pale pink. The iris is yellow or yellow-brown. The orbital ring is pink-purple. The underparts, rump and tail are white. The upperwing is slate-gray with a broad white trailing edge. The primaries are dark gray at the base, darkening to black toward the tip: P10 has a large white mirror, separated from the white tip by a black bar; P9 is similar, but often with only a partial mirror; P5-P8 have white tips merging with the white trailing edge, the tips separated by broad black bars from white crescents which terminate the paler basal section of the feathers. These crescents appear as an often-distinct pattern known as the "string of pearls," which (when distinct) is both diagnostic and delightful. The underwing is white, the primaries pale slate-gray, the trailing edge showing the same broad white bar with the primary pattern also visible. A "string of pearls" is therefore visible, but less distinct against the paler background. The legs and feet are pink, occasionally bright red-pink. Winter adults are as breeding, but with some gray-brown streaking to the crown, and heavy streaking to the nape and sides of the neck. There is also a dark streak through the eye. Juveniles are overall gray-brown, but paler fringing gives a scaly appearance. The underwing shows gray-brown coverts and pale gray flight feathers. The tail is dark brown. Second-winter birds have a gray back and white rump and uppertail-coverts (but the tail is still dark brown). Third winter birds have dark gray-brown overwings with the white trailing edge established. The juvenile bill is dark brown, becoming dull yellow with a dark tip by the second winter. The third-winter bill is dull yellow with a subterminal dark band and a small gonys spot. Downy chicks are brownish-black mottled pale gray.

Confusion species
None; the only dark-backed gull in its range.

▼ Adult Slaty-backed Gull in breeding plumage, Kamchatka.

Size
L: 24–26 in. (61–66 cm). WS: 4³/₄–5 ft. (145–150 cm). W: 3 lb. (1.35 kg).

Voice
Usual call is deep, hoarse *gak*. The long call is similar to, but higher than, that of the Great Black-backed Gull; in other words, a shorter, slower version of the Herring Gull's.

Distribution
Bering Sea. Breeds in far eastern Chukotka, on Kamchatka and on the northern coast of Sea of Okhotsk and on Commander Islands. Coastal, preferring cliffs, also found on bays with sandy beaches. Migratory, moving south of Japan, but non-migratory if ice conditions allow. Wintering birds are also coastal.

Diet
Omnivorous, taking fish and marine invertebrates, birds, chicks and eggs, and flying inland to hunt rodents.

Breeding
Gregarious or solitary. Often nests colonially. Displays as Great Black-backed Gull. Pair-bond monogamous and may be renewed. Nest set on rock pinnacles or the upper ledges of cliffs, or placed in thick vegetation of scrubby cliff, often some distance inland. Nest may be a mound of vegetation, but in thick vegetation may also be sparse, little more than a scrape in the substrate. Two to three olive or pale brown eggs, spotted or blotched black. Incubated for 26–28 days by both parents. Chicks semi-nidifugous and semi-precocial. Fed by both parents. Fledge at 40–45 days and are independent at that time. Breed at 4–5 years.

Taxonomy and geographical variation
Monotypic. Hybridizes with Herring Gulls of race *vegae*.

Sabine's Gull
Xema sabini

Together with Ross's and Ivory Gulls, Sabine's forms part of the trio of beautiful, elegant and elusive Arctic gulls.

Identification   See p. 257
A small, long-winged and fork-tailed two-year gull. Breeding adults have a dark gray hood extending from the upper nape to the throat. On the nape the hood has a thin black rim. The

short bill is black with a yellow tip, the gape is red. The iris is dark brown. The orbital ring is red, but often difficult to observe due to the overwhelming impression of an entirely black head. The underparts are white, occasionally tinged pink. The rump and uppertail are white. The tail is shallowly forked. The mantle, scapulars and back are blue-gray. The upperwing is tricolored, each color forming a triangle. Most lesser and median coverts, tertials and inner secondaries are blue-gray and form the inner triangle. The outer secondaries, most greater coverts, the outer lesser and median coverts and P1–P5 are white and form the middle-wing triangle. The outer primaries (and their coverts) form a black triangle; P1–P5 have small white tips (often worn away by late summer). The underwing is white, occasionally with pale gray triangles mirroring the upper dark triangles, and showing black tips on the primaries. The legs and feet are dark gray. Winter adults are as breeding, but the hood is lost except at the rear of the head, and what remains is blue-gray. Juveniles have brown or gray-brown crown and nape, the color extending to sides of throat and upper breast. On the upperparts, gray-brown replaces the blue-gray of breeding adults, but the wing triangles are otherwise maintained. The tail has a terminal black band. First-winter birds acquire a blue-gray mantle, back and scapulars, but maintain the gray-brown innerwing triangle. The black band on the tail is also retained. Downy chicks are dark brown-cinnamon above, buffish-cinnamon below.

Confusion species

First-year Black-legged Kittiwakes are similar but have a black terminal band on the tail and lack the striking dark hood.

Size

L: 10½–12½ in. (27–32 cm). WS: 36–40 in. (90–100 cm). W: 5¼–7½ oz. (150–210 g).

Voice

Usual call is a harsh, ternlike trill, *krr*. Long call is a slightly more melodious *keyrrr*.

Distribution

Circumpolar but very local. Breeds in northwestern and northeastern Greenland, in Svalbard, in northern

▶ Pair of Sabine's Gulls, Cambridge Bay.

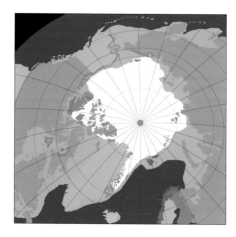

Chukotka and Wrangel, possibly also in southern Taimyr and the Kolyma Delta, western and northern Alaska, northern Yukon, Banks, Victoria and Southampton Islands and western Baffin Island. Coastal in summer. A true migrant, with Atlantic birds moving to the waters of the Benguela Current, off southwestern Africa, and the Humboldt Current, off northwestern South America. Wintering birds are pelagic and are rarely seen on coasts or inland.

Diet

Invertebrates (chiefly insects when feeding young) and small fish. More rarely takes chicks and eggs. Occasionally scavenges. Feeds on the sea by picking food items from the surface much as terns do; also feeds on mudflats like a wader.

Breeding

Solitary or in small flocks. Nests in loose colonies, often near Arctic Terns. Long call display as other gulls, but bill raised to near vertical. Courtship displays include head-tossing and feeding. Pair-bond monogamous and apparently long-lived. Nests are shallow depression in open ground, often unlined,

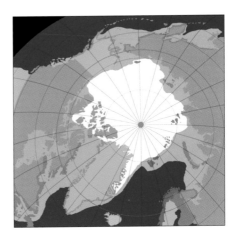

▲ Pair of *pollicaris* Black-legged Kittiwakes, St. Paul, Pribilofs.

sometimes lined with seaweed or vegetation. One to three brown eggs, lightly marked red-brown, incubated by both parents for 23–25 days. Chicks nidifugous and semi-altricial. Fed by both parents at first, chick stimulating regurgitation by pecking at yellow bill tip. Self-feeding after short period. Fledge in about 22 days. Thought to breed at 2 years.

Taxonomy and geographical variation
Monotypic, but up to four subspecies are recognized by some authorities.

Black-legged Kittiwake
Rissa tridactyla

Identification
See p. 258

A three-year gull with a short bill and short legs. Breeding adults have white heads. The bill is yellow, the gape orange-red. The iris is dark brown, the orbital ring red. The underparts, rump and tail are white. Tail is notched. Back, mantle and scapulars are gray. The upperwing is tricolored, the inner wing gray (as the mantle) with a white leading edge, the primaries pale gray, the wingtip black with small white tips on P6–P8, soon wearing to produce an all-black tip. The underwing is white. Legs and feet are black. Non-breeding and winter adults are as breeding, but with a dark gray crescent from ear-covert and, often, pale gray on nape. Bill is duller, often green-yellow, the orbital ring darker. Juveniles are as winter adults, but as well as gray ear-crescent there is a black band on nape and neck-sides (not meeting the front to form a necklace). On the upperwing, the median coverts and primaries P6–P10 are black, forming a conspicuous black M. Tail has a broad black terminal band. Bill is black. Juvenile plumage is maintained in first-winter, the M fading in first-summer, the bill becoming dark yellow. By second-winter essentially as winter adults. Downy young white.

Confusion species
The black wingtip is diagnostic against smaller white gulls. The black hood of Sabine's Gull is diagnostic for the only other gull with tricolored wings. Juvenile Sabine's can cause problems at a distance, but the back, mantle and scapular color is diagnostic.

Size
L: 15–16 in. (38–40 cm). WS: 3–4 ft. (95–120 cm). W: 10½–18¾ oz. (300–535 g).

Voice
Very vocal at breeding sites, the usual call being a repetition of the name *kitt-ee-wake*. Also a hoarse *kek-kek*. Mating display involves a choking call.

Distribution
Circumpolar. Breeds around Greenland (though absent from northwestern coasts), Iceland, Jan Mayen, northern Scandinavia and Svalbard. Breeds on all Russia's Arctic islands, at a limited number of sites on the Russian mainland, but common on Chukotka and Kamchatka. Breeds on the Bering Sea islands, western Alaska (but rare on the north coast) and eastern Canada, including eastern Baffin Island. Essentially pelagic, moving ahead of the sea ice in winter to feed in the north Atlantic and north Pacific.

Diet
Marine invertebrates and fish obtained by plucking from the surface, head-dipping and shallow diving by swimming bird.

Breeding
Gregarious at breeding cliffs where huge colonies form, less so in winter where small groups are seen (though these may aggregate into flocks if the fishing is good). Male display is with body and head held down, head and neck then jerked up and down as though the bird is choking. Male and female also show mutual head-bobbing, and the female begs for food. Usually nests on a cliff ledge. Nest is a shallow cup of mud and seaweed. Two cream eggs blotched red-brown; incubated by both birds for 25–32 days. Chicks nidicolous and semi-precocial. Fed by both parents bill to bill. Fledge at 35–50 days and are independent soon after. Breed at 4–5 years.

Taxonomy and geographical variation
Polytypic. The nominate race breeds in the north Atlantic; *R. t. pollicaris* breeds in the north Pacific. It is larger and darker, with a broader black wingtip.

Red-legged Kittiwake
Rissa brevirostris

Identification
See p. 258
A three-year gull with a short bill and short legs. Breeding adults are as Black-legged Kittiwake, but gray upperparts are darker, with less contrast between the pale innerwing and the darker outerwing. The black wingtip is broader and less conspicuous against the rest of the dark wing. The white band on the trailing edge of the wing is also broader. The legs and feet are bright red. Non-breeding and winter adults have an ear-crescent as the Black-legged, but it is much darker, and similar gray smudging to nape and sides of the neck. Otherwise winter birds are as breeding adults. Juveniles have an all-white tail (the only juvenile gulls to show this). The upperparts do not show the dark M of juvenile Black-legged. Alula and outer primary coverts of P6–P10 are black, adding a partial black leading edge to the black wingtip. The white trailing edge is much broader in the center, forming a white triangle on the trailing edge. First-winter/first-summer birds as juvenile, but second-winter birds are as winter adult. Downy young have white, buff and black upperparts, white underparts.

▲ Red-legged Kittiwake on the nesting cliff, St. Paul. Note the feet.

Confusion species
Red legs separate adult Red-legged Kittiwakes from Black-legged Kittiwakes. Juveniles resemble non-breeding and winter Sabine's Gulls but are much less strongly marked.

Size
L: 13³/₄–16 in. (35–40 cm). WS: 34–36¹/₄ in. (85–92 cm). W: 11¹/₄–16¹/₂ oz. (320–470 g).

Voice
Vocal at breeding sites, but has a high squeal unlike Black-legged Kittiwake. Mating display involves a choking call.

Distribution
Bering Sea. Rare, breeding only on Pribilof Islands, Buldir and Bogoslof Islands in the Aleutians and on the Commander Islands. Essentially pelagic, with wintering birds moving to the north Pacific.

Diet
As Black-legged Kittiwake. Red-legged Kittiwakes are unusual among gulls in being partially nocturnal feeders. Feed in deep water, usually beyond the continental shelf.

Breeding
Gregarious at breeding sites, less so in winter, but flocks form at good fishing sites. Male stands at nest site with his body horizontal, tail raised, head forward and down and bill open, making the choking call. Arriving female will call quietly and the pair will then call loudly in unison. Pair-bond is monogamous and apparently long-lived. Nest is set on a cliff ledge. The nest is a platform of mud, built by both birds. One, occasionally two, grayish-green eggs blotched dark brown; incubated by both birds for 25–32 days. Chicks nidicolous and semi-precocial (eyes closed and prostrate for about two days). Brooded and fed by both parents. Fledge at about 37 days, but remain at the nest site for several more weeks being fed. Probably breed at 4–5 years.

Taxonomy and geographical variation
Monotypic.

◄ Red-legged Kittiwake in flight, at sea off the Pribilofs.

Ivory Gull
Pagophila eburnea

Identification
See p. 258

A magical bird that appears, ghostlike, in icebound seas. A two-year gull. The only pure white gull. Adults are white, but the face is sometimes stained red after feeding on carrion. The bill is blue-gray with a yellow, orange or red tip. The gape is purple. Iris is dark brown, orbital ring red. Legs and feet black. Juveniles have a gray face, the color covering the eye, and dark brown speckling from the dark tips of the flight feathers and greater coverts. The upperparts, uppertail-coverts and underwing-coverts are similarly speckled, and tail has a narrow dark terminal band. Bill is dark gray with a pale tip. First-winter birds are as juvenile; first-summer birds lose much of the speckling, so second-winter birds are as adult or have minimal speckling. Downy young are pale gray.

Adult Ivory Gull in flight, Kongsfjorden, Svalbard.

Confusion species
None.

Size
L: 16–17 in. (40–43 cm). WS: 3½–4 ft. (108–120 cm). W: 16¼–24 oz. (450–680 g).

Voice
Usual call is a grating, ternlike, disyllabic *kree-arr*. Long call is a descending scream, *keeer*.

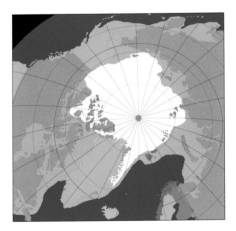

Distribution
Circumpolar, but the high Arctic only. Breeds in northwestern, northeastern and eastern Greenland, Jan Mayen, Svalbard, the Russian Arctic islands (but not southern Novaya Zemlya) and the northern Canadian Arctic islands (Banks, Parry, northern Baffin and Ellesmere Islands). Found at the floe edge and among drifting ice. Moves only with the advancing ice edge.

Diet
Marine invertebrates and fish. Also scavenges on carrion from Polar Bear kills and eats feces of bears and pinnipeds. Pecks from the surface or shallow plunge-dives for food; also wades.

Breeding
Gregarious, but not highly so, in winter, usually solitary in the breeding season, though loose colonies occur. Displays include long call (with head only to a horizontal position; the male also occasionally makes the long call in flight), head-tossing and courtship-feeding. Pair-bond apparently monogamous and long-lived. Nests on cliff ledges (sometimes far inland), but has been observed nesting on stony patches on sea ice. Colonial nest sites sometimes visible from a distance because of the growth of vegetation below. Nest is sometimes a large mass of seaweed, but occasionally made with little or no material; may be lined with vegetation and feathers. One to three (usually one to two) cream or buff eggs blotched red-brown, incubated by both birds for 24–26 days. Chicks nidicolous and semi-precocial. Brooded and fed by both parents, feeding by regurgitation at first, then bill to bill. Fledge at 30–35 days but remain and are fed at the nest site for several more weeks. Breed at 2 years.

Taxonomy and geographical variation
Monotypic.

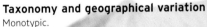

▶ Ivory Gulls feast on the remnants of a Ringed Seal killed by a Polar Bear. Kongsfjorden, Svalbard.

Ross's Gull
Rhodostethia rosea

Perhaps the most beautiful of all Arctic gulls and, together with the Ivory Gull, the most sought-after by birders.

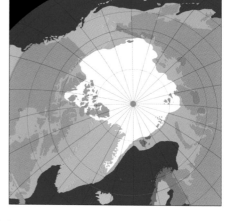

Identification
See p. 258

A small two-year gull. Breeding adults have white heads with, uniquely, a thin black necklace extending from throat to mid-nape (and wider toward nape). The small, thin bill is black, the gape bright red. The iris is dark brown, the orbital ring red. The underparts are white with a rosy pink tinge, strongest on the breast and belly. The rump and wedge-shaped tail are white, also with a rosy pink tinge. The mantle, scapulars and upper-wings are pale blue-gray, the wing having a broad white trailing edge, widening at the elbow to form a white triangle. The outer primary has a narrow black outer web, indiscernible except at very close range. Underwing pale blue-gray, showing the same white triangular trailing edge as upperwing. Legs and feet red. Wintering birds are as breeding, but black necklace reduces to a black streak on the sides of the neck, and the rosy-pink tinge is lost. Juveniles have brown crown and nape, smudges on the sides of the breast and a darker brown ear-spot. The mantle and scapulars are dark brown, fringed paler to give a scaly appearance. The upperwing has a dark brown W (or M) similar to that of a juvenile Black-legged Kittiwake. The outer primaries have black tips, which create an outer black trailing edge in contrast to the broad white edge of the inner wing. The end of the tail is black. The legs are pink. First-winter birds lose all brown color apart from the ear-spot and the fading upperwing W. First-summer birds acquire indistinct, incomplete necklace and rosy-pink tinge to breast. Second-winter birds are as non-breeding adults. Downy chicks are creamy buff with extensive black-and-chestnut blotching.

Confusion species
None.

Size
L: 11½–12¼ in. (29–31 cm). WS: 3–3¼ ft. (90–100 cm). W: 5–9 oz. (140–250 g).

Voice
Generally silent except during breeding. Usual call is soft, high *kew*. There are also a ternlike *kik-kik-kik* and a barking *du-ur*.

Distribution
Circumpolar, but very local. Has bred in northeastern Greenland and Svalbard, and at Churchill in southern Hudson Bay, but not established. May also have bred in Canadian high Arctic. Only known regular breeding sites are southern Taimyr, the Lena and Kolyma Deltas and Chukotka. Found on tundra or at the shoreline. Wintering birds chiefly in Bering Sea from Kamchatka to northern Alaska (the birds are seen at Barrow during the autumn, but are less common than they were). Wintering birds are pelagic, but they are also regularly seen at the shoreline.

▶ Displaying Ross's Gull, Churchill.

Diet
Breeding birds take insects, often feeding on tundra meltwater pools close to coast, but also at the shoreline or in shallow water when marine invertebrates and fish are taken. Feeds at shoreline, much as phalaropes, but also hovers over the water surface or paddles in soft mud. Winter diet is marine inverte-brates and fish.

Breeding
Gregarious, but not highly so, in winter. Nests colonially, but usually in relatively small numbers, rarely more than 20 pairs. Flight display includes vigorous pursuit at heights to 330 ft. (100 m), but ground displays are subdued, often little more than the birds facing each other with head and tail raised simultaneously and quiet calling. Pair-bond monogamous and thought to be seasonal. Nests on dry hummocks in marshland, often some distance inland. Nest is of grasses and other vegetation lined with leaves or lichen. Two to three olive eggs, brown- or gray-spotted; incubated by both parents for 20–23 days (up to 28 days in very cold springs). Chicks nidifugous and semi-precocial. Parent birds abandon nest soon after hatching, returning only to feed chicks. Fledge in the remarkably short time of 16–18 days, but not independent for a further 10–14 days. Breed at 3–4 years (rarely at 2 years).

Taxonomy and variation
Monotypic.

Sabine's Gull

br

ad win

br

Mew Gull

br

L. canus

ad win

1st-sum

br

Bonaparte's Gull

Slaty-backed Gull

br

ad win

ad win

L. g. kumlieni

L. glaucoides

br

ad win

L. glaucoides

Iceland Gull

1st-win

L. g. kumlieni

Thayer's Gull

br

PLATE 19: SMALL GULLS AND TERNS

Ivory Gull

br

Black-legged Kittiwake

br

Ross's Gull

br

Red-legged Kittiwake

br

Aleutian Tern

1st-win

ad win

br

juv

ad win

Arctic Tern

br

juv

Terns

Aleutian Tern in flight, Seward Peninsula. Note the white forehead.

The elegant, graceful Arctic Tern is one of the most delightful of Arctic species, not least because of the admiration evoked by its extraordinary migration to and from the Southern Ocean. It is one of two Arctic tern species, the other being the Aleutian Tern. Each is a member of the "black-capped" *Sterna* group and is an agile plunge-diver, with an elongated, narrow body and long, pointed wings. A third species, the Common Tern (*Sterna hirundo*), breeds on the coast of northwest Fennoscandia and on the western White Sea coast. A subspecies, *S. h. longipennis*, breeds in Kamchatka. It has a black bill and dark red, often black, legs. However, the Common Tern is not generally considered an Arctic bird.

Aleutian Tern
Sterna aleutica

Identification   See p. 258
Breeding adults have black crown, ear-coverts and upper nape. The lores are also black, the color extending to the eye, and, behind the eye, linking with the black crown. Forehead is white, narrow white lines extending from behind the eye. Cheeks are also white. Bill is black, iris dark brown. Throat is white, the remaining underparts mid-gray. Rump and deeply forked tail are white. Upperparts are mid-gray, the upperwing having thin white leading and trailing edges. Underwing is white with a gray bar across the secondaries. Inner primaries are gray, outer primaries dark gray. Legs and feet are black. Juveniles have a black crown streaked with cinnamon, cinnamon patches on the breast-sides and flanks, and dark brown upperparts, lesser and median coverts, fringed with cinnamon to produce a mottled cinnamon and black. Upperwing-coverts are mid-gray fringed white, the flight feathers mid-gray. Uppertail is gray. Downy chicks have dark-streaked gray-buff upperparts, white breast, dark gray underparts.

Confusion species
Breeding Arctic Terns have red bills and legs and lack the white forehead.

Size
L: 12½–13½ in. (32–34 cm). WS: 30–32 in. (75–80 cm). W: 3½–4 oz. (104–114 g).

Voice
Usual call is whistling *chif-chif*, reminiscent of waders rather than other terns. There is also a sharp *chit*.

Distribution
Bering Sea. Breeds in southern Chukotka, Kamchatka and the Commander Islands, western Alaska and the Aleutians, but is nowhere numerous. Pelagic, preferring coastal waters in summer, but also found on inland lakes. Migratory, moving to seas off southern China and the Philippines in winter.

Diet
Marine invertebrates and small fish. Food is usually taken from from the surface after hovering, but prey is occasionally caught by plunge-diving.

Breeding
Gregarious at all times, nesting colonially. Male display has not been well studied, but includes an upward spiral flight. Males maintain territories despite colonial nesting. Pair-bond is monogamous and probably long-lived, and is reinforced by courtship-feeding. Nests are in low vegetation at a coastal site, but sometimes near an inland pond. Nest is a depression with limited or no lining. One to three (usually two) yellow-gray or pale olive eggs, occasionally marked brown. Incubated by female only for about 22 days. Chicks are semi-nidifugous and semi-precocial. Can flee the nest and hide after one to three days. Not brooded by parents, so mortality high. Fed by both parents. Fledge at 25–31 days, but stay close to the colony for a further two weeks (being fed during this time) before dispersing. Breed at 2–4 years.

Taxonomy and geographical variation
Monotypic.

▼ Aleutian Tern on the nest, Seward Peninsula.

Arctic Tern
Sterna paradisaea

Identification See p. 258

Breeding adults have a black cap, either extending to the base of the upper mandible or with a thin white stripe between the cap and the mandible, below the eye and the nape. The rest of the head is white. The bill is bright red, the iris dark brown. The underparts are pale gray or blue-gray, with an abrupt demarcation between the white of the head and the breast. The upper body is blue-gray (usually bluer than the underparts), though perched birds usually appear uniform, apart from the rump and the long, deeply forked tail, which are white. Upperwing is silver rather than blue-tinged, the outer primaries black-tipped to give a thin black trailing edge to the outer wing. The underwing is white. The legs and feet are red. Non-breeding/winter adults are as breeding birds, but with a reduced black cap, the front crown and forehead being white, with ragged demarcation between the black and white because of black streaking. Bill, legs and feet are black. Some birds show a dusky bar on the upperwing lesser coverts. Juveniles are as non-breeding adults, but the front crown is often streaked buff. The upperparts are fringed white, giving a mottled gray and white look to the perched bird. Upperwing secondaries, inner primaries and greater covert tips are white, creating a broad white panel. The bill is black, often with a red base. The legs and feet are red, becoming black in first-year birds. Downy chicks are black and cinnamon above, white below.

Confusion species

None in Arctic range, but very similar to the Common Tern where the species overlap.

Size

L: 13–13¾ in. (33–35 cm). WS: 30–34 in. (75–85 cm). W: 3–4¼ oz. (90–120 g).

Voice

Highly vocal, particularly at breeding sites. The birds have a repertoire of calls, all variations of *kek-kek-kek* or, more often, the two-syllable *kee-arr*. The disyllabic call is frequently heard by observers approaching tern colonies as the birds wheel above and dive at them.

Distribution

Circumpolar, breeding throughout Greenland, Iceland, Jan Mayen, Svalbard, Scandinavia, Russia from the Kola Peninsula to the Bering Sea (including the Arctic islands) and across North America from Alaska to Labrador, including the Canadian Arctic islands. Migratory; the migration is the longest of any bird; some winter in the pack ice of the Southern Ocean, a round trip from the high Arctic of around 22,000 mi. (35,000 km). This journey allows the birds to enjoy two polar summers and to exploit the productivity of both polar seas.

Diet

Marine invertebrates and fish, usually obtained by plunge-diving. Arctic Terns are heavily piratized by skuas.

▲ Nesting Arctic Tern, Seward Peninsula.

Breeding

Gregarious at all times. Displays includes a high flight in which male bird ascends quickly, often carrying a fish, with an interested female following him. At the end of the flight (often at an altitude of several hundred feet) the pair take a gliding zigzag path to the ground. There is also a low flight, often seen at the start of pairing, but also when the pair is established, in which the male flies low past his intended mate. Pair-bond monogamous and apparently lifelong, reinforced by courtship-feeding. Nests colonially. Tern colonies are impressively noisy and characterized by the sudden, short-lived departure of most or all of the birds (so-called "dread" behavior). Nest is a shallow scrape on open ground, excavated by both birds. Two cream or buff eggs heavily blotched red-brown; incubated by both birds for 20–24 days. Chicks semi-nidifugous and precocial. Fed by both parents bill to bill. Fledge at 21–24 days, but not independent for further one to two months. This prolonged period is probably due to difficulty of learning plunge-dive technique; the early efforts of young terns usually are spectacularly unsuccessful. Breed at 2–5 years.

Taxonomy and geographical variation

Monotypic.

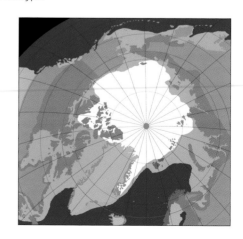

Auks

In all Arctic seas, the auks, members of the family Alcidae, represent the largest fraction of seabird biomass, with populations of some species measured in the millions. Auk adaptations include wings that allow both flight and effective underwater propulsion. However, this dual function requires short, relatively small wings – a morphological compromise that means that extant auks can swim, but not as efficiently as penguins, while a very high wing loading means fast, relatively inefficient and unmaneuverable flight that requires rapid wingbeats. Auk legs are set well back on the body, aiding streamlining underwater. However, unlike divers, which have similarly positioned legs, the shorter auks fare reasonably well on land. Most adopt an upright posture, though some, particularly the murrelets, tend to lie on their bellies rather than stand.

The underwater ability of auks is remarkable. They can dive as many as 20 consecutive times, with only about a minute's rest between them, and can reach depths of up to 197 ft. (60 m). An attested dive of one Thick-billed Murre reached 689 ft. (210 m), a depth only exceeded by the largest penguins. How auks prevent their lungs from collapsing under the pressure of such extreme depths and prevent the "bends" (the formation of nitrogen bubbles in the bloodstream) is not known. Auk bills are varied and differ according to preferred prey; those of the puffins also have a role in mating. Several colored plates encase the puffin bill during the breeding season, but are discarded during molting. During molt, larger auks lose the ability to fly, as the flight feathers are lost simultaneously; a progressive loss would extend the molt and extend the birds' compromised ability to fly, a cost avoided by a shorter, flightless period. Some auks have spectacular plumage in summer, especially the auklets and puffins; the Tufted Puffin has both a colorful bill and head plumes. Unusually, this ornamentation is present in both sexes.

Auks breed on remote sites, an adaptation to reduce losses to terrestrial predators; however, sea ice occasionally allows predators access to otherwise inaccessible islands. Auks are long-lived, which, together with the distance between feeding and breeding sites, means fewer chicks are raised than might be expected for birds of this size. For some species, only a single egg is laid. The chicks of some species are fed until full grown, either at the nest or at sea, but those of the Razorbill and the guillemots leave the nest when they are both small (about 25% of adults size) and flightless; they extend their wings, jump from the nesting ledge and glide towards, the sea. At some nest sites a proportion of chicks land short and, if uninjured, are forced to scramble desperately for the safety of the water while being pursued by Arctic Foxes, which take up station at the cliff base in anticipation of this annual harvest.

In addition to the species detailed below, there is one auk with a more southerly distribution that may occasionally be seen in Arctic waters. This is the Rhinoceros Auklet (*Cerorhinca monocerata*), which may be seen in the western Aleutians.

Great Auk
Pinguinus impennis

The Great Auk bred on remote Atlantic islands, particularly Funk Island near Newfoundland, islands off Iceland's southern coast and Scotland's northern shore. It stood 24–32 in. (60–80 cm) tall, with black upperparts and white underparts and had a very large bill similar to that of a Razorbill, with a large white patch between eye and bill. It was hunted for meat, oil and feathers in such numbers that extinction was probably inevitable long before the last authenticated pair were killed on the island of Eldey, off Iceland's southern coast, on June 3, 1844. The 1844 Eldey auk hunt was financed by a dealer in birds and eggs; it is ironic that having been brought to the edge of extinction by humans, the final extermination was a result of the rarity that the wholesale destruction had created. Though credible but not authenticated sightings of Great Auks occurred during the decade or so after 1844, it is generally acknowledged that the species was extinct by 1860.

Little Auks on Bear Island.

Dovekie (Little Auk)
Alle alle

Phylogenetically, the Dovekie is close to the guillemots and the Razorbill despite its physical similarities to the auklets. The Dovekie is the most numerous seabird of the North Atlantic and was an important source of food for Greenlanders, who pushed hundreds of them into sealskins, which retained their blubber, burying them whole under stones for the winter. The fermented auks were consumed in spring feasts.

Identification   See p. 281
Breeding adults have very dark brown or black heads, the color relieved only by a small white crescent above the eye. The short, stout bill is black, the iris dark brown (though the eye is impossible to distinguish from the black of the head unless the bird is extremely close). The neck and upper breast are black, with a strong delineation between the upper breast and the remaining underparts, which are white apart from black shadowing on the upper flanks. The mantle, scapulars, rump and uppertail-coverts are black, white tips on the outer scapulars creating white streaks on the perched bird. The tail is black, occasionally with white spotting at the tip. The upperwing is black with a white trailing edge on the secondaries (this forming a bar on perched bird). The underwing is silver-gray. The legs and feet are dark gray. Non-breeding adults are as breeding, but the upper breast, throat, neck-sides and face are white smudged very dark brown. There is often a dark, mottled band across the chest. Juveniles are as breeding adults, but the upperparts are more brown. Downy chicks are dark brown above, paler below.

Confusion species
None. Small size is diagnostic, though juvenile Atlantic Puffins are similar. Bering Sea birds may be confused with the local auklets, though the breeding plumage of the latter is usually diagnostic.

▼ Little Auks, Van Keulenfjorden, Svalbard.

Size
L: 6½–7½ in. (17–19 cm). WS: 16–19 in. (40–48 cm). W: 5–6 oz. (145–175 g).

Voice
Usual call is a rippling twitter, *kre-ri-ri*. There is also a soft *cluck*, and a hoarse *wep* from birds circling an intruder on the breeding site.

Distribution
North Atlantic, with small numbers in the northeastern Bering Sea. Breeds in north-western, central western and northeastern Greenland, Iceland, Jan Mayen, Svalbard, Franz Josef Land, Novaya Zemlya and Severnaya Zemlya. There is also a small colony on the west coast of Baffin Island, and others on the Diomede Islands and St. Lawrence Island in the northern Bering Sea. Little Auks are the most northerly of the auks, rarely seen except at sea, and then frequently near pack ice or near the breeding cliffs. Partially migratory, moving south to cold currents of the north Atlantic and north Pacific.

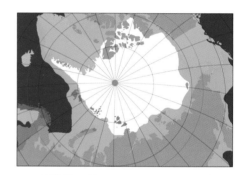

Diet
Almost exclusively planktonic crustaceans and larval fish obtained by diving, often in leads in the sea ice.

Breeding
Gregarious, highly so at breeding site, sometimes in vast

colonies (occasionally more than one million birds, though the St Lawrence Island colony currently contains no more than about six pairs), less so in winter where small flocks are more usual, though larger aggregations occur at good feeding sites. Flocks arriving at breeding site will circle, sometimes for hours, often making their twittering call, but occasionally silently. This is clearly display behavior, though its function is not understood. Pair-bond is monogamous and long-lived, perhaps lifelong. Paired birds bow to each other, wag heads, touch beaks and cluck. There is also a "butterfly" flight with slow, deliberate wingbeats. Nest is well hidden in a boulder field, occasionally in a crevice. Nest is of small pebbles, sometimes "lined" with lichen. Single white (often blue-tinged) egg, unmarked or sparsely brown-flecked; incubated by both birds for 28–31 days. Chick is nidicolous and semi-altricial. Brooded for two to four days. Fed by both birds, the chick taking food from a pouch in the adult's throat, the pouch developed in breeding adults for food transport. Fledges at 23–30 days and accompanies one adult (probably the male) to sea. Predation at this time from Glaucous Gulls and Arctic Skuas is high. First breeding age not known but assumed to be two to three years.

Taxonomy and geographical variation
Polytypic. The nominate race breeds everywhere except Franz Josef Land and presumably other Russian Arctic islands, and in the Bering Sea. Subspecies *A. a. polaris* breeds in these places. It is indistinguishable in terms of plumage, but is about 10% larger.

Razorbill
Alca torda

Identification See p. 281
Breeding adults have black heads, tinged brown on the face, with a thin white stripe from the eye to the bill. The large bill is black with a vertical, curved white stripe crossing the mandibles in front of the nostril, and is as sharp as the name implies. The iris is dark brown and difficult to see against the black head. The upper breast is black, strongly delineated from the remaining white underparts, the white plumage forming an inverted V toward the throat. The upperparts are entirely black, apart from a white trailing edge on the secondaries. The long tail is very dark brown-black. The underwing-coverts are white, the secondaries with a dark brown subterminal bar and white tips (forming a white trailing edge), the primaries dark gray with paler patches at the feather centers. The legs and feet are black. Non-breeding adults are as breeding, but the throat, face and neck-sides are white, occasionally smudged black, and the white line from eye to bill is lost. Juvenile and first-winter birds are as breeding adults, but much smaller and lacking the white vertical bill stripe. Downy chicks are dark gray-brown above, white below.

Confusion species
Similar to Thick-billed Murre, but heavy, marked bill and longer tail allow separation in the field.

▲ Razorbills of the race *islandica*. Iceland.

Size
L: 14½–15½ in. (37–39 cm). WS: 24¾–26¾ in. (63–68 cm). W: 22–28 oz. (620–800 g).

Voice
All calls are a variation of a growling *kurr*.

Distribution
North Atlantic. Breeds on southern Baffin Island, in northern Quebec and Labrador, central-western and southwestern Greenland, Iceland, Jan Mayen, Bear Island and in northern Fennoscandia. Small numbers have also become established on Svalbard. There are breeding colonies on the western White Sea coast, but the bird is absent from the rest of the Russian Arctic. Found in coastal and offshore waters. Partially migratory, with North American and Greenland birds moving to the coast of northeastern U.S. and Canada, European birds migrate to the Atlantic Ocean west of the British Isles, the North Sea, the Iberian coast and the western Mediterranean, again visiting both inshore and offshore waters.

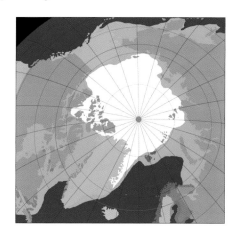

▲ Common Murres. The bird on the left is of the 'bridled' form. North Norway.

Diet
Primarily fish, mainly sand-eels *Ammodytes* spp., also takes capelin, herring and sprats by diving, also crustaceans. Dives as deep as 590 ft. (180 m), but more often about 80 ft. (25 m). Some Razorbills piratize Atlantic Puffins, flying below them and stealing fish from their bills.

Breeding
Gregarious at breeding sites, but less so when feeding and in winter. "Rafts" of birds form on the sea close to the breeding site. Birds swim together within these, with mutual head-shaking, preening and bill-nibbling. Bill-nibbling is also seen as a group behavior. On land Razorbills exhibit bill-vibrating, holding the head vertically and vibrating the lower mandible, usually as a greeting between a bonded pair. On land, male birds form "clubs" that females visit for mating. Pair-bonds are monogamous and long-lived, but there is a high rate of extra-pair copulation by both males and females, either at the "clubs" or with birds in adjacent territories. Nest is usually concealed in a crevice or beneath a boulder. Either no nest is made or a few pebbles are gathered. Single buff or brown egg, blotched black or dark brown; incubated by both birds for 32–39 days. Chicks nidicolous and semi-altricial. Brooded and fed by both parents, bill-to-bill with whole fish. Fledge in 14–24 days and leave for the sea when around 30% of adult weight. Male continues to feed chick for another 30 days. Breed at 4–5 years.

Taxonomy and geographical variation
Polytypic. The nominate race breeds throughout the range apart from on Iceland, the Faroes and the British Isles, where the smaller *A. t. islandica* breeds. The majority of the world's population of Razorbills (perhaps 70%) breeds on Iceland.

Common Murre
(Common Guillemot)
Uria aalge

Identification See p. 281
Breeding adults are patterned as Razorbill, but head, neck and upperparts chocolate brown rather than black, and the demarcation on the upper breast is an inverted U rather than an inverted V. The flanks show smudging with dark brown. The bill is black, the iris dark brown. In the north Atlantic, some birds are of the "bridled" form. These have a white orbital ring and a white line running from the upper rear of the eye toward the lower neck. In both Common Murres and Razorbills a narrow channel in the feathers leads away from the eye, presumably to aid the flow of water past the eyes when these larger auks swim. In "bridled" Common Murres this channel is picked out in white. The percentage of "bridled" birds increases to the north, varying from 0% in Iberia to 50% in Iceland, Svalbard and Novaya Zemlya. In the "non-bridled" form, the channel is darker brown, though the line of darker feathers is difficult to observe except in winter birds. The upperwing shows a white trailing edge on the secondaries, as in the Razorbill. The underwing is as the Razorbill, but with brown axillaries and brown mottling on the median coverts. The legs and feet are dark gray-brown. Winter adults are as breeding, but with white throat and cheeks (apart from the brown "bridle"). Juveniles are as small winter adults, but with the head speckled with white. Immatures are as winter adults. Downy chicks are dark brown above, white below.

Confusion species
Thick-billed Murre. Upperpart color is diagnostic when seen together, but solitary birds at a distance are difficult to distinguish. Common Murre has shorter wings and a longer, more tapered bill. The short tail, brownish upperparts and larger size distinguishes Common Murre from Razorbill.

Size
L: 1 ft. (38–41 cm). WS: 2 ft. (64–70 cm). W: 2–3 lb. (900–1,200 g).

Voice
Vocal at breeding sites. Calls are a variation of a hoarse, growling *aargh*.

Distribution
Circumpolar, but patchy. Breeds in southwestern Greenland, Iceland, Jan Mayen, northern Fennoscandia, Svalbard and the southern island of Novaya Zemlya. Absent from the remaining northern Russian coast and islands, but breeds on the eastern Chukotka coast and on Kamchatka. Breeds on Aleutians, Bering Sea islands and the western coast of Alaska, but not on the northern North American mainland or the Canadian Arctic islands, except for sites in Labrador. Found on both inshore and offshore waters, but avoids ice. Dispersive rather than migratory. Icelandic and Aleutian populations remain in local waters; other birds move to more southerly waters, where they join birds that have bred farther south. Wintering birds are also found on both inshore and offshore waters.

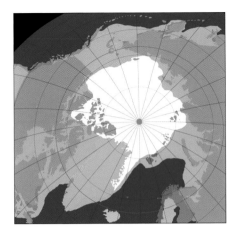

Diet
Chiefly fish, also pelagic plankton obtained by diving, usually to 65–165 ft. (20–50 m), occasionally to beyond 330 ft. (100 m).

Breeding
Gregarious at all times, but highly so at breeding sites. Rafts and clubs form as for Razorbills, and displays are very similar to that species. Paired birds also display mutual bowing as well as bill-clacking, in which bills are gently clashed in mock battle. Pair-bond is monogamous and long-lived, but as with the Razorbill, extrapair copulations may occur at the clubs. High nest-site fidelity. Nests on a cliff ledge or in crevices or cavities. Usually no nest, occasionally a few pebbles. A single pyriform egg, in color the most variable of any bird. This is presumably to help birds identify their own egg among the dozens on the same ledge, though it may also reflect the diet of the female. Base color varies from white to turquoise-blue and green, with scribbles and blotches of red or dark brown. Incubation by both birds, with egg held on tarsi, for 28–37 days. Chicks nidicolous and semi-altricial. Brooded and fed by both parents, bill-to-bill, with whole fish. Chick leaves nest site at 15–21 days before being fully fledged and weighing about 20% of adult weight. Chick is either led to sea by male bird at low sites, or glides to sea from cliff sites. Departs in the evening, but in the high Arctic (where there is no darkness) predation rates are high. On the sea the chick is cared for by the male until it is independent. Chicks fly at 50–70 days, but age at independence not known. Breed at 4–5 years.

Taxonomy and geographical variation
Polytypic. The nominate race breeds in eastern North America, Greenland, Iceland, the northern British Isles, and southern and central Norway. *U. a. hyperborea* breeds in northern Norway, Svalbard, and on Novaya Zemlya. It is darker than the nominate, almost black,

▶ Common Murres of race *hyperborea*, north Norway.

with mottling on the underwing. Race *U. a. inornata* breeds in the north Pacific. It is darker and larger than the nominate – it is the largest living auk, in fact – with longer wings and bill. Two other extralimital subspecies are also recognised.

Thick-billed Murre
(Brünnich's Gillemot)
Uria lomvia

Identification See p. 281
Breeding adults are patterned as Common Murre, but the upperparts are much darker, essentially black, though paler on the head where the feathering of the thin channel from the eye forms a black line. No "bridled" form has been observed. The flanks are unstreaked, and the upper breast demarcation between the white underparts and black neck and head forms an inverted V from the shoulders (rather than in the center as in the Razorbill). The bill is slightly decurved: it is black but has a paler streak, blue-gray to white, along basal edge of upper mandible. The iris is dark brown. The legs and feet are dark gray. Winter adults are as breeding, but with much more black on the head than is retained by the Common Murre, with only the lower cheeks and throat white. Juveniles are smaller versions of the breeding adults, but with upperparts speckled paler. Immature birds are as winter birds, but usually with more white on the face. Downy chicks are dark brown above, white below.

Confusion species
See Common Murre.

Size
L: 15½–17 in. (39–43 cm). WS: 26–29 in. (65–73 cm). W: 1¾–2½ lb. (800–1,100 g).

Voice
Similar repertoire to Common Murre, but basic call is more guttural.

Distribution
Circumpolar but patchy. Thick-billed Murre has a more northerly distribution than the Common Murre. Breeds on western, north-western and north-eastern Greenland, Iceland, Jan Mayen, northern Fennoscandia, Bear Island, Svalbard, the Russian Arctic islands, and some isolated parts of the northern Russian mainland. In the northern Pacific colonies occur on eastern Chukotka and Kamchatka, the Bering Sea islands

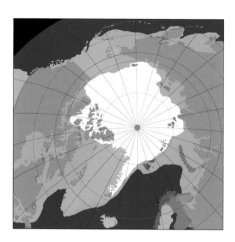

▲ A mixed colony of breeding guillemots on St. Paul, Pribilof Islands.

and the Aleutians. In North America there are colonies in western and northwestern Alaska, Baffin and Ellesmere Islands, northern Quebec and Labrador. Occurs in both inshore and offshore waters. Dispersive, moving to the north Atlantic (Newfoundland to north Scandinavia) and north Pacific (northeastern US to northern Japan) in winter, where habitat is as breeding birds.

Diet
Chiefly fish, but also marine invertebrates taken by diving after swimming with the head submerged. Very deep diving, but tends to dive 66–197 ft. (20–60 m). Winter diet tends to include more invertebrates than in summer.

Breeding
Gregarious in breeding season, less so in winter. Colonial nester; Atlantic birds tend to form separate colonies to Common Murre (though often mixed with other seabirds), but Pacific birds tend to form common colonies. Displays as Common Murre, but usually less flamboyant. No nest, laying egg on a bare ledge. Single pyriform egg is variable, though in general less so than for Common Murre, tending to be red-brown streaked on cream or buff. Incubated by both birds, with egg on tarsi for 30–35 days. Chick nidicolous and semi-altricial. Brooded and fed by both birds bill to bill with whole fish. Chick leaves nest at 15–30 days before being fully fledged when it weighs 20–25% of adult weight. As in Common Murre, the flightless journey to the sea is fraught with danger. Juvenile at sea is cared for by the male. Time to first flight probably as Common Murre. Breeds at 3–5 years, but some as late as 8 years.

Taxonomy and geographical variation
Polytypic. The nominate race breeds in the north Atlantic, from eastern Canada to Novaya Zemlya. *U. l. eleonorae* breeds east from Novaya Zemlya to the New Siberia Islands. It is paler than the nominate. *U. l. heckeri* breeds on Wrangel Island and Chukotka. It is as *eleonorae*, but with a larger bill. *U. l. arra* breeds in the north Pacific. It is darker and larger than the nominate.

▼ A party of Thick-billed Murre just off the floe edge, Baffin Bay, east of Bylot Island.

Black Guillemot
Cepphus grylle

Identification
See p. 281

Breeding adults are generally black tinged brown, apart from a white patch on the upperwing over all the coverts apart from the inner median and greater. This gives the perched bird a distinct white "shoulder." The underwing patch is larger, covering the primary coverts and auxillaries. The narrow channel from the eye is darker. The bill is black, the iris dark brown. The legs, feet and mouth are bright red. Winter adults are very different, being white overall apart from the upperparts, which are dark brown or black with wide white fringes. There is also dark mottling on the back and flanks. A rare variant has no white panel on the wings and retains a largely dark wing in winter. Juveniles are as the winter adult, but show much more dark mottling on the underparts and particularly on the head and nape, and less white on the upperparts. Immature birds are intermediate between juvenile and winter adult. Downy chicks are dark brown.

Confusion species
None in most of the range. In western Alaska, the Pigeon Guillemot is very similar, but has a dark bar across the base of the greater coverts (visible as a dark wedge on the perched bird) and lacks the white underwing patch. Juvenile and immature birds are virtually indistinguishable from their Pigeon Guillemot counterparts.

Size
L: 12–12½ in. (30–32 cm). WS: 20½–22¾ in. (52–58 cm). W: 10½–16 oz. (300–450 g).

Voice
A variety of high, piping whistles. There can be a short *pee-pee* or a drawn-out *pee-ooo*.

Distribution
Circumpolar. Breeds in western, northwestern and northeastern Greenland, Iceland, Jan Mayen, northern Fennoscandia, Svalbard, Russia's Taimyr Peninsula and the Russian islands of Franz Josef Land, Novaya Zemlya and Severnaya Zemlya; also east from the New Siberia Islands and adjacent coasts to eastern Chukotka, including Wrangel Island. In North America, breeds in northwestern and northern Alaska, Canada's northern coast from Yukon to Franklin Bay, on northern Hudson Bay and adjacent islands, western Baffin Island and southern Ellesmere Island. Occurs in shallow waters only. Has been seen fishing in pack ice leads to 88°N. Dispersive, but remains as far north as conditions allow in winter, with some birds resident.

Diet
Primarily a bottom feeder in water to 98 ft. (30 m), taking mostly fish, but opportunistic. Studies suggest that winter diet has a higher percentage of crustaceans.

▶ Black Guillemot in summer plumage, north Norway.

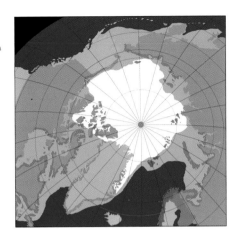

Breeding
Less gregarious than other auks, breeding in loose colonies and feeding in small flocks or alone in winter. Male displays in a strutting walk, with neck stretched and bill slightly down – a high-stepping walk on the toes. There is also mutual head-bobbing. Pair-bond is monogamous and long-lived. Nest is concealed in a crevice or beneath a boulder, often far inland (up to 2 mi./3 km), as bird takes flight easier than the larger auks. Nest is a scrape with minimal lining of available debris. Two (occasionally one) cream eggs, heavily blotched dark brown; incubated by both birds for 23–40 days. Chicks nidicolous and semi-altricial. Brooded and fed by both birds bill to bill with whole fish. Fledge at 31–36 days, leaving nest alone and flying to sea. Breed at 2–4 years.

Taxonomy and geographical variation
Polytypic but number of subspecies debated. Up to seven are recognized by some authorities, differing chiefly in the extent of white on winter plumage. *C. g. islandicus* breeds in Iceland and is darker in winter than *C. g. arcticus*, which breeds in Canada and northwest Greenland, and *C. g. mandtii*, which occurs on Svalbard. Other subspecies are largely extralimital.

Pigeon Guillemot
Cepphus columba

Identification See p. 281

Breeding adults as Black Guillemot, but only the inner greater coverts are white; the outer coverts are black with white tips, creating a black wedge on the white patch of the perched bird. In some races this partial wingbar takes different forms. The underwing shows no white patch, but may have paler patches. The slender bill is black, the mouth bright red. The iris is dark brown. The legs and feet are red. Winter adults are as Black Guillemot, but with more dark brown mottling on the upperparts, and the head speckled with dark brown. Juveniles and immatures are as Black Guillemot. Downy chicks are dark brown.

Confusion Species

See Black Guillemot.

Size

L: 12½–13½ in. (32–34 cm). WS: 22½–22¾ in. (58–65 cm). W: 14¾–19 oz. (420–540 g).

Voice

As with the Black Guillemot, the repertoire is a series of piping whistles.

Distribution

North Pacific. Breeds on eastern Chukotka, eastern Kamchatka, and the Kuril and Commander Islands, Aleutian Islands, and in places on western Alaska. Also breeds in southern and south-eastern Alaska. Found in sheltered, shallow waters. Less pelagic than the Black Guillemot, so absent from remote islands. Essentially resident, but moves south ahead of the sea ice.

Diet

Fish and marine invertebrates, obtained by bottom-feeding in depths of 33–66 ft. (10–20 m).

Breeding

Less gregarious than other auks, though breeds in colonies. Flocks fly over colonies at the start of breeding season and indulge in chases on waters close to the colony. Males and pairs defend larger territories than other auks, jabbing at

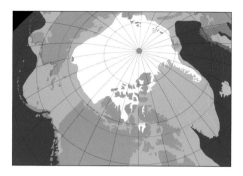

birds that intrude. Courtship display is mostly confined to bill-clacking and vocal duets. Pair-bond monogamous and long-lived. Nest is concealed in crevices or under boulders, driftwood and the like, but some birds excavate burrows or use old puffin burrows. Two cream eggs (rarely one), heavily flecked dark brown; incubated by both birds for 29–32 days. Chicks nidicolous and semi-precocial. Brooded and fed by both birds bill to bill with whole fish. Fledge at 35–40 days, leaving nest alone and flying to the sea. Breed at 1–2 years.

Taxonomy and geographical variation

Polytypic, but as with the Black Guillemot the validity of some of the five subspecies that have been suggested is debated. Suggested differences include the extent of black on the white upperwing patches. The nominate race breeds in eastern Chukotka and Kamchatka and in western Alaska. *C. c. snowi* breeds on the Kuril Islands and has a white patch divided by several (three or four) ragged dark bars. *C. c. adiantus* breeds on the Alaskan Peninsula and the Aleutians west to Atka Island. The white patch is divided into two by an extended dark wedge. *C. c. kaiurka* breeds in the western Aleutians and on the Commander Islands and is intermediate between *snowi* and *adiantus*. An extralimital subspecies, *C. c. eureka*, breeds south of the Alaskan Peninsula.

▼ Adult Pigeon Guillemot in breeding plumage, Cold Bay.

▲ Spectacled Guillemots taking off. Peter the Great Bay, Vladivostock, Russia.

Spectacled Guillemot
Cepphus carbo

A poorly known auk with a limited breeding range close to the Arctic boundary.

Identification
See p. 281
Breeding adults are as Black and Pigeon Guillemots, but larger and dark brown rather than black. There is a white eye-patch and two smaller white patches above and below the bill base. There is no white wing-patch. The bill is black, the iris dark brown. The legs and feet are red. Winter adults are as Black and Pigeon Guillemots, but more solidly dark on the upperparts. The underparts are white. Juveniles and immatures are as the Black Guillemot, but also more solidly dark on the upperparts. Downy chicks are dark brown.

Size
L: 15–16½ in. (38–42 cm). WS: 26–30 in. (65–75 cm). W: 22–25 oz. (620–700 g).

Voice
As Pigeon Guillemot.

Distribution
Far-eastern Russia. Breeds on coasts of the Sea of Okhotsk

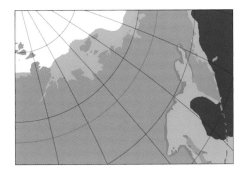

(including northwestern Kamchatka), southeastern China, eastern Korea, northern Japan and Sakhalin and Kuril Islands. Habitat as Black Guillemot. Resident, but northern birds move to southern breeding grounds.

Diet
Fish and marine invertebrates, especially crustaceans. A bottom-feeder in waters of 33–66 ft. (10–20 m).

Breeding
Behavior apparently much as Black and Pigeon Guillemots. Nest as in those species. Two eggs coloured as in those species. No data on incubation. Chicks nidicolous and semi-precocial. Thought to fledge at about 40 days. Probably breed at 3–4 years.

Taxonomy and geographical variation
Monotypic.

Kittlitz's Murrelet
Brachyramphus brevirostris

A small auk, Kittlitz's Murrelet has legs set far back on the body and very short tarsi, so it is a poor walker and can barely stand, usually lying on its belly while on land. Nocturnal at some but not all breeding sites.

Identification
See p. 282
Breeding adults have mottled gray and brown heads, with grayer crowns and ear-coverts. The black bill is short, the shortness emphasized by feathering that reaches beyond the nostril. The iris is dark brown. The underparts are also mottled gray-brown, but the brown is rather more golden. The central tail is black, the outer tail white. The upper- and underwings are uniformly dark brown. The legs and feet are dark brown. Winter adults have a gray crown, the rest of the head is white. The underparts are white with some gray-brown barring, occasionally forming a complete collar on the upper breast. The upperparts are gray or blue-gray, barred brown , with white patches on the scapulars that are prominent in the perched bird. The wings are uniformly gray-brown. Juveniles are as

▲ Kittlitz's Murrelet, Alaska.

populations fly south to winter with the resident birds of the Aleutians and southern Alaska. Winter birds found in similar habitat to summer.

Diet
Larval fish and marine invertebrates. Prey obtained by diving, but data are lacking.

Breeding
Habits little known. Breeds in very loose colonies. Nest is a scrape in bare tundra (which explains the cryptic plumage), occasionally furnished with small pebbles. Nest often 13 mi. (20 km) from sea and may be at elevations to 2,000 ft. (600 m), often set between snowfields. A single pale olive-yellow egg, spotted brown; incubation details and period unknown, but probably similar to Marbled Murrelet. Chicks nidicolous and semi-precocial. Fed small fish since adults and do not have carrying pouch (see Little Auk). Fledge at about 25 days, shedding down only in the last few hours before departing nest. Juvenile flutters alone to the sea, though it has been suggested that some from remote nests use streams and rivers to reach the sea. Breeding age unknown.

Taxonomy and geographical variation
Monotypic.

Marbled Murrelet
Brachyramphus marmoratus

A small auk, similar to Kittlitz's Murrelet. As in that species, the position and length of the legs means that the Marbled Murrelet cannot stand upright and frequently rests on its belly. The perched bird, particularly on the sea, often cocks its tail vertically. Marbled Murrelets are nocturnal at some breeding sites, though not at others.

Identification   See p. 282
Breeding adults have dark brown crown, nape and forehead, the color extending below the eye apart from a white patch forward of the eye. The rest of the face is white, heavily smudged with dark brown on the rear cheeks and streaked with dark brown below the eye. The throat has minimal streaking. The long, slender bill is black, the iris dark brown. The underparts are white, heavily spotted dark brown, particularly on the breast and flanks. The upperparts are dark brown, fringed chestnut on the mantle, and white and chestnut on the scapulars, giving a barred chestnut and dark brown appearance overall. The tail is dark brown. The upperwing and underwing are uniformly dark brown, though the underwing flight feathers are usually paler. Adults, however, are unusually variable in color, some are dark, others show more white on both under- and upperparts. Dissimilar birds often pair. The legs and feet are black. Winter adults are less variable in appearance. The crown, nape and forehead are dark blue-gray, the color again extending below the eye with a white patch in front of the eye. The underparts, including the undertail-coverts, are white with some gray barring on the flanks and a

winter adults, but the white of the head is extensively smudged gray-brown, with gray-brown barring on the underparts. The white scapular patch is also absent or much reduced. Downy chicks are buff, spotted black above, pale buffish gray below.

Confusion species
Very similar to Marbled Murrelet. Marbled is generally darker (though lighter birds are seen), has dark undertail-coverts and a longer bill. Winter birds differ only in the extent of dark feathers on the head.

Size
L: 7³/₄–9¹/₂ in. (20–24 cm). WS: 13³/₄–16 in. (35–40 cm). W: 7³/₄–9 oz. (220–260 g).

Voice
A soft groaning *urr* and a sharp, ducklike *quack*.

Distribution
Bering and Chukchi Seas. Rare. Breeds on Wrangel Island, eastern Chukotka and north-western Kamchatka, on the Aleutians, and in isolated colonies on the western and southern Alaskan coasts. The 1989 *Exxon Valdez* oil spill is thought to have killed 10% of the world population. Found at inshore locations, particularly sheltered bays. Northern

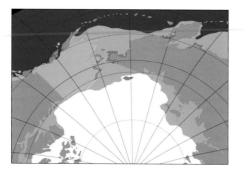

dark, usually incomplete, collar. The upperparts and tail are dark blue-gray, with large white patches on the scapulars. These, and the white sides of the rump, are conspicuous in the perched bird. Juveniles are as winter adults, but dark brown rather than dark blue-gray, and with dark brown barring on the flanks. Downy chicks are yellow and spotted dark brown above, gray below.

Confusion species
See Kittlitz's Murrelet.

Size
L: 8–10 in. (21–25 cm). WS: 13–15 in. (33–38 cm). W: 7½–H9¾ oz. (210–250 g).

Voice
Usual call is a high, gull-like squealing, *kleea-kleea*. There is also a sharp, high *kwep*.

Distribution
North Pacific. Breeds in southwestern Alaska, the Alaska Peninsula and the eastern Aleutians. Also breeds on the southern coast of Alaska. Across the Pacific, breeds on Kamchatka and on the coasts of the Sea of Okhotsk and Sakhalin. Prefers inshore waters in sheltered bays, but also found in faster waters between islands. Essentially resident in North America, but Asian birds move south to waters around southern Sakhalin and northern Japan, favoring similar habitat.

Diet
Fish and marine invertebrates, obtained by diving, but no data on depths.

Breeding
Solitary or in small groups. Marbled Murrelets nest in trees and have aerial displays related to the acquisition of suitable nest sites. One is a buzzing flight, the noise apparently produced by the wings, though the exact mechanism remains unknown. An alternative is a fast dive toward the prospective site, the wing noise increasing to a roar. Pair display seen on the sea, both birds pointing their bills upward while swimming side by side or

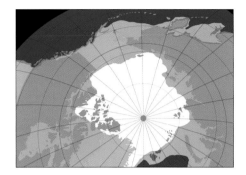

with one bird circling the other. North American birds seem to require old-growth trees, particularly those in boreal areas (such as southeastern Alaska) where epiphytes or ancient boughs create platforms large enough for the egg and bird. In Russia, the birds nest on moss and lichen platforms in taiga larches. Birds nest on ground in parts of range where trees are absent. Nest is depression in moss etc. or in a branch, or a scrape at ground sites. Single brown pale olive or yellow egg, spotted brown; incubated by both birds for 27–30 days. Chicks nidicolous and semi-precocial. Brooded constantly for first two days, fed by both birds bill to bill with whole fish. Fledge at 27–40 days, losing down just before leaving the nest. Chick is deserted by parents before fledging and makes its way to the sea alone. Breeding age unknown.

Taxonomy and geographic variation
Polytypic, but under review. The nominate race breeds in North America. *B. m. perdix* breeds in Asian Russia. It is 20% larger than the nominate, has a longer bill and the summer plumage differs; the head is brown, finely barred white; the throat white, finely barred brown; the underparts barred brown and white. The upperparts are brown, barred with darker brown. There is a white scapular patch mottled with brown. The upperwing is dark brown with paler barring, the underwing white, barred brown with gray-brown flight feathers. Winter adults are as the nominate, but gray-brown or gray with a brown tinge. Juveniles are as those of the nominate. Several authorities now split *perdix* from the nominate as a separate species, the Long-billed Murrelet (*B. perdix*).

▼ Marbled Murrelet, Alaska.

Ancient Murrelet
Synthliboramphus antiquus

As other murrelets, the Ancient Murrelet does not stand but lies on its belly when on land. If forced to run, it flaps its wings vigorously to maintain balance. At breeding sites, the birds are nocturnal, arriving about one and a half hours after sunset and departing one hour before sunrise. Forest-nesting birds often collide with tree branches as they arrive in darkness.

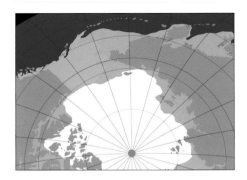

Identification
See p. 282

Breeding adults have black heads with a white-streaked crown, which gives the bird its name because of the resemblance to an old man's graying head. The crown color extends below the eye and onto the throat and upper breast as a bib, and the lower face and sides of the upper breast are white. The bill is dull yellow or pinkish-yellow with a black base and culmen. The iris is dark brown. The underparts and undertail-coverts are white. The upperparts and tail are uniformly slate-gray, apart from the upper back, which is darker with white streaking. The upperwing is also slate-gray, the primaries usually darker. The underwing has white coverts and slate-gray flight feathers. Legs and feet are pale blue. Non-breeding and winter adults are as breeding, but lack the black bib and instead are smudged mid-gray. The crown and back also have much less streaking. Juvenile and immature birds are as winter but with darker bills, no black bib or gray smudging on throat and no streaking on head and back. Downy chicks patterned as adults, with black head, gray upperparts and white underparts.

Confusion species

None. Ancient is similar to southern murrelets, but different from the two that share parts of its north Pacific range. Also similar to Little Auk (though unlikely ever to be seen together).

Size

L: 9–10¼ in. (23–26 cm). WS: 13¾–16 in. (35–40 cm). W: 6¾–8 oz. (190–230 g).

Voice

Extensive repertoire of trills and chips. Most common is a rasping *chirrup*.

Distribution

North Pacific. Breeds on islands off the south coast of Alaskan Peninsula, the Aleutian Islands, the Commander

▼ Ancient Murrelet on the sea.

Islands, northwestern and southeastern Kamchatka, at sites on the north coast of the Sea of Okhotsk, and on the Sakhalin and Kuril Islands. Found in shallow waters. Partially migratory. Aleutian birds move to southern Alaskan waters, birds from northern Russia move to waters off south-astern China, Japan, and Korea. There are breeding sites in these areas, and birds there are presumably resident or move a little way south. Wintering birds occur in the same shallow-water habitat.

Diet

North American birds take fish and crustaceans, chiefly krill. Russian birds seem to take a higher percentage of fish, but data are limited. Data on wintering birds also lacking, but what exists suggests that krill is the chief constituent of the diet. Prey is obtained by diving. Ancient Murrelets often do not land on the water on arrival, but dive in. Data lacking on dive depth, but assumed to be 33–66 ft. (10–20 m).

Breeding

Gregarious, but not highly so. Colonial breeder, but nest sites well dispersed if space available. Groups of birds gather on the sea near colonies and display by raising crown feathers or jumping up from the water and flopping back, with the lower wing trailing. Paired birds "chatter" to each other. Pair-bond monogamous and long-lasting. Nests are in burrows, either among tree roots in forest sites or under grass hummocks in treeless areas. Also nests in rock crevices and under boulders. Nest is sparsely lined with vegetation. Two olive or brown eggs speckled brown; incubated by both birds for 29–37 days. Chicks nidifugous and precocial. They are not fed by the parents. Chicks remain in the burrow for one to four nights (usually two), then leave. The parents precede them to the sea, first calling at the burrow entrance and repeatedly after, the chick running to the sound of the call. Siblings do not remain together. The parents may accompany a chick all the way to the sea. Chicks can swim and dive as soon as they reach the sea. On the water the family reunites and swims offshore, covering 13–25 mi. (20–40 km) in a non-stop swim of 12–18 hours. Chicks then fed by parents until fully grown. Fledge at 27–29 days and are probably independent at that time. Breed at 2–4 years.

Taxonomy and geographical variation

Polytypic. The nominate race breeds across range, except on Commander Islands, where *S. a. microrhynchos* occurs. It has a smaller bill and slight differences in plumage.

▶ Crested Auklet in breeding plumage, St. Paul, Pribilofs.

Crested Auklet
Aethia cristatella

Identification
See p. 282

Breeding adults have deep grayish-black heads and necks, with a forward-curved crest of the same color and white plumes drooping from behind the eye. The bill is bright orange and has basal tubercles of the same color. The male bill is stouter and the upper mandible more sharply downcurved than that of the female. The iris is white, sharply contrasting with the dark head. The underparts are mid-gray, slightly gray-brown toward the vent. The upperparts and tail are dark slate-gray. The upperwing shows black coverts, the flight feathers gray-brown with black tips. The underwing shows dark or mid-gray coverts and silver-gray flight feathers. The legs and feet are pale blue-gray. Winter adults are as breeding adults, but the bill is duller, sometimes orange-brown, and lacks the tubercles. The white eye plumes are lost, though the narrow channel from the eye is paler. Juveniles and immatures are as winter adults, but the crest is short, the bill black, the iris pale gray and the underparts paler. Downy chicks are dark gray.

Confusion species
Similar to the Whiskered Auklet, but the head ornamentation is diagnostic. Crested Auklets are also much larger.

Size
L: 9½–10½ in. (24–27 cm). WS: 16–18 in. (40–45 cm). W: 8–11½ oz. (230–330 g).

Voice
Silent in winter but vocal at breeding sites. Usual call is like the yap of a small dog. There are also hoots, and a pair will sometimes cackle at each other.

Distribution
Bering Sea. Breeds on the Aleutians and Bering Sea islands, on Chukotka near Providenya, at the northern end of Kamchatka (both eastern and western coasts), on the northern coast of the Sea of Okhotsk and on the Commander Islands and Sakhalin. Found inshore and offshore, but avoids pack ice. Wintering birds occur in a band across the north Pacific from northern Japan to the southern Alaskan Peninsula. Habitat as breeding birds.

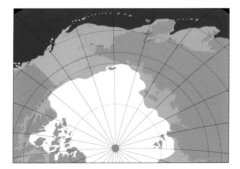

Diet
Predominantly crustaceans in breeding season, winter diet assumed similar. Birds sometimes congregate in huge numbers where tidal races or upwellings bring prey close to the surface.

Breeding
Highly gregarious at all times. Huge flocks occasionally overfly colonial sites in early breeding season. The enlarged male bill is used in competition for nest sites and females. Displaying males raise their nape feathers and call loudly. When bonded, birds nibble at the partner's bill and bury their bills in the partner's nape and neck feathers. Displaying pairs often attract other birds, the paired male jabbing with his bill to fend them off. Pair-bond monogamous and apparently long-lived, but extrapair copulations by both birds are frequent. Nests are placed on rock stacks, cliffs or boulder fields (to altitudes of 1,600 ft. (500 m)), where crevices or vegetation allow concealment. There is no nest, though a few pebbles may be gathered. A single white egg, incubated by both birds for 33–35 days. Chick nidicolous and semi-precocial. Brooded and fed by both birds, food carried in adult's throat pouch. Fledge at about 33 days. Chicks then leave nest site and fly to the sea, those falling short often being taken by predators. Chicks are independent at this time. First breeding thought to be at 3 years.

Taxonomy and geographical variation
Monotypic.

Least Auklet
Aethia pusilla

The smallest of the Auks, a bird that seems almost too fragile to survive the tough Arctic environment. Indeed, the Least Auklet cannot make headway against strong winds and can occasionally be seen moving backward while attempting to fly forward. Least Auklets are appealing little birds, standing upright on their toes and moving nimbly about on their cliff breeding sites.

Identification
See p. 281

Breeding adults have two morphs and intermediate forms, all with the same head and upperparts, but with differing underpart coloration. The head is dark gray or gray-brown apart from a white throat and a partial collar. There are short white forehead plumes, giving that area a streaked appearance, and longer white plumes behind the eye that curve towards the nape. The short, stubby bill is variable in color, from black with a red tip to red with a black base. There is a black knob on the culmen, varying in size from almost insignificant to very conspicuous. The iris is white. In pale morphs, the underparts are white with some dark spotting. In dark morphs, the underparts are dark gray or gray-brown with white spotting, with intermediate forms between these extremes. The upperparts and tail are dark grayish brown with white patches on the scapulars and tertials; these can form a solid bar along the base of the upperwing if the bird is seen from above. The upperwing is dark grayish brown, with pale fringing on the outer coverts and paler primaries. The underwing appears tricolored, with a dark leading edge on the lesser coverts, paler flight feathers and an even paler band between the two. The legs and feet are blue-gray. Winter adults are as breeding adults, but all forms have white underparts and the head-plume ornamentation and bill knob are lost. The bill is black. The white on the head is more extensive, as are the white scapular patches. Juveniles and immatures are as winter adults, with a pale gray eye. Downy chicks are dark grayish black.

Confusion species
None.

Size
L: 5½–6¼ in. (14–16 cm). WS: 11–12½ in. (28–32 cm). W: 2½–3½ oz. (70–100 g).

Voice
Silent at sea but vocal at breeding sites, where there is a repertoire of squeaks, high trills and chattering.

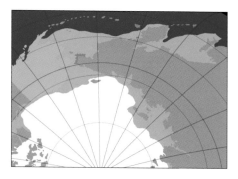

Distribution
Bering Sea. Breeds on islands off the southern Alaskan Peninsula, on the Aleutian, Bering Sea and Commander islands, on Chukotka near Providenya, islands near Kamchatka and in the Sea of Okhotsk and on the Kuril Islands. Essentially resident, but moves south ahead of the sea ice in a broad band across the Pacific, from northern Japan to the Alaskan Peninsula. Throughout the year, prefers tidal waters and upwellings, which bring prey within easier reach.

Diet
Crustaceans, chiefly copepods. Assumed to be a relatively poor diver and probably does not descend beyond about 50 ft. (15 m).

Breeding
Highly gregarious at all times. Arrivals and departures from breeding sites are synchronized, with huge, noisy flocks of birds wheeling over the area. There is intense competition for suitable nest crevices, resulting in frequent fights. Males call at sea; an attracted female will move close and touch bills, each bird extending its neck. On land males will crouch low and circle the female in a "rodent run," and the pair chatter to each other. Pair-bond monogamous and apparently long-lived, but each mate very likely to engage in extrapair copulation. Nests in crevices of sea cliffs or on scree slopes up to 0.6 mi. (1 km) from the sea. Some nests are well below the surface, though these are natural rather than excavated burrows. No nest; the egg is laid on bare soil or rock. Single white egg, incubated by both birds for about 30 days. Chicks nidicolous and semi-precocial. Brooded and fed by both birds from throat pouch. Fledge at 26–31 days and fly to the sea. Some weak chicks attempt to walk or do not make it to the sea and are highly vulnerable to predators. No apparent post-fledging care by parents. Thought to breed at 3 years.

Taxonomy and variation
Monotypic.

▼ Least Auklet, the smallest of the Auks. St. Paul, Pribilofs.

Parakeet Auklet
Aethia psittacula

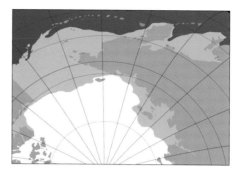

Identification
See p. 282

Breeding adults have dark grayish-brown heads with a long white plume curving down from behind the eye toward the nape. The bright red-orange bill is curiously shaped, the lower mandible almost semicircular. The iris is white. The head color breaks up on the throat, and the underparts, including the undertail-coverts, are white with dark gray or gray-brown smudging on the sides of the breast and flanks. The upperparts and tail are dark gray or gray-brown, the flight feathers occasionally tinged bronze. The underwing is dark grayish brown, the flight feathers paler. The legs and feet are blue-gray. Winter adults are as breeding, but the bill is duller, the facial plume smaller or absent, and the upperparts smudged white. Juveniles and immatures are as winter adults, but the bill is gray-orange and the iris gray. Downy chicks are dark gray.

Confusion species
None. The Crested Auklet is similar, but Parakeet Auklet's lack of forehead plumes and white underparts are distinctive.

Size
L: 9½–10¼ in. (24–26 cm). WS: 16½–18½ in. (42–47 cm). W: 8¾–12 oz. (250–350 g).

Voice
Silent at sea. Highly vocal at breeding sites. Usual call is a hoarse screech, repeated at length. Also a descending squeal.

Distribution
Bering Sea. Breeds on islands off southern Alaska, on the Aleutians, on Bering Sea and Commander Islands, on eastern and southern Chukotka, on islands in the Sea of Okhotsk and on the Kuril Islands. Partially migratory. Aleutian birds semi-resident, with northern birds moving south. Wintering birds are found in a broad band from northern Japan to the west coast of the U.S., north of California. Found on inshore and offshore waters throughout the year.

Diet
Jellyfish and soft zooplankton. The bill shape is assumed to be an adaptation to this prey, though underwater feeding has yet to be studied. Also takes fish larvae. Prey is found close to the surface, so Parakeet Auklets probably do not dive deeply.

Breeding
Not highly gregarious, feeding solitarily or in small flocks and breeding in loose colonies. Male chooses prominent rock and calls from it; interested females approach and, if pairing is accepted, join in the call. There is some bill-clacking and wing-raising, but the display is restrained. Pair-bond monogamous and possibly long-lived, with few extrapair copulations known. Nest is in a rock crevice or excavated burrow, with egg laid on to bare soil or rock. Single white egg, incubated by both birds for about 35 days. Chick nidicolous and semi-precocial. Brooded and fed by both birds from throat pouch. Fledge at 34–37 days and leave nest at night to fly to the sea. There is no post-fledging care. Probably breed at 3–4 years.

Taxonomy and geographical variation
Monotypic.

▼ Parakeet Auklets, St. Lawrence Island.

Cassin's Auklet
Ptychoramphus aleuticus

Identification See p. 282
Breeding adults have dark grayish-brown heads with a small white spot below the eye and a larger white crescent above. The long bill is black with a pale gray base to the lower mandible. The iris is white. The underparts are dark gray, with a white belly and undertail-coverts, the white areas somewhat variable. The upperparts are dark grayish brown, the underwing similar, but with a paler crescent across the inner-coverts. The legs and feet are blue-gray. Winter adults are as breeding, but slightly paler. Juveniles and immatures are as breeding, but with paler throats and dark brown iris. Downy chicks are mid-gray above, white below.

Confusion species
None.

Size
L: 7–8 in. (18–21 cm). WS: 12½–14 in. (32–36 cm). W: 5–7¾ oz. (140–220 g).

Voice
Silent at sea. Vocal at breeding sites, particularly at night with variations of a hoarse *nerreer*. There is also a sharp *kreer*.

Distribution
Aleutians and southern Alaska south to Baja California. Breeds on Buldir and other Aleutian islands, islands south of the Alaskan Peninsula and on Forrester Island off southeastern Alaska. Wintering birds found off southern Aleutian Islands and western United States. Pelagic year-round.

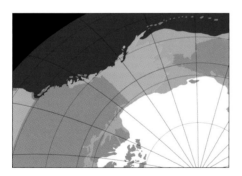

Diet
Feeds on zooplankton; also takes larval fish in dives down to 131 ft. (40 m).

Breeding
Solitary or in small groups. Nocturnal on breeding grounds, probably because of avian predators. Displays appear to include head-bobbing and wing-raising, but data are limited as activities are both nocturnal and, usually, underground. Pair-bond is probably monogamous and perhaps long-lived. Nests are almost exclusively on islands free of mammalian predators. The introduction of Arctic and Red Foxes on some breeding

▲ Cassin's Auklet in flight.

islands was disastrous for the resident Cassin's Auklet populations. Nest is in an excavated burrow or, rarely, in a rock crevice. Single white egg, incubated by both parents for 37–42 days. Chick nidicolous and semi-precocial. Brooded and fed by both birds from a throat pouch. Fledge at 35–46 days. Leave nest at night and apparently independent at that time. Breed at 2–3 years.

Taxonomy and geographical variation
Polytypic. The nominate race breeds throughout the range, except on southern Baja California, where the larger *P. a. australis* occurs.

Whiskered Auklet
Aethia pygmaea

Among the most ornamented of the auks, but less upright and less agile on land than the other auklets.

Identification See p. 282
Breeding adults have dark grayish-black heads with several ornamental plumes. On the forehead there is a forward-curved dark plume, longer but more wispy than that of the Crested Auklet. There is a white plume curving toward the nape from behind the eye (as in Least and Crested Auklets) and two white plumes in front of the eye, one downcurved back toward the nape, the other curved upward over the crown. The short, stubby bill is red with a paler tip to the upper mandible. The iris is white. The underparts are dark gray (paler than the head), gradually becoming paler on the belly, vent and undertail-coverts, the latter being white. There is some variability in the extent of white, but this can be difficult to see as perched birds lean forward, covering the area. The upperparts are dark gray (paler than the head but darker than the underparts), the upperwing dark grayish brown. The underwing shows dark gray coverts with paler flight feathers. The legs and feet are

▶ Whiskered Auklet in breeding plumage off the coast of Kamchatka. Note the spectacular plumes.

blue-gray. Winter adults are as breeding adults, but the facial plumes are vestigial and the bill is dull red. Juveniles and immatures are as winter adults, but few or no facial plumes and a gray iris. Downy chicks are black.

Confusion species
Similar to the Crested Auklet but smaller size, facial ornaments and posture are distinctive.

Size
L: 7–7³/4 in. (18–20 cm). WS: 13–14 in. (33–36 cm). W: 3¹/2–5 oz. (100–140 g).

Voice
Silent at sea but vocal at night at breeding sites. Usual calls are a kittenlike mewing and a sharp, repetitive *bee-deer*, *bee-deer*.

Distribution
North Pacific. The rarest of the northern auks. Breeds on islands in the northern Sea of Okhotsk, on the Kuril and Commander islands, and on a few of the Aleutian islands. Found on inshore waters at breeding sites. Essentially resident, but moves to offshore waters in winter. Often found in rough waters.

Diet
Crustaceans, obtained by diving, but depths unknown. Flocks form in areas of fast currents and rough water, presumably as these bring prey to the surface.

Breeding
Gregarious at all times. Rafts of birds form on the sea off breeding sites before nightfall, waiting to go ashore. Displays on sea are vocal, with paired birds swimming side by side with synchronous head waving. On land, males have vocal display; it is assumed that the white plumes are visible at night to aid the caller. Paired birds perform duet of *bee-deer* calls. Pair-bond assumed to be as other auklets. Colonial nester, often with other auklets. Availability of nest sites means that colonies are often well dispersed. Nest set in rock crevice or natural burrow. Egg laid on to bare soil. Single white egg incubated by both birds for about 35 days. Chick nidicolous

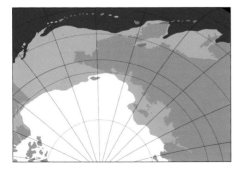

and semi-precocial. Brooded and fed by both birds from throat pouch. Fledge at 35–45 days, but fledged birds return to colony each night for about 6 weeks despite absence of parents. Probably breed at 3 years.

Taxonomy and geographical variation
Monotypic.

Atlantic Puffin
Fratercula arctica

Identification See p. 282
Breeding adults have black crown, nape and collar crossing the rear cheek. The rest of the face is white or pale gray, with a narrow channel running from the rear of the eye to the nape. At this point the black of the nape narrows and is divided by a thin gray line. The large bill is laterally compressed and conspicuously colored, the forward half red, the basal half blue-gray, these colors outlined and separated in yellow. The upper mandible has three vertical grooves. At the gape are yellow tubercles. The iris is brown, the orbital ring red. The eye is set in a triangle of dark bare flesh and has blue-gray horny appendages above and below. Below the black collar the underparts are white. The upperparts and tail are glossy black. The upperwing is black. The underwing shows gray-brown axillaries and broad bars of dark gray and silver-gray across the coverts. The flight feathers are dark gray. The legs and feet are red-orange. Winter adults lose the bill plates; the distal section becomes dull red, the basal section dull brown, showing a clear constriction as a result of plate loss. The tubercles and horny eye appendages are also lost, and the facial disk is gray, much darker in front of the eye. Other plumages are as breeding. Juveniles are as winter adults, but the bill is smaller laterally, the distal half dull red-brown, the basal half gray-brown. The legs and feet are pink. Downy chicks are dark brown with a white belly patch.

Confusion species
None.

▲ Nominate race Atlantic Puffins at a breeding colony, north Norway.

Size

L: 10¼–11½ in. (26–29 cm). WS: 18½–24¾ in. (47–63 cm). W: 13½–19½ oz. (380–550 g).

Voice

Silent at sea. Repertoire of calls based on a growl or grunted *arr*. These are occasionally strung together to form a call, once memorably described as sounding like a distant chainsaw.

Distribution

North Atlantic. Breeds in Labrador (with small colonies in northern Quebec and sout-western Baffin Island that may well become established), western Greenland, Iceland, Jan Mayen, northern Fennoscandia, Bear Island, Svalbard and Novaya Zemlya. Breeding birds prefer inshore waters. Migratory, moving to a broad band of the north Atlantic from Newfoundland and southern Greenland to the British Isles, the North Sea and the coast of Iberia and North Africa, including the western Mediterranean. Wintering birds are pelagic.

Diet

Fish and marine invertebrates, with a higher percentage of marine invertebrates in northern birds. Prey is obtained in dives to 50 ft. (15 m). Winter diet probably the same.

Breeding

Gregarious in the breeding season, but solitary or in small groups in winter. Rafts of birds form on the sea off breeding sites. Pairs form or reform in these rafts. On land, birds declare ownership of burrow with a "pelican walk": the bill is laid on the breast and a high-stepping walk is made around the burrow entrance, often in response to a rival pointing its bill vertically upward, presumably as a threat. Pair-bond is reinforced by bill-clacking after approach of one bird with body held horizontal and head-shaking from side to side. Pair-bond monogamous and renewed annually. Nest is placed in burrow excavated by the birds themselves, by Manx Shearwaters (*Puffinus puffinus*) or rabbits in areas where these are present. In the high Arctic, where frozen ground prevents burrow excavation, rock crevices or naturally concealed sites are used. These may also be used in colonies where suitable soil for burrows is in short supply. Burrows can be long, up to 7 ft./2 m (up to 50 ft./15 m recorded); the nest is a shallow scrape at its end. Single white egg streaked pale brown; incubated by both birds for 36–43 days. Chicks nidicolous and semi-altricial. Brooded and fed by both birds. Puffins famously accumulate numerous fish and carry them in their bills to the burrow. Many birds arrive at the colony together, presumably to thwart avian pirates. The transported fish are dropped to the floor of the burrow from where they are retrieved by chick. Studies suggest that about 2,000 fish are required to fledge a chick. Fledge at 38–53 days (but occasionally longer, even to 80 days) and leave the burrow at night. Breed at 5 years.

Taxonomy and geographical variation

Polytypic, but status of subspecies debated. The nominate breeds in North America, southwestern Greenland, Iceland, Scandinavia, Bear Island and the southern island of Novaya Zemlya. *F. a. naumanni* breeds in northwestern Greenland, Svalbard and the northern island of Novaya Zemlya. *F. a. grabae* breeds to the south of these two. The difference

▼ Nominate race Atlantic Puffins on the sea, Kjorholmane, Norway.

between the three races is size: *grabae* is smaller and *naumanni* larger than the nominate. Race *naumanni* is up to 70% heavier than *grabae* (about 1½ lb./650 g and 13½ oz./380 g respectively).

Horned Puffin
Fratercula corniculata

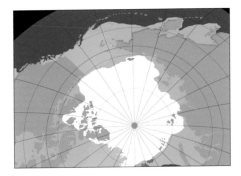

Identification
See p. 282

See p. 282

Breeding adults are similar to Atlantic Puffin, with glossy black upperparts and white underparts, black crown, nape and collar and white facial disk. However, the bill is much larger. The distal third of the bill is red (usually with a paler tip), the basal two-thirds are yellow. The distal one-third of the upper mandible has three to six vertical grooves. There is a red-orange tubercle. The iris is dark brown. The eye is set in a narrow, bare red ring from which a black horn of skin projects upward. Smaller horns are below the eye. From the eye a thin black line extends backward to the nape. The legs and feet are red-orange. Winter birds are as breeding, but the facial disk is gray, darker in front of the eye, and the ornamentation is lost. The basal upper mandible plate of the bill is lost so that the base looks very constricted. The distal third is dull red, the basal section dull brown. The tubercles are lost, the ring of flesh around the eye is brown and the horns are vestigial or absent. The legs and feet are dull pink. Juveniles are as winter adults, but the bill is smaller and dull brown (occasionally with a reddish tip), the facial disk forward of the eye much darker, and fleshy ring around the eye black. Downy chicks are dark brown.

Confusion species
None.

▼ Horned Puffin showing its distinctive horn above the eye, St. Paul, Pribilof Islands.

Size
L: 14–16 in. (36–40 cm). WS: 21½–24 in. (55–60 cm). W: 18–26½ oz. (500–750 g).

Voice
Silent at sea, and less vocal than the Atlantic Puffin at the breeding sites. Has low growls and groans as that species, but tending to be more rhythmic.

Distribution
Bering Sea. Breeds from eastern Chukotka to Kamchatka (and also on Wrangel Island, the shores of the Sea of Okhotsk and the Kuril and Sakhalin Islands), perhaps on the Commander Islands, Aleutian Islands and the Alaska Peninsula, Bering Sea islands and the western coast of Alaska. Also breeds (in small numbers) in southeastern Alaska. Breeding birds found on inshore waters. Partially migratory, with northern birds moving ahead of the sea ice. Winter birds are pelagic, found in a broad band of the north Pacific from northern Japan to coastal United States, extending northward to the floe edge.

Diet
Fish and marine invertebrates. Diving depth unknown, but probably similar to the Atlantic Puffin.

Breeding
Gregarious at breeding sites, where it forms colonies with Tufted Puffins and other auks, but less so in winter, though large flocks do sometimes form. Males defend their burrows and mates with the body thrust horizontally forward and the bill opened. Pair displays include head-flicking and billing display in which the birds face each other, bills together, and waggle their heads. Pair-bond monogamous and apparently renewed annually. Nest is in a rock crevice or beneath a boulder, though some pairs excavate burrows. Nest is a scrape, occasionally lined with vegetation or debris. Single white egg, lightly brown-spotted; incubated by both birds for 40–43 days. Chicks is nidicolous and semi-precocial. Brooded and fed by both birds. Diet entirely fish, several held in the bill in flight. Fledge at 37–46 days and leave the nest at night. No evidence of post-fledging parental care. Breeding age unknown, but assumed similar to Atlantic Puffin.

Taxonomy and geographical variation
Monotypic.

Tufted Puffin
Fratercula cirrhata

Identification See p. 282
Breeding adults are very dark brown or black apart from a white facial disk. The color is relieved only by some paler patches on the underwing. From above and behind the eyes, two long (up to 3 in./7 cm) sulphur-yellow plumes curve back over the nape. The lower mandible of the large bill is red. The distal two-thirds of the upper mandible is also red with up to four vertical grooves near the tips. The bill's basal third is dull yellow. There are red turbercules. The iris is pale gray, the eye surrounded by an area of bare red skin. There is a short, thin dark line from behind the eye. The legs and feet are orange. Winter birds are as breeding adults, but the underparts are paler and often have a few white spots. The facial disk is uniformly dark brown, the sulphur-colored plumes absent, the feathering behind the eye yellow-brown. Loss of the basal plate means the bill is constricted, but much less so than in the Horned Puffin. The distal two-thirds is dull orange-yellow, the basal third dark brown.

Juveniles are as the winter adults but with paler underparts and a paler patch from behind the eye toward the nape. The bill is smaller, the lower mandible and distal two-thirds of the upper mandible dull pale yellow, the basal third of the upper mandible dull brown. Downy chicks are dark brown above, paler below.

Confusion species
None.

Size
L: 14–60 in. (36–40 cm). WS: 24–26 in. (60–65 cm). W: 25–30 oz. (700–850 g).

▼ Tufted Puffin in breeding plumage, St. Paul, Pribilofs.

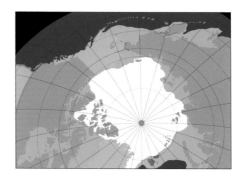

Voice
Silent at sea and not very vocal at breeding sites, with a limited repertoire of low, muffled groans.

Distribution
Bering Sea. Breeds on eastern Chukotka and in parts of Kamchatka, limited sites in the Sea of Okhotsk, and on the Sakhalin, Commander and Aleutian Islands, Bering Sea islands, western Alaska, Alaska Peninsula and southern and southeastern Alaska. Found on inshore waters during the breeding season. Partially migratory, with northern birds joining southern breeders in a broad band across the north Pacific from northern Japan to western United States. Wintering birds are pelagic, more so than wintering Horned Puffins.

Diet
Fish and marine invertebrates. Diving depths unknown, but presumably similar to Atlantic Puffin.

Breeding
Gregarious at breeding sites, when it forms loose colonies with Horned Puffins and other auks. Displays not well documented, but apparently similar to Horned Puffin with pairing and mating. Nests in a rock crevice or beneath a boulder, but birds often excavate burrows if the ground is unfrozen, usually around 7 ft. (2 m) long. Tufted Puffins also evict smaller auks to obtain suitable sites and will even fly up to 2,000 ft. (600 m) above sea level to acquire a good site. Nest is a scrape, often unlined. Single white egg, lightly speckled brown; incubated by both birds for 41–54 days. Chick is nidicolous and semi-precocial. Brooded and fed by both birds. Diet consists mainly of fish, delivered to chick in a similar fashion to other puffins. Fledge at 43–59 days and leave the nest-site at night. No evidence of any post-fledging parental care. Breeding age is unknown, but assumed to be similar to the other puffins.

Taxonomy and variation
Monotypic.

Black Guillemot

br

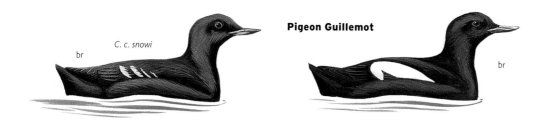

C. c. snowi

br

Pigeon Guillemot

br

Common Murre

br

Thick-billed Guillemot

br

Spectacled Guillemot

br

Razorbill

br

Least Auklet

br

Dovekie

br

PLATE 21: AUKLETS AND PUFFINS

br

Crested Auklet

br **Whiskered Auklet**

br

Parakeet Auklet

br **Cassin's Auklet**

Marbled Murrelet

Long-billed Murrelet
(B. m. perdix)

br

br

Kittlitz's Murrelet

br

br

Ancient Murrelet

Tufted Puffin

br

Horned Puffin

br

Atlantic Puffin

br

Owls

The owls or Strigidae are a remarkable group of hunting birds best known for their nocturnal behavior, although a number of species are active in daytime, especially those in regions with long days or even continuous daylight in summer. Owls have evolved features that enhance their ability to hunt at night, and most if not all of these are retained by diurnal species. Their flight feathers have unique soft fringes, so they provide lift for the bird while producing very little sound; owls therefore fly on effectively silent wings. This is especially important for species that rely on sharp-eared rodent prey. Owl eyes are large and tubular rather than spherical, and are set side by side. Tubular eyes enhance visual acuity, but reduce the field of view. To compensate, owls have remarkably flexible necks. An owl's vision is about three times better than that of a human observer.

Owls also have have excellent hearing, which augments vision in low-light conditions and sometimes functions as the primary or sole means of prey detection. The ears are generally asymmetric, and ear coverings can be adjusted to enhance sound reception. In some wholly nocturnal species, such as Tengmalm's Owl, the cranial bone structure is also asymmetric. The wide skull maximizes the sound delay to the ears, and the owl's facial disk also enhances sensitivity, the stiff feathers of the disk rim channeling sound in much the same way as the pinna, or outer ear, of a

▲ Tengmalm's Owl, Stavanger, Norway.

mammal. So good are owl ears at pinpointing sound that Snowy Owls and Great Gray Owls (*Strix nebulosa*) can hunt rodents beneath the snow without requiring visual cues. The outer toe is also reversible, increasing the area in which prey can be caught and improving grip. Prey is consumed whole, and indigestible parts are compressed into pellets, which are discharged through the mouth — the analysis of pellets gives much valuable information on an owl's diet.

There are only two truly Arctic species of owl, but five others inhabit the boreal forests just to the south. Three are circumpolar: Hawk Owl *Surnia ulula*, Tengmalm's Owl (*Aegolius funereus*) and Great Gray Owl. In the Nearctic, the Great Horned Owl (*Bubo virginianus*) breeds to the northernmost limit of the boreal forest; its Palearctic equivalent is the Eurasian Eagle Owl (*B. bubo*), which generally breeds in more southerly locations.

Snowy Owl
Bubo scandiacus

The Snowy Owl, along with the white-morph Gyrfalcon and Ross's and Ivory Gulls, is one of the most sought-after Arctic species. The evolution of the owl is thought to have followed a similar route to that of the Polar Bear, with a population of large brown owls (probably an ancestral form that also gave rise to the Great Horned Owl in North America) being isolated north of an ice sheet during a glaciation. However,

◄ Hawk Owl, a spectacular member of the boreal forest avifauna in both the Palearctic and Nearctic, Orre, Norway.

mitochondrial DNA analysis suggests that this speciation appears to predate that of the bear by a very long time, and probably dates to the late Pliocene.

Identification   See p. 298

Breeding males are entirely white; a few dark brown spots or bars may be on the crown, scapulars and upperwing-coverts. Breeding females have a white face, but the rest of the plumage is heavily barred dark brown; presumably this is cryptic for incubation. Both sexes have incomplete facial discs. Ear tufts are small and rarely seen. The bill is black and appears tiny because of the feathering. The iris is lemon- or golden-yellow. The claws are black. In general, Snowy Owls become whiter as they age. First-year birds show significant amounts of dark gray down until early winter, then males become as breeding females, which are much more heavily barred than non-breeding females. Chicks have two downs; neoptile is white, mesoptile is dark gray from day five or six.

Confusion species

None.

Size

L: 20¾–26 in. (53–66 cm). WS: 4⅝–5½ ft. (142–166 cm). W: 2¾–6½ lb. (1.2–2.9 kg).

Voice

Usually silent. The male has a low, hoarse hoot. The alarm call is a loud, grating *kre-kre*. Female alarm is similar but higher pitched.

Distribution

Circumpolar. Breeds in northwestern and northeastern Greenland, northern Scandinavia, northern Russia, including Novaya Zemlya (and perhaps Severnaya Zemlya) and Wrangel Island, western and northern Alaska and northern Canada

◄ Snowy Owl in flight, north Norway.

including the southern Arctic islands. However, population and distribution are dependent on prey numbers. Has bred on Iceland and Jan Mayen (where the absence of rodents will always limit potential breeding numbers), on the Shetlands, and probably Svalbard, other Russian Arctic islands and Canadian Arctic islands north to Ellesmere whenever numbers have increased following lemming irruption. Personal observation of Snowy Owl on the Pribilof Islands suggests that the range is erratic. Prefers low tundra often near coast, but found in mountains to 4,900 ft. (1,500 m) in Scandinavia. Generally resident, partially migratory and nomadic. Some North American birds move into the northern continental United States, European birds migrate to northern Germany and Poland, Asian birds to southern Russia and Mongolia. Wintering birds prefer open country.

Diet

Almost exclusively rodents, particularly lemmings. In winter can locate and catch rodents through 1 ft. (30 cm) of snow. Also takes insects, birds and larger mammals, and will also scavenge. When attacking hares, will grip with one foot and use the other as a brake in the snow or vegetation to tire prey. Has been seen to fish by lying beside water and thrusting out a foot to catch fish as it swims close by. Mainly hunts by scanning from perch, but also flies slowly over an area and can hover above the snow if listening for prey beneath. Although the owls hunt in the continuous daylight of the Arctic summer they prefer to hunt during the "night" hours. When there is darkness they are crepuscular, but they also hunt nocturnally in winter.

Breeding

Solitary and territorial. Male has a display flight in which wings are held in a V at the top of the stroke so he drops a short distance. On ground he assumes a remarkable position, sometimes called the "angel" position, with wings half-raised,

▼ Snowy Owl in summer, north Norway.

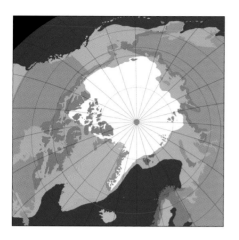

▲ Short-eared Owl, north Slope, Alaska.

head lowered, and tail fanned. Normally he adopts this after dropping a prey item, watching the female as she approaches. Pair-bond is usually monogamous, though polygyny has been observed. Bond is apparently for one breeding summer only, though owl pairs have been observed together in the winter. Nest is a scrape, usually on hummock or other feature above the snow. Clutch size highly variable (3–14), depending on prey abundance. White eggs are incubated by female only for 30–33 days. Female leaves nest rarely and briefly, being fed in position by male. Chicks nidicolous and altricial. Fed by female with food brought by male. Female feeds dead chicks to siblings. At about 16 days advanced young leave nest, hide locally and are fed by male while female tends remaining brood. Fledge at 43–50 days, but are not independent for another 10–20 days. Probably breed at 1 year.

Taxonomy and geographical variation
Monotypic.

Short-eared Owl
Asio flammeus

Identification

See p. 298

Breeding males have a buff facial disk, white on the eyebrow and below the beak surrounded by a darker ruff. The bill is black, the iris lemon- or golden-yellow. The eyes are enclosed in black patches. The short ear tufts are usually difficult to observe. The underparts are pale buff merging to white on the belly, vent and undertail-coverts, the whole streaked with dark brown, more heavily on the breast and throat. The undertail is white with dark brown chevron barring. The upperparts are tawny-buff, heavily streaked dark brown from crown to back, the scapulars more heavily streaked but fringed white, the rump less heavily streaked. The wedge-shaped tail is tawny-buff with dark brown chevron barring. The upperwing is tawny-buff, the flight feathers occasionally gray-tinged, with heavy dark brown and

some white spotting on the coverts, and heavy dark brown barring on the flight feathers. The outer primaries have a pale trailing edge and usually a bar-free patch at the base. There is a dark brown carpal patch. The underwing is cream with a black tip and a black carpal bar. Breeding females are as male, but deeper buff and, in general, heavier markings. Toes are yellow-gray, claws black. Juveniles are as breeding birds but darker overall, with less distinct facial features. Chicks have two downs: neoptile is buff above and white below, replaced at about five days by darker mesoptile down.

Confusion species
None.

Size
L: 13³/₄–16 in. (35–40 cm). WS: 3–3¹/₂ ft. (95–110 cm). W: 9³/₄–13¹/₂ oz. (280–380 g).

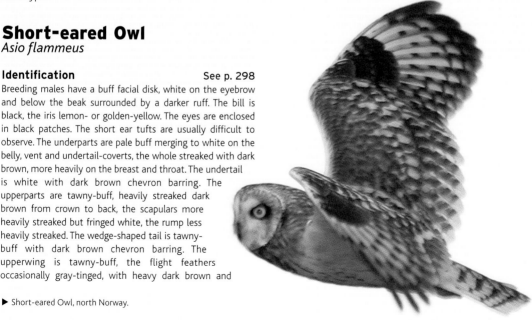

▶ Short-eared Owl, north Norway.

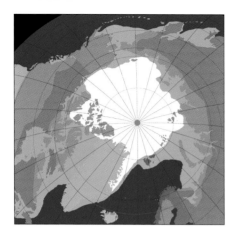

Voice

Silent except when breeding. Male display call is a muffled *oo-oo-oo*. Usual call of both sexes is a mournful *che-ef*.

Distribution

Circumpolar. Absent from Greenland, but breeds on Iceland, northern Scandinavia, across Russia including Kamchatka (but not to the northern coast), throughout Alaska, the Yukon and Northwest Territories, around Hudson Bay, in Labrador and on southern Baffin Island. As with Snowy Owl, range and population depend on prey irruptions. Found on tundra and in the boreal fringe. Northern birds are migratory, moving to northwestern and southern Europe, northern Black Sea, central Asia and northern United States. Birds winter in open country, cultivated fields and on coastal salt marshes.

Diet

Rodents, also birds and larger mammals. Preferred hunting method is a low-level quartering, alternating flapping and gliding, but will also hover and hunt from a perch.

Breeding

Solitary, but sometimes seen in small groups while migrating and in wintering areas. Territorial males display against intruders by raising wings high on upstroke and clashing them together on downstroke, occasionally while showing talons. Wing-clapping is also used to attract a potential mate, but after the clap the wings are held in position so the bird drops quickly before regaining height and clapping again. Courtship-feeding has also been observed. Pair-bond monogamous (but polygyny has been observed), seasonal only. Nest is a shallow scrape in thick vegetation, lined by female only, with vegetation. Clutch size is highly variable (3–13), depending on the prey population. White eggs are incubated for 24–27 days by female only, with male feeding her; male may occasionally incubate. Chicks nidicolous and altricial. If parents bring insufficient food, chicks will cannibalize siblings. Fledge at 24–27 days, but leave nest to hide in local area; fed by both parents. Juveniles can fly at about 35 days and are independent at about 60 days. Breed at 1 year.

Taxonomy and geographical variation

Polytypic. The nominate race breeds across Eurasia and North America; nine other subspecies are all extralimital.

Cuckoos

There are no Arctic members of the cuckoos or Cuculidae, but the Eurasian Cuckoo (*Cuculus canorus*) and Oriental Cuckoo (*C. saturatus*) both breed on Kamchatka.

Swifts and woodpeckers

There are no true Arctic swifts. The Common Swift (*Apus apus*) and Pacific Swift (*A. pacificus*) breed on the Kola Peninsula in the Palearctic. There are no Arctic woodpeckers either, though this group is diverse in northern boreal forests to the Arctic fringe. The Black Woodpecker (*Dryocopus martius*) breeds across boreal Russia and on Kamchatka. More southerly, but also breeding throughout Kamchatka are the Great Spotted Woodpecker (*Dendrocopos major*) and Lesser Spotted Woodpecker (*D. minor*). The White-backed Woodpecker (*D. leucotos*) is more southerly again, but it is also seen in Kamchatka, though rarely. The Kamchatka birds of these three latter species are considered endemic subspecies. The Eurasian Three-toed Woodpecker (*Picoides tridactylus*) breeds across the boreal zone of Eurasia, and its close relative the American Three-toed Woodpecker (*P. dorsalis*) breeds in forested parts of central and western Alaska and Canada. The Black-backed Woodpecker (*P. arcticus*), Downy Woodpecker (*P. pubescens*) and Hairy Woodpecker (*P. villosus*) are also found in the forests of central Alaska (though rarely), but they are more common in more southerly parts of Canada. More common in central Alaska, and breeding toward the timberline in Canada is the Northern Flicker (*Colaptes auratus*).

▼ Three-toed Woodpecker beside its nest-hole, southern Alaska.

Kingfishers

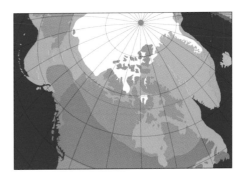

There is only one kingfisher that may be observed north of the Arctic boundary as defined here. This is the Belted Kingfisher of North America.

Belted Kingfisher
Ceryle alcyon

Identification
See p. 298

Breeding males have a dark slate-blue head with a distinctive crest. There are small white spots above and below the eye, but these are difficult to see at any distance. The large dagger bill is black, the iris dark brown. There is a white throat collar, the underparts below a dark slate-blue breast-band also white, with some dark blue smudging on the flanks. The undertail is banded dark slate-blue and white. The upperparts are dark slate-blue, the scapulars tipped white, the tail white streaked. The upperwing inner coverts and secondaries are dark slate-blue, tipped white. The primary coverts are darker, the primaries dark on the outer web, slate-gray on the distal inner web, white below. The underwing is white, smudged dark slate-blue on the coverts and with the outer sections of the flight feathers also dark slate-blue. Breeding females are as males, but have a second, narrower, chestnut breast-band and chestnut striping along the upper flanks. Legs and feet are dark gray or black. Juvenile males are as breeding male, but the breast-band is chestnut and blue and there is chestnut smudging on the flanks. Juvenile females are as breeding female but upper breast-band is chestnut and blue. There is no true down stage in the chicks, the feathers erupting to almost complete cover after 16–18 days.

Confusion species
None.

Size
L: 11–13¾ in. (28–35 cm), bill 2 in. (5 cm). WS: 18½–20½ in. (47–52 cm). W: 5–6 oz. (140–170 g).

Voice
Usual call is a harsh rattle, but there is also a more musical, trilling *trrrr*.

Distribution
Nearctic. Breeds on the Alaska Peninsula and western Alaska, though uncommon. Also found in central Alaska, central Yukon and Northwest Territories, and on southern Hudson Bay. Found on rivers, lakes, ponds and inshore coastal waters. Migratory, moving to southeastern Alaska and continental U.S. in winter.

Diet
Fish, but in times of scarcity will take crustaceans, mollusks, insects, small rodents, small birds and even berries. Fishes by diving head-first after its quarry.

Breeding
Solitary. Male defends a territory, which is used to attract a female. Pair-bond is reinforced by courtship-feeding and is monogamous and seasonal. Nest in burrows excavated in riverbanks of sand, clay or gravel. Both birds excavate, one bird digging, the other singing encouragement from a nearby perch. The burrow is 3–6 ft. (1–2 m) long and sloping upward. Five to seven glossy white eggs, incubated for 23–24 days by both birds but chiefly the female. Chicks are nidicolous and altricial. Brooded and fed by both birds, but female usually broods the young. Fledge at 27–29 days, but are fed for another three weeks before becoming independent. Breed at 1 year.

Taxonomy and geographical variation
Polytypic. The nominate race breeds in eastern North America. *C. a. caurina* breeds in Alaska and the Yukon. The wings of these northern birds are larger, but the difference is slight.

▼ Adult Belted Kingfisher.

Larks

There is only one breeding lark in the Arctic, the Horned Lark, though the nominate race of the Eurasian Skylark (*Alauda arvensis*) breeds in northern Fennoscandia, and another subspecies *A. a. pekinensis* occurs on Kamchatka.

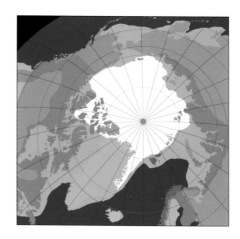

Horned Lark (Shore Lark)
Eremophila alpestris

Identification See p. 298

Breeding males have highly distinctive heads. The face and throat are pale yellow, with a black horseshoe through the eyes and bill and on to the cheeks. At the front of the crown is a black bar that ends in black tufts, the horns of the American name. The remaining crown is pink-brown. The bill is gray with a black tip, the iris brown. Below the throat is a deep black necklace. The underparts are white, smudged pink-brown on the flanks. The upperparts are pink-brown edged gray, becoming darker toward the rump so that the upper bird looks mottled pink, brown, dark brown and gray. The long tail is pink-brown in the center, dark brown on the sides, with white edges. The upperwing-coverts are as the upperparts, the flight feathers more uniformly dark brown or gray-brown. The underwing-coverts are white, the flight feathers gray. Breeding females are as male but overall duller, and lack the black horseshoe and necklace, these being pale gray. There are no horns. The legs and feet are black. Juveniles have a pale yellow throat The remaining head and upperparts are brown, heavily spotted paler or white. The upperwing-coverts are also heavily

▼ Horned Lark of the northeast Canadian race *arcticola*, Nunavut, Canada. Note the white stripe above the eye.

spotted. The underparts are white, heavily blotched dark brown on the breast and flanks. The bill, legs and feet are yellow-gray. Downy chicks are yellowish cream.

Confusion species
None.

Size
L: 5½–6½ in. (14–17 cm). WS: 12–13¾ in. (30–35 cm). W: 1–1½ oz. (30–45 g).

Voice
Usual call is a short series of weak chirps followed by rapid, rising warble, *pit-pit-pit pittle pittle tree*. Also a weak *see-tu*.

Distributions
Circumpolar. Absent from Greenland (though has bred there and may still do so in small numbers), Iceland, and Eurasian Arctic islands apart from the southern island of Novaya Zemlya. Breeds in northern Scandinavia and east across Russia to the Kolyma Delta north to the shoreline. In the Nearctic,

breeds throughout Alaska and northern Canada, including the Arctic islands north to Devon Island. Prefers stony, lichen tundra or drier shorelines. Migratory, with birds moving to southeastern Europe, southern Russia and central North America to join southern races in winter. Wintering birds are found on coastal dunes and salt marshes, and on arable land.

Diet
Breeding birds take insects and seeds. Wintering birds feed mainly on seeds.

▲ Horned Lark of the north Eurasian race *flava*, Norway.

Breeding
Gregarious away from breeding sites. A displaying male calls from a conspicuous perch to establish territory and advertise himself. He will follow an interested female closely, occasionally quivering his wings and assuming a horizontal posture, with the head well forward. There is also courtship-feeding. Pair-bond is monogamous and thought to be seasonal. Nest is on the ground, usually concealed in a tussock. Nest is a shallow depression excavated by female and lined with vegetation, with layer of softer lining (e.g., grass and willow down). Pebbles are often placed around the nest. Three to four cream eggs, heavily speckled dark brown; incubated for 10–11 days by female only. Chicks nidicolous and altricial. Brooded and fed by both parents. Chicks leave nest at 9–12 days and fly at 16–18 days. Age of independence is not known. Thought to breed at 1 year.

Taxonomy and geographical variation
Polytypic. Complex series of as many as 42 subspecies. The nominate race breeds in the northeastern Nearctic. The larger *E. a. arcticola* breeds in the northwestern Nearctic. Males of this race have chestnut nape, breast sides and rump, and a brighter yellow face, with a white throat and eyebrow-stripe; the female is as the nominate. *E. a. hoyti* breeds on Baffin Island and in northern Alberta. It has a pale yellow throat and a white eye-stripe. *E. a. flava* breeds in northern Eurasia. Males are paler than the nominate, with a yellow throat and white eyebrow-stripe, and have a smaller bill. Female is as the nominate. Other subspecies are extralimital.

◄ Horned Lark of the nominate race on the tundra of Churchill.

Swallows

The mosquito swarms that can turn summer into a nightmare for Arctic mammals and birds make the human observer long for the arrival of flocks of insect-eating birds. In Alaska, the Tree Swallow helps out. Other swallows may also be seen at the Arctic fringe. In the Nearctic, the Cliff Swallow (*Petrochelidon pyrrhonota*) is an uncommon visitor to western and northern Alaska and the eastern Aleutians. In the Palearctic, the Barn Swallow (*Hirundo rustica*) breeds in northern Norway and across Russia to the taiga limit, and in Kamchatka. The circumpolar Sand Martin (*Riparia riparia*) is uncommon in western Alaska and the western Aleutians, but more common close to the timberline across Canada, reaching the southern shores of Hudson Bay; this martin breeds across Eurasia, to northern Scandinavia, the taiga limit in Russia and throughout Kamchatka.

Tree Swallow
Tachycineta bicolor

Identification See p. 298
Adult males have a glossy blue crown extending to the bill base, below the eye and across the rear cheek to the nape. The short, needle-sharp bill is black, the iris dark brown. Underparts are white. Upperparts, from nape to uppertail-coverts and including inner coverts, are glossy blue; these and the crown sometimes having a greenish sheen. Tail is not deeply forked and is dark gray-brown. Upperwing (apart from inner coverts) and underwing are uniformly dark gray-brown. Adult females are patterned as males, but crown and upperparts are a dingy gray-brown, the crown color darker around the eye. Legs and feet are dark brown. Juveniles are as the females, but have a pale gray-brown band on the breast and the crown cap is not as extensive. The white of the throat forms a broad collar that tends to be gray-brown on the nape, where it can be indistinct. Chicks have only sparse down, with feathers erupting after six or seven days.

Confusion species
Juvenile birds are very similar to Sand Martins, but have a poorly defined breast-band.

Size
L: 5–6 in. (13–15 cm). WS: 13½–14½ in. (34–37 cm). W: ½–¾ oz. (18–22 g).

Voice
Usual call is a clear, whistling *twit-tweet*, but there is a repertoire of high twitters, including a repetitive *see-uw*.

Distribution
Nearctic. Breeds throughout Alaska (but uncommon in the north), in central Yukon and Northwest Territories, around southern shores of Hudson Bay, and in southern Quebec and eastern Labrador. Migratory, moving to southern United States, Mexico, and eastern coast of Central America. Breeding and wintering birds prefer wooded areas near water.

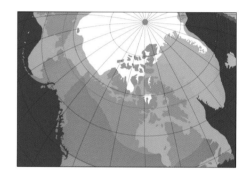

Diet
Insects and spiders, and will feed on vegetable matter in bad weather. Wintering birds also feed on berries, particularly the waxy *Myrica* berries.

Breeding
Gregarious, but not highly so. Displaying males stand vertically with bill pointing upward, the wings slightly drooped and flicking. Pair-bond monogamous, but the males may be polygynous. Nests in a tree cavities, also in buildings and nest boxes; the bird is often associated with human presence in remote areas. Curious nest sites, such as old oil drums, have been observed. The nest is of vegetation profusely lined with feathers, chiefly brought by the male. Two to eight (usually three to five) white or pale pink eggs, incubated for 14–15 days by the female only. Chicks nidicolous and altricial. Brooded by female only, but fed by both birds. Chicks are unable to thermoregulate effectively until about nine days. Fledge at 18–22 days, but are fed for about another three days before becoming independent. Breed at 1 year.

Taxonomy and geographical variation
Monotypic.

◀ Tree Swallow perching, Potter Marsh.

Pipits and wagtails

These slender-bodied passerines, which together form the family Motacillidae, are essentially an Old World insect- and seed-eating group. Wagtails are generally yellow and gray-black or gray-black and white; the pipits are more cryptically colored. The pipits are renowned for their display flights, with males climbing up to 330 ft. (100 m), then flying into the wind; the Nearctic Sprague's Pipit (*Anthus spragueii*) does this for as long as three hours, though males of most species display for a much shorter time before "parachuting" back to earth. In addition to the species described below, the Gray Wagtail (*Motacilla cinerea*) breeds on the Kola Peninsula, across central Russia and on Kamchatka, while the Citrine Wagtail (*M. citreola* breeds) around the White Sea. However, each is essentially a non-Arctic species.

American Pipit (Buff-bellied Pipit)
Anthus rubescens

Identification   See p. 298
Breeding adults have gray heads with a buff supercilium and lores. There is a lighter patch behind and below the eye, and a thin dark malar line separating the gray from the buff of the lower cheek and throat. The bill is dark gray. The iris is dark brown, the orbital ring white. The underparts are buff, heavily streaked with dark brown on the breast, with less streaking on the belly and vent (though it is heavy on the flanks). The upperparts are gray, finely streaked darker. The central tail is gray, bordered by black, then white outer feathers. The upperwings are dark gray, fringed buff, the coverts white tipped. The primaries are darker. The underwing is pale gray with buff patches on the inner coverts and at the base of the primaries. The legs and feet are dark pinkish brown. Non-breeding adults are as breeding, but head and underparts are white rather than buff. Juveniles are as non-breeding adults, but overall browner. Downy chicks are buff streaked black.

Confusion species
None in the Nearctic. Northeast Asian birds are similar overall to Pechora Pipit, though the latter is brown rather than gray.

Size
L: 6–7 in. (15–18 cm). WS: 9½–11 in. (24–28 cm). W: ½–¾ oz. (18–22 g).

Voice
Flight song is a clear rippling *tisp-tsi*, typical of pipits; birds in flight often emit a squeaky chirp. Alarm call is a high *wisp*.

Distribution
Nearctic but with a subspecies in Asian Russia. Breeds throughout Alaska, across mainland Canada to the northern coast and on southern Arctic islands (from Banks to Baffin). Also breeds in northwestern and western central Greenland. Russian population breeds in Chukotka and Kamchatka; occasionally encountered in western Alaska as a vagrant. Found on tundra, intertidal shores and salt marshes. Migratory, with Nearctic birds moving to southern United States and Central America, Asian birds to southern Asia, from Pakistan to Vietnam.

Diet
Terrestrial and freshwater invertebrates, and seeds. Also takes small crustaceans and mollusks by wading in shallow water. Winter diet is similar.

Breeding
Gregarious in winter with very large flocks forming, sometimes mixed with larks and longspurs. Solitary at breeding sites. Male

▼ Adult American Pipit, Churchill.

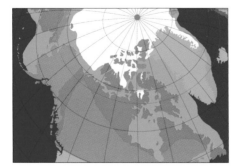

chases rivals and sings to establish territory and attract mate. Pair-bond monogamous and seasonal. Nests on the ground, in both wet and dry areas. Usually well-concealed nest is a depression, sometimes with no base material and often unlined, but may have a cup of twigs and a minimal lining of grasses, hairs and feathers. Four to seven pale grayish buff eggs, spotted red-brown; incubated for 13–15 days by female only. Chicks nidicolous and altricial. Brooded by female only but fed by both parents. Fledge at 13–15 days. Breed at 1 year.

Taxonomy and geographical variation
Polytypic. The nominate race breeds in northeastern North America and Greenland. *A. r. pacificus* breeds in Alaska and northwestern Canada. It is larger and paler than the nominate with yellow-buff underparts. *A. r. japonicus* breeds in Russia. When breeding it is more buff overall on the underparts with more delicate streaking, and has a much larger malar line. Another subspecies is extralimital.

Pechora Pipit
Anthus gustavi

Identification
See p. 298

Head and crown of the adults is streaked black and buff, and there is a pale buff supercilium. The lores and a patch in front of the eye are buff, with delicate gray mottling. The upper cheeks, ear-coverts and nape are light ochre, the nape finely streaked darker. The lower cheeks and throat are pale buff-white with a black malar line or patch. Upper mandible is dark brown, the lower paler, almost pinkish. Iris is dark brown. Breast and flanks are buff, becoming paler on the remaining underparts. The breast and flanks are heavily streaked dark brown, the remaining underparts unmarked or with some dark streaking. The upperparts are typically "pipit"; the mantle, scapulars and rump are black with broad buff or pale chestnut fringing. The central tail is dark brown, the outer tail black then off-white. The mantle shows symmetric broad white stripes on the perched bird. The upperwing is brownish chestnut, the coverts buff fringed, the flight feathers darker. The underwing-coverts and axillaries are gray-buff, the flight feathers darker. Legs and feet are usually dull pink, but may be grayish. Non-breeding adults are as breeding adults but are duller overall. Juveniles are as breeding birds but are less heavily streaked. Downy chicks are pale gray.

Confusion species
Overlaps with Red-throated Pipit throughout its range, and Meadow Pipit to the west. The white mantle stripes of Pechora are diagnostic with respect to the Meadow Pipit, while the red throat distinguishes the Red-throated Pipit.

Size
L: 5½–6 in. (14–15 cm). WS: 9–10 in. (23–25 cm). W: ¾ in.–1 oz. (20–26 g).

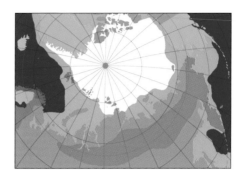

Voice
Song is series of not particularly musical trills broken by sharp cheeping *suurrrr-suurrrr-cheechee-suurrr*. A sharp *cheep* is also heard. The male rises very quickly and very high as it sings.

Distribution
Eastern Palearctic. Breeds from the Pechora River eastward to the Chukotka Peninsula, but only occurs to the northern coast in Chukotka. Breeds throughout Kamchatka and on the Commander Islands. Prefers heavily vegetated areas with tall sedges, particularly on riverbanks, but also found on boggy and scrub tundra. Migratory, wintering in Indonesia and the Philippines, where similar habitats are preferred.

Diet
Chiefly invertebrates obtained by ground foraging.

Breeding
Solitary or in small group. Male has song flight, interrupting this to join female on the ground. Pair-bond is assumed monogamous. Nests on ground in well-concealed area. Nest is constructed of grass and leaves lined with fine vegetation. Four to six olive-buff eggs, heavily marked dark red-brown; incubated by both birds for about 13 days. Chicks are nidicolous and altricial. Cared for by both parents. Fledge at

▼ Adult Pechora Pipit.

12–14 days and probably independent at that time or soon after. Thought to breed at 1 year.

Taxonomy and geographical variation
Polytypic. The nominate race breeds in northern Eurasia. *A. g. stejnegeri* breeds on the Commander Islands. It is larger and paler than the nominate, though the differences are subtle. Another subspecies is extralimital.

Meadow Pipit
Anthus pratensis

Identification

See p. 298

Adult crown and cheeks are olive or brown with heavy dark streaking on the crown. The supercilium is paler, often indistinct. The slender bill has a dark gray upper mandible, and a pink-yellow lower mandible, the entire bill often looking pinkish yellow. The iris is dark brown, the narrow orbital ring white. The throat and underparts are cream or pale buff, often brighter buff on the flanks. The breast and flanks are heavily streaked darker, with fewer streaks on the belly and vent. The undertail is unmarked. The upperparts are either olive or brown with black centers and buff fringing, giving the mottled brown, dark brown and buff appearance typical of pipits. The rump and uppertail-coverts are usually plain. The central tail is olive or brown, the outer feathers darker, then pale yellow-cream. The upperwing-coverts are as the back and mantle, the flight feathers darker and more uniform. The underwing-coverts are brown, fringed paler, the flight feathers uniformly darker. Legs and feet are yellow-brown. Non-breeding adults and juveniles are as breeding adults. Downy chicks are gray-brown above, bare below.

Confusion species
None over most of the range, but overlaps to the east with the Pechora Pipit. The white mantle stripes of Pechora Pipit are diagnostic.

Size
L: 5½–6¼ in. (14–16 cm). WS: 8½–10 in. (22–25 cm). W: ½–¾ oz. (18–24 g).

Voice
Male song is a long series of piercing *tsi* notes, the grouping and tempo changing. The alarm call is a double note, *tsi-itt*.

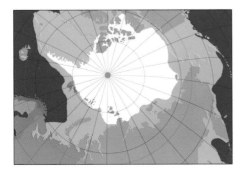

▲ Adult Meadow Pipit, north Norway.

Distribution
Breeds in southeastern Greenland, Iceland, Jan Mayen, northern Scandinavia and Russia east to the shores of the White Sea. Prefers low but complete vegetation cover, but also found on marshland, avoiding ice and snow. Migratory, moving to southern Europe, northern Africa, the Middle East and central Asia, where it prefers similar habitat but is also found at forest fringes.

Diet
Chiefly invertebrates found by ground foraging, but also takes some seeds.

Breeding
Gregarious during winter, but solitary in the breeding season. Male display flight is both territorial and an advertisement. The male often approaches interested female with a flight in which the wings beat slower and more shallowly. Courtship-feeding occurs to reinforce bond. Pair-bond usually monogamous (though polygyny observed) and may last for more than one season. Nests on the ground, concealed by vegetation. Nest is a cup of grasses and other vegetation lined with softer material, built by female only. Three to six eggs varying from almost pure white to uniform dark brown, with variable brown blotching; incubated for 13–15 days by female only or female mostly. Chicks nidicolous and altricial. Brooded and fed by both parents. Fledge at 10–14 days, but often leave nest before being capable of flight. Independent at flight. Breed at 1 year.

Taxonomy and geographical variation
Polytypic. Nominate race breeds throughout the range except in Ireland and western Scotland. There, *A. p. whistleri* breeds. It has redder upperparts and richer buff underparts.

Red-throated Pipit
Anthus cervinus

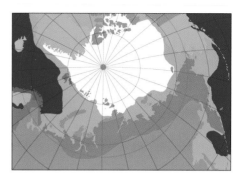

Identification See p. 298

Adults have a typical "pipit" plumage, but with distinctive heads and breasts. The head is normally orange-brown; some males have rufous heads, while most females are paler than "normal" males. The crown is streaked darker, there is a pale gray-buff patch on the ear-coverts and, often, a thin, dark malar line. The bill is brown, the base of the lower mandible pinkish. The iris is dark brown, the narrow orbital ring white. The upper breast is orange-brown, the remaining underparts pale buff-white, though the flanks are pale pink. Most males have relatively unmarked breasts, but heavily streaked flanks. Most females show much streaking on the breast, with a duller base colour. The upperparts are darker than other pipits, buff or gray-buff, but with dark centers which, despite paler fringing, gives an overall dark mottled look. The upperwing is dark brown, buff fringing on the coverts creating two narrow wing-bars. The flight feathers are uniformly dark brown. The underwing-coverts are buff, the flight feathers dark brown. The legs and feet are pink-brown or yellow-brown, but brighter pink in spring. Non-breeding adults lose the orange-brown head and breast color. Juveniles are as non-breeding adults. Downy chicks are dark-gray brown, bare below.

Confusion species

See Pechora Pipit.

Size

L: 5½–6¼ in. (14–16 cm). WS: 10–10½ in. (25–27 cm). W: ¾–⅞ oz. (20–24 g).

Voice

Song is based on a shrill, prolonged *twee, twee-twee-twee-twrrrroo-twee-twee*. There is also a long, squeaking *tsiii*.

Distribution

Palearctic, but small numbers also breed in the Nearctic. Breeds in northern Scandinavia and across Russia to Chukotka, north to the coast except on the Taimyr Peninsula. Breeds throughout Kamchatka. Also breeds in western Alaska. Prefers low shrubby or mossy tundra, but also found on marshland, forest fringes and on beaches, where it forages among exposed, drying seaweed, and to 3,300 ft. (1,000 m) in Scandinavia. Migratory, moving to central Africa and south-eastern Asia, where it is found on arable land, mudflats and grassland to 8,200 ft. (2,500 m).

Diet

Forages on the ground, chiefly for invertebrates but also feeds on seed. Will take water snails in marshland.

Breeding

Gregarious in winter, solitary at breeding sites. Male has song flight display, but female also has a slow, fluttering flight. On the ground the male has a courtship posture, assumed on a perch, with the head inclined at 45°. There is also courtship-feeding. Pair-bond is apparently monogamous, but lasts for one season only. Nest is on the ground, but well concealed, occasionally at the end of a tunnel excavated in a grassy hummock. Nest is a cup of grass and other vegetation lined with finer material. Built by female only. Two to seven cream, olive or brown eggs heavily blotched dark brown; incubated for 11–14 days by female only. Chicks nidicolous and altricial. Brooded and fed by both parents. Fledge at 11–15 days and are probably independent at that time. Thought to breed at 1 year.

Taxonomy and geographical variation

Monotypic.

▼ Adult Red-throated Pipit.

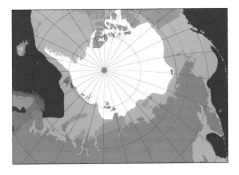

◀ Adult White Wagtail of the nominate race, Karelia, Finland.

Confusion species

None. Pied plumage and habit of wagging long tail are unmistakable.

Size

L: 6½–7½ in. (17–19 cm), tail 3–3½ in. (8–9 cm). WS: 10–12 in. (25–30 cm). W: ¾–⅞ oz. (20–25 g).

Voice

Usual call is monosyllabic *zit*, occasionally extended to two or three syllables, *si-ti* or *zi-ti-ip*. Male song is a lively twitter.

Distribution

Primarily Palearctic, but also in Greenland and western Alaska. Breeds in southeastern Greenland (near Ammassilak), Iceland, Jan Mayen, northern Scandinavia, and across Russia (north to the coast except on the Taimyr Peninsula) on the southern island of Novaya Zemlya, and on Wrangel Island. Breeds throughout Kamchatka. Also breeds irregularly in northwestern Alaska. The species also breeds throughout Europe and across central Asia. Huge range means a variety of habitats, but Arctic and sub-Arctic birds prefer areas of low vegetation near water or coastal sites. Northern birds are migratory, moving to central Europe, the Middle East and southern Asia. Wintering birds found in various habitats.

Diet

Invertebrates obtained by ground foraging or by short flights from the ground to take flying insects.

White Wagtail
Motacilla alba

Identification   See p. 298

Adult males have white heads with a black crown stripe starting above the eye and extending down the neck, broadening at the base of the neck. The bill is black, the iris dark brown. The throat is black, the color starting at the base of the lower mandible and extending to the lower cheek (separated from the nape color by a white patch) and to the breast. The remaining underparts are white, heavily smudged dark gray on the lower flanks. The back, mantle and scapulars are gray, strongly delineated from the black of the nape and becoming darker, then black, on the rump and uppertail-coverts. The central feathers of the long tail are black, the outer feathers white. The tertials are black, fringed white. The upperwing is black, the lesser and median coverts tipped white to give two short white wing-bars. The flight feathers are edged gray. The underwing is white. Adult females are as male, but less striking, the face smudged gray, the crown grayer, and tending to dark gray on the nape, the upperparts darker gray, the black bib and breast smaller and more broken. The legs and feet are black. Non-breeding males have pale gray crown and upperparts, a white throat apart from a small black crescent on the side, a smaller black breast patch, and a pale gray patch below and behind the eye. Non-breeding females and juveniles are as non-breeding males, but the gray crown extends to the forehead. Juveniles also have grayer underparts so that the bird looks duller overall. Downy chicks are gray above, bare below.

Breeding

Gregarious or solitary in winter, solitary at breeding sites. Male song is from a perch or sometimes from the ground. On the ground, the male points his head upward to expose his breast pattern. He will also bob his head and feather his wings as he zigzags toward a female, tilting his head to keep her in view, and occasionally raising the wing closest to her while dropping the other. Courtship-feeding not recorded. Pair-bond monogamous, but for one season only. Nest site is in natural hole or crevice, usually close to the ground. Nest is a cup of grass, roots and other vegetation, lined with finer material and feathers. Built by both birds but chiefly by female. Four to six eggs varying from white with brown speckles to heavily brown marked; incubated by both birds for 11–16 days. Chicks nidicolous and altricial. Brooded and fed by both birds (initially brooded by female only). Fledge in 11–16 days and are fed for further 4–7 days before becoming independent. Breed at 1 year.

Taxonomy and geographical variation

Polytypic. The nominate race breeds in Greenland, Iceland and northern Scandinavia. *M. a. dukhunensis* breeds in Russia east to the Yenisey Delta. It is paler gray than the nominate and has more white on the upperwing-coverts. *M. a. ocularis* breeds east of the Yenisey Delta and in northern Kamchatka. It is as the nominate, but with black stripe on the lores and through the eye to the nape. *M. a. lugens* breeds in southern Kamchatka and on the coast of the Sea of Okhotsk. It is similar to *ocularis*, but the upperparts are black rather than gray. It is now often regarded as a separate species, the Black-backed Wagtail (*M. lugens*). There are seven other extralimital races.

Yellow Wagtail
Motacilla flava

Identification   See p. 298

This description refers to the Scandinavian and north Russian subspecies *M. f. thunbergi*. Breeding males have slate-gray crown and neck, the rest of the head black with a vestigial or absent white supercilium. The bill is black, the iris dark brown, but often lost in the black face. The throat is pale yellow, occasionally with a thin white line separating it from the black face. The underparts are yellow with olive smudging on the sides of the breast (occasionally almost forming a complete band) and the flanks. The upperparts are olive green, the central tail dark gray, the outer feathers white. The tertials are dark gray, fringed white. The upperwing is dark gray, the coverts fringed and tipped pale greenish-yellow to create two thin, pale, partial wing-bars. The flight feathers are fringed gray on the inner web. The underwing-coverts are pale yellow, the flight feathers dark gray.

Breeding females have a light gray crown and nape, with a distinct white supercilium and a gray patch behind the eye that lies over the ear-covert. The underparts are as breeding male but paler, the upperparts as breeding male but duller. The legs and feet are dark slate gray. Non-breeding adult males are as breeding female, but crown and ear-covert patch are darker. Juveniles are as non-breeding female, but darker overall. Downy chicks are yellow-brown above, bare below.

Confusion species

None.

Size

L: 6½–7 in. (15–17 cm), tail 2–3 in. (6–7 cm). WS: 9–10½ in. (23–27 cm). W: ½–¾ oz. (16–20 g).

Voice

Generally silent except at breeding sites. Song is a high, musical *tsee-tsee-sirr*. Usual call is a sharp *seet*.

Distribution

Palearctic, but also breeds in western Alaska. Absent from Greenland and Iceland. Breeds in northern Scandinavia and across Russia to Chukotka, north to the coast except on the Taimyr Peninsula. Breeds throughout Kamchatka and on the western and northern coasts of Alaska. Also breeds in Eurasia south to Turkey and southern Russia. As with White Wagtail, the extensive range means an eclectic choice of habitat. Northern birds favor damp ground, including river and lake margins and coastal areas. Migratory, moving to central and southern Africa, India and Southeast Asia. Similar habitats are preferred (especially paddy fields in Asia).

Diet

Invertebrates, either obtained by ground-foraging or by a short flight from the ground or perch.

Breeding

Gregarious except at breeding sites. Male song display begins at perch. Bird then flies up, but soon returns to earth with wings drooped and tail lowered. Ground displays include male positioning himself in front of female with tail fanned and lowered, wings half open and bill open. There is also courtship-feeding. Pair-bond monogamous, but seasonal only. Nest site is on the ground concealed in vegetation. Nest is cup of grass

◀ Yellow Wagtail of the race *simillima*, Kamchatka.

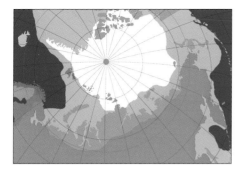

and other vegetation, lined with finer material. Built by female, occasionally assisted by male. 4–6 white, olive or brown eggs very variably marked; from unmarked to heavy brown streaking; incubated by both birds (but chiefly female) for 11–14 days. Chicks nidicolous and altricial. Brooded and fed by both parents. Fledge at around 16 days, but leave nest earlier. Not independent until around two weeks after fledging. Breed at one year.

Taxonomy and geographical variation

Polytypic. Thirteen subspecies described, most of which are extralimital. The nominate race breeds across central Europe from France to Urals. It has a grayish crown and nape, a white supercilium, gray cheek patches, a yellow throat and unmarked underparts. *M. f. thunbergi* (as described above) breeds in northern Scandinavia east to the Yenisey delta. *M. f. tschutschensis* breeds from the Kolyma river to Chukotka, and in western Alaska. It has a distinct white supercilium between the mid-gray crown, nape and cheek patches, and a white throat. The breeding range of *M. f. plexa* lies between that of *thunbergi* and *tschutschensis*; it interbreeds with both and represents an intermediate form. *M. f. simillima* breeds in Kamchatka. It is virtually indistinguishable from the nominate race but is greener overall. The eastern forms are now often considered a separate species, the Eastern Yellow Wagtail *M. tschutschensis*, of which *plexa* and *simillima* are subspecies.

Waxwings and dippers

The Bohemian Waxwing *Bombycilla garrulus* breeds in northern Scandinavia and northern Russia to Kamchatka, and also in central Alaska and Yukon and close to the south-western shore of Hudson bay.

Dippers are essentially sub-Arctic birds, but two species ranges reach to the Arctic boundary as described here. The American Dipper *Cinclus mexicanus* is a Nearctic species, common on the Alaska Peninsula, less common in the Aleutians and in western Alaska and rare in the north. The Brown Dipper *C. pallasii* is a Palearctic species that breeds throughout Kamchatka and on the Kuril Islands, and is usually found in upland areas. Both species have large preening glands to aid with the heavy waterproofing of the plumage that is required; these birds forage by walking in shallow water or by swimming underwater. American and Brown Dippers are remarkably cold-tolerant (as are other members of the genus), and they frequently feed beneath winter ice.

Wrens

The Troglodytidae or wrens are a New World family, the only Old World species being the Winter Wren *Troglodytes troglodytes*, which is thought to have spread from Alaska to Siberia and then colonised the Palearctic, reaching as far as Iceland, where it is a resident breeder. Although not an Arctic species, subspecies of Winter Wren are found in the Aleutian and Pribilof Islands, in Kamchatka, on the Commander Islands, and on the Kuril Islands. .

Irruptive Waxwings in winter. Central Norway.

PLATE 22: OWLS, KINGFISHERS, SWALLOWS, LARKS, PIPITS & WAGTAILS

Short-eared Owl
ad

Snowy Owl
♀

Belted Kingfisher
♂
♀

Tree Swallow
ad
ad
juv

Horned Lark
♂

American Pipit
br
ad win

Meadow Pipit
br

Pechora Pipit
ad win

♂ br

Red-throated Pipit

br
♂ br

M. F. thunbergi
♂ br

Yellow Wagtail

White Wagtail
ad

Not to scale

Varied Thrush
Ixoreus naevius

Identification See p. 305
A beautiful, strikingly colored thrush. Adult males have a lilac crown and nape, a broad, bright orange-brown supercilium curving down toward the nape base and a black forehead, the color continuing as a broad black stripe through and below the eye to the base of the nape. The bill is dark gray, the iris dark brown. The throat and upper breast are orange-brown, becoming paler, then white on the vent and undertail-coverts, with lilac smudging on the flanks and vent sides. Upperparts are lilac, the tail dark lilac. The upperwing is lilac with a short orange-brown bar on the lesser coverts, and a much broader one across the greater coverts. Flight feathers have orange-brown inner webs, the primaries tipped black. Adult females are as males, but more subdued, the eye-stripe pale lilac rather than black, the black breast band pale gray and the underparts paler. Upperparts are pale lilac, as is upperwing. Legs and feet are dull pink. Juveniles are as adult females, but even paler, the breast mottled pale lilac/orange. Downy chicks are brown-buff.

Confusion species
None.

Size
L: 9–10 in. (23–25 cm). W: 15–16½ in. (38–42 cm). W: 2½–2¾ oz. (75–85 g).

Voice
The song is a curious series of short, single-pitch whistles, the pitch rising gradually though the sequence and some notes are trilled. Also a short, harsh *chup* and a humming whistle.

Distribution
Nearctic. Breeds in all parts of Alaska except the extreme north and west, and along the northwestern Pacific coast. Prefers damp forests and forest fringes, but also found on marshes, tundra, and tidal flats. Migratory, moving farther down the western coast of the U.S.; similar habitat preferred in winter.

Diet
Insects, seeds and fruits. Wintering birds are fond of acorns.

Breeding
Solitary at all times, though loose flocks may be seen in winter.

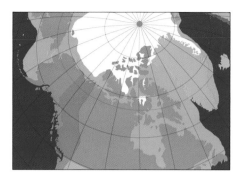

▶ Adult Varied Thrush

Male defends territory by singing and with threat display that involves raising the (unfanned) tail, lowering the wings and tipping the head forward. An alternative involves fanning the tail, lowering the head and opening the bill. Mating displays not noted, female presumably attracted to territory. Pair-bond apparently monogamous and seasonal. Nests in the fork of a tree, usually high above the ground. Nest is apparently built by female only; consists of twigs, bark and grasses lined with finer grass. One to five (usually three or four) pale blue eggs, unmarked or lightly brown-speckled; incubated for about 14 days by female only. Chicks nidicolous and altricial. Brooded by female but fed by both birds. Fledge at 13–15 days. Thought to breed at 1 year.

Taxonomy and geographical variation
Polytypic. The nominate race breeds in southeast Alaska and southern Canada. The paler and grayer race *meruloides* breeds in northern Alaska and northern Yukon east to the Mackenzie Delta. There is also one extralimital subspecies.

Chats and flycatchers
The sole Arctic representative of the Muscicapidae is the Northern Wheatear. Siberian Rubythroat (*Luscinia calliope*) and Red-flanked Bluetail (*Tarsiger cyanurus*) breed on Kamchatka, as does the Red-throated Flycatcher (*Ficedula parva*). The Dark-sided Flycatcher (*Muscicapa sibirica*) is a southern species, but it breeds in southern Kamchatka, as does the Gray-streaked Flycatcher (*M. griseisticta*).

Northern Wheatear
Oenanthe oenanthe

Identification See p. 309
Breeding males have pale blue-gray crown and nape, a white forehead and a narrow white supercilium. The lores are black and linked through and below the eye to a black cheek patch. The black is often separated from the pink-buff throat and broad blue-gray nape by a thin white stripe. Bill is black, iris dark brown. Underparts are pink-buff, usually paler than throat and paling to white on vent and undertail-coverts. Upperparts are pale blue-gray and nape, rump and uppertail-coverts white. Central tail is black, outer tail feathers white with a broad black terminal bar. Upperwing is black. Underwing-coverts and axillaries are black-fringed and tipped white, flight feathers

▲ Greenland Wheatear *leucorhoa* from south Greenland and (inset) nominate Wheatear from Norway. Compare the colour of the underparts.

pale gray. Adult females much plainer, with gray-brown crown, nape and upperparts. The supercilium is creamy buff, the lores and cheek patch dark brown. Underparts are usually richer buff, but may be much paler than in male. Upperwing is dark brown, underwing as the male but washed buff. Rump and tail are as the male. Legs and feet dark brown. Non-breeding birds similar to breeding; crown, nape and upperparts buff-brown, but rump and tail as breeding adults. Supercilium creamy buff, the lores and cheek patch as crown but darker. Underparts are pinkish buff, paler toward the tail. Upperwing is dark brown, all the feathers tipped and edged buff. Underwing is also washed buff. Non-breeding females are duller overall than males. Juveniles differ from adults, with dark brown upperparts mottled buff; the pale buff underparts have darker scaling. Bill, legs and feet are dark brown. Downy chicks dark gray above, bare below.

Confusion species
None.

Size
L: 5½–6¼ in. (14–16 cm). WS: 10¼–12½ in. (26–32 cm). W: ¾–1 oz. (20–28 g).

Voice
Male song is a short warble occasionally interspersed with mimicry of other species or sounds. The alarm call is a sharp *tek-tek*. There is also a high, whistling *heet*.

Distribution
Circumpolar, but patchy in the Nearctic. Breeds on all coasts of Greenland, but rare in the northeast. Breeds on Iceland, irregularly on Svalbard, and from northern Scandinavia to Chukotka; also on southern island of Novaya Zemlya. Breeds in western Alaska, on Baffin and southern Ellesmere, northern Quebec and Labrador. Found on both stony and shrubby tundra but also on beaches and mountain slopes; avoids forested areas. Migratory, with the entire population wintering in central Africa, birds preferring bare ground or rocky hillsides.

Diet
Insects and berries. Forages on the ground or pounces from perch. Flying insects taken by fluttering upward from the ground or by swooping from a perch.

Breeding
Solitary, but groups form during migrations. The male song is delivered in a labored upward flight, with wings beating in short bursts and tail fanned. At the top of the climb the bird hovers before diving back to earth. The male flies toward any female entering his territory, following her if she departs. He will crouch low, with tail fanned and head raised, and sing. Males also have a dancing display in which they leap about, sometimes over a female, with the tail fanned. The male may also stretch upward with the bill vertical, or may open his wings and run toward the female, his tail fanned and wings quivering. Courtship-feeding is rare. Pair-bond is monogamous (though polygyny recorded) and seasonal. Well-concealed nest in hole or crevice. Nest is a cup of vegetation lined with feathers. Four to seven white, occasionally lightly brown-speckled eggs, incubated by female mainly (or only) for 10–16 days. Chicks nidicolous and altricial. Brooded by female only for 5–6 days, then cared for and fed by both birds. Fledge in 10–21 days, but are not independent for a further 10–15 days. Breed at 1 year.

Taxonomy and geographical variation
Polytypic. The nominate race breeds in the Palearctic and in Alaska. Greenland Wheatear (*O. o. leucorhoa*) breeds in eastern Canada, Greenland and Iceland. It is as nominate, but larger, and both male and female have much richer buff underparts. Other races are extralimital.

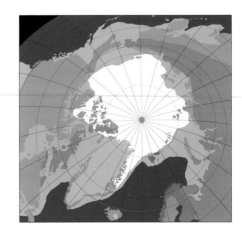

American Robin ♂

Gray-cheeked Thrush ♂

Varied Thrush ♀

♂ ad

♂ fall

♂

♀ 1st-fall

Dusky Thrush

♂ fall
T. n. eunomus

T. n. eunomus
♂

♀ 1st-fall
T. n. eunomus

Warblers, tits and chickadees

Fewer warblers breed in the Arctic than the observer might like: greater numbers might reduce the punishing number of mosquitoes that must normally be endured. Apart from the Arctic Warbler, Old World Warblers do not have ranges that extend to far north; this does at least spare the birder the difficulty of having to differentiate between very similar species, many of which are easily distinguished only by song.

The Willow Warbler (*Phylloscopus trochilus*) does invade the sub-Arctic, breeding as far north as the Lena and Kolyma Deltas and east to Anadyr, but this species is essentially a central Eurasian species. The Eastern Crowned Warbler *P. coronatus* also breeds north to the Kolyma Delta, but it too is primarily a central Asian species. The Dusky Warbler (*P. fuscatus*) breeds in southern Chukotka and parts of northern Kamchatka, but is a species of southern and eastern Asia. In addition to these species, Gray's Grasshopper Warbler (*Locustella fasciolata*), Middendorff's Grasshopper Warbler (*L. ochotensis*), Pallas's Grasshopper Warbler (*L. certhiola*) and Lanceolated Warbler (*L. lanceolata*) all breed in southern Kamchatka, while the Sedge Warbler (*Acrocephalus schoenobaenus*) breeds on the Kola Peninsula and the western shore of the White Sea.

▲ Adult Arctic Warbler of the nominate race *borealis*. Yamalo-Nenetsky, northern Russia.

Arctic Warbler
Phylloscopus borealis

Identification See p. 309

Breeding adults have dark olive crowns, a broad pale greenish-yellow supercilium terminating at the lore and a dark olive-brown eye-stripe, each stripe extending to the nape. The bill is dark brown, the base of the lower mandible yellow-brown. The iris is dark brown. The cheeks are olive-green, gently dappled paler. The throat is pale olive-yellow, the remaining underparts cream, suffused or streaked olive and yellow-olive to the upper belly. The flanks are smudged olive-brown, and the lower belly, vent and undertail unmarked cream. The upperparts are uniformly olive-green, the tail feathers darker at the tips. The upperwing-coverts are olive-brown with a narrow, pale yellow-green bar across the tips of the median coverts and another across the tips of the greater coverts; neither bar is distinct, and the median bar may be absent. The flight feathers are darker, fringed olive-brown on the inner web. The underwing-coverts are pale yellow, the flight feathers dark-olive-brown. The legs and feet are pale pinkish- or yellowish-brown. Non-breeding adults are as the breeding adults, but they are greener overall. Juvenile plumage is as adults, but the upperparts are more gray-brown than olive-brown. First-winter birds are as breeding adults but less gray Downy chicks are pale gray, initially on the head only.

Confusion species
None within the Arctic.

Size
L: 4½–5 in. (11–13 cm). WS: 6½–8½ in. (17–22 cm). W: ¼–⅓ oz. (8–11 g).

◀ Middendorff's Grasshopper Warbler, Kamchatka.

Voice

Male song is a fast and rhythmic *crecrecrecre*. Call is a short, sharp and very penetrating *dreek*, often noted as being very similar to that of a Eurasian Dipper (*Cinclus cinclus*), and unlike other *Phylloscopus*.

Distribution

Eurasia and western Alaska. Breeds in northern Scandinavia and across Russia to the Bering Sea, but infrequently to the northern coast, though has bred on Wrangel Island. Breeds around the Sea of Okhotsk, on Kamchatka and on the Kuril Islands. A forest dweller, though seen in thickets close to the edge of the taiga. Migratory, moving to the forests of south-eastern Asia for the winter.

Diet

Insects and other arthropods. Forages both in trees and bushes and on the ground, and will occasionally catch insects in flight.

Breeding

Solitary, but wintering birds are sometimes seen in small flocks. The male performs display song from high in a tree. An interested female will watch while slowly flapping her wings. Male may respond by flying to her and repeating wing-flapping. Male then suggests a nest site by moving to the site, plucking moss, and swinging from side to side. Pair-bond apparently monogamous, though polygyny reported, and probably seasonal. Nests in natural tree crevice or on the ground, often among tree roots. Nest is domed, built of grass and leaves lined with finer material. Three to seven white eggs lightly speckled red; incubated by female only for 11–13 days. Chicks nidicolous and altricial. Brooded by female only, but cared for and fed by both birds. Fledge in about 14 days and are independent at that time (though one study has suggested that parents continue to feed to about 28 days). Thought to breed at 1 year.

Taxonomy and geographical variation

Polytypic. The nominate race breeds across northern Eurasia. *P. b. kennicotti* breeds in Alaska. It has a shorter bill and some adults are much brighter, bright olive-brown above and yellow-green below. However, some adults are indistinguishable from nominate. *P. b. xanthodryas* breeds in Kamchatka and on the Kuril Islands. It is much brighter than either the nominate or *kennicotti* (though colour scheme similar) and has a broader bill. In Chukotka the nominate and *xanthodryas* interbreed.

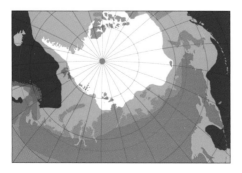

▲ Willow Tit, north Norway.

Tits and chickadees

Only one species of the "true" tits can genuinely be considered an Arctic bird, though several others are sub-Arctic. In the Palearctic the Coal Tit (*Periparus ater*) is found in southern Kamchatka. The Willow Tit (*Poecile montanus*) is found throughout Kamchatka; the resident subspecies *P. m. kamtschatkensis* is white apart from the black brown and bib and mid-brown upperwing. The Willow Tit also occurs in southern Chukotka. Some authorities suggest that the Willow Tit and the Nearctic Black-capped Chickadee (*Poecile atricapillus*) share a relatively recent common ancestor. The two are extremely similar, and are both similar to the Siberian Tit, though the ranges of the Siberian and Willow Tit overlap without apparent interbreeding. The Black-capped Chickadee breeds in central Alaska, but is uncommon in the west and absent from the north. This range is shared by the Boreal Chickadee (*Poecile hudsonicus*), a species that also breeds at the timberline on the southern shores of Hudson Bay.

Though not a true tit, the Long-tailed Tit (*Aegithalos caudatus*) breeds on Kamchatka. The Kamchatka birds are very pale birds, and are considered a distinct subspecies, *A. c. kamtschaticus*.

Siberian Tit
(Gray-headed Chickadee)
Poecile cinctus

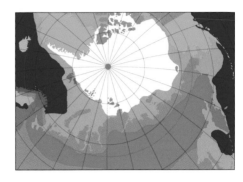

Identification See p. 309
Adults have dark chocolate crown and nape, the nape color forming a narrow strip. There is an indistinct black line through eyes and across the forehead at the base of bill. The rest of the face is white, extending to the sides of the nape. The bill and iris are both dark brown. There is a triangular black bib on the throat, its apex at the base of the bill. The underparts are white, with rust-brown breast sides, flanks, vent sides and undertail-coverts. The feathering of the underparts invariably looks puffed out. The upperparts are chestnut-brown, the tail dark gray. The upperwing is dark brown, the larger coverts and flight feathers fringed and tipped gray. The axillaries and underwing-coverts are gray-buff. The legs and feet are dark gray. Juveniles are as adults, but duller above and paler below. Downy chicks are gray-brown and have yellow bills.

Confusion species
May be confused with the Willow Tit where ranges overlap, but Willow Tit lacks the distinct contrast between the upperparts and the wings and, in eastern Russia, is much paler.

Size
L: 5–5½ in. (13–14 cm). WS: 7½–7¾ in. (19–21 cm). W: ⅓–½ oz. (11–13 g).

Voice
Song is an unmelodic buzzing, usually *che-che-che*, but occasionally with double syllables *che-err che-err*. Call is a softer *zee-du-du-du*. There is also a sharper *tsi*.

Distribution
Palearctic, but rare breeder in west and central Alaska. Breeds in northern Scandinavia and across Russia to Chukotka, but not to the northern coast. Breeds throughout Kamchatka. Found throughout the taiga but rarer at the forest edge, occasionally

▼ Adult Siberian Tit, Finland.

seen in scrub at southern edge of tundra. Prefers conifers, also found in deciduous trees. Resident or nomadic. Resident birds survive temperatures as low as -76°F (-60°C). At "higher" temperatures -40°F (-40°C) the birds find a tree hole for shelter, tuck in their heads and feet, and fluff out their feathers. The feathers have many barbs and barbules — up to 1,500/cu. in. (100/cm³) — allowing an insulating layer of still air to form. As the temperature drops towards -76°F (-60°C), the birds can also drop their body temperature by up to 50°F (10°C), thus entering a state of partial torpor. The birds need to consume around ¼ oz. (7 g) of food each day to maintain body temperature, and this must be gathered in a day that can be as little as four hours long (though, as noted below, the birds store food whenever possible). The survival of this little bird is one of the wonders of the Arctic.

Diet
Invertebrates and seeds. Takes caterpillars when available. Stores food at all times.

Breeding
Gregarious except at breeding sites. Male sings from a specific perch within territory. Mating displays little studied, but probably as other tits (i.e., wing-fluttering and bowing). Courtship-feeding definitely occurs. Pair-bond apparently monogamous, with pair staying in territory throughout the year. Nests in tree hole, either a natural cavity or old woodpecker hole. Nest has wood-chip base, then layers of moss and grasses. Built by female only. Six to 10 white eggs, lightly red-speckled; incubated by female only for 15–18 days. Chicks nidicolous and altricial. Cared for and fed by both birds. Fledge at 19–20 days, but are fed for a farther about 10 days or so before independence. Thought to breed at 1 year.

Taxonomy and geographical variation
Polytypic. Nominate race breeds in Asian Russia east of the Urals. *P. c. lapponicus* breeds in Scandinavia and European Russia. It is darker, particularly on the crown, which contrasts strongly with the upperparts. The flanks and undertail-coverts are pale cinnamon. There are other extralimital subspecies.

♂ br

Bluethroat

♀ br

1st-win ♂

♂ fall
O.o. leucorhoa

Northern Wheatear

br

♀ br

♂ br

1st-win

ad fall

Arctic Warbler

ad spring

br

Siberian Tit

Crows

The genus *Corvus* includes some of the most adaptable and versatile of birds, deriving from their undoubted intelligence. The largest *Corvus*, indeed the largest passerine, is the Raven, a true Arctic dweller. In Europe, Ravens were often seen as bad omens and harbingers of death, a reputation based largely on the fact they (and crows) scavenged on battlefield dead and gibbeted gallows victims. But Ravens were also seen more positively. Even today they "defend" the Tower of London (and therefore the monarchy), while in former times they had an integral part in the Viking pantheon. They remain an important part of the Creation myths of both Pacific Northwest Native Americans (appearing on totem poles) and of Inuit on both sides of the Bering Sea.

Jays and magpies, though essentially sub-Arctic, might be seen in Arctic areas. The Siberian Jay *Perisorius infaustus* breeds on the shores of the White Sea, near the Lena Delta, in western Chukotka and in Kamchatka, while the Gray Jay (*P. canadensis*) breeds in central Alaska (uncommon in the west and rare in the north), in central Yukon and the Northwest Territories, on the southern shores of Hudson Bay, and in southern Quebec and Labrador. The Common Magpie (*Pica pica*) breeds in northern Scandinavia through northern Russia to the Anadyr River and Kamchatka, while the possibly conspecific Black-billed Magpie (*P. hudsonia*) breeds in southern and central Alaska and the Yukon.

▼ Gray Jay sunbathing in Reindeer Moss. This generally sub-Arctic species can occur farther north. Churchill.

Common Raven
Corvus corax

Identification See p. 314

Adults are entirely black, glossed metallic purple, purplish-blue or even purplish-green depending on the light. The massive bill is black, the iris dark brown. Tail is wedge-shaped. In general, males are glossier purple than females. The legs and feet are black. Juveniles are as adult, but slightly matt black, particularly on the upperparts. Downy chicks are mid-brown.

Confusion species

If size is discernible none but Carrion Crow is also entirely black. Raven's wedge-shaped tail should distinguish the two.

Size

L: 1½–2 ft. (54–67 cm). WS: 4–5 ft. (120–150 cm). W: 2–3 lb. (1–1.35 kg).

Voice

More varied than might be imagined, though most are variations of the familiar gruff *croak*. There are higher, bell-like versions as well as softer, more musical forms. The basic form is *krok*, but the Inuit insist it is *kak*, because the first Raven was a man who, before setting out on a journey with colleagues, kept reminding them not to forget the blankets (*kak* in Inuktituk). His companions became so fed up that they ignored him, deliberately forgot the blankets, and then sent him to fetch them. In his panicky haste, he ran, then flew and became a Raven, still calling *kak*.

Distribution

Circumpolar. Breeds on both coasts of Greenland from the southern tip to the north. Breeds on Iceland, northern Scandinavia and across Russia to Chukotka, north to the coast except on the Taimyr Peninsula, but apparently absent from Arctic islands, though possibly on Wrangel. In North America, breeds throughout Alaska and across Canada, north to the coast and also on the Canadian Arctic islands. Found in all habitats, from mountains, forest edge and tundra and coast. Resident.

Diet

Omnivorous and opportunistic. Preys on mammals and birds and robs nests. Also takes mollusks and crustaceans at the shore, as well as berries and seeds, and will scavenge on carrion.

Breeding

Generally seen in pairs, though flocks of immature birds may occur. Pairing probably takes place in these flocks, though similar displays reinforce existing pair-bonds. Male has advertising displays,

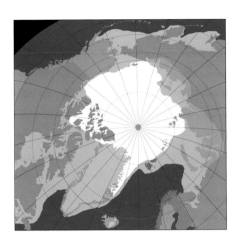

▲ Raven of the northern North American and Greenland race *principalis*, Unalaska.

raising feathers above the eyes to form "ears" or holding the head and throat feathers erect while opening the bill. Male also raises and fans the tail while drooping the wings. Pair-bond monogamous and probably lifelong. Nest site is high in isolated tree or on a cliff ledge. Nest is huge mass of sticks (up to 5 ft./ 1.5 m high and across) coated with mud (if ground unfrozen), then lined with grass, hair and other filamentous material. Four to six light blue or blue-green eggs, with black markings that range from minimal and delicate to heavy and blotched. Incubated by female only for 18–21 days. Chicks nidicolous and altricial. Cared for and fed by both birds. Fledge at 35–49 days, but often leave nest before capable of flight and are not fully independent for up to six months later. Breed at 2–3 years.

Taxonomy and geographical variation

Polytypic. The nominate race breeds in Eurasia east to the Yenisey River. Race *C. c. kamtschaticus* breeds east of Yenisey to Bering Sea and throughout Kamchatka. It is larger than the nominate. Race *C. c. varius* breeds in Iceland and the Faroe Islands. It too is larger than the nominate, with wings 10

percent longer and bill 15 percent to 20 percent longer, and its plumage is less glossy. Race *C. c. principalis* breeds in northern North America and Greenland. It is comparable in size to *varius*, but the feather base on the body is white. There are several other extralimital subspecies, in all cases differing in size and perceived glossiness.

Carrion Crow
Corvus corone

The Eurasian Crow occurs in two forms. The *corone* group is entirely black, the *cornix* group is gray and black. The *cornix* form is often called the Hooded Crow, particularly in the British Isles where both forms occur, as they do in other north European countries. The *corone* group occupies western Europe and eastern Asia, the *cornix* group is in Scandinavia, eastern Europe and European Russia. However, there are some significant outliers; Hooded Crows occur in Scotland and Ireland, for example, and Carrion Crows occur in southern Asia. How this distribution pattern arose remains the subject of debate. The evidence favors glacial separation of an ancestral form into three groups, the central one of which evolved the gray and black plumage, while the western and eastern groups remained black. The present distribution reflects this, with Scandinavian *cornix* birds having subsequently colonized the northern British Isles. Hybridization occurs along a narrow zone where the two forms meet, and hybrids seem to have reduced viability. Hence, Carrion and Hooded are regarded as separate species by several authorities.

Identification   See p. 314

Adult *corone* are entirely black, glossed blue or purple, sometimes green on the head. The bill is black, the iris dark brown. The legs and feet are black. Juveniles are as adults but "scrawny." Adult *cornix* have black head, throat and mid-nape,

◄ Pair of Ravens of the nominate race, Ytre Ryfylke, Norway. Note the diagnostic tail shape of the bird in flight.

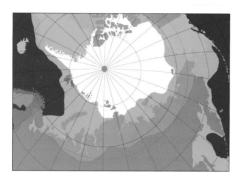

black wings and tail, and a black patch on the upper breast. The rest of the plumage is pale gray. Bill, iris, legs and feet as *corone*. Hybrid *corone* x *cornix* sometimes has a gray necklace, but more often dark gray underparts. The downy chicks of both groups are pale smoky-gray above, bare below.

Confusion species
For *corone*, see Raven; *cornix* has none.

Size
L: 18–20 in. (45–50 cm). WS: 3–3½ ft. (90–105 cm). W: 16–23 oz. (450–650 g).

Voice
All calls are based on a hoarse croak *kraa-kraa*, usually repeated several times. Some authorities claim that call of *corone* is "harder" than that of *cornix*, but this is debatable.

Distribution
Palearctic. Absent from Greenland and Iceland. Where *corone* and *cornix* occur together in northwest Europe, *cornix* is generally to the north. In Russia, the ranges are more complex: *cornix* breeds from the Kola Peninsula to the Yenisey River, *corone* east of Yenisey to Chukotka and throughout Kamchatka. Russian birds do not breed to the north coast

▼ Hooded Crow, north Norwegian coast.

except around the White Sea. Occurs in virtually all habitats, from tundra to forest edge to coast, though generally *cornix* occurs in more mountainous terrain than *corone*. Resident.

Diet
Highly adaptable; invertebrates and seeds, but also scavenges, takes small birds, robs nests and even kleptoparasitic on birds (especially raptors).

Breeding
Solitary or in small flocks at all times, though does not breed in colonies, as does the Rook (*Corvus frugilegus*). Male has seldom-seen display flight in which the wings perform an exaggerated arc on each beat. The male also has a head-bristling display similar to that of the Raven. Pair-bond monogamous and long-lasting. Nest site is high in isolated tree or, more rarely, on a cliff ledge. Nest is of twigs, decreasing in size as the construction rises, lined with bark, grass, hair and feathers. Built by both birds, or mainly by female with male supplying material. Three to six green eggs, variably marked (from almost blemish-free to heavily dark brown and black blotches). Incubated by female only for 18–19 days. Chicks nidicolous and altricial. Cared for and fed by both birds. Fledge at 28–38 days, but are not independent for further 20–30 days. Breed at 3–4 years.

Taxonomy and geographical variation
Polytypic. Nominate race *corone* breeds in British Isles and southern Europe. Race *orientalis* (part of the *corone* group) breeds east of Yenisey River. It is larger than the nominate. Race *cornix* breeds in northern Scandinavia and east to Yenisey. The Carrion Crow is split into two species by the BOURC; Carrion Crow *C. corone* and Hooded Crow *C. cornix*.

Spotted Nutcracker
Nucifraga caryocatactes

Often simply called the Nutcracker; however, the longer name is preferable to avoid confusion with the (non-Arctic breeding) Clark's Nutcracker (*N. columbiana*) of the western United States.

Identification See p. 314
Adults have dark chocolate crowns. The lores are white, as are the bristles that extend over the base of the upper mandible. The long, slender bill is black, the iris dark brown. The rest of the head, the back and underparts are chocolate brown, densely covered with white spots. Spot density decreases on the lower belly. The vent and undertail-coverts are white. The spot density also decreases toward the tail on the upperparts. The broad tail is chocolate brown with a white terminal band, broader towards the edges. The upperwing is dark brown, the lesser coverts paler and white spotted, the other coverts sparsely white spotted. The underwing-coverts are brown with white spots, the flight feathers unspotted and much darker. Legs and feet are black. Juveniles are as adult but duller, with gray bill and iris and pink-gray legs and feet. Chicks

▲ Spotted Nutcracker, Yakutia.

are naked for around seven days, then gray-white down above, bare below.

Confusion species
None.

Size
L: 12½–13¾ in. (32–35 cm). WS: 20–21½ in. (50–55 cm). W: 3½–6¼ oz. (100–180 g).

Voice
Generally silent, but has a loud, rasping *kraak* and also a softer babble.

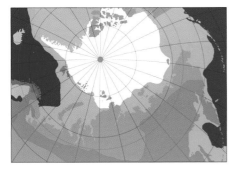

Distribution
Palearctic. Breeds in southern Norway, Sweden and Finland and across Russia from the Kola Peninsula to Chukotka (though not to the northern coast) and throughout Kamchatka. Boreal, but also found at the timberline. Resident, but also an irruptive migrant.

Diet
Nuts, seeds, invertebrates and, opportunistically, small vertebrates; omnivorous during irruptions. Caches food in summer and almost entirely dependent on this in winter.

Breeding
Solitary except during seed and nut season, when flocks form at feeding areas to collect food for winter caches. In display, the male ruffles his feathers, spreads his tail and either faces or walks around the female. Pair-bond apparently monogamous and long-lasting, reinforced by birds foraging together. Usually nests in conifers close to trunk, but occasionally uses deciduous trees and cliffs. Nest is of twigs and is built by both birds, but lined by female with grasses and lichen. Three to four white or pale green eggs with dark brown spots, incubated by both birds for 17–19 days. Chicks nidicolous and altricial. Cared for by both birds, and fed by both birds by regurgitation. Fledge in 23–28 days, but are not independent for up to further 12–15 weeks. Breed at 2 years or older.

Taxonomy and geographical variation
Polytypic. *N. c. macrorhynchus* (described above) breeds from the Urals to Chukotka and Kamchatka. The nominate breeds in southern Europe and European Russia. It has a shorter, stubbier bill. There are several other extralimital subspecies.

Nuthatches and Shrikes
The Eurasian Nuthatch (*Sitta europaea*) breeds across sub-Arctic Russia and throughout Kamchatka; on the Peninsula two subspecies breed, the Yakutian *arctica* to the north (and also in southern Chukotka) and the Kamchatkan *albifrons* to the south. Each is paler than the nominate race. No Nearctic nuthatches breed close to the Arctic boundary as defined here.

The Great Gray Shrike (*Lanius excubitor*) may be seen by Arctic travelers. It breeds in the Nearctic from western Alaska to the Atlantic coast, but it is usually limited to the sub-Arctic or Arctic fringe. It also breeds in Fennoscandia and across Russia to Chukotka, but again only to the Arctic fringe. The Brown Shrike (*L. cristatus*) is a Palearctic species, breeding eastward from central Siberia. It is a sub-Arctic species, but breeds throughout Kamchatka.

Starlings
The European Starling (*Sturnus vulgaris*), a common sight in European urban areas, breeds in Iceland and is now found over an increasing area of North America. Having been introduced into New York's Central Park in 1890, the species had reached the boundary of the Arctic by the 1970s and now breeds on the southern shores of Hudson Bay. As climate is believed to have stopped further advances to date, it may be assumed that if global warming continues the species will soon resume its northward expansion.

PLATE 25: CROWS

Carrion Crow

ad

ad
C. corone

ad
C. cornix

Carrion Crow
(C. corone)

Hooded Crow
(C. cornix)

ad

ad

Common Raven

ad

juv

ad

ad

**Spotted
Nutcracker**

New World warblers

New World warblers are more flamboyant than their Old World counterparts, making them easier both to observe and to identify in their breeding plumage. However, identification is no easier than for Old World species when considering winter plumage: *Dendroica* species are often called the "confusing Fall Warblers" because of the difficulty of distinguishing them. Most New World warblers are long-distance migrants, some almost doubling their body weights before setting off. Three *Dendroica* warblers and one other species breed within the Arctic boundary as defined here. Two other species are borderline Arctic species, Wilson's Warbler (*Wilsonia pusilla*) and the Orange-crowned Warbler (*Vermivora celata*) are common in south Alaska and on the Alaska Peninsula, and also occur on the southern shores of Hudson Bay. Wilson's Warbler also breeds on the Seward Peninsula and in Labrador. However, these are generally more southerly birds.

Blackpoll Warbler
Dendroica striata

Identification
See p. 319

Breeding males have a black crown extending to the lores and nape, the rest of the head white apart from a black malar stripe. The upper mandible and lower mandible tip are dark gray, the remaining lower mandible yellow-gray. The iris is dark brown. The underparts are white with black streaks on the sides of the breast and flanks, heaviest on the upper breast where they merge with the malar stripes. The upperparts are olive-gray heavily streaked black. The tail is black fringed gray, with large white mirrors on the three outer feather pairs (largest on the outer pair, smallest, occasionally absent, on the inner of the three). The upperwing is dark gray, but white tips to the median and greater coverts form two wingbars. The axillaries and underwing-coverts are pale gray or white, the flight feathers as the upperwing. Breeding females are duller, the crown and nape being pale olive streaked black, the supercilium buff-yellow, the face white, smudged olive-gray on the upper cheek. The underparts are white with a yellowish tinge. The streaking is much lighter and the malar stripe more broken. The upperparts are as breeding males, but olive-gray overall. The

legs and feet look yellow (a distinctive feature), usually darker in females than in male. Non-breeding adults have yellow-olive or gray-olive heads, with black streaking on the crown and a darker smudge on the cheek. The underparts are washed the same color on the breast and flanks, with streaking as breeding female. The upperparts are as breeding adults, but overall washed olive-green. Juveniles are as non-breeding adults, but the head is brighter olive-green and lacks the crown streaking. The breast and belly are yellow-green with no malar stripe and only faint streaking. The nape is gray, and there is less streaking on the upperparts. The bill, legs and feet are pink-brown. First-year non-breeding adults are as non-breeding adults. Downy chicks are pale gray.

Confusion species
None.

Size
L: 5–6 in. (13–15 cm). WS: 7½–9 in. (20–23 cm). W: ⅓–½ oz. (10–16 g).

Voice
Male song is a strident, rapid *sisisisi*, with occasional rapid trilling. Call is a sharp *chip*. There is also a buzzing *zzzz*.

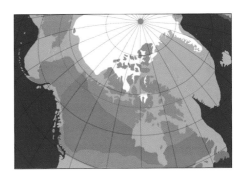

Distribution
Nearctic. Breeds throughout Alaska, but rarely in the north, across the Yukon and Northwest Territories (though not to the northern coast except at the Mackenzie Delta), around southwestern and southern Hudson Bay and in southern Quebec and Labrador. Favors woodland edges and tundra thickets. Migratory, moving to Central and South America, some birds making a very long flight to southern Chile and Argentina. Winter habitat similar to that of summer.

Diet
Insects and other invertebrates picked from foliage in the upper branches of trees and shrubs. Also takes fruits.

◄ Male Blackpoll Warbler singing to advertise his territory, Churchill.

Breeding

Males sing from a high perch to establish their territory and attract females. Pair-bond monogamous, though males with better territories may be polygynous. Bond is seasonal. Nests on the ground, near a tree or shrub. Nest is cup of twigs and lichen lined with grass and feathers. Three to five brown-speckled cream-buff or pale green eggs, incubated by female only for 11–12 days, with the male feeding her. Chicks nidicolous and altricial. Brooded by female only, but fed by both birds. Fledge at 8–10 days, but fed for about another 25 days before becoming independent. Breed at 1 year.

Taxonomy and geographical variation

Monotypic.

Yellow Warbler
Dendroica petechia

The most common, widespread and easily identified warbler in the North American Arctic. Often heard before it is seen as, despite the bright color, it can be elusive in thickets. Text refers to Arctic race *D. p. amnicola*.

Identification   See p. 319

Adult males have yellow head, the crown and nape usually greenish-yellow. The bill is black, the iris dark brown. The underparts are bright yellow with red-brown lines from breast to lower belly, the throat, vent and undertail-coverts unmarked. The upperparts are greenish-yellow, the tail darker, with yellow fringing. The upperwing is yellowish-olive, the flight feathers darker, but yellow fringing and tipping giving one or two short yellow wingbars, and giving an olive-yellow wing. Underwing-coverts are yellow, the flight feathers olive. Adult females are as male, but the red lines on the underparts are paler, narrower and often indistinct. Some birds have narrow white fringing on the primaries; all tend to be more olive on upperparts. The legs and feet are yellow-brown. Non-breeding adults are as breeding, but the red lines on the underparts of male are less distinct and overall the birds are brighter. Juveniles are as breeding adults, but drabber, with brownish wash on upper- and underparts. First-winter birds as juveniles, though some are washed gray-brown. Downy chicks are mid-gray.

▼ Male Yellow Warbler, Churchill.

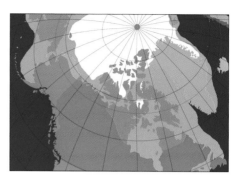

Confusion species

None.

Size

L: 4½–5 in. (11–13 cm). WS: 6½–7¾ in. (17–20 cm). W: ½–⅓ oz. (8–12 g).

Voice

Song is a sweet, cheerful series of double whistles *sweet-sweet-see-see-swee*, the ending emphatic. Call is a sharp *chip*. Flight call is a clear, sharp trill.

Distribution

Nearctic. Breeds throughout Alaska (though rare in the north), the Yukon and Northwest Territories, but rare in Nunavut. Breeds on the southern shores of Hudson Bay, in southern Quebec and Labrador. Prefers forest edge and thickets near streams, lakes and marshes. Wide breeding range, from Arctic to Caribbean and northern South America. Northern birds migratory, joining resident birds of extreme south. Same habitat preferred.

Diet

Insects and other invertebrates obtained by foraging in mid-height shrubs and thickets. Occasionally takes fruits.

Breeding

Gregarious on migration and in winter when flocks form, occasionally including other warblers. Highly territorial and solitary at breeding sites. Sings to establish territory. Male has numerous displays, including tail-spread, wings-out circling flight. It will also fly at potential rival, then circle away. When female approaches, male will chase her, but also performs a slow, almost stall-speed flight with exaggerated wingbeats. Pair-bond monogamous (though male may be polygynous) and seasonal. Nest built in fork of tree or shrub by female only. Nest is deep cup of grass or bark lined with fine grass, hair and feathers. Four to five pale gray or pale green eggs spotted or blotched olive-brown; incubated by female only for 11–12 days. Chicks nidicolous and altricial. Brooded by female only, but fed by both birds. Fledge at 8–10 days, but stay with parents for 9–13 days before becoming independent. Breed at 1 year.

Taxonomy and geographical variation

Polytypic. Races are divided into three groups, with the *aestiva* (yellow) group to the north of *petechia* (golden) and erithachorides (mangrove) groups. The petechia group includes the nominate, which breeds in the Caribbean, northern South America and Florida. D. p. amnicola breeds in northern Alaska, Yukon, Northwest Territories and Manitoba. In all, some 43 subspecies have been described, including four in southern Alaska. They differ subtly in color.

Yellow-rumped Warbler
(Myrtle Warbler)
Dendroica coronata

Identification
See p. 319

Breeding males have a yellow skullcap, the remaining crown and nape blue-gray. The short supercilium is white, separated by a black "tick" from a short white bar above the lore. A black patch covers the eye and upper cheek, extending to the side of the nape. There is a small white crescent beneath the eye. The bill is dark gray, the iris dark brown. The throat and sides of the neck are white. The underparts are white, this barely visible on the upper breast, which is extensively black-streaked. There is a yellow patch on the sides of the breast and flanks, into the pit of the wing, outlined by black streaking. The streaking is less pronounced on the belly, and absent on the vent and undertail-coverts. The upperparts are blue-gray, streaked black apart from the rump, which is bright yellow. The tail is dark blue-gray with white spotting on the outer three pairs. The upperwing is dark blue-gray with bluer fringing on all feathers, and white tips on the median and greater coverts, forming two white wingbars. The underwing-coverts are pale blue-gray, the flight feathers darker. Breeding females are patterned as males, but lack the yellow skullcap, have dark brown rather than black cheek patch, and both the upper- and underparts are washed brown. Legs and feet are dark brown or dark gray-brown. Non-breeding males are as breeding female, but retain a (reduced) yellow skullcap.

Juveniles are patterned as adults but lack yellow patches. The crown and throat are gray, streaked gray-brown. The underparts are as females, but the streaking is dark brown and less intense. The upperparts are browner overall. First-winter males are as non-breeding male. The bill is dark brown, the legs and feet paler than the adult. First-winter females are as the female, but head is mid-brown, the throat buff and the

underparts mid-brown tending to buff, the streaking dark brown and less intense. The upperparts are mid-brown, the yellow rump patch showing prominently. Downy chicks are pale brown.

Confusion species
None.

Size
L: 5–6 in. (13–15 cm). WS: 8–9½ in. (21–24 cm). W: ⅓–½ oz. (11–17 g).

Voice
Song is high, clear warbling seedl-seedl with little variation. Call is a hoarse chep. Flight call is a clearer, sharper tsit.

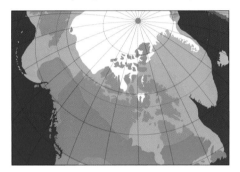

Distribution
Nearctic. Breeds in western and central Alaska, but less common in southwest and rare in the north. Breeds across the Yukon and much of Northwest Territories, south to southern Hudson Bay and north to southern Quebec and Labrador. Prefers coniferous or mixed woodland to the timberline and scrubby thickets beyond. Breeds to the southern United States, with migrating northern birds joining southern residents or moving to Central America and the Caribbean islands. The Yellow-rumped Warbler has the shortest migration of the northern Nearctic warblers and is also the hardiest of them; it is often seen in snowbound areas if sufficient food exists. Wintering birds are found in many habitats.

Diet
Insects and other invertebrates obtained by foraging in trees, but also takes flying insects in the air. Also feeds on seeds and berries, particularly in winter when berries become the chief or sole diet.

Breeding
Gregarious in winter but highly territorial and solitary at breeding sites. Male hops from perch to perch within his territory, fluffing out his feathers, raising his wings and erecting his crown feathers. He also displays his yellow rump patch and flicks his tail and wings to display his white and yellow patches. Pair-bond apparently monogamous and seasonal. Nests on the branch of a tree or shrub, usually high up (up to

◄ Adult Yellow-rumped Warbler, Great Slave Lake, Northwest Territories.

50 ft./15 m). However, will nest on the ground at tundra sites. Nest is cup of twigs, pine needles and grass built by female, though male may bring material. Nest is lined with grass and hair. Three to six (usually four to five) creamy white eggs speckled brown, incubated chiefly by the female for 12–13 days. Chicks nidicolous and altricial. Brooded by female only, but fed by both birds. Fledge at 10–14 days, but are fed for about a farther 14 days before becoming independent. Breed at 1 year.

Taxonomy and geographical variation
Polytypic. The nominate race breeds in Canada and the northern U.S. Some authorities consider Arctic birds to form a separate subspecies, *hooveri*. There are three extralimital subspecies.

Northern Waterthrush
Seiurus noveboracensis

One of the *Seiurus* New World warblers, all of which have streaked underparts and terrestrial habits, and so appear thrushlike at first glance.

Identification   See p. 319
Adults have dark olive-brown crown and nape, buff supercilium, (from bill base to nape), dark olive-brown eye-stripe and paler cheek patch. The bill is dark gray, the iris dark brown or sepia. The throat is off-white or pale yellow, the remaining underparts pale yellow, brighter on the flanks, yellow-brown on the sides of the breast and rear flanks, with a dark malar stripe and dark streaking or spotting from the throat to the lower belly. The spotting is heavier on the breast, absent on the vent and undertail-coverts. The upperparts, including the broad, square tail, are uniformly dark olive-brown, as is the upper-wing. The underwing is similar, but the coverts are paler than the flight feathers. Some birds wear to whitish rather than buff supercilium, and whitish rather than yellow underparts, others are whitish at all times. Legs and feet are pale pink or pink-brown. Downy chicks are dark gray; first molt is at 1 day.

Confusion species
Superficially similar to Buff-bellied Pipit and Gray-cheeked Thrush if viewing conditions are poor, but smaller and darker.

Size
L: 4³/₄–6 ft. (12–15 cm). WS: 8–10 in. (21–25 cm). W: ¹/₂–³/₄ oz. (16–20 g).

Voice
Song is a loud, clear chirping, falling in pitch. Call is a loud, sharp *chint*. There is also a buzzing *zwik* in flight.

Distribution
Nearctic. Breeds in western, southwestern and central Alaska, but rarer in the north. Breeds throughout the Yukon, then southward past Great Slave Lake to southern shores of Hudson Bay. Then northward to Quebec and Labrador. Prefers deciduous trees and scrubland close to lakes or streams, spending most of the time on the ground and even

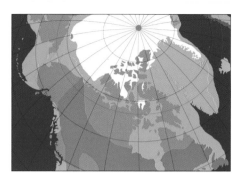

occasionally wading in shallow water. Migratory, moving to Central America, the Caribbean Islands and northern South America. Similar habitat preferred in winter.

Diet
Mainly insects; wintering birds take ants and beetles.

Breeding
Solitary, though large groups occasionally form on migration. Males sing to establish territory and to attract females. Pair-bond monogamous and seasonal with some evidence of polygyny. Nests on ground, concealed by old stumps or in tree roots, or in a moss-shrouded bank or clump of vegetation, often close to water. Nest is cup of vegetation, built by female only, lined with moss. One to five (usually four) brown- or gray-spotted white eggs, incubated by female only for about 12 days. Chicks nidifugous and semi-altricial. Brooded by female only, but fed by both parents. Fledge at 15–16 days, but leave the nest two to three days earlier, when they are unable to fly and hide in vegetation. Fed for a further 14–21 days before becoming independent. Thought to breed at 1 year.

Taxonomy and geographical variation
Now considered monotypic, though historically three races were recognized. Variations now thought too slight to justify subspecific separation.

▼ Adult Northern Waterthrush.

♂

♀

Yellow Warbler

♀ 1st-win

♂ br

♂ win

Northern Waterthrush

Blackpoll Warbler

ad

♀ br

Yellow-rumped Warbler

♀ br

♂ br

New World sparrows and buntings

Despite their name, New World Sparrows are not close relatives of the sparrows of the Old World (none of which are Arctic breeders, though the House Sparrow (*Passer domesticus*) breeds in Iceland and in Fennoscandia). The family to which New World sparrows belong, the Emberizidae, also includes the buntings. Ancestors of buntings almost certainly evolved in North America before crossing to Eurasia, probably via Beringia. Several New World sparrows and buntings breed in the Arctic, while a number of other species breed at the Arctic fringe. Lincoln's Sparrow (*Melospiza lincolnii*) breeds in central Alaska (though it is uncommon in the west and south-west), in northern Yukon and in the Northwest Territories. It also breeds around the southern shore of Hudson Bay and in southern Quebec and Labrador. The Dark-eyed Junco (*Junco hyemalis*) has a similar range, while the Song Sparrow (*Melospiza melodia*) only breeds as far north as southern Alaska, though it also breeds across the Aleutian chain and on the southern shore of Hudson Bay.

▲ Song Sparrow on Unalaska.

In the Palearctic, Little Buntings (*Emberiza pusilla*) occur in northern Sweden and Finland, and across Russia. Though essentially sub-Arctic, they can be found north of the timberline, though not in the far north. By contrast, the Rustic Bunting (*E. rustica*), which has a similar range, does not appear beyond the timberline. The Yellow-Breasted Bunting (*E. aureola*) breeds in Finland and has a similar Russian range. The Reed Bunting (*E. schoeniclus*) breeds in Fennoscandia and European Russia, but also throughout Kamchatka, while Pallas's Reed Bunting (*E. pallasi*) breeds in Asian Russia and, occasionally, in Kamchatka. Finally, the Japanese Gray Bunting (*E. variabilis*) breeds in southern Kamchatka.

American Tree Sparrow
Spizella arborea

Identification
See p. 332

A long-tailed, round-headed sparrow. Adult birds have a rufous cap and eye-line (behind the eye only), the rest of the head being gray or gray-buff. The bill is bicolored, the upper mandible dark gray, the lower mandible yellow with a dark tip. The iris is dark brown. The throat is gray, occasionally smudged pale rufous. There is a thin, dark malar stripe, but this is not always distinct. The underparts are gray, with ragged rufous patches on the sides of the breast, an isolated dark brown patch at the center of the breast, and extensive buff washing on the flanks. The vent is cream-buff. The upperparts are chestnut with darker streaking, the tail gray-brown, the outer feathers paler. The upperwing median coverts are gray-brown, the greater coverts chestnut, each with white tips, these forming two distinct wingbars. The secondaries are chestnut, fringed gray, the primaries dark gray-brown, fringed paler. The underwing-coverts are buff or buff-gray. The legs and feet are brown. Juveniles are as the adults, but the head is buff, streaked darker (though still with the rufous cap) and the breast and flanks are heavily dark-streaked. Chicks have sparse gray-brown down on the back and thighs.

Confusion species
None within the region. The rufous cap distinguishes American Tree Sparrow from possible confusion species.

Size
L: 5–6 in. (13–15 cm). WS: 8½–10 in. (22–25 cm). W: ½–⅞ oz. (13–25 g).

Voice
Usually silent, except during breeding season. Song is both

▼ American Tree Sparrow, Churchill.

▲ Adult American Tree Sparrow, Barren Lands, Northwest Territories. Note the distinctive rufous cap.

clear and sweet, a delightful *swee-swee-tsi-tsi*. The call is a curious *teedle-eet*.

Distribution
Nearctic. Breeds in central and western Alaska (though uncommon in the north), throughout the Yukon and much of mainland Northwest Territories (to the north coast in each of the latter two). Breeds on the shores of Hudson Bay and in northern Quebec and Labrador. Prefers shrubby tundra and dwarf conifers. Migratory, moving to the northern and central of the continental United States, where it is found at woodland edges and at the hedged boundaries of fields.

Diet
Seeds, berries and insects.

Breeding
Gregarious in winter, when birds join mixed sparrow flocks and roost communally. Highly territorial at breeding sites. Males sing to establish a territory and attract females. Pair-bond probably monogamous and seasonal. Nests on or near the ground, concealed by a tussock or by a mossy hummock on dry tundra. The nest is a cup of vegetation lined with grass and feathers. Four to five pale blue or green eggs speckled red-

brown; some of these, or excess eggs, may be dumped in other nests, especially those of the Savannah Sparrow. Eggs are incubated by female only for 11–13 days. Chicks nidicolous and altricial. Brooded by female only, but fed by both parents. Fledge at 8–10 days, but are fed for two or three weeks before becoming independent. Thought to breed at 1 year.

Taxonomy and geographical variation
Polytypic. The nominate race breeds east of the Mackenzie Delta. *S. a. ochracea* breeds in Alaska, along the Yukon and in the Mackenzie Delta. It is larger and paler than the nominate.

Fox Sparrow
Passerella iliaca

Identification See p. 332
A large, dark, bulky sparrow. The adult bird has a rufous and gray head, the patterning somewhat variable, but essentially the supercilium, a patch below the eye and a larger patch on the sides of the neck are gray, and the crown, ear-coverts and cheeks are rufous. However, there is often streaking, so the overall impression can be of a gray-and-rufous-streaked head (though the supercilium is usually distinct). The bill is yellow-brown, the lower mandible paler than the upper and more yellow. The iris is dark brown. The throat is white with broad rufous malar stripes. The underparts are white, the breast heavily spotted rufous, the spots forming a breast-band and striping that fades away on the lower belly, though continuing on the flanks. The undertail-coverts are also spotted rufous. The upperparts are streaked gray and rufous, the rump unmarked gray, the tail rufous. The upperwing is rufous, the median and greater coverts tipped buff to give two wingbars, the flight feathers fringed darker. Underwing-coverts are gray, splashed with rufous, the flight feathers darker. Legs and feet

▼ Adult Fox Sparrow of the nominate race, Nome, Alaska.

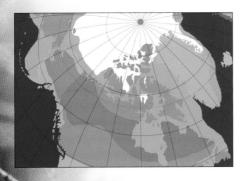

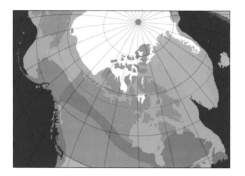

Polytypic and disputed. Some authorities consider the Fox Sparrow to be a single species with four subspecies across North America; others recognize up to 19 subspecies. The Red Fox Sparrow, which comprises the nominate race plus several similar subspecies, breeds in a band across the continent from western Alaska to the Labrador coast. The Sooty Fox Sparrow (*P. unalaschensis*) occurs in the Aleutians and southeastern Alaska. It is uniform brown above (varying from mid-brown to dark brown) and heavily brown spotted below. The other subspecies are extralimital.

are pale pink-brown. Juveniles are as adults, but the head and back are plain brown, rump and tail rufous, and underparts pale buff, heavily streaked brown. Downy chicks are gray-brown.

Confusion species
None within the region. Most Arctic Fox Sparrows are distinctively rufous.

Size
L: 6¼–7½ in. (16–19 cm). WS: 10–11 in. (25–28 cm). W: 1–1¼ oz. (28–38 g).

Voice
Usually silent except during breeding season. The song is arguably the finest of all the sparrows, a clear warbling *weet-weeto* with the pitch altering at each change of note. Call is a sharp, harsh *chip*.

Distribution
Nearctic. Breeds in central and western Alaska, the Yukon and Northwest Territories, on the southern shores of Hudson Bay and in central Quebec and Labrador. Prefers dense thickets, particularly in marshland, close to the forest edge. Migratory, moving to the eastern and western coasts of the United States, farther inland on the eastern side. Wintering birds occur in similar habitat.

Diet
Seeds, arthropods and small mollusks. The birds often forage on the ground, occasionally using a "double-scratch" where both feet are drawn back simultaneously to expose sub-surface food. Captures insects in the air. In winter, the birds chiefly feed on seeds, fruits and buds.

Breeding
Gregarious in winter with small flocks forming on migration. Solitary at the breeding sites. Male sings and chases rivals to establish territory. Male has wing-droop and wing-quiver mating displays. Pair-bond is monogamous and thought to be seasonal. Nests on the ground in thickets or low in trees or shrubs. The nest is built by female only; it is cup of twigs and grasses lined with grass and moss. Two to five pale blue-green eggs, spotted or blotched red-brown; incubated for 12–14 days by female only. Chicks nidicolous and altricial. Brooded by female only, but fed by both birds (though mostly by female). Fledge at 9–11 days. Thought to breed at 1 year.

Golden-crowned Sparrow
Zonotrichia atricapilla

Identification See p. 332
A large, rather plain sparrow. Adults have a yellow crown stripe, becoming paler toward the rear of the crown. On each side of the stripe are broad, very dark brown bands extending to the eye and almost to the nape. The nape and rest of the head are gray, the lores yellowish-gray. The bill is bicolored, the upper mandible dark gray-brown, the lower mandible paler and occasionally tinged yellow. The iris is brown. The underparts are gray, the flanks smudged buff or richly buff. The undertail is white. The upperparts are gray-brown, the back and scapulars streaked dark brown, the rump unmarked. The long tail is brown and slightly notched. The upperwing-coverts are rufous, the median and greater coverts tipped white to form two white wingbars. The flight feathers are gray-brown. The underwing-coverts are pale rufous. Non-breeding adults lose the broad dark crown side stripes, which become narrower and lighter. The legs and feet are pinkish-brown. Juveniles have a head pattern as adults, but the central crown stripe is buff-brown, the side strips gray-brown and not well defined against the overall gray-brown head. The upperparts are duller and more evenly brown, the underparts cream-buff with heavy dark spotting. First-winter birds are as non-breeding, but with

▼ Golden-crowned Sparrow, Cold Bay.

the head pattern poorly defined. Chicks have sparse gray down on crown and back. Feathers erupt at 3 days.

Confusion species
Harris's and White-crowned Sparrows are similar in shape, but they are distinctively marked and have pink bills.

Size
L: 6–7 in. (15–18 cm). WS: 8 1/2–10 in. (22–25cm). W: 3/4–1 1/4 oz. (22–35 g).

Voice
Vocal at all times. Song is a series of three descending whistles, *seee-seee-seee*, often written as "oh dear me" (or even as "three blind mice"). Call is a loud, harsh *chink*.

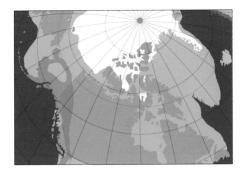

Distribution
Nearctic. Breeds in the Aleutians (to Unimak Island) and western Alaska, but uncommon in central Alaska and rare in the north. Limited Canadian range, extending southward only across southern Yukon and into British Columbia. Usually found in thickets or dwarf conifers close to the forest edge. Migratory, moving to the western coast of the United States, where it is found in thickets and field hedgerows.

Diet
Omnivorous, taking buds, seeds and terrestrial arthropods, and vegetable matter in winter.

Breeding
Gregarious on migration and in winter, but territorial at breeding sites. Males sing to establish a territory, raising their golden crowns as a threat to invaders. Once established, the pair forages together. Pair-bond is monogamous and probably seasonal. Nest is set in shrubs or other cover. The nest is a cup of grasses and twigs, lined with fine grass and hair, apparently constructed by the female only. Three to four pale blue or pale green eggs speckled or spotted red-brown; incubated by female only for 11–13 days. Chicks

nidicolous and altricial. Brooded by female only, but fed by both parents. Fledge at 9–11 days, but apparently stay with parents for longer. Breed at 1 year.

Taxonomy and geographical variation
Monotypic.

Harris's Sparrow
Zonotrichia querula

Identification
See p. 332

The largest of the New World Sparrows. Adult bird has black crown, face and throat, the frontal color extending back to the eye. There is a dark eye-stripe, sometimes curving down and then back toward the front of the head to form a semicircle around a gray-brown ear-covert/cheek-patch. However, this crescent is often ill-defined or absent, though the gray-brown patch is still visible. The rest of the head is gray, the nape brown. The bill is pink, the iris brown. The throat is black. A thin, ragged black necklace separates the head from the white underparts. A small, ragged black bib is below the necklace, and there are very dark brown or black smudges on the flanks. The mantle and scapulars are brown, streaked dark brown. The rump is gray-brown and unmarked. The tail is brown and slightly notched. The upperwing is brown (often chestnut), the median and greater coverts white-tipped to form two white wingbars. The secondaries are brown, the primaries darker. The underwing-coverts are pale brown. The legs and feet are pale pinkish-brown. Non-breeding adults maintain the black face and crown, but the head becomes pale chestnut and the facial crescent darker. Juveniles have a plain brown head, with hints of the adult dark facial crescent. The forehead and crown are streaked darker. The throat is white, streaked black. The underparts are white or pale buff, heavily spotted with brown.

▼ Harris's Sparrow, Hood River, Nunavut, Canada.

There is a black bib. The upperparts are as the adult, but pale chestnut. First-winter birds are as the non-breeding adults, but the black crown is smaller and less distinct, the throat white and defined by dark brown malar stripes and a ragged necklace. The underparts are unmarked white, apart from a smudged black bib and dark flecks on the flanks. Chicks have sparse gray down.

Confusion species
None.

Size
L: 6¼–7½ in. (16–19 cm). WS: 9–11 in. (23–28 cm). W: 1¼–1½ oz. (35–45 g).

Voice
Vocal at all times. Song is a series of clear whistles on the same pitch, *seee-seee-seee*. The call is a harsh *chip*.

Distribution
Nearctic. Breeds in a broad band across Canada from the Mackenzie Delta to southwestern Hudson Bay. Prefers the forest edge, but often seen far north on the tundra in vegetated river valleys. Migratory, moving to south-central United States, where it occurs in field hedges, low scrub and at the woodland edge.

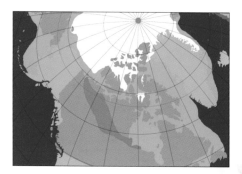

Diet
Omnivorous. Takes fruits and seeds, conifer needles and terrestrial arthropods. Winter birds have a similar diet.

Breeding
Gregarious in winter with large flocks forming, but solitary at the breeding sites. No known displays, but male presumably defends his territory by singing. Pair-bond apparently monogamous and seasonal. Nest is a scrape in the ground, a layer of moss and lichen covered with dry grass, apparently constructed by female only. Three to four eggs ranging from pale to dark green, spotted or blotched brown; incubated by female only for 12–14 days. Chicks nidicolous and altricial. Brooded by female only, but fed by both parents. Fledge at 8–10 days, but leave the nest before hiding locally, and are fed for another two weeks. Thought to breed at 1–2 years.

Taxonomy and geographical variation
Monotypic.

Savannah Sparrow
Passerculus sandwichensis

Identification See p. 332
A small, streaked sparrow. Adults have two brown crown stripes separated by a white, brown-streaked crown, with a brown stripe from the rear of the eye and brown ear-coverts. There is usually a yellow supercilium and lore spot, but on some individuals these can be indistinct. The bill is pink-brown, the upper mandible darker than the lower. The iris is dark brown. The throat and sides of the neck are white, divided by dark brown malar stripes. The underparts are white or pale buff, with dark brown streaking on the breast and flanks. The back, mantle, scapulars and rump are brown, streaked darker, the feathers fringed paler to give an overall mottled appearance. The notched tail is brown, sometimes paler on the outer feathers. The upperwing is brown, darker on the flight feathers; the median and greater coverts are paler tipped to give two, often indistinct, wingbars. The underwing-coverts are gray-brown. Some birds are washed rufous overall, others washed gray. The legs and feet are pink or pink-brown. Juveniles and First-winter birds are as the adults, but the head pattern is less distinct and there is more streaking on both the under- and upperparts. Chicks have sparse gray down on crown and back, then gray down at 5–6 days.

Confusion species
None. The streaked plumage and yellow lores are distinctive.

Size
L: 5½–6¼ in. (14–16 cm). WS: 8½–10 in. (22–25 cm). W: ¾–⅞ oz. (16–24 g).

▼ Adult Savannah Sparrow, Victoria Island.

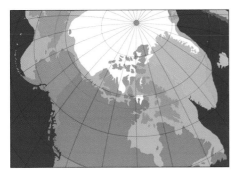

Voice

Vocal in the breeding season. Song is a series of buzzes that descend in pitch, often begun with shorter notes *ti-ti-tsee-tsee*. Call is sharp, high *seet*.

Distribution

Nearctic. Breeds throughout Alaska and northern Canada and on the southern Arctic islands (e.g., Victoria Island). Also breeds through southern Canada and the northern United States. Prefers open country, usually damp tundra or near pools in drier areas. Resident, partially migratory or migratory, depending on location. Migrants head for United States, Central America and Caribbean Islands, where they occur on fields and other open areas.

Diet

Omnivorous. Takes seeds, fruits and invertebrates, almost exclusively obtained by foraging on the ground, but will also feed on insect larvae from low branches.

Breeding

Gregarious in winter, though does not flock with other sparrows, but solitary at breeding sites. Male sings from an exposed perch to secure territory; this and flights around territory help attract female. Pair-bond is monogamous in the northern extremes of the range; southern males are polygynous. Nest is on the ground, usually well hidden, but sometimes in surprisingly open country. Nest is a cup of local vegetation lined with fine grasses, constructed by the female only. Two to six pale green, pale blue or cream eggs, spotted or speckled brown; incubated by female only for 10–12 days. Chicks nidicolous and altricial. Brooded chiefly by female, but fed by both parents, almost exclusively with insects. Fledge at 9–12 days and disperse immediately. Breed at 1 year.

Taxonomy and geographical variation

Polytypic. The nominate race breeds in the Aleutians and on the Alaska Peninsula. It is the largest of the 21 subspecies identified by some authorities. *P. s. athinus* breeds in the rest of Alaska and across northern Canada to Hudson Bay. It is as the nominate, but smaller. There is a clinal variation in size across the Alaska Peninsula from the large nominate to the smaller *athinus*. *P. s. labradorius* breeds east of Hudson Bay. It is darker and more heavily streaked on the underparts. The remaining subspecies are extralimital.

White-crowned Sparrow
Zonotrichia leucophrys

Identification See p. 332

Adult has a white crown stripe extending from just behind bill. To each side are broad black stripes that meet at the bill. The broad supercilium is white and there is a narrower black stripe from the rear of the eye. The lore is black. The remaining head and the nape are gray or gray-brown. The bill is pink or pink-yellow. The iris is dark brown. The underparts are gray and unmarked, the throat and upper breast paler, the flanks brown. The mantle and scapulars are brown, fringed paler giving the upperparts a streaked appearance. The rump is gray-brown and only lightly streaked. The long tail is unmarked gray-brown and slightly notched. The upperwing is brown, the median and greater coverts tipped white to give two white wingbars. The underwing-coverts are gray-brown. Legs and feet are yellow-brown. Juveniles do not have the adult head pattern, the head instead pale brown, streaked darker overall. The underparts are buff and heavily streaked. First-winter adults have head pattern as adult, but with buff median crown stripe and supercilium, and dark brown lateral and eye-stripes. Chicks have sparse mid-gray down on crown and back.

Confusion species

The white crown is diagnostic from other species of New World sparrows. Juveniles may be confused with Savannah Sparrows, but they are plainer and lack the yellow lores.

▼ Adult White-crowned Sparrow of race *gambelii*, Nunavut, Canada.

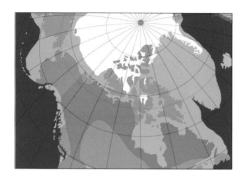

Lapland Longspur
(Lapland Bunting)
Calcarius lapponicus

Identification
See p. 333
A long-winged, stout-billed bunting. Breeding males have a black head with a buff-white supercilium that extends to the side of the nape, then curves to return toward the throat before continuing on to the breast. The bill is yellow or even orange, with a small black tip. The iris is brown. The black of the head continues over the throat and breast, separated into a bib by the two buff-white breast-side stripes. The rest of the underparts are white, often unmarked, but sometimes with black streaks on the flanks. The nape is bright chestnut. The upperparts are pale chestnut, streaked black, the streaks forming lines on the mantle, but breaking up as spotting on the rump. The tail is dark brown, fringed buff. The upperwing-coverts and tertials are black, fringed pale chestnut and tipped white to form two wingbars. The flight feathers are dark brown, fringed buff. The underwing is pale gray. Breeding females lack the bold head pattern, the crown instead being dark brown, the cheeks and ear-coverts dark brown. The throat is white with a ragged black malar stripe. The upper breast is dark brown. The underparts are cream rather than white. The nape and upperparts are as in breeding males, but more subdued. The legs and feet are dark brown or black. Non-breeding males are as the breeding female, but the crown is speckled buffish dark brown, the face pale chestnut, and the breast patch much more smudged. The upperparts are more chestnut-washed than those of the female, the greater coverts forming a distinct chestnut panel. The bill is paler. Non-breeding females are as breeding females but tawnier overall, particularly on the head and upper breast. The chestnut panel on the upperwing greater covert is as non-breeding male. Juveniles are as non-breeding females, but paler. Downy chicks are dark brown to yellowish-buff.

Confusion species
None for breeding males, but female and non-breeding birds are similar to Smith's Longspurs. The buffish underparts of Smith's Longspurs are diagnostic.

Size
L: 6–7 in. (15–18 cm). WS: 8½–10 in. (22–25 cm). W: ⅞–1¼ oz. (24–34 g).

Voice
Sing throughout the year, but especially vocal in the breeding season. Song is variable, but usually starts with several clear whistles, then a descending series of buzzes, *ti-tizeee-zeee-zeee*. Call is a sharp *pink*.

Distribution
Nearctic. Breeds throughout Alaska (though uncommon in the north) and across mainland Canada to the northern coast, but absent from the Arctic islands. Prefers thickets close to the forest edge, but also seen in more open areas. Migratory, moving to southern United States and Mexico, where similar habitat preferred.

Diet
Seeds and arthropods (chiefly insects), usually found by foraging on the ground. Winter birds take seeds, buds, fruits and arthropods.

Breeding
Gregarious in winter but solitary at the breeding sites. Male establishes a territory by singing and chasing rivals. Pair-bond is monogamous and seasonal. Nests above ground (e.g., on a tussock) if a suitable site is available, otherwise constructed on the ground. Nest is a cup of grass and twigs lined with dry grass and hair made by female only. Three to seven green, blue-green or blue eggs, spotted and blotched red-brown; incubated by female only for 10–14 days. Chicks nidicolous and altricial. Brooded by female only, but fed by both parents. Fledge at 8–10 days, but fed for 8–10 days more before becoming independent. Breed at 1 year.

Taxonomy and geographical variation
Polytypic. The nominate race breeds in eastern Canada westward to central Manitoba. *Z. l. gambelii* breeds from central Manitoba westward. It has a white median crown-stripe extending to the bill, and the lores are pale gray. The bill is either orange-pink or orange-yellow. There are three other extralimital subspecies.

▶ Recently fledged Lapland Bunting, south Greenland.

▶ Adult male Lapland Longspur of the race *subcalcaratus* in breeding plumage, southern Greenland.

Size
L: 5–6¼ in. (15–16 cm). WS: 10–11 in. (25–28 cm). W: ³/₄–1 oz. (20–30 g).

Voice
Vocal at all times. Song is a repeated series of tinkling notes, *fretle-titi-free-free*. Call is a rattling *pic-tic*.

Distribution
Circumpolar. Breeds along the western coast of Greenland from southern tip to Thule, and on the southeastern coast. Rare in the northeast. Breeds in northern Scandinavia and across Russia, north to the coast and on the southern island of Novaya Zemlya, the New Siberia Islands and on Wrangel Island. In North America, breeds throughout Alaska, on Bering Sea islands and across Canada, including Arctic islands north to Ellesmere. Found on tundra, preferring shrubby and damp areas, avoiding stony or bare ground. Migratory, with Eurasian birds moving to a broad belt across eastern central Europe and southern Russia, and North American and Greenlandic birds moving to the southern United States. Wintering birds favor broad, flat moorland or cultivated fields.

Diet
Insects in the breeding season, supplemented by seeds, which form the main winter diet. Forages mainly on the ground or in low bushes, but will jump to catch flying insects.

Breeding
Gregarious at all times, but less so at breeding sites. Male song is often performed in flight, the bird rising to about 33 ft. (10 m) then parachuting back to earth with wings held high. On the ground, the male stands with bill raised to display the black throat and chases females who enter territory. Females have been observed to beg, but courtship-feeding appears rare. Pair-bond is monogamous, of unknown duration, but polygyny has been observed and in some adjacent pairs shared parentage results in shared feeding of young. Nests on the ground, on a dry spot in a damp area, usually sheltered or concealed by vegetation. Avoids stony ground. The nest is a cup of grass or lichen that incorporates numerous *Lagopus* grouse feathers, built by female only. Three to seven dark brown eggs, streaked black; incubated by female only for 11–13 days. Chicks

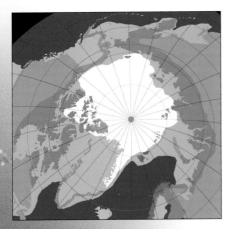

▼ A Lapland Longspur nest with four eggs, St. Lawrence Island.

nidicolous and altricial. Brooded mainly by female, fed mainly by male. Fledge at 8–11 days, but leave nest before capable of flight, and are independent in a further 7–10 days. Breed at one year.

Taxonomy and geographical variation

Polytypic. The nominate race breeds in Eurasia east to the Kolyma Delta. *C. l. alascensis* breeds in eastern Eurasia, Alaska and Canada east to the Mackenzie Delta. It is paler with almost no chestnut tinge. *C. l. subcalcaratus* is found from the Mackenzie across Canada, and on Greenland. It is larger and heavier, with a longer bill and wings. *C. l. coloratus* breeds on the Commander Islands. It is larger than the nominate and much darker. *C. l. kamtschaticus* occurs on Kamchatka. It is dark as *coloratus*, but its size is as the nominate. Some authorities combine the nominate with *subcalcaratus* and also *coloratus* with *kamtschaticus*.

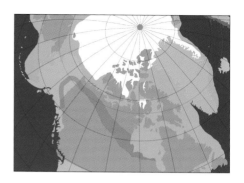

Smith's Longspur
Calcarius pictus

Identification`   See p. 333

A long-tailed buffish bunting. Breeding males have a dark brown and black crown, sometimes flecked white at the rear, a white supercilium and lores, a black stripe from the rear of the eye, white ear-coverts and a broad black band from the eye around the white ear, which meets the black eye-stripe and black crown. The bill is brown-yellow, darker at the top, the iris brown. The nape, throat, neck-sides and underparts are unmarked rich buff-ochre, the throat and neck-sides separated from the black face band by thin white stripes. The upperparts are black, fringed buff to give the impression of streaking. The tail is dark buff-brown, the two outer feathers white. The upperwing lesser coverts are black (anterior) and white (posterior), the remaining coverts dark brown, the median and greater coverts tipped white to give

wingbars. The flight feathers are dark brown. The underwing is uniformly gray-brown. Breeding females are as the males, but the head is dark brown and buff rather than black and white, the upperparts duller and more gray-brown and the underparts finely streaked brown. The legs and feet are brown to dark brown. Non-breeding males are as breeding, but head color is dark brown, the whole finely streaked so that the bold pattern is much less distinct. The underparts are finely streaked brown. Non-breeding females are as non-breeding males, but paler. Juveniles are as non-breeding males, but with heavier streaking on the underparts. Chicks are naked apart from buff down on the crown and back.

Confusion species

None for breeding males. Buffish underparts of females and non-breeding males distinguish from Lapland Buntings.

Size

L: 5½–6¼ in. (14–16 cm). WS: 10–10½ in. (25–27 cm). W: ¾–1 oz. (20–28 g).

Voice

Song is a high-pitched warble, *tee-tee-swee-zeet*. Call is a sharp, rattling *tic-tic* similar to that of the Lapland Longspur. There is also a nasal buzz.

Distribution

Nearctic. Rare in central and northern Alaska. Breeds in northern Yukon and Northwest Territories, then in a thin band southward to and around southern Hudson Bay, as far as its junction with James Bay. Prefers damp tundra close to the timberline. Migratory, moving to central and southern United States, where it favors short grassland such as golf courses.

▼ Adult male Smith's Longspur in breeding plumage.

Diet
Chiefly seeds, but insects during the summer. Forages mostly on the ground.

Breeding
Gregarious in the winter, loosely so at the breeding sites. Male sings from an elevated perch at the breeding sites, but territories are very loose, with those of several males overlapping. The males will chase one another, but tolerate one another more than might be expected. Both sexes are polygamous, and no pair-bonds are formed. When the female is ready to lay, she will mate with two or three males repeatedly (up to 350 times each week). Males also mate with two or three females. Males often attempt to guard a female, but this usually fails. Nests on dry ground, usually close to a hummock. The nest is a cup of grasses lined with hair and *Lagopus* grouse feathers, constructed by the female only. Four pale green or gray-green eggs, dotted, streaked and blotched dark purple-brown; incubated by the female only for 12–14 days. Chicks are nidicolous and altricial and usually the brood has several fathers. Brooded chiefly by female, but males have been observed to brood. Fed by both female and male birds. Chicks leave the nest at 7–9 days, but are not fledged until around 12 days and are fed until about three weeks, when they become independent. Breed at 1 year.

Taxonomy and geographical variation
Monotypic.

▼ Adult male Snow Bunting in breeding plumage, Bylot Island.

Snow Bunting
Plectrophenax nivalis

Identification   See p. 333
The most northerly breeding passerine. A Snow Bunting has even been observed at the North Pole (from a surfacing U.S. Navy submarine). Breeding males have white heads. The bill is black, the iris dark brown or black. The underparts are white. The mantle and scapulars are black, the lower back, rump and uppertail-coverts white, but heavily splattered black. The central tail is black, the outer three feathers white, thinly fringed black on the outer web. The upperwing shows black tertials, alula, tips of greater primary coverts and primaries. The remaining wing is white. The underwing is white apart from the black primary tips. Breeding females are as the male, but the black is replaced with brown and the head is dusted with dark brown spots or speckles. The legs and feet are dark gray. In non-breeding males, the black is replaced with pale rufous. The head has a dark brown crown, the nape and cheek are rufous. There is a (usually incomplete) rufous breast-band and rufous smudging on the flanks. The bill is yellow-brown.

Non-breeding females are as non-breeding males. Juveniles have head, back and underparts gray-brown (apart from white vent and undertail-coverts), with broad darker streaks (black on the upperparts) or, occasionally, mottling. The bill is brown. First-winter adults are as the winter adults, but the head is more uniformly rufous. Downy chicks are dark gray above, bare below.

Confusion species
McKay's Bunting is similar, but much whiter.

▲ Adult female Snow Bunting near Kongsfjorden, Svalbard.

Size
L: 6¼–7 in. (16–18 cm). WS: 12½–15 in. (32–38 cm). W: 1–2 oz. (30–45 g).

Voice
Song is musical *twee-turee-twee-turiwee*. Call is a loud, high *tweet*. There is also a hoarse buzz.

Distribution
Circumpolar. Breeds on the eastern and western coasts of Greenland to the far north, on Iceland, Jan Mayen, Bear Island and Svalbard, in northern Scandinavia and across Russia including all the Arctic islands, on eastern Kamchatka, the

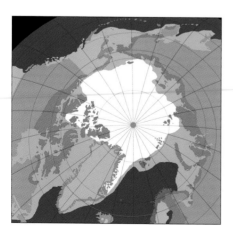

Commander Islands, Bering Sea islands and the Aleutians, and western and northern Alaska and northern Canada including all the Arctic islands. Found on rocky tundra, coastal tundra and cliffs. Often found close to northern settlements and is sometimes seen on nunataks (isolated rock outcrops). Migratory, though some Icelandic birds as well as Pribilof and Aleutian birds are resident. Eurasian birds move to Scotland and a broad band across central Europe (east from Denmark and Germany) and southern Russia, North American birds move to western Canada, the eastern seaboard of Canada and the northern United States. Birds from northeastern Greenland migrate, as might be expected, to Europe as far east as the Caspian Sea, but birds from southeastern Greenland move to the Great Lakes area of North America. This apparent anomaly makes sense if a globe is studied rather than an atlas. Winter birds occur on moorland, cultivated land and on beaches.

Diet
Chiefly seeds, but also invertebrates in the breeding season. Young birds are fed exclusively on invertebrates. Forages on the ground, occasionally on low branches.

Breeding
Typically gregarious in winter, forming solitary pairs in the breeding season. Male sing from the ground or from a prominent boulder to establish a territory. If a female enters the territory, the male stands in front of her, stretches his wings, fans his tail and turns to reveal his black pattern. He then pursues her to display again if she walks or flies away. Pair-bond is monogamous (polygamy observed in pairs at low latitudes, but in the high Arctic the pair must concentrate on a single brood as both time and food are limited). Pair-bond duration unknown. Nest set in a rock crevice, a "cave" in the scree at the base of a slope or under a boulder. Snow Buntings also nest in buildings in northern settlements and have been observed to use not only nest boxes but also old tin cans and even a frozen human corpse. Nest is a cup of grass and other vegetation lined with grass and feathers, constructed by female only; nests are sometimes reused. Four to six cream eggs, speckled or blotched red or black; incubated by female only for 12–13 days. Chicks nidicolous and altricial. Fed and cared for by both parents. Fledge in 10-17 days, but may leave nest before capable of flight. Fed for a further 8–12 days before becoming independent. Breed at 1 year.

Taxonomy and geographical variation
Polytypic. The nominate race breeds across North America, in Greenland, Svalbard and northern Fennoscandia. *P. n. vlasowae* breeds from the White Sea to the Bering Sea. It is paler than the nominate, with females less brown on the head and breast. The nominate and race *vlasowae* interbreed near the White Sea. *P. n. townsendi* breeds on the Commander Islands, the Pribilofs and on the western Aleutians east to Adak Island. It is larger with a heavier bill, but otherwise as *vlasowae*. The nominate and *townsendi* interbreed on the Aleutians. *P. n. insulae* breeds in Iceland. It is darker than the nominate, having more black on the wings and tail. The female of this race is also darker brown.

McKay's Bunting
Plectrophenax hyperboreus

Identification
See p. 333

A rare species with a population believed to number less than 6,000. Breeding males have white heads, underparts and upperparts. The bill and iris are black. The tail is white apart from the central two-four rectrices, which are black-tipped. The upperwing is white apart from a black alula and tertials, and black tips on the outer five primaries. The underwing is white. Breeding females are as male, but with some rufous speckling of the crown and forehead, and black streaking of the back. The legs and feet are dark brown. Non-breeding males have a rufous crown, ear-patch and smudging to the shoulder. Non-breeding females are as non-breeding males, but the rufous patches are darker. Juveniles have crown, back and breast mottled gray-brown, the back being black fringed buff, the rump brown and the bill yellow-brown. First-winter adults are as winter adults, but usually darker. Downy chicks are dark gray above, bare below.

Confusion species
Similar to Snow Bunting but much whiter.

Size
L: 6¼–7½ in. (16–19 cm). WS: 13½–16 in. (34–40 cm). W: about 2 oz. (45 g).

Voice
As Snow Bunting.

Distribution
Bering Sea islands. Breeds on Hall and St. Matthew Islands and, rarely, on the Pribilof Islands. Prefers upland, rocky tundra. Migratory, moving to the western coast of Alaska, from Nome to Cold Bay.

Diet
As Snow Bunting.

Breeding
As Snow Bunting.

Taxonomy and geographical variation
Monotypic. Formerly considered a subspecies (*P. nivalis hyperboreus*) of the Snow Bunting, but now generally considered to form a separate species.

Icterids
There are no Arctic members of this group, but two species, the Red-winged Blackbird (*Agelaius phoeniceus*) and Rusty Blackbird (*Euphagus carolinus*) must be mentioned. The Red-winged Blackbird breeds in the southern Northwest Territories and close to the southern shores of Hudson Bay, while the Rusty Blackbird has a more extensive northern range, breeding throughout Alaska (though it is nowhere common and is rare in the north), in the Yukon and Northwest Territories, around the southern shores of Hudson Bay and in Quebec and Labrador.

◄ Adult male McKay's Bunting, St. Paul.

PLATE 27: NEW WORLD SPARROWS

ad

Golden-crowned
Sparrow

ad

White-crowned Sparrow

ad
Z. l. gambelii

Savannah Sparrow

ad

**Harris's
Sparrow**

ad

ad
S. a. ochracea

**American Tree
Sparrow**

ad

Fox Sparrow

ad

ad

Sooty Fox
Sparrow
(P. unalaschensis)

PLATE 28: LONGSPURS AND BUNTINGS

♂ br

♀ br

juv

Lapland Bunting

♂ br

♀ br

Smith's Longspur

♀ br

Snow Bunting

♂ br

♀ br

♂ br

McKay's Bunting

Finches

The current distribution of finches implies an Old World origin, with New World species probably having crossed Beringia in an similar manner to the arrival of buntings in Eurasia, albeit in opposite directions. As a contrast to buntings, the finches generally prefer the seeds of dicots, opening them with the sharp edge of the lower mandible. One of the great joys of observing finches is watching them manipulate seeds with bill and tongue, flicking shards of husk away as the seed is reached and swallowed.

Several finch species familiar to European observers may be seen at the Arctic fringe in eastern Russia. Hawfinches (*Coccothraustes coccothraustes*) breed in southern Kamchatka; Eurasian Bullfinches (*Pyrrhula pyrrhula*) breed throughout Kamchatka, while Bramblings (*Fringilla montifringilla*) and Common Rosefinches (*Carpodacus erythrinus*) breed not only throughout Kamchatka, but also across Russia's Arctic fringe. Bullfinches and Bramblings also breed in northern Fennoscandia. A species that reaches the Arctic boundary that is far less familiar to European birders is the Oriental Greenfinch (*Carduelis sinica*), which breeds in southern Kamchatka.

Common Redpoll (Mealy Redpoll)
Carduelis flammea

Identification See p. 340
A small, brown-streaked finch. Breeding males have a red forecrown, with the rear crown and nape tawny brown, streaked darker. The lores are black, and there are small black patches above and below the bill. The forehead is buff. The rear cheek and ear-coverts are gray-brown, the supercilium paler. The bill is yellow-brown, the culmen and gonys black. The iris is dark brown. The front cheek, throat, breast and upper belly are rose-pink, fringed buff or white. The lower belly, vent and undertail-coverts are cream-buff, with dark brown streaking on the lower flanks and undertail. The upperparts are tawny, lined dark brown. The rump and uppertail-coverts are paler and unmarked or faintly lined dark brown. The tail is dark brown. The upperwing is dark brown, the median and greater coverts tipped pale buffish white to form two wingbars. The underwing-coverts and axillaries are pale gray. Breeding females are as breeding male, but have little or no rose-pink on the underparts. Non breeding males have much reduced rosy-pink on underparts and are paler overall. Non-breeding females are as breeding. Juveniles are as females, but lack the red cap and are more heavily streaked overall. First-winter males acquire the red cap, but lack the rose-pink underparts. Downy chicks are mid-gray.

Confusion species
Very similar to the Hoary Redpoll, but the latter is paler and less brown-washed, and the rose-pink underparts of the male Common Redpoll are deeper and brighter. The undertail-coverts of Common Redpoll are streaked, while those of the Hoary Redpoll are unmarked or only minimally streaked.

Size
L: 4½–5½ in. (11–14 cm). WS: 7¾–10 in. (20–25 cm). W: ⅓–½ oz. (11–18 g).

Voice
Song comprises call note and short trills, *chet-chet-chet-tweerrr*. Call is a hard, metallic *chet*. There is also a rapid, rattling *chichichi*, often heard in paired birds.

Distribution
Circumpolar. Breeds on the west coast of Greenland from the southern tip to Thule and on the east coast, but rare in the northeast. Breeds on Iceland, in northern Scandinavia and across Russia, but to northern coast only at the White Sea and in Chukotka. Breeds throughout Alaska (but uncommon in the north), and across the north Canadian mainland, but only on western Baffin Island. Seen on all forms of tundra, but chiefly on treeless ground if the area also has Hoary Redpolls, as the latter occupy Arctic Willow and birch. Some Greenlandic and most Icelandic birds are resident. Elsewhere partially migratory, some Greenland birds staying in Iceland, others joining Eurasian birds in northern and central Europe. Asian-Russian birds move to

▼ Common Redpoll, Yamalo-Nenetsky.

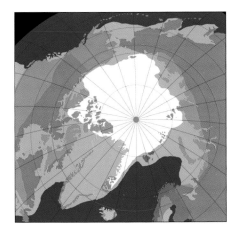

Japan and southeastern China, North American birds to southern Canada and northern United States. However, some Alaskan birds stay as far north as Fairbanks during the winter. Wintering birds occur on moors and heathland, and at the edges of woodland areas.

Diet
Seeds, foraged in trees and shrubs or on the ground, but also takes flower buds and invertebrates in summer.

Breeding
Gregarious at all times, less so at breeding sites. The male sings from a perch or in flight to establish a territory and advertise himself. When a female enters his territory he will chase her, each bird giving a rattling call. On the ground the male presents his side to female, then may take a short flight and return. Courtship-feeding occurs when the female begs with an open bill and wings quivering. Pair-bond is probably monogamous and seasonal only. Nest set in a tree or shrub and so, depending on site, can be at ground level or up to 13 ft. (4 m). Nest is a cup of twigs and grass, lined with finer material including hair and feathers; constructed by female only. Four to six light blue-green eggs, speckled red-brown; incubated by female for 10–12 days. Chicks nidicolous and altricial. Cared for and fed by both birds (initially with the male giving food to the female). Fledge at 9–14 days, but may leave nest before being capable of flight. Fed for a further 10–14 days before becoming independent. Breed at 1 year.

Taxonomy and geographical variation
Polytypic. The nominate race breeds in northern Eurasia and mainland North America. *C. f. rostrata* breeds in Greenland, northern Labrador and on Baffin Island. It is larger and darker. Birds on Iceland are usually separated into an endemic subspecies, *C. f. islandica*. They are paler, and are very similar to nominate race Hoary Redpoll. A further race, *cabaret*, breeds in southern Scandinavia, throughout the British Isles and in central Europe. This is often considered a separate species, the Lesser Redpoll.

▶ Hoary Redpoll of race *exilipes*, Seward Peninsula.

Hoary Redpoll (Arctic Redpoll)
Carduelis hornemanni

Identification   See p. 340
Breeding males have red caps, black lores and small black patches at the upper and lower bill base. The rest of the head is pale gray or gray-brown, finely streaked darker on the crown, nape, ear-coverts, chin and throat. The bill is yellow-gray with a black culmen and gonys. The iris is dark brown. The upper breast is pale rose-pink, the remaining underparts cream with dark gray-brown streaks on the sides of the breast and flanks. The remaining underparts are unmarked. The upperparts are cream, with dark gray-brown streaking except on the rump and uppertail-coverts. The tail is dark gray. The upperwing is dark gray, the median and greater coverts white-tipped to form two wingbars. The underwing-coverts and axillaries are white, the remainder dark gray. Breeding females are as breeding males, but the breast lacks the rose-pink tinge, and the head and upperparts are washed buff. The legs and feet are dark brown. Non-breeding males lack the rose-pink breast. Non-breeding females are as breeding. Juveniles lack the red cap, the head being cream-buff streaked darker, the underparts more heavily streaked, the tail feathers fringed paler and the wing dark gray-brown rather than gray. First-winter birds are as winter adults, but washed brown on the upperparts. Downy chicks are mid-gray.

Confusion species
See Common Redpoll.

Size
L: 5–6 in. (13–15 cm). WS: 8–11 in. (21–28 cm). W: ⅓–½ oz. (11–16 g).

Voice
Less vocal than Common Redpoll, but voice identical. Some authorities claim that on average the Hoary voice is lower and

softer than that of the Common, but variability is such that this is debatable.

Distribution

Circumpolar. Breeds on the western coast of Greenland, but scarce, and in northeast, where it is rarer. Breeds in northern Scandinavia and across Russia, but to northern coast only at the White Sea and in Chukotka (though also breeds on southern island of Novaya Zemlya and on Wrangel Island). Breeds in western, northern and central Alaska and across northern Canada to Hudson Bay, around Ungava Bay and on the eastern Arctic islands of Baffin and Ellesmere. Found on Arctic Willow tundra. Resident or partial migrant, moving short distance only, to southern Scandinavia, sub-Arctic Russia and southern Canada, choosing similar habitat.

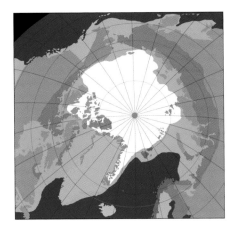

Diet

Mainly seeds of willow and birch, but also grass seeds and invertebrates in summer.

Breeding

Gregarious at all times, wintering birds sometimes flocking with Common Redpoll. Male sings to attract female and also sings when close to her. Male also courtship-feeds female by regurgitation. Pair-bond probably monogamous and seasonal. Nest set in dwarf willow or birch, usually close to the ground (but up to 7 ft./2 m if tree is tall enough; in the high Arctic the nest is inevitably at ground level). Nest is a cup of twigs and grass lined with hairs and feathers. Three to six brown-speckled light blue-green eggs, incubated by female only for 11–12 days. Chicks nidicolous and altricial, cared for and fed by both birds by regurgitation. Fledge in 9–14 days and thought to be independent in another two weeks. Thought to breed at 1 year.

Taxonomy and geographical variation

Polytypic. The nominate race breeds in Greenland and eastern Canada (including Baffin and Ellesmere islands). *C. h. exilipes* breeds throughout the rest of the range. It is smaller and paler.

▲ Adult male Pine Grosbeak of race *leucura*, Churchill.

Pine Grosbeak
Pinicola enucleator

Identification See p. 340

A very large, long-tailed finch. Breeding males have red heads with black lore, black at the base of the bill, a pale gray crescent below the eye and an indistinct dark brown crescent around the ear-coverts. The bill is dark gray, the iris dark brown. The underparts are red, becoming gray on the lower belly, vent and undertail-coverts, the flanks smudged gray, with pale fringing on some feathers to give a vague gray scalloping. The mantle is red-brown with dark brown chevrons, the rump and uppertail-coverts dark gray, fringed red. The tail is dark brown to black. The upperwing is dark brown to black, the marginal coverts fringed pink, the median and greater coverts tipped white to give two white wingbars. The underwing is mid-gray. Breeding females are patterned as males, but the head color varies from russet to golden-yellow, the underparts and upperparts are golden-yellow scalloped gray. Juveniles have brown-yellow heads and upperparts and pale gray-brown underparts. The wings and tail are paler, the upperwing with two indistinct buff bars. First-winter adults resemble breeding females, but male is duller, and female much less yellow. Legs and feet are dark gray; those of juveniles and first-winter birds may be tinged pink. Downy chicks are dark gray, rapidly becoming browner.

Confusion species

None.

Size

L: 7–9 in. (18–23 cm). WS: 12½–17½ in. (32–37 cm). W: 1¾–2 oz. (50–60 g).

Voice
Song is a delightful series of clear, melodic whistles, more a yodel than a warble. Call is a loud *tee-you, tee-you*.

Distribution
Circumpolar. Breeds in northern Scandinavia and across Russia to the timberline. In North America, breeds throughout Alaska to the timberline (but uncommon everywhere and rare in the north), and to the timberline across Canada, including the southern shores of Hudson Bay and southern Labrador. Found in both deciduous and conifer forests. Either resident and partially migratory, with some Eurasian birds moving to central Scandinavia and to the southern Russia taiga belt, North American birds to moving to southern Canada and northern U.S. Found in both deciduous and conifer forests in winter.

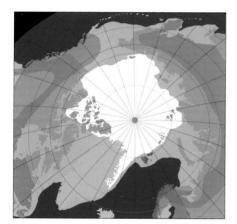

Diet
Buds and seeds, but also shoots and berries of a wide range of tree species. Also takes invertebrates, including flying insects in the breeding season.

Breeding
Gregarious in winter, solitary at breeding sites. Both adults sing, though male song from an exposed perch is most clearly an advertisement. Male also assumes horizontal position with drooped wings and tail-flicking. Courtship-feeding is a regular feature of pairing. Pair-bond apparently monogamous and seasonal. Nest set relatively low (up to 13 ft./4 m) in a conifer. Nest is mass of twigs and grass lined with moss and lichen, constructed by female only. Three to five light blue-green eggs blotched black, incubated by female only for 13–14 days. Chicks nidicolous and altricial. Cared for by both birds and fed by both birds from gular pouches on each side of the tongue, these developing during the breeding season. Fledge at 13–18 days, but are fed for a further 21 days before becoming independent. Thought to breed at 1 year.

Taxonomy and geographical
Polytypic, with some authorities recognizing as many as 11 subspecies. The nominate breeds in northern Eurasia east to the Yenisey River. *P. e. pacata* breeds east of the Yenisey to the

Kolyma and on the western shores of the Sea of Okhotsk. It has a shorter bill than the nominate. *P. e. kamtschatkansis* breeds in Chukotka, on the northern shores of the Sea of Okhotsk and throughout Kamchatka. It has an even smaller bill. *P. e. leucura* (which may incorporate several subspecies) breeds across North America from central Alaska to the Atlantic coast. It is larger and paler than the nominate. *P. e. flammula* breeds in southwestern Alaska (primarily the Alaska Peninsula and Kodiak Island). It is larger and more orange than the nominate.

Gray-crowned Rosy-finch
Leucosticte tephrocotis

Until 1983, the various forms of north Pacific Rosy-finch were considered to be subspecies of a single species. At that time, the Nearctic and Palearctic birds were separated into different taxa, though the taxonomy remains confused.

Identification See p. 340
This description refers to the Aleutian subspecies *L. t. griseonucha*. Breeding males have black forehead, the color extending downward between the eye and the upper mandible. The remaining head is silver gray. The iris is brown, the bill dark gray or black, the throat black. There is a strong delineation between the head and throat and the chocolate-brown breast. The breast color merges into the mid-brown belly, becoming red-brown, occasionally pink-brown towards the vent. The undertail is dark gray-brown. The flanks are lightly streaked dark brown. The lower nape, back and scapulars are tawny brown, streaked black because of black feather shafts. The rump, uppertail-coverts and notched tail are gray-brown, with darker tips and often a pink wash. The upperwing is mid-brown with pink tips so that from above the wing has two pink covert-bands. The primaries are also pink-edged so the outer wing appears brown, washed pink. The underwing

▼ Gray-crowned Rosy-finch of race *griseonucha*, Unalaska.

shows dark brown coverts but pale pink-gray flight feathers, which appear translucent. Breeding females are as males, but duller overall. Non-breeding adults are overall duller and brown, rather than pink, washed and they do not have the distinctive black head color (it is dark gray and ragged). The bill becomes yellow. Juveniles are as non-breeding adults, but lack any crown color, and pale feather edging gives a "scaly" appearance. Chicks have gray down.

Confusion species
None.

Size
L: 5½–7 in. (14–18 cm). WS: 12½–14½ in. (32–37 cm). W: ¾–⅞ oz. (20–25 g). Pribilof birds: length up to 8½ in. (22 cm) and weight 1½–2 oz. (40–60 g).

Voice
Song is a sharply rising and crescendoing *chew* that rapidly falls and quietens.

Distribution
Nearctic northern Pacific. Breeds in central and southwestern Alaska, on the Aleutians and on the Pribilofs. Rare in northern Alaska and northern Bering Sea islands. Also breeds in southern Alaska, Yukon and British Columbia, and Pacific Northwest of United States. Prefers upland or tundra areas, but found at coast in Aleutians. Some authorities claim the species is the highest-nesting bird in North America (in the Rocky Mountains). Pribilof and Aleutian birds are resident; central Alaskan birds migrate as far as northern California. Winter birds occur in open country, again mostly upland.

Diet
Chiefly seeds, but also insects and buds. Catches insects by pecking from vegetation and on the wing. Winter diet is similar.

Breeding
Gregarious in winter, solitary at breeding sites. Male sings to establish territory, but also threatens rivals with open bill and ruffled feathers. However, territory limited to area immediately surrounding nest. Male displays on the ground, waving wings and calling. Established pair nibble bills, and female begs for food. Pair-bond is monogamous and seasonal, but male guards female attentively, suggesting that extrapair

▲ Gray-crowned Rosy-finch of race *umbrina*, St. Paul, Pribilofs.

copulation may sometimes occur. Nests in crack in cliff. Aleutian birds frequently nest in crevices in buildings. Nest is large mass of vegetation lined with fine grass, hair and feathers. Two to six white or cream eggs, unmarked or sparsely speckled red-brown; incubated by female only for 12–16 days. Chicks nidicolous and altricial. Probably brooded by female only, but fed by both birds. Fledge at 15–22 days but are fed for a further period before independent. Breed at 1 year.

Taxonomy and geographical variation
Polytypic, but see also Asian Rosy-finch below. The nominate race breeds in Alaska's Brooks Range, in Yukon, and to the south. It is lighter brown than *griseonucha*, and the upper body color continues on the head and nape to eye level. *L. t. griseonucha* (described above) breeds on the Aleutian Islands and western Alaska Peninsula. *L. t. umbrina* breeds on the Pribilof Islands. It is darker and much larger than *griseonucha*. *L. t. littoralis* breeds in central Alaska to the western coast, southwestern Yukon and the Cascade Mountains. It is smaller than other forms with a smaller bill, and is paler and brighter than *griseonucha*. There are three extralimital subspecies.

Asian Rosy-finch
Leucosticte arctoa

Identification See p. 340
Very similar to the Gray-crowned Rosy-Finch, but the head is overall dark gray, rather than showing a distinct dark forehead. The nape is pale gray with a rosy tinge. The remaining plumage is as the Gray-crowned Rosy-finch, but it is washed silver on the underparts and upperwings.

Confusion species
None.

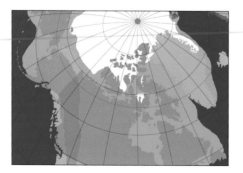

▲ Wintering Asian Rosy-finches in Japan. These birds are of the northeast Asian race *brunneonucha*.

Size

L: 5½–7 in. (14–18 cm). WS: 12½–14½ in. (32–37 cm). W: ³/₄–⁷/₈ oz. (20–25 g). Commander Island birds: length up to 9 in. (22 cm) and weight 1½–2 oz. (40–60 g).

Voice

As Gray-crowned Rosy-Finch, but softer.

Distribution

Palearctic northern Pacific. Breeds in upland areas of a north-south band of Siberia from the Lena Delta to the northern coast of the Sea of Okhotsk, and in a band from that coast westward to central Siberia. Breeds throughout Kamchatka and on the Commander and Kuril Islands. Prefers upland or tundra areas, but found at coast in islands. Migratory, moving to southern Siberia east to China and Japan. Winter birds occur in open country, again mostly upland.

Diet

As Gray-crowned Rosy-finch.

Breeding

Poorly studied. Gregarious in winter. Displays probably very similar to those of Gray-crowned Rosy-finch. Nests in crevices in rocky outcrops. Nest as Gray-crowned Rosy-finch. Usually 4–5 white, rose-tinged eggs, incubated by both birds, but mostly female for about 15 days. Chicks nidicolous and altricial. Probably brooded by female only, but apparently fed by both birds. Probably fledge at about 20 days. Thought to breed at 1 year.

Taxonomy and geographical variation

Still debated. Most authorities consider Palearctic birds to form a single species (the Asian Rosy-finch) with the nominate race breeding in the Altai Mountains and Mongolia, with subspecies elsewhere. Formerly the birds of Chukotka, Kamchatka and the Commander and Kuril Islands were regarded as a separate species, the Arctic Rosy-finch (*L. pustulata*), but most now consider this a subspecies, *L. a. brunneonucha*.

The birds of the Commander Islands provide an intriguing taxonomic puzzle. Some authorities lump them with the *brunneonucha* subspecies of Asian Rosy-finch; others split them off as a separate subspecies, *L. a. maxima*; and others consider the birds on the Commander Islands to form a subspecies of the Gray-crowned Rosy-finch. These birds are as large as the *umbrina* Pribilof race of Gray-crowned Rosy-finch (and larger than the Aleutian race, *griseonucha*). Genetic studies are needed to clear up this confusion.

In addition to the races discussed, there are five extralimital subspecies of Asian Rosy-finch.

A rosy-finch on the Commander Islands — possibly Asian, possibly Gray-crowned.

PLATE 29: FINCHES

Pine Grosbeak
♂

Common Redpoll
♂
♀

♂
C. h. exilipes
♀
C. h. exilipes

juv
C. h. exilipes

Hoary Redpoll
♂

Gray-crowned
Rosy-finch

♂
L. a. brunneonucha

Asian Rosy-finch

♂
L. t. griseonucha

♀
L. a. brunneonucha

Field guide to
Arctic Mammals

Shrews

The shrews or Soricidae are insectivores; they are the only members of the order Insectivora to have Arctic representatives. Arctic shrews belong to the subfamily Soricinae, the "red-toothed" shrews, so-called because of the red tips to their teeth. These are the result of iron-rich enamel, reflecting the tough nature of the diet of the animals. The Arctic species are all in the genus *Sorex*.

Shrews are tiny mammals with small eyes that are often difficult to distinguish as they are hidden in the fur. Vision seems to be poor. However, as shrews often hunt underground, either in their own tunnels or those of rodents, vision is less important than the senses of smell and hearing, which are acute. The nose is long, pointed and mobile, but the ears are often much less visible, particularly in *Sorex* species. Some *Sorex* generate ultrasound, using it as a basic navigational tool and as an echolocation system for finding prey.

Shrews have extraordinarily high metabolic rates, in part because they have the highest ratio of surface area to volume of all mammals. Heart rates of up to 1,000 beats per minute have been measured. These measures are invariably from frightened animals; so high does the heart rate rise that shrews may die when stressed (attributed to "fright," which is true even if not technically the exact cause of death), something to bear in mind if shrews are captured in the field. Capture is unlikely, however, as the animals are extremely elusive. There have been few studies of wild shrews, and much of our knowledge of their

biology comes from the study of captive animals. These studies are limited to very few species, so much of the information given in this section is sparse, particularly for the rarer Arctic species.

Because of their high metabolic rate, shrews must consume prodigious amounts of food each day. Although consumption depends on ambient temperature, on average a shrew must consume its own body weight in food daily, and lactating females consume perhaps double their body weight. Consequently, a shrew's life is spent in a whirl of foraging, with only short rest periods since the animal may die of starvation if it does not feed for more than a few hours. Shrews' perpetual hunger, combined with an unpleasant bite, has given these mammals a reputation as greedy and aggressive, which is the basis of the derogatory term "shrew-like," often applied to mean-spirited persons. Some shrews produce a neurotoxin in their salivary glands, which is delivered along a groove between the lower front incisors — hence the nasty bite. The venom is similar to that of cobras, though much less toxic. It can kill mice in minutes, and animals as large as rabbits may die, but most humans experience only local swelling and discomfort, though some individuals may experience more unpleasant allergy symptoms.

The front incisors are enlarged, forming excellent grasping and shearing "tools" for catching and eating prey. The rest of the teeth are not easily categorized, though the length of the tooth row is often diagnostic. Shrews could not survive the enforced starvation of tooth shedding, so the first (milk) set of teeth is resorbed by the fetus, and shrews are born with teeth

▼ Common Shrew, a sub-Arctic species.

that must last them a lifetime. Tooth wear is a guide to the age of a shrew; the few that survive predation and the constant physiological stress of a high metabolism will die of starvation when the teeth wear out. Because of their high food intake, the shrew's digestive tract is both simple and short, designed to reduce throughput time. Most shrews also re-ingest feces. The shrew will regularly grasp its hindfeet with the forefeet and licks its anus to stimulate the extrusion of the rectum. This takes place after the intestine is empty of fecal material and appears to be important in the production of certain vitamins.

Despite the impression of being perpetually hungry, shrews do occasionally cache food. The cache may be of live food; shrews are capable of immobilizing invertebrates, though the exact mechanism is debated. The shrew may cause paralysis with a bite to a specific nerve center; alternatively neurotoxins may be responsible, or perhaps it is a combination of the two. Shrews are catholic in their diet, taking not only insects but also earthworms and snails, amphibians, fish (chiefly by the water shrews, though other species take fish opportunistically) and small mammals, including smaller shrews. This wide dietary range helps explain why several shrew species are able to coexist in the same area, with diets comprising different fractions of the available prey types. This ability for different species to share rather than compete for resources may explain why there are so many shrew species (with new ones still being discovered). Very short lifetimes with large litters also promote rapid evolution and speciation. In many species, large numbers of subspecies have been identified, though the morphological differences are generally slight. Differentiating similar species is difficult enough, so subspecies are not discussed in the descriptions below.

A high metabolic rate also means that Arctic shrews cannot hibernate; it is not possible to reduce the metabolic rate to a level at which the slow consumption of fat stores would not lead to starvation. Some northern species shrink their skeletons and internal organs to reduce energy demand. They also increase their metabolic rate, because although both their fur and the snow beneath which they hunt are good insulators, heat loss remains significant. Despite these adaptations, however, a significant proportion of shrew populations is likely to die of starvation during the winter. This is compensated for by rapid rates of reproduction. Average gestation time is 20 days, with lactation lasting about the same time. Even in the high Arctic, two litters are possible each year of between four and 11 young, though one litter is more usual. Both males and females often die after their first breeding season, largely because of tooth wear, so the winter population is largely of immature animals, the survivors breeding in the spring.

Most Arctic shrews are solitary, meeting only to mate. They are promiscuous, so the young of a litter may have different fathers. Young shrews, born in a nest of grasses, are altricial. Male shrews suffer prior to mating, taking bites and a range of high-pitched squeals that usually cause intruding shrews to retreat away from the female. The male opens neck glands to exude an odor that, if he is lucky, ultimately makes the female receptive. Shrews also have other scent glands on their sides, but those seem to release chemicals that are defensive rather than mate-enticing; even dead shrews often remain uneaten, as few predators can tolerate their taste.

In the Palearctic a number of shrews are sub-Arctic. The Common Shrew (*Sorex araneu*) is found in northern Scandinavia, the Kola Peninsula and the shores of the White Sea. The Pygmy Shrew (*S. minutus*) and European Water Shrew (*Neomys fodiens*) have similar ranges, though they are not found in the far north of Fennoscandia. The Water Shrew also has a more limited White Sea range. In the eastern Palearctic the Flat-skulled Shrew (*S. roboratus*) breeds from central Siberia to the Sea of Okhotsk, but not to the north coast, except, perhaps, in limited numbers to the east of the Lena Delta. The European Least Shrew (*S. minutissimus*) is found throughout the taiga and on Kamchatka. The Eurasian Dusky or Taiga Shrew (*S. isodon*) breeds in a narrow belt of central Sweden, in central Finland, across Russia's taiga belt and throughout Kamchatka. The rare Siberian Large-toothed Shrew (*S. daphaenadon*) is found across central Siberia and throughout Kamchatka, while the Kamchatka Shrew (*S. camtchaticus*) occurs around the shores of the Sea of Okhotsk and throughout Kamchatka.

In the Nearctic the Arctic Shrew (*S. arcticus*) belies its name by breeding in the Canadian timber belt, including the southern shore of Hudson Bay. The American Pygmy Shrew (*S. hoyi*) breeds across North America from central Alaska to Labrador, but again in the timber belt. The American Water Shrew (*S. palustris*) has a patchy distribution, covering areas of the timber belt, including the southwestern corner of Hudson Bay and southern Quebec and Labrador. One subspecies, the Glacier Bay Water Shrew (*S. p. alaskanus*), breeds in southeastern Alaska (this is split as a full species by some authorities). Finally, the Alaskan Tiny Shrew (*S. yukonicus*) is confined to small areas of the Yukon and Susitna river valleys.

Eurasian Masked Shrew
Sorex caecutians

Identification
See p. 347
The upper pelage is dark golden-brown, the underparts silver-white with a strong delineation between the two. The feet are white with fine silver hairs, the brown tail long and ending in a tuft.

Confusion species
The Flat-skulled Shrew is much longer, while Portenko's Shrew is much smaller. The Tundra Shrew has a distinctive tricolored pelage.

Size
TL: 3–4½ in. (75–115 mm). T: 1⅛–1¾ in. (30–45 mm). W: ¹⁄₁₀–1¼ oz. (3–8 g).

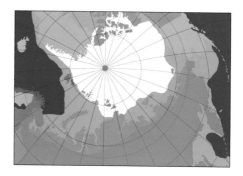

Distribution
Palearctic. Breeds in northern Fennoscandia and across Russia from the Kola Peninsula to Chukotka, but not to north coast. Breeds throughout Kamchatka. Found on tundra and in taiga.

American Masked Shrew
Sorex cinereus

Identification   See p. 347
The commonest Nearctic species. Pelage is brown or gray-brown above, paler below, the delineation less precise than in the European Masked Shrew. The feet are brown. The tail is brown above, paler below and tipped black, sometimes with a black tuft. Mainly nocturnal. Young American Masked Shrews form "caravans," a chain of shrews, with the first holding the mother's rump in its mouth and each subsequent youngster similarly gripping the one in front. Such caravans help the female move her young if the nest is endangered. The grip of the young shrew is tenacious, the youngsters maintaining their hold even if the female is lifted off the ground.

Confusion species
The Barren-ground Shrew has a shorter tail and pale patches on its sides.

Size
TL: 3–5 in. (75–125 mm). T: $1\frac{1}{8}$–2 in. (30–50 mm). W: $\frac{1}{12}$–$\frac{1}{5}$ oz. (2.5–5.5 g).

Distribution
Nearctic. Breeds in Alaska to the western coast and on the Aleutians, and north to the Brooks Range. Breeds near the Mackenzie Delta, but otherwise restricted to the timberline to the southern shore of Hudson Bay, then north along the timberline of Quebec and Labrador. Found in both wet and dry areas. Primarily boreal, but also found in tundra shrub.

Barren-ground Shrew
Sorex ugyunak

Identification   See p. 347
Closely related to the American Masked Shrew and the shrews of the Bering islands.The upper pelage is brown, the flanks and underparts paler, with a sharp delineation between the two. The feet are brown. The tail is brown above, paler below and ends with a buffish, light brown tuft. In winter the pelage is darker, but the sharp contrast between the upper body and paler underparts remains.

Confusion species
See American Masked Shrew.

Size
TL: 3–$4\frac{1}{8}$ in. (75–105 mm). T: $\frac{7}{8}$–$1\frac{1}{8}$ in. (22–30 mm). W: $\frac{1}{10}$–$\frac{1}{5}$ oz. (3–5.5 g).

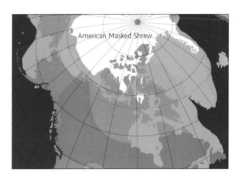

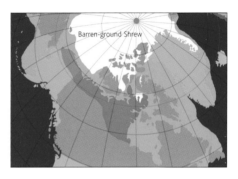

Distribution
Nearctic. Breeds in northern Alaska and across northern Canada, including the Boothia Peninsula, to the western shore of Hudson Bay. Absent from the southern shore of Hudson Bay and northeastern Canada. Prefers damp sedge-grass tundra and willow or birch thickets.

Pribilof Shrew
Sorex hydrodamus

In about 1840 Russian scientists collected two specimens of a shrew from "Unalaska." Though at first assumed to be Unalaska Island in the Aleutians, no shrew has been found there since the sale of Alaska to the U.S. The Russians used "Unalaska" as a collective term for the Bering Sea islands; shrews have been found on St. Paul Island, one of the Pribilof Islands, though rarely. A related species has also been found on St. Lawrence Island. It

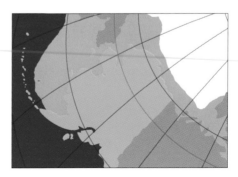

is conjectured that at a time of lower sea levels during periods of glaciation, an ancestral shrew population spread across Beringia, with populations becoming isolated on certain islands. Populations on small islands are vulnerable to extinction because of their small size and limited food resources, which may be why populations are now known only on St. Paul and St. Lawrence. However, it is also possible that other populations have yet to be discovered, such is the secretive nature of these tiny mammals. One such population might even exist on Unalaska Island.

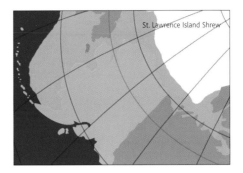

Identification   See p. 347
Upper pelage brown, underparts paler. The tail is bicolored, brown above, paler below. The feet are brown. The ears are more prominent than in most shrews.

Confusion species
None. The only shrew on St. Paul.

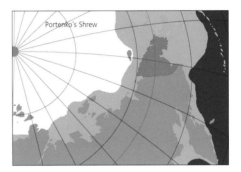

Size
TL: 3½–3⅞ in. (88–97 mm). T: 1¼–1½ in. (32–37 mm). W: ¹⁄₁₀–¹⁄₇ oz. (3–4 g).

Distribution
Nearctic. St. Paul Island, Pribilofs.

St. Lawrence Island Shrew
Sorex jacksoni

A little-known and virtually unstudied species. Believed to be part of the *cinereus* group of *Sorex* shrews (which includes Barren-ground and Pribilof Shrews, and several species from Siberia), with which it apparently shares a number of common features.

Identification   See p. 347
Pelage is bicolored, as in others of the *cinereus* group, brown above and buff or buff-gray on the flanks and underparts. The tail is also bicolored, brown above, paler below. The feet are pale brown.

Confusion species
None.

Size
TL: 3¾–4¼ in. (94–107 mm). T: 1¼–1½ in. (32–37 mm). W: ¹⁄₇–¹⁄₆ oz. (4–5 g).

Distribution
Nearctic. St. Lawrence Island.

Portenko's Shrew
Sorex portenkoi

Identification   See p. 347
Very similar to the St. Lawrence Island Shrew and other Beringian species. Upper pelage is brown with yellow-brown flanks and pale gray underparts. The tail is bicoloured, brown above, paler below. The feet are pale brown.

Confusion species
The Tundra Shrew is a little larger but the two are virtually indistinguishable.

Size
TL: 3½–4 in. (90–100 mm). T: 1¼–1½ in. (32–37 mm). W: ¹⁄₁₀–¹⁄₆ oz. (3–4.5 g).

Distribution
Palearctic. Northeastern Chukotka.

Tundra Shrew
Sorex tundrensis

Identification   See p. 347
Some authorities believe this species to be a northern subspecies of the Arctic Shrew (*S. arcticus*). The upperparts of the body and head are dark brown, the flanks pale gray-brown and the underparts pale gray. The tail is bicolored, brown above, paler below. The feet are pale brown. In winter the tricolored pelage becomes bicolored, the flanks becoming pale gray, as for the underparts.

Confusion species
None. The tricolored pelage is distinctive.

Size
HB: 3⅛–4¾ in. (80–120 mm). T: ¾–1⅜ in. (20–35 mm). W: ¹⁄₆–⅓ oz. (5–10 g).

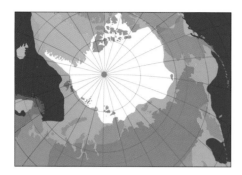

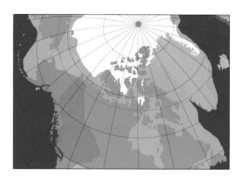

Distribution

The Asian and Alaskan Arctic. Breeds in Siberia east of the Pechora River, north to the northern coast almost throughout, except on the Taimyr Peninsula. In North America breeds on the Aleutian Islands, in western, central and northern Alaska and, to a limited extent, in northern Yukon. Prefers dry tundra, particularly areas dotted with birch and willow thickets, but also occurs in grasslands.

Dusky Shrew
Sorex monticolus

Identification   See p. 347

The upperparts are brown, usually red-brown, the underparts paler and often silver-washed. There is no clear delineation between the colors. The tail is bicolored, brown above, paler below. The feet are a pale brown. In winter the pelage is darker.

Confusion species

The Dusky Shrew is browner and larger than the American Masked Shrew.

Size

TL: 3³/₄–5¹/₂ in. (95–140 mm). T: 1¹/₈–2³/₈ in. (30–60 mm). W: ¹/₆–¹/₃ oz. (5–10 g).

▼ Northern Bat in flight, Finland.

Distribution

Nearctic. Breeds in southwestern and central Alaska, southern and (less commonly) northern Yukon and southern parts of the Northwest Territories. Prefers damp tundra and taiga; often found beside streams with thickets of willow or birch trees.

Bats

Given the paucity of available roosts, the lack of potential prey for much of the year and the rigors of the Arctic winter, it is no surprise that there are no Arctic breeding bats. However, there are hardy species in both the Nearctic and the Palearctic that may be found as far north as the timberline. In the Palearctic, Brandt's Bat (*Myotis brandtii*) breeds in southeastern Kamchatka and across the Russian taiga belt, while the Northern Bat (*Eptesicus nilssoni*) breeds in northern Scandinavia, across the Russian taiga and in southeastern Kamchatka. The Northern Bat hibernates in winter, and there is some evidence that Brandt's Bat makes limited migrations south.

In the Nearctic, the Little Brown Bat (*M. lucifugus*) breeds in central and southern Alaskan forests and across the Canadian taiga, including forests close to the southern shores of Hudson Bay. These bats hibernate in winter. The Hoary Bat (*Lasiurus cinereus*) breeds in Canadian forests from the Great Slave Lake, east, and is found surprisingly far north on both western and eastern Hudson Bay and in Quebec and Labrador. Though some Hoary Bats hibernate, most migrate south.

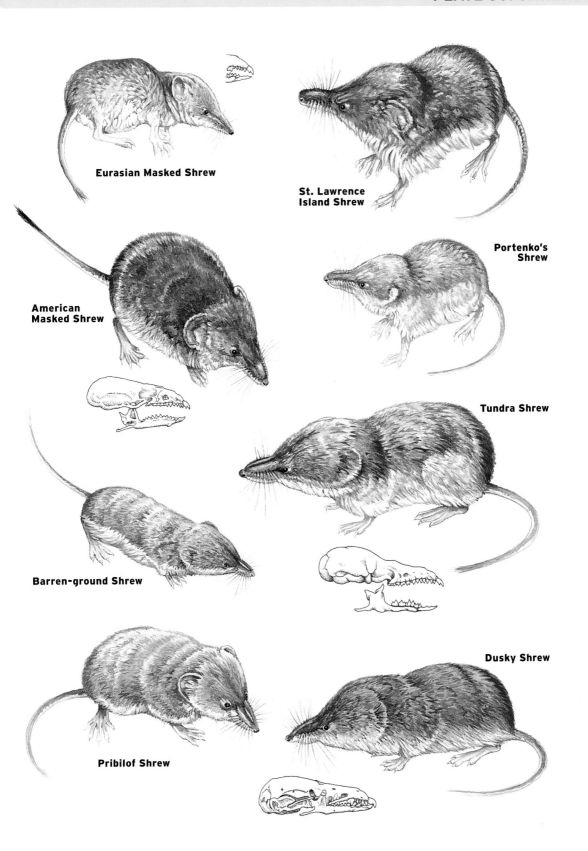

Eurasian Masked Shrew

St. Lawrence
Island Shrew

Portenko's
Shrew

American
Masked Shrew

Tundra Shrew

Barren-ground Shrew

Dusky Shrew

Pribilof Shrew

Rodents

Comprising more than 40% of all species, with members inhabiting virtually all habitats, rodents are arguably the most successful of all mammals. They are also important ecologically, not only as the protein source of choice for many carnivorous mammals and birds, but as distributors of seeds and of fungal spores. Only relatively recently has the importance of the latter been recognized. Certain plants are only able to extract nutrients from the soil when benevolent fungi (mycorrhizae) invade their root systems; rodents transferring spores to areas where they were absent therefore allows plants to invade and flourish. Set against such benefits are the problems caused to people by rodents, by direct competition for food, in nuisance value and as disease vectors. Rodent infestations can ruin crops, particularly stored crops; not only will rodents consume stored grain, but they will spoil what remains with urine and feces. In some agricultural communities, crop and storage losses can be as high as 90%, and it has been estimated that overall annual crop losses to rodents amount to 50%. Also, it is estimated that rodent-borne diseases have caused more human deaths than all the wars of history.

Rodents vary in size from the many small forms weighing as little as ¼ oz. (7 g) to the Capybara (*Hydrochoreus hydrochaeris*), which can weigh 155 lb. (70 kg), 10,000 times heavier. Most are terrestrial, though some are aquatic and have webbed feet. Rodent tails vary from the short, almost vestigial tails of hamsters, through the prehensile tail of the Eurasian Harvest Mouse (*Micromys minutus*) to the flattened, rudderlike tails of beavers. Rodents also include the porcupines, whose appearance is very different from the familiar rodent form. Yet all rodents share the same basic morphology, including a pair of sharp incisors in each jaw. These grow continuously, requiring the animal to gnaw to maintain incisor length, as elongating incisors would eventually prevent the animal from feeding. This characteristic increases the nuisance value of rodents to people, and has given them their name, from the Latin *rodere*, "to gnaw."

Rodents eat a variety of foods. A few are carnivorous, but most eat diverse plant materials, including tree bark, leaves, fruits and seeds. Herbivorous rodents have a large appendix in which bacteria aid the digestion of cellulose. The constituents of cellulose can only be absorbed in the upper gut, but must also be processed there before they can be treated in the appendix. Therefore, rodents practice refection, the re-ingestion of material excreted from the anus. Much of the reingested matter is excreted a second time, as the hard, dry pellets familiar to anyone whose house has accommodated mouse lodgers.

Mice and Rats

Of the three primary rodent pests to humans, the House Mouse (*Mus musculus*), Brown Rat (*Rattus norvegicus*) and Black Rat (*R. rattus*), the first two are found in association with people even in the Arctic, though the Black Rat is not, perhaps preferring the more equitable climate of the temperate world. Brown Rats have occasionally been observed living independently of humans, in Svalbard for example, but such "feral" populations do not survive the prolonged Arctic winter.

Apart from these commensal species, there are no Arctic mice or rats, though some are sub-Arctic. In the Palearctic the Northern aBirch Mouse (*Sicista betulina*) occurs along the shores of the White Sea. In the Nearctic the Deer Mouse (*Peromyscus maniculatus*) is found to the treeline and so may be seen close to the southern shores of Hudson Bay and in northern Quebec and Labrador. The Meadow Jumping Mouse (*Zapus hudsonius*) is found in southern Alaska and to the southern shores of Hudson Bay.

Porcupines

One further rodent that may be seen north to the timberline across North America from central Alaska to Labrador, and even occasionally on the tundra if there is dwarf willow or dwarf alder, is the North American Porcupine (*Erethizon dorsatum*). Though not strictly an Arctic species, porcupines are found in the Arctic National Wildlife Preserve, as well as in more southerly Alaskan locations.

◀ Spruce Squirrel, a sub-Arctic species that can occur in Arctic areas, Denali, Alaska.

◄ American Beaver, Norther Ontario. Note the dark brown pelt.

American Beaver
Castor canadensis

Identification See p. 366
The pelage of dense underfur and long guard hairs is rich dark brown overall, with some animals darker, almost black. The blunt muzzle is usually paler. The naked tail is long and flattened into a scaly paddle. The tail is used as both paddle and rudder, and also as a "fifth" leg; beavers stand on their hind legs and tail when gnawing trees, and walk on the hind legs with the tail as a prop when carrying material in their forelegs to the top of their dam. The ears and eyes are small, the legs short and the feet webbed.

Dental formula: 1/1, 0/0, 1/1, 3/3 = 20 teeth.

Confusion species
The Eurasian Beaver is usually paler and more red-brown, but may be dark brown or black. In reality, the two species can really only be distinguished by the shape of the skull, which is of no value in the field. The Muskrat is much smaller and has a tail that is flattened laterally.

Size
HB: 30–36 in. (75–90 cm). T: 11–15 in. (28–38cm). SH: 12–24 in. (30–60 cm). W: 31–77 lb. (14–35 kg).

Communication
Limited repertoire of grunts and hisses. The tail is also used to slap the water. This acts as a warning to family members if a predator is near, but may also be used if a strange beaver invades the territory. The tail-slap usually brings a response from the intruder, which gives the resident information on its size and likely threat. Beaver territories are highly prized and are marked out by scent produced not only in the preputial glands, but from anal scent glands. Beavers do not have "standard" mammalian genitalia; instead the anal and urogenital orifices opening into a common cloaca. The scent glands secrete into the cloaca and are smeared onto mounds of earth and vegetation at strategic points on the borders of the territory. Beavers are highly territorial, and conflicts between rivals can escalate to serious fights in which the loser may be badly wounded or even killed.

Distribution
Nearctic (but introduced into the Palearctic). Breeds to the timberline across North America. Found on rivers and streams. Beavers are largely aquatic, though young adults may travel on land when dispersing, and all animals forage on land.

Diet
Herbivorous and primarily nocturnal. In summer Beavers feed on leaves, roots and grasses, but also on twigs and bark. The animal's caecum aids digestion of wood, and beavers practice refection. In winter the animals feed on branches that have been cached, often underwater, during the summer, though they also consume fat stored in the body and tail, and can also

Beavers

The two species of beaver are both sub-Arctic, as their lifestyles require the presence of trees so they cannot survive beyond the treeline. However, beavers are likely to be seen by Arctic travelers close to the northern limits of the forest and by those who venture to Alaska's Denali National Park. The animal (or its pelt) played an important role in the exploration of the northern coastline of North America. The Hudson's Bay Company was set up to exploit the fur-bearing animals of northern Canada and was soon exporting 100,000 beaver pelts annually. The richness of the area led to conflict between Britain and France, just as it had previously led to battles between the French and the indigenous Canadians, and also to exploration. Although the British Royal Navy mapped many of the islands of Arctic Canada, exploration of the mainland was, in large part, the work of Hudson's Bay Company staff.

Beaver pelts were important economically in Europe too: the coat of arms of the city of Irkutsk in Siberia includes a beaver, an acknowledgment of the animal's contribution to the city's prosperity. As well as fur, beavers have also been hunted for food (they are large animals) and medicine; castoreum, a secretion of the preputial glands that discharge into the animal's urethra, includes salicin, the basis of aspirin, and has been used as a medicine since at least the time of Hippocrates.

Today the range of the Eurasian Beaver (*Castor fiber*) is much reduced. It is believed that the population of the species was little more than 1,000 in the early years of the 20th century. Though in a much healthier position now, the Eurasian Beaver's range is still patchy; it is found in central Scandinavia and in isolated areas of sub-Arctic Russia. American Beavers have also been introduced into Finland and northwestern Russia. The two forms do not interbreed.

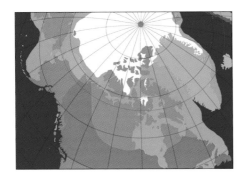

reduce their metabolism. Such caches are vital for northern American Beavers as ice may cover their ponds. Animals at the southern limit of the range do not cache food. Life in the semi-darkness of the lodge during the frozen days of winter leads to a breakdown of the Beaver's circadian rhythms and the creation of a "beaver day" of 26–29 hours.

Breeding

Social, living in family groups of up to 12 animals, but more usually five or six. The family will hold a territory that may be as little as 1,640 ft. (500 m) of rich riverside habitat, but as much as 4 mi. (6 km) in poor habitat. The territory will also extend away from the river, covering several square miles. Beavers fell trees and collect mud and rocks to create dams, which are usually placed at narrow sections of the river. Dams can be up to 13 sq. ft. (4 m) high, 20 ft. (6 m) thick at the base and up to 330 ft. (100 m) long, though they are usually smaller. The dam is not watertight; water flows through and over it, making the dam less susceptible to destruction if the river volume increases, but water backs up behind it to form a pond. In this the beavers build a lodge, a conical structure of branches and the like, with an underwater entrance to an above-water living area. There is usually also a separate dining

▼ This mound of sticks and branches is an American Beaver Lodge. Denali, Alaska.

area. Food is cached at a different location. Occasionally beavers may burrow into banks for their homes. Again the entrance will be underwater. Within their ranges American Beavers may excavate the beds of streams to form canals for ease of movement since they are much better adapted to swimming than walking. They may even divert streams for the same purpose. Trees of up to 4 ft. (1.2 m) in diameter may be felled, but contrary to popular myth these are not then hauled to the dam site. Only small trees are hauled in, the succulent upper branches being stripped before the trunk is used in the dam. Beavers are also not capable of controlling the direction of fall of trees (another myth). It is just that as most trees overhang rivers because of the natural sloping of banks, they tend to fall in the right direction. Underwater the American Beaver's ears and nose close and a membrane covers the eyes. The lips also close behind the incisors so the animal can manipulate branches without ingesting water.

The damage to trees is severe, but the preferred species — aspen, willows and cottonwoods — grow readily from the remaining stump, so the beavers are actually practicing a form of coppicing. When the pond silts up, the territory is abandoned. Ultimately the area may revert to forest, or a "beaver meadow" may be created on the silted pond. Some authorities maintain that much of the meadowland of North America derives from beaver meadow.

Beavers are monogamous, though polygyny has been (rarely) observed, but the pair is usually of different ages as a new mate is taken when the existing one dies. One to six (usually two to four) kits are born after a gestation of 100–110 days. The kits are precocial and swim within hours; weaned at around 3 months. The family unit is the breeding pair, the current year's infants and young from the previous one or two years, though the latter are often driven away when each year's young are born. Females breed at 2 years, males at 3, but these ages depend on the gaining of a territory. When young disperse in search of partners and territories, they may travel up to 155 mi. (250 km).

Taxonomy and geographical variation

Polytypic. Up to 24 subspecies though morphological differences between them are minimal.

Squirrels and marmots

There are no Arctic squirrels of the family Sciuridae, but several species may be found at the treeline. In the Palearctic the Eurasian Red Squirrel (*Sciuris vulgaris*) breeds in northern Scandinavia, across Russia and on Kamchatka. In the Nearctic the Spruce Squirrel (*Tamiasciuris hudsonicus*), also known as the American Red Squirrel, and the Northern Flying Squirrel (*Glaucomys sabrinus*) breed to the timberline from Alaska to Labrador.

Marmots, the largest sciurids, are also the largest true hibernators, spending as much as nine months underground each year. With the exception of the Groundhog (*Marmota monax*), they are also social animals, living in family groups in excavated burrows from which they emerge in spring or early summer to graze on local vegetation, storing fat for the coming winter. In the Palearctic the Alpine Marmot (*M. marmota*) is, as the name suggests, an alpine rather than northern species. In the Nearctic the Hoary Marmot (*M. caligata*) has a similar habitat in mountainous parts of central and southern Alaska and southern Yukon. The Groundhog is more southerly, but breeds close to the southern shores of Hudson Bay. There are two other species of marmot, one in each hemisphere, that are more truly Arctic.

Black-capped Marmot
Marmota camtschatica

Identification
See p. 366

The upper pelage is brown, with a distinctive black or dark brown cap, which covers not only the crown but also the nape, and extends below the eye. The fur is soft and thick, and individual hairs are often black-tipped to give a flecked appearance. The underparts are paler, often bright yellow-red.

Dental formula: 1/1, 0/0, 2/1, 3/3 = 22 teeth.

Confusion species
None.

Size
HB: 20–21½ in. (50–55 cm). T: 4–6 in. (10–15 cm). W: 6½–11 lb. (3–5 kg).

Communication
A shrill whistle.

Distribution
Palearctic. Rare and patchy in upland areas (to 6,235 ft./1,900 m) of northeastern Siberia. Found in the mountains and tundra of Baikal, the Upper Yana and Kolyma Rivers, in north central Kamchatka and in parts of central and northern Chukotka.

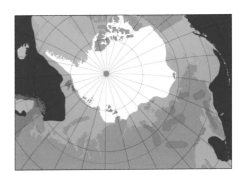

Diet
Herbivorous, grazing on tundra and alpine vegetation.

Breeding
Social. Spends considerable time underground in burrow systems, which may extend over 330 ft. (100 m) and go deep below the permafrost. Because of the harshness of the northern environment and the litter size, female marmots cannot accumulate bodily reserves to breed annually. Breeding takes place within the winter den. Three to 11 (usually four to six) young are born after a gestation of about 32 days. Litter sizes are large because of predation and winter

◀ Hoary Marmot, a sub-Arctic species, Alaska.

survival rates. It is estimated that about 80% of males and about 50% of females do not survive to breed. The young stay with their parents until they are 2 years old, the family hibernating together.

Taxonomy and geographical variation
Monotypic.

Alaska Marmot
Marmota breweri

Identification See p. 366
Pelage is gray with silvery guard hairs. The back, rump and hind legs are often darker than the upper body. The head is also darker. The broad tail is brown with a black tip.
   Dental formula is 1/1, 0/0, 2/1, 3/3 = 22 teeth.

Confusion species
None.

Size
HB: 16–20 in. (40–50 cm). T: 5–7 in. (13–18 cm). W: 5½–8¾ lb. (2.5–4 kg).

Communication
A shrill whistle.

Distribution
Nearctic. Breeds in the Brooks Range, Alaska, particularly on the northern slopes. There are unconfirmed reports of breeding up to the northern coast.

Diet
Herbivorous, grazing on tundra and alpine vegetation.

Breeding
Social. Excavates both summer and winter burrows. Summer burrows are usually in boulder fields; this provides a degree of protection from Brown Bears, which find digging among the boulders difficult. Boulders also provide the marmots with lookout posts for seeing eagles

and other predators. Winter burrows are excavated on windswept ridges and they are plugged with mud, vegetation and feces, which freeze hard. In spring the wind sweeps the slope of snow and allows the plug to melt, freeing the occupants. The marmots spend nine months in the winter den. Two to six young are born after a gestation of 30 days. As with the Black-capped Marmot, the young stay with their parents for two years.

Taxonomy and geographical variation
Monotypic. Formerly believed to be a subspecies of the Hoary Marmot, the Alaska Marmot is now considered a separate species.

Arctic Ground Squirrel
Citellus parryi

Only one of the numerous Nearctic ground squirrels breeds in the Arctic — the Arctic Ground Squirrel, which also occurs in the Palearctic. In the Palearctic the Siberian Chipmunk (*Tamias sibiricus*) breeds to the timberline, its range including southern Chukotka and northern Kamchatka.

▼ Arctic Ground Squirrel, Cold Bay.

Identification
See p. 366

See p. 366

Pelage is tawny, the upperparts flecked buff and white. The head is darker on the crown, redder on the forehead and nose and with a pale cream or buff eye-ring. The tail (which is shorter than some Nearctic ground squirrels, but longer than other Eurasian sousliks) is tawny above, paler below, often with a black tip.

Dental formula: 1/1, 0/0, 2/1, 3/3 = 22 teeth.

Confusion species
Smaller and browner than the Alaska Marmot, the range of which overlaps.

Size
HB: 10–13¾ in. (25–35 cm). T: 3–6 in. (7.5–15 cm). W: 18½–30 oz. (530–850 g).

Communication
Vocal. The alarm call is a shrill whistle, but there is also a *chick-chick* call that gives the animal its Inuit name, *sik-sik*. The Eurasian name *souslik* derives from the same root. There is reason to believe that the whistle is used in response to avian predators, the *chick-chick* to terrestrial predators, but the latter is also used, in a quieter form, "conversationally." Fleeing run with tail held erect as signal to conspecifics.

Distribution
Nearctic and Palearctic, but not circumpolar. Breeds in Chukotka and Kamchatka, in northern Alaska and northern Canada to the eastern shores of Hudson Bay. Absent from Canada's Arctic islands. Found on dry tundra from the coast to upland areas.

Diet
Primarily herbivorous, grazing on tundra vegetation, seeds and roots, but also takes fungi, insects, birds' eggs and carrion (one delightful tale has a squirrel removing more than its own body weight of meat from a dead Caribou during the course of one day). Males also kill and eat young they have not fathered.

Breeding
Colonial, with colonies of up to 50 animals. The animals excavate burrow systems. Males are territorial and will attempt to mate with all females within the territory, defending them against rival males. Fights are frequent and serious injuries occur. The energy cost of fighting and the injuries sustained

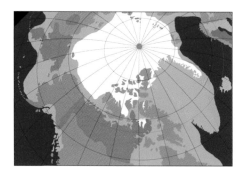

▲ Arctic Ground Squirrel, Yttagran Island.

mean that many males do not survive the subsequent winter. Females may form groups (perhaps kin groups) as a way of defending their young from unrelate males. Males also defend their territories after the cessation of mating activities, also presumably to help their young survive. Five to 10 altricial young are born after a gestation of about 25 days. The eyes open at 3 weeks and they are weaned at 4 weeks. At 6 weeks they go above ground for the first time. They are cared for by the female for another one to two weeks, by which time they are about 80% adult weight. Now capable of defending themselves against marauding males, they become independent and are ready to breed when they emerge from first hibernation. Hibernation takes place in a part of the burrow blocked off from colonial areas, the animal preparing a hollow ball of grasses inside which it sleeps. The hibernation chamber also has a store of seeds, but these seem not to be for periods of waking, but for consumption just before spring emergence, as breeding begins almost right away.

Taxonomy and geographical variation
Polytypic. Many subspecies are recognized in both North America and Asia, but differences from the nominate race, which breeds from the Mackenzie Delta to Hudson Bay, are minimal.

Microtines

Voles and lemmings make up the majority of the rodent subfamily Microtinae and are the most northerly of all rodents, with many species being true Arctic dwellers. The microtines are also of major ecological importance, converting the short-term abundance of Arctic plant life into a protein source that sustains the smaller mammalian carnivores and many bird species. For example, Snowy Owl numbers are locked into microtine population cycles, years of abundance (lemming years) leading to sharp rises in predator numbers.

Both voles and lemmings are small, stocky animals with small ears and eyes, short tails (particularly in lemmings) and 16 teeth (two pairs of incisors and 12 molars, three on each side of the upper and lower jaws). Most microtines, and all *Microtus* species, have continuously growing molars that allow them to feed on tough vegetation. They are herbivorous (though the Muskrat, the largest microtine, also eats mollusks) and do not hibernate, spending the winter foraging in tunnels beneath the snow, which provides an insulating blanket against the cold of the Arctic winter. In general, both male and female microtines are solitary and aggressively territorial, marking their boundaries with feces and scent from a variety of glands. In defining territories the sexes have differing motives. Females compete for areas that are rich in food, while males compete for access to many females. Gestation is only about 20 days. The young are altricial, but they are weaned at three weeks. Sometimes this is simply because the mother is pregnant again; females made pregnant when they are lactating may have a slightly longer gestation period, perhaps 24 days. In general parental care is by the female only, though in two southern vole species the males do contribute. In some species young females can breed at three weeks, though in northern species first breeding is usually much later. Even in Arctic species several litters are produced each year and the young of the first litter will probably breed in the same summer. Because of their distribution and population densities, voles and lemmings can be vectors of diseases that affect humans, though infections are rare. In particular microtines carry the protozoan *Giardia lamblia*, which causes acute diarrhea, and the bacteria that causes tularaemia (also known as rabbit fever), a lymphatic disease. Giardia can be difficult to avoid as it occurs in apparently clean water; water must be treated to eliminate it. Tularaemia is more problematic as it is a serious, sometimes fatal disease.

There are many species of microtines, often with numerous subspecies and overlapping ranges. In the species sections below, only Identification, Size and Distribution are considered. In general, diet and breeding are similar in all species, as is communication: a series of high chattering and squeaks, with scent glands used to define territories. Confusion species are not discussed; pelage, size and distribution usually allow identification, but often the characteristics that unambiguously define very similar species are of little or no value in the field. The taxonomy of microtines, which have very small ranges, is very complex. All are polytypic with numerous subspecies. In northern species there is a further complication; some island microtines are considered distinct species rather than subspecies. In general, taxonomy and geographical variation is not discussed in the descriptions below.

Voles

In the Palearctic the Field Vole (*Microtus agrestis*) breeds in northern Scandinavia and on the southern Kola Peninsula, while the Eurasian Water Vole (*Arvicola terrestris*) breeds in northern Scandinavia, on the Kola Peninsula, around the White Sea and north to the coast as far east as Pecherskoya Bay. Colonies of the Sibling Vole (*M. rossiaemeridionalis*), a northern and central Palearctic species, have been found on Svalbard, probably introduced accidentally from ships. The species appears to have become established, surviving the Arctic winter better than other introduced rodents and counteracting high winter mortality by having up to four litters during the short summer. Animals from the early litters apparently breed when they are as young as one month of age.

In the Nearctic the Eastern Heather Vole (*Phenacomys ungava*) and Southern Red-backed Vole (*Clethrionomys gapperi*) breed north to the southern shores of Hudson Bay and, on the eastern side of the Bay, in central Quebec and Labrador.

Gray-sided Vole
Clethrionomys rufocanus

Identification See p. 364
Pelage very distinctive, with gray flanks and a broad chestnut band on the forehead, crown, nape and along the back to the base of the tail. Underparts and feet are pale gray. The tail is chestnut brown above, gray below.

Size
HB: 4½–5½ in. (11–13.5 cm). T: 1–1½ in. (2.5–4 cm). W: ½–1¾ oz. (15–50 g).

Distribution
Palearctic. Breeds in northern Scandinavia and across Russia, but only to the north coast on the Kola Peninsula and east to Baydaratskaya Bay. Breeds throughout Kamchatka and in southern Chukotka to the shores of the Bering Sea. Prefers mountainous terrain. Builds a round nest of grass under winter snow with tunnels leading from it. Summer nest is concealed in tree roots, but may be at a surprising height in a tree hole.

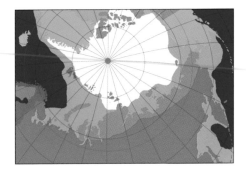

Northern Red-backed Vole
(Ruddy Vole)
Clethrionomys rutilus

Identification See p. 364

Pelage very distinctive, with pale golden-brown flanks and broad red-brown band from the forehead, across the crown and nape and back to the base of the tail. The underparts and feet are cream or pale buff. The tail is golden brown above, cream below and has a small terminal tuft.

Size
HB: 3–4½ in. (8–11 cm). T: 1–1¼ in. (2.5–3.5 cm). W: ½–1½ oz. (15–40 g).

Distribution
Circumpolar. Breeds in northern Scandinavia and across Russia, where range is as the Gray-sided Vole. In North America breeds throughout Alaska and northern Canada east to Hudson Bay. Canadian range extends to northern coast, including Boothia

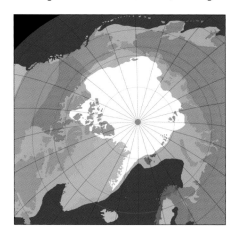

Peninsula, but does not include Arctic islands. Found throughout forest belt, also on tundra. Often found in human habitations, where it behaves as House Mouse (*Mus musculus*), sharing dwellings. Nest of available vegetation made in burrow, among tree roots or in tree holes. In winter the voles often nest communally.

Singing Vole
Microtus miuris

Identification See p. 364

Pelage variable, but usually dark brown above, tawnier on flanks and gray-buff underparts. The crown often shows patches of gray, and there are usually pale tawny ear-spots. The tail is brown above, paler below. Acquired its name because adults occasionally sit in exposed places and "sing" a high, trilling song. This may be an alarm call for young voles, as the singing usually takes place when litters have been weaned. The voles make hay balls, some of them huge (up to 8 gal./30 L), which are placed above ground and provide food in winter.

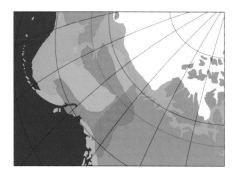

Size
HB: 4¼–5 in. (10.5–13 cm). T: ¾–1⅜ in. (2–3.5 cm). W: 1–2 oz. (25–55 g).

Distribution
Nearctic. Breeds in northern and southern Alaska to the west coast, but absent from most of the central State, from the Alaska Peninsula and the Aleutian Islands. Also breeds in central Yukon. Prefers dry tundra, but may be found on riverbanks. Also found in mountain areas and forests.

Insular Vole
Microtus abbreviatus

Identification See p. 364

Very similar to the Singing Vole, from which it probably evolved. Pelage is paler than Singing Vole, with brown upperparts, yellow-brown flanks and pale buff underparts. The ear-tips and cheeks are buff. The tail is bicolored. Insular Voles have a remarkably short breeding cycle; pups are altricial, but they have fur at six days, eyes are open at 11 days and they are weaned at 15 days.

Size
HB: 4½–5¾ in. (11–14.5 cm). T: 1–1¼ in. (2.5–3 cm). W: 1½–2½ oz. (45–75 g).

Distribution
Nearctic. Found only on Hall and St. Matthew Islands in the Bering Sea.

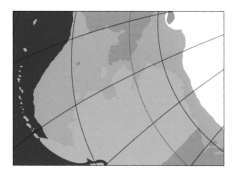

▲ Insular Vole, Hall Island, Alaska. This individual is singing.

Narrow-headed Vole
Microtus gregalis

Identification
See p. 364

Upper pelage varies from light ochre to dark brown with characteristic darker spotting and white tips to individual hairs that give an overall silvery appearance. There is a dark stripe extending from the back of the head to the upper back. The stripe is particularly prominent in young voles. The underparts are pale grayish brown. The tail is bicolored with a terminal tuft. The name derives from the head shape; the skull is narrow, particularly between the eyes. This is diagnostic.

Size
HB: 4³/₄–6 in. (12–15 cm). T: 1¹/₄–2 in. (3–5 cm). W: 1³/₄–2³/₄ oz. (50–80 g).

Distribution
Palearctic. A patchy distribution across Russia, breeding close to the coast of the White Sea and east to the Ob Delta, from Khatanga to the Kolyma Delta. The largest populations are on the steppes and mountains of Kazakhstan and Kirghizstan, where the vole is found to 11,483 ft. (3,500 m). Highly colonial, excavating complex mazes of shallow tunnels. Prefers dry tundra.

North Siberian Vole
Microtus hyperboreus

The taxonomy of this species is debated. The voles breed in north-central and northeastern Siberia. Some authorities consider these to represent two species, with the North Siberian Vole in the northeast and Middendorf's Vole *M. middendorfi* in the northcentral region; others consider the voles to be one species with two subspecies. In the field the two are essentially identical.

Identification
See p. 364

The upper pelage is gray-brown, often with a reddish wash. The underparts are silver-gray, occasionally washed yellow. The tail is bicolored.

Size
HB: 4³/₄–6 in. (12–15 cm). T: 1³/₈–2¹/₄ in. (3.5–5.5 cm). W: 2–3 oz. (55–85 g). The vole has a long tail, up to 25% of the total length.

Distribution
Palearctic. Breeds in Russia from the Ob River (and a short distance west of it) to the western edge of Chukotka, but only reaches the northern coast near the Lena and Kolyma Deltas. Found in dry tundra and boggy areas. Colonial, excavating shallow burrows in dry places and tunnels among tussocks in wetter areas. Occasionally constructs grass "burrows" among shrubs, some to heights of 13–16 ft. (4–5 m).

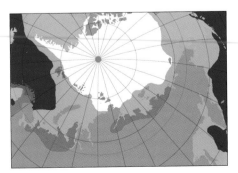

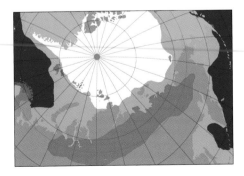

Tundra Vole
Microtus oeconomus

Identification

See p. 364

A large vole with a relatively long tail. Pelage is dark brown above with buff flecking. Color becomes paler on the flanks and pale buff on the underparts. The feet are pale gray-brown, more silvery in winter. Tail is gray-brown above, paler below.

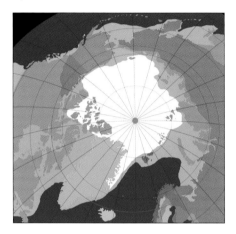

Size
HB: 3¼–6¼ in. (8.5–16 cm). T: 1–3 in. (2.5–8 cm). W: 1–2¼ oz. (25–65 g). American Voles tend to be longer and heavier, but with a shorter tail.

▼ Tundra Vole, St. Lawrence Island.

▲ Tundra Vole, Alaska.

Distribution
Circumpolar. Breeds in northern Scandinavia and across Russia, up to or near the northern coast except on the Taimyr Peninsula. Breeds throughout Kamchatka. In North America, breeds throughout Alaska and the Yukon, to the northern coast. Prefers damper tundra. If the animal's burrow system is damp, it will build its nest above ground. The species is primarily nocturnal in summer, but diurnal in winter. The Latin species name, *oeconomus*, means "housekeeper" (and is also the root of "economic"), referring to the storage of seeds and rhizomes by these voles to supplement their winter diet. In Alaska these stores may be sizable and are sometimes exploited by the Inuit.

Meadow Vole
Microtus pennsylvanicus

Identification

See p. 364

The most widespread American Vole. Pelage is red or dark brown above and on the flanks. with pale gray-brown underparts. Tail is uniformly dark gray-brown. The feet are dark gray. Winter fur is grayer. Meadow Voles are claimed to be the world's most prolific mammals. The gestation period of 20 days is followed by a 14-day lactation period, but the female can mate again within hours of giving birth, and so can give birth within a week of weaning a litter. One captive female produced 17 litters in one year. With litter sizes of 3–10 (usually 3–5), the birth rate and population growth rate can be phenomenally high. The animals are very clean, using

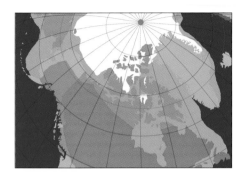

communal toilet areas to keep burrows free of waste. In winter the voles often nest communally. The voles squeak or stamp with their hindfeet to warn conspecifics of approaching danger.

Size

HB: 3½–5¼ in. (9–13 cm). T: 1³⁄₈–2½ in. (3.5–6.5 cm). W: 1–2½ oz. (30–70 g).

Distribution

Nearctic. Breeds in central Alaska, but not to either the western or northern coasts. Breeds in northern Yukon, but more southerly farther east to the western coast of Hudson Bay. Breeds around Hudson Bay, reaching northern Quebec and Labrador on the eastern side. Usually found in damp areas, often near rivers or lakes. Occasionally occurs in drier areas.

Taiga Vole
Microtus xanthognathus

Identification See p. 364
A large vole. The pelage is dark brown or gray-brown above, paler below and with a prominent yellow-brown cheek-patch. In some animals the snout is also yellow-brown; these individuals tend to have less prominent cheek-patches.

Size
HB: 6–7 in. (15–18 cm). T: 1½–2⅛ in. (4–5.5 cm). W: 3½–6 oz. (110–170 g).

Distribution
Nearctic. Breeds in central Alaska, northern Yukon and the

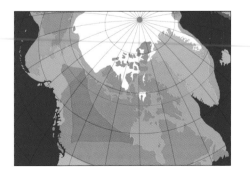

boreal belt to the southwestern shore of Hudson Bay. Found at the timberline, in both forest and on tundra, preferring damp *Sphagnum* moss areas. The voles seem to prefer new growth and tend to colonize areas where fire has created a new, rather than successional, habitat. This means that the distribution is patchy and variable, making the vole elusive.

Lemming Vole
Alticola lemminus

Identification See p. 364
Pelage is thick and gray-brown overall, including tail, which ends with long bristles. Winter pelage is much lighter and may even be white.

Size
HB: 4¾–5 in. (12–13 cm). T: ¾–1 in. (2–2.5 cm). W: ¾–1½ oz. (20–45 g).

Distribution
Palearctic. Found in a broad semicircular belt that starts from the Lena Delta, curves south toward the northern shore of the Sea of Okhotsk, then curves north into Chukotka, reaching the Bering Sea as far north as Cape Dezhnev. A second belt follows the western shore of the Sea of Okhotsk, then heads inland toward the northern tip of Lake Baikal.

Muskrat
Ondatra zibethicus

Identification See p. 366
The largest and most visible vole. The name derives from the odor of the scent glands used to define territories. Pelage is rich red-brown above, becoming paler on the flanks and much paler on the underparts. The feet are gray, as is the naked tail. The tail is laterally compressed (about three times as deep as it is wide) as an aid to swimming, as the Muskrat is primarily aquatic. The feet are also partially webbed. The hindfeet are longer than the forefeet and have stiff hairs on the toes, both adaptations for swimming. Swimming Muskrats may be confused with beavers if only the head is above surface, but the size and paddle tail of the beaver are diagnostic if more of the animal is visible. Muskrats are excellent swimmers and can stay submerged for up to 15

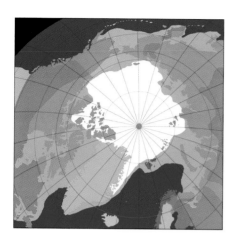

minutes, traveling long distances underwater. The dense underfur provides insulation, the pelage trapping air as an aid to both insulation and buoyancy. However, heat loss can be a problem, particularly in winter, and in lakes they create floating platforms on which they can feed out of the water. Though herbivorous, Muskrats also eat fish and mollusks and even young waterbirds.

Size
HB: 9½–16 in. (24–40 cm). T: 7½–11 in. (19–28 cm). W: 1¼–4 lb. (600–1,800 g).

Distribution
Circumpolar. Originally Nearctic, found from western Alaska to Labrador, but not to the northern coast. Valued for their fur (musquash), Muskrats were farmed in Europe and escapes have produced breeding populations in Scandinavia and across Russia. Prefers freshwater rivers and lakes, but occasionally found at the coast. Excavates burrows in riverbanks or lake margins. May also build lodges in marshy areas. From these they may excavate canals to facilitate movement about

▼ Swimming Muskrat, Great Slave Lake, Northwest Territories.

▲ Muskrat, Great Slave Lake, Northwest Territories. Note the long, flattened tail.

territory. Muskrats are highly territorial; females will kill other females and their litters to gain a territory, and defend it aggressively. Males also assist, as Muskrats are more monogamous than other vole species. However, males offer little other parental care. Although gestation and weaning are much as other voles, Muskrats take longer to mature, as might be expected from their larger size. Muskrat populations are cyclical, following six- or 10-year cycles, the longer cycle in northern ranges. The reason for these cycles is not understood.

Lemmings

Contrary to popular belief, lemmings do not commit mass suicide, but the myth is so powerful that it is still frequently heard, a story too good to be untrue. The myth involves the exquisitely colored Norway Lemming (*Lemmus lemmus*), a sub-Arctic species, though it does breed in northern Scandinavia and on the Kola Peninsula. Similar population surges occur in other microtine species, but their mass migrations are less spectacular than those of the Norway Lemming. The reasons for the cyclical population surges in some microtines are poorly understood. It may be due to a sudden drop in predation, or it may be climatic; an early spring and abundant food can mean a swift increase in population, as the animals breed quickly and population growth can be rapid. Whatever the cause, the large population needs to disperse, so migrations occur. The Norway Lemming is a particularly intolerant species, highly aggressive to conspecifics. Trapping of migrating animals has shown that a very high proportion are immatures. It is likely that these have been driven away by older lemmings. The topography of Norway, with its narrowing valleys, means that the migrating animals are thrown together. Conflicts would inevitably occur and these might lead to the panic that is an apparent feature of

the migrations. When they reach lakes or the sea, the animals at the front, forced by pressure from behind, start swimming. Swimming out to sea appears suicidal to the human observers, but, of course, the lemmings have no idea that they will never reach the far shore.

Siberian Brown Lemming
Lemmus sibiricus

Identification See p. 365

Very similar in size and habits to the Norway Lemming, which it replaces on eastern European and Asiatic tundras. The pelage is similar, but more subdued. Basic color is brown-yellow, with a thick black stripe on the head and back. The winter pelage is the same color, but with thicker fur. As with the Norway Lemming, breeding can involve prodigious numbers, with 3–4 broods annually, each of 5–6 young. This species has "lemming years."

Size

HB: 4½–5½ in. (11–14 cm). T: ½–1 in. (1.5–2.5 cm). W: 2–4¼ oz. (60–120 g).

Distribution

Palearctic. Breeds on the northern coast of Russia from the

▼ Norway Lemming, north Norway.

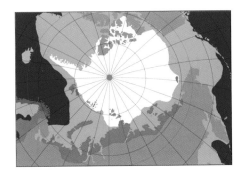

White Sea to the Kolyma Delta, including the Taimyr Peninsula. Also breeds on Novaya Zemlya, the New Siberia islands and on Wrangel Island.

American Brown Lemming
Lemmus trimucronatus

Identification See p. 365

Formerly considered a subspecies of Siberian Brown Lemming, which it closely resembles, but now considered a separate species. Pelage is tawny with buff and darker brown flecking, paler on the flanks and paler again on the underparts. The head and neck are often gray-brown rather than tawny, and older animals show a distinctive rusty patch on the lower back. Cyclical population surges every three to four years, but no mass migrations as seen in Norway Lemmings, though the animals do appear above ground in greater numbers (perhaps a limited dispersal), where they are easy prey for avian and terrestrial predators.

Size
HB: 4½–5½ in. (11–14 cm). T: ¾–1¼ in. (2–3 cm). W: 2½–4 oz. (70–115 g).

Distribution
Nearctic. Breeds in western and northern Alaska and across

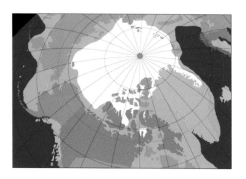

northern Canada to the western shore of Hudson Bay. Also breeds on the southern Arctic islands from Banks to Baffin, and on islands in the Bering Sea. Some authorities believe that the brown lemming of the Pribilof Islands, *L. t. nigripes*, is a separate species. Found on all tundra forms, but in greater abundance on damp tundra with grasses, sedges and mosses.

Wood Lemming
Myopus schisticolor

Identification See p. 365
A small, stocky lemming. Pelage is uniformly dark gray, with paler underparts. Adults develop a rusty patch on the lower back (as in the brown lemmings), but this is much more indistinct. Very short tail. Much less aggressive to conspecifics than Norway Lemming, with which it overlaps.

Size
HB: 3–4½ in. (8–11.5 cm). T: ⅓–¾ in. (1–2 cm). W: ¾–1½ oz. (20–45 g).

Distribution
Palearctic. Breeds in southern Scandinavia, but more northerly in Russia, though only to the north coast near the White Sea

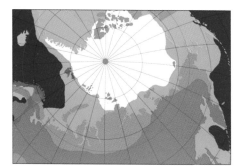

and the Lena and Kolyma Deltas. Breeds throughout Kamchatka, but largely absent from Chukotka. Prefers damp, moss-covered conifer forest floors, excavating tunnels through the moss, but also found on damp, mossy tundra.

Northern Bog Lemming
Synaptomys borealis

Identification See p. 365
A small animal that resembles a mouse, apart from the tail, which is bicolored as in many voles. The pelage is gray-brown above, with occasional patches of gray and of red-brown and gray below.

Size
HB: 4–4¾ in. (10–12 cm). T: ½–1 in. (1.5–2.5 cm). W: ⅞–1¼ oz. (25–35 g).

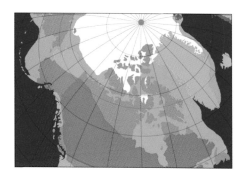

Distribution
Nearctic. Breeds in central and southern Alaska, and across central Canada to the southern shores of Hudson Bay. On the eastern side of the Bay, the Northern Bog Lemming breeding range is more northerly, though it does not extend to the northern coasts of Quebec and Labrador. Though extensive, the distribution is very patchy. Northern Bog Lemmings do not undergo the cyclical population changes of other lemmings, the reasons for which are unclear. The patchy distribution of this species has led to the evolution of a number of subspecies.

Collared Lemmings
Collared lemmings belong to the genus *Dicrostonyx*, the name deriving from the Greek "forked claw", a reference to the growth of a double claw in winter to aid digging in the snow. The pad between the third and fourth toes hardens and enlarges, fusing with the claws to form a forked double claw. The name "collared" derives from the collar seen on the pelage of most species. If the collar is paler than the upper body color, it may be visible as a complete band, but often it merges with the upper body color and so is visible only as a chest band. The number of collared lemming species has been debated for years. Authorities generally agree on five species.

Arctic Collared Lemming
Dicrostonyx torquatus

Identification See p. 365

Pelage is variable. In general red-brown on the back, usually more gray-brown toward the lower back and on the head, and with a dark dorsal stripe from the head to the tail. This stripe is usually conspicuous, but may be inconspicuous or, occasionally, conspicuous only on the lower back. The collar is pale gray or gray-buff. However, some animals are gray-brown. Occasionally red-brown patches on the flanks. The underparts are paler, often pale buff or gray-buff. The feet are pale gray or pale-gray buff. The tail is as the back at the base, but with a whiter tip. In winter the animals turn white.

Size

HB: 4¾–6 in. (12–15 cm). T: ⅓–¾ in. (1–2 cm). W: 1¾–2½ oz. (50–75 g), but heaver in winter (up to 4 oz./110 g).

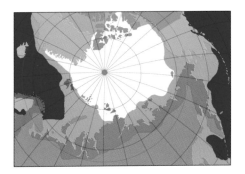

Distribution

Palearctic. Breeds from the eastern shores of the White Sea to Chukotka and eastern Kamchatka. Breeds to the northern coast and on the southern island of Novaya Zemlya, Severnaya Zemlya and on the New Siberia Islands. Found on all forms of tundra, but prefers drier, rocky ground. Colonial, excavating shallow burrows. If the opportunity arises, female lemmings will kill the young of nearby females, presumably to ensure a better food supply for their own litter. The subspecies that breed on Russia's Arctic islands have been proposed as separate species, particularly *D. t. ungulatus*, which breeds on Novaya Zemlya.

Wrangel Lemming
(Vinogradov's Lemming)
Dicrostonyx vinogradovi

The lemmings of Wrangel Island were once considered a race of the Arctic Collared Lemming, but they are now considered a separate species by most authorities.

Identification See p. 365

Pelage is pale gray with gray-cream patches. Collar is paler, but often very indistinct because of overall pale coloration. Ears are chestnut brown. In general the dorsal stripe is absent, though

▲ Wrangel Lemming, Wrangel.

it may be visible in younger animals. The underparts are washed yellow.

Size

HB: 5½–7½ in. (14–19 cm). T: ½–1 in. (1.5–2.5 cm). W: 2–3 oz. (60–90 g), but considerably heavier in winter.

Distribution

Very rare, breeding only on Wrangel Island.

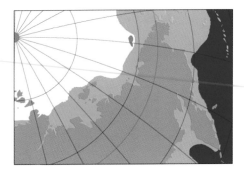

Greenland Collared Lemming
(Northern Collared Lemming)
Dicrostonyx groenlandicus

Identification   See p. 365
Very similar to the Arctic Collared Lemming, but grayer and with buff flanks and chest, and a pale gray head. Turns white in winter. The change in color coincides with the first snows of winter, which led the North American Inuit to call the lemmings *kilangmiutak*, meaning "drops from the sky."

Size
HB: 4–6 in. (10–16 cm). T: ½–¾ in. (1–2 cm). W: 1–2 oz. (35–55 g), but heavier in winter (up to 4 oz./110 g).

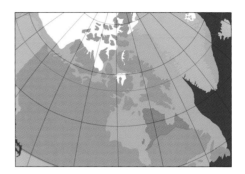

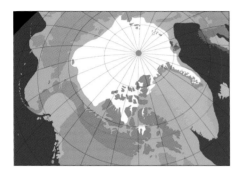

Distribution
Nearctic. Breeds in northeastern, northern and northwestern Greenland. In North America breeds in western and northern Alaska, and on the northern Canadian mainland east to Hudson Bay. Breeds on all of Canada's Arctic islands to northern Ellesmere Island. Found on all forms of tundra, but prefers dry, rocky tundra.

The lemmings of the Aleutian Islands are larger, lack the double claw and do not turn white in winter. Some authorities classify them as a subspecies, *D. g. unalascensis*, but others consider this taxon as a separate species; *unalascensis* is taken by some as referring only to the lemmings breeding on Unalaska, with other subspecies on the other Aleutian and Bering Sea islands.

Labrador Collared Lemming
(Ungava Lemming)
Dicrostonyx hudsonicus

Identification   See p. 365
Pelage is gray-brown above (though some individuals are red-brown) with a thin black dorsal stripe and red-brown patches close to the ears. In adult animals the dorsal stripe can be very indistinct. The underparts are pale gray, often separated from the upperparts by a pale brown band. The collar is red-brown, but often indistinct. In winter the pelage is white.

Size
HB: 5–5½ in. (12–14 cm). T: ¾–1 in. (2–2.5 cm). W: 1½–2¾ oz. (45–80 g).

Distribution
Nearctic. Breeds on the Ungava Peninsula of northern Quebec and Labrador, and on several of the islands of eastern Hudson Bay, e.g., Belcher and King George Islands. Found on all forms of tundra, but prefers dry, rocky tundra. The Labrador Collared Lemming probably descends from the Greenland Collared Lemming, with the ancestral populations of the two species being separated by the expansion of the forest belt.

Richardson's Collared Lemming
Dicrostonyx richardsoni

Identification   See p. 365
Pelage is dark red-brown above, becoming paler on the flanks and with buff or buff-gray underparts. There is a dark dorsal stripe, often indistinct in adults. There are often pale red-brown cheek and ear-patches. Collar is red-brown, and so only visible on the chest.

Size
HB: 4–5½ in. (10.5–14 cm). T: ⅓–½ in. (1–1.5 cm). W: 1–3 oz. (35–90 g).

Distribution
Nearctic. Breeds close to the western shore of Hudson Bay. Overlaps with the range of Greenland Collared Lemming, but does not appear to interbreed with that species (or to produce fertile offspring if it does). It is assumed that Richardson's evolved from the Greenland Collared Lemming, the two populations presumably separated during the Ice Ages.

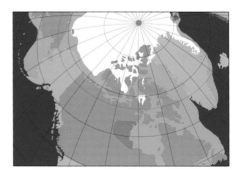

PLATE 31: VOLES

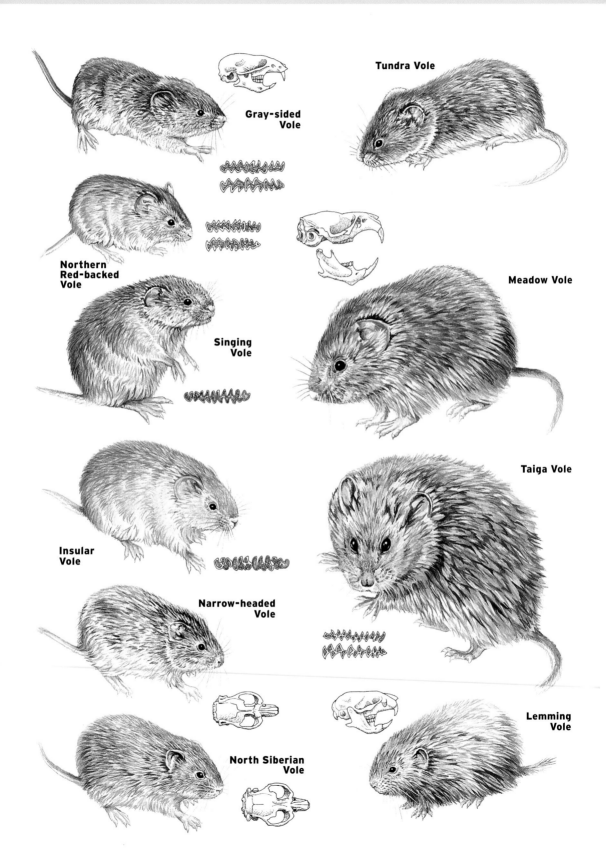

Gray-sided Vole

Tundra Vole

Northern Red-backed Vole

Singing Vole

Meadow Vole

Insular Vole

Taiga Vole

Narrow-headed Vole

North Siberian Vole

Lemming Vole

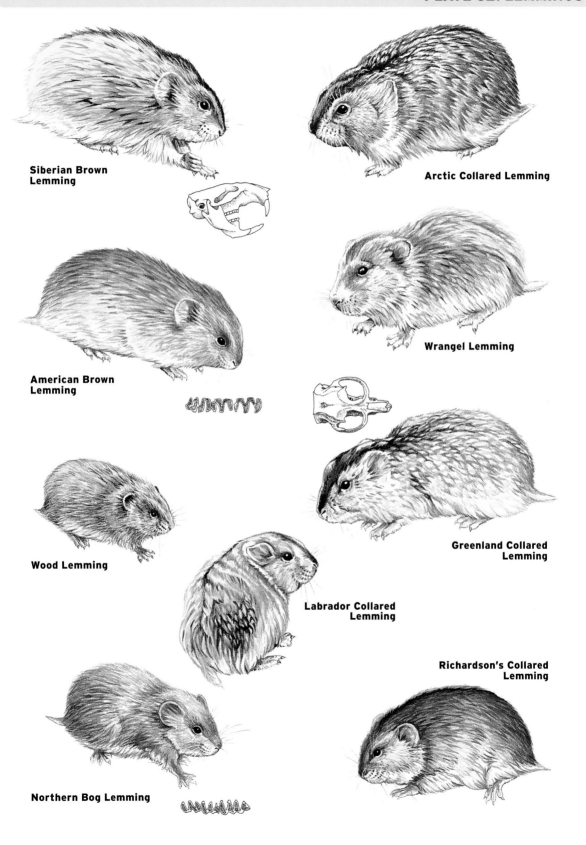

Siberian Brown
Lemming

Arctic Collared Lemming

American Brown
Lemming

Wrangel Lemming

Wood Lemming

Greenland Collared
Lemming

Labrador Collared
Lemming

Richardson's Collared
Lemming

Northern Bog Lemming

PLATE 33: LARGER RODENTS AND LAGOMORPHS

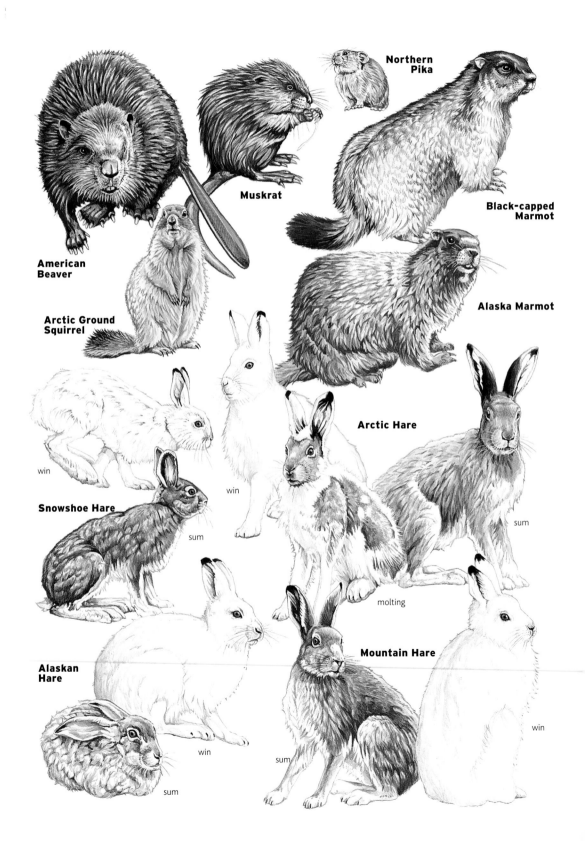

Northern Pika

Muskrat

Black-capped Marmot

American Beaver

Arctic Ground Squirrel

Alaska Marmot

Arctic Hare

win

win

Snowshoe Hare

sum

sum

molting

Alaskan Hare

Mountain Hare

win

win

sum

sum

Lagomorphs

The lagomorphs — rabbits, hares and pikas — differ from rodents in having a second pair of smaller incisors known as peg teeth that lie behind the first pair. Rabbits and hares have large ears and long back legs that evolved to give them the speed required to escape predators in open country; some hares can reach speeds of more than 44 mph (70 km/h). They have excellent excellent vision and a broad field of view due to both eye position and a flexible neck. By contrast, the much smaller pikas look like rodents and behave in similar ways.

Hares and rabbits differ in the strategies they use to escape predators. Hares attempt to outrun them, while rabbits make a rapid dash to cover or into a burrow. Hares do not construct burrows, though Snowshoe and Arctic Hares occasionally dig into deep snow. Consequently leverets (young hares) are born above ground and are necessarily precocial. Young rabbits are born below ground and are altricial. Leverets are left in concealed positions and are usually visited just once a day to be nursed. Suckling lasts only about five minutes. Hare milk has, consequently, a very high fat and protein content. Male hares may protect their young from attack by other females intent on reducing competition for their own litter, but otherwise do not contribute to the raising of leverets. All lagomorphs practice refection, the redigestion of "first-pass" fecal material, which has not been fully digested within the caecum. The "second-pass" fecal material is in the form of hard, black currantlike balls.

Pikas

All but two species of pika are Asian. The two non-Asian species breed in North America; one of these, the Collared Pika (*Ochotona collaris*) is found in southern Alaska and Yukon. Of the Asian species, most have a southerly range, though some are alpine animals. Only one species is northern, and it is a true Arctic dweller. This species is also responsible for the generic name of these animals; *pika* is the name given to them by the Tungus of Siberia because of the distinctive call.

Northern Pika
Ochotona hyperborea

Identification   See p. 366
Pelage is uniformly brown or dark brown, occasionally with darker patches on the sides of the neck and a darker wash to the lower back. There is a white stripe around the periphery of the ear. The feet are darker brown than the main pelage. The tail is inconspicuous. The whiskers are very long (up to 2 in./5.5 cm) which helps distinguish Northern Pikas from Altai (*O. alpina*), Daurian (*O. daurica*), and Mongolian (*O. pallasi*) Pikas where they overlap. In winter the thicker fur varies from gray-brown to reddish-brown, with underparts paler than the upperparts.

Dental formula: 2/1, 0/0, 3/2, 2/3 = 26 teeth.

Confusion species
Larger ears and the absence of a tail distinguish Northern Pikas from voles. If the observer is lucky enough to see the animal feeding, the side-to-side motion of the jaws is also diagnostic, as the only other species with a similar feeding method are the hares.

Size
L: 5–7½ in. (13–19 cm). W: 2–7 oz. (55–200 g).

▼ Northern Pika, Chukotka.

Communication

Relatively vocal, with a shrill *peeka*. Also communicates by scent.

Distribution

Palearctic. Breeds in Russia east of the Yenisey River, north to the coast except on the Taimyr Peninsula and south into Mongolia. Breeds throughout Chukotka and Kamchatka. Found in both mountainous and tundra areas.

Diet

Herbivorous, grazing on available tundra vegetation. Harvest vegetation in the summer to create haypiles, used in winter to supplement food obtained by tunneling beneath the snow. These haypiles are concealed beneath stones or in natural depressions.

Breeding

Colonial, sometimes with very large numbers of animals. Excavates burrows, but will also use natural shelters under stones or fallen trees. Two to six altricial young born after a gestation of around 30 days. Weaned after 30 days and achieve adult size at 40–50 days. If circumstances allow, females may produce more than one litter annually. In general Northern Pikas do not breed until 1-year-old.

Taxonomy and geographical variation

Polytypic. Various subspecies identified, though the differences are marginal. Whether the pikas of central Siberian, currently placed as subspecies *O. h. turuchanensis*, actually form a separate species is under debate.

Snowshoe Hare
Lepus americanus

Identification   See p. 366

Summer pelage is uniformly red-brown above with pale grey-brown underparts including the chin. The ears are relatively small for a hare and black-tipped. The tail is red-brown. The winter pelage is white apart from the black ear-tips. In both summer and winter, the guard hairs define the color, as the underfur remains pale gray-brown or yellow-brown. These color changes explain the occasional name of Varying Hare. The hind feet are very large (snowshoe like), an adaptation to allow the hare to move more easily over soft snow. A very fast runner (up to 25 mph/40 k/h claimed) and can bound up to 10 ft. (3 m) to avoid predators.

Dental formula is 2/1, 0/0, 3/2, 3/3 = 28 teeth.

Confusion species

None; the range rarely overlaps with other Arctic hares, though Snowshoe and Arctic Hares are found on the southern shore of Hudson Bay. The relatively small ears and large hind feet are diagnostic.

Size

HB: 13 in. (30–45 cm). Ear length: 3½–4 in. (9–10.5 cm). W: 2–5 lb. (0.9–2.2 kg).

▲ Snowshoe Hare in summer, Churchill.

Communication

Essentially silent, but squeals when attacked. Communication between adults is by scent from glands at the groin and under the chin, and by urination.

Distribution

Nearctic. Breeds from Alaska to Labrador. Differs from other hares in being boreal, rarely seen beyond the timberline (indeed, rarely seen far from cover). Found in both dense and sparse forest, and in both dry and wet areas.

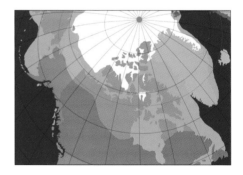

Diet

Herbivorous, feeding on a variety of plants. In winter the hares feed on twigs and bark. Will eat meat if available and has even been known to eat its own kind. Nocturnal, occasionally seen at dawn and dusk. During the day the hare hides in thick vegetation to elude its numerous predators. The hares create and maintain trails through their territories that lead to good feeding sites.

Breeding

Solitary, though small groups form at feeding sites and larger groups are occasionally seen in winter. During the mating season males are much less tolerant. Fights may occur with significant bite wounds inflicted. Male hares, though not highly territorial, have territories of up to 10 acres (4 ha) that overlap with those of several females, all of whom he will attempt to mate with. Other males will attempt to do likewise. Females occasionally trailed by several males who drum with their hind feet for attention and compete with each other in leaping battles. One to seven (usually two to four) leverets are born after a gestation of 34–40 days. They are weaned after around four weeks and achieve adult size within three to five months. Even at the northern limit of range, female Snowshoes usually have more than one litter annually. Breed at 1 year.

Snowshoe Hare populations are cyclical and synchronized over wide areas. The cycle is of around 10 years and, as with other small-mammal cycles, is not well understood. It is conjectured that, as for other species, the cycle is driven by food availability and predation; the hare population increases, food becomes short and high population density allows disease to spread rapidly, which, with starvation, causes numbers to plummet, assisted by increased predation as predator numbers rise in step (though lagged) with the hare population. When hare numbers are low, vegetation recovers from overgrazing and predator numbers fall, allowing the hare population to rise again.

Taxonomy and geographical variation
Polytypic, with some 15 subspecies described, most of them extralimital. In general differences are marginal, though the southern subspecies do not become white in winter.

Arctic Hare
Lepus arcticus

Identification
See p. 366

Variable pelage. In southern parts of the range, the summer pelage is gray or gray-brown, usually frosted white. To the north the hares are often white at all times. Winter pelage of southern hares is white. Unlike the Snowshoe Hare, the fur of Arctic Hares is white to the skin. The tail is white at all times; the ear-tips and the inner ear are black. The large feet are heavily furred. There are long claws on all four feet. When

approached the hares initially stand on hind legs to observe. Leverets are pale gray at birth, but soon take adult coloring. When chased the hares hop on their hind feet in a kangaroo-like fashion, reaching speeds of mor than 37 mph (60 k/h). They are also excellent swimmers.

Dental formula: 2/1, 0/0, 3/2, 3/3 = 28 teeth.

Confusion species
None.

Size
HB: 16–24 in. (40–60 cm). Ear length: 3–4 in. (7.5–10.5 cm). W: 5½–14 lb. (2.5–6.5 kg).

Communication
Silent. Squeals when attacked. Communicates mainly by scent.

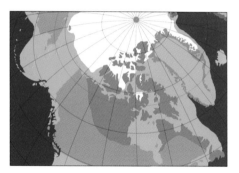

Distribution
Nearctic. Breeds on central and northern coasts of both eastern and western Greenland, but rare on the southern coasts. Breeds on Canada's Arctic islands to northern Ellesmere, and on northern mainland Canada east of the Mackenzie Delta to Labrador. Absent from Alaska. Mainland

▼ Arctic Hares in northeast Greenland. These hares retain their white coats year-round.

▲ Young Arctic Hare on the run, Cambridge Bay.

range extends to southwestern coast of Hudson Bay. Found on open tundra. Often seen sheltering from the wind in the lee of rocks. In winter Arctic Hares occasionally burrow into the snow, excavating short tunnels to dens that offer shelter from the intense cold. Introduced to Svalbard in the 1830s, but failed to thrive despite attempts to nurture the population; extinct on the island by the 1950s.

Diet
Herbivorous, taking vegetation in summer, twigs and bark in winter. Digs in snow with its claws to find winter food, often enlarging the feeding hole by pushing snow away with nose. Will eat meat if it is available and has been seen on sea ice looking for trapped seaweed. Fur trappers often find that traps baited for Arctic Foxes have caught hares tempted by the bait meat. Often nocturnal, so observable only at dawn and dusk, but active at all hours during periods of perpetual daylight.

Breeding
Usually solitary, but groups are often seen. These are usually small, but aggregations of several hundred have been observed. Males compete to mate with many females, but have no part in raising the leverets. Two to eight precocial leverets born, after gestation of 50–53 days, in a "nest" formed by the female stamping down local vegetation, usually in the shelter of a boulder. Female feeds her litter for short time, usually about five minutes but often less, once every 24 hours. She stands upright watching for danger as the gray leverets form a semicircle around her. At 3 weeks the leverets attain adult coloring and feed independently, though they are not weaned until 8 weeks. Breed at 1 year.

Taxonomy and geographical variation
Polytypic, with nine subspecies. Different subspecies inhabit most of the Canadian islands and isolated areas of Greenland.

Alaskan Hare (Tundra Hare)
Lepus othus

Identification
See p. 366

Summer pelage is red-brown, paler below, with a darker crown. The ears are bicolored, the front half as the body, the rear half white. The ear-tips are dark brown or black, this maintained in winter. The tail is also white. The hind feet are large and the feet are heavily clawed. The winter pelage is white and, as for the Arctic Hare, the fur color extends to the skin.

Dental formula: 2/1, 0/0, 3/2, 3/3 = 28 teeth.

Confusion species
The Alaskan Hare shares characteristics with both the Arctic and Snowshoe Hares, the summer pelage being as the Snowshoe, the winter as the Arctic. It is separated by range from the Arctic Hare, but overlaps in southern Alaska with the Snowshoe Hare. Distinguished from the Snowshoe by the tail, which is white at all times.

Size
HB: 20–24 in. (50–60 cm). Ear length: 2¾–4 in. (7–11 cm). W: 9–15 lb. (3.9–7 kg).

Distribution
Nearctic. Breeds in southwestern, western and northern Alaska. Found on tundra in northern and northwestern part of range, but also in forests in southern parts of the range. The population appears to be decreasing for unknown reasons.

Communication
As Snowshoe and Arctic Hares.

Diet
Herbivorous. Digs in snow with large claws to expose twigs, bark and other plant material in winter.

Breeding
Solitary, but forms groups in winter and during the mating season. Five to seven leverets born after a gestation of about 46 days. On tundra birth is usually in a natural depression. In forests or thickets, birth is in concealed place. Females nurse the leverets for five to nine weeks, a long period for hares. As a consequence the leverets grow rapidly, attaining adult weight at four months. Breed at 1 year.

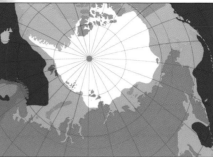

▲ Alaskan Hare.

Taxonomy and geographical variation

Polytypic. The nominate race breeds in north of range. *L. o. poadromus* breeds to the south and is more boreal. Otherwise the two are essentially identical. Alaskan Hare can only be reliably distinguished from Arctic and Mountain Hares by skull characteristics, and some authorities consider all three to be conspecific.

Mountain Hare
Lepus timidus

Identification See p. 366

Summer pelage dark brown or gray-brown, paler below and with gray or white tail. The ears are black-tipped. Winter pelage is white, but fur is not white to body, the underfur being slate-gray or blue-gray. This is occasionally visible as blue-gray flank patches. Animals in northern Siberia are white at all times.

Dental formula: 2/1, 0/0, 3/2, 3/3 = 28 teeth.

Confusion species

None, though in southern part of range may be confused with European Hare (*L. europaeus*), which has longer ears and a brown tail.

Size

HB: 18–24$\frac{1}{2}$ in. (45–61 cm). Ear length: 2$\frac{3}{4}$–4 in. (7–10 cm). W: 4$\frac{1}{2}$–13 lb. (2–5.8 kg).

Communication

Silent. Squeals when attacked. Female clicks with her teeth to warn leverets to stay still.

Distribution

Palearctic. Breeds in northern Scandinavia and across Russia from the Kola Peninsula to Chukotka, and throughout Kamchatka. Breeds to the northern Eurasian coast, but absent from all Arctic islands. As with the Arctic Hare, was introduced

to Svalbard in the 1930s, but failed to establish a viable population. Found on tundra.

Diet

Herbivorous. Nocturnal grazer on available vegetation. Feeds during the day in snowstorms.

Breeding

Solitary, but groups form at feeding sites and during the mating season (up to 100 animals). One to five leverets born after a gestation of 50 days. Birth is in depression formed by stamping local vegetation, but may also be in a burrow. Burrows are those of other animals, but hares have been observed digging or enlarging burrows. As with other northern hares, the female nurses the young once daily. Leverets are weaned at 3 weeks, gain adult size rapidly, and breed at 1 year.

Taxonomy and geographical variation

Polytypic, with numerous subspecies recognized.

▼ Mountain Hare in winter coat.

Ungulates

The ungulates or hoofed animals are divided into odd- and even-toed groups, the latter being by far the larger of the two. None of the odd-toed ungulates or Perissodactlya, a group that includes horses, tapirs and rhinoceroses, are Arctic breeders, though some may have occurred in Arctic regions in the past. Of the even-toed ungulates or Artiodactyla, members of two families, the Cervidae or deer and the Bovidae, a family that includes cattle, sheep and antelopes, breed in the Arctic. The Eurasian Wild Boar (*Sus scrofa*), a member of the pig family Suidae, breeds to the shores of Russia's White Sea.

Caribou (Reindeer)
Rangifer tarandus

Domesticated in Scandinavia and areas of Russia, truly wild Eurasian caribou now occur only in Russia, though feral herds are also found in Scandinavia. They have never been domesticated in North America, where huge herds still roam the northern tundra. The common name for the animal derives from a Native American name, usually rendered *xalibu*, meaning "pawer," from the animal's habit of using its hooves to expose food.

Unlike any other deer, Caribou of both sexes grow magnificent multibranched, semi-palmated antlers. These are asymmetrical, and unlike the left- or right-handedness of humans, the asymmetry is not consistent from year to year. The antlers grow annually within velvet, a sheath of skin with a rich blood supply. When the velvet is shed, it hangs in shreds from the antlers. Ultimately bone-dissolving cells invade the antler base and the antlers are shed, by males in early winter after the rut, by females in spring, though pregnant females keep theirs as late as calving (as an aside, the early winter shedding of antlers by males means that the Christmas red-nosed Reindeer is much more likely to be Rachel than Rudolph). The evolution of antlers has intrigued scientists for many years. At first it was assumed that they evolved as weapons, and males do indeed lock antlers during the annual rut. But those contests are a trial of strength rather than a true battle; biologists now favor the idea that antlers signal the quality of an animal to the opposite sex, and so enhance mating prospects. Studies show that the offspring of parents with large antlers grow faster, because the mother's milk is richer, and can move quicker and at an earlier age. Big antlers therefore indicate good genes. The downside of large antlers are the energetic requirements of their growth. To satisfy these, a Caribou must choose fertile areas for feeding, and this both limits habitat suitability and necessitates annual migrations. In practice, though, the extensive distribution of the species means that their browse is much less limited than might be expected.

Most Caribou form huge herds, which, while minimizing the chances of an individual falling prey to predators, increases competition for resources. It is suggested that the antlers of female Caribou allow them to compete with males that might otherwise evict them from feeding areas. Tundra females would be particularly prone to piracy, as they have to excavate holes in the snow to reach food. Woodland Caribou (*R. t. granti*) browse lichen from trees, so piracy offers no advantage, and their females often do not have antlers.

Identification   See p. 381
Pelage is dark brown or gray-brown, paler on the underparts, buttocks and feet (and occasionally with a broad, pale collar).

▼ A small herd of Caribou of the nominate race, northern Norway.

The muzzle and forehead are usually darker. Winter pelage is much paler, often cream or light buff in northern animals. The winter color change is aided by the growth of long guard hairs that are usually white-tipped; these hairs are hollow and so add a layer of insulating air. There is a fringe of longer hairs on the throat. The tail is short and of limited value against mosquitoes and other insect pests (so the animal's primary defense is to head for windier spots or to rest on snowfields, where the cooler air reduces insect flight abilities). The feet are the widest of any deer, and the dewclaws, vestigial in most deer, are well developed; these are adaptations for walking on snow. Walking Caribou make a characteristic click as tendons in the feet stretch across bony nodules. The hooves are sharp-edged to provide greater traction on ice and rock. In winter the hoof pads shrink and harden, and become covered by hair that grows in tufts between the toes. The animal then walks on the outer rim of the hoof, protecting the vulnerable pads from the frozen ground. The iris is dark orange-brown.

Dental formula: 0/3, 0–1/1, 3/3, 3/3 = 32–34 teeth.

Confusion species
None.

Size
HB: 5½–7¼ ft. (1.7–2.2 m). T: 4–7¾ in. (10–20 cm). SH: 2½–4 ft. (80–120 cm). W: 130–330 lb. (60–150 kg).

Communication
Generally silent. Cows communicate with their newborn calves with a repertoire of low grunts. Bulls bellow loudly during the rut.

Distribution
Circumpolar. Breeds in western and northern Greenland, on Svalbard and across Russia, sporadically to the northern coast (e.g., on Taimyr Peninsula and around the Lena and Kolyma Deltas). Breeds on the southern island of Novaya Zemlya, the New Siberia Islands (these islands were discovered when a hunter saw a herd crossing the sea ice to the mainland and realized they must have come from an island) and on Wrangel Island (where they have been introduced). Domesticated Caribou have been introduced to Iceland, where the species is now feral and established in the east of the island.

In the Nearctic, breeds throughout Alaska and northern Canada, including the Arctic islands north to Ellesmere Island (note that the animals of the Belcher Islands are Eurasian Caribou introduced in 1978). Island Caribou are resident or partially migratory, mainland animals are migratory. Island Caribou are largely restricted to tundra, but mainland animals can migrate from tundra to forest (and back), though some are confined to forests. Caribou use traditional calving grounds, with some migratory herds traveling 3,100 mi. (5,000 km) annually between these and the winter feeding grounds. Sometimes the animals will travel more than 60 mi. (100 km) each day, though 15–40 mi. (25–65 km) is more usual. Migrating animals travel at around 4 mph (7 km/h). Migrations may cross rivers; Caribou are excellent swimmers, traveling at around 2 mph (32 km/h) in water, though they

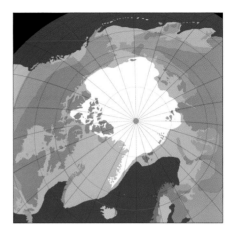

can swim at up to 6 mph (10 km/h) in short bursts. Barren-ground Caribou (*R. t. groenlandicus*) crossing Bathurst Inlet have been observed swimming 6 mi. (10 km) shore to shore.

Diet
Herbivorous, browsing on tundra vegetation or on arboreal or terrestrial lichens in forests. Feeds extensively on Caribou Moss (*Cladonia rangiferina*), which is actually a lichen. The animals locate the lichen beneath the snow by smell. Caribou are vulnerable to thaw-freeze conditions that may leave terrestrial lichens under a blanket of impenetrable ice. Digging for terrestrial lichens in the snow is energy-intensive, while the browse is energy-poor, so excavated holes are extremely valuable. As noted above, protection of such holes may explain why female Caribou have antlers. Caribou have been seen eating lemmings in "lemming years," but this behavior is rare. They also eat shed antlers to obtain minerals for antler growth.

Breeding
Subspecies range from occasionally solitary (Peary Caribou [*R. t. pearyi*], Svalbard Caribou [*R. t. platyrhynchus*] through "semi-gregarious" (Woodland Caribou, which form small groups) to gregarious (the huge herds of Barren-ground Caribou and, pre-domestication, the Eurasian Caribou [*R. t. tarandus*]. However, highly gregarious animals often form much smaller groups when not migrating. The annual rut is in autumn, when males stop feeding to form and maintain harems. Fights are frequent, but these are ritualized and rarely result in injury, merely the retreat of the weaker of the two males. After the rut, bull Caribou can be exhausted and often fall prey to Wolves. As the bulls shed their antlers at this time, it has been suggested that females retain theirs for longer to signal to wolves that they are not weakened males.

During the spring migration to the calving grounds, cows and yearlings lead the way, with the bulls following behind and lagging farther back as the migration proceeds. The two sexes have different imperatives; cows need to reach the open tundra where they can calve in relative safety, as Wolves and Brown Bears do not, in general, follow them out onto the tundra (there are tundra wolves and bears, but fewer of them), while the bulls need to linger where the feeding is richest as

◄ Caribou of the endemic Svalbard race *platyrhynchus*. Note the short legs and small stature; following millenia of isolation on Svalbard, these deer are well on the way to becoming true dwarfs. Dwarfism often occurs in populations of larger mammals on islands.

nominate and with *fennicus*; others believe that nominate Caribou formerly bred in Kola, and that the present form is a wild nominate/domesticated Caribou/*fennicus* cross.

There are several subspecies that have evolved on the islands and peninsulas of the region. Peary Caribou (*R. t. pearyi*) breeds on the northern Canadian Arctic islands. It is smaller and paler than the nominate and tends to be solitary or form small herds of three to five animals. While searching for winter food, *pearyi* will cross sea ice between the islands of Arctic Canada. These movements have brought the animals into contact with Barren-ground Caribou on the Canadian mainland and interbreeding has occurred. It is now thought that the genetically purest stock of *pearyi* are found on the Queen Elizabeth Islands. *R. t. platyrhynchus*, the Svalbard Caribou, is similar to *pearyi*. It is a short-legged form, dark as the nominate in summer, but almost white in winter. As with *pearyi*, it is solitary or forms small herds. The distance of the Svalbard archipelago from mainland Scandinavia means that there has been no interbreeding with continental animals. The animals of Russia's Arctic islands (Novaya Zemlya and the New Siberia Islands) are also considered a subspecies, *R. t. pearsoni*, though regular gene flow with mainland populations has limited differences from the nominate, leading some authorities to question whether subspecific designation is appropriate. By contrast, the subspecies status of the Caribou of the Kamchatkan Peninsula is unequivocal; these are *R. t. phylarchus*. As with some other of the peninsula's mammals (for instance, the Brown Bears), Kamchatka's Caribou are larger than those of other populations. Race *phylarchus* is as much as 50% larger than the nominate, though the domesticated animals of the native Koryak people are of "normal" size, suggesting that they derive from Caribou from elsewhere in Russia.

▼ Caribou on the move, Barren Lands, Northwest Territories.

they must build up their strength for the autumnal rut. The urgency of the cows to reach the calving grounds is such that calves born early, and therefore along the migration route, may be left behind by their mothers. At the calving grounds, the cows divide into small groups to give birth. A single calf is born after a gestation of 210–240 days. Twins are occasionally born to Eurasian Caribou, but they are extremely rare in Nearctic Caribou. Calves are precocial, walking at about one hour (and able to run several miles/kilometres within two hours) and growing rapidly on the richest milk (about 20% fat) produced by any deer, or indeed by any terrestrial mammal. The first hour is critical, however; the calf needs to dry or to be licked dry to prevent it from freezing to death. Calves are weaned at 4–6 weeks. Females usually give birth annually, but may miss a year if their body reserves are low. Females usually breed at two years. Males are also sexually mature at this time, but competition from older males may prevent them breeding.

Taxonomy and geographical variation

Polytypic. The nominate race is the Eurasian Caribou. (*R. t. groenlandicus*), the Barren-ground Caribou, breeds in Greenland and in the tundra regions of North America. It is paler than the nominate. The Woodland Caribou *R. t. granti*, breeds in North America's boreal forest. It is as dark as the nominate but has a distinctive broad white collar on the neck, shoulders and chest, and also has larger antlers. The Palearctic equivalent is *R. t. fennicus*, the Forest Caribou, which breeds in the forests of east-central Finland and adjacent European Russia to the shores of the White Sea. Hybridization of *fennicus* with domesticated nominate race Caribou has occurred, and fencing has been erected to prevent this. However, cross-breeding at the boundary of the two forms has caused such concern that purebred Forest Caribou have been released into a protectorate in southern Finland in an attempt to preserve the race. Opinion on the provenance of the Caribou of Russia's Kola Peninsula is divided. Over the last 100 years or so, there have been introductions into this area as well as cross-breeding with *fennicus*. Some authorities believe that there may once have been a native subspecies, but this has now completely hybridized with the

Moose (Elk)
Alces alces

The differences of nomenclature between European and American naturalists are mostly trivial, as it is usually easy to remember both and confusions are minimal. However, this is not true in the case of *Alces alces*. In Europe, this animal is called the Elk, the name deriving from the old Germanic appellation *elch*, but in North America, the Elk is a different animal. Also known as the Wapiti, the North American Elk (*Cervus canadensis*) is very similar to the Red Deer (*C. elaphus*) of Europe and eastern Asia. *Alces alces* is known in North America as the Moose, a name derived from the Algonquin word for "twigeater." Some European biologists also use this name, adding to the confusion.

Moose are dangerous, particularly females with calves. The animals lash out with their front hooves. These are sharp, and arrive at the victim with the full force of a 1,100 lb. (500 kg) animal behind them, a blow that can result in serious injury or death. Moose are also very quick, reaching speeds of around 35 mph (55km/h), and they have even been seen to overtake canoes in which two men were paddling furiously.

Identification   See p. 381

The world's largest extant deer, and apart from the very largest bears, the largest terrestrial species in the Arctic. Normally seen within forests when their apparent size can seem small relative to the trees, Moose seen on the tundra reveal their true proportions — they are huge. The coarse body pelage is dark brown or dark gray-brown, the underparts paler, the legs pale gray-white or gray-brown. Moose have very long legs, which may be an adaptation to deep snow in winter; they are also useful for evading predators such as Wolves, with the Moose trotting easily over obstacles that require the pursuer to make an energy-sapping jump. The tail is surprisingly short for an animal pestered by seasonal insects. The snout is bulbous and a large pendant "bell" hangs from the throat. The function of this bell is unknown, but bull moose spatter the bell with urine-soaked mud during the rut. The ears are large and can rotate through 180°, giving the animal excellent hearing. Males have huge, palmate antlers with numerous tines; the antlers may weigh up to 66 lb. (30 kg) and have a spread of around 7 ft. (2 m). Unlike the antlers of all other deer, Moose antlers grow laterally rather than vertically. Antler velvet is shed in late summer, antlers in December-February. The iris is dark orange.

Dental formula: 0/3, 0–1/1, 3/3, 3/3 = 32–34 teeth.

Confusion species
None.

Size
HB: 6½–9½ ft. (2–2.9 m). T: 2¾–4 in. (7–10 cm). SH: 5–7¼ ft. (1.5–2.2 m). W: 660–1,800 lb. (300–800 kg).

Communication
A very deep, low mooing. In rut both sexes have a higher, rather nasal squeal. Coughs when alarmed.

▶ Moose resting deep in the boreal forest, northern Sweden.

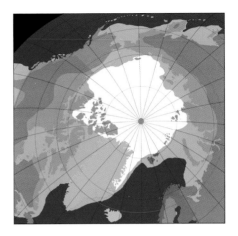

Distribution
Circumpolar. Absent from Greenland, Iceland and the Arctic islands. Breeds in Fennoscandia (but not to the northern coast) and across Russia to the northern coast west of the Ob River, but not east of this. In the Nearctic, breeds in Alaska, but not to the northern coast or on the Aleutians. Breeds throughout Yukon, in southern Northwest Territories and on the eastern shore of Hudson Bay through central Quebec/Labrador. Essentially boreal, preferring marshland in summer, but drier ground in winter; also found on the tundra. Many animals are resident, but some are migratory, moving up to 90 mi (150 km) between wintering grounds and summer calving grounds. Despite the association of Moose with forests, the animals will actually travel far out onto the tundra if browse is available.

Diet
Herbivorous, browsing shoots and twigs of trees (especially pines) and aquatic plants. Winter browse is low in sodium, so Moose, as other deer, need salt in spring. They obtain this from aquatic plants such as *Potamogeton* pond weeds; not only will they submerge their heads to browse, but Moose have even

▲ Female Moose of the race *gigas* with her calves. Seward Peninsula.

been observed to dive up to 13 ft. (4 m) to take the weeds. It is thought that Moose build up a store of sodium in the rumen, one part of the multi-chambered stomach that all ruminants have. This is an adaptation to help these mammals deal with plant cellulose; Moose have a four-chambered stomach. Photographs of Moose, particularly bulls, standing belly-deep in water, often with a tangle of vegetation in their antlers, have become iconic and representative of the Alaskan wilderness. Moose go into water not only to feed, but also to cool off. The huge fermentation pit that is the animal's stomach is a heat source, and as Moose do not perspire they can overheat. Moose are often victims of road traffic, as in winter they use snowplowed roads, which are easier to negotiate than the deep snow of the forest, and also because they are prone to licking the salt occasionally spread on winter roads. One particularly interesting aspect of the animal's autumnal diet appears to affect Scandinavian Moose rather than North American animals. Scandinavian Moose feed on fermenting apples, if they are available, becoming belligerently drunk and menacing cyclists and walkers.

▼ Musk Oxen, Oestersletten, northeast Greenland.

Breeding

Moose are much less gregarious than other deer, particularly the Caribou, which forms herds of tens of thousands. They are generally solitary, though small, mixed herds occasionally form in winter under the leadership of an older female. Territorial, with both males and females holding territories that can be 1–8 sq. mi. (2–20 km²) and are marked by urine. During the autumnal rut, Moose use their hooves to scrape a pit in which they urinate, splashing urine-soaked mud onto the belly and flanks. They also urinate onto their hind legs. Female Moose call loudly to attract males. One, occasionally two, rarely three, calves are born after a gestation of about 285 days. Calves can follow their mother in 1–3 days, but do not begin to browse until 4–6 weeks. Calves stay with their mother until she is ready to give birth again. At that time, she evicts them from her presence. Breed at 4–5 years. Females are capable of bearing calves for many years, but the physical effort of growing antlers takes a toll on bulls, which may only be in prime mating condition for two to three years.

Taxonomy and geographical variation

Polytypic. The nominate race breeds in Eurasia. The larger, darker *A. a. gigas* breeds in Alaska and the Yukon. *A. a. andersoni* breeds from the Yukon to the west of Hudson Bay. It is smaller than the nominate, though marginally so, and is of a similar color. *A. a. americana* breeds east of Hudson Bay. It is smaller than the nominate and a beautiful mahogany-brown. A fifth subspecies, the gray-brown *A. a. shirasi*, is extralimital, breeding in the northern Rocky Mountains.

Musk Ox
Ovibos moschatus

With their straggling hair, occasionally so long it all but obscures the short legs, and huge horns, Musk Oxen are among the most recognizable of all Arctic species. Musk Oxen are nervous and suspicious. Lone animals are particularly nervous,

as they are vulnerable to Wolf predation. Approaching naturalists are watched closely and charged if they stray too close. Most charges are terminated when the observer turns and runs, but being caught by a charging Musk Ox is likely to result in serious injury. As a defence against Wolves, Musk Ox herds form circles, the adults facing outward, calves at the center. This strategy is very effective and the Wolves will go hungry unless they can provoke the Musk Oxen into breaking the circle and fleeing. Even then, if the Musk Ox herd remains cohesive, the Wolves have difficulty in isolating an individual. Musk Oxen have been known to pick up Wolves with their horns, throw them and then stamp on them. However, the defensive circle is a poor strategy against a human with a rifle, and Musk Ox populations have been severely depleted wherever hungry people have shared their territory.

The ease of slaughter of Musk Oxen by hunters has led to population crashes in many parts of the animal's range. In northeastern Greenland, where Norwegian fur trappers were active in the 1920s and 1930s, Musk Oxen were almost exterminated. The successful sovereignty claim by Denmark over what the Norwegians termed Eirik Raudes Land led to a virtual cessation of hunting, and numbers have increased again. Ironically, the increase was partly because the Norwegians had killed off most of the area's Wolf population and so limited natural predation of the Musk Oxen. A similar slaughter of oxen in the Canadian Arctic led to government protection of the species in 1917 and was the primary reason for the creation of the Thelon Game Sanctuary in 1927.

▲ This old bull Musk Ox has been abandoned by the rest of its herd. Kapp Petersens, northeast Greenland.

Identification   See p. 381

A large, stocky, oxlike bovid. The pelage is dark brown and dark gray-brown, but with a paler saddle. The muzzle is also paler. The legs, too, are paler, but they are often hidden or partially hidden by the long straggling guard hairs, which appear to be in a constant state of molt. Individual guard hairs are up to 28 in. (70 cm) long. The fine underfur is claimed by many to be the finest wool in the world. Known by the Inuit word *qiviut*, it is highly prized for the manufacture of (very expensive) small items of clothing, chiefly scarves. The hooves are broad, with a sharp outer rim and a softer inner rim, allowing the animal to be surprisingly agile on rock. The large head is crowned by huge horns emanating from a forehead boss, similar to that of a buffalo. The horns sweep down from the boss, then curve up and forward.

Dental formula: 0/3, 0/1, 3/2–3, 3/3 = 30–32 teeth.

Confusion species

None.

Size

HB: 6–8¼ ft. (1.8–2.5 m). T: 4–4¾ in. (10–12 cm). SH: 3–5¼ ft. (90–160 cm). W: 485–881 lb. (220–400 kg), males occasionally to 1,320 lb. (600 kg).

Communication

A typically bovine bellow. The animals also communicate by spraying urine on the guard-hair fringe. The musky smell of this gives the animal its name.

Distribution

Essentially Nearctic. Breeds in western and northern Alaska, though these are introduced animals (originally released near Fairbanks, then on Nunivak Island in 1935), as the native stock was eliminated by hunting in the 1860s. Greenlandic animals were released with the intention of recreating the original distribution. Breeds on the extreme northern rim of mainland

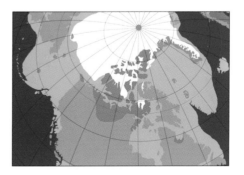

Canada west of Hudson Bay and on western and northern Arctic islands. Absent from Baffin Island, but a small herd breeds near Ungava Bay in Quebec. Breeds in northeastern and northern Greenland. Has also been reintroduced to northwestern and western Greenland. Absent from Iceland. Was introduced to Svalbard, where it almost certainly never occurred naturally, but that population is now believed to be extinct. Has also been introduced to Scandinavia and Russia, but populations are small. Tundra dweller. Resident or partially migratory. Musk Oxen roam in search of food, but some have a distinct summer-winter movement of up to 50 mi. (80 km). Wintering animals move slowly to conserve energy and often huddle together when resting. Musk Oxen swim rivers during migrations in search of food, and may also swim to evade Wolves.

Diet

Tundra vegetation, primarily Arctic Willow and birch, but also herbaceous plants. In winter, browses on lichens, twigs and any available grasses, choosing hilltops where the snow is blown away to expose the browse. Musk Ox will paw at frozen ground to reach food; they also occasionally smash at the icy surface with their noses to break through the windblown crust and so expose the surface for pawing. As with Caribou, Musk Oxen are vulnerable in thaw-freeze conditions.

Breeding

Gregarious, but herd sizes variable because of the scarcity of browse and predation. Herds can reach 50 animals, but 5–12 is more common. In general the presence of Wolves increases herd size. Smaller groups usually include a dominant male with a harem of females and some immature animals. During the rut, the dominant male may have his authority tested. Threat postures are enough to put lesser males to flight, but two evenly matched males may compete in a spectacular trial of strength, rushing at each other at speeds to about 25 mph (40 km/h) and banging heads.

One calf (rarely two) born after gestation of about eight months. Calves are precocial; they can stand and suckle within minutes of birth. Young calves are "piglike" and have an endearing habit of hiding under the guard-hair skirt of their mother when startled. Calves may suckle until they are 15–18 months old, the availability of milk aiding survival during the calf's first winter. Females breed at three years and in general give birth biennially, though the exact timing depends on the quality of the local browse; annual birthing has been observed Males breed at 4–6 years depending on the competi-tion. They grow throughout their lives, which may be between 20 and 25 years long.

Taxonomy and geographical variation

Perhaps polytypic. Some authorities identify several subspecies, but this is disputed, since many populations have been introduced. In general it is thought that the nominate race breeds on Greenland and mainland North America, with *O. m. wardi* breeding on Canada's Arctic islands. Race *wardi* is darker, but the difference lies within the range of nominate coloration.

Dall's Sheep
Ovis dalli

Dall's and Snow Sheep were once considered to be subspecies of the North American Bighorn Sheep (*Ovis canadensis*). The two are now considered to be separate species, but they share many characteristics with each other and with the Bighorn Sheep.

Identification See p. 381

Pelage is white, but one subspecies is gray-brown with pale underparts, buttocks and inside legs. Some sheep are "gray phase" with silver-gray backs and outer legs but white head, neck, shoulders, chest and buttocks. Intermediate forms are also seen. The hooves are black, the tail very short. The horns curve back from the forehead, then grow strongly downcurved with forward-pointing tips. They are thinner than those of the Bighorn Sheep and more heavily corrugated on the outer keel. The horns range from yellow-brown to tawny-brown. Ram's horns are up to 3 ft. (100 cm) long. Ewes have smaller, straighter horns up to 10 in. (25 cm) long. Horn growth rings indicate sheep's age. The iris is yellow-orange.

Dental formula: 0/3, 0/1, 3/3, 3/3 = 32 teeth.

Confusion species
None.

▼ Female (right) and young Dall's Sheep. Turnagain Arm, Alaska.

◀ A flock on a steep, rocky cliff — classic Dall's Sheep country, Alaska.

Breeding
Gregarious, but rams and ewes are rarely together except during the autumn rut. Rams do not hold territories, moving around to find, then hold, estrus ewes, defending them against other rams until mating, then moving on to find another female. Rams compete by bashing their horns in a trial of strength, the run toward the opponent beginning with the ram standing up on its hind legs to add extra momentum. The sound of the crash of competing rams carries over several miles/kilometres. One, rarely two, precocial lambs born after a gestation of 170–180 days. Weaned at 3–5 months. Ewes breed at two or three years and give birth annually. Rams are sexually mature at 2–3 years, but first breeding is dependent on the local competition.

Taxonomy and geographical variation
Polytypic. The nominate race breeds throughout most of the range. *O. d. stonei*, Stone's Sheep, breeds in the southern Yukon region. It is darker in color, gray-brown with lighter underparts. Some authorities also recognize *O. d. kenainesis* breeding on the Kenai Peninsula. It is smaller than the nominate, but a similar color.

Size
HB: 4¼–6 ft. (1.3–1.8 m). T: 2¾–4½ in. (7–11 cm). SH: 3–3½ ft. (90–105 cm). W: 110–242 lb. (50–110 kg).

▼ Male Dall's Sheep sport impressive horns. Denali, Alaska.

Communication
A "standard" sheep bleat.

Distribution
Nearctic. Breeds in upland Alaska and Yukon. Partially migratory, usually moving up to 20 mi. (30 km) between summer and winter ranges. The sheep exhibit high fidelity to these ranges. Prefers steep, precipitous ground.

Diet
Herbivorous, taking a range of available vegetation, but primarily grasses in summer and lichen in winter. Dig through the snow to find winter browse but, as with Caribou, are vulnerable to thaw-freeze conditions. In spring, the sheep follow the retreating snow to feed on succulent new growth.

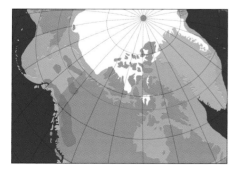

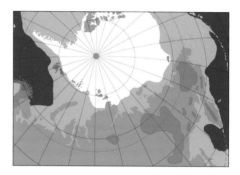

◀ Adult Snow Sheep, Kamchatka.

Communication
A "standard" sheep bleat.

Distribution
Palearctic. Breeds in upland areas of eastern Siberia, including Chukotka and Kamchatka, where it is rare. Resident, but moves in search of browse.

Snow Sheep
Ovis nivicola

Identification   See p. 381
Pelage variable, usually brown with paler underparts insides of legs and rump patch. The rump patch is often white and may spread onto the lower back. The forelegs are usually darker. The horns are curved as for Dall's Sheep rams, and are similarly massive in the ram.
    Dental formula: 0/3, 0/1, 3/3, 3/3 = 32 teeth.

Confusion species
None.

Size
HB: 5¼–6 ft. (1.6–1.8 m). T: 2¾–4¾ in. (7-12 cm). SH: 32–40 in. (80-100 cm). W: 154–220 lb. (70–100 kg), but specimens to 308 lb. (140 kg).

Diet
Ground vegetation (e.g., grasses, herbs), the foliage of shrubs and deciduous trees, the needles of coniferous trees, and lichens.

Breeding
Gregarious, forming small herds of up to 20 animals outside the breeding season. Breeding biology is poorly understood, but assumed to be similar to that of Dall's Sheep.

Taxonomy and geographical variation
Polytypic. The nominate race breeds in Kamchatka. Two other subspecies are recognized, *O. n. alleni*, the Yakutian Snow Sheep of eastern Yakutia, and *O. n. koriakorum*, the Koryak Snow Sheep of northern Kamchatka and southern Chukotka. The claimed differences refer to pelage color, but these lie within the range of pelages seen in nominate Snow Sheep and are dismissed by some authorities.

◀ Adult Snow Sheep molting into
summer coat, Kamchatka.

Caribou

♂

R. t. granti

♀

R. t. granti

R. t. platyrhynchus

♀

R. t. platyrhynchus

♂

♀

♀

R. t. pearyi

♂

R. t. pearyi

Moose

♂

♀

Musk Ox

Snow Sheep

♂

♀

Dall's Sheep

lamb

♂

♀

Carnivores

Carnivores, members of the large mammalian order Carnivora, include some of the most largest, most spectacular and charismatic of all Arctic species. Most carnivores have an enlarged fourth upper premolar and first lower molar, which together form an efficient shear for cutting into meat; these teeth are referred to as the carnassials. The Carnivora is broadly split into two major groups, the fissipeds or terrestrial carnivores, and the pinnipeds, a group that includes the seals, sea lions and walrus that are considered separately. Fissiped families with Arctic representatives include the Canidae (dogs), Ursidae (bears), Felidae (cats) and Mustelidae (weasels and allies).

Dogs

In Alaska, Coyotes (*Canis latrans*) have been observed as far west as the Alaskan Peninsula, on the northern shore of Bristol Bay and in the Brooks Range, but in both Alaska and Canada the Coyote is essentially sub-Arctic.

Gray Wolf
Canis lupus

Few animals evoke such strong emotions as the wolf. For many people, the Wolf epitomizes the wilderness, and there is strong support not only for its preservation but also for its reintroduction into areas in which it has been extirpated. However, for a greater number the very name evokes a fear and loathing out of all proportion to any genuine danger presented by these wonderful canids. The native peoples of the north did not share the modern distaste of the wolf, with wolves frequently being the animal familiar of shamans. Arctic and sub-Arctic Native Americans did not view the wolf as

▼ Male wolf of race *nubilus*, Barren Grounds, Northwest Territories.

dangerous, and in many areas considered it totemic, though there are instances of wolves being killed to provide skins for clothing, or, less often, because the wolf hunted similar, perhaps sparse, prey. High Arctic Inuit were aware of the wolf and its hunting methods: when police were first introduced to Canadian Inuit settlements, the locals called them *amakro*, meaning wolf, because the police stood in the background observing, watching for mistakes, as wolves do. The similarities of pre-industrial humans and wolves — both living in family groups, using cooperative hunting with strategies based on patience and cunning — mean that it is no surprise that when wolves were domesticated they became companions and partners, rather than servants or slaves.

Early Europeans also viewed the wolf positively. A female wolf was said to have nurtured Romulus and Remus, and was therefore instrumental in the birth of Roman civilization, while Viking lords often took the name *Ulf* (as do modern Scandinavians). But by the early medieval period, things had changed, the wolf becoming a malevolent presence, the change reflected in a host of tales in which the animal is represented as deceitful, greedy, ferocious and, most significantly, dangerous. Of course, for medieval European farmers the wolf represented a real threat to domestic stock, and the more that farmers encroached on the wolf's territory and reduced the numbers of its natural prey, the more sheep and goats the wolf was forced to take. In the battle between wolf and human, there could be only one winner. In northern and most of western Europe the wolf population has been systematically destroyed. The last English wolf was killed in the early 16th century. In Scotland, forests were torched to destroy the final remnant populations, which were gone by the mid-18th century. In Scandinavia wolves were eliminated from Sweden in 1966 and from Norway in 1973. Numbers were also reduced to the verge of extinction in Finland, but recolonization from Russia prevented total extirpation. With changing attitudes, the wolves that have now recolonized Sweden and then Norway through Finland have been protected, though persecution continues and the populations

▲ An alpha male of race *arctos*. White Wolves are restricted to the high Arctic. This one is shedding its coat. Ellesmere Island.

hover on the edge of survival. It would be ironic if Fennoscandia were to be successfully repopulated from Russia, given the present position of abuse of the animal in that country. Hunting licenses are annually granted for the killing of about 35% of the population, according to the best estimates by the few Russian wolf biologists, and these licenses include the hunting of wolves within nature reserves.

Early European settlers to North America took their prejudices with them, but these new Americans became even more fanatical in their hatred of the wolf. It seems that faced with a country of awesome size and wildness, the newcomers equated the eradication of the wolf with the taming of the wilderness, and set about the task with vigor. Only relatively recently has the change in public attitude allowed the reintroduction of the wolf to Yellowstone National Park. The suggestion that wolves be reintroduced to Scotland has elicited much less enthusiasm. Populations who would sign petitions to set up tiger reserves in rural India are far less keen on the idea of wolves on their own doorsteps. This represents another problem, that of perception. Although wolf attacks on humans have occurred, these are, in general, by dog-wolf crosses or by rabid animals. Attacks by thoroughbred wolves are exceedingly rare. Wolves are generally curious, but never threatening. But the belief prevails that wolves are dangerous. Attacks on domestic stock are also relatively rare unless habitat destruction has decimated natural prey, but even then the beliefs of farmers are invariably an exaggeration. The problem is that facts are not allowed to get in the way of a well-held prejudice; in the relationship between wolves and humans, it is beliefs and superstitions that dominate.

Identification
See p. 410
The Gray Wolf is the largest wild dog. The pelage is usually gray, but can vary (particularly in North American animals)

from almost black to white. Usually the pelage is a mix of colors, with darker fur above, often dark gray or black toward the tip of the tail, and paler underparts. The legs may also be darker on the outer surface. There is often darker fur on the nape, forehead and muzzle, with paler patches on the cheeks. White Wolves are found in northern Canada and the Canadian Arctic islands, in Greenland and areas of Arctic Russia, in particular the Arctic islands, though data on Russian wolves are sparse. Cubs are dark gray and brown above, paler below and on the legs. White wolf cubs are pale gray. Wolves have deep yellowish orange eyes and a greenish-orange eye-shine.

Dental formula: 3/3, 1/1, 4/4, 2/3 = 42 teeth.

Confusion species
Wolves are larger than Coyotes and run with the tail held high rather than held down.

Size
HB: 3–5 ft. (90–150 cm). T: 12–20 in. (30–50 cm). SH: 2–3 ft. (65–80 cm). W: 66–175 lb. (30–80 kg).

Communication
The Gray Wolf's howl is one of its most famous features. Howling helps packs to reform, distinguishes pack members from outsiders, defines boundaries and may also reinforce pack bonds. Lone wolves howl to identify where the pack is by listening for the response, but such howls are usually quieter so as not to attract the attention of hostile neighboring packs. Gray Wolves do not only howl; they have a range of vocalizations including barks, growls and whimpers. Barks are often used as short-range signals. Growls are an aggressive

vocalization, while whimpering is used to beg for food, to indicate submission or by fearful or injured animals. Pack territories are marked by urine on landmarks such as prominent rocks or tree stumps. Territory size depends on prey density and can be as small as 40 sq. mi. (100 km²) for a pair of wolves in an area of high prey density or as large as 5,800 sq. mi. (15,000 km²) for a large pack with limited prey. Territories also depend on prey species; North American Gray Wolves largely dependent on Caribou have more fluid territories, as fixed territories would be of limited value with migratory prey.

Distribution

Circumpolar. Breeds in northeastern and northern Greenland. Absent from Iceland and Svalbard. Breeds in Fennoscandia (but rare) and across northern Russia, including the southern island of Novaya Zemlya, the New Siberia Islands and Wrangel Island (though the presence of Gray Wolves on Russia's Arctic islands is conjecture rather than fact; the wolf has been savagely persecuted in northern Russia, and distribution and population are poorly understood). Breeds throughout Alaska and across Canada including (probably) all Arctic islands with sufficient prey species. White Wolves are found in the high Canadian Arctic (including the mainland near, for instance, Bathurst Inlet), in Greenland and in northern Russia. Whether wolves migrate from their breeding territories depends on the

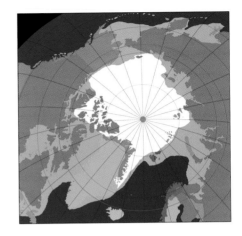

▼ Adult female Gray Wolf, Finnish Karelia, close to the Russian border.

movements of prey. Where prey is seasonal, the wolves may move, but where prey is resident, in the high Arctic for example where prey species include Musk Oxen and Arctic Hares, wolves are also resident.

Diet

Variable, depending on prey species within the wolves' territory. Gray Wolves will take prey opportunistically, attacking animals as large as Moose or as small as rodents and birds. They also regularly feed on carrion. Gray Wolves hunt singly, in pairs or in packs, depending partly on opportunity and partly on pack size. For instance, in the high Arctic, prey numbers may restrict the wolf population and "packs" may comprise a pair of animals or even a single wolf. Gray Wolves locate prey by tracking, scent or sight, or by luck. Once located, tactics depend on prey numbers and size. A single wolf will chase down small prey (rodents, hares), but larger prey requires more caution. Moose and Musk Oxen will stand and face an approaching wolf or pack, and are sufficiently dangerous to pose a real threat, as a blow from a hoof or antler is capable of inflicting serious damage. A single Moose or Musk Ox can usually face off a single wolf, but may be vulnerable to a pack. A herd of potential prey can often see off a pack, forming a defensive wall behind which young animals stand. Large Musk Ox herds often form a circle with the young in the middle. If the prey stands firm, the wolves usually retreat fairly quickly, though standoffs lasting up to four hours have been observed. The aim of the wolves is to cause the herd to run. They can then run into the herd, biting at flanks and seeking out a young or weak animal on which the pack then concentrates. However, if the running herd remains cohesive, the wolves may find it difficult to isolate a single animal. Chases are usually over within 1–2 mi. (1–2 km), though wolves have the stamina for longer chases; single wolves having been observed to chase deer for more than 13 mi. (20 km). After a successful kill, wolves will gorge on meat, caching any remaining food.

Breeding

Gray Wolves are social animals living in packs that form cohesive, extended family groups. However, pack cohesion can break down in packs that are territorial but that hunt Caribou as they move through the wolves' territory during migration. Packs form when a mature male and mature female from separate packs meet, form a breeding pair and establish a viable territory. Pack sizes vary with prey size, prey density and wolf mortality. A pack can contain as few as two wolves or as many as 30 (exceptionally up to 60). Pack sizes in general are much smaller for high Arctic Wolves.

The pack is dominated by the alpha pair of breeding adults; the remaining pack members are non-breeding adults and immature offspring of this pair, and, occasionally, unrelated wolves from other packs. In general only the alpha female breeds, but cases where several females produce litters have been observed. In most parts of the Gray Wolf range, the female produces a litter each year, though in the high Arctic this may not be the case, fetuses being resorbed in years of low prey density. Mating takes place during female estrus. Between one and 11 (usually 6–7 in the low Arctic, often 1–2 in the high Arctic) altricial pups (weighing about 1 lb./500 g) are born after a gestation of 60–65 days in a concealed den, either in a natural cave or crevice or in one excavated by the female. The pups are mobile at 20–24 days, but have no coordinated movement until about 35 days. Weaning is at 60 days. The pups then move from the den to "rendezvous" sites where they can be active. They are fed by regurgitation by all members of the pack, stimulating feeding by licking at the mouth of the adults (as domestic dogs do). Adults also feed the young with prey that they have carried back to them in their mouths. Pups are almost full-grown at nine months and usually breed at 2 years, though this time may be constrained by pack dynamics. In many cases, a strong 2-year-old male will cause a split in the pack, the male taking younger, currently non-breeding females to start a new pack. Males may also leave the pack on their own, though contrary to the common phrase "lone wolf" such solitary animals are rare; in most cases, a dispersing male will join another pack (itself an uncommon event, as most packs will drive off or even kill a strange wolf) or entice females from another pack to join him.

Taxonomy and geographical variation

Polytypic. The nominate race breeds in northern Europe. *C. l. arctos* breeds in the high Arctic of Canada and in Greenland. It is paler and larger, with larger teeth than the nominate; it is very similar to *C. l. albus*, which breeds on the tundras of northern Russia. *C. l. occidentalis* breeds in Alaska, along the Yukon and in Northwest Territories west of the Great Slave Lake. It is larger than the nominate, but with a similar head and tooth size. *C. l. nubilus* breeds in mainland Canada east of the Great Slave Lake and on Baffin Island. It is very similar to the nominate. There are a number of other extralimital subspecies.

▲ Adult blue-morph Arctic Fox foraging, St. Paul, Pribilofs.

Arctic Fox
Alopex lagopus

The Arctic Fox is among the best adapted of all terrestrial mammals to the harsh Arctic climate. The ears, muzzle and limbs are small, while the large, bushy tail acts as an insulating blanket around the curled-up animal. The fur is extremely thick and covers the soles of the feet. In winter, guard hairs can be inches thick, and these, combined with a dense undercoat, enable the fox to maintain a body temperature of 104°F (40°C) in ambient temperatures as low as -76°F (-60°C). The luxuriant coat makes the animal look much larger than it is; the coat also led to its merciless pursuit by fur trappers; indeed, fur-trapping was one of the driving forces behind European colonization of northern Canada and Siberia. Overtrapping drove the fox to the verge of extinction in many areas. The trappers' greed had ramifications for other species as well. The introduction of Arctic Foxes to the Aleutian Islands, for example, had disastrous consequences for several populations of ground-nesting birds.

Identification   See p. 410

Arctic Foxes occur in two forms. In one, the so-called white morph, the summer pelage is gray-brown above, paler below and usually on the tail. In winter, this form turns white. The second form, known as the blue fox, is dark chocolate-brown or dark blue-gray in summer and paler blue-gray in winter. In general, white-morph foxes are continental while blue foxes are found on islands. However, mixing occurs because of the winter roaming of animals, and litters may comprise pups of both forms. Captive breeding has shown that the blue morph is dominant. Pups are uniformly dark brown, the blue or white morphs being identifiable at about two weeks. The iris of both forms is deep golden or orange-yellow.

Dental formula: 3/3, 1/1, 4/4, 2/3 = 42 teeth.

Confusion species
None.

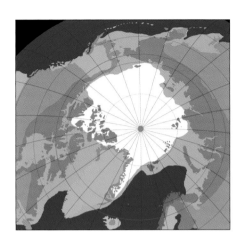

▲ Fearless and inquisitive, this young Arctic Fox has only recently left the safety of the den for the first time. Mackenzie Bay, northeast Greenland.

Size

HB: 21½–30 in. (55–75 cm). T: 10–18 in. (25–45 cm). SH: 10–13¾ in. (25–35 cm). W: 6½–20 lb. (3–9 kg).

Communication

A range of hoarse, sharp barks and yelps. Also communicates with ear and tail position, tail movement and lip retraction.

Distribution

Circumpolar on both mainland and on islands, including northern Greenland, Ellesmere Island and Svalbard. Breeds on Iceland following escapes from fur farms in the 1930s. Although the species colonized Jan Mayen by way of the sea, the population there is now extinct. Resident but migratory if prey density falls. Some foxes travel a very long way; tagged individuals have traveled more than 620 mi. (1,000 km) over two years and have even changed continents (moving from Russia to Alaska). Foxes caught on ice floes when sea ice breaks

up can also travel great distances. Where both Red and Arctic Foxes occur, the larger Red will drive the Arctic out. The Red Fox cannot thrive in areas of sparse prey, so far-northern latitudes favor the Arctic Fox. The northern limit to the Arctic Fox is therefore defined by the availability of food, while its southern limit is defined by the range of the Red Fox.

Diet

Chiefly rodents, but also birds and eggs, berries and fish. Has been seen to patrol beaches searching for crustaceans and fish marooned in rock pools, and to stir freshwater with a paw to attract fish. Will venture onto sea ice to sniff out Ringed Seal pups. Despite the assumption that most Ringed Seal pups fall prey to Polar Bears, predation by foxes is actually significant. In one study in the Beaufort Sea, foxes took over 25% of the year's seal pups. Will also take carrion such as dead whales. Arctic Foxes patrol the area at the foot of bird cliffs looking for eggs and fallen hatchlings, and also for juvenile auks that do not make it to the sea on their first flight. Foxes will also venture up or down cliffs in search of accessible nests. Food is cached in periods of surplus. In winter, carrion is the main food; Arctic Foxes trail Polar Bears on the sea ice to eat the

▼ White-morph Arctic Fox in winter. It is eating part of a Ringed Seal, probably a Polar Bear's leftovers, Kongsfjorden, Svalbard.

remains of seal kills (and also, occasionally, bear feces), and they trail wolves on land for the same prey reason. These activities must be pursued circumspectly, as both bears and wolves will kill and eat foxes. When there is a choice, Arctic Foxes are largely nocturnal.

Breeding
Solitary or in pairs, though groups of foxes may occasionally be seen, feeding on a dead whale for example. Small family groups have also been noted (e.g., a male and several females). The additional animals may be young adult "helpers" from earlier litters. Territorial in the summer; both sexes mark boundaries with urine and feces on prominent tussocks or rocks. Breeding dens are constructed in light soils (e.g., on eskers) and are often used over successive years. Some den sites may have been in continuous use for centuries. Most dens have several entrances (4–12), but dens that have been used over generations can be vast, with up to 100 entrances, and visible for some distance because of the luxuriant growth resulting from tilling of the soil and manuring by fox droppings. Usually dens are some distance apart (with territories of > 12 sq. mi./30 km^2), but in years of high fox population, breeding pairs may be much closer, even sharing the same esker. Arctic Foxes also breed in natural dens and, in high population years, may even breed in the open in the absence of suitable sites. Five to 12 altricial pups (up to 20 in "lemming years" when the lemming population explodes) are born after gestation of 50–57 days. Eyes open at 14–16 days. Stronger siblings may kill and eat weaker ones if food is scarce. Weaned at 4–10 weeks, but do not leave the den until around 15 weeks. Pups reach maturity at about 9 months and breed at 1 year.

Arctic Fox numbers are strongly related to prey numbers. In lemming years, the fox population rises dramatically. If the lemming population is much reduced the following year, as is likely, then the foxes, which need around 4,000 lemmings during the breeding season, may have fewer pups; they may even not breed at all. Large numbers of foxes from the previous year may starve during their first winter.

Taxonomy and geographical variation
Polytypic, but the differences between the three subspecies are slight and complicated by dispersion and migration. Island populations (e.g., on the Bering Sea islands) are more discrete, but even then the differences between nominate and *A. e. pribilofensis* (on the Pribilofs) and *A. e. hallensis* (on Hall and St. Matthew islands) are marginal.

Red Fox
Vulpus vulpus

Identification See p. 410
The Red Fox is the most widespread and abundant carnivore in the world. Its pelage is a beautiful red-brown above and on the bushy tail. The tail usually has a white tip. The large, pointed ears have black backs. The upper lip, chin and breast are buff or white, the underparts buffish cream. The feet and

▲ Adult Red Fox, Churchill.

much of the legs are black. There are several color forms, though the standard color is seen in the majority of the total population. One color phase is a paler version of the standard "red." Another is the so-called "cross" fox, an overall darker animal, the name originating from a dark back and shoulders that form a prominent dark "cross" shape. The tail and head are also usually darker, though the white tail tip is maintained. Cross foxes can represent 45% of the local population in Canada. Another variation, the silver fox, is all black (or almost so; the cheeks and muzzle are paler), but with white-tipped guard hairs that give it a shimmering silver sheen. The Samson fox lacks guard hairs and so appears much "woollier." In North America another form, known as the bastard fox, is blue-gray overall, similar to the blue-morph Arctic Fox. All forms have a golden or orange-yellow iris. The eye shine is blue or white, but may be reddish at some angles. Cubs are uniformly dark brown, but with white tip to the tail.

Dental formula: 3/3, 1/1, 3/4, 3/3 = 42 teeth.

Confusion species
None.

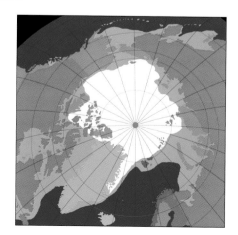

Size
HB: 21½–36 in. (55–90 cm). T: 12–19 in. (30–48 cm). SH: 13¾–16 in. (35-40 cm). W: 9–22 lb. (4–10 kg).

Communication
The usual call is a doglike bark, but also has an unearthly scream, usually from the female (or vixen), occasionally from the male (or dog). Non-vocal communication involves ears, mouth, lips and tail positions.

Distribution
Circumpolar. Breeds in northern Scandinavia (but absent from Svalbard) and throughout northern Russia, but only on the southern island of Novaya Zemlya. In North America, breeds throughout Alaska and across northern Canada, including the southern Arctic islands. Found wherever there is an adequate food supply. Resident, though as with other carnivores, Red Foxes will move if prey becomes scarce.

Diet
Omnivorous, taking rodents, hares, birds and eggs, but also insects, earthworms, fish, berries and carrion. When possible Red Foxes are nocturnal, and they are almost exclusively nocturnal in temperate regions. Essentially opportunistic, but hunts rodents using a remarkable "rodent leap" to pounce on them. This involves springing from a crouched, stalking position, going up and forward to arrive above the prey, and landing on it. Food is cached in times of plenty.

Breeding
Solitary or in small family groups. Groups usually comprise a dog and several vixens that are often relatives; they act as "helpers" during the raising of the alpha vixen's cubs. The group holds a territory, marking it with urine and feces in prominent places, but also with scent from glands on the feet and near the mouth, the latter rubbed onto vegetation. The copulation tie may last up to 90 minutes. Dogs may also mate with subordinate females who conceive, then lose the cubs in late-term abortion, presumably to keep breeding options open until the alpha vixen gives birth. The vixen gives birth in a den that she may dig, but that she may have fashioned from the burrow of another species. Four to seven (but up to 12) altricial cubs born after a gestation of 52–53 days. Eyes open at 11–14 days. Weaned at 8 weeks. Young are full-grown at 6 months and females may breed at 1 year.

Taxonomy and geographical variation
Polytypic. Red Foxes were formerly classified as two species, *V. vulpes* in the Old World and *V. fulva* in the New, but today they are considered one species, with as many as 48 subspecies. Arctic races include *alascensis* in most of Alaska, the Yukon and Northwest Territories, *harrimani* on Kodiak Island, *kenaiensis* on the Kenai Peninsula and *beringiana* in northeast Siberia. Color variants are generally more varied among the Nearctic races.

Adult Red Fox, north Norway.

adult seals by stealth or by patience at their breathing holes in the ice. During the summer, as the sea ice breaks up, the success rate of kills drops for more southerly Polar Bears, perhaps to one seal every five days, and, ultimately, to the point where the return on the time and energy invested becomes unwarranted. The bears then make for land, where they eat kelp and berries until the ice reforms. They are usually inactive at this time, especially on warm days, as this reduces energy loss and prevents overheating.

Breeding

Solitary, but groups form near an abundance of food, such as a whale carcass, and during periods of enforced fasting waiting for ice to form. In the main such aggregations are peaceful, with bouts of play-fighting rather than genuine aggression. When seeking a mate, male bears are very aggressive to other males and will also kill cubs if they encounter them, which allows them to mate with the mother. Males finding a female ready to mate will try to maneuver her into a non-feeding area to minimize the likelihood of interference from other males. Ovulation must be induced, a process requiring the bear to mate several times over a period of days; otherwise fertilization will not occur. Females will mate with another male if the first is displaced.

Mating occurs in spring and early summer, but implantation of the blastocyst is delayed until late autumn. The female excavates a maternity den in drifting snow on land close to the coast, though in some places (such as on the Beaufort Sea), females den in permanent ice 124–186 mi. (200–300 km) offshore. The maternity den is usually a single chamber, but some multi-chambered dens have been observed. One to three (usually two, rarely four) cubs are born; this can be 200–250 days after mating, though due to delayed implantation the true gestation is about 60 days. The altricial cubs weigh around 20 oz. (600 g) at birth, are around 16 in. (40 cm) long, and are covered in very fine hair (about 3/4 in./2 cm long), which gives the mistaken impression that they are naked. Their eyes open at about 25 days. The female undergoes torpor during the winter, including throughout birth. She does little direct caring, though her body temperature is maintained in case she must suddenly defend her cubs. The den protects the cubs from the harsh Arctic winter outside. The cubs feed from their mother while she remains dormant; Polar Bear milk has a fat content of 33% (higher than in any other bear and comparable to that of cetaceans; only seals produce richer milk) and a solids content of about 48%. During the winter, the mother may lose up to 50% of her body weight. Because of the timing of the formation of the sea ice in southern Hudson Bay and in James Bay, pregnant females in that area may go for as long as eight months without feeding, giving birth and feeding their cubs during that period.

Mother and cubs emerge from the maternity den in March or April, at which time the cubs weigh between 11 and 44 lb. (5 and 20 kg). Emergence is timed to coincide with the arrival of the year's "crop" of Ringed Seal pups. The bears feed on pups for about four months. Ringed seal pups are 50–75% fat, and some bears will lay down enough fat to survive for the rest of the year on that catch alone.

▲ Seal-pup hunting Polar Bear style, Agardhbukta, Svalbard. The bear launches itself upward, using its momentum to punch through the snow in search of a seal-pup den underneath.

Cubs stay with their mother for about 30 months, at which point she is ready to mate again. Females are therefore ready for mating every three years. As there are approximately equal numbers of male and female bears, this effective 3:1 ratio between bears that are ready to mate of each sex explains the fierce competition for females among males. Male Polar Bears breed at four years, females at 3–7 years.

Taxonomy and geographical variation

Probably monotypic, though, as noted above, distinct populations exist, apparently with little interchange between them.

Brown Bear
Ursus arctos

In terms of recorded maximum specimen weights, male Brown Bears of the Kodiak subspecies *U. a. middendorffi* are heavier than male Polar Bears, and would stand taller, though the differences are marginal, and individuals of some subspecies are much smaller.

Identification See p. 410

Pelage is uniformly dark brown, though some individuals are paler (even very pale or gray-brown) and others may be almost black. The muscle-hump at the shoulders is very prominent in many individuals. Adult bears are usually darker on the flanks than elsewhere. Immature bears usually have a pale collar. As with Polar Bears, Brown Bears have both underfur and guard hairs and are capable of withstanding very low temperatures, the reason for winter denning being the lack of available winter food. In general, Brown Bears have a concave head profile (a "dish face"). The ears are small and rounded, the tail virtually non-existent. The iris is golden or orange-yellow. The claws are very large, those on the front paws about twice the length of those on the rear paws. On average the front claws are about 3½ in. (9 cm) long, but may be up to 5 in. (12 cm). The claws are slightly downcurved at the tips; they are usually dark brown, but may be paler, occasionally even ivory; in general, the claws of older bears are paler than those of immatures. Some bears have paler tips to the guard hairs, which gives them a "grizzled" appearance (hence the name Grizzly Bear). However, some Grizzlies may be so pale overall that this is barely discernible.

Brown Bears are very powerful and surprisingly quick (up to 37 mph, or 60 km/h) over short distances. They are also aggressive in certain circumstances (e.g., females with cubs, particularly if the observer comes between mother and cubs). Brown Bears are also unpredictable; attacks on people are often blamed on thundery weather or even perfumes. In practise, the likely cause is surprise encroachment on territory, or appearance in a favored feeding area. The problem is that the human observer cannot understand the bear, and the bear certainly does not understand the observer. An aggressive bear will snap its teeth, salivate so that it appears to be frothing at the mouth, lay its ears back and growl or "woof" (rapid exhalations believed to be associated with deep breaths that allow the bear to "taste" who you are). If an attack occurs, the standard wisdom is to assume a fetal position and stay motionless.

Dental formula: 3/3, 1/1, 2–4/2–4, 2/3 = 34–42 teeth.

▼ Grizzly Bear in spring. Denali, Alaska.

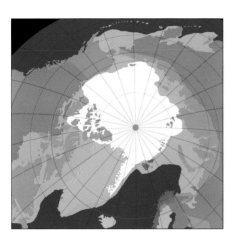

▲ Brown Bear of the race *piscator*, Kamchatka.

Confusion species

None. The heavy thick-set body shape of Brown Bears, together with the rounded ears and uniformly colored muzzle, distinguish the darkest bears from Black Bears.

Size

HB: 5½–9 ft. (1.7–2.8 m). T: 2¼–8 in. (6–21 cm). SH: 3–5 ft. (90–150 cm). W: male 330–880 lb. (150–400 kg), up to 2,205 lb. (1,000 kg) for Kodiak Bears, female 175–440 lb. (80–200 kg).

Communication

Repertoire of deep grunts. Females calling young have a plaintive bleat.

Distribution

Circumpolar. Absent from Greenland and Arctic islands, except perhaps Banks Island. Breeds in northern Scandinavia and across Russia, but not to the northern coast. It is likely that the majority of the world's population of bears live in Russia. Breeds throughout Alaska and in extreme northern Canada east to northwestern Hudson Bay. Brown Bears are found both south of and above the timberline, the latter often referred to as Barren-ground Bears. Resident, with a period of winter torpor. The body temperature of torpid bears is lowered only by a few degrees, but the heart rate is significantly reduced, from 40–70 beats/minute to about 10 beats/minute. Dens are excavated (or appropriated) in dry, well-drained areas, usually south-facing and set where a good layer of insulating snow is likely to accumulate. Dens are often dirt-floored, but may have a covering of grass and tree branches. Some dens have entrance tunnels.

Diet

Omnivorous, but chiefly plant material such as leaves, flowers, tubers, roots, mosses and berries in season. It is estimated that, on average, vegetation provides at least 50% of the bear's annual food intake. Also eat insects (tearing open dead logs to reach ants and other insect larvae), mammals and fish. Mammals are taken opportunistically, but also hunted, including rodents dug out of burrows, and Elk chased down on soft snow with a windblown or frozen crust through which the ungulate falls but which will support the bear; Brown Bears are very quick over short distances. Prey fish famously include spawning salmon on the rivers of Alaska and Kamchatka. Brown Bears have also been observed on sea ice eating the remains of Polar Bear kills and even, rarely, killing seals. Coastal bears frequently explore beaches, where they dig for shellfish and search for tide-borne carrion. Brown Bears are nocturnal where human disturbance is high, but otherwise diurnal. When fattening up in preparation for winter torpor, Brown Bears may increase their body weight by up to 30%. Brown Bears have good eyesight, comparable with that of humans, excellent hearing and an equally good sense of smell.

Breeding

Solitary, but will feed colonially on salmon rivers, though such groups are not without conflict in disputes over fish. Brown Bears are highly territorial, scratching trees and scent-marking to define their areas. They defend these areas, the size of which can cover 77–770 sq. mi. (200-2,000 km²) or males and about half that for females, depending on productivity. A male territory will overlap that of several females. Males are aggressive in defending their territories and in seeking, or defending, access to females. A male will mate with several females each year, but females will also mate with more than one male if the opportunity presents itself. Most encounters between male bears do not end in fights. The less dominant bear will usually sit and lower its head in response to the stare of a standing, dominant male. However, fights do occur between comparable males, which can result in significant injuries and even death. A bear killed by another may be partially eaten by the victor. Mating is in early summer, with ovulation induced by copulation, but implantation of the blastocyst is delayed until November, when the female enters winter torpor. Females excavate a den on a well-drained slope where a layer of insulating snow is likely to occur. Natural dens (e.g., caves, hollows among tree roots) are also used. One to four (normally two) cubs are born in the winter den about 225 days after mating (implantation delay means true gestation period is about 60 days). Cubs are altricial, but covered in fine silver hair, and weigh around 18 oz. (500 g). This weight increases to 11–15 lb. (5–7 kg) by the time the cubs emerge from the den. Within the den, the cubs feed from their torpid mother, with lactation lasting (in total) 18–30 months. During birthing and nursing the female may lose 40% of her body weight. One characteristic that Brown Bears share with Black Bears is that a female will abandon a single cub if she deems it reproductively more profitable to mate again and so raise two or three cubs the following year.

The cubs stay with their mother for two or three years, denning with her during those winters they share. The female chases her cubs away when she is ready to mate again. Sibling sub-adult bears stay together at first and usually den together during their first winter apart from their mother. Young females become solitary when ready to mate for the first time, usually at five years. Males become solitary when they first seek mates, but must first find and hold territories. Females may breed at four years, but seven or eight years is more usual. Males are not usually in a position to mate until they are fully grown, at 7–8 years.

Taxonomy and geographical variation
Polytypic. Up to 200 subspecies have been suggested at various times, but most authorities now consider the nominate race to breed over most of the range. *U. a. horribilis*, the Grizzly

▼ Female Brown Bear of the nominate race, eastern Karelia, Finland.

Bear, occurs in central Alaska and inland Canada. It is smaller than the nominate and has the distinctive "grizzled" appearance. By contrast, *U. a. middendorffi*, the Kodiak Island Brown Bear, is considered to be the largest, though bears of Chukotka (*U. a. beringianus*) and Kamchatka (*U. a. piscator*) are also very big; Kamchatkan bears are usually darker than those of Alaska. Brown Bears once occurred to the east of Hudson Bay, in northern Quebec/Labrador. Found on both tundra and within the northern forest belt, never numerous and apparently very large and fierce, these bears seem to have become extinct in the early 20th century. All other races are extralimital.

American Black Bear
Ursus americanus

The most common bear; population estimates suggest that there are twice as many American Black Bears than there are of all other bear species combined, a consequence of their great adaptability. The annual mortality rate from hunting is staggering, perhaps as high as 30,000 animals, though this rate does not appear to have reduced the population. One appalling statistic suggests that 90 percent of American Black Bears older than two years die as a result of human activity, either from shooting, trapping or from being struck by vehicles.

Identification See p. 410
Despite the name, the pelage of American Black Bears can be white (in, for example, the Kermode Bear (*U. a. kermodei*) of west-central British Columbia, which chiefly occurs on offshore islands), blue-gray (the Glacier Bear (*U. a. emmonsii*) from Glacier Bay, Prince William Sound) or brown (bears in Alaska range from pale cinnamon to a dark brown that is close to the "standard" color of Brown Bears). In Kermode and Glacier Bears, the muzzle can be as the pelage, though in most forms it is light brown. Brown and black forms often have a white chest patch. The ears are much longer and are more triangular than those of Brown Bears. The iris is dark orange.

Although American Black Bears are much less aggressive and dangerous than Brown Bears and usually retreat from humans, it is unwise to assume this, particularly if the bear is a female with cubs.

Dental formula: 3/3, 1/1, 2–4/2–4, 2/3 = 34–42 teeth.

Confusion species
In general, color and size are diagnostic. However, large brown American Black Bears are very similar to small Brown Bears. The pale muzzle and straight muzzle profile, as opposed to the concave muzzle profile of Brown Bears, and the lack of a shoulder-muscle hump are diagnostic.

Size
HB: 4½–6½ ft. (1.4–2 m). T: 3–5½ in. (8–14 cm). SH: 24–36 in. (60–90 cm). W: male 132–330 lb. (60–150 kg), female 88–176 lb. (40–80 kg), but specimens of males (882 lb./400 kg) and females (510 lb./230 kg) have been recorded.

Communication

A repertoire of grunts and growls. Contented bears also hum quietly with an enginelike drone.

Distribution

Nearctic. Breeds in the forests of Alaska and Canada, though rarely seen north of the timberline. However, to the east of Hudson Bay where there are no Brown Bears, American Black Bears are found on the tundra of northern Quebec and Labrador. Also found in the continental United States. Both male and female defend territories, the size depending on food availability. Male ranges are 23–39 sq. mi. (60–100 km²) and frequently overlap those of up to 15 females, as well as those of other males, so competition for females occurs. American Black Bears are dispersive; cubs leave their mothers, traveling up to 124 mi. (200 km) to find their own territories. Bears scratch trees and scent-mark to define territories, but in readiness for winter torpor will travel great distances (up to 125 mi./200 km) to secure food before returning "home." As in Brown Bears, the body temperature falls only slightly during winter torpor, but the heart rate falls significantly. Wintering dens are usually beneath fallen trees in hollow trees, or in caves, but bears will occasionally excavate their own dens. The den is lined with vegetation.

Diet

Omnivorous, but less carnivorous than Brown Bears. Primarily a herbivore, taking buds and shoots in spring and summer and nuts and berries in autumn, when huge amounts are consumed in readiness for winter torpor. Supplements diet with insects, obtained by ripping open ant nests and decaying logs, and by overturning boulders. An expert climber; the curved claws give the bear excellent purchase, and it will climb to reach beehives to feed on honey. Will take animals opportunistically, being fast enough over short distances to catch young animals in spring. Raids birds' nests and will take fish in areas where Brown Bears are absent. Also feeds on carrion and is now notorious for raiding garbage dumps and campsites. At campsites, the bears will even break into vehicles to steal food.

Breeding

Usually solitary, but forms hierarchical groups in areas of abundant food. As noted above, males hold territories that overlap those of many females. Mating takes place in June or

▲ Adult American Black Bear, Northern Ontario.

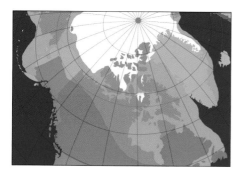

July, with delayed implantation of the blastocyst. One to five (usually two) cubs are born in the winter den around 215 days after mating (true gestation is about 55 days). At birth the altricial cubs weigh 7–16 oz. (200–450 g). Lactation lasts nine months. The cubs stay with their mother for about 18 months (including one winter spent in a shared den) before being forced to disperse. Females therefore breed every two years. Brown Bears will kill Black Bears, and foraging female American Black Bears will therefore send their young into a tree for their protection. Male cubs seek their own territory, but female cubs may share, in part, their mother's; the older female not only tolerates her offspring, but shows occasional signs of affectionate familial ties. Females breed first at 4–6 years (though two years and ages of up to nine years have been recorded). Males can breed at 3–4 years, but continue to grow until they are around 10 years old; the age of first breeding depends on the degree of territorial competition.

Taxonomy and geographical variation

Polytypic, with many subspecies, usually best identified by color, such as the Glacier Bear (*U. a. emmonsii*) and the Kermode Bear (*U. a. kermodei*) within the Arctic, and, extralimitally, *U. a. cinnamonium*, the Cinnamon Bear of Colorado and Wyoming. Most authorities consider the nominate race to breed in Alaska and throughout northern Canada, but subspecies have been proposed for Alaska's Kenai Peninsula and for the southern Yukon.

Cats

Though cats, members of the family Felidae, are found worldwide (except in Antarctica, Australia and Madagascar), they are generally thought of as a warm-country carnivore group, mainly because the best-known big cats are found in Africa and India. But cats can also survive in cold climates; the Siberian Tiger (*Panthera tigris altaica*) occurs as far north as southern Siberia, as does the Amur Leopard (*Panthera pardus orientalis*), while the Snow Leopard (*P. uncia*) lives among the snows of the high Himalayas, and in the New World the Puma (*Felis concolor*) lives at altitude in both the Rockies and the Andes. However, no cats are truly Arctic, though both the Old and New World Lynx species may be seen beyond the timberline. Like other species of felids, the Lynxes have sharp eyes and hearing and are quick and agile hunters.

Eurasian Lynx
Lynx lynx

Identification   See p. 410
A long-legged and heavy-bodied medium-sized felid. The pelage is yellow-brown above, paler or cream below, with a black tip to the end of the short tail. There are frequently dark spots or blotches, densest on the frontal section of all four legs. The crown is streaked black and there are black streaks on the cheeks. Long hairs on the rear cheeks and neck form half-collars. The muzzle and chin are paler. There are prominent ear tufts. The feet are relatively large, ideal for supporting the animal's weight when walking on snow. In winter, the pelage is thicker and paler. The iris is yellow; the name lynx comes from a Greek word meaning "to shine," a reference to the eyes of these cats.
   Dental formula: 3/3, 1/1, 2–3/2, 1/1 = 28–30 teeth.

Confusion species
None.

Size
HB: 2½–4¼ ft. (80–130 cm). T: 4½–10 in. (11–25 cm). SH: 2–2½ ft. (60–75 cm). W: 39½–55 lb. (18–25 kg).

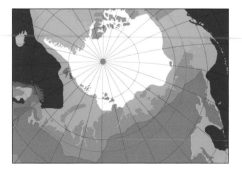

▲ An adult Lynx of the rare Siberian *wrangeli*. Note the distinctive ear-tufts.

Communication
A series of catlike howls.

Distribution
Palearctic. Rare in central Scandinavia. Breeds across Russia, though only to northern coast near the White Sea. Breeds in southern Chukotka and throughout Kamchatka. Primarily a forest animal, but also found on tundra close to the forest edge and in mountains. Resident through the year.

Diet
Wholly carnivorous, taking rodents, hares, small (often young) deer and ground birds (e.g., *Lagopus* grouse). On Kamchatka, Eurasian Lynx hunt Snow Sheep. Prey is stalked then taken after a final rush, or ambushed. Food that cannot be eaten immediately is cached.

Breeding
Solitary, but mated pair stays together during the early stages of cub-raising. The territory sizes of both males and females depend on prey density and can be as small as 4 sq. mi. (10 km²) or as large as 115 sq. mi. (300 km²). Lynxes have dens in a hollow

tree or beneath tree roots. Mating takes place during the winter, with kittens born in late spring. One to five (usually two to three) altricial cubs, born after 60–65 days gestation. Eyes open at 16–17 days. Lactation lasts between two and five months, and kittens stay with their mother for about one year. The male is evicted from the den by the female when the kittens are born, but brings food to the female for about two months. Breed at 2–3 years.

Taxonomy and geographical variation
Polytypic. The nominate race breeds throughout Scandinavia and western and central Russia. *L. l. wrangeli* breeds in eastern Siberia. It tends to be a little larger than the nominate, but the difference is slight. There are several other extralimital subspecies.

Canadian Lynx
Lynx canadensis

Identification
See p. 410

In form very similar to the Eurasian Lynx, but overall gray or gray-brown and with denser dark flecking on the upperparts. The winter pelage is grayer and much thicker. The iris is dark orange-yellow.

Dental formula: 3/3, 1/1, 2/2, 1/1 = 28 teeth.

Confusion species
None.

Size
HB: 26–43½ in. (65–110 cm). T: 2–5 in. (5–13 cm). SH: 20–26 in. (50–65 cm). W: 17½–37½ lb. (8–17 kg).

Distribution
Nearctic. Breeds in Alaska except on the Yukon-Kuskokwin Delta and on the the southern Alaska Peninsula. Rarer in the north. Breeds in Yukon, Northwest Territories, Quebec and Labrador, but not to the northern coast. Primarily a forest animal, but also occurs to the north of the timberline. Resident.

Diet
Primarily the Snowshoe Hare. Canadian Lynx populations show a 10-year cycle, which is linked to, but slightly offset from, a similar hare population cycle. Studies suggest that 80% of the Lynx diet is comprised of Snowshoe Hares. Will also take other prey, including squirrels, beavers, deer and ground bird species such as *Lagopus* grouse. As with the Eurasian Lynx, hunts by stalking or ambush.

Breeding
As Eurasian Lynx.

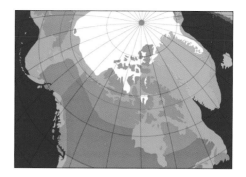

Taxonomy and geographical variation
Polytypic. Once thought to be a subspecies of the Eurasian Lynx, but now recognized as a distinct species. The nominate race breeds throughout the range except on mainland Labrador, where *L. c. subsolanus* is found. As with the subspecies of Eurasian Lynx, the differences are slight.

▼ Adult Canadian Lynx running over snow. Note the very large paws. These allow the animal to walk on soft snow without sinking, an essential adaptation for hunting fleet-footed prey in winter.

Mustelids

The Mustelidae is the most diverse of the world's carnivore families. It includes the smallest carnivore in the world, the Weasel, females of which can weigh as little as ⁷/₈ oz. (25 g); another mustelid, the 100 lb. (45 kg) Sea Otter, is almost 2,000 times heavier. Mustelids have long, slender bodies and short legs, which allows them to follow prey into burrows, although this is less of an advantage for the larger mustelids, particularly the Wolverine. However, this arrangement increases body surface area relative to mass, so metabolic rate must increase to maintain body temperature. As a consequence, food intake must rise; lactating Weasels must consume around 60% of their body weight daily.

The mustelid head is flattened and wedge-shaped, tapering distinctly toward the muzzle. Mustelids are aggressive and highly effective hunters, particularly the smaller species; size for size, Weasels are probably the most formidable carnivores on Earth. It has been suggested that weasels are such effective hunters that their absence from an area may help to precipitate a "lemming" year; if there are few weasels, the rodent population increases exponentially as rodent reproduction outstrips the weasel catch. The weasels then breed swiftly to "catch up," but rodent dispersal means that the increased weasel population is forced to take prey from a fast-diminishing population, leading to a collapse in the rodent population.

In general, mustelids are solitary and highly territorial, marking their boundaries with scent from the anal glands. In the skunks, secretions from these glands can be sprayed as a foul-smelling deterrent to attackers. There are no Arctic skunks, though the Striped Skunk (*Mephitis mephitis*) occurs in the forests around James Bay. There are a number of other sub-Arctic mustelids. In the Palearctic, the Pine Marten (*Martes martes*) breeds in north-central Scandinavia, the southern Kola Peninsula and around the White Sea, while the European Mink *Mustela lutreola* also breeds around the White Sea. In the Nearctic, the American Marten (*Martes americana*) breeds in the forests of Alaska and central Canada to the southern shores of Hudson Bay.

Least Weasel
Mustela nivalis

Identification See p. 411
A tiny mustelid. Has a typical mustelid cylindrical body, short legs and flattened, wedge-shaped head. Pelage is chestnut brown above, white below, usually with clear delineation between the two. As with other Arctic species, the animal has short, fine underfur and long guard hairs. The tail is entirely chestnut, the feet entirely white (including furred soles). The bicoloring extends to the head, with the chin and lower lip being white. In winter, the pelage is entirely white. The iris is dark orange-brown, but the eye appears black and beadlike, particularly against the winter pelage. When above ground, frequently stands on hind legs to survey area.
Dental formula: 3/3, 1/1, 3/3, 1/2 = 34 teeth.

Confusion species
Distinguished from the Short-tailed Weasel by its smaller size and lack of a black tip to tail.

Size
HB: male 7–8 in. (18–21 cm), female 6¼–7 in. (16–18 cm). T: male 1–1½ in. (2.5–4 cm), female ³/₄–1¼ in. (2–3 cm). W: male 1³/₄–2 oz. (40–55 g), female 1–1½ oz. (30–45 g).

Sexual dimorphism is a feature of mustelids, but it is extreme in the case of the Weasel, where the male may be as much as twice the weight of the female. This dimorphism may be a response to prey availability, the two sizes meaning that males can take larger prey and so do not compete with the females. Males could also be larger to increase their capacity for holding territories and competing for females.

Communication
Usual call is a high, rippling squeak. Also hisses or barks when alarmed.

Distribution
Circumpolar. Absent from Greenland and Iceland, but breeds in northern Scandinavia and across Russia, though absent from Svalbard and the Russian Arctic islands. Breeds

▼ Adult Weasel of the race *rixosa* outside a maternity den, Canada.

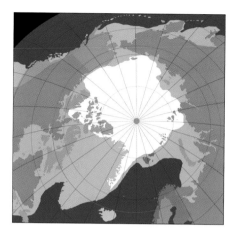

throughout Alaska, but not on the Bering Sea islands or the western Aleutians, and across northern Canada, but absent from the Canadian Arctic islands. Found in all habitats where prey is available. Resident.

Diet

Primarily rodents, but will take birds and eggs. Must eat about 30% of its body weight daily. Feeds at all times of day and night, chasing rodents in their burrows or in tunnels beneath the snow. Kills with a bite to the base of the skull. A Weasel can travel at near-normal running speed carrying a dead rodent that weighs

as much as half the Weasel's body weight. Caches food if surplus prey taken, which is particularly important to breeding females as it reduces the time spent away from their young.

Breeding

Solitary and territorial. Territory size depends on prey density, but that of the male is usually 17–62 acre (1–4 ha), overlapping several female territories (of 2½–10 acre, or 4 ha each). Weasel dens are often originally those of rodent victims and are lined, particularly the maternity dens, with the plucked fur of rodent kills. Weasels do not have delayed implantation and breed in spring. 1–6 altricial kits are born after a gestation of 34–37 days. Eyes open at around 25 days. Lactation lasts 20–30 days. Kits can kill prey at around 45 days and leave their mother at 60–70 days. The male does not contribute to the raising of the young and there is no permanent pair-bond. Females are sexually mature at four months, males at eight months. In years of abundant prey, weasels will have two litters. In lemming years, they may breed continuously.

Taxonomy and geographical variation

Polytypic. The nominate race breeds in northern Eurasia and, some authorities consider, in northern North America; however, most split the Nearctic animals into two subspecies. These are *M. n. rixosa*, which breeds east of the Mackenzie Delta, and *M. n. eskimo* which breeds in Alaska and the Yukon. Differences between these races and the nominate are slight.

Short-tailed Weasel (Stoat)
Mustela erminea

Identification See p. 411

Has the typical mustelid cylindrical body, short legs and flattened wedge-shaped head. The tail is long, despite the name Short-tailed Weasel, which allows comparison with the Nearctic Long-tailed Weasel (*Mustela frenata*). Pelage is chestnut brown above, cream below, with strong delineation between the two. The tail is chestnut with a distinct black tip. The feet are chestnut. The lower lip and chin are as the underparts. In winter, the pelage is entirely white apart from the black tail-tip. Winter animals are known as ermine in both Europe and North America. In Britain, ermine skins were used to create the upper sections of cloaks worn by members of the House of Lords, the tail-tips providing the black spots in the otherwise milk-white cloaks. However, not all ermine are white, notably on the Pacific coast of North America, where the animal's winter pelage is sandy brown. The eye is dark orange-brown. Short-tailed Weasels can be very curious, especially in remote areas, approaching humans closely and peering at them. If the observer is quiet and unthreatening, Short-tailed Weasels may go about their business, but they are very busy animals and quick movers, so not easy to observe at length or in great detail without patience.

Dental formula: 3/3, 1/1, 3/3, 1/2 = 34 teeth.

◀ Adult Short-tailed Weasel, Victoria Island. They often stand up on their hind legs to check out a potential predator.

Confusion species
See Least Weasel.

Size
HB: male 6¼–12 in. (16–30 cm), female 5–10 in. (13–25 cm). T: 2¾–4 in. (7–10 cm). W: male 2½–6 oz. (70–170 g), female 1–3 oz. (30–90 g). Extreme sexual dimorphism, with male about twice the weight of female. European Short-tailed Weasels tend to be larger in southern parts of the range, with measured weights to 15½ oz. (440 g).

Communication
Usual call is a shrill *kree, kree* when surprised or excited. Also chatter when together.

Distribution
Circumpolar. Breeds on Greenland wherever lemmings are found. Absent from Iceland and Svalbard. Breeds in northern Fennoscandia and throughout Arctic Russia (though absent from the Arctic islands, though this is likely to be an absence of observation, as in general there are Short-tailed Weasels wherever there are enough rodents). Breeds throughout the North American Arctic, including Canada's Arctic islands and northern Ellesmere Island. In general, European Short-tailed weasels do not live above the timberline except on parts of the Siberian coast. By contrast, Nearctic Short-tailed Weasels are among the most northerly of all the mustelids.

▼ Adult Short-tailed Weasel in summer coat, north Norway.

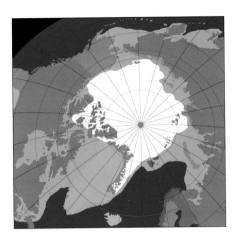

Diet
A fearless predator that will tackle animals up to 10 times its own body weight. Feeds on rodents, lagomorphs and birds. Kills with canine bite to the base of the skull or neck. Short-tailed Weasel will opportunistically kill more prey than can be immediately consumed, caching the remainder for leaner hunting times.

Breeding
Territorial, but with marked differences during the breeding season. Adults mark their territories with feces often tainted with musky secretion from the anal sacs. During the breeding season, females maintain territory, but male tends to become non-territorial, with his range overlapping that of several females. In a remarkable breeding cycle, the male mates with suckling female young at the nest. Young, pregnant females (which become sexually mature at about five weeks) delay implantation of the blastocyst for around 280 days, giving birth the following year. Nest sites, and dens of adults outside breeding season, are often in rodent dens and are usually lined with fur from their victims. Five to 12 altricial kits born after a true gestation of 21–28 days. Kits are covered in fine fur and have a temporary, thicker dark brown mane that the mother takes between her teeth to move them. It is likely that scent glands below this mane allow males to identify and mate with young females. Kits are weaned at five weeks and are independent at around 12 weeks.

Taxonomy and geographical variation
Polytypic. The nominate race is the European animal, but many subspecies have been identified, particularly in North America, though most of these are extralimital. Differences between the subspecies are usually limited to size, but these size differences can be marked. In North America the largest animals are those that occur in the north, with North American Arctic animals, on average, comparable to or larger than European Arctic animals. However, even the largest North American animals are only half the size of the largest south European (and British) Short-tailed Weasels.

American Mink
Mustela vison

Identification
See p. 411

Has the typical mustelid cylindrical body, short legs and flattened, wedge-shaped head. The soft pelage is a lustrous dark brown. American Mink have repeatedly escaped from European fur farms over the last century; color mutations that are the product of captive breeding are discernible in many American Mink, including cream, blue, "silver" (a glossy blue-gray) and shades of brown. The tail is bushy. There is a white patch on the lower lip and, in about 20 percent of animals, the top lip has a similar patch. Females occasionally have white patches on the nape from mating bites. The feet are semi-webbed. The iris is dark orange-brown.

Dental formula: 3/3, 1/1, 3/3, 1/2 = 34 teeth.

Confusion species
Although the American Mink and European Mink (*M. lutreola*) look almost identical, DNA analysis shows that they are not closely related, and they do not interbreed. In general the American Mink is larger and has displaced the European Mink from areas where the two overlap. Now almost extinct in Europe, European Mink breed across European Russia to the shores of the White Sea. European Mink always have a white upper lip, but as some American Mink show this, it is not a reliable identification feature. In the field, only range is a sure indicator of species, but as American Mink spreads east this will become less dependable.

Size
HB: 12½–18 in. (32–45 cm). T: 5–9 in. (13–23 cm). W: 1–2¾ lb. (0.6–1.2 kg).

Communication
Usually silent. Gives a loud scream when alarmed. Catlike purr when mating.

Distribution
Circumpolar. Originally Nearctic only, breeding throughout Alaska, but rare in the north and absent from Bering Sea and Aleutian islands; also in Yukon, in central Northwest Territories,

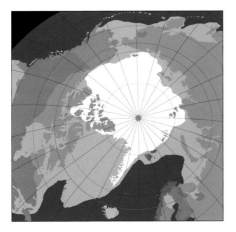

▲ American Mink, north Norway.

the northwestern, southern and northeastern shores of Hudson Bay, and central Quebec/Labrador. Now also breeds in Iceland and Scandinavia, where it has become established after escaping from fur farms. Prefers fresh, slow-moving rivers, ponds and marshland, but also found at the coast. Resident.

Diet
Carnivorous and opportunistic. Semi-aquatic, feeding on fish, crustaceans, amphibians, rodents and birds. In general, takes more rodents than the European Mink, which relies more on amphibians. Release of fur-farm American Mink in Britain has led to a drastic reduction in the population of Water Vole (*Arvicola terrestris*). In North America, the primary prey of the mink is the Muskrat. Unlike weasels, American Mink do not cache food: if surplus prey are taken, the preferred parts of each are eaten and the rest is discarded. Feed nocturnally, but diurnal sightings are not uncommon. Despite being semi-aquatic, American Mink do not see well underwater and often view their prey from the surface before diving to take it.

Breeding
Solitary and territorial. Territories tend to be linear (0.6–4 mi., 1–6 km, depending on productivity) along rivers or lakeshores. Marshland territories to 25 acres (10 ha). Territories marked with scent from anal glands by anal dragging or by depositing feces, and also with scent from glandular patches on the throat and breast. Mink often take over Muskrat dens, lining them with grass, and feathers or fur from prey. Females usually use Muskrat dens as maternity dens. Both males and females are polygamous, with paternity for a litter determined by the last male to mate with a female. Breeding is variable in northern latitudes, with varying lengths of delayed implantation (13–50 days). Four to seven altricial kits born after a true gestation of 30–32 days. Lactation lasts 35–40 days. Male takes no part in rearing offspring, the female teaching the kits to hunt. Kits disperse at around 14 weeks and breed at 1 year.

Taxonomy and geographical variation
Polytypic, with some 14 subspecies. Arctic races include the large *ingens* in Alaska and *melampeplus* in Kenai, both of which have been domesticated for the fur trade. The nominate race breeds in southeast Canada and the Appalachians.

Sable
Martes zibellina

A marten of the boreal forests. Essentially sub-Arctic, but found in Kamchatka and Chukotka.

Identification See p. 411

See p. 411

Has the typical mustelid body and head shape. Luxuriant pelage varies from almost black to golden brown, but is usually dark brown, relieved only by paler nose, cheek patches and bib. The tail is short and bushy. The soles of the feet are covered in thick hairs. The iris is dark orange.

Dental formula: 3/3, 1/1, 4/4, 1/2 = 38 teeth.

Confusion species
None.

Size
HB: 13¾–21½ in. (35–55 cm). T: 3¼–7 in. (12–18 cm). W: 2–4½ lb. (0.9–2 kg).

Communication
Usually silent, but has a catlike howl.

Distribution

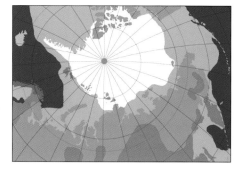

Palearctic. Breeds patchily in eastern Siberia, southern Chukotka, and throughout Kamchatka. Numbers have been severely depleted by fur trapping and habitat destruction. A forest dweller, but much more likely to be seen on the forest floor than in the trees. Usually found close to flowing water.

Diet
Carnivorous, taking squirrels and other boreal forest rodents, birds and fish, particularly salmon. Primarily nocturnal, but may be seen during the day. A very agile tree climber, but, as noted above, more likely to be seen on the ground.

Breeding
Solitary, with territories of 0.7–10 sq. mi. (2–25 km²), depending on prey density. Territories are smaller in pine forests than in larch woodlands. Delayed implantation can lead to a time between mating and birth of almost 12 months, though true gestation is only 28–30 days. One to five altricial kits cared for by female only. Weaned at around seven weeks. Sexually mature at around 15 months.

Taxonomy and variation
Polytypic. The largest of the races is *M. z. camtshadalica*, which breeds throughout Kamchatka.

Sable, eastern Russia.

Wolverine (Glutton)
Gulo gulo

The largest member of the Palearctic mustelids (in the Nearctic, the Sea Otter is, in general, larger). The alternative name in Europe, Glutton, is the basis of the species' scientific name and is based on a supposed reputation for greed. The Wolverine suffers from a bad press, some of which may be justified. It takes bait and trapped animals from the traps of fur trappers. It has a reputation for the "cruelty" of its killings, but seems no worse than, for instance, domestic cats in this regard. The Sámi people claim that a satiated Wolverine catching a Reindeer will gouge out the deer's eyes so that it cannot move, returning when hungry to kill and feed on the still-fresh animal. In the absence of significant competition from Wolves, this strategy might work, but historically Wolves and Wolverines have shared ranges. This, together with the known propensity of Wolverines to dismember larger prey and cache it in well-separated places, argues for the story being nothing more than negative propaganda; the Reindeer-herding peoples of eastern Siberia do not tell this tale.

Identification   See p. 411
Adults are short-legged, heavy animals with bushy tails and a relatively short mantle, the head more similar in shape to a Polecat (*Mustela putorius*) than to a European Badger (*Meles meles*). The pelage is dark brown, with yellowish-brown stripes from behind the front leg across the lower flank to the rear, and across the base of the tail. There are similarly colored patches between the eyes and the ears. The ears are small. The iris is dark brown or black.

The legs are short, the paws large. The pawprint shows five digits, but is similar to that of a Wolf if only four digits register. Wolverines have partially retractable claws. In snow

▲ Adult Wolverine in Finnish Karelia, close to the Russian border.

the Wolverine usually bounds, with front and hind feet landing together, so it leaves a track with all four feet within a limited area. The scat is long and twisted (6 in., or 15 cm long, ¾ in., or 2 cm diameter) and noticeably full of hair.

Dental formula: 3/3, 1/1, 2–4/2–4, 1/2 = 30–38 teeth.

Size
HB: 30–40 in. (75–100 cm). T: 4¾–6 in. (12–15 cm). SH: 16–18 in. (40–45 cm). W: 35–65 lb. (16–30 kg).

Communication
Angry Wolverines hiss and growl. Breeding pairs and family groups have a narrow range of grunts and squeals.

Distribution
Circumpolar. Breeds in northern Scandinavia and across Russia

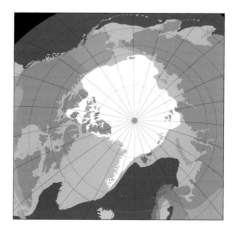

from the Kola Peninsula to Chukotka, but does not occur on Russia's Arctic islands. In North America, breeds throughout Alaska and northern Canada including most Arctic islands.

Diet
Although Wolverines have a reputation for ruthless killing, in reality they are generally scavengers rather than hunters, feeding on the carcasses of animals that have succumbed to the rigors of the Arctic winter. They will, however, opportunistically attack animals as large as Elk, Reindeer and Snow Sheep, as well as taking smaller prey such as rodents, birds and eggs, and they will supplement their diet with berries and vegetation. Surplus meat is cached, occasionally retrieved up to six months after storage.

Breeding
Highly territorial. Males hold a territory of 230–385 sq. mi. (600–1000 km²), which overlaps the ranges of two or three females, each of which holds a territory of 20–135 sq. mi. (50–350 km²). Wolverines tirelessly patrol their territories, marking boundaries by raking trees with their claws or with secretions from anal scent glands. The scent is detectable by neighboring animals over many miles/kilometres. Evidence suggests that neighbors time their border patrols to avoid conflict, as territorial disputes can result in serious injury. Mating occurs in late spring or early summer, but delayed implantation means that females give birth the following year, in late winter or early spring. Maternity dens are usually in caves, hollow trees and the like, but they may be excavated into the snow. One to five (usually two to three) altricial kits are born after a true gestation of around 50 days. Kits are nursed for 8–10 weeks. Male kits usually disperse at the start of the next breeding season, but female kits may stay within their mother's range, occasionally for a protracted period. As Wolverines do not live to a great age (6–12 years), older females may inherit a mother's territory. Young probably breed at 1–2 years, with females giving birth annually.

Taxonomy and geographical variation
Polytypic. The nominate race breeds in Eurasia. *G. g. luscus* breeds in North America. The differences are marginal and some authorities believe the species to be monotypic.

▼ Despite their fearsome reputation, Wolverines get most of their food from scavenging.

Eurasian River Otter
Lutra lutra

Identification See p. 411
Has the typical mustelid body and head shape, but with a broad muzzle and relatively small ears. Pelage is dark brown above, cream below, with ragged delineation between the two. On the face the cream color extends to the lower ear. Tail is long, thick at the base and tapering to the tip, and uniformly dark brown. All feet are fully webbed. The iris is dark orange-brown. The muzzle has many stiff vibrissae, which are tactile and help locate prey in murky waters. The ears and nostrils close when the otter dives.

Dental formula: 3/3, 1/1, 4/3–4, 1/2 = 36 or 38 teeth.

Confusion species
Swimming otters are distinguished from American Mink by their smooth action and a consistent U-shaped wake. Mink are much less fluid swimmers, having a jerky action that creates turbulence. On land, otters are much larger and have a much longer tail.

Size
HB: 24–36 in. (60–90 cm). T: 34³/₄–18 in. (35–45 cm). SH: 12 in. (30 cm). W: 15¹/₂–37¹/₂ lb. (7–17 kg).

Communication
Usually silent. Call is a high whistle, but there is also a repertoire of less frequently heard hisses and growls.

Distribution
Palearctic. Breeds in northern Fennoscandia and across Russia, but only to the northern coast near White Sea. Breeds in southern Chukotka and throughout Kamchatka. Found mainly in freshwater with good vegetated banks for holts and cover, but coastal otters also hunt in saltwater, preferring rocky shores. Dispersive. Concerns were expressed about the effect of introduced American Mink on Eurasian Otter populations, but these were overstated; the otters are dominant wherever the ranges overlap. Eurasian Otters are, however, very vulnerable to pollutants, particularly agricultural runoffs.

Diet
Fish, crustaceans and other invertebrates, amphibians, rodents and birds. Mostly taken in the water, but will also take prey on

▲ A Eurasian Otter tucks into an eel, north Norway.

land. Although the otter has dense underfur and its guard hairs trap an insulating layer of air, water is an excellent conductor of heat, and the otter has a large surface area for heat loss. The metabolic rate is therefore high and otters must consume around 15 percent of their body weight daily in food.

Breeding
Solitary, with males holding linear territories of up to 50 mi. (80 km), females to 25 mi. (40 km). Otters do not scent-mark their territories except with "spraints" left at specific sites. These defecations have a characteristic "sweet" smell from a secretion excreted with them, very different from the foul-smelling feces of American Mink. Otters construct holts, dens in natural cavities or tunneled into banks. The entrance is often below the waterline with an air shaft for ventilation. There are also resting places outside the holt, often called couches, among vegetation. Unlike their Nearctic cousins, Eurasian River Otters do not have delayed implantation. One to five (usually 2–3) altricial cubs are born after a gestation of 61–63 days. Eyes open at 35 days, weaned at four months, but taken into the water at about three months. The male takes no part in cub rearing. Cubs may remain with their mother for up to one year, but are capable of breeding at 1 year.

Taxonomy and geographical variation
Polytypic. The nominate race is found throughout the Arctic.

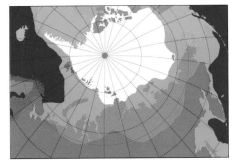

American River Otter
Lutra canadensis

Identification
See p. 411

Very similar to the Eurasian Otter. Pelage is rich dark brown above, pale creamish brown below, with a silvery sheen on the breast. Lower jaw and cheeks are pale brown, this extending to the base of the ear. All four feet are fully webbed. The iris is dark orange-brown.

Dental formula: 3/3, 1/1, 4/3, 1/1 = 34 teeth.

Confusions
As for European Otter in distinguishing from the American Mink.

Size
HB: 26–30 in. (65–75 cm). T: 12–20 in. (30–50 cm). SH: 12 in. (30 cm). W: 11–30 lb. (5–14 kg).

Communication
Usually silent, but has a sharp whistling call.

Distribution
Nearctic. Breeds throughout Alaska, but rare in the far north and absent from the Aleutian islands and the islands of the Bering Sea. Breeds in Yukon, Northwest Territories (but not to the northern coast), around Hudson Bay and throughout Quebec and Labrador (again not to the northern coast). Found in rivers and at the coast. Resident.

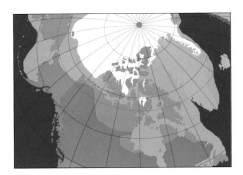

Diet
Fish, crustaceans and other invertebrates, amphibians, rodents and birds. Mostly taken in water, but travels surprising distances on land. Will pursue Muskrats into their tunnels to kill them, and apparently preys on Beavers. Has been observed deliberately holing a Beaver dam, then cruising the pond catching fish and amphibians exposed by the diminishing water level. Primarily nocturnal.

Breeding
Solitary, males and females holding linear territories as small as 0.6 mi. (1 km), but also very much larger territories if the prey density is low. However bachelor males do occasionally form groups of up to 12 individuals. Otters mark their territories with anal scent glands. Usually take over Muskrat or Beaver dens, or use a hollow tree or some other natural crevice.

▲ Young American Otters play in the snow.

The den will usually have underwater entrance and be lined with vegetation. Rarely excavate their own dens. Exercise delayed implantation of up to 12 months if conditions are unfavorable for breeding. One to five (usually two to three) altricial, but fully furred kits born after a true gestation of around 60 days. Eyes open at about 20 days, weaned at about three months, but are swimming at 6–9 weeks. Disperse at around six months. Females are sexually mature at two or three years. Males probably similar, but do not breed until they hold territories, which may be at 5–7 years if competition is fierce.

Taxonomy and geographical variation
Polytypic, with up to 24 subspecies identified.

Sea Otter
Enhydra lutris

With their delightful habits — floating on their backs and using their chests as dinner tables, attaching kelp fronds to themselves as anchors while they sleep, and holding their young in their forepaws — and teddy-bear looks, Sea Otters are probably the "cutest" of all Arctic animals. They are rivalled only by newly emerged Polar Bears, but getting too close to a baby Polar Bear is not recommended.

Sea Otters are marine mammals, but they have no blubber layer beneath the skin and so rely on their fur to keep warm. They are meticulous in grooming, as the fur traps air that acts as an effective insulator, and any problem with the fur not only prevents air trapping but allows water to reach the skin, with resultant rapid cooling. As a consequence, Sea Otters are extremely vulnerable to oil spills; the *Exxon Valdez* disaster of March 1989 killed 2,000 or more animals, while some estimates put mortality at around 5,000. They died not only of hypothermia when contaminated fur lost its insulating properties, but also of kidney and liver failure; in their desperate attempts to restore their fur, they ingested oil that then poisoned them.

Identification See p. 411
Pelage variable because of the color of both underfur and guard hairs. Sea Otters have the densest fur of any mammal, the hairs of the underfur reaching around 7,00 sq. in. ($45,000/cm^2$) and a total of around 800 million on the entire body. Sadly, the animal was hunted to the edge of extinction for this wonderfully luxuriant and warm fur. The hairs of the underfur are 1/4 in. (6 mm) long, while the guard hairs, which represent about 1.5 percent of the total number of hairs, are 1 1/2 in. (4 cm) long. The underfur color varies from mid-brown to vary dark brown, but the guard hairs can be silver or shades of brown or black, so that overall the otter can vary from silver through shades of brown to almost black. But as the animal is invariably seen in water, the effect of water on the fur and light reflecting from the water can make the true color difficult to observe. In general, the head, and particularly the muzzle, is paler, sometimes buff or even cream-buff. The head color tends to become more silver with age. The ears are small and rounded, the tail long and flat. The paws of Sea Otters differ markedly from those of other otters. The rear paws have evolved into flippers similar to those of seals, with full inter-toe webbing. Claws have been retained on all toes. The front paws are similar to those of other otters, as a high degree of manual dexterity is required to handle prey. However, the digits are enclosed in a mittenlike structure, presumably an adaptation to the cold of the marine environment. The morphology of the feet means that Sea Otters are far less agile on land than other otters; indeed, they appear clumsy on occasions. The iris is dark orange-brown, but the eyes look black against the pale head.

Dental formula: 3/2, 1/1, 3/3, 1/2 = 32 teeth.

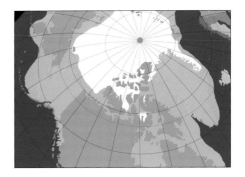

Confusion species
None.

Size
HB: 3½–5 ft. (1.1–1.5 m). T: 10–18 in. (25–45 cm). W: 33–99 lb. (15–45 kg).

Communication
Usually silent, but has a piping whistle as other otters. Cubs have a shrill scream.

Distribution
Bering Sea. Formerly found on the sea coast of North America from California to the western tip of the Aleutians, and from the Commander Islands along the Kamchatka coast to the Kuril Islands and Hokkaido. Fur-trapping reduced both the range and the population dramatically, but reintroductions in North America are allowing the original range to be re-established, though it remains patchy in the United States apart from in Alaska. An entirely marine species, preferring shallow sheltered bays and inlets. Usually only seen on land during storms.

Diet
Primarily marine invertebrates but also some fish. Particularly fond of abalone, squid, sea urchins and crabs. Clams and mussels are opened by bashing them against a rock placed on the chest until they crack, then using the powerful jaws and teeth to prise open the shell. Occasionally one shellfish will be used as an anvil on which to crack another. Crabs are dismembered, claws first, then legs. Prey is taken by diving, sometimes to 65–98 yd. (60–90 m), but usually much shallower. Because of their marine environment and lack of a blubber layer, Sea Otters have high metabolic rates and must eat around 25 percent of their body weight daily to survive.

Sea Otters will hit abalones with a rock to dislodge them from the substrate. Abalones are remarkably tenacious; it is judged that their suction foot exerts a pressure of greater than 4,000 times their body weight (which can be up to 2 lb./1kg) so the otter has to bash long and hard, some abalones requiring several dives (of 30–60 seconds each) before they are prised loose. The otter can make repeated use of a particularly useful rock, using it on successive forages. Clams are dug from seabed sediments, the otters excavating craters to find them, with the craters being gradually enlarged. Sea Otters effectively regulate the populations of prey species in the areas they inhabit. This has led to conflict between the otters and commercial shellfishers. However, wherever otters have not recovered from overhunting, sea urchins have overgrazed the kelp forests, and this removal of the basic building brick of the local food web has led to a degree of species poverty.

Breeding
Males hold territories, but those without territories, and females, are occasionally colonial, forming "rafts" of animals that can range in size from five individuals to several hundred. Sea Otters have no anal scent gland, as these would be of limited use in the sea; males defend coastal territories of up to 80ha by patroling borders that are apparently defined relative to landmarks. Females move in and out of these territories, the otters being polyandrous, though females usually limit their mates to 1–3 males. A single cub is born after a gestation of about 120 days, but there may be delayed implantation, as the time from mating to birth can vary from 4–9 months. There is no den; the female gives birth in the water. A Sea Otter cub is more precocial than cubs of other otters, but it cannot swim or dive. It can, however, float and is left at the surface when the mother dives to obtain food. The cub is held by the female on her chest as it suckles. When it is too large to fit neatly, it lies crosswise to her, the pair forming a T. Cubs are weaned at roughly six months (though this is highly variable, ranging from 2–11 months), but stays with the female for about one year. Females usually give birth annually. Females usually breed at 3–5 years. Males are sexually mature at 5–7 years but do not breed until they hold territories, which may be several years later.

Taxonomy and geographical variation
Polytypic. The nominate race breeds throughout the Arctic part of the species range. Two extralimital subspecies are recognized on the western seaboard of the United States.

▼ Sea Otter in typical "backstroke" pose, Resurrection Bay.

PLATE 35: LARGE CARNIVORES

Arctic Fox

blue morphs

win

sum

win

sum

"White" Wolf

Gray Wolf

"cross"

"silver"

Polar Bear

"blue"

Red Fox

V. a. emmonsii

ad
V. a. cinnamonium

ad

ad
V. a. kermodei

Brown bear

American Black Bear

Eurasian Lynx

ad
V. arctos

ad
V. a. horribilis

Canadian Lynx

Short-tailed Weasel

sum

Least
Weasel

win

Sable

win

sum

American Mink

Eurasian
River Otter

Wolverine

American
River Otter

Sea Otter

Pinnipeds

The suborder Pinnipedia, the seals, sea lions and Walrus, is divided into two superfamilies, Phocoidea and Otarioidea. The Phocoidea contains only one family, the Phocidae or true seals. The Otarioidea contains two families, Otariidae or eared seals (which includes fur seals and sea lions) and the Odobenidae, consisting of just one species, the Walrus. All pinnipeds are carnivores in both senses of the word; they belong to the order Carnivora. Their evolution is still debated and the group may well be paraphyletic. Most authorities consider that the Phocidae evolved from a mustelidlike ancestor, while the ancestors of the Otariidae were bear- or doglike. However, DNA testing suggests that the two families are actually closer than had been supposed.

Adaptations for a life at sea

The Phocidae are well adapted for marine life. They have spindle-shaped bodies, lack external ears to minimize drag, have hind flippers (shaped much like the tail flukes of whales) that provide the power for swimming and have short front flippers, which are usually held tight to the body when the animal is diving or swimming but which can act as fins to aid steering. Body insulation is provided by blubber, with the ancestral fur reduced to a few coarse hairs. On land the hind flippers of true seals are next to useless, and locomotion is an ungainly wriggle aided by the front flippers.

By contrast, the sea lions are reasonably mobile on land, as they can rotate their hind flippers underneath their bodies and, aided by these and their long front flippers, can achieve a turn of speed that can surprise an inquisitive observer who gets too close. In these mammals it is the front flippers that provide most of the propulsion in water. Sea lions and fur seals rely in part on fur for insulation; the underfur of fur seals is luxuriantly thick, which led to their near-extinction due to zealous overhunting. Fur seals and sea lions have external ears and less pointed faces, and in general are not as well adapted to life at sea as the true seals, although fossil evidence suggests that their ancestors took to the seas around the same time or even before those of the true seals. As a consequence of using fur for insulation, fur seals and sea lions are chiefly animals of temperate waters. However, the Walrus, the sole member of the second otarioid family the Odobenidae, is a true Arctic specialist, and it has blubber insulation similar to the true seals, though it shares the reversible hind flippers of the sea lions and fur seals.

All pinnipeds have vibrissae (whiskers), which are used in prey detection. Experiments with blindfolded Harbor Seals have shown that the seals can still hunt successfully without vision. It is believed that the vibrissae detect minute hydrodynamic changes in the water — in other words, they are able to detect the wakes of fish and other underwater animals.

The sea lions and fur seals are colonial, highly so in the case of the fur seals, but the true seals are generally solitary for most of the time. Antarctic seal pups are dark, but in general Arctic seal pups are born with a covering of soft white fur, or lanugo, though there are exceptions to this; these too, though, are usually partially white. Presumably this coloration acts as a camouflage against terrestrial carnivores when the pups are on the ice in the weeks after birth.

▼ Walruses basking on sea ice, Fosterbukta, northeast Greenland.

Seals

Phocids are a predominantly polar and subpolar marine group, but there are some startling exceptions, including the Baikal Seal (*Pusa sibirica*), which lives in the freshwater of Lake Baikal, the inland but saltwater Caspian Seal (*Pusa caspica*), and the *Monachus* Monk Seals of the Mediterranean, Hawaii and the Caribbean (through the last is probably extinct).

Ringed Seal
Pusa hispida

The most numerous of all Arctic mammals with a population estimated at around six million. Ringed Seals are small for polar seals; this may be an adaptation for the use of birthing caves, which can never be very large.

▲ Ringed Seal on the sea ice of Kongsfjorden, Svalbard.

Identification See p. 429

The pelage is dark gray or gray-brown dorsally, with a mosaic of pale gray rings that give the seal its name. The rings are smaller or absent on the head. Ventrally the pelage is silver, silver-brown or gray-brown, the flippers the same color or darker. The front flippers have large claws used for scraping away at breathing holes in the ice. The head is "catlike," with the muzzle shorter than those of other phocids, which tend to the more "doglike." Ringed Seal pups are white, molting at around eight weeks to dark silver-gray dorsally, lighter ventrally and to adult pelage at one year.

Dental formula 2-3/1–2, 1/1, 4/4, 0–2/0-2 = 26–38 teeth.

Confusion species

In the Bering Sea, the Spotted Seal is of similar size and shape, but it tends to be browner, and with dark spots rather than the distinctive rings of the Ringed Seal.

Size

HB: 4¼–5½ ft. (1.3–1.7 m). W: 100–240 lb. (45–110 kg).

Communication

Usually silent, but with a limited repertoire of grunts and barks. During the mating period, male Ringed Seals give off a pungent scent from glands on the muzzle and under the front flippers. Polar Bears rarely take males during the mating period because they find the scent repulsive.

Distribution

Circumpolar. Found at the ice edge throughout the Palearctic and Nearctic. Also found in three freshwater locations: Lake Ladoga in Russia and Lake Saimaa in Finland (both close to the Gulf of Finland) and Lake Nettilling on Baffin Island's western coast. The Lake Ladoga population is substantial (around

5,000) and stable, but that of Lake Saimaa is small (around 200) and highly vulnerable. Both Lake Ladoga and Lake Saimaa are connected to the sea, but no evidence suggests that the seals venture along these connective waterways. It is assumed that ancestral populations either migrated to the lakes or have been isolated by landscape changes. The highest numbers of Ringed Seals are found in eastern Russia, around the Bering Sea and in the Nearctic. There is also a substantial population in the Sea of Okhotsk. By contrast, there are much smaller populations on eastern Greenland, on Svalbard and in western Russia. There is also a small population in the Baltic Sea. Freshwater populations are resident; marine populations move with the advances and retreats of the floe edge. In winter Ringed Seals occasionally reach the northern coast of Iceland.

Diet

Fish and crustaceans, the proportions of each apparently

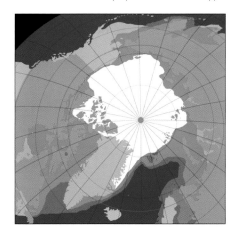

varying with the season. Arctic Cod (*Boreogadus saida*) seems to be eaten almost exclusively in winter and is the chief food source at all times, supplemented by isopods and amphipods in spring and by euphausiids in summer. Ringed Seals dive for prey in open water and beneath the sea ice. Diving beneath the ice requires breathing holes, which are kept open by chewing the surrounding ice or by scraping with the claws of the front flippers. The seals venture far from their breathing holes while diving, and it is unclear how they regain them. Several breathing holes are maintained to reduce the chances of predation or being caught short. Breathing holes have been found in ice up to 7 ft. (2 m) thick. The seals occasionally hollow out resting chambers in the accumulated snow on the ice close to a breathing hole. Dives may last 20 minutes, but are usually much shorter (4–8 minutes). Ringed Seals are known to reach depths of up to 130 ft. (40 m) and may reach 295 ft. (90 m).

Breeding

Solitary, though occasionally form small groups. Adults seem to be territorial, though interactions between hauled-out seals are rare, except when groups form during the annual molt. Then as many as 100 seals may be seen together at a lead. Pair-bond appears monogamous, though this may be because of a lack of opportunity, and polygamy may be common in populations of high density. Mating, which apparently takes place underwater, occurs in spring after the females give birth (and while they are still suckling the current year's young). Females practice delayed implantation of two to three months, and give birth in the subsequent spring after an effective gestation of around 270 days. The female excavates a birthing chamber above the sea ice, choosing a pressure ridge close to a breathing hole as a starting point, the snows of later winter and early spring adding further coverage. Freshwater females may dig in snowbanks beside the lake. Within the den, a single precocial pup around 2 ft. (65 cm) long and weighing 10 lb. (4.5 kg) is born. The female excavates tunnels away from the birthing chamber to reduce the chances of predation. Polar bears can smell seals and pups

▲ A seal hole through the ice, Kongsfjorden, Svalbard.

through the snow and will attempt capture by crashing through the snow roof. It is estimated that predation by bears and by Arctic Foxes accounts for around 50% of each year's pups. Pups can swim, but do not do so until they are weaned at 5–7 weeks, by which time their weight has increased to 22–27 lb. (10–12 kg). Male seals take no part in the rearing of the young. Both males and females breed at 7 years.

Taxonomy and geographical variation

Polytypic. The nominate race breeds in the high Arctic, but the Baltic Sea (*P. h. botnica*), Lake Ladoga (*P. h. ladogensis*), Lake Saimaa (*P. h. saimensis*) and Lake Nettilling (*P. h. soperi*) populations are given subspecific status, as are the seals of the northern Bering Sea, (*P. h. krascheninikovi*), and the Sea of Okhotsk, (*P. h. ochotensis*). The differences between the subspecies are generally marginal, and relate to skull size and shape, but *ladogensis* is smaller, while the lanugo of *saimensis* is gray.

Ringed Seal on the ice, Kongsfjorden, Svalbard.

Ribbon Seal
Phoca fasciata

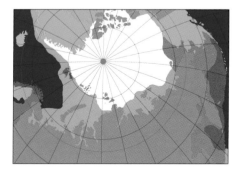

▲ Adult male Ribbon Seal on the ice — an unmistakable and beautiful seal species, Bering Sea.

Identification See p. 429

The male pelage is dark brown with four distinct broad bands of pale gray and cream, one around the neck, two around the front flippers (almost meeting on the breast) and a fourth around the lower abdomen. The flippers are dark brown. Females have the same pattern, but the bands are much less distinct as the body color is buff-brown. The head is "doglike." Pups are white at birth, becoming gray at around five weeks. The color bands appear at about two years of age. Ribbon Seals defy the generalization that phocids are slow and cumbersome out of the water; they are very rapid on the pack ice, using the front flippers, a sinuous motion of the rear end and the fact that ice is virtually friction-free to achieve a surprising speed over short distances.

Dental formula: 2–3/1-2, 1/1, 4/4, 0–2/0–2 = 26–38 teeth.

Confusion species
None.

Size
HB: 5–5½ ft. (1.5–1.7 m). W: 154–187 lb. (70–85 kg).

Communication
Male Ribbon Seals have an air sac at the posterior end of the trachea, close to where it bifurcates to form the bronchi, which inflates over the ribs on the animal's right side. The air sac is much less developed in females. This air sac is a communication aid for mating males, used to announce their presence to females or to rival males. Underwater recordings reveal a series of huffing noises and a characteristic long whistle of decreasing frequency.

Distribution
Bering Sea. The Ribbon Seal is found on pack ice far from land in the Bering Sea and southern Beaufort Sea, and also in the Sea of Okhotsk. Rarely seen close to land and assumed to be pelagic outside the breeding period.

Diet
Fish, cephalopods and crustaceans. Little is known of the diving abilities of Ribbon Seals.

Breeding
The social life of Ribbon Seals is poorly understood. Seems to be usually solitary or in small groups. Males assumed to be polygynous. Single pup (about 3 ft./90 cm long, weighing 122 lb./10 kg) born on the ice after gestation of around 280 days, with assumed delayed implantation following mating during lactation or immediately upon weaning. Pup has white or pale gray lanugo. The female suckles her pup for three to four

weeks, then abruptly departs, leaving the pup, by then weighing 55–66 lb. (25–30 kg), to fend for itself. Both males and females breed at three to 5 years.

Taxonomy and geographical variation

Unclear. Probably monotypic, but Bering Sea and Sea of Okhotsk populations may not interbreed and so may be subspecifically distinct.

Harp Seal
Phoca groenlandica

The annual slaughter of pure white, doe-eyed Harp Seal pups off Canada's eastern coast became an international issue in the 1980s. Today the seals are still hunted, but less for their skins and more for their oil, which is rich in omega-3 fatty acids. The hunt is now controlled and carried out to manage numbers, as local fishermen fear competition from an increasing seal population. However, it should be noted that the Newfoundland banks cod fishery has declined mainly as a consequence of human action, by both international and local fishermen, rather than seal predation.

Identification See p. 429

Adult males are silver-gray with dark gray and black upper muzzle, crown and cheeks, with black lines after which the seal is named on the back and flanks. The "harp" is actually on the flanks, the two harps linked across the back so that the total design is more of a "saddle" shape. Adult females are patterned as the males, but the head and back/flank patch are paler. In females, both the head and body pattern may be broken, appearing as a collection of spots. The base color of males and females may also be different, and change as the animal ages, varying from silver-gray to green-gray. Pups have white lanugo. It is the annual harvesting of the pure white Harp pups with their saucerlike black eyes that brings the animal to public notice. Pups molt to a silver-gray pelage with dark gray spotting and blotching at about four weeks, the adult pattern appearing at about four years. Head shape is neither dog- or catlike, but has a distinct "Roman" nose.

Dental formula: 2–3/1-2. 1/1, 4/4, 0–2/0-2 = 26–38 teeth.

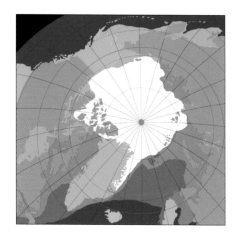

Confusion species

None, though immature Harp Seals are similar to young Harbor and Ringed Seals.

Size

HB: 5$\frac{1}{2}$–6$\frac{1}{4}$ ft. (1.7–1.9 m). W: 254–309 lb. (115–140 kg).

Communication

A vocal seal with an extensive repertoire of grunts. These vary across the three breeding populations.

Distribution

North Atlantic and Palearctic. Found from the eastern Canadian Arctic islands (east of Peel Sound) to the Laptev Sea. The infamous pup harvesting occurs on the sea ice of the North Atlantic near Newfoundland. Three distinct breeding populations of Harp Seals exist: off Newfoundland, off Jan Mayen and in Russia's White Sea. Harp Seals follow the ice edge north in summer and south in winter, some animals traveling up to 3,105 mi. (5,000 km) annually. Newfoundland breeders spend summers to the west of Greenland's Cape

▼ Porpoising Harp Seals, northeast Greenland. This behavior, whereby the animal leaps from the water as it swims, allows the animals to breathe without loss of speed; penguins and dolphins also regularly porpoise.

◀ Basking Harbor Seal of the nominate race, Kjorholmane, Norway.

Harbor Seal
Phoca vitulina

Identification
See p. 429

Pelage is silvery-gray, occasionally buff with an extensive dark gray; dark gray-brown or dark brown spotting dorsally and on the crown and nape. There are usually fewer ventral spots. The hind flippers are dark gray or gray-brown, the front flippers paler. Pelage is variable with region. Most pups are similar in color to the adults, having shed their white lanugo coat before birth, but some pups, particularly in the northern reaches of the range, are born with white coats, shedding these within a few days. Head is "doglike."

Dental formula: 3/2, 1/1, 5/5 = 34 teeth.

Confusion species
In the North Atlantic, the Gray Seal is larger and has different head shape. In the North Pacific, the Spotted Seal is smaller, usually has a browner pelage and has more spots that are more uniform.

Size
HB: 4–6¼ ft. (1.2–1.9 m). W: 100–300 lb. (45–135 kg).

Communication
Usually silent, but has a limited repertoire of barks and grunts. Makes a low click underwater, but it is unclear whether this is echolocation to detect prey, or for communication, perhaps as a threat to an approaching seal.

Farewell, Jan Mayen breeders near eastern Greenland and White Sea breeders from Svalbard to eastern Russia. Porpoising herds of Harp Seals on the move are one of the great sights of the Arctic seas.

Diet
Fish, particularly Capelin (*Mallatis villosus,*) and crustaceans. Adults dive to as deep as 655 ft. (200 m) to feed, though most dives are much shallower.

Breeding
Gregarious, though some old males are solitary. Some males are apparently polygynous, but the usual bond is serially monogamous. A single precocial pup (about 3 ft./90 cm long, weighing 13–22 lb./6–10kg) is born after a gestation of about 230 days, but with delayed implantation, as mating takes place in the water soon after the females give birth. Birth takes place on the ice, sometimes in aggregates of tens of thousands of females. The pups gain weight rapidly on the fat-rich milk (fat content is around 42%). At 10 days, when the pup weighs about 77 lb. (35 kg) — representing a weight gain of 5 lb. (2.5 kg/day) — the female leaves and the pup must fend for itself from that point onward. Female departure is a necessity; she has lost up to 50% of her body weight and must feed. Both males and females breed at four to six years.

Taxonomy and geographical variation
Probably polytypic. Newfoundland, Jan Mayen and White Sea populations have minor morphological differences. DNA analysis shows that Newfoundland animals are possibly distinct from other populations.

Distribution
Circumpolar. Found in coastal waters off southern Greenland, Iceland, northern Scandinavia and Svalbard north to Prinz Karls Forland, but absent from northern Russia. Found in the northern Pacific and southern Bering Sea from Kamchatka to southern Alaska, and in the waters of eastern Canada, including Hudson Bay, northern Quebec and Labrador and around southern Baffin Island. Harbor Seals usually avoid ice, but they can occasionally be seen on ice floes if their preferred

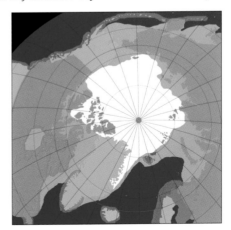

feeding area has limited haul-out sites. Resident, but moves in response to changes in prey density. Journeys of up to 620 mi. (1,000 km) have been recorded for tagged individuals.

Diet
Varied, taking fish, crustaceans, cephalopods and mollusks as available. There is some evidence that individuals may preferentially select one prey type. Harbor Seals have been recorded diving to 1,476 ft. (450 m), but this is exceptional as these seals are normally limited to shallow coastal waters, diving to 100 ft. (30 m).

Breeding
Solitary in the water, but gregarious when hauled out, with groups of several hundred animals forming at pupping or molting sites. However, even in apparently peaceful groups there is constant grumbling as neighbors try to protect their personal space. Harbor Seals are not gregarious in the way that, for instance, Walrus are. Some evidence suggests that males defend territories close to breeding sites, and males certainly compete for females, as they often show scarring to the neck. Females also defend their pupping area. Males are either polygynous or serially monogamous. Mating occurs soon after the year's pup is born, following delayed implantation. A single, precocial pup (2–3 ft./70–95 cm long, weighing 20–24¼ lb./9–11 kg) is born after a gestation of around 240 days. Pups are born on ice floes, sandbanks or on the shore, and can swim after just a few hours, an adaptation to minimize the risk of predation. Pups can dive almost from the first swim and are pushed underwater by their mother if danger threatens. Pups are weaned at 3–6 weeks and abandoned at that time. Females breed at 4–6 years, males at 5–6 years.

Taxonomy and geographical variation
Polytypic. The nominate race is found in the eastern Atlantic, including Iceland. *P. v. concolor* lives in the western Atlantic around Greenland and eastern Canada. The pelage of this form tends to be blue-gray with very dark black spots. There are some freshwater populations, landlocked in the Upper and Lower Seal Lakes of northern Quebec, close to the eastern shore of Hudson Bay. These animals tend to be darker than *concolor* and are considered a separate subspecies, *P. v. mellonae. P. v. richardsi*, the Pacific Harbor Seal, is found in the northeast Pacific, from the Aleutians and southern Alaska along the western seaboard of the United States as far south as California. It is larger than the nominate, but has similar coloring. *P. v. stejnegeri* is found in the northwest Pacific from Hokkaido to eastern Kamchatka and the Commander Islands. It is the largest of the Harbor Seal races, and shows the most definite sexual dimorphism, males being much larger than females; *stejnegeri* usually have a dark pelage.

Spotted Seal
(Largha Seal)
Phoca larga

Once thought to be a subspecies of the Harbor Seal, the Spotted's scientific name derives from the seal's name in the language of the Tungus people of the western Sea of Okhotsk. Many prefer the name Largha as the principal common name, Spotted Seal, can cause confusion — Spotted Seal is sometimes used for the Harbor Seal in Europe.

Identification See p. 429
Adult pelage is pale gray, gray-brown or mid-brown dorsally, paler ventrally with heavy, uniform dark brown or black spotting. The hind and front flippers are usually darker and may show some spotting. Pups are born with a white lanugo coat, which is shed for adult coloration after two to four weeks.
Dental formula is 3/2, 1/1, 5/5 = 34 teeth.

Confusion species
See Harbor Seal.

Size
HB: 5–5½ ft. (1.4–1.7 m). W: 175–240 lb. (80–110 kg).

Communication
A limited repertoire of barks and grunts.

Distribution
North Pacific and Bering Sea. Found in the Sea of Okhotsk and from Kamchatka to the coast of western Alaska, southward to

▼ Harbor Seals of the race *richardsi*, Tracy Arm, Alaska.

▲ Spotted Seal, Sea of Okhotsk. Note the spotted pelage.

the Aleutians and north to the Chukchi and Beaufort Seas. Also occurs along the Kuril Islands and on Hokkaido. Usually found on or near the pack ice in winter, spending the summer in open water, but also seen in shallower coastal waters.

Diet
Fish, cephalopods and crustaceans. Apparently dives as deep as 984 ft. (300 m).

Breeding
Normally solitary, but groups form when the seals are moulting. Unusually for seals, "family" groups form on the pack ice. The seals are seasonally monogamous, the male joining the female around the time she gives birth and remaining with her until the current year's pup is weaned, at which time he mates with her. Male, female and pup are therefore seen together, but the male might not be the father. The precocial single pup (28 ft./85 cm long and weighing 22 lb./10 kg) is born on the ice, or more rarely on a sandbar or beach. Eight main breeding areas are known, including the southeastern Bering Sea from the

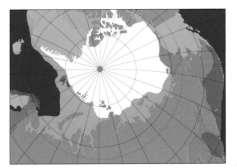

Pribilofs to Bristol Bay, the southwestern Bering Sea off Kamchatka, the Gulf of Anadyr and the northern sea of Okhotsk. Gestation period is unknown, but assumed to be around 240 days with delayed implantation. Pup weaned at 4 weeks, by which time it weighs around 62 lb. (28 kg). In contrast to Harbor Seals, Spotted pups are poor swimmers and spend almost all their time on the ice until weaned. Breeding age assumed to be as Harbor Seal.

Taxonomy and geographical variation
Poorly understood. There may be little interbreeding between Spotted Seals from the various breeding areas, and this separation my be subspecifically significant. It is known that the population near Hokkaido is around 33 lb. (15 kg) heavier and 4 in. (10 cm) longer than more northerly populations.

Gray Seal
Halichoerus grypus

A sub-Arctic rather than Arctic species, but found on the Labrador coast, the southern and western coasts of Iceland and from northern Scandinavia east to the White Sea.

Identification See p. 429
The largest of the northern phocids. Adult males are dark gray or gray-brown overall (though usually darker dorsally than ventrally) with light gray patches. Adult females are the reverse; light gray with darker patches. Head shape is very different from other true seals, being straight from crown to nose, i.e. "horselike." Muzzle is wide and heavy. Pups are born with white lanugo coat, which is shed at 4–6 weeks.
Dental formula: 3/2, 1/1, 5–6/5 = 34–36 teeth.

Confusion species
Coloration is very similar to that of Harbor Seal, but Gray Seal is larger and the head shape is diagnostic. If the observer is close enough, the nostrils are also diagnostic. Those of the Gray Seal are separated, while Harbor Seal nostrils almost join at the base.

Size
HB: 7–11 ft. (2.1–3.3 m). W: 275–660 lb. (125–300 kg). Gray Seals show the largest degree of sexual dimorphism of the northern phocids (or of any member of the Phocidae apart from the *Mirounga* elephant seals), with the males up to three times larger than the females.

Communication
Vocal, particularly at pupping and molt sites. Males have a low huffing, females an eerie howl. Pups have a human babylike cry.

Distribution
North Atlantic. Three populations have been identified. On the North American coast the seals breed from Labrador's Cape Chidley to Cape Cod in the United States. Another population breeds on the western and southern coasts of

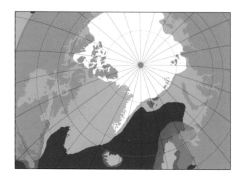

▲ Gray Seal in the swell near a rocky coast, north Norway.

Iceland, around the British Isles, on the west coast of Norway and around the coast of northern Fennoscandia. The third population breeds in the Baltic. Gray seals are absent from Greenland. Found in shallow coastal waters. Partially migratory, moving to favored feeding and molt sites.

Diet
Fish and cephalopods, also occasionally take birds.

Breeding
Solitary except at pupping and molting sites when they are highly gregarious, though maintaining a personal space. Males defend harems rather than territories. Very successful males may mate with up to 10 females. Often males show scarring on the neck from conflicts over females. A single precocial pup

(3–3½ ft. /90–105 cm long, weighing 30 lb./14 kg) is born in colonies that may number up to 50,000 females. In the North Atlantic, the pups are born on sandbanks or on the shore, but in the Baltic they are born on the ice. Pups have a cream-white lanugo coat. Gestation is around 240 days with delayed implantation. Pups are weaned at 16–21 days and swim at that stage. However, some pups remain on land (or on the ice) for up to four weeks, eating nothing throughout that period. This behavior is not understood. Females breed at 4–5 years. Males are sexually mature at 6 years, but rarely breed until they are at least 8 years old, because they cannot maintain harems against larger males before then.

Taxonomy and geographical variation
Polytypic. Subspecies are identified by geography and pupping time — morphological differences are minor. The nominate race breeds on the North American coast and pups in January and February. *H. g. atlanticus* breeds in the northeastern Atlantic and pups in September to December. *H. g. balticus* breeds in the Baltic and pups in February and March. Both eastern subspecies are significantly smaller than the nominate.

▼ Gray Seals, north Norway. This may well be a harem.

Bearded Seals haul out on the last of the winter ice, Magdalenafjorden, Svalbard. The Gullybreen glacier is in the background.

Bearded Seal
Erignathus barbatus

As with Polar Bears, the livers of Bearded Seas are so rich in vitamin A that they can be toxic to humans. A small percentage of seals (about 5%) are infested with the parasite that causes trichinosis, assumed to be acquired by eating crustaceans that have scavenged on infected animal carcasses. Eating raw seal meat can pass this disease to humans.

Identification
See p. 429
The largest Bearded Seals are as heavy as Gray Seals, but are not as long. Adult pelage is gray-brown or brown, darker dorsally than ventrally and with some dark blotches. The head is small compared to the large, rotund body (making the seal look even fatter) and "doglike" face, though the muzzle is blunter than that of other "doglike" seals. This seal has a profusion of long vibrissae that curl when dry, giving the mustached facial-hair look that explains the name. The front flippers are square. They are used to stir up bottom sediments in search of food, the long whiskers then aiding prey detection in the murky, sediment-filled water. Pups shed their white lanugo coat *in utero* and are born with a coat of dense, long blue-gray or gray-brown lanugo, which soon molts into the adult pelage. As pups join their mother in the water soon after birth, this lack of a camouflaged coat does not lead to an increased risk of predation. The dentition is rudimentary and loose, with older animals often missing teeth.

Dental formula: 3/1–2, 1/1, 4/4, 0–2/0–2 = 26–38 teeth.

Confusion species
None. Size and "beard" are diagnostic.

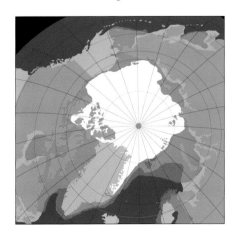

▲ Adult Bearded Seal on the ice off the coast of Svalbard. Note the long whiskers, which are used to detect benthic invertebrates.

Size

HB: 7–8 ft. (2.2–2.5 m). W: 400–660 lb. (200–300 kg). Unusually, females are slightly larger than males.

Communications

Males have a long vibrating whistle, which ends as a loud sigh, the call often made underwater. It can be heard from several miles away and advertises their presence to rival males and potential mates. It is not clear whether females whistle in the water, but they do not appear to do so when hauled out.

Distribution

Circumpolar. Found throughout northern waters, and also in Hudson Bay and the Sea of Okhotsk. Usually found around pack ice, but occasionally in shallow coastal waters. Rarely seen on land. Resident, but moves with the ice edge.

Diet

Benthic animals of all kinds. Canadian seals apparently eat more fish than European and Bering Sea animals, which tend to consume more crustaceans and mollusks. Mollusk shells are rarely found in Bearded Seal stomachs, suggesting that they obtain the meat by suction, as does the Walrus. Bearded Seals are known to feed at night. Dives to 920 ft. (280 m) have been recorded, but most are only to about 65 ft. (20 m).

Breeding

Solitary; groups are rarely seen. Males are apparently monogamous, but may be opportunistically polygynous. Single precocial pup (about 4 ft./120 cm long and weighing 66–88 lb./30–40 kg) born on the ice after a gestation of around 240 days with delayed implantation. Twins have been observed, but females producing twins do not apparently

breed in the second year, so the overall reproductive rate is as for those producing a single pup annually. The pup joins its mother in the water soon after birth. The pup is weaned at 12–18 days, by which time it weighs around 200 lb. (90 kg). The female then abandons it. Females breed at 6 years, males at 6–7 years.

Taxonomy and geographical variation

Polytypic. The nominate race breeds in the North Atlantic. *E. b. nauticci* breeds through North America to central Siberia. The differences are slight; some authorities suggest that the species is monotypic.

Hooded Seal
Cystophora cristata

Identification See p. 429

The heaviest of the northern true seals. Adult pelage is silver-gray with extensive mottling of dark brown or black patches, which tend to be longer on the back and flanks. The head is "doglike," but this shape is partially obscured by the hood of the name. This is a sac of skin, an enlarged extension of the nasal cavity, which forms a proboscis that hangs over the mouth in males, but is much less pronounced or absent in females. The hood can be inflated to form a large black cushion or blister that spreads from the forehead over the mouth. Males can also extrude and inflate the internasal septum membrane. This extrudes from one nostril, usually the left, as a red balloon. The inflation mechanisms of hood and balloon are dissimilar: the hood requires closed nostrils, the balloon an open nostril. Consequently, both hood and balloon cannot be inflated simultaneously. However a "half-hood" and balloon can be inflated, to grotesque effect. Although the hood and balloon are used in mating displays, they are also inflated if the seal is surprised by an observer (perhaps in anxiety or as a threat) and, occasionally, by resting seals, for no apparent reason. The hood develops in males from the age of four years. Hooded Seal pups lose their lanugo *in utero*, and are born with a pelage that is dark blue-gray dorsally (hence the occasional name of "blue backs"), cream ventrally. The pup spends time on the ice after being abandoned by its mother, so the reason for the shedding of the camouflaged coat is not apparent.

Dental formula: 2/1, 1/1, 4/4, 1/1 = 30 teeth.

Confusion species

None. Size and colour are distinctive, as are the inflated hood and balloon.

Size

HB: 6½–9½ ft. (2–2.9 m). W: 320–770 lb. (145–350 kg). Significant sexual dimorphism; males are almost twice as heavy as the females, though they are only about 25% longer. Recorded male weights have exceeded 880 lb. (400 kg).

Communication

Vocal repertoire of loud roars, particularly by the male during the mating season. The male hood and balloon are also used, both to attract females (when, presumably, the size of each is a sign of the male's quality) and to threaten rival males (when size indicates maturity). The hood increases in size with age and physical size until the male is around 15 years old; these seals have a lifespan of around 35 years. Underwater, the seals emit a rapid series of clicks, and the males also emit pulses of low-frequency sound.

Distribution

North Atlantic. Found on the eastern seaboard of North America from Newfoundland to Lancaster Sound, but rarely west of Labrador's Cape Chidley or north into Smith Sound. Found in the northwestern Atlantic around Iceland's northern coast, Jan Mayen, Svalbard and Bear Island, and rarely as far east as Franz Josef Land. Found in dense pack ice during breeding and molting, otherwise in the open sea. Partially migratory, moving between molting and breeding sites and the open sea. Rarely seen on land.

Diet

Benthic or deep-water fish, cephalopods, crustaceans and mollusks. Dives to around 980 ft. (300 m).

Breeding

Solitary, though groups form at favored moulting sites. The largest of these are in the Denmark Strait and off north-eastern Greenland. In the mating season, "family" groups of male, female and current year's pup form as male waits for female to be receptive. Other males may also gather, the principal suitor maintaining aggressive "ownership" of the female. Males are probably opportunistically polygynous. Specific breeding areas have been identified to the north of Jan Mayen, close to northern Newfoundland, in the Gulf of St. Lawrence and off Greenland's southwestern coast from Nuuk to Maniitsoq. A single precocial pup (3–3¼ ft./90–100 cm long, weighing 30–50 lb. (15–25 kg) is born on an ice floe after gestation of around 250 days and a period of delayed implantation. The pup can swim and dive after a few days and gains weight at a prodigious rate, doubling its birth weight within four days. This phenomenal weight gain (up to 15 lb./7 kg per day) is aided by the production of lipase enzymes in the pup's saliva, which allow digestion of milk fats to start in the mouth and stomach rather than only in the small intestine as in most mammals. Hooded Seal milk is around 60% fat. The weight gain is necessary, as at four days the female abandons the pup, mating again soon after. Four-day weaning is the shortest period of any mammal. Following weaning, the pup stays on the ice for several weeks. As the pups can swim and dive if necessary, this delay (also seen in other true seals) is not understood. Females breed at 4–5 years. Males are sexually mature at five years, but are rarely able to breed until they are much older.

Taxonomy and variation

Probably polytypic, though the differences between seals of different breeding areas are marginal.

Hooded Seal on the pack ice between northeast Greenland and Svalbard.

Sea lions

Since they lack insulating layers of blubber, most eared seals are found in temperate waters, but one sea lion and one fur seal are found at the edge of the Arctic.

Steller's Sea Lion (Northern Sea Lion)
Eumetopias jubatus

The largest of the eared seals, named after Georg Wilhelm Steller, the naturalist on Bering's expedition to the North Pacific. Steller's is the most northerly sea lion. Unlike other eared seals, it does have a layer of blubber, so it relies less on its fur for thermoregulation. Concerns have been expressed in recent years about this sea lion; numbers on the Russian side of the Bering Sea have plummeted by about 90% over the last 40 years. A reduction of 80% has been seen on the American side of the sea; the species will be extinct within 50 years if present trends continue, though biologists are unsure as to the reasons for the decline.

▲ Male Steller's Sea Lion, Resurrection Bay. Note the "mane."

Identification See p. 429
Adult pelage varies from buff to red-brown, usually darker dorsally than ventrally and tending to become lighter with age. The flippers are dark gray or black. The head is "doglike." Male Steller's develop thickened, muscular necks, over which grows a mane of coarse hair (after which "sea lions" are named). Pups have a darker pelage, which molts to the lighter adult color after about two years.

Dental formula is 3/2, 1/1, 4/4, 1/1 = 34 teeth.

Confusion species
None.

Size
HB: 6½–11½ ft. (2–3.5 m). W: 440–2,200 lb. (200–1000 kg). Extreme sexual dimorphism, with males three to four times heavier than females and 50% longer.

Communication
Very vocal, with a repertoire of grunts and roars; male voices are much deeper than female's. The males defend harems with an array of threatening postures.

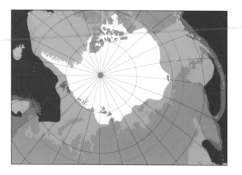

Distribution
Bering Sea. Found in the western Sea of Okhotsk and across the southern edge of the Bering Sea from Kamchatka through the Commander Islands (where Steller first described it, on Bering Island) to the Aleutians and southern Alaska. Also found on the Kuril Islands and along the eastern seaboard of North America as far south as California. In British Columbia the population has been culled in response to pleas from fishermen, so the animal is rare away from Russia and Alaska. Usually found in coastal waters, often close to breeding sites. These are usually rocky, but may be sandy beaches. Out of the breeding season may occur up to 560 mi. (900 km) from shore, but usually sticks to the continental shelf. Rarely seen on ice floes.

Diet
Fish and cephalopods. Local fishermen often complain of the devastating effect of colonies on salmon and pollock populations, but these claims are exaggerated. Apparently dives to no more than 164 ft. (50 m). Also takes Northern Fur Seal pups and small adult seals.

Breeding
Females gregarious at all times; males solitary except in the breeding season. At the breeding sites, which are exciting, noisy places, males form and defend a harem of up to 30 females. The strain of this reduces male life expectancy to about 25 years, while females may reach 30 years or more. The reward for the male is the fathering of many pups. A single precocial pup (rarely twins), about 3 ft. (1 m) long and weighing 40–48 lb. (18–22 kg), is born after a gestation of about 240 days with delayed implantation. The pup stays with its mother until the following year when a new pup is born. Some females actually continue to suckle the previous year's pup. Instances of suckling to 18 months have been recorded, with one observation of a 3-year-old immature still suckling. As the pup grows, the female

spends more time away from the breeding site feeding. The pups may then supplement milk with crustaceans, but they are essentially not weaned for at least 12 months. Females breed at 3–6 years. Males are sexually mature at 6 years, but do not breed until they are capable of maintaining a harem.

Taxonomy and geographical variation
Monotypic.

Northern Fur Seal
Callorhinus ursinus

One of only two northern fur seals (the other is the Guadalupe Fur Seal, *Arctocephalus townsendi*), and the only one whose range extends to the edge of the Arctic.

Identification
See p. 429

Male pelage is a rich dark brown; females are gray-brown dorsally, pale chestnut-gray ventrally. The luxuriant coats are reflected in the generic name, derived from *kallos rhinos* or beautiful skin, and in the history of the species, which was ruthlessly exploited by trappers in the 19th century; the original population on the Pribilofs was reduced from about three million to 300,000 or fewer. The underfur of the seal has around 8,800 hairs/sq. in. (55,000 hairs/cm^2); only Sea Otters have denser fur. So dense is the fur that water does not reach the skin even if the seal scratches itself underwater. Male seals become darker with age and develop thickened necks and shoulders and a mane of coarse hair. The seals have small heads with stubby snouts; head size is most noticeable on males in comparison to their large bodies. The hind flippers are very long, the largest of any eared seal. These aid the seals to achieve an impressive turn of speed, catching the unwary observer off guard. Pups (2 ft./60–65 cm long and weighing 9–13 lb./4–6 kg) have black pelage, which molts to silver gray dorsally, paler ventrally, during the late summer, and becomes gray-brown during the first winter.

Dental formula: 3/2, 1/1, 4/4, 2/1 = 36 teeth.

Confusion species
None.

▼ Female Northern Fur Seals, St. Paul, Pribilofs.

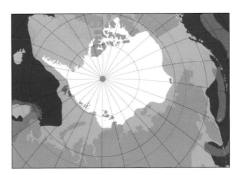

Size
HB: 4–7 ft. (1.2–2.1 m). W: male 285–595 lb. (130–270 kg), female 66–110 lb. (30–50 kg). Extreme sexual dimorphism; males are up to five times heavier and around 70% longer than females.

Communication
Very vocal. Males have a deep bellow, females a mellower grunt. Pups are also highly vocal, as they must be as they wander through the vast breeding sites and are found by females by voice alone, though females also recognize pups by smell at close quarters. Males make visual threats to trespassing strangers.

Distribution
Northern Pacific. Found in the Sea of Okhotsk and across the Pacific from Japan to the Californian coast, but chiefly in the southern Bering Sea. The primary breeding sites are on the Pribilof and Commander Islands (and Bogoslof Island, where the seals began to breed in the 1970s), where 90% of the animals breed. The rest breed on the Kuril Islands, Robben Island in the Sea of Okhotsk and San Miguel Island off California. Of these many island sites, the most important are the Pribilofs (with 70% of the population) and Commander Islands (15%). Outside the breeding season the seals migrate into the North Pacific. The population of seals dropped dramatically in the 20 years from the late 1960s to the late 1980s for reasons not understood, but possibly because of commercial harvesting and commercial fishing, the latter reducing seal prey species drastically. Harvesting was banned in 1988 and the population is now apparently stable.

▲ A male Northern Fur Seal bellows his dominance, St. Paul.

Diet

Primarily fish, also cephalopods. Fish species are chiefly herring, flounder and sand eel. Also take a few salmon. Seals feeding on the continental shelf feed mainly during the day, while those in pelagic water dive at night. Most dives are shallow (50–165 ft./ 5–50 m) but they can reach 520 ft. (250 m).

Breeding

Solitary except at the breeding sites, where the seals are highly gregarious and huge aggregations form. The breeding sites are sandy or rocky beaches on which dominant males maintain harems of up to 50 females, which they defend vigorously. Real fights are relatively rare but brutal. A single precocial pup (21–26 in./55–65 cm long, weighing 9–11 lb./4–5 kg) is born after a gestation of about 240 days with delayed implantation. Females have a bifurcated uterus, alternating between the two chambers in successive years. The female stays with the pup continuously for about eight days, then mates again. After mating, females alternate feeding trips of two to seven days with nursing the current year's pup. During their progress from the beach and through shallow water, the females are harassed by males who have not formed harems. Pups are weaned at 5–6 months. They are then abandoned, spending a short time at the breeding site before venturing into the sea and heading for the North Pacific. Females breed at 3–5 years. Males are sexually mature at 4–5 years, but rarely breed before they are 10 years old. The draining effect of maintaining a harem shortens the male lifespan; few live past 15 years, while females may live to 25 years or more.

▶ Atlantic Walruses, northeast Greenland.

Walruses

The walruses evolved from the eared seals some 20 million years ago. The fossil record suggests that walruses were once a dominant form of pinniped, but gradually the group's fortunes declined to leave just a single species. The Walrus is a true Arctic specialist, and high on the wish list of all who travel to the area to observe its wildlife.

Walrus
Odobenus rosmarus

Identification See p. 429

See p. 429

The largest of all Arctic pinnipeds and second in size only to the elephant seals. Adult pelage color varies with blood flow to the skin. In the water, or recently emerged, Walruses can be very pale, light gray or gray-brown. But when hauled out, blood is pumped to the skin to aid cooling and the animal becomes pink. The skin is loose with many folds, and males have many nodules near the neck and shoulders, which probably serves as armor in mating conflicts. Walrus skin is thick (up to 2 in./4 cm on the neck) and tough, and was used by the Inuit to cover summer houses because of its durability. Walrus blubber can be 6 in. (15 cm) thick, though on average it is only half that thickness. The head is small relative to the huge body. The eyes, too, are tiny, and there is no external ear. The upper canines are massively extended to form tusks. Above the tusks, Walruses have many rows of very sensitive, stiff white vibrissae.

The tusks are used to make or maintain holes in the ice and to aid hauling out, and give the Walrus its genus name (*Odobenus*, from *odontes baino*, "tooth walker"). The species name derives from *ros maris*, "sea rose," a reference to the animal's color and maritime habitat; the common name descends from the Norse *hvalross*, "whale horse."

Walruses have a pair of internal pharyngeal sacs extending from the neck along the back. These can be inflated with air from the lungs; they help the animal float when resting at sea (as Walruses have negative buoyancy) and also seem to act as a resonator for underwater vocalizations. Walrus calves shed their lanugo coats *in utero* and are born with a pelage that is darker than that of adults.

Dental formula: 2–3/1–2, 1/1, 4/4, 0–2/0–2 = 26–38 teeth.

Confusion species
None.

Size

HB: 7¹/₂–11³/₄ ft. (2.3–3.6 m). W: 1,540–4,410 lb. (700–2,000 kg). Extreme sexual dimorphism: males are about 50% heavier and about 20% longer than females. Tusk length: Atlantic subspecies (nominate), males to 30 in. (75 cm), females to 24 in. (60 cm). Pacific subspecies *divergens*, males to 40 in. (100 cm), females to 30 in. (75 cm). In general, female tusks are circular in cross-section (male tusks are elliptical) and more slender. In older animals the tusks are often chipped or broken.

Communication

Silent except at breeding sites, where a variety of barks and growls are made. Underwater male Walruses make a clear, bell-like noise at breeding sites. As many as 15 distinct vocalizations have been identified. Males also use their tusks in displays against rivals. In general, showing the tusks is sufficient to see off less well-endowed males. However, males of comparable size may fight. The considerable thickness of the skin means that many wounds are superficial, but older males frequently show extensive battle scars on the neck.

Distribution

Circumpolar. Breeding sites are in northwestern and north-eastern Greenland, on Svalbard, Franz Josef Land, Novaya Zemlya and around the Laptev Sea. The Laptev Sea is especially favorable for Walrus: it is ice-free in summer to 77°N, and areas remain ice-free throughout the winter. Walruses in the Laptev can live much farther north than in the neighboring North American Arctic, and they have been seen more than 435 mi. (700 km) further north than their Nearctic cousins. Other breeding sites include the northern Bering Sea, Chukchi Sea (including Wrangel), Baffin Island and the islands to the north of Hudson Bay, particularly near Igloolik. In spring Walruses are found among pack ice. In summer and early autumn they haul out on the shore to molt. The same haul-out sites are used

▲ Pacific Walrus, Chukotka. Note the red hue to the skin. This is caused by capillaries close to the surface filling with blood to help keep the animal cool on land.

annually. At other times they are found in open water, though even then they are rarely observed more than 10–12 mi. (15–20 km) from the shore or ice edge. Walruses follow the ice edge, moving north with it in summer and south in winter.

Diet

Benthic animals, particularly mollusks. Wear patterns on vibrissae and tusks suggest that the Walrus stands on its head in the sediments on the ocean floor, feeling for prey with the highly sensitive whiskers. The Walrus also emits jets of water to clear the sediment and expose hidden prey. The meat of mollusks is obtained by suction. Walrus have a powerful suck, which explains why few mollusk shells are found in their stomachs. Some observers have also seen Walruses crushing shells between their front flippers, then ingesting the meat. The Walrus suck is also used in surprise attacks on birds resting on the surface of the sea; Inuit tell of watching Walrus coming up beneath the birds and sucking them under, and also of Walrus killing Beluga. Walrus also occasionally eat young seals. For their more usual benthic diet, Walruses dive to 165 mi. (50 m). Not only do they restrict blood circulation when diving, pumping blood to the brain and the heart at the expense of the extremities, but the heart rate also reduces. When the animal surfaces, temporarily exhausted, the pharyngeal (throat) pouches expand to form a "flotation collar," allowing the animal to rest without exertion and holding the head above even stormy waters. These pouches are larger in males and act as resonators for the bell-like sounds emitted underwater.

Breeding

Highly gregarious. Single Walruses are rarely seen, as even

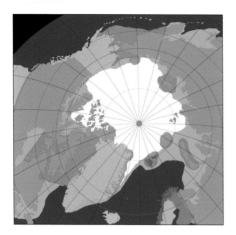

outside the breeding season they usually travel in groups. If seen, a solitary animal is probably male. When hauled out, the animals are both colonial and highly social, preferring to lie close to, or on, others rather than seeking their own space. Mating is polygynous; males display their size to assembled females, and vocalize both above and below water. Males also compete with one another for prime display sites. This mode of display is similar to the "lekking" of some birds. The single precocial calf (rarely twins), 3–4 ft. (1–1.2 m) long and weighing 100–165 lb. (45–75 kg), is born after a gestation of about 12 months, with a delayed implantation of three to four months. Females give birth only every two to three years, so the reason for delayed implantation is unclear. The calf is suckled for up to two years (by which time the tusks are visible, but they are only 2 in./5 cm long) and may stay with its mother even after weaning, perhaps until it is 4 years old. Young females then join female groups, while young males congregate with other males. Their sheer size, the potential damage from the tusks and the thickness of the skin make mature Walruses immune to Polar Bear attack, but younger Walruses are vulnerable to any bear willing to risk the wrath of the mother, who will defend the calf for as long as she can. Such raids by bears were once considered apocryphal, but have been filmed on Wrangel Island and near Igloolik. In the water, Walrus are a threat to the bear rather than

the reverse. They can also apparently hold their own against Orcas; the Inuit claim that cupping the hands at the water surface and shouting with them to cause a Walruslike underwater bellow will cause nearby Orcas to scatter in alarm. Females breed at 5–6 years. They may breed every two years initially, but this becomes every three years as they age. Males are sexually mature at 8 years, but do not usually breed until they are 10–15 years old.

Taxonomy and geographical variation

Polytypic. The nominate race breeds in the north Atlantic. *O. r. divergens* breeds in the Bering Sea and represents the majority of the world's Walruses, comprising 90% of the total population of some 225,000 animals. The Atlantic population represents around 8%, the Laptev population, 2%. Race *divergens* is larger, has a wider head and longer, often bow-shaped tusks (hence the scientific name *divergens*, "divergent"); the tusks may bow away from each other and even diverge so the tips are much farther apart than the bases. The tusks of Atlantic Walruses are parallel. Animals in eastern Canada are smaller than the nominate and may form a distinct subspecies. Laptev Sea Walruses may also form a separate subspecies; they are smaller than *divergens*, but are generally larger than Atlantic animals and again have larger tusks.

Sirenians

In 1741, when shipwrecked on Bering Island, Georg Wilhelm Steller identified an unknown, gigantic sirenian, later named Steller's Sea Cow (*Hydrodamalis gigas*). This whale-sized animal lacked teeth and had only a small head and flippers. It lived in shallow, inshore waters where it fed on kelp. It was slow and provided an abundance of good-quality eating, a lethal combination. By 1768 no animals could be found on either Bering or Copper Islands (the only two of the Commander Islands on which it had been encountered), and it is assumed to have been hunted to extinction. The animals might have survived for a little longer on other, more isolated, islands, but either way this gentle giant — by far the most northerly sirenian — is long extinct.

▼ Atlantic Walruses shuffle into the sea, Nordaustlandet, Svalbard.

PLATE 37: PINNIPEDS

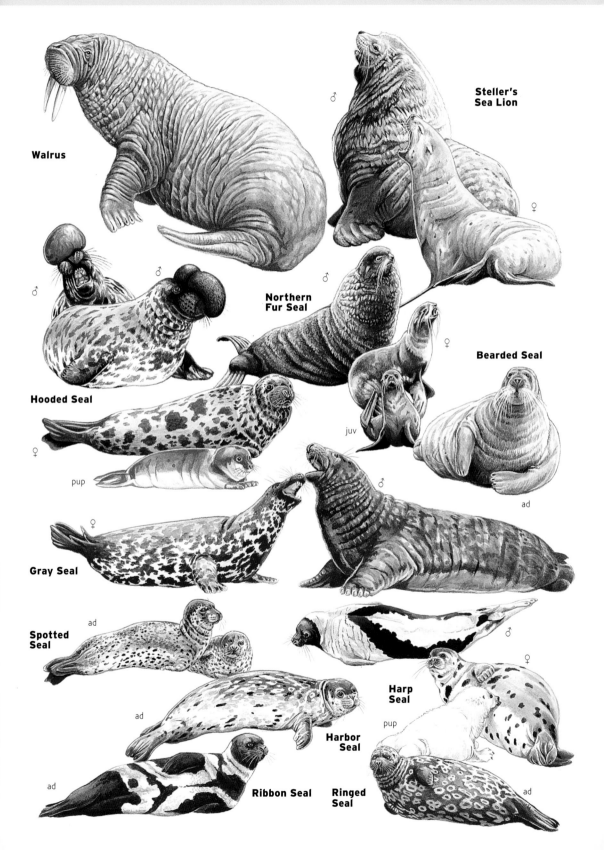

Walrus

Steller's
Sea Lion

♂

♀

♂

Northern
Fur Seal

♂

♀

Bearded Seal

Hooded Seal

♀

pup

juv

ad

♀

Gray Seal

♂

Spotted
Seal

ad

♂

Harp
Seal

♀

ad

Harbor
Seal

pup

ad

Ribbon Seal

Ringed
Seal

ad

Cetaceans

Although pinnipeds are extremely well adapted to their marine environment, females must come ashore to give birth, most species mate on land and all spend periods out of the water resting or during molting. The evolution of the cetaceans has led to the elimination of these landbound requirements.

Cetaceans have some similar adaptations as pinnipeds in terms of body streamlining, with the reduction of protuberances; the male genitalia are retained within the body cavity, and external ears are absent, with the ear opening being a tiny hole about the size of a match head. Cetaceans have additional morphological and physiological changes necessitated by full-time immersion. The front flippers have become modified to be supremely efficient paddles, while the hind limbs have either disappeared entirely (in toothed whales) or are vestigial and lie within the body (in baleen whales). The standard mammalian tail of cetaceans' terrestrial ancestors has become a muscular twin-fluked tail of limited flexibility but enormous power. Some cetaceans have also evolved dorsal fins to aid stability. Hair has been virtually eliminated, with insulation instead provided by thick subcutaneous blubber.

Due to the buoyancy of water, the cetacean skeleton does not have to overcome gravity, so it can be much less bulky. Honeycombed whale bones are remarkably light compared to those of terrestrial mammals. The bones have a hard outer shell covering a spongelike inner one with numerous blood vessels, and a marrow rich in oil; when whales were hunted, about 30% of the oil obtained from a carcass came from the bones. Though strong enough to act as anchors for the whale's huge muscles, some whale bones are so light that they float in water. By contrast, the rostrum bones in the heads of certain beaked whales are among the densest bones known.

The eyes are relatively tiny. In part this is because vision is less useful underwater, particularly to baleen whales, which trawl for food rather than pursuing their prey, but may also be due to their use in navigation. Many whales are known to "spyhop," raising their heads out of the water, apparently to view the local area. Small eyes, acting as pinhole cameras, allow a greater depth of focus and may assist the whales, which often stay close to shore, to locate land features.

Because of the reduced value of vision underwater, the toothed whales, which feed on highly mobile prey or at depths where light barely penetrates, have evolved echolocation. The exact way in which whales transmit and receive sounds is not fully understood. They lack true vocal cords, so sound is thought to be generated by the compression of air sacs in the larynx or blowholes. Many toothed whales have a "melon," an oil-filled organ in the forehead, which may be an echo receiver or an acoustic lens. The head of the Sperm Whale holds a vast reservoir of spermaceti oil, for which, in part, the whale was once hunted.

Breathing and diving

The cetacean nostrils lie on top of the head, allowing breathing without the need to expose the entire head, which would increase drag. Breathing is also explosive: a huge volume of air is exhaled, then inhaled in just a few seconds. For example, Fin Whales exhale and inhale about 3,900 gal. (15,000 L) of air in just two seconds. Whales also extract more oxygen from a set volume of air than any other mammals; 10%–12% against 4% in humans, for example. They also use a greater percentage of their lung capacity than other mammals, exchanging about 90% of the volume each breath, compared to about 15% in humans.

Pod of Orcas, Prince William Sound.

Not only must cetaceans come to the surface frequently to exhale and inhale, which creates problems for Arctic marine mammals because of the extent of ice cover, but they must store oxygen for relatively long periods if they are to feed successfully. Storing a large supply of air in the lungs has its problems. The full lungs would increase buoyancy and make the animal vulnerable to the bends, caused by nitrogen dissolved in the blood forming gas bubbles on decompression as the animal rises toward the surface. Marine mammals overcome this by using an oxygen "store," myoglobin, in the muscles, which releases oxygen during a dive. At the huge pressures of deep dives, the lungs of cetaceans collapse, forcing air into the nasal passages, where nitrogen absorption is not possible.

Caring for young

Perhaps the most important cetacean adaptation for a fully marine existence is the existence of contractile muscles associated with the delivery of milk from the mammary glands. Normal suckling would require the young whale to spend protracted periods underwater. The muscles mean that the mother whale squirts milk into her infant, allowing a large quantity of milk to be transferred at each suckling. Another reproductive adaptation is that whale calves are born tail first, the mother ushering her newborn to the surface for its first breath as soon as the head appears. Despite the intuitively obvious advantage of this birthing method, there are reliable observations of baleen whale calves being born head first.

Feeding

Cold Arctic waters are oxygen-rich. They are also nutrient-rich from the huge inflow of the rivers of North America and Asian Russia. The combination makes the Arctic seas among the most productive on Earth, and a magnet for whales, which are at their most diverse in the Arctic and sub-Arctic. Toothed whales have jaws lined with teeth, but one group of cetaceans has developed an entirely different method of feeding from this "standard" mammal model. The baleen whales have a series of keratinous plates that hang from the roof of the mouth. Baleen plates are not modified teeth, nor do they grow from the whale's gums; they are an independent structure. Baleen is smooth, but the inner edges abrade to form "bristles." The bristles of the plates overlap to form a sieve. Baleen whales feed on plankton, taking in water and then squeezing it against the plate sieves with the huge tongue so that food is trapped while the water escapes.

Baleen whales use two methods of feeding. Some swim slowly forward and allow their sieves to extract food continuously, while others take huge gulps of water, usually locating places rich in prey beforehand. Sievers include the Right and Bowhead Whales; these have huge heads to allow space for large baleen plates. Gulpers include the Blue, Fin and Humpback Whales: these have pleats or furrows of skin on the lower jaw, which allow the mouth to expand to engulf vast quantities of water at each gulp. These furrows give this group of whales their common name, *rorqual*, from a Norwegian word for pleated. One species, the Sei Whale, feeds with a combination of sieving and gulping, while the Gray Whale differs by sieving bottom sediments. Because of their feeding method, baleen whales do not need to use echolocation. Baleen whales differ from toothed whales not only in their feeding structures and methods, but also because they have two nostrils rather than just one.

Many cetaceans, to a lesser or greater extent, slap the surface of the water with their flippers or flukes, and breach, whereby they hurl themselves out of the water. The Humpback Whale is famous for these behaviors, and the sight of a 30-ton whale rising clear of the water is one of the great sights of the sub-Arctic. But to the north of the breaching Humpbacks, this behavior is, astonishingly, repeated by the apparently habitually slow and ponderous Bowhead Whale, which can weigh up to 80 tons.

Toothed whales

The majority of whale species belong to the suborder Odontoceti. Though the Sperm Whale is a huge animal, most species are relatively small and highly maneuverable, an adaptation for catching small, mobile prey, i.e., fish and cephalopods. The suborder contains 10 families of which five, the dolphins, porpoises, single-toothed whales, beaked whales and the Sperm Whale, include Arctic or sub-Arctic species.

Many of the Odontoceti are surface-feeders, and they are countershaded, dark dorsally and white ventrally. This cryptic pattern makes the animal less visible to prey species who invariably view it from below against the sky, and also to potential predators. Few present-day whales have predators other than humans, but Orca pods will attack other whales, and there have been other large marine predators in ancient times.

Much has been made of the intelligence of toothed whales, and of dolphins in particular. The cetaceans have relatively large brains, but the ratio of brain mass to overall body mass (which is probably a better indicator of intelligence) suggests that most cetaceans, particularly the baleen whales, are not especially gifted. However, for some dolphin species the ratio is close to that of chimpanzees (*Pan* spp.).

In addition to the species described below, both the Atlantic White-sided Dolphin (*Lagenorhynchus acutus*) and Pacific White-sided Dolphin (*L. obliquidens*), though essentially animals of temperate waters, may be seen at the Arctic boundary. Atlantic White-sided Dolphin is sometimes seen off Iceland's southern shore and off northern Scandinavia, while the Pacific White-sided Dolphin may be seen off the Aleutians, the Commander Islands and southern Kamchatka. The Bottlenose Dolphin (*Tursiops truncatus*) is found in both the Atlantic and Pacific, but more rarely as far north as the two White-sided Dolphins. Cuvier's Beaked Whale (*Ziphius cavirostris*) has a similar range to the Bottlenose Dolphin.

Orca (Killer Whale)
Orcinus orca

Identification
See p. 454

The largest of the dolphins. Adults are large black-and-white cetaceans with prominent dorsal fins. Skin is black dorsally, but with a pale gray saddle behind the dorsal fin. The chin and throat are white, the white continuing ventrally. At the flippers the white ventral band narrows, but behind them it expands, forming irregularly shaped patches on the flanks. Ventral surface of flukes is also white, and there is an oval white patch behind the eye. The shape of this patch distinguishes individuals. The flippers are paddle-shaped, the tail flukes forming a shallow V. In males the dorsal fin is tall and triangular, in females it is short and sickle-shaped. Can swim up to 37 mph (60 km/h), but usually swims at 3–6 mph (5–10 km/h). Ten to 14 (usually 12) pairs of large conical teeth in each jaw.

Confusion species
None.

Size
HB: males 20–30 ft. (6–9 m), females 13–21 ft. (4–6.5 m). W: male 4–7 t., female 3–4 t. Male dorsal fin is 3–7 ft. (1–2 m) high.

Communication
The white head patch is probably a visual signal. Orcas also emit clicks of 1–25 minutes duration, in a frequency range to around 80 kHz; also whistles and pulses of sound. It is thought that the clicks allow echolocation, but the other sounds are for communication within a pod. A specific repertoire of sounds is made by a particular pod, and though these are comparable to those of other pods, a pod "dialect" is discernible. Orcas also spyhop, breach and slap the water surface with flippers or flukes.

Distribution
Circumpolar. Found in the north Atlantic and north Pacific to the ice edge. Orcas are found in all the world's oceans, and in the Southern Ocean as far south as the pack ice. Usually considered the most widespread of the cetaceans. In general pods appear to be confined to a "home" range of up to 580 sq. mi. (1,500 km²), but they may travel long distances in search of prey. Young Orcas seem to stay within a pod for life, but pod-splitting also occurs and there must be immigration to minimize inbreeding.

Diet
Fish, cephalopods, pinnipeds, and other cetaceans. In Antarctica, Orcas take penguins and in the Arctic they also

◀ Breaching Orca, British Columbia.

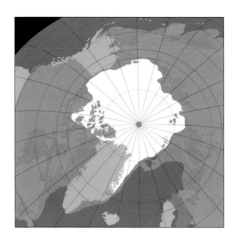

▲ White-beaked Dolphin off the coast of Iceland.

take avian prey opportunistically. Dives to 820 mi. (250 m) have been recorded. At Peninsula Valdez in Argentina, Orcas have been filmed deliberately beaching to take fur seals as well as hurling captured seals into the air with their tails. In the Arctic, seals will leave the water for the shore or an ice floe in panic at the approach of Orcas, and smaller cetaceans head for shallow water and hide among the rocks.

Orcas hunt as a group, circling fish shoals to form tight balls of fish, then plunging into them, and they will pursue larger cetaceans, such as Gray Whales in the Bering Sea. Often Orcas will eat only the tongue of a Gray Whale adult or calf that they have killed. This also seems to be the case for other baleen whales. Orcas harass larger whales, taking bites from the flanks and tail, and they may kill them by forcing them underwater until they drown. Orcas have been observed to take moose and deer swimming across narrow channels, and to spyhop to find seals on ice floes, then tipping the floe. However, despite legends, this does not seem to have happened to humans on ice floes, and though kayakers have reported close encounters, no attacks have been recorded.

Breeding
Highly social; pods of up to 40 Orcas form, with observed aggregations of several hundred. However, pairs of Orcas and even solitary animals are not uncommon. Pods are led by a mature female. The female's group members are related to her and help with calf raising. Females may mate with solitary males. Females give birth to a single calf (6½–8 ft./2–2.5 m long, weighing about 1,350 lb./60 kg) after a gestation of 12–16 months. The calf is weaned at 12 months, but stays with its mother for several years. Females breed for the first time at 8–10 years and give birth every five years or so. Males are sexually mature at around 15 years.

Taxonomy and geographical variation
Unclear, but probably polytypic. There is minimal intermixing of populations between various parts of the range, and adaptations for prey and conditions in specific areas have almost certainly produced subspecies.

White-beaked Dolphin
Lagenorhynchus albirostris

Identification   See p. 454
Highly variable, but basically black dorsally with a pale gray or white patch behind the dorsal fin. This patch diffuses into the black dorsal color rather than being delineated, and extends toward, but does not reach, the tail stock and onto the flanks. On the flanks are pale gray or white stripes, narrower at the head end. The stripes are occasionally discontinuous, forming white patches on the front and rear flanks. Some individuals also have irregular white patches below and behind the eyes. As with the rump patch, the stripe is diffuse rather than sharp-edged, and toward the tail stock merges with the rump patch. The prominent beak is white, though individuals with black beaks are known in the northwestern Atlantic. The dolphin is white ventrally, becoming pale gray toward the tail stock. The dorsal fin is sickle-shaped and taller in the male. The tail is notched, the flukes with a concave trailing edge. The flippers curve backward and narrow toward the tip. There are 44–56 teeth in each jaw.

Confusion species
The Bottlenose Dolphin, which overlaps in the southern part of the range, is very similar but lacks the white flank stripe and gray rump patch.

Size
HB: 7–9 ft. (2.2–2.8 m). W: 350–530 lb. (160–240 kg), but weights to 770 lb. (350 kg) have been recorded.

Communication

Poorly known, but emits echolocation clicks and various whistles as other dolphins. White-beaked Dolphins breach and engage in periods of very fast swimming, the latter believed to be a form of communication.

Distribution

North Atlantic. The most northerly of the smaller dolphins, reaching the southern shores of Svalbard and the Barents Sea, though more southerly in the colder, western Atlantic where it is rarely seen north of Labrador or southwestern Greenland. Despite their northerly range, these dolphins are poor ice travelers and many become entrapped in pack ice and die. Essentially a continental shelf feeder, also seen in deeper waters. The dolphins are fond of riding the bow waves of powered craft.

Diet

Fish, cephalopods and benthic crustaceans. Cooperative feeding has been observed. White-beaked Dolphins have a relatively thick layer of blubber, allowing them not only to travel to the far north, but also apparently to dive deep, as benthic species form a high proportion of the diet.

Breeding

Gregarious; groups of 10–20 often seen and aggregations of up to 1,000 animals have occasionally been observed, but pairs also seen frequently. White-beaked Dolphins are athletic, sometimes leaping high above the water. Breeding biology poorly known. Single calf born after about 10-month gestation. Twins have been recorded, but apparently only a single calf is reared. Calf is 3–4 ft. (1–1.2 m) long, weight not known, probably around 35 lb. (15 kg). Breeding ages unknown.

Taxonomy and geographical variation

Monotypic, but west and east Atlantic populations are probably better considered separate subspecies.

Harbor Porpoise
Phocoena phocoena

Now rare and considered vulnerable. Tends to feed inshore and close to the seabed and may consequently be trapped in gillnets. Deaths are mainly of young and female animals, and so are apparently an important factor limiting population. The lifespan of the Harbor Porpoise is relatively short — 13 years, often less, and some females may only produce three or four calves, so mortality in nets may have a dramatic effect. Reduction of prey stock by overfishing is also a factor.

Identification See p. 454

Dark grey, diffusing into pale gray on the flanks. Pale gray ventrally. Lacks the beak of dolphins, but blowhole is prominently depressed, so that head suggests a "Roman nose." Distinctive gray line from rear of the jaw to the flippers, which are short and dark gray. The dorsal fin is short and triangular, with a distinct concave trailing edge. The tail flukes have a distinct notch. Each jaw has 44–56 teeth. Rarely bow-rides or breaches.

▲ Harbor Porpoise, Iceland.

Confusion species

Lack of beak and smaller dorsal fins distinguish porpoises from dolphins. Harbor Porpoise distinguished from Dall's Porpoise by diffuse rather than abrupt color change on the flanks.

Size

HB: 4–6¼ ft. (1.3–1.9 m). W: 110–145 lb. (50–65 kg), but weights up to 210 lb. (95 kg) recorded.

Communication

Pulsed sound at very high frequencies (100 kHz or even higher) with short duration of around 6 seconds, which implies a well-developed echolocation ability. Also emits pulses at lower frequencies, apparently as communication to others in the group.

Distribution

Circumpolar. Essentially sub-Arctic, but in north Atlantic found around Iceland, northern Scandinavia and east to Novaya Zemlya, around southern Greenland and off the Labrador coast; and in the north Pacific from southern Kamchatka across the Aleutian chain to southwestern and southern Alaska. Coastal, preferring bays, estuaries and harbors. Found in more open water in winter.

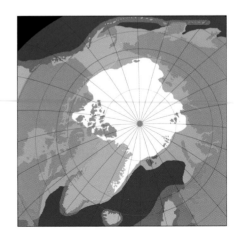

Diet
Fish, particularly schooling fish (and especially herring) and crustaceans. Dives to 330 ft. (100 m), usually only to 165 ft. (50 m). Little evidence of cooperative feeding, though group feeding is observed.

Breeding
Solitary or found in groups of four to six animals. Aggregations of several hundred porpoises have been observed, but these appear to be loose feeding groups that quickly disperse. Single calf (length 28–32 in./70–80 cm, weight 11–18 lb./5–8 kg) born after gestation of around 11 months. Weaned at 8 months, but calf stays with mother until she is ready to give birth again. Females give birth every one to two years. Males and females are sexually mature at 3–5 years.

Taxonomy and geographical variation
Monotypic, but Atlantic and Pacific populations are probably separate subspecies.

Dall's Porpoise
Phocoenoides dalli

Identification
See p. 454

A robust porpoise with a small head. Black but with large white patches on flanks stretching from just in front of the dorsal fin almost to the tail stock, and continuous ventrally. There are also variable white patches on the dorsal fin, and on the trailing edges of both flippers and flukes. A variant (or possibly subspecies), True's Porpoise, has the white flank and ventral patch extending from the flippers toward the tail stock, and usually a mostly white dorsal fin with a black base. Adult males have a dorsal hump forward of the dorsal fin. The dorsal fin is triangular and hooked at the top. The flippers are small and positioned well forward. The caudal peduncle is keeled above and below, and the flukes are notched. The flukes of calves have a concave trailing edge, and are uniformly gray. The fluke shape alters with age. Female flukes are straight-edged but notched; male flukes are convex. Each jaw has 44–56 teeth. Dall's Porpoises are very fast swimmers, reaching speeds of 38 mph (60 km/h) or more, with an erratic swimming pattern, changing direction frequently. They often bow-ride ships.

Confusion species
The distinct division between the white-and-black areas and the contrast of white and black distinguishes Dall's Porpoise from the Harbor Porpoise.

Size
HB: 6 1/4–7 3/4 ft. (1.9–2.4 m). W: 375–465 lb. (170–210 kg).

Communication
Poorly studied. Assumed to be much as the Harbor Porpoise.

Distribution
North Pacific. Found in the Sea of Okhotsk and from

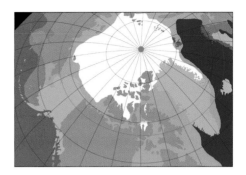

Kamchatka to Alaska, though not extending far north into the Bering Sea. Rare to the north of Hall and St. Matthew Islands. Found in both coastal and more open water.

Diet
Schooling fish and squid. Some suggest that feeding is chiefly nocturnal, perhaps a response to the prey moving closer to the surface at night; Dall's Porpoise has relatively thin blubber for so northerly a cetacean and many avoid deep dives.

Breeding
Social, forming small groups of 2–12 animals, but groups may coalesce and then disperse. Some evidence of age and sexual separation in groups. Single calf (length 3 ft./1 m, weight 24 lb./11 kg), born after gestation of 10–11 months. Calf stays with mother until she gives birth again, though lactation seems to last only four to five months. Female Dall's Porpoises

▼ Dall's Porpoises, Kenai Fjords National Park, Alaska.

give birth annually. Females are sexually mature at 3–4 years, males at 4–5 years.

Taxonomy and geographical variation

Disputed. Most authorities think that the species is monotypic and that True's Porpoise is simply a variant of "normal" color pattern. Others consider True's to be a subspecies, *P. d. truei*, as it primarily occurs only in the Sea of Okhotsk and off southern Kamchatka.

Beluga
Delphinapterus leucas

One of only two species of the family Monodontidae, the single-toothed whales, both of which are true Arctic dwellers.

Identification   See p. 454

Adults are entirely creamy white (the name derives from the Russian "white"). There is no dorsal fin, but a small triangular ridge is visible in many individuals. The lack of a dorsal fin is perhaps due to the animal's northerly range, where a fin would be likely to be damaged when feeding under the ice or moving near the ice edge. The head is broad. Above the mouth is a distinctive "melon," which becomes larger with age. The melon is fluid and can change shape, presumably by the animal moving air within sinus cavities. Why Belugas do this is not understood. The flippers are short and rounded. Calves are uniformly gray, becoming white only when they are about six years old. Belugas have unfused cervical vertebrae, allowing the head to turn and nod, a very unusual feature in cetaceans. Each jaw has 16–22 teeth. Belugas swim at 3–9 mph (5–15 km/h).

Confusion species

None.

Size

HB: 10–16 ft. (3–5 m). W: 1,100–3,300 lb. (500–1500 kg).

Communication

Very vocal, with a repertoire of whistles, squeak and bell-like "rings" which can often be heard above the water; early sailors called Belugas "sea canaries." There are also high-frequency clicks used in echolocation. Some evidence that Belugas use sonar to find breathing holes in the ice. Belugas spyhop and occasionally roll on their sides.

Distribution

Circumpolar, though rare or absent in the Greenland Sea. Found near Svalbard and east from there along the Russian Arctic coast to the Chukchi Sea. Also found in the Bering Sea and the Arctic waters of North America to eastern Greenland and in Hudson Bay. Belugas that feed on the Bering Sea coast of Chukotka head through the Bering Strait to molt in the Mackenzie Delta. Five distinct populations have been identified within this overall range.

In winter Belugas are found in polynyas and at the ice edge. In summer occurs in both coastal and deep waters. Found at river mouths during the annual molt, when the warmth and low salinity of the mixed fresh and saltwaters may aid molting; shallow water also allows the whale to rub off old skin on the riverbed. The congregation of Belugas at the Churchill River in southwestern Hudson Bay has led the town of Churchill to term itself the "Beluga Capital of the World" (it claims the title "Polar Bear Capital of the World" in the autumn). Belugas occasionally become trapped when the pack ice closes behind them or seals the entrance to a bay or fjord: such open water traps are called *savssats* by the Inuit, who have used them to hunt the whales. The Belugas can keep the water open, but if the hole in the ice becomes small they may fall prey to Polar Bears. As well as hunting Belugas in savssats, native peoples also hunted the whales in the shallow waters of molt sites, where Belugas are occasionally stranded by ebb tides. These animals tend to lie very still until the rising tide releases them, as flailing attempts to regain the water could signal their plight to a Polar Bear. Polar Bears find Belugas easier to hunt in shallow water than in a savssat, where they must kill the whale but somehow drag it onto the ice. In shallow water, the bear bites at the whale's blowhole, disabling it immediately so that its meal of skin and blubber can be consumed with minimal effort. Stranding also has other dangers; the whales can be burned by the sun on bright days.

Diet

Schooling fish, cephalopods and crustaceans. Belugas feed in both shallow waters and by diving to depths of up to 2,625 ft. (800 m).

Breeding

Social, usually in groups of 5–20, coalescing to form aggregations of up to 1,000 Belugas at favored molting sites. Outside the breeding season, the groups usually comprise females and calves, all probably related. Mating apparently

◀ Beluga spyhopping, Northwest Territories.

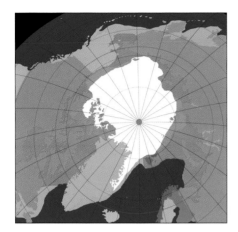

to grow when the animal is 2–3 years old (occasionally at 1 year) and grows continuously. Very old males may have tusks 10 ft. (3 m) long that weigh as much as 22 lb. (10 kg). The tusk may be used aggressively but seems to be primarily a signal, indicating male quality. Females only rarely have a tusk. Narwhal calves are uniformly mid-gray, becoming darker with scattered white blotching until they reach maturity. Thereafter the animals become paler and old animals can be almost white. Narwhals swim at 3–9 mph (5–15 km/h).

Confusion species
None.

Size
HB: 11½–18 ft. (3.5–5.5 m) excluding tusk. W: 1,765–3,530 lb. (800–1,600 kg).

Communication
Narwhals whistle over an extensive frequency range (300–10 kHz). Their echolocation clicks have a twin range, 500–5 kHz and 12–24 kHz. Females use a low-frequency moan to communicate with their calves. The male tusk is also used in communication. Narwhals have been seen to cross tusks, but never actually to "fence" with them. Nevertheless, broken tusks and scarred animals imply that fights do occur, presumably over access to females. However, animals also use the tusk in a much gentler way, laying it across the back of another animal in what appears a tactile gesture. Narwhals occasionally spyhop.

▼ Adult male Narwhal, source of legends, Baffin Island.

polygynous. A single calf (5–5¼ ft./1.5–1.6 m long and weighing 175–220 lb./80–100 kg) is born after a gestation of 14 months. The calf is nursed for up to two years, females giving birth every three years. Females are sexually mature at 4–7 years, males at 8–9 years.

Taxonomy and geographical variation
Probably polytypic, as distinct breeding populations have been identified, though poorly studied. Size also differs across the range; Hudson Bay Belugas are smaller and western Greenland Beluga larger than their Atlantic relatives.

Narwhal
Monodon monoceros

One of the world's most remarkable animals, with an extraordinary tusk, whose function is still debated. The tusk is almost certainly the source of the unicorn legend; tusks may have been washed ashore, though people such as the Pomores of northern Russia may have encountered Narwhals on fishing trips to Novaya Zemlya or even Svalbard. Evidence suggests that knowledge of the Narwhal was deliberately suppressed to promote the legend and so enhance the value of tusks. The whale's name is Norse in origin; *nár hvalr*, "corpse whale," because the skin color suggests that of a dead man.

Identification See p. 454
Adult skin is mottled blue or dark gray and white, the mottling usually more extensive dorsally then ventrally. The melon, which overhangs the upturned mouth, is usually uniformly dark gray. There is no dorsal fin, and the dorsal ridge is marked only by a dark line. The flippers are short and square. The flukes are convex in males, less so, or even straight, in females. There are only two teeth, both in the upper jaw. In females these often do not erupt during the animal's lifetime. In males the left tooth pushes through the lip to form a tusk. Usually this has a leftward spiral (counterclockwise from the whale's eye view), the tusk axis being straight. Occasionally the axis is twisted or vaguely spiraled. In some males the right tooth also erupts: double-tusked narwhals are very rare. The tusk begins

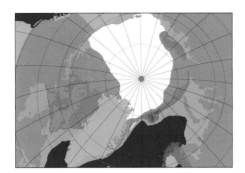

Distribution
North Atlantic. Found in the eastern Palearctic from east of Peel Sound to the western coast of Greenland, rarely south of the southern tip of Baffin Island or into southern Hudson Bay. In the eastern Atlantic, found east of northeastern Greenland, including Svalbard, Franz Josef Land, northern Novaya Zemlya, Severnaya Zemlya and New Siberia Islands. However, due to overhunting, the Narwhal is rare in the eastern Atlantic, and rarer still around Svalbard and in the Russian Arctic. Has been recorded in Chukchi and Beaufort Seas, but those are clearly extralimital records. Found at the ice edge or in pack ice. Predictable annual movements, which have allowed native hunters to target them. Narwhal skin (*muktuq*) is considered a great delicacy (tasting vaguely of hazelnut). May become trapped in small holes in the ice if wind moves the pack, or if sea ice is forming quickly. At such times they may become a target for Polar Bears.

Diet
Fish, cephalopods and crustaceans. Having no teeth, Narwhals suck prey into the mouth and swallow it whole. Despite occasional references to the contrary, Narwhals do not use their tusks to spear fish. The worn tips of many Narwhal tusks have suggested to some authorities that they may be used to disturb bottom sediments in a search for food. However, females without tusks feed well enough. Narwhals seek prey at all levels from the surface to the bottom, diving as deep as 3,280 ft. (1,000 m) and staying underwater for up to 25 minutes.

Breeding
Solitary or in groups of 4–20 animals in winter; aggregations of up to 1,000 observed in summer. The groups are usually females and calves (the whole group often related) or animals of the same sex and age. Aggregations form in spring for breeding. Single calf (5–5³/₄ ft./1.5–1.7 m long, weighing about 175 lb./80 kg), born after gestation of 14–15 months. Calf is weaned at 12–20 months, probably staying with its mother until she is about to give birth again. Females give birth every two to three years. Females are sexually mature at 5–8 years, males at 11–13 years.

Taxonomy and geographical variation
Probably polytypic as the western and eastern Atlantic populations do not intermix, and within these areas there are distinct populations that may be subspecifically distinct.

Baird's Beaked Whale
Berardius bairdii

The longest of the beaked whales. Rare, with a population of probably a few tens of thousands at most.

Identification   See p. 454
Adult skin is dark grayish brown with numerous white ventral patches. The melon is prominent above the long beak. The lower jaw is longer than the upper and the two anterior teeth of the four in the jaw are visible when the mouth is closed. They glint in sunlight and may therefore be diagnostic. Older whales, which are usually darker, show numerous scars over their bodies (denser dorsally), which show as white lines. The scars are assumed to be inflicted by the teeth of conspecifics. The dorsal fin is small with a straight or falcated trailing edge. The flippers are broad and rounded. The flukes are not notched and have a shallow concave trailing edge.

Confusion species
Larger than Stejneger's Beaked Whale, but rather similar in color. If visible, the teeth of the two species are diagnostic.

Size
HB: 36–43 ft. (11–13 m). W: 9–12 t.

Communication
The whales breach and slap the water with their flippers.

▼ Pair of Baird's Beaked Whales. The prominent beak is an adaptation for catching squid and other cephalopods.

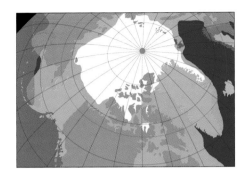

Vocalizations are unknown, but they are probably similar to those of other toothed whales.

Distribution
North Pacific. Found north of a line from Japan to Baja California, as far north as the Sea of Okhotsk and the Pribilof Islands. A deep-water species.

Diet
The beak is an adaptation for grasping squid, but deep-sea fish are also taken. The whale apparently feeds on or close to the ocean bed at depths to 10,000 ft. (3,000 m).

Breeding
Social, usually travelling in groups of up to 50. Reproductive biology is not well understood, and the scant existing evidence suggests anomalous behavior; males mature faster than females (contrary to the cetacean norm), outnumber females

and may help care for weaned calves so that females can breed more frequently. Other research suggests that both males and females achieve sexual maturity at 8–10 years. Single calf (about 15 ft./4.5 m long, of unknown weight but possibly many hundred pounds) born after unknown gestation period, though specimens taken in hunts suggest a period of 10–17 months.

Taxonomy and geographical variation
Monotypic.

Stejneger's Beaked Whale
Mesophodon stejnegeri

Known from a single skull found on Bering Island and described in 1885, but not seen again until 1994 when a group of four stranded on Adak Island in the Aleutians. Almost nothing is known of the species' biology.

Identification See p. 454
Skin is dark gray overall. Females are paler ventrally and on the lower jaw. Males are paler on the lower jaw and ventrally as far as the flipper. Some specimens appear gray-brown. Both male and female have gray-brown cap, which extends below the eye. The beak is slightly upturned. The whale has two tusklike teeth in the lower jaw, set about 8 in. (20 cm) back from the beak tip and protruding well above the upper jaw. The teeth are 8 in. (20 cm) high, 4 in. (10 cm) wide and 1³/₄ in. (2 cm) thick. The dorsal fin is small and triangular, the trailing edge falcated. The flippers are small and taper to a rounded end. The flukes are not notched, the trailing edge straight but upturned at the extremities. Older whales often have scars, which appear as white lines and are especially extensive on males, suggesting that wounds are inflicted in battles over females, though some may be shark-inflicted.

Confusion species
Smaller than Baird's Beaked Whale; tusklike lower jaw teeth diagnostic.

Size
HB: 18 ft. (5.5 m). W unknown.

Communication
Unknown.

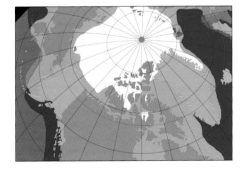

Distribution
Found in a curved band of the North Pacific from Japan to the Aleutians and down to northern California. In the Bering Sea, found north to southern Chukotka, but much more southerly on the North American side.

Diet
Analyses of stomach contents show both fish and squid, including deep-sea squid species that imply foraging at great depths.

Breeding
Unknown; presumably similar in most respects to Baird's Beaked Whale. Calves are about 7 ft. (2.2 m) long at birth.

Taxonomy and geographical variation
Monotypic, though lack of information on the whale's biology means this may well be incorrect.

Northern Bottlenose Whale
Hyperoodon ampullatus

Identification   See p. 454
Variable skin color, from dark brown through gray-brown to greenish brown, paler ventrally with cream or cream-buff blotches. The whales become paler with age, some becoming buff or even pale buff. The melon is very prominent and creamy-white from the crown to the forehead. Below it is a

dolphin white beak. There are two V-shaped grooves on the throat. The dorsal fin is small (about 1 ft./30 cm) and triangular, with a falcated trailing edge. The flippers are short, the leading edge curved so that the flipper appears tapered. The flukes are not notched, the trailing edge is straight or shallowly concave, but with sharply upturned tips. There are small vestigial teeth in the upper and lower jaws, but in older males a pair of teeth erupt at the tip of the lower jaw. Stalked barnacles occasionally attach to these teeth.

Confusion species
Beak and color are similar to the Bottlenose Dolphin, but the Northern Bottlenose Whale is twice as long and has a much less prominent dorsal fin.

▼ Northern Bottlenose Whale, Nova Scotia.

Size
HB: 23–31 ft. (7–9.5 m). W: 7–9½ t.

Communication
Uses high-frequency echolocation, but communication sounds unknown. Breaches and lobtails (slams of the tail onto the water surface) more often than the other beaked whales. Also spyhops occasionally.

Distribution
North Atlantic. Seen as far north as the summer ice edge at northeastern Greenland and Svalbard, though not as far north in the Davis Strait. Does not extend east into the Russian Arctic or Hudson Strait. Prefers deep waters. Moves with the ice, but populations are resident in more southerly parts of the range.

Diet
Primarily deep-sea squid such as *Gonatus fabricii,* also deep-sea fish. Can stay submerged for up to two hours and apparently reaches depths of up to 4,920 ft. (1,500 m).

Breeding
Solitary or in small groups, usually of 4–10 animals, with aggregations of up to 50 observed, often females with calves, or animals of similar age or sex. Males apparently polygynous. Single calf (10–11½ ft./3–3.5 m long, weight unknown) born after gestation of around 12 months. Calf is weaned at 12

▲ Young Sperm Whale, North Atlantic.

months, with females giving birth every two years. Males mature sexually earlier (at 7–9 years) than females (4–11 years).

Taxonomy and geographical variation
Specific breeding populations near Svalbard, Norway, Iceland, and Labrador suggest that subspecies may exist, but intermixing of these populations may occur.

Sperm Whale
Physeter macrocephalus

The largest of the toothed whales, and one of the least understood, despite its legendary status, stemming from Herman Melville's classic novel, *Moby Dick.* At 20 lb. (9 kg) the brain of the Sperm Whale is the largest of any animal.

Identification See p. 455
Characterized by a massive, square-cut head, constituting 25%–30% of the total length, and a more slender body. The head contains up to 530 gal. (2,000 L) of spermaceti oil, much prized by early whalers, but whose function is still not understood. Suggestions include use as a sonic lens, amplifying or concentrating either outgoing sound waves (with which to stun its prey) or incoming echoes (to aid prey location in the

murky depths to which the whale dives). Alternatively the spermaceti may help regulate nitrogen absorption, or, more likely, act as a buoyancy regulation system; the organ's oil solidifies when cold water flows into nasal passages, pulling the whale downward, water is then expelled and the oil is warmed by the blood, so it becomes more buoyant and aids the whale's ascent.

The skin is dark gray, with occasional white patches and, normally, white lips. Surfacing whales often appear more gray-brown. Moby Dick was, of course, white, and truly leucistic (as opposed to albino). Sperm Whales are known. The skin is wrinkled and often scarred. Scarring results from disputes with conspecifics, as well as encounters with Giant Squid (*Architeuthis* spp.) in the ocean depths. The lower jaw is long and narrow, and holds 18–25 conical teeth in each half. These teeth grow to around 10 in. (25 cm) and were historically carved by whalers to create scrimshaw. The teeth fit into sockets in the upper jaw when the mouth is closed. The upper jaw is toothless or occasionally has a few rudimentary teeth. The dorsal fin is small, thick and rounded, and behind it there is a series of bumps along the dorsal ridge toward the tail stock. The flippers are short and triangular with a rounded tip. The flukes are notched, with a straight trailing edge. Sperm Whales show the tail flukes before deep dives. The blowhole is set toward the front of the head and to the left. The blow is forward and left, at an angle of 45°. Usually swims at 2–4 mph (4–6 km/h), but can reach up to 16 mph (25 km/h).

The horny beaks of squid are indigestible and irritate the stomachs of the whales. To counteract this, the whales secrete a resinous substance that coats the beaks. Coagulated masses of this material are eventually egested by the whales, and were also vomited out by harpooned whales. The masses are ambergris, a highly prized material used in the perfume industry that floats and that can therefore be retrieved from the ocean surface.

Confusion species
None. Blow is diagnostic, as is size and shape of head.

Size
HB: male 36–61 ft. (11–18.5 m), female 26–43 ft. (8–13 m). W: male 13–85 t., female 2–30 t. The most extreme sexual

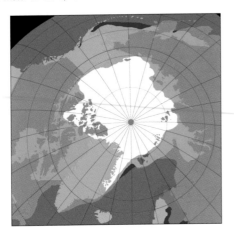

dimorphism of all cetaceans: males weigh up to three times more than females.

Communication
Emits pulsed clicks over a very wide frequency range (between 10 Hz and 30 kHz). Lower-frequency sounds carry over tens of miles and may be addressed to conspecifics rather than related to hunting prey. Sperm Whales spyhop, breach and lobtail, and may taste the secretions of conspecifics excreted into the water.

Distribution
Circumpolar. Found in all oceans, north and south to the ice edges. However, in the Arctic the Sperm Whale is rare in the far north, though it does occur off northeastern Greenland, Bear Island and in the Barents Sea, and in the Davis Strait and the southern Bering Sea. A deep-diving pelagic animal. Migratory, with seasonal movement to warmer waters.

Diet
Primarily squid, also fish. Despite the huge teeth, Sperm Whales feed mostly by using suction. Sperm Whales have become entangled in cabling at depths beyond 3,280 ft., (1,000 m) and have been sonar-tracked to more than 6,560 ft. (2,000 m), staying submerged for up to 90 minutes, but most dives are shallower and shorter.

Breeding
Social, with small pods (usually containing 4–10 animals) of related females and calves, or of bachelor males. Females probably remain in the pod of their birth for their entire lives. The pods may aggregate to groups of about 25 whales, and groups of up to 100 have been seen during migrations and at good feeding sites. Individuals in a pod will attend a sick or injured member, creating a "marguerite" formation in which healthy pod animals place their heads close to the sick one, their bodies radiating like the spokes of a wheel. This formation was utilized by whalers to increase their catch. Healthy animals attracted by the distress calls of one whale are a possible cause of mass strandings. This is likely to be true of other species of cetaceans.

Within pods of females with calves, other females will tend the calves of mothers while they deep-dive for food, and communal suckling is also apparently practiced. Older, sexually active males occasionally form small pods, but are usually solitary. In general solitary males travel further north (and south) and are therefore more likely to be seen in Arctic waters. Competition for females can lead to fierce combat. Single calf (about 14 ft./4 m long and weighing around 1 ton) born after gestation of 16–17 months. Twins have been observed but are rare, and it is not clear whether both survive. The calf is suckled for at least two years and often longer. The birthing interval is five to six years. Females are sexually mature at 7–12 years, males at 18–19 years, though they rarely breed before they reach 25.

Taxonomy and geographical variation
Believed to be monotypic, but widespread distribution means there are likely to be subspecies.

Baleen whales

The scientific name of the second, and smaller, group of whales, the Mysticeti, derives from "mustachioed whales," a reference to the huge plates of baleen that hang from the roof of the mouth of these beasts. The Mysticeti or baleen whales represent only about 10% of all whale species, but they form about 50% of the species in the Arctic. Baleen whales trawl the rich polar waters for both plankton and fish. The Mysticeti comprises three families, the Balaenopteridae or rorquals, the Eschrictidae, which includes just the Gray Whale, and the Balaenidae or right whales, all of which have Arctic representatives.

▲ The Blue Whale. The waters around the whale are clouded with zooplankton.

25% of the total length, and is broad and flat. Each side of the mouth has 250–400 black baleen plates, each about 2½ ft. (80 cm) long and 1½ ft. (50 cm) wide. There are 70–120 throat pleats. The dorsal fin is small and falcated, and set far back on the body. The pectoral fins are long and pointed. The blow is narrow and very high, up to 30 ft. (9 m). The tail flukes usually only just break the surface before deep dives and occasionally may not be seen at all. Blue whales feed at

Blue Whale
Balaenoptera musculus

The largest animal on Earth and quite possibly the largest ever, bigger than even the largest dinosaurs. The specific name, *musculus*, means "little mouse," which could be evidence of humor by Linnaeus, or a mistranslation of "muscle." Overhunting has drastically reduced the population of Blue Whales, though numbers are slowly recovering. The current population is estimated at around 11,000 animals, about 15% of the pre-hunting population.

Identification   See p. 455

A massive animal, very long but narrow. The skin is blue-gray with occasional white blotching. The head constitutes about

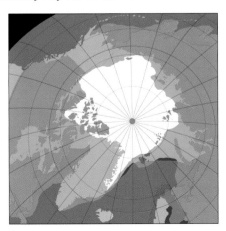

13–16 mph (21–25 km/h), cruise at 3–19 mph (5–30 km/h) and can reach speeds of around 31 mph (50 km/h).

Confusion species

Apart from the Humpback Whale, which is usually straight-forward to identify, the rorquals can be problematic to distinguish. Color and the high blow are diagnostic. Blue whales are shyer than other rorquals.

Size

HB: 72–102 ft. (22–31 m). W: 73–170 t. Southern Ocean Blue Whales are larger than their northern relatives, with lengths to around 108 ft. (33 m) and weights to 230 t., though the giant whales that were killed during the early days of rorqual hunting do not seem to have reappeared now that the species is fully protected. Time may tell, though; these whales are relatively long lived.

Communication

Repertoire of clicks, sound pulses and "moans" in the frequency range 14 Hz–30 kHz. Lower frequencies are assumed to be communication with conspecifics, while the higher range is possibly echolocation to aid navigation. Low frequency sounds are the loudest of any animal (about 200 dB) and can travel for several thousand miles through the water. Adult Blue Whales are not known to breach, though young Blues have been seen breaching. Spyhopping is not recorded.

Distribution

Found in all oceans. Migratory, moving from summer feeding grounds in polar waters to subtropical waters for breeding.

Diet

Primarily plankton, obtained by gulping. Presumably takes other marine creatures during huge gulps. Large Blue Whales consume around 6 tons of plankton daily. Blue Whales do not seem to feed at their tropical breeding grounds.

Breeding

Once formed large groups, but depressed numbers from overhunting means that the whales are now seen as solitary individuals or in groups of two to four animals. Little is known of breeding behavior. Single calf (23–26 ft./7–8 m long, weighing 2.5–4½ t) born after gestation of around 11 months. The calf puts on weight at a rate of about 100 lb. (90 kg) per day (almost 9 lb./4 kg per hour) and increases in length by 1½ in. (4 cm) per day, fuelled by 160 gal. (600 L) of fat-rich milk; weaned at 6–8 months. Females give birth every two to three years. Males and females reach sexual maturity at about 5 years, historically perhaps much later, but overhunting appears to have reduced the age of first reproduction (probably leading to the reduced size of mature whales).

Taxonomy and geographical variation

Polytypic. The nominate race is found in the northern hemisphere. *B. m. intermedia* is the larger, Southern Ocean subspecies. The Pygmy Blue Whale (*B. m. brevicauda*) of the southern Indian Ocean grows to about 65 ft. (20 m) with a maximum weight of

▲ A Fin Whale breathes out off the coast of Jan Mayen.

around 80 t., and has a shorter caudal peduncle. Some authorities consider this a full species rather than a subspecies.

Fin Whale
Balaenoptera physalus

The second largest of the great whales, and probably the most abundant, with population estimates of more than 100,000, of which perhaps 40% are in the northern hemisphere.

Identification See p. 455

Massive, long and narrow. The skin is slate-gray dorsally, paler (even white) ventrally. There is often a pale swirl on the right side of the head and pale V on the back behind the head. These patterns can be used to distinguish individuals. The asymmetry of the head swirl is mirrored in the coloration of the lower jaw, which is dark on the left and white on the right. The reason for this asymmetry is not understood. One speculation is that it may be effective camouflage at a distance from schooling fish,

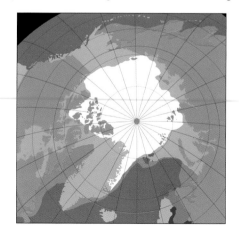

and that the whales turn sideways when they reach the fish to enhance the camouflage effect of "white below, dark above." A different explanation is that the whale can choose to circle fish clockwise or anti-clockwise, presenting a white jaw to frighten and herd the fish, a black one for camouflage. There are 280–480 dark greenish-black baleen plates on each side of the mouth (those on the right much paler), each about 2 ft. (70 cm) long and 1 ft. (30 cm) wide. There are 70–110 throat pleats. The dorsal fin is small and falcated, and set far back on the body. There is a well-defined dorsal ridge from the fin to the tail stock (hence the whalers' name "razorback" for the Fin Whale). The pectoral fins are long and pointed, the tail stock notched and with shallow concave trailing edges. The blow is high, up to 20 ft. (6 m), and narrow. The tail rarely breaks the surface before a deep dive. Fin Whales feed and cruise at similar speeds to Blue Whales, but may be faster in short bursts.

Confusion species
Pale ventral area is diagnostic. From above the Fin Whale head is V-shaped; Blue Whale head is more U-shaped.

Size
HB: 60–80 ft. (18–24 m). W: 55–85 tons.

Communication
Similar to Blue Whale, with low-frequency moans and high-frequency clicks. Low-frequency sounds are more songlike than those of the Blue Whale. As with Blue Whales, the low-frequency sounds travel enormous distances underwater. Fin Whales rarely breach and spyhopping is not recorded.

Distribution
Found in all oceans. Appears less migratory than the Blue Whale; tagging information suggests that some populations are more or less resident (though others move considerable distances). Some observations suggest that while some whales move south from northern waters in winter, others move in the opposite direction. Absent from tropical waters.

Diet
Plankton and small fish, taken by gulping.

Breeding
Solitary or in pairs, more rarely in groups of up to 30 animals. Little is known of breeding behaviour. Single calf (20 ft., or 6 m long, weighing 2–3 tons) born after gestation of around 11 months. Weaned at 6–8 months. Females calve every two to three years. As with Blue Whales, the age of sexual maturity appears to have been reduced by overhunting and is now 4–6 years for both males and females.

Taxonomy and geographical variation
Probably polytypic, with northern and southern subspecies and, perhaps, subspecies in distinct range areas, e.g., the Mediterranean.

Sei Whale
Balaenoptera borealis

The name is pronounced "sigh" rather than "say" and derives from the Norwegian for pollock, believed to be a principal prey of the species.

Identification See p. 455
The skin is mid-gray or dark gray dorsally, paler (occasionally cream-white) ventrally with numerous oval gray or white scars, thought to result from attacks by the Cookie-cutter Shark (*Isistius brasiliensis*), which is known to take oval-shaped chunks of blubber from great whales. A longitudinal ridge on the top of the head runs from the tip of the snout to the blowhole. There are 300–400 white-fringed black baleen plates on each side of the mouth, each about 28 in. (70 cm) long and

▼ Sei Whale Calf, North Atlantic.

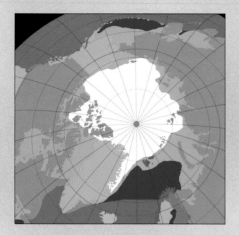

1½ in. (4 cm) wide. There are 30–80 throat pleats. The falcated dorsal fin is larger than those of either the Blue or Fin Whales and closer to the head than in those species. The pectoral fins are small and pointed. The flukes are notched, the trailing edge straight with upturned tips. The blow is about 10 ft. (3 m) high and columnar. Often, because of the forward position of the dorsal fin, it is visible when the whale blows. The tail flukes are not shown before a deep dive. Swimming speeds are similar to those of Blue and Fin Whales.

Confusion species
Dorsal fin, size and relatively short blow column are diagnostic.

Size
HB: 39–52 ft. (12–16 m). W: 10½–19 t. Females are significantly larger than the males, by up to 40% by weight, though only 5% by length.

Communications
Poorly documented. Low-frequency moans and high-frequency (16–28 kHz) clicks are known. Sei Whales rarely breach, and spyhopping is not recorded.

Distribution
Found in all oceans. Tends to travel less far north (and south) than the Blue and Fin Whales, rarely seen north of Jan Mayen, Labrador, southeastern Greenland or the Aleutians. Migratory, feeding in northern waters in summer and moving to tropical waters in winter to breed.

Diet
Unique among the rorquals in feeding both by gulping and by skimming. Takes plankton, fish and copepods. Studies in the North Atlantic suggest that the copepod (*Calanus finmarchius*) is a favored prey.

Breeding
Social, often seen in small groups, though pairs and solitary whales are seen. Little is known about breeding behavior. Single calf (15 ft./4.5 m long, weight 1,540 lb./700 kg) is born after gestation of 10–11 months and weaned at 6–7 months. Females give birth every two to three years. Both males and females achieve sexual maturity at 6–8 years.

Taxonomy and geographical variation
Polytypic. The nominate is the northern race. *B. b. schlegelii* is found in the Southern Ocean; *schlegelü* tends to be larger, but there is considerable overlap.

Minke Whale
Balaenoptera acutorostrata

Identification
See p. 455

Smallest of the Arctic baleen whales, with a sleek body and a flattened head with a pointed snout so that from above the head forms a sharp V-shape. There is a prominent mid-nostril ridge. The skin is dark gray dorsally, diffusing into white patches on the flanks and white ventrally, with gray mottling on the flank patches. Usually several dark gray ventral bands close to the tail stock. Some individuals show a white patch on the right side of the upper jaw, as in the Fin Whale. Some whales also have a pale chevron on the back behind the head. There are 230–360 cream or white baleen plates on each side of the mouth, each up to 1 ft. (30 cm) long and 5 in. (12 cm) wide. There are 50–70 throat pleats. The dorsal fin is tall and falcated, and set far back on the body. The pectoral fins are long and tapered, and have a broad, white diagonal stripe on the upperside and are white on the lower side. This pattern is diagnostic. The flukes are notched, the trailing edge shallowly concave. The blow is indistinct and shallow (rarely higher than 6½ ft./2 m). As with the Sei Whale, the dorsal fin is visible when the whale blows. The flukes are rarely shown on sounding.

Minke Whale in the sunshine of midnight, Spitsbergen.

▲ Humpback Whale diving, Lynn Canal, Alaska.

Confusion species

The white pectoral fin band and underside, and the white baleen plates are diagnostic if visible, as is the lack of a columnar blow and the small size. More likely to be confused with Northern Bottlenose Whale than the larger rorquals.

Size

HB: 26–34½ ft. (8–10.5 m). W: 10–12 t.

Communication

The least vocal of the rorquals, with a repertoire of low-frequency (80–200 Hz) grunts and a curious ratcheting at around 850 Hz. Also emits higher-frequency clicks (4–7.5 kHz). Occasionally spyhops and breaches.

Distribution

Circumpolar. Found far north in Davis Strait In the north Atlantic, less far north in the western Atlantic, though occasionally seen near Svalbard and often in the Barents Sea. Minke Whales have become entrapped in wind-driven pack ice. In the North Pacific, found throughout the Bering Sea and into the Chukchi Sea. More likely to be seen in coastal waters than the other rorquals, but usually migrates from northern summer feeding grounds to southern breeding grounds through deep waters.

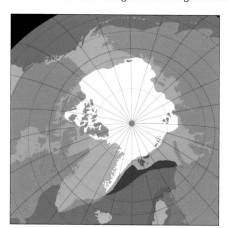

Diet

Fish, squid and plankton, taken by gulping.

Breeding

Social and breeding biology poorly known. Usually seen alone or in groups of two to four animals. A single calf (8–9 ft./2.5–2.8 m long, weighing 770 lb./350 kg) is born after a gestation of 10 months. The calf is weaned at 6 months, the shortest time for any rorqual. Most females give birth every year and so are pregnant and lactating simultaneously. Both males and females are sexually mature at about 7 years.

Taxonomy and geographical variation

Polytypic. The nominate race breeds in the north Atlantic. *B. a. scammoni* breeds in the north Pacific and is larger. Subspecies are likely in the eastern and western North Atlantic. Minke Whales were formerly believed to breed in all the world's oceans, but the southern race is now believed to be a distinct species, the Antarctic Minke (*Balaenoptera bonaerensis*). A third form, the Dwarf Minke that occurs off Australia, is smaller than either of the others, but its taxonomy is unclear.

Humpback Whale
Megaptera novaeangliae

Identification See p. 455

The skin is uniformly dark gray or black with variable white patches or larger areas ventrally. The front sections of the upper and lower jaws have a variety of knoblike protuberances, each of which encloses a stiff hair, which is believed to aid in

▲ Breaching Humpback Whale — a spectacular and unforgettable sight, Lynn Canal, Alaska.

detecting prey or current movements in the water. The skin often shows the oval scars of Cookie-cutter Shark (*Isistius brasiliensis*) attacks. There are 270–400 dark gray or black baleen plates in each side of the mouth, each up to 26 in. (65 cm) long and 6 in. (15 cm) wide, and 14–35 throat pleats. The falcated dorsal fin is small and mounted on a hump, usually more easily visible in front of the fin. This hump, which is prominent when the whale arches its back before diving, gives the species its common name. Some whales show a series of bumps along the dorsal ridge behind the dorsal fin. The pectoral fins are very long, up to 17 ft. (5 m), often 30% of the whale's total length. They have both a distinctive black-and-white pattern above and below, and a knobbly leading edge. The color and edge patterns are highly individual and can be used to identify particular whales. This is also true of the flukes, which have a similar black-and-white pattern, though they are more often dark gray above and distinctly patterned below, and a ragged, concave trailing edge. The flukes are usually prominently shown before sounding. The blow is bushy and up to 10 ft. (3 m) high. Humpbacks are slow swimmers, usually traveling at 1–3 mph (2–6 km/h), but are capable of bursts to around 19 mph (30 km/h).

Confusions
May be confused with other baleen whales at a distance, but the long pectoral fins and bicolored flukes are diagnostic.

Size
HB: 36–59 ft. (11–18 m). W: 30–55 t.

Communication
The eerie, ethereal "song" of male Humpbacks is famous. It comprises a complex series of whistles and tones — after human speech the most complex of any animal vocalization — which is similar for the males within a given population but changeable. The songs can be heard over long distances, though these distances are relatively short, about 90 mi. (150 km) or so, compared to the low-frequency thumps of the other baleen whales. They may last for up to 30 minutes or more, and are sometimes repeated over days. The songs, usually in a frequency range <4 kHz, are too long and complex to be for anything other than communication. Male singing may serve to attract females, or it might be targeted at other males in competition for breeding rights. Research suggests that whales that move toward the singer are generally male rather than female, favoring the competing-male explanation, but the evidence is not conclusive. The whales also emit clicks in the frequency range 2–7 kHz and bursts of extremely loud noise, up to 190 dB. The clicks appear to be in a range suitable for echolocation; the noise bursts are at an intensity that would damage the hearing of humans, and they perhaps stun, confuse or terrify fish. As well as these sounds, Humpbacks have visual displays; breaching, lobtailing and slapping the water with their long pectoral fins. Some breach repeatedly, and some hoist the pectoral fin like a sail. This may be a visual signal, (e.g., proof of breeding quality,) or it may simply be to cool the whale in warmer waters.

Distribution
Found in all the world's oceans. In the Atlantic, Humpbacks are seen as far north as Svalbard, but rarely east of the Barents Sea. In the Pacific, they are seen in the Bering Sea. In the Southern Ocean, the whales reach the ice edge. Coastal rather than pelagic. Migratory; Atlantic Whales congregate in the Caribbean in winter to breed, Pacific Whales move to waters off Hawaii or Mexico. Not all whales migrate every year.

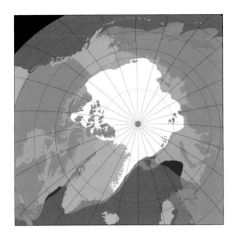

Diet

Plankton, cephalopods and schooling fish. Humpbacks are gulp feeders. The whales also use bubbles to concentrate schooling fish. Individual whales spiral upward while exhaling a stream of bubbles from their blowholes. The hollow cylinder of bubbles forces the fish together, and the whales then lunge into them to feed, or they may stun the fish by slapping them with flukes or fins. Humpbacks also employ bubble-netting; whales in a group rise in a circular formation, releasing bubbles, then lunge up and out of the water to gulp in the herded prey. Humpbacks also occasionally use clouds of bubbles, releasing large numbers of bubbles in one go, seemingly confusing fish, which herd together in panic and rise with the cloud, becoming trapped between it and the surface. The whales also turn the white side of their large pectoral fins toward the fish, further alarming and corraling them. The cloud technique is favored by Atlantic Humpbacks, the net by Pacific animals. Bubble-netting is usually assumed to be a cooperative feeding technique, but sometimes only one or two in the whale group actually release bubbles, and it may be that the remaining whales in the group are pirates, closing in rapidly when they hear the bubbles being released to get a free feed with minimum effort. Humpback Whales do not feed at the winter breeding grounds.

Breeding

Social, with groups of up to 20 animals forming for feeding and breeding. Otherwise solitary or in small, unstable groups. During mating, many males may gather around one receptive female, the bumping for position occasionally leaving scars. More serious fights involving ramming and tail slashing also occur. A single calf (13–15 ft./4–4.5 m long, weighing 1,435 lb./ 650 kg) is born after a gestation of 12 months and nursed on 53 gal. (200 L) of fat-rich milk daily. As with the other large baleen whales, the production of the milk takes a toll on the female's reserves; some lose a third of their body weight while suckling. The calf is weaned at 6–12 months, usually staying with its mother for at least a year. Females are highly protective of their calves. Females give birth every two to three years, but may reproduce annually when young. Males and females are sexually mature at 4–5 years.

Taxonomy and geographical variation

Probably polytypic. Atlantic and Pacific feeding groups congregate to breed and so mix genetically, but there may be little mixing between the oceans or between northern and southern populations.

Gray Whale
Eschrichtius robustus

The Gray Whale is the only living representative of its family. Once though to have split from the other baleen whales long ago, DNA analysis suggests a more recent separation. Phylogenetically, Gray Whales are intermediate between rorquals and right whales, and they exhibit some characteristics of each.

Identification See p. 455

The skin is mottled dark gray, light gray, and white, with extensive barnacle clusters on the head and anterior back. All whales collect barnacles, but in Gray Whales the colonies are unusually large, and whereas the other whales chiefly offer a ride to the Acorn Barnacle (*Coronula balaenaris*), the Gray Whale is also host to its own species, *Cryptolepas rachianecti*. Within the whale's barnacle colonies are numerous "whale lice" (actually *Cyamus* spp. amphipods), pale, spiderlike creatures about 1 in. (2 cm) across. These lice also infest other whales. There are 130–180 cream or pale yellow baleen plates on each side of the mouth, each up to 1½ in. (50 cm) long and 10 in. (25 cm) wide. There are only two to five throat pleats. There is no dorsal fin, merely a small, triangular dorsal hump. From this, a series of small bumps run along the dorsal ridge to the tail stock. The pectoral fins are broad and paddle-shaped. The flukes are also broad. They are notched with a straight if ragged trailing edge with upturned tips, and often have colonies of barnacles. The flukes are prominent when the whale sounds. The blow is vertical, about 13 ft. (4 m) high and opening into a bushlike cloud. The Gray Whale blow is very loud. During their long migrations Gray Whales swim at up to 6 mph (10 km/h).

Confusion species

The lack of a dorsal fin distinguishes the Gray Whale from the rorquals, the slender shape from the right whales. The feeding behavior of Gray Whales stirs up clouds of sediment and small creatures, and the whales are therefore usually accompanied by flocks of gulls looking for a meal.

Size

HB: 36–50 ft. (11–15 m). W: 17½–38½ t.

Communication

Pulsed sounds at 12 kHz, presumably for echolocation. There is also a repertoire of lower-frequency thumps and groans. The whales often spyhop, and practice a semi-breach in which they partially emerge before splashing back down again. This can be repeated many times. Full breaching has also been observed. In recent years the coastal habits of the whales has made them

▲ Young Gray Whale, North Pacific.

a popular target for whale-watchers and the animals seem to enjoy the attention, coming close to boats and allowing themselves to be scratched and patted. They will even place their heads on shallow craft. This behavior is in marked contrast to the highly aggressive behavior shown to early whalers, who named the Gray Whales "devil fish."

Distribution

North Pacific. There was formerly an Atlantic population of Gray Whales; the animals fed off Iceland and Greenland and migrated as far south as the Bay of Biscay, but this population became extinct in the 18th century, probably due to overhunting by Basque whalers. In the Pacific in summer, the whales are found as far north as the Chukchi and Beaufort Seas as well as throughout the Bering Sea. Gray Whales have one of the longest migrations of any animal; the Bering Sea whales

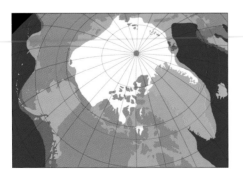

move some 6,200 mi. (10,000 km) to the lagoons of Baja, California, and the Gulf of California and back each year. On migration the whales move continuously, day and night, apparently without sleeping. A second, smaller population of whales is found in summer in the Sea of Okhotsk. This group also migrates, to waters off southern China. The whales are essentially coastal, rarely seen far offshore. The whale's coastal migration made the species easy to catch. Shore-based whalers in the 19th century, operating from the west coast of the United States, preferentially took pregnant females and females with calves as they were the easiest to pursue. As a consequence the population crashed, but fortunately it has recovered well.

Diet

Primarily feeds by filtering benthic amphipods, isopods, polychaete worms and mollusks from bottom sediments. The whales turn on to their sides and trawl through the sediment, invariably with their right sides in the substrate, sucking in prey and debris. The whales gouge furrows 6½–10 ft. (2–3 m) deep in the ocean floor, which helps to bring nutrients to the surface of the ocean sediment and promote the health of the habitat. Why the whales rarely use their left sides is unknown. Mid-water and surface-feeding also takes place.

Breeding

Solitary, usually single whales or females with calves. Several males will cluster around a female at breeding sites, and mixed-sex groups also form. Gestation is apparently exactly 12 months, as mating and birth take place in the same lagoons. However, there is some evidence that no fetal growth takes place at the end of the pregnancy, so gestation may be shorter, with a delayed birth. The single calf (16 ft./5 m long and weighing 1,433–1,540 lb./650–700 kg) accompanies its mother on the long migration north. The calves are vulnerable to Orca attack on this journey. The calf is weaned at 6–7 months and is independent before the long migration south. Females give birth every two years. Males and females are sexually mature at 5–11 years.

Taxonomy and geographical variation

Probably polytypic. There appears to be no mixing of the eastern and western Pacific populations.

Right Whales

Right Whales were so-called because they were the "right" ones to kill. They were slow and could be easily overhauled by a rowing boat, they floated when dead, making them easier to transport to ships or shore, and they yielded huge amounts of baleen and blubber. This combination, though right for the whalers, was wrong for the whales and led to their virtual extinction. Despite full protection, the populations of the three species of large Right Whales have not recovered well and measure only a few thousand individuals. Some authorities consider that full recovery of the species may not occur and that extinction in the medium to long term is probable, and perhaps inevitable for the Northern Right Whale, due to the inbreeding depression that must be occurring in the small remaining population.

The larger Right Whales share characteristics that differ from those of the rorquals. They have an arched rostrum, resulting in a bow-shaped mouth rather than the rorqual straight mouth; their baleen plates are consequently much longer. Right Whales also have no throat pleats, feeding by skimming rather than gulping; there is also no dorsal fin. Of the

three large Right Whales, two are Arctic dwellers. The third, the Southern Right Whale (*Eubalaena australis*), was once thought to be conspecific with the Northern Right Whale, but is now considered a separate species.

Northern Right Whale
Eubalaena glacialis

One of the world's rarest cetaceans. Reliable population figures are difficult to calculate, but the Atlantic population is estimated at no more than 300–400, while the Pacific population may be as few as 100. Even if these are under-estimates, the species is critically endangered. There appears to have been no increase in population since the species was protected.

Identification See p. 455

See p. 455

Large and rotund. The skin is black with variable white patches ventrally. The animal's head has a number of callosities, raised crusted areas of skin (usually white, occasionally yellow or pink) infested with barnacles, whale lice and other parasites. The callosities are above the eyes, on the upper and lower lips on on the head; they have stiff hairs growing from them, but their function is unknown. They are not, as might be inferred from the infestations, caused by the parasites, as callosities are observed in fetal whales. The shape and size of the patches allow observers to identify individuals. The blubber is up to 2 ft. (60 cm) thick and contributes 40% of the total weight. There are 220–260 black baleen plates on each side of the mouth, each up to 9 ft. (2.7 m) long and 1 ft. (30 cm) wide. Pectoral fins are triangular and very broad at the base. Flukes are broad, deeply notched and have a concave trailing edge. Tail usually raised before sounding. Blow is high (up to 16½ ft./5 m) and V-shaped. The whale rarely exceeds 6 mph (10 km/h).

Confusion species

None. Little range overlap with the Bowhead Whale, which is

▼ Northern Right Whale, Bay of Fundy. Note the callosities encrusted with extensive barnacle growth.

the only species that shares its characteristics. The head callosities are diagnostic.

Size
HB: 49–59 ft. (15–18 m). W: 60–109 t.

Communication
Several low-frequency (160–500 Hz) moans and grunts. Also occasional short pulses of sound at about 2 kHz. Despite its size and apparent slowness, Northern Right Whales occasionally breach. They also spyhop.

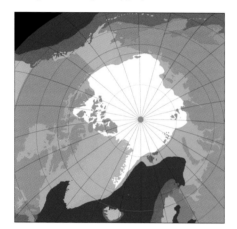

Distribution
Circumpolar. The Atlantic population is divided into two subpopulations, in Iceland/Norway and Labrador/Maine. The Pacific population is chiefly found from Japan to Kamchatka and in the Sea of Okhotsk, but some animals are found to the west, near the Aleutians and southern Alaska and as far south as California. The whales apparently migrate south to breeding grounds in summer. Mainly pelagic.

Diet
Plankton obtained by skimming. This feeding technique is solitary, but feeding groups of up to 150 whales have been observed at good feeding sites such as Canada's Bay of Fundy. This concentration would seem to represent a good chance for mating for a species that otherwise is spread thin across a vast ocean; however, the Bay is threatened by industrial developments, which consequently threaten the whales.

Breeding
Solitary or in small, unstable groups. At breeding sites several males may cluster around a receptive female. The female may mate with successive males; the males apparently use sperm competition as a technique for successful breeding, as they have the largest testes of any mammal: Northern Right Whale testes can weigh 1,985–2,205 lb. (900–1,000 kg). The whales copulate in all seasons, but this is assumed to have a social function as calves are always born in winter. A single calf (13–15 ft./4–4.5 m long and weighing 1,985 lb./900 kg) is born after a gestation of 12 months. The calf is weaned and

independent in 12 months, though some remain with their mothers for two or even three years. Females give birth every two to four years. Males and females are sexually mature at 4–10 years.

Taxonomy and geographical variation
Possibly polytypic. The lack of gene flow between the Atlantic and Pacific populations has led to suggestions of a nominate race in the Atlantic and a separate subspecies, *E. g. japonica*, in the North Pacific, but the differences, though not well documented, are apparently marginal.

Bowhead Whale
Balaena mysticetus

Identification See p. 455
These most Arctic of baleen whales are named on account of their massive heads (which make up 35–40% of their total length) and huge bow-shaped mouths. The skin is black with a collection of white marks on the back, usually toward the tail stock, which may be caused by scarring from banging against ice. Bowheads can break through ice 8–24 in. (20–60 cm) thick. There is a prominent triangular bump in front of the blowholes, and a depression behind them. The lower lip is white with black spotting. Older individuals also have white areas on the lower back and tail stock and on to the flukes, which become whiter with age. Based on evidence from the discovery of ancient harpoon heads in whales butchered after modern-day hunts, Bowhead Whales can live to well over 100 years. Ages consistent with these have been suggested by analyzing the ratio of two stereoscopic isomers of the amino acid aspartic acid, a constituent of the lens protein of the Bowhead's eye. From both studies, ages of up to 200 years have been conjectured; this would suggest that Bowhead Whales rival the Giant Tortoises (*Geochelone* spp.) as the longest-lived animals on Earth.

The pattern of spots and the dorsal scarring allow individuals to be identified. There are 230–360 baleen plates in each side of the mouth, each up to 15 ft. (4.5 m) long (the longest of any baleen whale) and 16 in. (40 cm) wide. The pectoral fins are triangular, with rounded tips, very broad at the base. The flukes

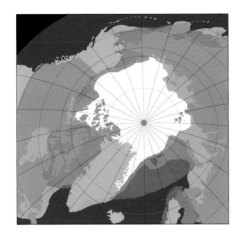

are deeply notched, with a shallow concave trailing edge. The flukes are raised before sounding. The blow is V-shaped, directed forward and sideways, and up to 17 ft. (5 m) high. Bowheads swim slowly, at about 4 mph (6 km/h).

Confusion species
None.

Size
HB: 49–61 ft. (15–18.5 m). W: 73–97 t.

Communication
Extensive repertoire of musical grunts and moans at 100–800 Hz. There are also pulsed tones at higher frequencies (up to 3.5 kHz). These are almost certainly an echolocation system, allowing the whales to navigate through pack ice. As with the Northern Right Whale, Bowheads occasionally breach, despite their large size. They also slap the water with their flukes and spyhop.

Distribution
Circumpolar, occurring in the western Atlantic around Baffin Island and in northern Baffin Bay and Smith Sound, northern Hudson Bay, the eastern Atlantic from northeastern Greenland to Novaya Zemlya, including the waters around Svalbard, and the north Pacific, including the Sea of Okhotsk, the Bering Strait and the Chukchi and Beaufort Seas. The Pacific population is believed to number 6,000–9,000, with another 300 whales in the Sea of Okhotsk, but these could be overestimates. The Atlantic stock has been depleted by hunting, with only 450 animals remaining on the western side and perhaps fewer than 100 to the east. Usually found at the ice edge. Pelagic, but does occur in coastal waters. Migrates with the ice edge and to more southerly breeding areas in winter.

Diet
Skim-feeds for planktonic copepods, amphipods and euphausiids. Usually feeds alone, but groups gather at favored feeding grounds, and these may form a line to sweep an area. Also dives to feed, staying underwater for up to an hour. Some dives are to the seabed.

Breeding
Social, but only in small groups. As with the Northern Right Whale, the testes of male Bowheads are very large, implying sperm competition. Several males will gather around a receptive female and she presumably mates with more than one male. Social copulations outside of the breeding season have also been noted. A single calf (13–15 ft./4–4.5 m long and weighing 1,985 lb./900 kg) is born after a gestation of 12–14 months. The calf is weaned at 6 months, but stays with its mother for at least a year. Females give birth every two to four years. Age of sexual maturity poorly known, probably up to 15 years.

Taxonomy and geographical variation
Probably polytypic because of the lack of gene flow between Pacific and Atlantic populations.

▼ Bowhead Whales, Isabella Bay, Baffin Island.

PLATE 38: SMALLER CETACEANS

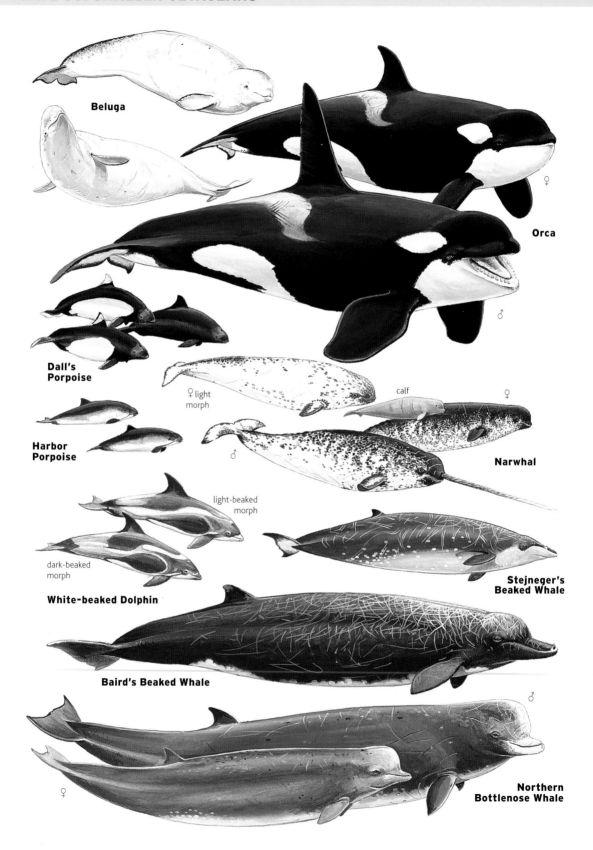

Beluga

Orca

♀

♂

Dall's Porpoise

Harbor Porpoise

♀ light morph

calf

♂

♀

Narwhal

light-beaked morph

dark-beaked morph

White-beaked Dolphin

Stejneger's Beaked Whale

Baird's Beaked Whale

♂

Northern Bottlenose Whale

♀

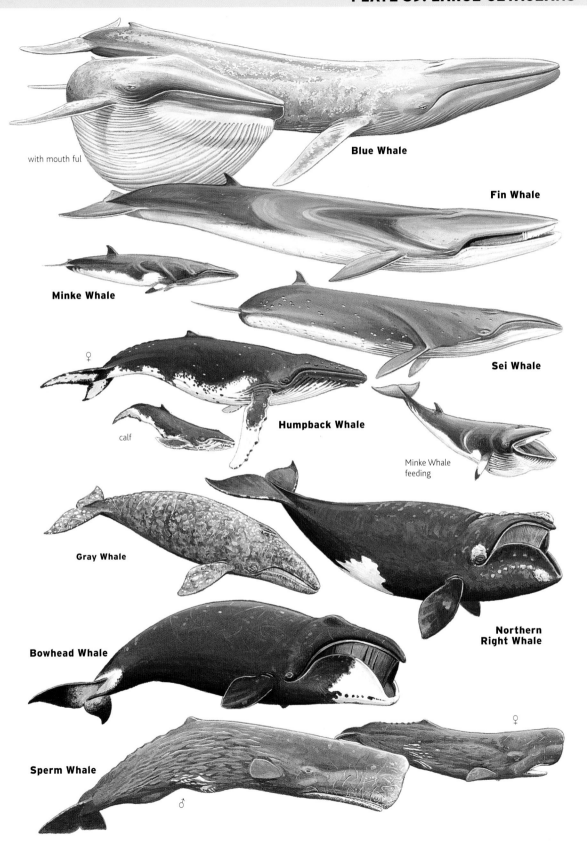

with mouth ful

Blue Whale

Fin Whale

Minke Whale

Sei Whale

♀

Humpback Whale

calf

Minke Whale
feeding

Gray Whale

Northern
Right Whale

Bowhead Whale

♀

Sperm Whale

♂

A visitor's guide to the Arctic

With Arctic travel one of the growth industries of international tourism, any guide to the region will be quickly out of date. In the sections below, brief details are given on the countries and regions that constitute the Arctic rim. Some general principles on travel are also given, but specific details are largely omitted. The guide starts with Iceland and heads east.

Iceland

Iceland lies between 63.5°N and 66.5°N, just below the Arctic Circle. The Circle passes through the island of Grimsey off the northern coast and close to the extreme northeastern tip of the mainland. The nearest significant landmass is Greenland, 180 mi. (290 km) to the west. The island is about 185 mi. (300 km) from north to south and 310 mi. (500 km) from east to west, and covers 39,770 sq. mi. (103,000 km²). The mean temperature in the capital, Reykjavik, is 30°F (-1°C) in January and 52°F (11°C) in July. The climate is variable; guidebooks usually note that if visitors to Iceland do not like the weather, they need only wait a few minutes, as it will change. Of course, the reverse also holds; if the weather is good, in a few minutes it will be poor.

Iceland's population is only 300,000, many of whom live in Reykjavik, and so it is largely empty. This has aided the setting up of many national parks, though these are primarily intended to protect the unique landscape rather than the wildlife. Travel to the island is straightforward. Icelandair and, increasingly, other airlines offer flights from major European cities and from a few North American cities, too. Road travel is slow outside the main cities as the roads are gravel, but the network is good. Car hire is expensive, but readily available. All main towns and cities have hotels and there are many good campsites. Wilderness camping is allowed. For the wildlife observer Iceland has the distinct advantage of being mosquito-free.

The interior of the island is an unforgiving place, particularly during the winter. This coastal distribution of much of the population means that there is a coastal road, allowing visitors access to the many excellent birding sites. Iceland has no indigenous mammals. Brown and Black Rats as well as House and Wood Mice have been accidentally introduced. Reindeer have been deliberately introduced, though numbers remain small, and populations of American Mink and Arctic Fox have become established from fur-farm escapees. Iceland is the only place in Europe where Harlequin Ducks and Barrow's Goldeneyes nest. The island also has a small population of gray-phase Gyrfalcons and is regularly visited by migrating Greenlandic white Gyrs. Good bird sites include the Látrabjerg sea cliffs, at the western tip of Iceland's northwestern landmass, most easily reached after a flight to Isafjördur, which is one of the largest seabird nesting areas in the north Atlantic. There is also Lake Myvatn, where Harlequin Ducks and Barrow's Goldeneyes nest. South Iceland has one of the world's largest colonies of Great Skuas, near the Skaftafell National Park. The Reykjanes Peninsula, southwest of Reykjavik, has a huge Gannet colony on the offshore island of Eldey. Finally, the lake in downtown Reykjavik is also good for ducks.

Jan Mayen

Jan Mayen lies at 71°N, 8°30'W, about 370 mi (600 km) northwest of Iceland. The island is Norwegian territory. It is spoon-shaped, about 35 mi. (55 km) long and 12 mi. (20 km) wide at its widest point, narrowing to around 12 mi. (2.5 km) at its narrowest point, and covers an area of 145 sq. mi. (375 km²). The "spoon" section of the island is dominated by Beerenberg, a 7,470 ft. (2,277 m) active volcano, whose last significant eruptions were in 1970 and 1985, but which has active fumaroles at all times. The island comprises lavas from a history of eruptions, colonized by mosses, liverworts and around 70 flowering plants. The "greening" of the black lava fields is fascinating for ecologists, and offers one of the most spectacular sights in the Arctic. The beaches of black sand are littered with the bleached trunks of trees that have arrived after a long journey by ice and water current from the rivers of Siberia. The mean temperature is 23°F (-5°C) in January and 41°F (5°C) in July, the climate kept relatively mild by the ocean. The island is often cloud- or mist-shrouded because of the high relative humidity; some years see as few as five clear days. The island is also frequently windswept.

Apart from the occasional Polar Bear, the only terrestrial mammal was the Arctic Fox, with a high proportion of blue-phase animals, though this population is now thought to be extinct. Of bird species, Fulmars occupy the island throughout the year, and other species arrive to breed.

Jan Mayen is occasionally visited by Arctic cruise ships, particularly those returning to Europe from northeastern Greenland. Although the island's stations are permanent and are provisioned by air, the few flights are always full, so visitors must either use the cruise ships or make their own voyages. Permission for traveling independently must be obtained before the trip.

Svalbard

Svalbard ("cold coast") is the name of the archipelago of islands lying between 74°N and 81°N. The archipelago , which is Norwegian territory, includes Spitsbergen, the best known of the islands, and the name often erroneously used when people actually mean the entire island group. Spitsbergen is the largest island, accounting for 14,670 sq. mi. (38,000 km²) (62%) of the archipelago's total land area of 23,630 sq .mi. (61,200 km²). Other islands include Nordaustlandet, northeast of Spitsbergen, the second largest of the group at 5,600 sq. mi. (14,500 km²) (24% of land area). Off Spitsbergen's east coast are Edgeøya and Barentsøya, to the

▲ Ivory Gulls, high on any birder's wish-list, can be seen on Svalbard.

behavior has been the decision to restrict where snow scooters may travel, particularly on Spitsbergen's eastern coast. A map is available that shows visitors where unescorted snow scooter travel and escorted group travel are allowed and where all snow scooter travel is forbidden. In general, travel close to Longyearbyen and Ny Ålesund is allowed, as is travel from Longyearbyen to Barentsburg and Pyramiden. Travel on Spitsbergen's eastern coast, near Agardh Bay, and north from there to Wichebukta, is restricted to escorted groups. To further protect this magnificent wilderness, a number of national parks have been set up, covering the northwest of the island from Krossfjorden to Woodfjorden, Prins Karls Forland, the north side of Isfjord, the head of Isfjord, Spitsbergen south of Van Keulenfjorden, the land south of Barentsburg, northeast Spitsbergenern and the islands of the eastern archipelago.

Despite these provisos, Svalbard remains the most accessible high-Arctic destination, with scheduled air services from Oslo and Tromsø. Once there, the landscapes are stunning and the wildlife is magnificent.

Bear Island

Bear Island, a Norwegian territory, lies at 74°30'N between the northern coast of Norway and Svalbard. It is roughly triangular, the base at the northern end, the apex to the south, the main axis aligned roughly N–S. It measures about 12 mi. (20 km) north to south, 9 mi. (15 km) east to west (across the triangle's base), and covers 69 sq. mi. (178 km²). Geologically it is part of the Svalbard Archipelago. Due to wave action the island is heavily eroded, with steep cliffs virtually everywhere, some rising to 1,312 ft. (400 m). It is low-lying, so before the era of GPS sailors could easily pass it, especially when the island was covered with clouds. An alternative name, Island of Mists, reflects the prevalence of cloud cover. Standing where relatively warm and humid continental air masses meet cold Arctic waters, this is no surprise; in July mist shrouds the island for much of the time. Bear Island's mean temperature ranges from 41°F (5°C) in July to 19°F (-7°C) in January. The relatively shallow waters around the island are among the most productive of the Barents Sea, which, together with the steep cliffs, make it an important nesting site for seabirds. Some of the island's colonies are among the biggest in the northern hemisphere. Bear Island is also important as a staging post for the Svalbard populations of Barnacle, Brent and Pink-footed Geese on their autumn migration. Of mammals, only the Arctic Fox is resident.

Bear Island is now a nature reserve, and though access is not actually restricted, there is no possibility of aircraft landing, and sea journeys must be privately organized, although Arctic cruise ships, usually on their way to or from Svalbard, occasionally stop at the island.

Fennoscandia

Fennoscandia — mainland Scandinavia and Russia's Kola Peninsula — lies to the south of the Arctic as defined in this book, though in midwinter it is hard to persuade visitors that they are not in the "Arctic." particularly as they are north of

northeast of which is Kong Karls Land, itself an archipelago of three small islands and a collection of islets. Off Spitsbergen's west coast is Prins Karls Forland, while off the northern coast are smaller islands, including Moffen and Amsterdamøya, the latter famous for its whaling station during the early years of Svalbard whaling. Finally, off Nordaustlandet's northeastern coast is Kvitøya, White Island, where the Andrée balloon expedition team died. Svalbard's mean temperature is 14°F (-10°C) in January and 41°F (5°C) in July.

Tourism on Svalbard has expanded, particularly over the last decade when the available accommodation for visitors in Longyearbyen changed from a campsite close to the airport and a basic guest house in town to five-star hotels serving haute cuisine. The change is not to everyone's taste, as it has been accompanied by a massive increase in tourist-related businesses. Where once a handful of snow scooters took the genuinely interested in search of views and wildlife, now squadrons conduct day trips for thrill-seekers. In the town, shops selling tourist trinkets abound. The impact on the landscape and wildlife of Svalbard has thankfully been minimized. The ruts of wheeled vehicles take decades to disappear so they are banned, meaning that summer travel must be made by ship or on foot. Ships usually explore the western coast of Spitsbergen, returning from a point at about 80°N, or they circumnavigate the island. Other islands of the archipelago are rarely visited; many are off limits due to their importance as Polar Bear denning sites, and others (e.g., Kvitøya) are usually too difficult to reach because of sea ice. The increase in the number of ships has caused problems with tourists ransacking historic sites for souvenirs, but that now seems to be under better control. In winter, out of sight of authority, some visitors still fail to realize that chasing a Svalbard Reindeer on a snow scooter means that the fun of a few minutes is exchanged for a life-threatening run for the animal; so precarious are the winter survival prospects of the animal that the energy lost in such a chase could mean the difference between life and death. One outcome of this the Arctic Circle. Because of the relative ease of travel both to and around the region, the northern areas of Norway, Sweden and Finland provide a fine introduction to "Arctic" scenery and climate, and a number of the terrestrial mammals and birds observed here have distributions that extend to the true Arctic. The fjords of northern Norway, especially Varangerfjorden, accessible from Kirkenes, are excellent for both breeding birds and migrants. Across the border in Russia, the devastation caused by unrestricted industrialization is apparent in the swathes of dead trees downwind of the nickel and copper smelters of Russia's Kola Peninsula. In Sweden and Norway, the national parks of Sarek, Padjelanta, Dividal and Øvre Pasvik include some of the finest scenery in Europe. Though less spectacular, northern Finland (especially the Lemmenjoki National Park) with its lakes and forests is equally good for birds. In this area can be found the now-rare Brown Bear, Eurasian Lynx and Wolf, as well as the elusive Wolverine.

Though still north of the Arctic Circle, the Lofoten Islands lie well south of the Arctic as defined here, but they are well worth visiting for their spectacular coastal scenery. The islands are a starting point for whale-watching trips in the northern Norwegian sea; species include Orca, Sperm and Minke Whales, and occasionally larger rorquals.

▲ Far-eastern Curlew, one of the sub-Arctic specialities of southern Kamchatka.

Russia

Russia has an Arctic region that extends from its border with Finland in the west, to the Bering Sea in the east, just a few miles from Alaska. Yet for much of this vast distance the mainland does not lie in the Arctic as defined here, the deep cold of the Siberian winter being moderated by warm summers. As a consequence, only a relatively narrow section of the mainland is truly Arctic, though all of the country's northern islands are.

Despite perestroika, travel within Russia is still difficult, though the development of services for independent travelers is improving all the time. Having Russian-based organizations assist with travel eases the problems of acquiring visas and the occasional burdens of bureaucracy, and it is likely to be the best way for the Arctic wildlife enthusiast to travel for some years to come. The best Russian Arctic destinations, the islands, still require visitors to join an organized cruise as there are no airports, while the use of helicopters from the mainland is prohibitively expensive if available, which is often not the case due to lack of machines or local bureaucracy. Chukotka and Kamchatka are notable exceptions, where private enterprise now allows travel for individuals and parties with itineraries based around the traveler's requirements rather than those of the bureaucracy.

An increasing number of ship-based tours are now available to the western Arctic islands (Franz Josef Land and, to a lesser extent, Novaya Zemlya and Severnaya Zemlya) and to Wrangel Island, and specific birdwatching tours are also available to some of the large river deltas, where visitors can observe Siberian White Cranes and other rare Russian breeding endemics. Chukotka is the breeding ground of the Spoon-billed Sandpiper, one of the Arctic's more exotic bird

species. It is now possible to fly to Anadyr to stay in well-placed huts close to the breeding sites of north Bering Sea birds and inland species. Kamchatka is also opening up, with tour operators from both on and off the peninsula offering tours that allow visitors to enjoy the scenic highlights of, for instance, the Kronotsky Reserve, which covers the Valley of the Geysers and the Uzon Caldera, as well as allowing more exotic, customized trips. Kamchatka offers the possibility of sightings of Snow Sheep, Black-capped Marmots and Black-billed Capercailles, while Steller's Sea Eagles and Spotted Nutcrackers are near-certainties.

Visitors to the Russian Arctic can expect summer temperatures of 39–50°F (4–10°C) (and much higher in southern Kamchatka), and winter temperatures as low as -22°F (-30°C).

Alaska

Alaska is the easiest destination for independent travel, as car hire is readily available in many of the most interesting destinations, such as Barrow, Cold Bay and Nome; quad bikes can be hired on St. Lawrence Island, visitors to Pribilof are offered an out-and-back transfer service, and on St. Paul one of the best auk watching sites is within walking distance of the town, while boat trips from Dutch Harbor help search out the elusive Whiskered Auklet. Transport is less readily available in Denali National Park, and some magnificent country can only be reached by aircraft and walking, but in general the species of interest can be observed in the most accessible areas.

Within the state, a realization of the extraordinary scenic beauty and importance of Alaska has led to the creation of a number of national parks and national wildlife refuges and these will be mentioned, where appropriate in the sections below. Details of all the refuges, together with access information, is available as a leaflet from the U.S. Fish and Wildlife Service, U.S. Department of the Interior. The leaflet is available from tourist outlets in all the main towns.

In the north of the state, Barrow is the most readily accessible town, with scheduled flights from Anchorage via Fairbanks. It is also an excellent centre from which to base a trip, as both Steller's and Spectacled Eiders breed there, and breeding birds from Russia are also seen frequently. The autumn "invasion" of Ross's Gulls, which was such a feature of Barrow has declined significantly in recent years; the gulls are now rarely seen in large numbers and are becoming increasingly rare as the ice moves farther north.

To the west, Nome is equally accessible, and visitors may see Bluethroats and Bristle-thighed Curlews as well as Aleutian Terns. To the north of Nome, on the northern side of the Seward Peninsula, the Bering Land Bridge National Preserve is excellent for breeding and migrating birds as well as for sea and terrestrial mammals. The Preserve can be reached by chartered aircraft from Nome and Kotzebue. To the south of Nome across Norton Sound is the Yukon Delta National Wildlife Refuge, which includes the deltas of both the Yukon and Kuskokwim Rivers. Offshore is Nunivak Island, which is a separate refuge. Regular flights reach St. Mary's, on the Yukon River, Bethel, on the Kuskokwim and Mekoryuk on Nunivak Island, but to reach deep into the Preserves from these, the traveler must charter flights or walk. Birdwatchers visit in spring and autumn in the hope of sighting McKay's Bunting, whose summer breeding sites are more difficult to reach. In summer, Black Brants, Emperor Geese and Spectacled Eiders breed in the Preserve.

Farther south is the Togiak National Wildlife Refuge and the adjacent coastal Cape Newenham Wildlife Refuge, with upland tundra and excellent coastal sites. The closest town is Dillingham, which is also the starting point for trips to the Walrus Islands State Game Sanctuary. Most travelers visit Round Island, a famous haul-out for the Pacific subspecies of Walrus and a nesting area for Pacific auks. Access to the island is controlled, so permission must be sought. Travelers must also be entirely self-sufficient and unfazed by an unexpected extension to their visit, as bad weather frequently makes landings impossible.

On the road that heads east then south from Anchorage toward Seward, Potter Marsh is a good bird site, and Elk are often seen there. Farther on, look out for Dall's Sheep on the cliffs close to Beluga Point. A turn left to Whittier reaches boat trips in Prince William Sound where there are Sea Otters and Pacific auks. Visitors on boat trips from Seward into Resurrection Bay visit a Steller's Sea Lion colony, usually see Sea Otters and pass directly below the Pacific auk colonies. Homer, reached by turning off the Seward Road, is well known for its winter congregations of Bald Eagles. Homer Spit is also good for waders and wildfowl, including Black Turnstones, the three scoters, and Harlequin Ducks.

On the Alaskan Peninsula, accommodation and vehicle hire are possible at Cold Bay, where the main wildlife interest is the Izembek National Wildlife Refuge. The lagoon here includes more than 44,475 acres (18,000 ha) of Eelgrass, more than 50% of the world's total acreage of this important plant. Each year the Eelgrass attracts some 200,000 geese. More than 95% of the world population of Black Brants stops here to feed before their flight south. On the Aleutian chain, only Dutch Harbour is readily accessible, with boat trips from there offering a chance to see Whiskered Auklet, which breed on the uninhabited Uniaga Island to the west, and feed on the Chelan Banks. Unalaska is excellent for Bald Eagles, and Ravens abound here, but other birdlife is more elusive, though the Aleutian subspecies of the Common Teal can usually be found, as can the Gray-crowned Rosy-finch.

North of the Aleutian chain lie the Pribilof Islands of St. Paul and St. George. The islands are reached by a flight from Anchorage, which requires good visibility for landing and good bladder control by the passengers. There is a hostel on each island that will accommodate visitors and guides, who assist in moving visitors around the island to the best wildlife viewing sites and are also happy to offer information. The islands are excellent for Pacific auks and seabirds, including Red-legged Kittiwakes and for the occasional Asian rarity. St. Paul is the primary breeding ground of the Northern Fur Seal, with vast herds of seals occupying a few beaches during the breeding period.

North of the Pribilofs are St. Matthew and Hall Islands, on which McKay's Buntings breed. Each island is difficult to access and requires specific permission. St. Lawrence Island, to the north, is easier to get to; flights link Savoonga and Gambell to Nome. Of the two, Gambell is the more usual destination as it is renowned for its birdlife, particularly migrating species. As Chukotka is only some 50 mi. (80 km) away, Asian species are frequent visitors.

Though technically not a part of the Arctic as defined here, few travelers will visit Alaska and not drive north from Anchorage to see Mount McKinley or visit the Denali National Park. The Park was set up to protect the exquisite scenery around the peak as well as the mammals and birds. There are 37 mammal species, including Grizzly Bears, and more than 130 bird species have been identified there.

With such a vast area, mean temperature ranges are not entirely helpful, but in general in the north of the state they will range from 41°F (5°C) to -13°F (-25°C), in the south from 50–51°F (10–15°C) to 14°F (-10°C).

Canada

Canada's northern islands represent a large fraction of the land area of the Arctic. Because of the vagaries of the world's climate, the "Arctic" also extends much farther south into mainland Canada than it does into mainland Russia. The combined area of the Yukon and Northwest Territories, together with Nunavut, represents 40% of Canada. As a consequence, a realistic overview of the country is beyond the scope of this book. Only brief notes on the area's national parks and major wildlife sites are given below. Travel to the Canadian Arctic usually involves charter flights and, consequently, a good deal of preparation, but more recently

Russian ice-breaker cruises have been venturing into the area, offering trips through the Northwest Passage.

In the northwest of the country, Inuvik is readily accessible and from it charter flights visit Herschel Island. The island is used by Caribou as a calving ground. Bowheads and Belugas swim close to the island as they migrate, and migrant waterfowl stop here to feed before continuing south. On the nearby mainland, Vuntut National Park is a vast wetland plain, comprising around 20,000 shallow lakes and ringed by mountains. The park is a habitat for Brown Bears, Elks and Muskrats, and the breeding ground for waterfowl and waders. Vuntut is also on the migration route of the Porcupine Caribou herd to and from their traditional calving grounds in the Ivvavik National Park. The Ivvavik lies to the north, sharing its southern border with Vuntut Park. It may also be possible to visit the Anderson River Delta Bird Sanctuary to the east of Inuvik. This sanctuary, with the bird sanctuaries on Kendall Island north of the Mackenzie Delta and those on Banks Island, were set up to protect the tidal flats that are important to breeding and migrating waterfowl and waders.

Another bird sanctuary at Cape Parry, on the mainland east of the Anderson Delta, protects a major fraction of the western Arctic's population of Brünnich's Guillemots. East of Cape Parry, Tuktut Nogiat National Park Reserve protects the calving grounds of the Bluenose Caribou herd and has impressive canyon scenery. On Banks Island, a bird sanctuary covers a huge area of the western island, while to the north, Aulavik National Park encompasses the valley of the Thomson River and Castel Bay, and was set up to protect one of the largest concentrations of Musk Oxen in the Arctic, as well as Wolves and other terrestrial mammals, the sea mammals of the northern coast and many species of waterfowl and waders.

Heading east from the Northwest Territories, beyond Bathurst Inlet (crossed annually by the Bathurst Caribou herd) is the Queen Maud Migratory Bird Sanctuary, the most important breeding site of Ross's Goose. At least 90% of the world population of these geese are thought to nest within the reserve. South of the Queen Maud reserve is the Thelon Wildlife Sanctuary, established in 1927 to preserve a remnant Musk Oxen population. Eastward, in the northern part of Hudson Bay, is Southampton Island, which has two bird sanctuaries, again principally for migratory and breeding waterfowl; Harry Gibbons Sanctuary near Bay of God's Mercy and East Bay Sanctuary at the northern end of the Bell Peninsula to the east of Coral Harbour. There are scheduled flights to Coral Harbour, but travel on the island can be difficult. To the east of Southampton Island, the newest Canadian national park, Ukkuksiksalik, encompasses Wager Bay, a habitat for Nunavut's largest concentration of Peregrine Falcons. At the other end of Hudson Bay in James Bay, there are bird sanctuaries on Akimiski Island and in the nearby Hannah and Boatswain Bays.

On southern Baffin Island, at Cape Dorset on the southern tip of the Foxe Peninsula, there is a bird sanctuary, while south-east of the Foxe Peninsula, on the exotically named Meta Incognita Peninsula, the Katannilik Territorial Park has Caribou and Wolves, and a bird population that includes waterfowl, waders, grouse and Gyrfalcons. Another important site lies northwest of Iqaluit, on the coastal plain south of the Koudjuak River. Here, in 1927,

the Canadian biologist Dewey Soper first located the breeding grounds of the blue phase of the Snow Goose. The bird sanctuary named in his honor has the largest breeding colony of Snow Geese in the world. There are also other waterfowl and waders, and Caribou in the adjacent Bowman Wildlife Sanctuary to the south. On the eastern coast across from the Dewey Soper Reserve is the Auyuittuq National Park with its remarkable granite peaks. At the northern end of Baffin Island, the Sirmilik National Park covers two areas of the island and Bylot Island, making up one of Nunavut's largest and most biodiverse parks. Within the park, 30 species of bird breed, including colonies of Snow Geese, auks and seabirds. Bylot Island also has white-morph Gyrfalcons, and Cape Hay, on the northern island, is an excellent viewpoint for cetaceans migrating into Lancaster Sound. Access to the park is via the townships of Pond Inlet and Arctic Bay. East of the Sirmilik, the Prince Leopold Migratory Bird Sanctuary covers both the island of that name and the northeastern tip of neighboring Somerset Island, where more than 300,000 pairs of auks and seabirds breed.

Farther north, the Polar Bear Pass National Wildlife Area on Bathurst Island has become famous for its use by Polar Bears during their spring and autumn traverses of the island. However, the reserve was set up to protect an important wetland area that is a breeding habitat for Snow Geese and Thayer's Gulls, as well as other waterfowl and seabirds, and for waders. Finally, at the northern end of Ellesmere, the Quttinirpaaq National Park encompasses a vast area of this magnificent island, taking in the fjords of the northern and eastern coast (the eastern coast separated from northern Greenland by the narrow Robeson Channel), and Lake Hazen, the largest high-Arctic lake. The entire park lies north of the 80th parallel. The Park is home to Peary Reindeer and white Wolves, and to a thriving population of Arctic Hares. More than 20 species of high-Arctic birds breed within the park. Cruises using Russian ice-breakers often travel to Tanquary Fjord at the Park's southern rim, making a thrilling passage between eastern Ellesmere Island and Axel Heiberg Island.

Though this brief overview of Nunavut's parks and reserves highlights the most important wildlife, and some of the best scenery, in the territory, a vast area of high Arctic lies outside them, which is equally pristine and worthwhile. Igloolik, a tiny island close to the entrance to the Fury and Hecla Strait, is reached by scheduled flights from Iqaluit and is renowned for Bowhead Whales and Walruses. Pond Inlet, at the northern end of Baffin Island, is not only a useful entry point for the Sirmilik National Park, but also excellent for Narwhals, which can be viewed from the floe edge in Baffin Bay. Charter flights from Resolute can be made to Cunningham Inlet on northern Somerset Island, where Beluga congregate, and to Eureka on Ellesmere Island, where years of research have shed light on the behavior of high-Arctic white Wolves. Cambridge Bay, at the southern end of Victoria Island, is reached by scheduled flights from Yellowknife. It is a good place to see Musk Oxen, Sabine's Gulls and other wildlife. The same is true of the Hudson Bay townships of Rankin Inlet, Repulse Bay and Coral Harbour, while history beckons at Gjoa Haven on King William Island, where Roald Amundsen wintered in 1903 in his journey through the Northwest Passage.

In southern Canada, Churchill, Manitoba, is one of the most easily accessible and entrancing wildlife destinations in the Canadian Arctic. In the spring and early summer, several thousand Belugas congregate in the Churchill River to molt, leading the town to claim the title of "Beluga Capital of the World." During the autumn, Polar Bears marooned on Hudson Bay's southern coast move to Cape Churchill to await winter's freeze; the numbers involved have led the town to claim the title of "Polar Bear Capital of the World" as well. Add the remarkable bird life and it is easy to see why Churchill attracts visitors in droves. The Wapusk National Park has recently been set up to protect the bears of this area of southern Hudson Bay. Park lands cover a coastal strip from west of Cape Churchill to the Nelson River. The Park therefore protects one of the most important bear denning sites in the world. Access to the Park is controlled, but operators in Churchill are able to offer tours.

In Ontario, James Bay has the southernmost population of Polar Bears (on the same latitude as London), which come ashore when the sea ice melts and await its autumnal refreezing. Female bears also den on the shores of the Bay. The Bay can be reached by train from Toronto via Cochrane (the train called, to no one's surprise, the Polar Bear Express), which reaches Moosonee.

On the eastern side of Hudson Bay lies the last of mainland Canada's Arctic. In Quebec, the region above the 55th parallel is Nunavik, comprising a series of scattered Inuit coastal villages on the shores of the Ungava Peninsula, lapped by the waters of the Hudson Strait and Hudson Bay itself. The largest of these villages is Kuujjuaq at the southern edge of Ungava Bay. Essentially a land of low-lying, flat tundra, the region is bordered on the east by the Torngat Mountains, which extend into Labrador. Nunavik's tundra is the habitat of huge Caribou herds. The George River herd is the largest, with more than 700,000 animals. Two other herds, the Leaf River and the much smaller Torngat Mountain herd, raise the total number of animals in Nunavik to at least one million. Travel to the region is limited, but scheduled flights from Quebec cities reach Kuujjuaq and many of the villages of the Ungava Peninsula.

Between the Torngat Mountains and the sea in northern Labrador live the Sikumiut Inuit, whose ancestors hunted sea mammals on the ice of the Labrador Sea and Caribou on the inland tundra. Negotiations are currently underway between the people and the Canadian government to transfer ownership of an area of northern Labrador, with a view to creating an equivalent to the Inuit lands of Nunavut and Nunavik. It is hoped that once an agreement has been reached, a national park to protect the Torngat Mountains will also be created. As with Nunavik, travel within the area is limited, but scheduled flights reach Nain and there is a coastal ferry to the town. Flights to Labrador are occasionally weatherbound, particularly on the last stretch from Goose Bay to Nain, so travelers must be patient and remain flexible.

Quoting temperatures for Canada as a whole is pointless because of its size, but summer visitors to Churchill can expect a mean of 59°F (12°C) with places to the north cooler, while winter visitors should prepare for temperatures as low as -22°F (-30°C).

Greenland

Greenland is the largest island on Earth, with an area of 850,000 sq. mi. (2.2 million km^2). It extends from just below the 60th parallel at Kap Farvel north to 83°40'N at Oodaaq Island, the most northerly land so far discovered (and probably to exist). The distance from Kap Farvel to Cape Morris Jessup, the northern-most point on the mainland, is 1,660 mi. (2,670 km). More than 80% of Greenland's area (695,000 sq. mi., or 1.8 million km^2) is covered by an ice cap, the Inland Ice, which is up to 7,900 ft. (2,400 m) thick and represents the second-largest ice sheet on Earth after that covering Antarctica.

There are scheduled air services to Kulusuk and Constable Point (near Scoresbysund) on the east coast, and to towns on the west coast as far north as the U.S. services base at Thule, from Iceland and the Scandinavian countries. Within the country, the Greenland airline Grønlandsfly has fixed-wing and helicopter services between the main towns. Flying is the only realistic way of getting around the island for most travelers, as apart from a few miles in each of the towns there are no roads. Ships and boats offer the only alternative. In winter, snow scooters can be used, of course, but in winter there is much less wildlife to see, although the scenery is still stunningly beautiful. Visitors are therefore restricted to walking from the towns, or they need to charter flights, from Iceland for the eastern coast, or from Canada for the western one. Such flights are not without difficulty in arranging, as Greenland is a foreign country to the pilots of both Canada and Iceland, so international regulations apply and may limit the willingness of some operators. If chartering is not an option, Greenland's main towns are still worth visiting, as the scenery close to them is excellent, though wildlife may be in short supply as the locals still hunt for food regularly.

Greenland has few protected areas, but each is worthwhile. Melville Bay in the northwest is an important breeding area for species including Sabine's Gulls, white-morph Gyrfalcons and Ringed Seals. Pride of place, though, must go the Northeast National Park, at 270,000 sq. mi. (700,000 km^2) the largest park in the world. This vast area is the last great wilderness in the lands bordering the northeast Atlantic, and is truly magnificent. It is also an important wildlife reserve, with Polar Bears, Musk Oxen, Wolves, Arctic Hares, Northern Collared Lemmings and all of the North Atlantic pinnipeds. These include Walruses, which have been hunted to extinction in other parts of the island, so now only two haul-out areas in the national park remain. Breeding waterfowl include Barnacle Geese. Tour ships now regularly visit the park.

With such a vast area, suggesting temperature means for Greenland might appear pointless, yet the range is actually surprisingly narrow; southern January temperatures average around 5°F (-15°C), while those of the north of the island are around -22°F (-30°C), and July averages are 46°F (8°C) and 41°F (5°C) respectively. The northeastern coast of Greenland, as with west-central Ellesmere Island, is well known for its beautiful summers, with stable high pressures and periods of warm, sunny weather. Temperatures at these times sometimes exceed 68°F (20°C).

Index

This index gives the common, alternative common and scientific names of species with full entries in the field guide sections of this book. Plates are given in *italics*.

▼ Arctic Hare molting into summer coat, Churchill.